The
St. Martin's
HANDBOOK

The
St. Martin's
HANDBOOK

Andrea Lunsford
Ohio State University

Robert Connors
University of New Hampshire

ST. MARTIN'S PRESS   New York

Senior Editor: Mark Gallaher
Developmental Editor: Marilyn Moller
Project Editor: Denise Quirk
Manuscript Editor: John Elliott
Editorial Assistant: Virginia Biggar
Production Supervisor: Julie Power
Text Design: Helen Granger/Levavi & Levavi, Inc.
Cover Design: Darby Downey

For information, write:
St. Martin's Press, Inc.
175 Fifth Avenue
New York, NY 10010

ISBN: 0-312-00264-5

Acknowledgments

The American Heritage Dictionary, Second College Edition. Copyright © 1985 by
Houghton Mifflin Company. Reprinted by permission.

J. Bland. "Spelling and Pronunciation—Hints for Foreigners," from a letter published
in London *Sunday Times*, January 3, 1965, from J. Bland. Cited by McKay and Thompson in "The Initial Teaching of Reading and Writing," *Program in Linguistics and
English Teaching*, paper 3, University College, London, and Longmans Green and Co.,
Ltd., London and Harlow, 1968, page 45.

James M. S. Careless, *Canada: A Story of Challenge*. Copyright © 1970 by St. Martin's
Press, Inc. Reprinted by permission of Macmillan of Canada, a division of Canada
Publishing Corporation.

"Chicken Soup: It Might Help Your Memory." From *Newsweek*, December 1, 1986.
Copyright © 1986, Newsweek, Inc. All rights reserved. Reprinted by permission.

E. E. Cummings, "Me up at does." Copyright © 1963 by Marion Morehouse Cummings, reprinted from *Complete Poems 1913–1962* by E. E. Cummings by permission
of Harcourt Brace Jovanovich, Inc.

Acknowledgments and copyrights are continued at the back of the book on
pages 758–59, which constitute an extension of the copyright page.

Preface

The story of *The St. Martin's Handbook* began in 1983. In the course of investigating the history of writing instruction, we came across some information about teaching composition that, though at first simply amusing, led us to a series of compelling questions. We discovered, for instance, that in the late nineteenth century, professors at Harvard perceived that their students had great difficulty distinguishing between the use of *shall* and *will*, and that in the 1930s, American students persistently misused *would* for the simple past. How quaint, we thought; look at how much student writers and their problems have changed.

We intuitively assumed that such changes must have taken place, but what exactly were they? This question took on greater significance as we focused our investigation on the history and development of composition textbooks. As part of that research, we found that the first edition of John C. Hodges's *Harbrace College Handbook* (1941) was based on an analysis of over 20,000 student papers written in the 1930s. So, we reasoned, that book reflected the writing problems of students of the time, problems that were decidedly different from how to use *shall* and *will*. How might the problems faced by our students, fifty years later, have changed?

With something of a shock, we realized that we didn't know. Further investigation showed us not only that Hodges's research seemed to be the last serious effort of that kind but that his handbook was still organized exactly as it had been in 1941. Since subsequent college handbooks had necessarily responded to that book, we realized with some surprise that the world of composition handbooks was still being tacitly guided by conceptions of error patterns that were almost a half century old.

We set out, then, to discover what patterns of error actually characterize student writing today, and which of these patterns seem most important to their instructors. To answer this question, we gathered a nationwide sample of over 20,000 student essays that had been marked by instructors and carefully analyzed a scientifically stratified sample of them, eventually identifying the twenty error patterns most characteristic of student writing today. As you might imagine, we got some provocative results.

Most intriguing to us is the fact that many of these errors relate in some way to visual memory—wrong words, wrong or missing verb endings, missing or misplaced possessive apostrophes, even the *its/it's* confusion—which suggests that students today may well be less familiar with the visible aspects of writing than students once were. Part of the effect of an oral, electronic culture seems to be, then, that students do not automatically bring with them the visual knowledge of writing conventions that text-wise writers possess and use effortlessly.

This problem of visualization was most pronounced in terms of spelling errors, which occur—by a factor of 300 percent—more frequently than any other error. Interestingly enough, the words students most often misspell are homonyms, words that sound alike but have different meanings and spellings. These findings support our other data linking error patterns to visual memory and suggest that the visual aspect of spelling is particularly important, that in a world of secondary orality we need to find ways to help students visualize their language.

Our research also revealed that many errors are governed not so much by hard and fast rule as by rhetorical decisions involving style, tone, and rhythm. Among others, such errors include the omission of a comma after an introductory element, inappropriate shift in verb tense, and misuse of commas with restrictive and nonrestrictive elements. This finding suggested to us that students need help writing prose that is not only mechanically correct but rhetorically effective as well. Doing so, we believe, demands that they view the tools of writing—grammar, punctuation, mechanics—as having rhetorical force and as being based on choices they must learn to make.

Armed with this information, we set out to create a textbook that would address the needs of students at the end of the twentieth century. The result is *The St. Martin's Handbook*. In many ways it is a traditional handbook, with all the requisite materials on the writing process, grammar, punctuation, mechanics, and research. In other respects, however, it charts new territory, extending writing instruction in features not found in any other handbook. Among its distinctive features are the following:

Special attention to the twenty most common errors. An introductory chapter entitled "Learning from Your Errors" offers practical guidelines for recognizing, understanding, and revising each of the top twenty errors that our research identified. This chapter also serves as an index, with cross-references to all the places in the book where students can find more help on each error. Especially helpful, we hope, will be step-by-step guidelines that show students how to check their own drafts for each error and then how to revise accordingly.

In presenting these errors, we have tried always to give a clear message about "correctness" *along with* realistic discussion of actual usage. Without oversimplification, our goal has been to help students know *what to do*. Most important, we present errors as opportunities for improving skills, as something to be examined in context and learned from rather than as blots to be eradicated. We ask students not simply to amass information about errors but to analyze the sources and consequences of those errors in their own writing—to build, if you will, a theory about how to improve their writing based on a close study of the errors that they make.

Attention to writing, not just to correctness. We feel strongly that students need practice in *writing*, not only in revising incorrect sentences. Like all composition handbooks, *The St. Martin's Handbook* provides guidance in checking and revising a draft for correctness; unlike most others, however, it also offers ample opportunity for student writing, in guided-writing and imitation exercises that get students to stretch their writing muscles, and in revising exercises that send them back into their own writing.

This attention to writing informs every chapter in the book, including those dealing with grammar and mechanics. In the chapter on adjectives and adverbs, for instance, we ask students to focus not only on how to use adjectives and adverbs correctly but also on the more compelling question of why and in what circumstances to use them at all. In the chapter on end punctuation, we provide rules for using periods, question marks, and exclamation points, and in addition, we ask students to try revising a piece of their own writing for sentence variety, using declarative, interrogatory, and exclamatory structures. In other words, we have tried to present grammar and mechanics as something to use for a writing purpose, not simply to use "correctly."

And because we believe that students learn best by reflecting on the rhetorical characteristics of what they have written, we show them how to keep a writing log—for recording their efforts at using grammatical structures, listing troublesome spelling words, jotting down noteworthy examples or images for future use. As a feature, the writing log is completely optional, but we recommend it as a means of helping students to reflect systematically on their own writing.

Systematic attention to reading. Because we see writing and reading as inextricably linked, we have included reading instruction throughout the text. Not only is there extensive guidance to help students read observantly and critically—whether evaluating a draft, an argument, a paragraph, or a source—but in addition, we present reading as one more tool that can help improve writing skills. Almost every chapter includes a special exercise asking students to "read with an eye for" some structure or element they are learning to use as writers—verbs, semicolons, hyphens, and so on. These exercises ask them to study passages from famous essays (and sometimes, poems) or from drafts of their own or other student work. In addition to the obvious benefits of studying expert use of basic rhetorical elements, such exercises will, we hope, help build students' visual knowledge of writing and writing conventions. Many of these exercises ask students then to try to imitate something in the passage—in other words, to step from their reading into writing.

Five chapters on the research process. Nowhere do students need more thorough instruction in how to move back and forth between reading and writing than in the writing they do based on sources. For this reason, *The St. Martin's Handbook* concentrates not simply on helping students produce a "research paper," but on how they might use research for many writing purposes. We show students how to approach all sources with a questioning eye, to assess source materials critically, not just to find them and use them. Like all handbooks, we give detailed instruction in quoting, paraphrasing, and summarizing; unlike others, however, we also show students how to discover patterns in the many discrete bits of data they find. With step-by-step guidelines in synthesizing data and drawing inferences, we help them to use their research in support of their own written arguments.

Focus on student writing throughout. To illustrate the points made throughout this text, we have drawn most of our examples and exercises from the 20,000 essays gathered for our research. These are not handy-dandy examples manufactured by textbook authors but illustrations of conventions and error patterns as they really exist in student writing today. As such, these examples reflect the writing needs our students have as well as their interests. In addition, we have included seven full-length student essays.

A link with the most commonly studied essays. We have also drawn on examples from professional writing. And since we know that many of you use a handbook along with a reader, we have deliberately taken these from the essays most often included in composition readers—that is, from the essays your students are likely to be reading as they use this handbook. Many of these examples serve as models for imitation, as prompts for writing, or as occasion for readerly response. Such passages will of course serve as memorable examples; more important, however, they will provide the larger rhetorical context so often missing in most other handbooks. An index of authors and titles lists all the professional examples included in this book.

The greatest possible accessibility. As we worked on this book, we spoke with hundreds of colleagues about handbooks. Among the many concerns we found was one very common one—that a handbook must be accessible, that it has to be easy to get in and out of quickly. In then studying other handbooks, we noted that all put grammar, punctuation, and mechanics in easily accessible form, with many numbered headings, but that in no handbook were the rhetorical chapters as easy to use. Chapters on the writing process and on specific writing assignments were not set up to be dipped into quickly; they had to be read like chapters. In an attempt to make the rhetorical chapters in our handbook easier to use, we have deliberately added many more headings and put much of the information in list form. Many are in the form of questions, which we hope will guide students in making necessary rhetorical choices. Our goal here is for users of this book to be able to use it easily and quickly. Our greatest hope is that our readers will spend less time with our text and, as a result, have more time to contemplate their own.

Practical, helpful ancillary materials. Accompanying *The St. Martin's Handbook* are some companion materials we hope will facilitate its use: *The St. Martin's Workbook*, by Lex Runciman; an *Evaluation Manual* with diagnostic and competency tests and writing assignments, by Edward M. White; a *Guide to Teaching Writing*, by Robert Connors and Cheryl Glenn; transparency masters, prepared by

Roger C. Graves; and additional exercises on disk, available for IBM-compatible systems. Especially exciting, we think, is *The St. Martin's Hotline*, a complimentary "pop-up" reference system available for both IBM-compatible and Macintosh systems. The handbook is available in both the student edition and an *Annotated Instructor's Edition*, prepared by Cheryl Glenn, Roger C. Graves, R. Gerald Nelms, and Dennis Quon, that includes practical and interesting information about using the handbook and about teaching writing.

Acknowledgments

We have been aided by an amazingly imaginative team. *The St. Martin's Handbook* has been a collaborative effort in the best and richest sense of the word. We are particularly indebted to Nancy Perry and Marilyn Moller of St. Martin's Press. From the beginning, Nancy supported both the research that underlies this book and our efforts to translate that research into a useful tool for instructors and students. Marilyn, whose efforts as developmental editor on this project have been above and beyond the call of any duty we have ever known, has earned our deep respect and gratitude. Jean Smith believed in this project, and has made the really extraordinary efforts made by St. Martin's on our behalf possible. Virginia Biggar, Kay Fleming, Alicia Mahaney, Susan Manning, Kim Richardson, Richard Steins, and Lynne Williams at St. Martin's all provided indispensable help at every stage. And Denise Quirk has worked so hard and on so many aspects of this project that we simply could not have gotten along without her. In addition, John Elliott, Marcia Muth, and Tyler Wasson provided editorial help on the original manuscripts that often emerged from their careful surgery transformed.

We are also more than grateful to the many instructors and students whose work we have depended on. First of all we wish to thank the many instructors who sent in essays:

Alabama: Rosemary M. Canfield, Troy State University; Charles R. Craig, Alabama State University; Stephen Glosecki, University of Alabama at Birmingham; Peggy Jolly, University of Alabama at Birmingham; Kris Lackey, Auburn University; Jane Latture, Jefferson State Junior College; Ronald E. Smith, University of North Alabama; *Arizona:* Delmar Kehl, Arizona State University; Vera Kielsky, Arizona State University; Lisa Miller, Phoenix College; Beth Stiefel, Northern Arizona University; *Arkansas:* Joyce Dempsey, Arkansas Technological University; *California:* Victoria Babcock, University of

California at Santa Barbara; Gwen Brewer, California State University at Northridge; Gary Brown, San Diego State University; Stanford Carlson, Grossmont College; Dennis Chaldecot, California State University at San Jose; Elena J. Cleef, University of California at Santa Barbara; Michael P. Collings, Pepperdine University; David Dickson, Sierra College; Antoinette Empringham, El Camino College; Diane Goodwin, College of San Mateo; Helen Gordon, Bakersfield College; W. Greenstein, Long Beach City College; Susan K. Hahn, University of California at Santa Barbara; Sherri Hallgren, University of California at Berkeley; Linda Humphrey, Citrus Community College; Malcolm Kiniry, University of California at Los Angeles; Michael Kramer, University of California at Davis; Robert E. Lend, University of California at Irvine; Arlene Lighthall, Miracosta College; Annette P. Lynch, Mount San Antonio College; Elizabeth Macey, Santa Ana College; Bruce McIver, University of California at Santa Barbara; David Madden, California State University at Sacramento; Charlotte Montandon, San Jose City College; Richard L. Moore, San Joaquin Delta College; Lawrence Parker, Mount San Antonio College; MeMe Riordan, City College of San Francisco; Ann Rothschild, University of California at Davis; Rodney Simard, California State College at Bakersfield; Mark Snowhite, Crafton Hills College; Cheryl Walker, Scripps College; Katherine Watson, Orange Coast College; Nancy Watts, Cuesta College; Jacqueline Webber, American River College; Leonard Weiss, College of Marin; *Colorado:* Edward A. Kearns, University of Northern Colorado; Jeane Luere, University of Northern Colorado; *Connecticut:* Srilekha Bell, University of New Haven; Gerald S. Coulter, Central Connecticut State University; Anne Greene, Wesleyan University; Lyda E. Lapalomara, South Connecticut State University; Mikail M. McIntosh, University of Connecticut; Mariann Russell, Sacred Heart University, David Sonstroem, University of Connecticut; *District of Columbia:* Judith Nembhard, Howard University; *Florida:* Sharon Cleland, Florida Junior College at Kent; Roger Drury, University of Florida; Dorothy P. Harris, Okaloosa-Walton Junior College; Lynn Hicks, Central Florida Community College; Mary Sue Koeppel, Florida Community College-South; Marcelle C. Lovett, University of North Florida; James F. O'Neil, Edison Community College; Hugh G. Paschal, Hillsborough Community College; April E. Riley, University of Florida; Steve Rubin, University of South Florida; Leora Schermerhorn, Seminole Community College; Gerald Schiffhorst, University of Central Florida; Jewell Sterling, Palm Beach Junior College; Carlos Valdes, University of Florida; *Georgia:* William Dodd, Augusta College; Tony Grooms, Macon Junior College; Patricia B. Handley, Macon Junior College; Donna Jones, Georgia Southern College; Marguerite P. Murphy, Georgia State University; Huey Owings, West Georgia College; Joseph J. Popson, Macon Junior College; John Presley, Augusta College; Lorie Roth, Armstrong State College; William R. Thurman, Georgia Southwestern College; *Idaho:* Okey Goode, Lewis-Clark State College; Richard Hannaford, University of Idaho; Gordon

Hinds, Boise State University; George Ives, North Idaho College; Scott Samuelson, Ricks College; *Illinois:* Steven Craig, Illinois State University; Marcia Gealy, Northwestern University; Edwina Jordan, Illinois Central College; Carolyn S. Kropp, Southern Illinois University; J. G. Lidaka, Northern Illinois University; Fred Robbins, Southern Illinois University; *Indiana:* Robert Habich, Ball State University; Jane Haynes, Ball State University; Stephen Heady, Indiana State University; Barry Kroll, Indiana University; John Lowe, Saint Mary's College; Rai Peterson, Ball State University; Mary C. Suttinger, Purdue University at Calumet; Keith Walsh, Indiana University; *Iowa:* Nancy K. Barry, University of Iowa; *Kansas:* Carol Ann Barnes, Kansas State University; James Bridson, University of Kansas; Donna Campbell, University of Kansas; Mary Grace Foret, Johnson County Community College; Patrick Giebler, Colby Community College; Myra Hinman, University of Kansas; Linda Hughes, Washburn University of Topeka; Beth Impson, University of Kansas; Linda Livingston, Dodge City Community College; Fred Terry, University of Kansas; Cheryl Hofstetter Towns, Colby Community College; Thomas Zelman, University of Kansas; *Kentucky:* George Cheatham, Eastern Kentucky University; Lou-Ann Crouther, Western Kentucky University; Katherine Fish, Cumberland College; *Louisiana:* Patricia Bates, Louisiana State University at Shreveport; Sara Burroughs, Northwestern State University of Louisiana; Robert H. Garner, Southern University in New Orleans; William Holditch, University of New Orleans; David H. Jackson, Centenary College; John Fleming McClelland, Northeast Louisiana University; Adelaide McGinnis, Delgado Community College; Mary Sue Ply, Southeastern Louisiana University; Ben Rushin, Delgado Community College; *Maine:* Alan Lindsay, University of Maine at Orono; *Maryland:* Jane Donawerth, University of Maryland; Jade Gorman, University of Maryland; Margaret Reid, Morgan State University; Margaret Wolfe, Anne Arundel Community College; *Massachusetts:* Priscilla Bellairs, Northern Essex Community College; Lila Chalpin, Massachusetts College of Art; James Dean, Tufts University; Patsy MacDonald, Northeastern University, Patricia Skarda, Smith College; *Michigan:* Alice Forer, University of Michigan at Flint; James C. Hines, Mott Community College; Geraldine Jacobs, Jackson Community College; Rowena Jones, Northern Michigan University; J. L. McDonald, University of Detroit; Robert Merkel, Monroe County Community College; Leslie Prast, Delta College; Kathleen Rout, Michigan State University; Maureen P. Taylor, Kalamazoo Valley Community College; *Minnesota:* Phyllis Ballata, Lakewood Community College; Gail Jardine, Rochester Community College; David L. Wee, Saint Olaf College; *Mississippi:* Faye Angelo, Hinds Junior College; De Lois Gatis, Northeast Mississippi Junior College; Tommy Ray, University of Mississippi; *Missouri:* Norma Bagnall, Missouri Western State College; Sally Fitzgerald, University of Missouri at St. Louis; Paul Jones, Northwest Missouri State University; Elizabeth Otten, Northeast Missouri State University; Pearl Saunders, St. Louis Community

College; David Slater, Northwest Missouri State University; **Montana:** Rachel Schaffer, Eastern Montana College; **Nebraska:** Jean Ferguson, University of Nebraska at Lincoln; Marge Holland, Wayne State College; **Nevada:** Terese Brychta, Truckee Meadows Community College; **New Hampshire:** W.C. Spengemann, Dartmouth College; **New Jersey:** Naomi Given, Middlesex County College; Harlan Hamilton, Jersey City State College; Albert Romano, Hudson County Community College; **New York:** Efrain Acevedo, Cornell University; Donna Allen, Erie Community College; Joyce Benson, Alfred University; Fred Blomgren, Monroe Community College; Diana Bloom, Mercy College; Ren Draya, Borough of Manhattan Community College, CUNY; Mary Erler, Fordham University; Richard Fabrizio, Pace University; W. Speed Hill, Lehman College, CUNY; Mary Anne Hutchinson, Utica College; Carol Kushner, Onondaga Community College; Carol Kusner, SUNY at Cortland; Morgan Jones, SUNY at New Paltz; Milton Levy, Kingsborough Community College, CUNY; Joyce Maggio, Suffolk County Community College; Carolyn McGrath, SUNY at Stony Brook; Rosa Lou Novi, SUNY at New Paltz; Astrid M. O'Brien, Fordham University at Lincoln Center; April Selly, College of St. Rose; Ilene Singh, College of Staten Island, CUNY; Karyn Sproles, SUNY at Buffalo; John Stinson, SUNY at Fredonia; Eve Maria Stwertka, SUNY at Farmingdale; Maeruth P. Wilson, SUNY at Buffalo; **North Carolina:** Mark Branson, Davidson County Community College; Jean Chase, Central Piedmont Community College; James Cuthbertson, Johnson C. Smith University; John Ebbs, East Carolina University; Terry J. Frazier, University of North Carolina at Charlotte; Kelly Griffith, University of North Carolina at Greensboro; Jay Jacoby, University of North Carolina at Charlotte; Rebecca W. Nail, Winston-Salem State University; Theresa Norman, Western Carolina University; Mary F. Stough, Davidson College; Mark Thomas, University of North Carolina; **Ohio:** Jutta Bendremer, University of Akron; Rosa I. Bhakuni, University of Akron; Leslie F. Chard, University of Cincinnati; Joyce R. Durham, University of Dayton; Bruce L. Edwards, Bowling Green State University; Jeffrey Hogeman, University of Cincinnati; Ann K. Jordan, University of Cincinnati, Clermont College; Barbara Langheim, University of Cincinnati; Christine H. Lavik, Lakeland Community College; Ulle Lewes, Ohio Wesleyan University; Nancy Kammer Peters, University of Cincinnati; William Pratt, Miami University; Deborah Roberts, University of Cincinnati; Janet Samuelson, University of Akron; Michael Shea, Miami University; Jacquie Skrzypiec, University of Akron; **Oklahoma:** Stanley Cameron, East Central University; Emily Dial-Driver, Rogers State University; Betty Gonul, East Central University; **Oregon:** Marna Broekhoff, University of Oregon; Warren Howe, Mountain Community College; John Miller, Umpqua Community College; Baxter Wilson, Portland State University; **Pennsylvania:** Ted Atkinson, Edinboro University of Pennsylvania; Rosemarie A. Battaglia, Kutztown University; William W. Betts, Indiana University of Pennsylvania; Terry P. Caesar, Clarion University of Pennsylvania; J. C. Condravy, Slippery Rock University; Elizabeth Curry, Slippery Rock University; Colleen Lamos, University of Pennsylvania; George Mower, Community College of Allegheny County; Gerald Siegel, York College of Pennsylvania; *Rhode Island:* David Hoch, Rhode Island College; Ira Schaeffer, Community College of Rhode Island; *South Carolina:* Ellen Arl, University of South Carolina at Sumter; Hallman B. Bryant, Clemson University; Bonnie Devet, University of South Carolina at Columbia; Larisa Garrison, Clemson University; Linda S. Schwartz, University of South Carolina-Coastal Carolina College; Sharon E. Spangler, Clemson University; Tom Waldrep, University of South Carolina at Columbia; Harriet S. Williams, University of South Carolina at Columbia; Laura Zaidman, University of South Carolina at Sumter; *South Dakota:* Ruth Foreman, South Dakota State University; John Taylor, South Dakota State University; *Tennessee:* Betty Hawkins, Volunteer State Community College; Charles H. Long, Memphis State University; Douglas Morris, David Lipscomb College; John Paine, Belmont College; Sue Palmer, Austin Peay State University; Stephen Prewitt, David Lipscomb College; David Worley, Lincoln Memorial University; Sally Young, University of Tennessee at Chattanooga; *Texas:* Bruce C. Autry, Lamar University; Suzanne Blaw, Richland College; Cleo Congrady, Alvin Community College; Barbara Craig, Del Mar College; Allen Billy Crider, Alvin Community College; Carl Fowler, Amarillo College; Charles Gongre, Lamar University; Perry E. Gragg, Angelo State University; Debra Hower, Texas A & M University; Glenda Hicks, Midland College; Henry Hutchings, Lamar University; Reba Kochersperger, North Harris County College; Joyce McEwing, Texas Southern University; Mary Jean Northcut, Richland College; Fred A. Rodewald, Stephen F. Austin State University; Vivian Rudisill, San Antonio College; Anne Sandel, Wharton County Junior College; Michael C. Sotterwhite, Texas Tech University; Lana White; West Texas State University; Terry Wiggs, Southwest Texas State University; Robert M. Wren, University of Houston; *Utah:* Kate Begnal, Utah State University; Kathryn Fitzgerald, University of Utah; Marne Isakson, Utah Technical College at Orem; Joyce Kinkead, Utah State University; Jan Ugan, Utah State University; *Vermont:* Francine Page, St. Michael's College; Cameron Thrull, University of Vermont; Arthur Tishman, University of Vermont; Rhoda Yerburgh, Vermont College; *Virginia:* Mary Balazs, Virginia Military Institute; Margaret Brandon, Thomas Nelson Community College; Elizabeth S. Byers, Virginia Polytechnic Institute and State University; John Lee, James Madison University; Stan Poole, University of Virginia; Michael Smith, Virginia Polytechnic Institute and State University; *Washington:* Debbie Kinerk, Tacoma Community College; Chris Kellett, University of Washington; Denis Thomas, Central Washington University; Jeff Wagnitz, Grays Harbor College; Carl Waluconis, Bellevue Community College; *West Virginia:* Stephen Warren, Fairmont State College; *Wisconsin:* Sue Beckham, University of Wisconsin at

Stout; James Plath, University of Wisconsin at Milwaukee; Jean P. Rumsey, University of Wisconsin at Stevens Point; Katherine White, University of Wisconsin at Stevens Point.

We also wish to thank the following colleagues who participated in focus groups held in the planning stages of this book: Joy Allameh, Eastern Kentucky University; Chris Burnham, New Mexico State University; Michael Cohen, Eastern Kentucky University; Don Richard Cox, University of Tennessee; Corrine Dale, Belmont College; Joyce Durham, University of Dayton; James David Earnest, Murray State University; Thomas L. Erskine, Salisbury State College; George D. Gopen, Duke University; Patricia H. Graves, Georgia State University; Edward Lotto, Lehigh University; Timothy P. Martin, Rutgers University; Mary Ellen Pitts, Memphis State University; Janet Samuelson, University of Akron; Barbara Sowders, Eastern Kentucky University. For their time and their many helpful suggestions we are grateful. Among our own students, Melissa Bloise, Laura Brannon, Leah Clendening, Amy Dierst, Elizabeth Lyon, Julie Slater, Colleen Starkey, and Tracy Vezdos all provided essays and other writing examples. Their good work is reflected in many, many pages of this book.

And we are especially appreciative of the many colleagues who painstakingly reviewed our manuscript and shared their thoughts on our efforts and on handbooks in general. Their incisive comments, queries, criticisms, and suggestions have improved this book immeasurably:

    John Algeo, University of Georgia
    Rise Axelrod, California State University at San Bernardino
    David Bartholomae, University of Pittsburgh
    Ray Brebach, Drexel University
    Douglas Brent, University of Calgary
    Monika Brown, Pembroke State University
    Barbara Carson, University of Georgia
    Charles Cooper, University of California at San Diego
    Edward P. J. Corbett, Ohio State University
    Cornelius Cronin, Louisiana State University
    Carol David, Iowa State University
    Angus Dunston, University of California at Santa Barbara
    Joyce Durham, University of Dayton
    Lisa Ede, Oregon State University
    Thomas Gaston, Purdue University
    Helen Gilbart, St. Petersburg Junior College

Jennifer Ginn, North Carolina State University at Raleigh
Patricia H. Graves, Georgia State University
Franklin Horowitz, Teachers College, Columbia University
Carl Klaus, University of Iowa
Edward Kline, University of Notre Dame
Janice Lauer, Purdue University
Edward Lotto, Lehigh University
David Mair, University of Oklahoma
Charles Meyer, University of Massachusetts at Boston
Michael Moran, University of Georgia
Patricia Murray, DePaul University
Lee Odell, Rensselaer Polytechnic Institute
MeMe Riordan, City College of San Francisco
Mike Rose, University of California at Los Angeles
Jane Stanhope, American University
Laura Stokes, University of California at Davis
William J. Vande Kopple, Calvin College
Harold Veeser, Wichita State University
Suellyn Winkle, Santa Fe Community College
Linda Woodson, University of Texas at San Antonio
Richard Zbaracki, Iowa State University

Finally, we are indebted to some special friends and colleagues: Charles Cooper, who provided invaluable advice about conducting the research; Mike Rose, who offered support and encouragement throughout; Douglas Brent, whose advice on research writing helped us immensely, Melinda Bako, Beverly Bruck, Sabina Foote, Heather Graves, Sue Lape, Jaime Mejia, Roxanne Mountford, Jon Olson, Dori Stratton, Kimberly Town, and Kelly Vezdos, who provided additional research, helped with assorted and sundry clerical tasks, and gave us smiles when we most needed them; the faculty and graduate students at Ohio State who helped us to organize and analyze the 3,000-paper sample—in particular, David Frantz, Murray Beja, and Michael Rupright; and, always, Lisa Ede, our critical reader and good friend extraordinaire.

We could go on and on and on, for we are fortunate (beyond our wildest dreams, as our mentor Ed Corbett would say) to be part of a true scholarly and academic community, one characterized by compassion, by commitment to students, by a celebration of learning. We are grateful to be among you.

Andrea Lunsford
Robert Connors

A Note to Students

Our goal in writing *The St. Martin's Handbook* has been to produce a book that will guide you to becoming competent and compelling writers, a book that you can use easily and efficiently throughout your college years.

We began work five years ago by examining a scientifically selected sample of more than 20,000 essays written by students from all areas of the country—students probably pretty much like you. We discovered the kinds of writing errors you are most likely to make and studied the twenty most common error patterns in detail. Throughout this book you will find guidance on those patterns. You will find help first of all in the chapter immediately following, one we call "Learning from Your Errors." This chapter will help you to analyze your own error patterns and especially to recognize, analyze, and overcome any of the twenty most common ones in your own writing.

Throughout this text, we ask that you look at errors in the context of your own writing, that you become accustomed to carefully analyzing your own prose. In almost every chapter, we will not only provide explanations and opportunity for practice, but also we will be asking you to apply the principles presented directly to your own writing. If you follow our directions, they will guide you in becoming a systematic self-critic—and a stronger writer. And since writing and reading in many ways go hand in hand, many chapters will also offer you a chance to read with an eye for various logical or stylistic or conventional aspects of writing, often in the work of some of the finest American and English writers. Sometimes you will be asked to try to imitate their sentences. As your writing improves, so will your reading.

Chapters 1–5 will guide you through the process of expository and argumentative essays—from your first choice of a topic to your final typed essay. Chapters 6–36 provide thorough discussion of writing conventions—grammar, punctuation, and mechanics. These chapters provide examples and practice to guide you in mastering such conventions and in learning to use them appropriately and effectively.

Next come chapters that will help you understand, carry out, and use research in your writing; examine the writing of your chosen discipline; and practice taking essay examinations or producing job application letters and résumés.

This book has been designed to make its information as easy as possible to find and use. You can find what you are looking for by consulting the table of contents, the subject index, or the index of authors and titles. Once you find the correct chapter, you can skim the many headings. If your instructor uses our codes in marking your essays, you can find the code symbols at the top of each page. Even the exercises can be "used" easily, for we include at the end of the book answers to many of them, to allow you to check your understanding as you work.

Because we assume you will be consulting this book regularly when you are revising your drafts, we wish to call to your attention the many sections designed to help you *check* various elements and structures. Especially notable are guidelines to help you to check for—and revise—each of the twenty most common error patterns; to make these easy to find, we have marked them with a small red chevron: ➤

For those who compose on a computer, we offer the complimentary *St. Martin's Hotline*, a "pop-up" reference system available for IBM-compatible and Macintosh systems.

Finally, we'd like to call your attention to a small feature you might find valuable, a writing log. We urge you to keep a log as a repository of materials from and for your own writing—notable anecdotes, exemplary phrases, memorable images, troublesome words or structures. Procedures for keeping a log are described in 1c, and exercises throughout this text suggest materials to add to it. Keeping a log can help you to examine and contemplate your own writing.

We hope that this book will prove to be a useful reference. But in the long run, a book can be only a guide. You are the one who will put such guidance into practice, as you work to become a precise, a powerful, and a persuasive writer. Why not get started on achieving that goal right now?

Andrea Lunsford
Robert Connors

Contents

Part VII
UNDERSTANDING MECHANICAL CONVENTIONS   483

Part IX
ACADEMIC WRITING   637

Learning from Your Errors

Many people who are not instructors or students tend to think of "correctness" in writing as an absolute. There are hard and fast "rules," they believe, and if all of those rules are followed, correct writing will result. Errors in writing result from not following these "rules," which are handed down from time immemorial and set out in grammar books and handbooks like this one. Learning to write, for these people, is learning the rules.

Instructors and students know different. They know that there are "rules," all right, but that the rules change all the time. "Is it okay to use *I* in essays for this class?" asks one student. "My high school teacher wouldn't let us." "Will more than one comma splice flunk an essay?" asks another. "Must I have three paragraphs on each page?" asks a third. These students know that rules clearly exist, but that they are part of a social transaction between writers and readers that is always shifting and thus needs constantly to be explored.

Research has shown how much that transaction has changed in the last century alone. Mechanical and grammatical questions that no longer concern us at all used to be perceived as extremely important. In the late nineteenth century, for instance, instructors at Harvard told us that the most serious writing problem their students had was an inability to distinguish between the proper uses of *shall* and *will*. Similarly, split infinitives seemed to many instructors of the 1950s a very serious problem, but ever since the starship *Enterprise* set out "to boldly go" where no one has gone before, split infinitives have wrinkled fewer brows.

These examples of shifting standards are not meant to suggest that there is no such thing as "correctness" in writing—only that correctness always depends on some context. Correctness is not so much a question of absolute right or wrong as a question of how a writer is perceived by an audience. As writers, we are all judged by the words we put on the page. We all want to be regarded as competent and careful, and formal errors in our writing work against that impression. As one very famous writing instructor put it, errors make unintentional demands on readers, drawing their attention to something from which they will gain no mental reward.* The world judges us by our mastery of the conventions we have agreed to use, and we all know it. As Robert Frost once said of poetry, trying to write without honoring the conventions and agreed-upon rules is like playing tennis without a net.

So fluency in writing means having something to say and saying it in the way most appropriate to a given audience and context. One assumption this book makes is that you already have important things to say and that as you learn more and more about the subjects you study in college, you will have more and more to say. A second assumption is that you want to master the conventions used in academic writing. Since you already know the vast majority of these conventions, the most efficient way to proceed is to focus on those conventions that are still unfamiliar or puzzling. Achieving this practical focus means identifying, analyzing, and overcoming *patterns of conventional error* in your writing.

Almost all writing problems follow a pattern. If you have ever gotten back an assignment covered with red marks, the task of figuring out how to solve all the problems no doubt seemed somewhat daunting. Each mark seemed to point to a separate error, and there were dozens of them. But if rather than considering each mark separately you try to fit them together into patterns, you will nearly always find one or two major kinds of errors. From, say, twenty different problems, you have cut your job down to only a few.

Make the effort, then, to take control of your own writing by seeking out your own patterns of error and learning from them. This task does not mean becoming obsessed with errors to the exclusion of everything else in your writing. A perfectly correct essay is, after all, a limited and limiting goal. You want to aim for a perfectly persuasive and enlightening essay—that also happens to be correct.

You should, in fact, *not* concern yourself with correctness at every stage of writing. Concentrating on errors during planning or drafting can inhibit you from writing freely. Instead, worry about errors

---

* Mina P. Shaughnessy, *Errors & Expectations* (New York: Oxford UP, 1977).

when you revise and edit. If your instructor comments on your early drafts, study them to identify patterns you follow.

Keep a record of your error patterns, perhaps in a writing log. If you find that you tend to leave off verb endings, for example, keep a list of the endings that have given you trouble; and check your drafts against that list as you proofread. Concentrate on one error pattern at a time. Dealing with errors systematically in this way is the best possible way of conquering them once and for all.

This handbook will help you take control of those writing conventions that give you trouble. Research conducted for this book has revealed much about the error patterns typical of college students today, and this chapter addresses those errors. Analysis of a scientifically determined sample taken from more than 20,000 freshman and sophomore essays from around the United States has shown which errors you are most likely to make—and which ones your instructor is most likely to mark. From this analysis comes some very interesting determinations about student writing, and especially about student errors.

First, spelling errors are by far the most common, by a factor of more than three to one. Because they are so plentiful, the words found to be most often misspelled are given in a separate list, which you can find in Chapter 22. Second, instructors do not always mark all errors; some error patterns clearly strike them as more serious than others. Whether your instructor comments on one of your writing problems in a particular assignment will depend on his or her judgment about how serious it is and what you should be dealing with at the time. Finally, not all errors are even seen as errors. In fact, some of the patterns identified in the research are considered errors by some instructors but stylistic options by others. This finding confirms the belief that "correctness" is really defined by a transaction between readers and writers. This book describes the nature of this transaction, noting those areas where agreement is widespread and others where it is not. You, of course, are a part of the transaction. As a writer, you will constantly need to consider the expectations of your readers and to make decisions about the appropriateness of certain writing conventions. For much of your college writing, your primary reader will be your instructor, and so if ever you are uncertain about whether something is appropriate (or, correct), you should take the opportunity to discuss it with him or her.

Here, in order of occurrence, are the twenty most common error patterns among college students in the late 1980s.

1. Missing comma after an introductory element
2. Vague pronoun reference
3. Missing comma in a compound sentence
4. Wrong word
5. Missing comma(s) with a nonrestrictive element
6. Wrong or missing verb ending
7. Wrong or missing preposition
8. Comma splice
9. Missing or misplaced possessive apostrophe
10. Unnecessary shift in tense
11. Unnecessary shift in pronoun
12. Sentence fragment
13. Wrong tense or verb form
14. Lack of agreement between subject and verb
15. Missing comma in a series
16. Lack of agreement between pronoun and antecedent
17. Unnecessary comma(s) with a restrictive element
18. Fused sentence
19. Dangling or misplaced modifier
20. *Its* / *it's* confusion

Statistically, these twenty are the errors most likely to cause you trouble. A brief explanation and examples of each one are given in this chapter, and each error pattern is cross-referenced to at least one place elsewhere in this book where you can find more detail or additional examples.

▌1. Missing comma after an introductory element

When a sentence opens with an introductory word, phrase, or clause, readers usually need a small pause between the introductory element and the main part of the sentence. Such a pause is most often signaled by a comma.

INTRODUCTORY WORD

Frankly⌃we were baffled by the committee's decision.

INTRODUCTORY PHRASE

In fact, the Philippines consist of more than eight thousand islands.

To tell the truth, I never have liked the Mets.

Because of its isolation in a rural area surrounded by mountains, Crawford Notch doesn't get many visitors.

INTRODUCTORY CLAUSE

Even though I provided detailed advice for revising, his draft became only worse.

Short introductory elements do not always need a comma. The test is whether the sentence can be easily understood without one. The following sentence, for example, would at first be misunderstood if it did not have a comma—readers would think the introductory phrase was *In German nouns,* rather than *In German.* The best advice is that you will rarely be wrong to add a comma after an introductory element.

In German, nouns are always capitalized.

➤ For guidelines on checking for commas after introductory elements, see page 425. For more on commas and introductory elements in general, see 6c, 15c, 20b, and 27a.

▌ 2. Vague pronoun reference

A pronoun like *he, she, it, they, this, that,* or *which* should refer clearly to a specific word (or words) elsewhere in the sentence or in a previous sentence. When readers cannot tell for sure who or what the pronoun refers to, the reference is said to be vague. There are two common kinds of vague pronoun reference. The first occurs when there is more than one word that the pronoun might refer to; the second, when the reference is to a word that is implied but not explicitly stated.

POSSIBLE REFERENCE TO MORE THAN ONE WORD

Before Mary Grace physically and verbally assaulted Mrs. Turpin, ~~she~~ *the latter*

was a judgmental woman who created her own ranking system of people

and used it to justify her self-proclaimed superiority.

Transmitting radio signals by satellite is a way of overcoming the problem

of scarce airwaves and limiting how ~~they~~ *the airwaves* are used.

REFERENCE IMPLIED BUT NOT STATED

The troopers burned an Indian camp as a result of the earlier attack.
This *destruction of the camp* was the cause of the war.

They believe that a zygote, an egg at the moment of fertilization, is as

deserving of protection as the born human being, but ~~it~~ *such an assertion* is totally un-

provable scientifically.

➤ For guidelines on checking for vague pronoun reference, see page
244. For more on pronoun reference, see Chapter 11.

▋3. Missing comma in a compound sentence

A compound sentence is made up of two (or more) parts that
could each function as an independent sentence. These parts may be
linked by either a semicolon or a coordinating conjunction (*and, but,
so, yet, nor, or, for*). When a conjunction is used, a comma should
usually be placed before it to indicate a pause between the two thoughts.

The words may sound simple, but "I do" means a complex commitment

for life.

We wish dreamily upon a star, and then we look down to see what we have stepped in.

In *very* short sentences, this use of the comma is optional if the sentence can be easily understood without it. The following sentence, for example, would be misunderstood if it did not have a comma—readers would think at first that Meredith was wearing her feet. The best advice is to use the comma before the coordinating conjunction, since it will always be correct.

Meredith wore jeans, and her feet were bare.

➤ For guidelines on checking for commas in compound sentences, see page 427. For further discussion and examples, see 6d1 and 27b.

■ 4. Wrong word

"Wrong word" errors range from simple lack of proofreading, like using *should* for *would*, to mistakes in basic word meaning, like using *prevaricate* when you mean *procrastinate*, to mistakes in shades of meaning, like using *sedate* when you mean *sedentary*. Many errors marked "wrong word" are *homonyms*, words that are pronounced alike but spelled differently, like *their* and *there*.

A knowledge of computers is ~~inherent~~ *assumed* in this office.

Mark noticed the ~~stench~~ *fragrance* of roses as he entered the room.

Paradise Lost contains many ~~illusions~~ *allusions* to classical mythology.

➤ For guidelines on checking a draft for wrong words, see page 397. For additional, more detailed information about choosing the right word for your meaning, see 22a, 23c2, and 25b.

■ 5. Missing comma(s) with a nonrestrictive element

A nonrestrictive element is a word, phrase, or clause that gives additional information about the preceding part of the sentence but does not restrict or limit the meaning of that part. A nonrestrictive element is not essential to the sentence; it can be deleted without changing the sentence's basic meaning. To indicate that it is not essential, it is always set off from the rest of the sentence with a comma before it and, if it is in the middle of the sentence, after it as well.

Marina‚who was the president of the club‚was first to speak.

Louis was forced to call a session of the Estates General‚which had not

met for 175 years.

The bottom of the pond was covered with soft brown clay‚a natural base

for a good swimming hole.

➤ For guidelines on checking for commas with nonrestrictive elements, see page 431. For additional explanation, see 27c.

▌ 6. Wrong or missing verb ending

The verb endings -s or (-es) and -ed (or -d) are important markers in standard edited English. It is easy to forget these endings in writing because they are not always pronounced clearly when spoken. In addition, some dialects do not use the -s ending in the same way as standard edited English.

uses
Eliot use feline imagery throughout the poem.

I runs a mile every morning before breakfast.

dropped
The United States drop two atomic bombs on Japan in 1945.

imagined
Nobody imagine he would actually become president.

An -s (or -es) ending must be added to a present-tense verb whose subject is a singular noun; the personal pronouns *he, she,* or *it*; and most indefinite pronouns (such as *anyone, each, everybody, nobody, nothing, someone*). The ending is not added to a verb whose subject is a plural noun; the personal pronouns *I, you, we,* or *they*; and indefinite pronouns that have a plural meaning (such as *both or few*). The past-tense and past-participle forms of most verbs must end in -ed (or -d).

➤ For guidelines on checking for verb endings, see pages 189 and 192. For more on verb endings, see pages 187–190, 8b, 8c, and 9a.

∎ 7. Wrong or missing preposition

Many words in English are regularly used with a particular preposition to express a particular meaning; for example, we *agree to* a proposal, *agree with* another person, and *agree on* a price for something. Using the wrong preposition in such expressions is a common error. Because most prepositions are so short and are not stressed or pronounced clearly in speech, they are also often left out accidentally in writing.

The bus committee is trying to set a schedule that will meet the needs

of most people who rely ~~in~~ *on* public transportation.

Nixon compared the United States ~~with~~ *to* a "pitiful, helpless giant."

She received a dishonorable discharge for refusing to comply ~~to~~ *with* army

regulations.

In his moral blindness Gloucester is similar ~~with~~ *to* Lear.

Dennis found the shaving soap *in* the medicine cabinet.

➤ For guidelines on checking a draft for wrong or missing prepositions, see page 288. For additional information about choosing the correct preposition, see 6b6.

∎ 8. Comma splice

A comma splice occurs when two or more clauses that could each stand alone as a sentence are written with only a comma between them. Such clauses must be either clearly separated by a punctuation mark stronger than a comma—a period or semicolon—or clearly connected with a word like *and* or *although*, or else the ideas they state should be combined into one clause.

Westward migration had passed Wyoming by *;* even the discovery of gold

in nearby Montana failed to attract settlers.

I was strongly attracted to her, *for* she had special qualities.

Having
~~They always had~~ roast beef for Thanksgiving / ~~this~~ was one of their family traditions.

➤ For guidelines on checking for comma splices, see page 257. For additional information about ways to avoid or revise comma splices, see Chapter 13.

◼ 9. Missing or misplaced possessive apostrophe

To show that one thing belongs to another, either an apostrophe and an -s or an apostrophe alone is added to the word representing the thing that possesses the other. An apostrophe and -s are used for singular nouns (words that refer to one thing, such as *leader* or *Chicago*); for indefinite pronouns (words like *anybody, everyone, nobody, somebody*); and for plural nouns (words referring to more than one thing that do not end in -s, such as *men* and *women*). For plural nouns ending in -s, such as *creatures* or *fathers*, only the apostrophe is used.

child's
Over-ambitious parents can be very harmful to a ~~childs~~ well-being.
Yankees'
Ron Guidry has been one of the ~~Yankees~~ most electrifying pitchers.

➤ For guidelines on checking for possessive apostrophes, see page 458. For additional, more detailed information on use of the apostrophe to indicate possession, see page 175 and 30a.

◼ 10. Unnecessary shift in tense

An unnecessary shift in tense occurs when the verbs in a sentence or passage shift for no reason from one time period to another, such as from past to present or from present to future. Such tense shifts confuse the reader, who must guess which tense is the right one.

cries
Joy always laughs until she ~~cried~~ at that episode of *Dynasty*.
slipped   Fell
Lucy was watching the great blue heron take off when she ~~slips~~ and ~~falls~~ into the swamp.

Each team of detectives is assigned to three or four cases at a time. They ~~will~~ investigate only those leads that seem most promising.

The representative had begun his speech when a young man in blue jeans ran up to the podium. He ~~shoves~~ *shoved* a shaving-cream pie in the speaker's face.

➤ For guidelines on checking for unnecessary shifts in tense, see page 248. For more on shifting tenses, see 12a, and on using verb tenses in sequences, see 8g.

∎ 11. Unnecessary shift in pronoun

An unnecessary pronoun shift occurs when a writer who has been using one kind of pronoun to refer to someone or something shifts to another for no reason. The most common shift in pronoun is from *one* to *you* or *I*. This shift often results from an attempt at a more formal level of diction, which is hard to maintain when it is not completely natural.

When one first sees a painting by Georgia O'Keeffe, ~~you are~~ *one is* impressed by a sense of power and stillness.

If we had known about the ozone layer, ~~you~~ *we* could have banned aerosol sprays years ago.

➤ For guidelines on checking a draft for unnecessary pronoun shifts, see page 251. For additional information about shifts in pronouns, see 12d.

∎ 12. Sentence fragment

A sentence fragment is a part of a sentence that is written as if it were a whole sentence, with a capital letter at the beginning and a period, question mark, or exclamation point. A fragment lacks one or both of the two essential parts of a sentence, a subject and a complete verb; or else it begins with a subordinating word, which means that the idea it expresses depends for its meaning on another sentence.

LACKING SUBJECT

Marie Antoinette spent huge sums of money on herself and her favorites. *Her extravagance helped*
~~Helped~~ to bring on the French Revolution.

LACKING COMPLETE VERB

The old aluminum boat *was* sitting on its trailer.

BEGINNING WITH SUBORDINATING WORD

We returned to the drugstore, *where* ~~Where~~ we waited for the rest of the gang.

➤ For guidelines on checking for sentence fragments, see page 266. For additional, more detailed information on sentence fragments, see Chapter 14.

▌13. Wrong tense or verb form

Errors that are marked as being the wrong tense or verb form include using a verb that does not indicate clearly that the action or condition it expresses is (or was or will be) completed—for example, using *walked* instead of *had walked* or *will go* instead of *will have gone*. In some dialects of English, the verbs *be* and *have* are used in ways that are not used by most other native speakers of the language; these uses may also be labeled as the wrong verb form. Finally, many errors of this kind occur with verbs whose basic forms for showing past time or a completed action or condition do not follow the regular pattern, like *begin, began, begun* and *break, broke, broken*. Errors may occur when a writer confuses the second and third forms or treats these verbs as if they followed the regular pattern—for example, using *beginned* instead of *began* or *have breaked* instead of *have broken*.

Ian was shocked to learn that Joe *had* died only the day before.

The poet *is* ~~be~~ looking at a tree when she ~~have~~ *has* a sudden inspiration.

Florence Griffith Joyner has ~~broke~~ *broken* many track records.

The Greeks ~~builded~~ *built* a wooden horse that the Trojans ~~taked~~ *took* into the city.

➤ For guidelines on checking verb tenses, see page 201. For additional, more detailed information about verb tenses and forms, see 6b1, Chapter 8, and 9a–9i.

▌ 14. Lack of agreement between subject and verb

A subject and verb must agree, or match. In many cases the verb must take a different form depending on whether the subject is singular (one) or plural (more than one): *The old man is angry and stamps into the house* but *The old men are angry and stamp into the house.* Lack of agreement between the subject and verb is often just a matter of leaving the -*s* ending off the verb out of carelessness and failure to proofread, or of following a dialect that does not use this ending (see Errors 6 and 13). Sometimes, however, it results from particular kinds of subjects of sentence constructions.

When other words come between subject and verb, a writer may mistake a noun nearest to the verb for the verb's real subject. In the following sentence, for example, the subject is the singular *part*, not the plural *goals*.

A central part of my life goals ~~have~~ *has* been to go to law school.

Other problems can arise from subjects made up of two or more parts joined by *and* or *or*; subjects like *committee* or *jury*, which can take either singular or plural verb forms depending on whether they are treated as a unit or as a group of individuals; and subjects like *politics* and *measles*, which look plural but are singular in meaning.

My brother and his friend Larry commutes every day from Louisville.

The committee ~~was~~ *were* taking all the responsibility themselves.

Politics ~~have~~ *has* been defined as "the art of the possible."

Subjects that are pronouns cause problems for many writers. Most indefinite pronouns, like *each, either, neither,* or *one* take singular verb forms. The relative pronouns, *who, which,* or *that* take verbs that agree with the word the pronoun refers to.

Each of the items in these designs ~~coordinate~~ *coordinates* with the others.

Johnson was one of the athletes who ~~was~~ *were* disqualified.

Finally, some problems occur when writers make the verb agree with a word that follows or precedes it rather than with the grammatical subject. In the following sentences, for example, the subjects are *source* and *man.*

His only source of income ~~were~~ *was* his parents.

Behind the curtains ~~stand~~ *stands* an elderly man producing the wizard's effects.

➤ For guidelines on checking for subject-verb agreement, see page 219. For additional, more detailed information about subject-verb agreement, see pages 187–189 and 9a–9i.

▌ 15. Missing comma in a series

A series consists of three or more parallel words, phrases, or clauses that appear consecutively in a sentence. Traditionally, all the items in a series are separated by commas. Many newspapers and magazines do not use a comma before the *and* or *or* between the last two items, and some instructors do not require it. Check your instructor's preference, and be consistent in either using or omitting this comma.

Sharks eat mostly squid, shrimp, crabs, and other fish.

You must learn to talk to the earth, smell it, squeeze it in your hands.

➤ For guidelines on checking a draft for series commas, see page 434. For more on parallel structures in a series, see 19a, or on using commas in a series, see 27d.

16. Lack of agreement between pronoun and antecedent

Most pronouns (words like *I*, *it*, *you*, *him*, *her*, *this*, *themselves*, *someone*, *who*, *which*) are used to restate another word (or words), so that that word does not have to be repeated. The word that the pronoun replaces or stands for is called its antecedent. Pronouns must agree with, or match, their antecedents in gender—for example, using *he* and *him* to replace *Abraham Lincoln* and *she* and *her* to replace *Queen Elizabeth*. They must also agree with their antecedents in referring to either one person or thing (singular) or more than one (plural)—for example, using *it* to replace *a book* and *they* and *them* to replace *fifteen books*.

Most people have few problems with pronoun-antecedent agreement except with certain kinds of antecedents. These include words like *each*, *either*, *neither*, and *one*, which are singular and take singular pronouns; antecedents made up of two or more parts joined by *or* or *nor*; and antecedents like *audience* or *team*, which can be either singular or plural depending on whether they are considered a single unit or a group of individuals.

Every one of the puppies thrived in ~~their~~ *its* new home.

Neither Jane nor Susan felt that ~~they~~ *she* had been treated fairly.

The team frequently changed ~~its~~ *their* positions to get varied experience.

The other main kind of antecedent that causes problems is a singular antecedent (such as *each* or *an employee*) that could be either male or female. Rather than use masculine pronouns (*he*, *him*, and so on) with such an antecedent, a traditional rule that excludes or ignores females, a writer should use *he or she*, *him or her*, and so on, or else rewrite the sentence to make the antecedent and pronoun plural or to eliminate the pronoun.

Every student must provide his *or her* own uniform.

~~Every~~ *All* ~~student~~ *students* must provide ~~his~~ *their* own ~~uniform~~ *uniforms*.

Every student must provide ~~his own~~ *a* uniform.

> For guidelines on checking for pronoun-antecedent agreement, see page 223. For additional, more detailed information about pronoun-antecedent agreement, see 9j–9m.

17. Unnecessary comma(s) with a restrictive element

A restrictive element is a word, phrase, or clause that restricts or limits the meaning of the preceding part of the sentence; it is essential to the meaning of what precedes it and cannot be left out without changing the sentence's basic meaning. Because of this close relationship, it is *not* set off from the rest of the sentence with a comma or commas.

An arrangement,/for orchestra,/was made by Ravel.

Several groups,/opposed to the use of animals for cosmetics testing/ picketed the laboratory.

People,/who wanted to preserve wilderness areas/ opposed the plan to privatize national parks.

The vice-president succeeds,/if and when the president dies or becomes incapacitated.

Shakespeare's tragedy,/*Othello*,/deals with the dangers of jealousy.

In the last of the preceding examples, the appositive is essential to the meaning of the sentence because Shakespeare wrote more than one tragedy.

> For guidelines on checking for unnecessary commas with restrictive elements, see page 440. For additional, more detailed information about restrictive phrases and clauses, see 27c and 27i1.

■ 18. Fused sentence

Fused sentences (sometimes called run-on sentences) are created when two or more groups of words that could each be written as an independent sentence are written without any punctuation between them. Such groups of words must be either separated into two sentences, by using a period and a capital letter, or joined together in a way that shows their relationship, by either adding words and punctuation or by rewriting completely.

Klee's paintings seem simple⟨, but⟩ they are very sophisticated.

The current was swift⟨. He⟩ he could not swim to shore.

She doubted the value of meditation⟨; nevertheless,⟩ she decided to try it once.

➤ For guidelines on checking for fused sentences, see page 257. For more detailed information about ways to revise fused sentences, see Chapter 13.

■ 19. Misplaced or dangling modifier

A misplaced modifier is a word, phrase, or clause that is not placed close enough to the word it describes or is related to. As a result, it seems to modify some other word, phrase, or clause, and readers can be confused or puzzled.

They could see the eagles swooping and diving⟨With binoculars,⟩

He had decided he wanted to be a doctor⟨When he was ten years old,⟩

Slowly and precisely⟨I⟩ watched the teller count out the money,

The architect ⟨only⟩ wanted to use pine paneling for decoration.

⟨Rising over the trees⟩ the campers saw a bright red sun,

The woman bought ⟨the painting⟩ from the shop that depicted a Chicago street scene.

A dangling modifier is a word, phrase, or elliptical clause (a clause from which words have been left out) that is not clearly related to any other word in the sentence. The word that it modifies exists in the writer's mind, but not on paper in the sentence. Such a modifier is called "dangling" because it hangs precariously from the beginning or end of the sentence, attached to nothing very solid.

A doctor should check your eyes for glaucoma every year if *you are* over fifty.

Looking down the stretch of sandy beach, *one sees* people ~~are~~ lying face down trying to get a tan.

As *a* male college student, *M* many people are surprised ~~at my~~ *that I,* support ~~for~~ the draft.

➤ For guidelines on checking for misplaced and dangling modifiers, see page 281. For additional, more detailed information on misplaced and dangling modifiers, see 15a and 15c.

▌ 20. *Its / It's* confusion

The word *its*, spelled without an apostrophe, is the possessive form of *it*, meaning "of it" or "belonging to it." The word *it's*, spelled with an apostrophe, is a shortened form of *it is* or *it has*. Even though an apostrophe often indicates a possessive form, in this case the possessive form is the one *without* the apostrophe.

The car is lying on its side in the ditch.

It's a white 1986 Buick.

It's been lying there for two days.

➤ For guidelines on checking *its* and *it's*, see page 459. For more on *its* and *it's*, see 22b and 30b.

1

PART ONE

The Writing Process

1. Understanding the Writing Process

A significant part of any college education involves reading and writing, two primary means of sharing knowledge. Of course, no one can complete college without doing an enormous amount of reading, and more and more people in education, business, and the professions now realize that the ability to write effectively is just as important as the ability to read well. In fact, research shows that writing encourages and enhances certain kinds of learning, and even that some kinds of complex thinking may be impossible without it. Writing, then, is not an artistic talent that only a lucky few possess, but an essential and powerful means of discovering what you know and of expressing that knowledge in communicating with others. As one author says:

> . . . writing is foremost a mode of thinking and, when it works well, an act of discovery. I write to find out what I believe, what seems logical and sensible to me, what notions, ideas, and views I can live with.
> —JOSEPH EPSTEIN

If you can read this text, you have the potential to be a writer of just the sort Epstein describes. There is nothing mysterious about the process of writing, and writers are not born with any special power. Writers simply explore observations and ideas on paper and care about the ways that their readers respond to their written words.

In order to write successfully, however, it helps to understand how the writing process works and how to develop a method that works for you. Charlotte W., for example, sits down at the typewriter a few hours before an essay is due and frantically pounds out a draft. Her essays often touch on interesting ideas, but they are so disorganized and full of grammatical errors that the effect of the ideas is lost. Peter

G. works terribly hard to put every comma in place and spell every word correctly, and his papers are letter-perfect—but rarely do they have anything to say. Although these writers put very different amounts and kinds of effort into their writing, neither is gaining much intellectual reward or academic credit. Looking carefully at the way they *go about* writing, at their processes of writing, should help them to see why they aren't writing effectively and to make the kinds of changes that will lead to better essays and greater rewards. Because the writing process is complex and directly related to the quality of the finished piece of writing, the next several chapters will focus on the various parts of that process.

1a. Recognizing the recursive parts of the writing process

The mental processes that actually accompany the writing process are tremendously complex. They are, moreover, so subtle and so lightning-fast that we are only now beginning to learn how they all interact. But we *do* know that writers always set and shift and reset a series of goals as they write. These goals range from those as large as "try to make the reader laugh here" or "explain that concept" to ones as small as "use a semicolon instead of a period here to make this section less choppy." Researchers often describe the process of writing as seamless and **recursive**, meaning that its goals or parts are constantly flowing into and influencing one another, without any clear break between them. The shifting set of goals may focus one moment on deciding how to organize a paragraph and the next moment on using knowledge gained from that decision to revise the wording of a sentence. Repetitive, erratic, and often messy, writing does not proceed in nice, neat steps: first an idea; then a plan; then an introduction, body, and conclusion. In fact, these "steps" often take place simultaneously, in a kind of spiraling sequence, with planning, drafting, and revising all taking place throughout the process of writing. A writer may get an idea for a conclusion while drafting the introduction, or may plan one paragraph while revising the previous one.

In any case, writers seldom pay conscious attention to these constantly shifting goals and recursive patterns. Ideally, writing can be like riding a bicycle; with practice the process becomes more and more automatic. As you become more practiced as a writer, more and more of the goal-juggling you do will become automatic. Like an experienced cyclist, you will be able to pay attention to the big things—oncoming traffic, the view, the route you're taking—without thinking too consciously about changing gears or moving your feet or stopping at red lights.

Instructors who study the ways writers work most effectively find it useful to think of the writing process as a series of recursive activities: **planning**, during which the writer finds information and prepares to write; **drafting**, during which the writer puts down on paper a version of the essay; and **revising**, during which the writer works with the draft to improve it. But these activities seldom, if ever, occur in a linear sequence, with one following another. Rather, writers move back and forth—planning, drafting, planning some more, revising, drafting, revising, planning a little more—until the writing is complete. Though the following sections discuss planning, drafting, and revising in that order, remember that in the process of writing these activities are always interwoven.

▌ 1. Planning

Effective writing does not just happen. Of course, you can merely sit down, dash something off, and call it writing, but writing worth reading usually starts with a nagging question or puzzle or idea that requires planning: thinking, investigating, organizing, and generally getting ready to write. While planning continues throughout the writing process, it is often the way a writer begins.

Depending on the writing task, planning can last a few minutes or several months. If you have to write a one-page essay in class about a member of your family, you will probably jot down a few notes, put them in order, and start writing very quickly. If, on the other hand, you have six weeks to prepare a fifteen-page paper on U.S.–Soviet relations, you will need to do some research and explore the topic thoroughly before deciding exactly what you want to say.

Planning includes everything you do as you prepare to draft: thinking about your purpose, exploring a topic, coming up with a working thesis, gathering materials, deciding how to appeal to your audience, and developing a strategy for organizing the writing. Your organizational plan may be a short list or a long, detailed outline accompanied by a tall stack of research cards. Whatever shape your planning takes, it will act as your guide as you draft your essay. Your planning and thesis may well shift as you draft, but just having them there will help you to keep on course, or at least to remember where you are headed. The process of planning is examined in detail in Chapter 2.

2. Drafting

Drafting is the central part of writing—the one element in the process that can never be skipped or avoided. As one student put it, drafting is "where the rubber meets the road," the time when you try your ideas out in writing.

Writing habits are, of course, as variable as writers. Some people can work on a draft only in complete silence; others need music playing. Some must be completely alone, while others work best in a crowded library. Some prefer to produce a draft in one long, sustained burst of energy; still others work more slowly, taking breaks after drafting each section.

As much as anything, drafting represents a process of exploration. The great British writer E. M. Forster once wrote, "How can I know what I think until I see what I say?" Indeed, some kinds of understanding come only from trying to express your ideas for others—in writing. No matter how thoroughly you explore your topic while planning, you will discover more about the topic while drafting your essay. Sometimes these new insights will cause you to turn back—to change your organizational plan, to bring in more information, to approach the subject from a new angle, or to rethink your appeal to your audience. Drafting, then, is *not* merely "putting your ideas down on paper." More often than not, drafting also involves coming up with new ideas or completely reshaping your concept of what you are trying to achieve in the essay. And since writing is indeed a recursive activity, this moving back and forth among planning, drafting, and revising is just what one would expect.

Some writers make drafting more difficult than it needs to be by trying to make their writing come out perfectly the first time. Agonizing over every sentence, word, and quotation mark can make drafting a lengthy, painful, and unsatisfying process. In fact, such agonizing often prevents effective writing. It is much more fruitful to view drafting as just that—the process of working out a *first draft*, which explores thoughts, expresses ideas, and tries out examples. The goal of drafting is not a final copy, or even a version good enough to show anyone else. Smooth sentences, the ideal word choice, and the right punctuation can come later; in your first draft, just try to express your thoughts clearly.

If your planning has been productive, the drafting stage may go almost as quickly as you can write. Maintaining momentum, without getting sidetracked by any one question or problem, is one of the most important skills a writer can develop. Problems may well crop up—questions to be answered, new areas to be explored—but these can be considered once the draft is finished. First you need to produce a draft. A thorough discussion of drafting appears in Chapter 2.

▎ 3. Revising

With your first draft, you have a version of your essay before you, and the rest of your work will be devoted to making sure it says what you want it to say. Doing so requires careful rereading and analysis of the draft with an eye toward establishing a systematic plan for revising.

Re-vision means literally "to see again." It means looking at a draft with a critical eye—seeing it anew and deciding if it accomplishes the goals you originally set out to accomplish. Some writers at first think revising is a matter of simply correcting misspellings, inserting commas, and typing up the result. Such tasks are important, but true revision is something more. It requires hard work, much harder and more demanding than fixing misspellings and commas, for it may mean eliminating whole sections, moving paragraphs, writing new sentences, doing additional research, or even choosing a new topic and starting all over again.

In fact, because it can be complex and quite extensive, revising more closely resembles drafting than it does editing or proofreading, the final steps of the writing process. With editing and proofreading, you make your essay ready for the world, which means it must meet those conventions of written form known as "correctness." Sentence structure, spelling, punctuation—all must meet conventional standards. Even editing, however, may lead you to reconsider a sentence, a paragraph, a transition, or an organizational pattern—and you may find yourself planning or drafting once again. Chapter 3 explores revising in some detail and provides a blueprint for successful revising and final editing.

In addition to your own analysis of the draft's strengths and weaknesses, you may want to get responses from other people. The analysis you do on your own is important, of course, because no one knows as well as you what you are trying to say. Other readers, however, can be just as important in helping you to reexamine the thesis, the organization, the argument, the diction, the tone, the thoroughness with which the essay is developed.

All writing assumes a particular audience of readers—even if only the writers themselves. Revising can be made easier and more productive if you can actually make use of an audience, be it your friends, your classmates, or your instructor. Other people have a distance that is very difficult for writers to achieve; we are always attached to what we write, especially right after we have written it. Getting comments and criticisms from others is a way of seeing your work through new eyes, and it should be a part of every writer's process.

▌ 1b. Reading with an eye for writing

One good way to improve your writing is by paying close attention to what you read, taking tips from writers you especially admire. In the words of William Faulkner, "Read, read, read. Read everything—trash, classics, good and bad, and see how they do it." Throughout this handbook, we will be taking time to "see how they do it," examining the work of well-known writers to see what they do with the strategies and structures we ourselves will be practicing.

In addition, most chapters include exercises asking you to read a passage with an eye for some element in the writing—adjectives, subordination, whatever. These exercises should help you learn to use these elements in your own work—and might lead you to insights about how you can make your own writing more accurate and powerful.

FOR EXAMINING YOUR OWN READING PROCESS

The writer Anatole Broyard once cautioned readers about the perils of "just walking through" a book.* A good reader, he suggested, "stomps around" in a book—underlining passages, scribbling in the margin, noting any questions or comments.

How would you describe yourself as a reader—avid? hurried? meticulous? relaxed? what else? Do you annotate the text as you read, or are you careful never to write in a book? What role does reading play in your life as a student and as a writer?

---

* Anatole Broyard, "The Price of Reading Is Eternal Vigilance," *New York Times Book Review*, 10 Apr. 1988, pp. 11–12.

▮ 1c. Examining your own writing

One of the best ways to improve your process of planning, drafting, and revising is to make the effort to analyze it from time to time. You can do this most systematically by keeping a **writing log**, a notebook in which you jot down your thoughts about a writing project while you are working on it or after you have completed it. Studying these notes will help you identify patterns of strength and weakness in your writing process, and sharing the writing log with your instructor or your classmates may yield some helpful advice on how you can write more efficiently and effectively.

Although you may not have thought very much about how you go about planning and producing an essay, you probably already have your own characteristic process of writing. Examining and understanding this process can help you make it work to your advantage. To get started on thinking about and evaluating your own writing process, answer the following questions. If you are keeping a writing log, you might record your answers as the first entry.

FOR EXAMINING YOUR OWN WRITING PROCESS

1. How do you typically go about preparing for a writing assignment? Describe the steps you take, including rereading the assignment, asking questions about it, talking to instructors or friends, jotting down ideas, gathering information, and so on. How far in advance of the due date do you usually begin working on the assignment?
2. When and where do your best ideas often come to you?
3. Where do you usually do your writing? Describe this place. Is it a good place to write? Why, or why not?
4. What materials do you typically use when writing? Pen or pencil and note pad, typewriter, word processor, something else?
5. Describe your typical drafting process. Do you finish a draft in one sitting, or do you prefer to take breaks? How many drafts do you usually go through before the final one? Why?
6. If you "get stuck" while writing, what do you usually do to get moving again?
7. How do you typically go about revising, and what does your revising include? What are the things you think about most as you revise?
8. What would you say is most efficient and effective about your writing process?
9. What is least efficient and effective about your writing process?
10. What specific steps could you take to improve your writing process?

2. Planning and Drafting

Planning and drafting begin the moment a writer starts to think about a topic, question, or idea that will result in a piece of writing. And the process ends only after revising and editing, when the writer passes on the finished product for response by an instructor or some other intended audience. This chapter takes a close look at how planning and drafting work in practice.

▌ 2a. Deciding to write

Often the decision to write is made for you: you must take an essay examination at 10 A.M.; the editor of your newspaper sets a specific deadline; a professor announces that an essay will be due next Tuesday; your employer asks for a full report on a complex issue by the next management meeting. But even in such situations, consciously *deciding to write* is an important step to take. Here is why. Experienced writers report that making up their minds to begin a writing task represents a big step toward actually getting the job done. You can use this insight to your advantage, determining not to put off a writing assignment but to meet it head-on by consciously deciding to get to work on it.

Experienced writers also tell us that when a topic is not assigned but left open, the best way to choose one is literally to let the topic choose you. That is to say, those subjects that compel you—that puzzle, intrigue, or even irritate you—are likely to engage your interests and hence encourage your best writing. Even with assigned topics, you can often look for some aspect of the topic that is particularly compelling. Once you start to *wonder* about a topic, you are at the point of having something to write about.

This advice is not meant merely to encourage you to start early on any writing task. Rather, it suggests that you broaden your definition of writing to include your earliest thoughts on a topic and that you move deliberately from those early thoughts to begin writing. This conscious decision to begin working toward a draft represents an important though seldom discussed point in the writing process. And it is a decision that only you, the writer, can make.

■ 2b. Understanding writing assignments

Most on-the-job writing addresses specific purposes, audiences, and topics: a group of chemists and biologists produces a report on food additives for the federal government; an editorial assistant composes a memo for an editor summarizing the problems in a new manuscript; a team of psychologists prepares scripts for videos intended to help large corporations deal with alcoholism among employees. These writers all have one thing in common: specific goals. They know exactly why and for whom they are writing.

College writing assignments, in contrast, may seem to appear out of the blue, with no specific purposes, audiences, or topics. In extreme cases, a college writing assignment may be only one word long, as in a theater examination that consisted of the single word "Tragedy!" At the opposite extreme come assignments in the form of fully developed cases, often favored in business, commerce, and engineering courses. Such cases are very specific: you could, for example, be asked to assume the role of a civil engineer who is to evaluate various proposals for constructing a bridge and report the results of your evaluation to your superiors.

In between the one-word assignment and the fully developed case lies a wide spectrum of assignments and topics. You may get assignments that specify purpose but not audience—to write an essay arguing for or against capital punishment, for example. Or you may be given an organizational pattern to use—to compare and contrast, for example—but no topic. Because each assignment is different, and because comprehending a topic is crucial to your success in responding to it, you should always make sure you understand the assignment as fully as possible. Consider the following questions as you analyze any assignment:

- *What, exactly, does this assignment ask you to do?* Look for words like *analyze, classify, compare, contrast, describe, discuss, define, explain,* and *survey.* These are key terms, and you should be sure you understand what task they set. Remember that these words may differ in meaning among disciplines—*analyze* might mean one thing in literature and something rather different in biology.

- *What knowledge or information do you need to fulfill this assignment?* Do you need to do any research? See 2f and 2g for ways of assessing your own knowledge and gathering additional information.

- *How can you limit—or broaden—the topic or assignment to make it more interesting?* Is there any particular aspect of the topic in which you have special interest or knowledge? Be sure to check with your instructor if you wish to redefine the assignment in any way.

- *What are the assignment's specific requirements?* Consider length, format, organization, and deadline. Being sure of such things will help you not only to respond properly to the assignment but also to know the scope expected. Your instructor is not likely to expect library research for a paper due in twenty-four hours, for example. If no length is designated, you should ask for some guideline.

- *What is your purpose as a writer in this assignment?* Do you need to demonstrate knowledge of a certain body of material, or do you mainly need to show the ability to express certain ideas clearly? See 2c for a discussion of ways to assess purpose.

- *Who is the audience for this piece of writing?* Does the writing task tell you to *assume* a particular readership besides your instructor? See 2d for a discussion of ways to assess your audience.

Once you can answer these questions, you will have gone a good way toward exploring an assignment and making it one you can accomplish.

EXERCISE 2.1

The following assignment was given recently to an introductory psychology class: *Discuss in an essay the contributions of Jung and Freud to modern clinical psychology.* What would you need to know about the assignment in order to respond successfully? Using the set of questions in 2b, analyze this assignment.

2c. Deciding on purposes

The writing of college essays, reports, and other papers almost always involves dual or multiple purposes. On one level, you are writing to establish your credibility with your instructor, to demonstrate that you are a careful thinker and effective writer. Fulfilling this purpose means considering your instructor's expectations very carefully, a concern addressed in detail in 2d. But good college writing also accomplishes some other, more individual purpose that the writer has in mind. In fact, the best writing you do in college will be writing that in some way achieves a goal or goals of your own, that says as clearly and forcefully as possible what you think about a topic of importance to you, and what you have to say to readers about this topic. For example, if you are writing an essay about abortion, your purposes might be to share your knowledge of the topic with your readers, to persuade them to support or oppose legalized abortion, or even to clarify in your own mind the medical information about abortion or the moral debate over it. If you are writing a profile of your eccentric grandfather, you might be trying to amuse your readers at the same time that you are paying tribute to someone who was important to you.

In ancient Rome, the great orator Cicero noted that a good speech generally fulfilled one of three major purposes: to delight, to teach, or to move. Although the world has changed mightily in the two thousand years since Cicero, our purposes when we communicate with one another remain pretty much the same: we seek to *entertain* (delight), to *inform and explain* (teach), and to *persuade or convince* (move). Most of the writing you do in college will address one or some combination of these purposes, and it is thus important for you to be able to recognize the overriding purpose of any piece of writing. If, for example, an American history professor asks you to explain the web of causes that led up to the 1964 Civil Rights Act (primary purpose: to explain) and you respond by writing an impassioned plea for a new civil rights act (primary purpose: to persuade), you have misunderstood the purpose of the assignment.

For most college writing, you should think in terms of purposes rather than one single purpose. Specifically, you should consider **purpose** in terms of the *assignment,* in terms of the *instructor's expectations,* and in terms of *your own goals.*

The assignment

Is the primary purpose of the assignment to entertain, to explain, to persuade—or some other stated purpose? What does the primary purpose suggest about the best ways to achieve it? If you are unclear about the primary purpose, have you talked with your instructor or other classmates about it? Are there any secondary purposes to keep in mind?

The instructor's expectations

What are the instructor's purposes in giving this assignment—to make sure you have read certain materials? to determine whether you understand certain materials? to evaluate your thinking and writing abilities? to determine whether you can evaluate certain materials critically? What can you include in your essay to fulfill these purposes?

Your own goals

What are your purposes in carrying out this assignment—to respond to the topic adequately and accurately? to meet the instructor's expectations? to learn as much as possible about a new topic? to communicate your ideas as clearly and forcefully as possible? What can you include in your essay in order to achieve these goals?

EXERCISE 2.2

Choose one of the following assignments and describe its various purposes. If your instructor allows, this exercise may be done in small-group discussions, with one group member taking notes and reporting to the rest of the class.

1. Compare two book-length biographies of Herman Melville.
2. Discuss the controversies surrounding the use of genetic engineering to change characteristics of unborn children.
3. Write about a person who has been important in your life, and describe why he or she has affected you strongly.
4. Support or attack the latest presidential request for military funding.
5. Analyze the use of headlines in a group of twenty advertisements.
6. Describe a favorite spot in your college town.

EXERCISE 2.3

Consider a writing assignment you are currently working on. What are its purposes, in terms of the assignment, the instructor, and you, the writer?

▌ 2d. Considering audiences

Although you may sometimes write only to yourself (as in diaries or personal journals, lists of things to do, and so on), most of your college writing will be addressed to others. An important part of your writing process, therefore, involves thinking about your **audience**—who your readers are. Skilled writers consider their readers carefully; in fact, one of the characteristic traits of a mature writer is the ability to write for a variety of audiences, using language, style, and evidence all appropriate to particular readers.

The key word here is *appropriateness:* just as a funeral director would hardly greet a bereaved family with "Howdy, customers," neither would you be likely to sprinkle jokes through an analysis of child abuse written for a PTA group. Why not? Because such behavior would be wildly inappropriate in that context and because your good sense would lead you to consider the nature of your audience and to address them in an appropriate way.

For much of your college writing, an instructor may serve as the primary audience. You may, however, sometimes find yourself writing for others: lab reports addressed to your class, business proposals addressed to a hypothetical manager, or in one American history class, a letter to a seventeen-year-old living in the year 1775. Every writer can benefit from thinking carefully about who the audience is, what the audience already knows or thinks, and what the audience needs and expects to find out. The following questions will help you begin to think in such careful ways about the audience for your writing.

- *Who is your audience?* Your boss? Other college students? Scientists? People already sympathetic to your views? People unsympathetic to your views? Potential voters? The general public?
- *What do you need to be sensitive to in your audience's background?* Think in terms of level of education, geographical region, age, sex, occupation, cultural heritage, and special interests.
- *What does your audience value?* Think in terms of qualities such as brevity, originality, honesty, wit, thriftiness, and so on. What goals and aspirations do they have?
- *What is your audience's stance toward your topic?* What are they likely to know about the topic? What preconceived views might they have?
- *What is your relationship to the audience?* Is it student to instructor? friend to friend? subordinate to superior? superior to subordinate? citizen to community? anything else?

Thinking systematically about your audience will help you decide what sort of organizational plan to follow (which one would be easiest for a particular audience to understand, for example), what information to include or to exclude, and even what specific words to choose. If you

15

are writing an article for a magazine for nurses about a new drug prescribed to prevent patients from developing infections from intravenous feeding tubes, you will not need to give much information about how such tubes work or to define many terms. But if you are writing about the same topic in a pamphlet given to patients when they check into the hospital, you will have to give a great deal of background information and define any technical terms or, better yet, use other words altogether. For writing intended to persuade, such as a newspaper column advocating a tax increase to pay for school construction, a writer in a community with many parents of young children might assume a fairly sympathetic audience and try to emphasize the benefits to the children that new schools would provide. In a community with many elderly people living on fixed incomes, on the other hand, a writer would anticipate resistance to higher taxes. Therefore, the column might express understanding of and sympathy with this point of view before arguing the case for building more schools; it might also emphasize the meeting space or recreational facilities new schools could provide for all of the community's citizens.

EXERCISE 2.4

In order to experiment with how considerations of appropriateness for a particular audience affect what you write, describe the last cultural or social event you especially enjoyed to three different audiences: first to your best friend, then to your parents, then to a group of high school students attending an open house at your college. Then describe the differences in content, organization, and wording that the differences in audience led you to make.

▌ 2e. Exploring a topic

The point is so simple that we often forget it: we write best about topics we know well. One of the most important parts of the entire writing process, therefore, is exploring your topic, surveying what you know about it and then determining what you need to find out.

You may already have a good system for exploring topics you wish to write about. If so, use it and share it with friends and members of your class. If you have no particular personal system, however, this chapter provides a brief description of strategies designed to help you explore a topic. These strategies can be very useful in getting you started in your thinking about a topic and in helping you determine what you already know—and indeed in helping you solve problems that crop up later in the writing of an essay. The strategies include brainstorming, freewriting, looping, and questioning.

1. Brainstorming

Used widely in business, industry, and engineering, **brainstorming** involves tossing out ideas—often with several other people—in order to find new or fresh ways to approach a topic. You can adapt brainstorming to writing, however, by quickly writing down everything that occurs to you about a topic. All you need is a pen or pencil and a blank sheet of paper. Give yourself a time limit—five minutes, perhaps—and write down in list form *every* word or phrase that comes into your mind about your topic. Just put down key words and phrases, not sentences. No one has to understand the list but you. Don't worry about whether something will be useful or not. Just get it *all* down. When the time is up, stop and read over your list. If anything else comes to you, add it to the list. Then reread, looking for repetitions and patterns in the list, for clusters of interesting ideas, or for one central idea. Brainstorming can work well alone, but it is particularly effective with a group of between three and five people. You may want to get together with several members of your class to brainstorm about one another's topics—and you may well be surprised at what good ideas can come from such spontaneous discussion.

2. Freewriting

Freewriting is a kind of structured brainstorming, a method of exploring a topic by writing about it—or whatever else it brings to mind—for a certain number of minutes *without stopping*. Set a time limit, begin by thinking about your topic, and then simply let your mind wander and write down everything that occurs to you—in complete sentences as much as possible.

Continue writing *without stopping* for your set length of time (ten minutes maximum to begin with). Don't stop for anything; if you can't think what to write next, you can write "I can't think of what to write next" over and over until something else occurs to you. Then stop and look at what you've written. You are sure to find much that is unusable, irrelevant, or nonsensical. But you may also find important insights and ideas that you didn't even know you had. Writing has a way of jogging loose ideas, and seeing a word or idea appear before you on paper will often trigger others.

17

❙ 3. Looping

Looping is essentially a form of directed freewriting that narrows or focuses a topic in five-minute stages, or "loops." As in freewriting, you first write whatever comes to mind when you think of your topic, basically following the free flow of your thoughts. Then you follow a central thread of those thoughts wherever it leads you. Here is how to do looping:

1. With your topic in mind, spend five minutes freewriting *without stopping*. This is your first loop.
2. Stop and look back at what you have written. Find the strongest or most intriguing thought. This is your "center of gravity," which you should summarize in a single sentence; it will become the starting point of your next loop.
3. Starting with the summary sentence from your first loop, spend another five minutes freewriting. This second loop circles around the center of gravity in the first loop, just as the first loop circled around your topic. Look for a center of gravity within this second piece of freewriting, which will form the basis of a third loop.
4. Keep this process going until you have discovered a clear angle on your topic or have expressed something about it that you can pursue in a full-length essay.

❙ 4. Mapping

Mapping is a way of generating ideas using a visual scheme, or map. It is especially useful for finding relationships among the main parts of a broad topic. To create a planning map, start with a blank piece of paper, and write down your topic in the middle of the page. Circle it. Then write down the main parts of your topic; circle each one and connect it to the topic in the center. Next think of any ideas, details, examples, or facts relating to each main part; write them down, circle them, and attach each one to the main parts with a line.

Continue associating from each new circle until you can't think of any more details, creating a visual map of your topic. Some terms will generate outward and some will just come to a dead end, but you will end up with various information trails to follow and many useful connections among ideas. Mapping is an especially useful way of developing various subtopics in an essay. At the top of the facing page you can see a representation of a map.

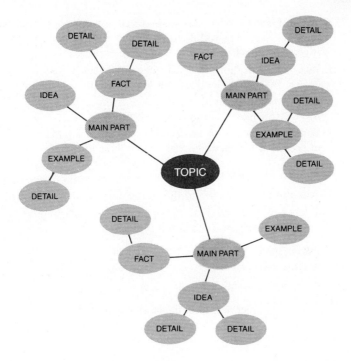

5. Questioning

The strategies presented thus far for exploring topics are all informal and based on freewheeling association of ideas. But there are more formal and structured ways of approaching topics that involve **asking**—and answering—particular **questions**. Such questions will help you probe a topic, look at it from varying perspectives, and generate ideas about it. The following are several widely used sets of questions designed to help you explore your topic. Of course, you can also make up your own questions to use.

Questions to describe a topic

Originally developed by Aristotle and refined by modern scholars, the following questions can help you explore any topic by carefully and systematically describing it.

1. *What is it?* What are its characteristics, dimensions, features, and parts? What does it look like?

2. *What caused it?* What changes occurred to create your topic? How is it changing? How will it change? What part of a changing process is your topic? What may it lead to in the future?
3. *What is it like or unlike?* What features differentiate your topic from others? What analogies does your topic support?
4. *What is it part of?* What larger system is your topic a part of? How is your topic related to this larger system?
5. *What do people say about it?* What reaction does your topic arouse in people? What about the topic causes those reactions?

Questions to explain a topic

This is the well-known question set of *who, what, when, where, why,* and *how.* Widely used in news reporting, these questions are especially useful to help you explain a topic.

1. *Who* is doing it?
2. *What* is at issue?
3. *When* does it begin? When does it end?
4. *Where* is it taking place?
5. *Why* does it occur?
6. *How* is it done?

Questions to persuade

When your purpose is to persuade or convince, answering the following questions developed by the modern philosopher Stephen Toulmin can help you think analytically about your topic.

1. What CLAIM are you making about your topic?
2. What GOOD REASONS support your claim about the topic?
3. What UNDERLYING ASSUMPTIONS support the reasons for your claim?
4. What BACKUP EVIDENCE do you have or can you find to add further support to your claim?
5. What REFUTATIONS can be made against your claim?
6. In what ways is or should your claim be QUALIFIED?

Systematically using any of these strategies will be helpful, for doing so will get you thinking seriously about your topic—and putting those thoughts on paper. So don't be discouraged if your first attempts at looping or answering questions about a topic fail to produce timeless prose or revolutionary ideas. Be persistent, and these exploratory systems should begin to show results.

For an essay describing a favorite spot in her college town, Colleen Starkey, a student at the University of New Hampshire, began with brainstorming to explore a favorite spot, the bagel restaurant where she worked. Here are her brainstorming notes:

March 17th '83	CR, P, Oat, onion,
Ports—since 7/85	Cart April—Oct
May 1982—initial idea	2 am—open
Warren—full time	soups & quiches came later
Ithaca—consultant	bakery case
from bagel bakery	
	Horizontal mixer
Wkly shipments	Vertical mixer
	Bagel machine
per-day wholesale ave. 150 doz	
Durham 120 doz	Boiled—1 min
Ports. 50 doz	550 degrees F—15 min
	malt, salt, yeast, water

Brainstorming helped Colleen to get an idea of what she might have to say about the Bagelry. In order then to find out whether she really knew enough to write about the place, she decided to try describing it. She did this by writing out answers to the questions for describing shown above. Look at what she wrote:

1. What is the Bagelry? a restaurant that specializes in bagels, beverages, and sweets. small, contemporary, like a bakery, with a long counter. popular with students from UNH.
2. What caused the Bagelry? a couple from New York moved to Durham and realized there was a market for bagels here. already it has grown to two stores, the one in Durham and a branch in Portsmouth.
3. What is the Bagelry like or unlike? it's a little like a New York coffee shop, but because it's in Durham it's quite unlike a typical New York bagel shop—neater, less cluttered. I guess it's also basically similar to most bakeries that bake on the premises.
4. What is it part of? it's in a mall in downtown Durham. it's not far from a Burger King. but—and perhaps this is most important—it's part of everyday life for many students at UNH.
5. What do people say about the Bagelry? that it has great bagels. some say they'd have trouble getting through the morning without a wake-up bagel.

EXERCISE 2.5

Choose a topic that interests you, and explore it by using two of the strategies described in 2e. When you have generated some material, you might try comparing your results with those of other members of the class to see how effective or helpful each of the systems was. If you have trouble choosing a topic, use one of the working theses in Exercise 2.6.

▮ 2f. Establishing a working thesis

A **thesis** states the main idea of your essay. Most kinds of college writing contain a thesis statement, often near the beginning of the essay, which functions as a promise to the readers—to let them know what will be discussed. Though you will probably not have a finished thesis when you begin to write, you should establish a tentative **working thesis** early on in your writing process. The word *working* is important here, as the working thesis may well be modified, clarified, or otherwise changed as you write. In spite of the fact that it will probably change, a working thesis is important for three main reasons: (1) it directs your thinking, research, and investigation and thus keeps you on track; (2) it helps you to focus on a particular point about the topic; (3) it provides concrete questions to ask about purpose and audience (helping you see, for example, what you must do to design a thesis for a particular audience).

A working thesis should have two parts: a topic part and a comment part. The **topic** part states the topic, while the **comment** part makes an important point about the topic. Here are some examples.

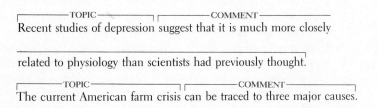

A successful working thesis has three characteristics. It should be potentially *interesting* to your intended audience. In its language, it should be as *specific* as possible; and it must limit and focus a topic enough to make it *manageable*. You can evaluate a working thesis by checking it against each of these criteria. For example:

Preliminary working thesis

The theory of "nuclear winter" is being debated around the globe.

INTEREST The topic itself holds interest, but it seems to have no real comment attached to it. The thesis merely states a bare fact, and there seems no place to go from here except to more bare facts.

SPECIFICITY The thesis is fairly clear, but not very specific. Who is debating the theory? What does it mean to these people? What are the larger implications of this debate? What does the writer think of the theory, or the debate?

MANAGEABILITY The thesis is not manageable: it would require research in many countries and in many languages and would be beyond the capacities and time limits of most if not all students.

ASSESSMENT The topic of this thesis is very general and needs to be narrowed by a workable comment before it will be useful. Right now the field of investigation is too large and vague. This preliminary thesis can be narrowed into the following working thesis:

Working thesis

Scientists from several different countries have challenged the "nuclear winter" theory and claimed that it is more propaganda than science.

Throughout this chapter and the next, we continue to follow the writing process of Colleen Starkey as she works her way through one writing assignment. For that essay, she produced the following preliminary working thesis:

The Bagelry is a Durham restaurant popular with everyone.

When Colleen subjected this working thesis to the tests of interest, specificity, and manageability, she found that her thesis was manageable but was deficient in both interest and specificity. It contained only a statement of fact and did not make any real comment on the topic. After considering the problem, Colleen decided to show in what ways the Bagelry was unusual for a small New England college town. She then wrote the following working thesis:

Set in the college town of Durham, New Hampshire, the Bagelry offers authentic bagels in an atmosphere much like the small coffee shops and cafés that line New York City streets.

23

EXERCISE 2.6

Choose one of the following preliminary working theses, and, after specifying an audience, evaluate the thesis in terms of interest, specificity, and manageability. Revise it as necessary to meet these criteria.

1. Drug abuse presents Americans with a big problem.
2. Abortion is a right.
3. Othello is a complex character whose greatest strength is, ironically, also his greatest weakness.
4. The Reagan Supreme Court decided many cases less conservatively than you might have expected.
5. White-collar crime poses greater danger to the economy than more obvious forms of street crime.

EXERCISE 2.7

Using the topic of the assignment you chose in Exercise 2.2, write a preliminary working thesis. Evaluate it in terms of interest, specificity, and manageability, and then revise it as necessary to create a satisfactory working thesis.

▍2g. Gathering information

Many of your writing assignments will call for some research. Your instructor may specify that you research your topic and cite your sources; or you may find that you do not know enough about your topic without doing some research. You may need to do research at various stages of the writing process—early on, to help you define your topic, or at a later point to find examples in support of your thesis— but usually you will want to consider what additional information you might need once you have defined a working thesis.

If you find it necessary to do research, you should probably begin with those resources closest to hand: your instructor, who can help you decide what kind of research to do, and your textbooks, which may include a bibliography or list of references. Basically, you can do two kinds of research: library research and field research.

Before going to the library you should try to think of general subject headings to check; then look in the card catalog, encyclopedias, periodical indexes, and bibliographies for specific materials. You may want to ask advice from a librarian. Consider field research: observation, interviews, or questionnaires. In Chapter 3, for instance, we will see how Colleen Starkey uses observation and interviews to find much good concrete detail for her essay about the bagel business.

Detailed discussion of how to conduct both library and field research are given in Chapter 38. Once you determine you need to research your topic further, turn to that chapter for detailed guidelines.

2h. Organizing information

Exploring a topic and gathering information can provide essential data for an essay, but the data are *raw*—and not very helpful—until they are organized. Even as you are finding information, therefore, you should be thinking about how you will group or organize that information in your writing, how you will make your data accessible and persuasive to your readers.

At the simplest level, writers can group information in three ways: according to principles of **space** (*where* bits of information occur spatially); according to principles of **time** (*when* bits of information occur, usually chronologically); or according to principles of **logic** (*how* bits of information are related). The ways you group your information in an essay will ultimately depend on your topic, purpose, and audience.

1. Organizing information spatially

If the information you have gathered is *descriptive*, you may choose to organize it spatially (see 2e for questions that help you describe a topic). Using **spatial organization** allows the reader to "see" your information, to fix it in space. A report on the library's accessibility to students in wheelchairs, for example, might well group information spatially. In describing the spaces in the library that are most often used and evaluating their accessibility to a student in a wheelchair, the writer would most certainly present information spatially—one room or space or area at a time. In this case, the description of the student's progress through various library spaces might even be accompanied by a map. (See 5c for examples of information organized spatially.)

2. Organizing information chronologically

You are probably already very familiar with **chronological organization,** since it is the basic method used in stories, cookbooks, and instructions for assembling or using various products. All of these kinds of writing group information according to when it occurs in some process or sequence of events. Reports of laboratory studies and certain kinds of experiments also use chronological ordering of information.

25

A student studying the availability of motorcycle parking in a campus lot ordered his information chronologically at least once in his proposal, to show the times when motorcycles entered and exited the parking lot and thus to identify peak periods of demand for parking spaces. This student chose to present this information in narrative (story) form, using chronological order to build tension as the minutes tick by and the lot gets more and more crowded, the drivers more and more frustrated. He could have altered the narrative order, however, and told his story backwards (using a kind of flashback technique). If you choose to use a narrative or story form for presenting information, you will probably use chronological order, but reversing that order— or starting "in the middle" and then going back to the beginning—can provide effective methods of organizing data as well.

Chronological order is especially useful in **explaining a process,** step by step by step. A biology report, for instance, might require describing a frog's process of circulation. An essay for an anthropology class might include an explanation of the rituals of initiation into the tribe in an Indian culture. If you decide to organize information about a process in chronological order, you can test whether your explanation is clear and precise by asking a fellow student to read the explanation and report how easy (or hard) it is to follow the steps of the process.

3. Organizing information logically

In much of the writing you do in college, you will find it appropriate to organize information according to some set of logical relationships. The most commonly used **logical patterns** include *illustration, definition, division/classification, comparison/contrast, cause-effect,* and *problem-solution.* (See 5c for examples of information organized logically.)

Illustrating points

Often much of the information you gather will serve as examples to **illustrate a point.** An essay discussing how one novelist influenced another might cite a number of examples from the second writer's books that echo themes, characters, or plots from the first writer's works. An appeal for donating money to the Red Cross might be organized around a series of examples of how such money will be used. If you use illustration in writing intended to persuade or convince, arrange the examples in order of increasing importance, for maximum effect.

Defining terms

Many topics can be developed by **definition:** by saying what something is—and is not—and perhaps by identifying the characteristics that distinguish it from things that are similar or in the same general category. A magazine article about poverty in the United States, for example, would have to define very carefully what it meant by poverty—what level of personal income, household assets, or other measure defined a person, family, or household as poor. A student essay about Pentecostalism for a religion class might develop the topic by explaining what characteristics separate Pentecostalism from related religious movements, such as fundamentalism or evangelicalism.

Dividing and classifying

Division means breaking a single item into its parts; **classification** means grouping many separate items according to their similarities. Dividing a topic involves beginning with one object or idea and discussing each of its components separately. An essay about the recruiting policies of the United States military, for instance, might be organized by dividing the military into its different branches—army, air force, and so on—and then discussing how each branch recruits volunteers. Classifying involves putting items or pieces of information into categories. A writer discussing the student organizations on a college campus would probably call on classification as a way of organizing the information, classifying students' groups into service, academic, and social groups or into male, female, and mixed groups. If you have been reading histories of the eighteenth century in preparation for an essay on women's roles in that time, and you have accumulated dozens of pages of notes in the process, you could begin to organize this mass of undigested information by classifying it: information related to women's education, women's occupations, women's legal status, and so on.

Comparing and contrasting

Comparison focuses on the similarities between two things while **contrast** highlights their differences, but the two are often used together. Asked to read two chapters in an introductory philosophy text (one on Plato and the other on Aristotle), to analyze the information presented, and to write a brief response, a student might well use an organizational framework based on comparison and contrast. The student could then organize the response in one of two ways: by presenting all the information on Plato in one section and all on Aristotle in

27

another *(block comparison)* or by alternating back and forth between Plato and Aristotle, looking at particular characteristics of each *(alternating comparison)*.

Analyzing causes and effects

Cause-effect analysis either examines why something happens or happened by looking at its causes or looks at a set of conditions and explains what effects result or are likely to result from them. A chemistry report on an experiment combining a mix of chemicals in several different ways, for instance, suggests moving from causes to effects. On the other hand, a newspaper article on the breakdown of authority in inner-city schools might well be organized by focusing on the effects of the breakdown and then tracing those effects back to their causes.

Considering problems and solutions

Moving from a **problem** or set of problems to a **solution** or solutions presents a natural and straightforward way of organizing certain kinds of information. The student studying motorcycle parking, in fact, decided to structure the overall organization of his data in just this way: he identified a problem (the need for more parking) and then offered two possible solutions to the problem. Many assignments in engineering, business, and economics call for a similar organizational strategy. One economics professor recently asked students to gather information on the latest slide in the stock market and to use that information to give advice to investors who lost money. The information students gathered first defined the problem the investors faced and then formed the basis for potential solutions.

EXERCISE 2.8

Using the topic you chose in Exercise 2.2, identify the most effective means of organizing your information. Write a brief paragraph explaining why you chose this particular method (or methods) of organization.

EXERCISE 2.9

Identify which method or methods of organization you would recommend for students who are writing on the following topics—and why.

1. The need for a new undergraduate library.
2. The autobiographical elements in Virginia Woolf's *To the Lighthouse*.
3. How to improve your writing.

4. Education to prevent the spread of AIDS.
5. The best places to study on campus.

■ 2i. Writing out a rough plan

A writer who has carefully organized information is a writer who already has a rough plan for a draft, a plan that should then be written down. Our student who wrote about some possible solutions to the motorcycle parking problem on campus organized all his data and developed the following rough plan. Notice that his plan calls for several organizational strategies within an overall problem-solution framework:

INTRODUCTION

give background to problem (use *chronological order*)
give overview of problem (use *division*)
state purpose—to offer solutions

BODY

present proof of problem in detail (use *illustration*)
present two possible solutions (use *comparison*)

CONCLUSION

recommend that first solution be scrapped for reasons of (a) cost (b) space (c) relative disadvantages
recommend that second solution be adopted and summarize benefits of doing so

While an informal plan worked well for this writer, you may wish to prepare a more formal outline such as the one illustrated in Chapter 39. Whatever form your organizational plan takes, however, you may want or need to change it as you begin drafting. Writing has a way of stimulating thought, and you may find yourself getting new ideas in the process of drafting, ideas you could pursue effectively. Or you may find that you need to go back and reexamine some information or gather more information.

Colleen Starkey, whom we last saw exploring her topic and organizing the information she generated, worked with an informal outline. Outlining before writing is sometimes difficult, but Colleen was able to generate the following outline on the basis of her exploratory work for her essay on the Bagelry.

```
 I. Introduction
    set picture—atmosphere
    describe it as a bagelry straight from the metropolis
    of NYC
II. Making bagels is their forte
    who—bakers
    what—all varieties (12)
    when—am and pm bake
    how—procedure—ingredients, baking time
    Business outside of store
III. Extra added specialties
     assorted sandwiches
     spreadables
     Bagel chips
     knishes
     pastries (6 layer—brownies, cakes)
     soups
 IV. A place for all to enjoy
     pleases tastes from plain to extravagant
     young to old
     NY'er to New Englander
     Health food nut to junk food junky
     meals and desserts
     Place to eat authentic . . . in NH
```

This informal outline shows elements of spatial order, description, process explanation, and illustration: she depicts the restaurant (spatial order and description); gives the procedure for making bagels (process explanation); and tells about the specialties of the house (illustration). On the basis of the above rough plan, Colleen began to draft her essay about the Bagelry.

EXERCISE 2.10

Write out a rough plan for an essay supporting the working thesis you developed in Exercise 2.7.

2j. Producing a draft

Most of us are in some sense "producing a draft" the moment we begin thinking about a topic. One writer reports that his best ideas for opening essays almost always come to him in the shower, another that she "practices" writing versions of paragraphs or sentences in her head while driving to and from work. At some point, however, we commit our thoughts to paper, sitting down with pen, typewriter, or word processor to produce a draft.

No matter how good your planning, investigating, and organizing have been, chances are that you will want and need to alter some things as you draft. This fact of life leads to a first principle of successful drafting: be flexible. If you see that your rough plan is not working as you begin drafting, do not hesitate to alter it. If some information now seems irrelevant, leave it out, even if you went to great lengths to obtain it. Through the entire drafting process, you may need to go back to some point you have already been through: you may learn that you need to do more research, or that your whole thesis must be reshaped, or that your topic is too broad and should be narrowed. The writing process is primarily a learning process, and you will continue planning, investigating, and organizing throughout the whole of that process. You may want to ask your instructor or a classmate to help you by reading drafts and telling you if your direction seems clear and effective.

Definite principles of drafting are hard to come by, because we actually know very little about how writers produce drafts. What we do know suggests that there may be almost as many ways to produce a successful draft as there are people to do it. Nevertheless, you can profit by learning as much as possible about what kind of situation is likely to help you produce your best writing. You can do so by considering a few simple questions: *Where* are you most comfortable and productive writing (in your room, in the library)? *When* are you most comfortable and productive writing (in the morning, late at night)? *Under what conditions* are you most comfortable and productive writing (with complete quiet, with "background" music, wearing jeans)? *What rituals* seem to help you produce good writing (exercising beforehand, sharpening pencils, cleaning up the room, scheduling breaks or treats)?

Once you have learned as much as you can about the atmosphere most conducive to your best writing, make every effort to do your drafting in that atmosphere. A few other practical tips about the drafting process may be helpful to you:

- *Have all your information close at hand and organized according to your organizational plan.* Having to stop to search for a piece of information can break your concentration or distract you in unhelpful ways.
- *Try to write in bursts of at least ten to twenty minutes.* Writing can provide its own momentum, and once you get going the task becomes easier.
- *Don't let small questions bog you down.* As you write, questions will come up that need to be answered, but unless they are major ones, make a tentative decision and move on.
- *Stop writing at a place where you know exactly what will come next.* Doing this will help you get started easily when you return to the draft.
- *Remember that a first draft need not be perfect.* In order to keep moving and get a draft done, you often must sacrifice some fine points of writing at this stage. Concentrate while drafting on getting your ideas across as clearly as possible. Don't worry about anything else, and don't stop writing.

Here is Colleen's first draft.

The Bagelry

It is a chilly fall morning. Many of the cars on [1] the road are covered with a thick crisp frost—a sure sign that another cold New England winter is on its way. To brighten this early morning and take the chill out of this fall day, many will start the day off with a piping hot cup of coffee and a fresh warm bagel straight from the oven. Although set in the college town of Durham, NH, the "Bagelry" offers authentic bagels in an atmosphere much like the small coffee shops and cafes that line NY city streets.

Making bagels is Warren and Elise Daniels' forte. [2] Having moved from Queens, NY, to the southeastern section of NH they saw a market for the traditional bagel. Even bakeries are a rarity in this area. With a store in Durham and Portsmouth they must make hundreds of dozens of bagels to satisfy the needs of both stores. Along with providing for their stores, they also sell bagels wholesale. Around Durham they supply the university and off-campus living areas—like the Greek houses. Deliveries are also made as far north as Portland, ME, and as far south as Manchester, NH.

A typical day at the Bagelry starts at 4 o'clock in 3 the morning. The first batch of bagels are prepared for the morning bake. One hundred to one hundred and twenty dozens of bagels are made for retail sales on the average. Approximately seventy dozens of bagels will be prepared for wholesale. All cooking and baking is performed at the Durham location. The Portsmouth store calls in its orders daily.

While most people are still sound asleep, the bakers 4 at the bagelry are busy making bagels before the sun rises. One hundred pounds of flour is used at a time to make the dough needed. Water and other ingredients are added. The dough is prepared in a huge mixer (approx. 6 ft. x 6 ft. x 4 ft.). Once the dough reaches the proper con- sistency it is transferred to another contraption that actually makes and shapes each individual bagel. It is the bakers' job, at this point, to put the bagels in rows on large flat boards. After all bagels have been put on boards they are stacked on portable racks and covered with cloth sheets to stand and rise. (The Baker knows the batch has risen when an uncooked bagel, like those rising, has begun to float in a pot of hot water on the stove.) After the bagels have risen they are refrigerated until they are baked. The first step in cooking the bagels is what makes them authentic NY style. Unlike the frozen type bagels one can buy in the supermarkets, these bagels are boiled before they are baked. This is done to give a special gloss to the outside of the bagel and a lighter—fluffier

consistency to the inside. After being boiled for approx.
5 mins., the bagels are placed on large baking boards and
put into a four shelf oven set at 500 degrees F and baked
for 15–20 mins. By seven a.m., the time the store opens,
hundreds of fresh hot bagels are ready for the craving
customer.

There are 12 varieties of bagels to choose from. 5
(If by chance your favorite is sold out when you arrive,
never fear for there is an afternoon bake as well.) The
types of bagels served range from the old stand–bys to
one actually invented by the proprietors. As you walk
into the Bagelry you can see all the bagels aligned, in
wire baskets, in this order; Garlic, Onion, Wheat, Egg,
Rye, Salt, Pumpernickel, Poppy, Oat, Sesame, Plain, and
Cinnamon Raisin. While plain is the old safe stand–by,
onion and cinnamon raisin seem to be the most popular.
The oatmeal bagel was actually created by one of the owners
Elise Daniels. This type has attracted a large following
as well.

There are extra added specialties that the Bagelry 6
serves. Along with selling bagels by the dozens, one can
get a bagel plain, toasted, with cream cheese or assorted
spreadables, or even done up like a sandwich. Gallon tubs
of cream cheese based spreads are prepared as needed.
A variety of taste options are open to the customer. If
you don't feel like cream cheese or butter, why not try
veggie spread, garlic and herb spread, lox spread, walnut
and raisin spread, cream cheese and chive spread, or olive
spread. If the customer feels the need for something more
substantial—there is a whole menu of assorted sandwiches
that can be made on the bagel of your choice. These sand–
wiches are combinations created by Elise Daniels that use
a variety of meats, cheeses, spreads, and vegetables.

Also available to the customer are fresh baked 7

quiches, breads, cakes, knishes, brownies, and delicious
but fattening 6-layer bars. One can also indulge in hot
or cold soups with a side order of bagel chips. The problem
of thirst has not been forgotten nor neglected. At the
Bagelry there are hot and cold drinks, carbonated and non-
carbonated beverages as well as seasonal specials like
hot mulled cider or thirst quenching lemonade.

    All in all, the Bagelry is a place for all to enjoy. 8
It pleases all tastes from plain to extravagant. One can
obtain any or all of the three meals consumed daily
(Breakfast, lunch and dinner foods are available). This
restaurant/bakery has fast, accommodating, pleasant
service. And it's the only one of its kind in this New
England area. If you ever have a craving for an authentic
NY bagel, the Bagelry is for you.

EXERCISE 2.11

Write a draft of an essay from the rough plan you worked on in Exercise 2.10.

▌ 2k. Reflecting on your writing process

    Finishing a draft provides a good opportunity to sit back, relax, and reflect a bit on your drafting, and to make an entry in your writing log if you are keeping one (see 1b). With the experience of writing still fresh in your mind, you can note down what went well, what gave you problems and why, what you would like to change or improve. Here are the entries Colleen made in her writing log:

1. *How did you arrive at your topic?* One of our choices was to "describe a favorite spot in your college town." From that general topic, I started brainstorming. I brainstormed for about five minutes and came up with a list of spots I liked or had an interest in. The Bagelry seemed like a natural thing to write on because I work there, know its workings, and could research it easily and talk about it in detail.

2. *When did you first begin to think about the assignment?* When the essay was first assigned, I began to think of ways I could write about things. After I spoke with my instructor, I knew that a good, clear description of the place would be important.

3. *What kind of planning or investigating did you do?* I interviewed the bakers and the owners of the Bagelry and took notes of what they said. I then set up an outline before beginning to write. (I like to use outlines before I write. A lot of the other people in the class don't like outlines, I know, but I like them.)

4. *How long did it take to complete your draft (including time spent gathering information)?* Interviewing the owners and bakers took a few hours. I came up with the first draft in two days. I used Day 1 to organize and collect ideas. In my case, this meant coming up with a list of possible things to include in the paper and then working out an outline of the paper. On Day 2, I sat down and actually wrote out the first draft at one sitting. That took about two hours.

5. *Where did you write your draft? (Briefly describe the setting.)* I wrote my draft in my own room sitting at my desk. It is a quiet atmosphere and a comfortable setting for me.

6. *Who is the audience for this piece of writing?* At first the general public was my audience. I had no specific age group or category of people in mind. Now that I've talked to other friends and my instructor about this draft, I think of the audience more as the readers of *Granite State Profiles* or *New Hampshire Monthly*.

7. *What is your relationship to the audience?* Primarily that of an informant, telling them something they didn't know before. Also maybe that of an entertainer. I want them to enjoy reading the paper.

8. *What do you see as the major strengths of your draft?* If I succeed, it makes people want to go get bagels!

9. *What do you see as the major weaknesses of your draft?* As of right now, lack of quotations from owners and workers, and more vivid description of the inside of the store itself.

10. *What would you like to change about your drafting process?* Nothing . . . ? Honestly, I'd like to be able to work more quickly.

FOR EXAMINING YOUR OWN WRITING PROCESS

Using the preceding questions on the writing process or the questions in 1b, record the planning and drafting activities you went through as you prepared for and wrote the draft of your essay in Exercise 2.11. Make this an entry in your writing log if you are keeping one.

3. Revising and Editing

"There's only one person a writer should pay attention to," says author William Styron. "It's the reader. And that doesn't mean any compromise or sell-out. The writer must criticize his or her own work as a reader." Author Doris Lessing elaborates on what this writer/reader must do in the advice she always gives to beginning writers: "learn to trust your own judgment, learn inner independence, learn to trust that you will sort the good from the bad. . . ." These experienced writers know first-hand the power that self-criticism and self-confidence bring to the task of **revising**. If you have analyzed your own process of writing, you probably know whether you tend to revise extensively and when you tend to make any revisions. Perhaps you also know what kinds of revisions you typically make. And a careful look at any essay you have submitted to an instructor will reveal how well you edited the paper. You may, however, have thought of revising and editing as one and the same thing; after all, both involve changes in a draft. The distinction between the processes of revising and editing, however, is one that will be useful as you become a more powerful and efficient writer.

Revising involves reenvisioning your draft—taking a fresh look at how clearly your thesis is stated and how persuasively it is developed, how logical your organization is, how varied your sentences are, how appropriate and memorable your choice of words is. In each case, you will be rethinking your aims and methods in terms of your original purpose and audience and of all you have learned during work on the essay. Revising may call for changes both large and small. You may need to reshape sentences, rethink sections, gather more information to support a point, perhaps even do some further exploratory writing.

Editing, on the other hand, involves fine-tuning your prose, attending to details of grammar, punctuation, and spelling. You might think of editing as the dress rehearsal for a written "performance"; as you edit, you work toward making your essay ready for public presentation. This chapter will explore the processes of revising and editing and provide you with a systematic plan for making the best use of these processes in your own writing.

3a. Getting distance before revising

The ancient Roman poet Horace advised aspiring writers to get distance from their work by putting it away for nine years. "Destroy whatever you haven't published," he wrote. "Once out, what you've said can't be stopped." If such advice seemed impractical to the Romans, it seems just about impossible to those writing in the late twentieth century. You have schedules to follow, deadlines to meet, examinations to take, graduation ceremonies to qualify for. Nevertheless, Horace's advice holds a germ of truth: the more time and distance you give yourself between the writing of a draft and its final revision, the more objectivity you will gain and the more options you will have as a writer. Even putting the draft away in a folder for a day or two will help clear your mind and give you some distance from your writing.

3b. Rereading your draft

If you give yourself—and your draft—a rest before revising, you will need to take time to review the draft by rereading it carefully for meaning, by recalling your purpose, and by considering your audience.

1. Rereading for meaning

Effective writers are almost always effective readers, particularly of their own writing. You can best begin revising, then, by finding a quiet and comfortable place to reread your draft carefully. For this reading, don't worry about small details. Instead, concentrate on your meaning and how clearly you have expressed it. If you see places where meaning seems unclear, note them in the margin.

2. Remembering your purpose

After rereading, quickly note the main purpose of the essay and decide whether it matches your original purpose. At this point, you may want to go back to your original assignment to see exactly what it asks you to do. If the assignment asks you to "prove" something, make sure you have done so. If you intended to propose a solution to a problem, make sure you have not simply analyzed the problem instead.

3. Considering your audience

Gaining some distance from your draft should help you think clearly about how appropriate the essay is for your audience. Is the language formal or informal enough for the audience? Will the audience be interested and be able to follow your discussion? What objections might the audience raise to the essay?

EXERCISE 3.1

Take twenty to thirty minutes to look critically at the draft you prepared in Exercise 2.11, rereading it carefully, checking how well the purpose is accomplished, and considering how appropriate the draft is for the audience. Then write a paragraph-length description of how you would go about revising it.

3c. Getting critical responses to your draft

Rereading and reviewing purpose and audience will allow you to take a good, critical look at your draft. In addition to your own critical response to your writing, however, you may want to get responses from friends, roommates, or classmates. Although you may trust your friends or classmates to do a thorough job for you, remember that they probably don't want to hurt your feelings by criticizing your writing. You can help by convincing them that constructive criticism is what you need, that trying to protect you by not mentioning problems does you no good.

But even honestly critical readers need to know where to focus their responses. In some cases, you may get exactly the advice you need by asking a quick, direct question: "What do you see as my thesis?" Be sure to pose questions that require more than yes/no answers. Ask readers to tell you in detail what they see, and then compare their reading to what you see. Merely asking "Is my thesis clear?" will not tell you nearly so much as "Would you paraphrase my thesis so I can see if it's clear?"

You may even want to provide a series of written questions for your readers. Following are some questions that might serve as guidelines for evaluating a draft. They can be used to respond to someone else's draft or to evaluate one of your own.

Questions for reviewing a draft

1. *Introduction:* What does the opening accomplish? How does it catch the reader's attention? How else might the essay begin? Can you suggest some better way of opening?

2. *Thesis:* Paraphrase the thesis of the essay in the form of a promise: "In this paper I will . . ." Does the draft fulfill the promise made by the thesis? Why, or why not?

3. *Supporting points:* List the main points made in the draft, in order of presentation. Then number them in order of interest to you, noting particularly parts that were *not* interesting to you or material that seemed unnecessary or added on for no reason. Review the main points one by one. Do any need to be explained more fully or less fully? Should any be eliminated? Are any confusing or boring to you? Do any make you want to know more?

4. *Organization:* What kind of overall organizational plan is used—spatial, chronological, or logical? Are the points presented in the most useful order? What, if anything, might be moved, deleted, or added? Can you suggest ways to make connections between paragraphs clearer and easier to follow?

5. *Paragraphs:* Which paragraphs are clearest and most interesting to read, and why? Which ones are well developed, and how are they developed? Which paragraphs need further development? What kinds of information seem to be missing?

6. *Sentences:* Number each sentence. Then reread the draft, and choose the three to five sentences you consider the most interesting or the best written—stylistically effective, entertaining, or memorable for some other reason. Then choose the three to five sentences you see as weakest, whether boring, bland, or simply uninspired. Are sentences varied in length, in structure, and in their openings?

7. *Words:* Mark words that are particularly effective—those that draw vivid pictures or provoke strong responses. Then mark words that are confusing or unclear. Do any words need to be defined? Are verbs active and vivid?

8. *Tone:* How does the writer come across in the draft—as serious, humorous, satiric, persuasive, passionately committed, highly objective? Mark specific places in the draft where the writer's voice comes through most clearly. Is the tone appropriate to the topic and the audience? Is the tone consistent throughout the essay? If not, is there a reason for varying the tone?

9. *Conclusion:* Does the essay conclude in a memorable way, or does it seem to end abruptly or trail off into vagueness? If you like the conclusion, tell why. How else might the essay end?

10. *Final thoughts:* What are the main strengths and weaknesses in the draft? What surprised you—and why? What was the single most important thing said?

Colleen Starkey, whose writing process we followed in Chapter 2, received the following responses from classmates to her draft. (Her draft appears in 2j.) Note that the first respondent followed the preceding list of questions very closely, answering almost every one in detail, while the other one gave much shorter and more generalized answers.

RESPONSE ONE

1. *Introduction:* Your introduction is good because it brings people to the scene. Maybe you should mention the Bagelry a little sooner to make sure that the readers know that you are going to talk about it all through the paper. It seems as if you are describing Durham. Another way of getting the reader's attention would be to start with the sights and smells inside the Bagelry—especially the aromas of the bagels and other goodies as they're baking. Or you could begin with the Danielses arriving in New Hampshire, seeing a market for bagels, and deciding to capitalize on it.

2. *Thesis:* "In this paper I will describe how/where a person can enjoy an authentic NY bagel in Durham, NH." Yes—fulfilled the thesis because you fully described the Bagelry.

3. *Supporting points:* (1) Danielses moving from NY; (2) size and scale of the Bagelry's operation; (3) how bagels are made; (4) varieties of bagels (5) bagel spreads and sandwiches; (6) other food and drinks. Interesting to me: how big the business is; how many different kinds of bagels are made; the variety of things the Bagelry sells. The Danielses might be interesting if they were developed more. Uninteresting to me: exactly how bagels are made. The point you could develop more perhaps is how the Bagelry is situated in such a small, quaint New England town and how it services it.

4. *Organization:* Overall organizational plan seems to be division—giving a sense of the scope of the business and how it got started and then discussing different aspects of how it operates and the products it sells. Order of points seems OK, but there are a few problems. Paragraph 3 starts out with the idea that work at the Bagelry begins early in the morning, but then you go on to other kinds of information before coming back to the early-morning idea at the beginning of the next paragraph. Also, in the conclusion you introduce an idea that hasn't been mentioned before—the Bagelry's "fast, pleasant, accommodating service." This idea needs to be either developed more or cut out. At the beginning of paragraph 2, you need

41

a clearer transition from the introduction—maybe mention the owners' move from New York right away.

5. *Paragraphs:* Even though I wasn't very interested in it, the paragraph on how bagels are made had a very clear chronological development that was easy to follow. Paragraph 2 needs more information about how the Danielses came to New Hampshire and opened the Bagelry and how it grew to its present size.

6. *Sentences:* I especially liked the second sentence of the introduction, the first sentence of paragraph 3 and the second and fourth sentences of paragraph 5. They all read smoothly and give interesting details. The other sentences in paragraph 3 seem weak—they just recite facts and statistics in a dull way, and it sounds as if the same sentence is being repeated again and again. Also, the first sentences of paragraphs 5 and 6 both start out with "There are" and don't arouse much interest. Except for paragraph 3, there's a good variety of length, structure, and openings.

7. *Words:* The words I thought were especially effective were *crisp* in the introduction, *contraption* and *gloss* in paragraph 4, and *delicious but fattening* and *indulge* in paragraph 7. I liked the word *craving* in the last sentence of the conclusion, but *the craving customer* sounds odd at the end of paragraph 4. I don't know what lox and knishes are. A couple of years ago I didn't even know what a bagel was—do you think most people in New Hampshire do?

8. *Tone:* The tone seemed objective, but at the same time you were trying to persuade people to like the Bagelry and its products. The persuasive tone comes through most in the sentences where you address the reader directly as *you,* especially the last sentence of the conclusion. The tone is consistent and I guess it's OK, even though sometimes it starts to sound like a commercial.

9. *Conclusion:* The conclusion is pretty good, but you should concentrate on the fact that the Bagelry is in a small town but is a "taste of NY."

10. *Final thoughts:* Strong points: It makes me want a bagel! There's a lot of colorful and mouthwatering detail. Weak points are just the listed information and description. Add more of your personality to it.

RESPONSE TWO

1. *Introduction:* The opening of this paper makes me hungry! I love the Bagelry! The lead draws me into the descriptive narrative on the Bagelry with sights, sounds, and taste sensations. It is great! Gives me a nice feel of NY and Durham.

2. *Thesis:* "In this paper I will describe how the Bagelry serves authentic NY bagels in a New England college town." You accomplished this nicely—but you also showed us how the Bagelry works.

3. *Supporting points:* The information on the whole was relatively new and informative to me. Good. Maybe you could pretend you were a bagel and write from that point of view. I would like to feel the culture and romance of bagels more. Even though I'm from a Jewish home, I can still remember what it was like to eat lox and cream cheese on a bagel for the first time. Your paper changes to a nearly scientific mode in its body. The intro. is great—description of cars, the smell of fresh dough, the warmth of the oven, and so on.

4. *Organization:* The paper organization is OK, I guess. I like the opening paragraphs best. Perhaps the paper would read better if the description were more involved and not so generalized—smells, taste-comparisons, textures, sights.

5. *Conclusion:* The essay concludes effectively. Perhaps you could let the reader know more about a NY delicatessen, Bagel Nosh, or bagelry. Colleen, perhaps you might consider playing up the role of the Bagelry in our small New England college town.

As these responses demonstrate, different readers react in very different ways to the same piece of writing. They do not always agree on what is strong or weak, effective or ineffective; they may not even agree on what the thesis is. In addition, you may find that you simply do not agree with their advice. As the author, the authority on what you want to say, you must decide what advice to follow and how best to do so. In examining responses to your writing, you can often proceed efficiently by looking first for areas of agreement ("everyone was confused by this sentence—I'd better review it") or strong disagreement ("one person said my conclusion was 'perfect' and someone else said it 'didn't conclude'—better look carefully at that paragraph again").

On the basis of broad areas of agreement in the responses she received, Colleen decided on the following changes: (1) to add more sensory details, since this description depends on appealing to the readers' senses; (2) to concentrate more on the Bagelry's location and its connection to New York, since the respondents like the idea of a "taste of NY"; and (3) to add more personal opinion in response to one reader's suggestion for "more personality."

Colleen also got some advice from her instructor. After noting that her topic seemed appropriate for readers of a local magazine, he suggested that she begin to consider the readers of such a magazine as her audience and that she add some quotations from the owners as well as some more information about the atmosphere of the restaurant. With these tips, Colleen saw that she needed to do more research on the Bagelry. She decided to interview the owners, bakers, and customers and to spend some time observing the restaurant, trying to see what made it so attractive to people in the area.

EXERCISE 3.2

Using the questions listed in 3c as a guide, analyze the draft you wrote in Exercise 2.11.

▌ 3d. Evaluating the thesis and its support

Once you have studied the responses to your essay and considered advice from all sources available to you, reread your essay once more, paying special attention to your thesis and its support. Check to make sure your thesis sentence contains a clear statement of the *topic* that the essay will discuss and a *comment* explaining what is particularly significant or noteworthy about the topic. As you continue to read, ask yourself how each sentence and paragraph relates to or supports the thesis. Such careful rereading can help to eliminate irrelevant sections or details or to identify sections needing further explanatory details or examples. If some points need more support, look back at your exploratory work and at suggestions from those who responded to your essay. If necessary, take time to gather more information and to do further exploration of ideas (see 2e).

EXERCISE 3.3

After rereading the draft you wrote in Exercise 2.11, evaluate the revised working thesis you produced in Exercise 2.7, and then evaluate its support in the draft. Identify points that need further support, and list those things you must do to provide that support.

▌ 3e. Analyzing organization

One good way to check the organization of a draft is by outlining it. You may have written an outline *before* the draft, but your organization may well have changed as you drafted. Drawing up an outline *after* the draft is finished allows you to evaluate the organizational plan as it actually exists in the draft. After numbering paragraphs in the draft, read through each one, jotting down its main idea or topic in a sentence or phrase. Then examine your list, and ask yourself the following questions:

- What organizational strategies are used? spatial? chronological? logical? Are they used effectively?
- Do the main points clearly relate to the thesis and to one another?
- Can you identify any confusing leaps from point to point?
- Can you identify clear links between paragraphs and ideas? Do any others need to be added?
- Have any points been left out?
- Are any of the ones included irrelevant?

Colleen briefly outlined her draft in the following way:

1. Thesis: The Bagelry offers authentic NY-style bagels in an atmosphere much like that of the small shops that line NY streets.
2. Warren and Elise Daniels saw a market in SE NH for bagels and now have a two-store franchise that also makes wholesale deliveries in the area.
3. Typical day—average daily sales—all baking done at Durham.
4. Process of how bagels are made and cooked.
5. Variety of bagels offered.
6. Types of spreads and sandwiches available.
7. Baked goods, desserts, soups, beverages.
8. Conclusion: The Bagelry is fun for any and all!

Colleen's outline helped her to see some problems in the first three paragraphs. First of all, she saw that the link from paragraph 1 to paragraph 2 might be weak. In fact, the first sentence of paragraph 2, *Making bagels is Warren and Elise Daniels' forte*, comes as a bit of a surprise to the reader—the Danielses are not linked to anything in paragraph 1 except the word *bagels*. To strengthen the transition, Colleen decided to add a new sentence linking the Danielses clearly to the Bagelry and also reemphasizing the New York connection.

```
    . . . Although set in the college town of Durham,
NH, the "Bagelry" offers authentic bagels in an atmosphere
much like the small coffee shops and cafés that line NY
city streets.
```

"This NY connection is no accident," said the Bagelry's
~~Making bagels is Warren and Elise Daniels' forte.~~
owner, Warren Daniels.
Having moved from Queens, NY, to the southeastern section
, Warren and his wife, Elise,   in an area where
of NH they∧saw a market for the traditional bagel∧ Even

bakeries are a rarity⊙~~in this area.~~ . . .

In addition, Colleen sensed that there was a leap or gap between paragraphs 2 and 3. As she said, "Paragraph 2 introduces the Danielses—and then they disappear." She decided to add more information on them, including some quotations from an interview she decided to conduct, and several other new sentences.

EXERCISE 3.4

On the basis of Colleen's list of paragraph points, evaluate the organization of the rest of her first draft (in 2j). Begin by answering the questions given in 3e.

EXERCISE 3.5

In checking the rest of the paragraph transitions in Colleen's first draft, did you find any others that were weak or missing? If so, suggest at least two ways of strengthening or adding each one.

3f. Reconsidering the title, introduction, and conclusion

First and last impressions count. In fact, readers remember the first and last parts of sentences—and of essays—better than anything else. For this reason, it is wise to pay careful attention to three important elements in an essay—the title, the introduction, and the conclusion.

1. The title

A good **title** gives readers information, draws them into the essay, and even gives an indication of the writer's view of the topic. It is an important device for defining what the essay will be. Colleen's original title, "The Bagelry," was accurate enough but not vivid or particularly intriguing. Following a suggestion from a reader of her first draft, she changed it to "A Taste of New York City in Downtown Durham." This revision establishes the implied comparison between New York and the small New England town and sets up expectations about just what the "taste of New York" might be.

▌ 2. The introduction

A good **introduction** accomplishes two important tasks: first, it draws readers into the essay, and second, it clearly states the topic and makes some comment on it. It contains, in other words, a strong lead, or a "hook," and often an explicit thesis as well. The most common kind of introduction opens with a general statement about the topic and then goes into more detail, leading up to a statement of the specific thesis at the end. A writer can also introduce an essay effectively with an *intriguing quotation*, an *anecdote*, a *question*, or a *strong opinion*. (See 5e for a fuller discussion and examples of various kinds of introductions.)

Colleen's original draft contained a fairly effective lead—a word picture of a fall morning in a small New England town, a picture her readers liked. But because it did not establish the connection between the Bagelry and New York as clearly as she wanted, she decided to add a sentence to do so: *Although bagels are not exactly a traditional New England breakfast, they have become a part of life for many people in southern New Hampshire.*

▌ 3. The conclusion

Like introductions, **conclusions** present special challenges to a writer. If a good introduction captures readers' attention, sets the scene, and signals what is to come, a good conclusion leaves readers satisfied that a full discussion has taken place. Often a conclusion will begin with a restatement of the thesis and then end with more general statements that grow out of it; this pattern reverses the common general-to-specific pattern of the introduction. Writers can also draw on a number of other ways to conclude effectively, including a *provocative question*, a *quotation*, a *vivid image*, a *call for action*, or a *warning*. If you look at the essay you are preparing now, you may find other means of concluding effectively. (See 5e for a fuller discussion and examples of various kinds of conclusions.)

Colleen signaled that she was drawing to a close—*all in all,*— then summed up the points she had made, and finally ended with an appeal to her readers: *If you ever have a craving . . . for an authentic NY bagel, the Bagelry is for you.* She felt that her conclusion was sufficiently clear, but she decided that the last sentence lacked punch. To make the sentence more emphatic, she revised it thus: *So if ever you have a craving for an authentic New York bagel, the Bagelry can satisfy your desire.*

EXERCISE 3.6

Review Colleen's draft in 2j, and compose an alternative conclusion. Then write a paragraph commenting on the strengths and weaknesses of the conclusion she actually used.

3g. Examining paragraphs, sentences, words, and tone

In addition to the large-scale task of examining the logic, organization, and development of their essays, effective writers look closely at the smaller elements: paragraphs, sentences, and words. Many writers, in fact, look forward to this part of revising because its results can often be very dramatic. Turning a bland, forgettable sentence into a memorable one—or finding just exactly the right word to express a thought—can yield great satisfaction and confidence.

1. Examining paragraphs

Paragraphing serves the reader by visually breaking up long expanses of writing and by signaling a shift in topic or focus. Readers expect a paragraph to develop an idea or topic, a process that almost always demands several sentences or more (see 5a). The following guidelines can help you evaluate your paragraphs as you revise:

1. Look for the topic or main point of each paragraph, whether it is stated or merely implied. Then check to see that every sentence serves to expand or support the topic.
2. Check to see how each paragraph is organized—spatially, chronologically, or by some logical relationship such as cause-effect or comparison-contrast. Then determine whether the organization is appropriate to the topic of the paragraph and if it is used fully to develop the paragraph. (See 5c and 5d.)
3. Count the number of sentences in each paragraph, noting those that have only a few. Do these paragraphs sufficiently develop the topic of the paragraph?

In paragraph 3 of her draft, for instance, Colleen counted six sentences. And of these sentences, the last four really did very little to develop the topic introduced by the first sentence of the paragraph, the beginning of a typical day at the Bagelry. When she looked to paragraph 4, Colleen saw the topic of "a typical day" further developed there. She decided, therefore, to put the sentences relating to this topic into a single paragraph along with more information describing a typical early morning in the Bagelry; information that did not develop that topic was moved to other paragraphs. Her revision of these paragraphs is shown below.

> A typical day at the Bagelry starts at 4 o'clock in the morning~~,~~ *when* ~~The~~ first batch of bagels ~~are~~ *is* prepared for the morning bake. ~~One hundred to one hundred and twenty dozens of bagels are made for retail sales on the average. Approximately seventy dozens of bagels will be prepared for wholesale. All cooking and baking is performed at the Durham location. The Portsmouth store calls in its orders daily.~~
>
> ~~While~~ most people are still sound asleep, *one of* the *five official* bakers *begins the task of preparing the dough.* ~~at the bagelry are busy making bagels before the sun rises.~~ *He starts with* ~~One~~ hundred pounds of flour~~,~~ ~~is used at a time to make the dough needed. Water and other ingredients are added.~~

EXERCISE 3.7

Choose two other paragraphs in Colleen's draft in 2j, and evaluate them using the guidelines listed above. Write a brief paragraph in which you suggest ways to improve the development or organization of these paragraphs.

▌ 2. Examining sentences

Sentences are the soldiers of prose, ideally marching forward in an orderly and impressive way that keeps readers engaged and ready for more. As with life, variety is the spice of sentences. You can add variety to the life of your sentences by looking closely at their length, structure, and opening patterns.

Varying sentence length

Too many short sentences, especially one after another, can sound like a series of blasts on a car horn—or like an elementary school textbook—while a steady stream of long sentences may bore or confuse readers. Most writers aim for some variety of length, then, breaking up a series of fairly long sentences with a very brief one, for example. In looking at her conclusion, Colleen found all of its sentences roughly the same length: twelve, eight, twelve, seven, ten, fourteen, and sixteen words. In revising, she decided to join sentences one through four into one twenty-six-word sentence, with three briefer sentences remaining at the end. If you read the draft version and revised version aloud, you should be able to hear the difference in rhythm the greater variety of length makes. (See 20a for detailed guidelines for checking sentence length in your own writing.)

```
                                          everyone
        All in all, the Bagelry is a place for all to enjoy,
      pleasing
  It pleases all tastes from plain to extravagant. One can
              at
  obtain any or all of the three meals, consumed daily
                                             m
  (Breakfast, lunch, and dinner, foods are available). This
  restaurant/bakery  has  fast,  accommodating,  pleasant
  service.  And it's the only one of its kind in this New
              So
  England area. If you ever have a craving for an authentic
  NY bagel, the Bagelry is for you.
                        can satisfy your desire.
```

Varying sentence structure

The simple sentence is the most common kind of sentence in modern English, but using all simple sentences can sound very dull. On the other hand, constant use of compound sentences may result in a singsong or repetitive rhythm, while long strings of complex sentences may sound, well, overly complex. The best rule is to strive to vary your sentences; see 20c for advice on ways to do so. Paragraph 3 of Colleen's draft could use some work on sentence variety, since all six of its sentences were simple. Colleen eventually decided that this paragraph should be completely revised and merged with paragraph 4, but she did revise sentences one and two to turn sentence two into a subordinate clause and hence create one complex sentence rather than two simple sentences. You can see the original two sentences along with her revision at the top of the facing page.

A typical day at the Bagelry starts at 4 o'clock in
the morning. ⌃*when* The first batch of bagels is prepared for
⌃*what is known as* the morning bake.

Varying sentence openings

If anyone has ever noted that your writing seemed "choppy," the cause of the problem probably lay in lack of variety in sentence openings. Most sentences in English follow subject-predicate order and hence open with the subject of an independent clause, as does the sentence you are now reading. But opening too many sentences in a row this way results in a jerky, abrupt, or "choppy" rhythm. You can vary sentence openings by beginning with a dependent clause, a phrase, or a subordinating conjunction. (See 20b for more information on ways of opening sentences.) Colleen's first paragraph suffered from a very jerky rhythm, probably because every one of its sentences opened with a subject. See how in the example that follows revising some of the openings improved the flow and made the entire paragraph easier to read.

It is a chilly fall morning. Many of the cars on
the road are covered with a thick crisp frost—a sure sign
that another cold New England winter is on its way. ⌃*Many*
will start the morning off with a piping hot cup of coffee
and a fresh warm bagel straight from the oven to brighten
this early morning and take the chill out of this fall *day,*
Although day. ⌃Bagels are not exactly a traditional New England
breakfast, ~~but~~ they have become a part of life for many
people in southern New Hampshire.

Checking for sentences with *it is*, *there is*, *and* there are

As you go over the sentences of your draft, look especially carefully at the ones beginning with *it is*, *there is*, or *there are*. In many cases, such as the first sentence of Colleen's draft (*It is a chilly fall morning*), which helps to create the setting for her essay, these phrases are perfectly good ways to start a sentence. But they can easily be overused or misused. You don't know what *it* means, for instance,

3g rev REVISING AND EDITING

unless the writer has already pointed out exactly what *it* stands for (see 11c). A more subtle problem with these openings, however, is that they may be used to avoid taking responsibility for a statement. Look at the following two sentences:

> It is necessary to raise student fees.
>
> The university must raise student fees.

The first sentence avoids responsibility by beginning with the weak *It is*—and fails to tell us *who says* it is necessary.

Many writers use *it is, there is,* and *there are* openings not to avoid responsibility but just because they are easy ways of getting a sentence going. But they are often unnecessary, and using them gives the important opening spot of a sentence to a vague, weak word (*it* or *there*) and the most overused verb in the English language (*be*). Usually a sentence will be much stronger if it is rewritten to begin another way. For example, *It is known that radon causes cancer* can be rewritten as *Radon is known to cause cancer.*

EXERCISE 3.8

Here are two sentences from Colleen's draft that open with *there are*. Find at least two ways to rewrite each one to eliminate the *there are* openings:

1. There are twelve varieties to choose from.
2. There are extra added specialties the Bagelry serves.

EXERCISE 3.9

Choose a paragraph of your own writing, and analyze it for variety of sentence length, sentence structure, and sentence openings. Then write a revised version of your paragraph.

3. Examining words

To an even greater extent than their paragraphs or sentences, writers' word choice, or diction, offers an opportunity for them to put their personal stamp on a piece of writing. As a result, writers often study their diction very carefully, making sure they get the most mileage out of each word. Because word choice is highly individual, general guidelines are hard to define. Nevertheless, the following questions should help you become aware of the kinds of words you most typically use.

1. Are the nouns primarily abstract and general or concrete and specific? Too many abstract and general nouns can create boring prose. To say that you bought a new car is much less memorable or interesting than to say you bought a new convertible or a new Porsche. (See Chapter 25.)

2. Are there too many nouns in relation to the number of verbs? The *effect* of the *overuse* of *nouns* in *writing* is the *placing* of too much *strain* on the inadequate *number* of *verbs* and the resultant *prevention* of *movement* of the *thought.* In the preceding sentence, one tiny form of the verb *be* (*is*) has to drag along the entire weight of all those nouns. The result is a heavy, boring sentence.

3. How many verbs are forms of *be?* If *be* verbs account for any more than about a third of your total verbs, you are probably overusing them. (See Chapter 8.)

4. Are verbs *active* whenever possible? Passive verbs are harder to read and remember than active ones. *The student's question was answered* is not as easy to understand or remember as *Professor Corbett answered the student's question.* The first sentence calls attention to the act of answering, which is hard to visualize since apparently no one is around to do it—the question is simply there, being answered. The second sentence, however, points our attention to the concrete presence of a particular person answering the question. The passive voice has many uses (see Chapter 8), but in general your writing will be stronger, more lively and energetic, if you use active verbs.

▌4. Examining tone

Word choice is closely related to **tone,** the attitude toward the topic and the audience that the writer's language conveys. In examining the tone of your draft, you need to consider the nature of the topic, your own attitude toward it, and that of your intended audience. Check the use of slang, jargon, and emotional language and the level of formality to see whether they create the tone you want to achieve (humorous, serious, impassioned, and so on) and whether that tone is an appropriate one given your audience and topic. You may even discover from your tone that your own attitude toward the topic is different from what you originally thought. (See Chapter 26.)

EXERCISE 3.10

Turn to 2j, read paragraphs 6 and 7 of Colleen's draft, and describe the tone you think she achieves. Does the tone seem appropriate to readers of a local magazine and to the topic she chose? What changes in wording would you recommend and why? Then revise the two paragraphs to create what you consider an appropriate tone.

▌ 3h. Editing

Because readers expect, even demand, a final copy that is clean and correct in every way, and because you want to put your very best foot forward in any formal writing you do, you need to make time for thorough and careful **editing.** You can make editing somewhat systematic by keeping a personal checklist of editing problems. All writers have personal trouble spots, problems that come up again and again in their writing. You may already be aware of some of your own trouble spots and will probably have others pointed out to you by instructors. Paying attention to the *patterns* of editing problems you find in your writing can help you overcome errors.

After identifying any typical trouble spots in your writing and getting advice on editing from this handbook, organize the information you have gathered in a systematic way. To begin, list all the errors or corrections marked on the last piece of writing you did. Then note the context of the sentence in which each error appeared. Finally, try to derive a guideline that will tell you what to look for to spot future errors of the same kind. You can broaden these guidelines as you begin to find patterns of errors, and you can then add to your system every time you write and edit a draft. Here is an example of such a checklist.

MARKED ERRORS	IN CONTEXT	LOOK FOR
wrong preposition	*to* for *on*	*to*
spelling	*to* for *too*	*to* before adjectives, adverbs
fragment	starts with *when*	sentences beginning with *when*
spelling	*a lot*	*alot*
missing comma	after *however*	sentences opening with *however*
missing apostrophe	*Michael's*	all names
missing apostrophe	*company's*	all possessive nouns
tense shift	*go* for *went*	use of present tense
fragment	starts with *while*	sentences beginning with *while*
spelling	*sacrifice*	*sacrafice*
comma	after *for example*	*for example*

This writer has begun to isolate patterns, like her tendency to write sentence fragments beginning with subordinating conjunctions (*when* and *while*), her trouble with apostrophes in possessives (*company's* and *Michael's*), and her tendency to skip commas after introductory elements. Some sorts of errors, such as the use of wrong words or misspellings, may seem so unsystematic that you may not be able to identify patterns in an editing checklist. (If spelling presents a special problem for you, keeping a separate spelling checklist as explained in Chapter 22 can help, or you may have a program that checks spelling as part of a word processor package.) But keeping an editing checklist will gradually allow you to identify most of the error patterns that trouble you. And since keeping up your editing checklist takes only a few minutes for each piece of writing, doing so is well worth the time.

EXERCISE 3.11

Using several essays you have written, establish your own editing checklist based on the one on the facing page.

▌ 3i. Proofreading the final draft

As a writer, you need to make your final draft *errorless*. You can do so by taking time for one last, careful **proofreading,** which means reading to correct any typographical errors or other slips, such as inconsistencies in spelling and punctuation. To proofread most effectively, read through the copy *aloud*, making sure that punctuation marks are used correctly and consistently and that all sentences are complete and no words are left out. Then go through again, this time reading *backwards* so that you can focus on each individual word and its spelling. This final proofreading aims to make your written product letter-perfect, something you can be proud to put your name on.

You have already seen a number of the revisions Colleen made in her draft. Following is the edited and proofread version she turned in to her instructor. If you compare her final draft with her first draft, you will notice revisions of both the content and the writing. For example, she eliminated details about the Portsmouth store, about the bagel-making process (paragraph 4 was just too long), and about the beverages. As for the writing, she eliminated a shift between *you* and *one* and strengthened her wording. In the conclusion, for instance, she changed *extravagant* to *adventurous* (a term more appropriate to patrons of a bagel restaurant) and *has* to *boasts*, a more specific word.

A Taste of New York City in Downtown Durham

It is a chilly fall morning. Many of the cars on the road are covered with a thick, crisp frost—a sure sign that another cold New England winter is on its way To brighten this early morning and take the chill out of this fall day, many of the drivers and their passengers will start the morning off with a piping hot cup of coffee and a fresh, warm bagel straight from the oven. Although bagels are not exactly a traditional New England breakfast, they have become a normal part of life for many people in southern New Hampshire ever since the Bagelry opened its doors six years ago. Set in the college town of Durham, New Hampshire, the Bagelry offers authentic New York–style bagels in an atmosphere much like that of the small coffee shops and cafés that line the streets of New York.

"This New York connection is no accident," said the Bagelry's owner, Warren Daniels. Having moved from the New York City borough of Queens to the southeastern section of New Hampshire, Warren and his wife, Elise, saw a market for the traditional bagel in an area where even bakeries are a rarity. With help from a bagel consultant in Ithaca, New York, they set out to bring bagels to New Hampshire. Their dream became reality on March 17, 1983, the day the Bagelry opened its doors. It wasn't long before their business was booming—and they now supply the campus dining halls, the Memorial Union pub, the Greek houses, and most supermarkets in the area.

A typical day at the Bagelry starts at four o'clock in the morning, when the first batch of bagels is prepared for what is known as the morning bake. While most people are still sound asleep, one of the five official bakers begins the task of preparing the dough. The baker starts with one hundred pounds of flour. Other ingredients include yeast, malt, and salt, but no preservatives, sugar, or fat. In fact, bagels are actually less fattening than other kinds of bread.

All the ingredients are blended together in an enormous horizontal mixer. Once the dough reaches the proper consistency, it is transferred to another contraption—creatively labeled the Bagel Machine—that actually makes and shapes each individual bagel. This machine measures out three-ounce pieces of dough, forms them into rings, and pushes them down a large metal chute onto a canvas conveyor belt. At this point, the baker puts the bagels in rows on large flat boards. When all bagels have been put on boards, the boards are stacked on portable racks and covered with cloth sheaths to allow the bagels to rise.

The first step in cooking the bagels is what makes them authentic New York style. Unlike the frozen bagels for sale in supermarkets, these bagels are boiled before they are baked, a step that gives an attractive gloss to the outside and a lighter, fluffier consistency to the inside. After being boiled for approximately one minute, the bagels are baked at 550°F for fifteen to twenty minutes. At this time the aroma of hot, fresh baked goods fills the Bagelry. You can smell the yeast of dough rising and the strong tang of garlic and onion bagels.

The Bagelry offers twelve varieties of bagels to choose from, ranging from the old standbys to one actually invented by the proprietors. (If by chance your favorite is sold out when you arrive, try later in the day, for there is an afternoon bake as well.) As you walk into the Bagelry, you can see all the types aligned in wire baskets. First comes halitosis heaven, Garlic and Onion; for the more mellow palate, there are Wheat, Egg, and Plain. Rye, Pumpernickel, and Oat cater to the health-conscious customer, followed by Sesame, Poppyseed, and Salt. Cinnamon Raisin brings up the rear and offers something on the sugary side for those with a sweet tooth. While Onion and Cinnamon Raisin seem to be the most popular, the oatmeal bagel, created by Elise Daniels, has attracted a large following as well. "I enjoy experimenting a lot with ideas at home," she said. "I'm constantly investigating new cookbooks and possible recipes."

Elise is largely responsible for the Bagelry's enticing menu, which includes many variations on the basic bagel. Along with bagels by the dozen, you can get a bagel toasted, with cream cheese or assorted spreadables, or even done up like a sandwich.

Also available are fresh baked knishes—another New York specialty, consisting of dough with meat, cheese, and other fillings—as well as various quiches, breads, cakes, brownies, and delicious but fattening six-layer bars. In addition, you can indulge in hot or cold soups with a side order of bagel chips.

But along with its large, assorted menu of tasty treats, the Bagelry has something more to offer—atmosphere. It is a quiet, serene shop that is well lighted and comfortably decorated, with bright white walls and a clean appearance. The Bagelry serves a large number of people, yet it offers quiet spaces to converse with friends or read without distraction. You can slip back to a far corner, bagel and coffee in hand, and settle down with a complimentary national or local paper—or you can sit under hanging plants in the front enjoying the comforts of the indoors while gazing at the outdoors.

The relaxed atmosphere is very welcoming to the frazzled business executive and the "always-on-the-go" college student. Quite often, area businesspeople will hold informal interviews at the Bagelry, and during finals time each semester, many students can be seen studying there. A majority of customers are regulars.

All in all, the Bagelry is a place for everyone to enjoy, pleasing all tastes from plain to adventurous, at all meals—breakfast, lunch, and dinner. This restaurant/ bakery boasts fast, accommodating, pleasant service. And it's the only one of its kind in this area of New England. So if ever you have a craving for an authentic New York bagel, the Bagelry can satisfy your desire.

3j. Using a word processor when revising and editing

If you have access to a word processor, you may want to take advantage of it as you revise, edit, and proofread. A word processor allows you to move sentences, paragraphs, and even whole sections of your essay around easily, so that you can experiment with various possibilities. You can also use a word processor to identify misspelled words and various other problems. (See Chapter 45 for a detailed discussion of how you can use a word processor as you write.)

EXERCISE 3.12

Using the guidelines presented in this chapter, revise, edit, and proofread the draft you wrote in Exercise 2.11.

FOR EXAMINING YOUR OWN WRITING PROCESS

While your revising, editing, and proofreading are still fresh in your mind, answer the following questions. Make your answers an entry in your writing log if you are keeping one.

1. How did you first begin revising?
2. What kinds of comments on or responses to your draft did you have? How helpful were they and why?
3. How long did the revising process take? How many drafts did you produce?
4. What kinds of changes did you tend to make—in organization, paragraph development, sentence structure, wording, adding or deleting information?
5. What worried you most as you were revising?
6. What pleased you most?
7. What would you most like to change about your process of revising, and how do you plan to go about doing so?

4. Understanding and Using Argument

Some 2,400 years ago, Aristotle noted that we need to understand the art of language use (which he called rhetoric) in order to create meaning, to express meaning clearly, and to defend ourselves against others who would use language to manipulate us. Those needs are no less pressing today as we approach the twenty-first century than they were for Aristotle and the Greeks in the fourth century B.C. In fact, written language surrounds us more than ever before, and this language—advertisements, news stories, memos, reports—not only competes for our attention but argues for our agreement. Even supposedly abstract and uncontroversial subjects like mathematics depend to a large extent on successful **argument**: language whose purpose is to persuade. As two professors point out in a recent book, the common idea that mathematics represents an absolute, abstract level of truth is in fact a myth. "Mathematics in real life is a form of social interaction," the authors note, in which "proving" anything involves a mixture "of calculations and casual comments, of convincing argument and appeals to the imagination."* Since argument so pervades our lives, we need to understand and be able to use the strategies of effective argument. In this chapter, you will practice these "survival arts" of recognizing, understanding, and using written arguments.

---

*Phillip J. Davis and Reuben Hersh, *Descartes' Dream: The World According to Mathematics* (Boston: Houghton Mifflin, 1988).

▌ 4a. Recognizing argument

In a way, all language use is argumentative. Even when you greet someone warmly, you wish to convince the person that you are genuinely glad to see him or her, that you value the person's presence. In this sense we are immersed in argument the way we are immersed in air: advertisements argue that we should buy their products; clothing argues that we should admire or respect the people inside; our friends argue—through their actions, their language, even their personal style—that we should accept and value them. Even the apparently objective reporting of newspapers and television has strong argumentative overtones: by putting a particular story on the front page, for example, a paper "argues" that this subject is more important than others, or by using emotional language and focusing on certain details in reporting an event, a newscaster tries to persuade us to view the event in a particular way. What one reporter might call *public assistance*, for example, another might call *welfare*, and yet another, the *dole*. We could legitimately find an argumentative "edge," therefore, wherever we find meaning in language. This chapter will look at written arguments, and specifically at ways writers can provide convincing support for their assertions.

Of course, argument is not always necessary. If everyone can agree on the truth of a statement, no argument is needed. For instance, saying that personal ownership of computers in North America has increased in the last twenty years makes a factual statement that should not produce an argument. On the other hand, saying that computers pose dangers to mental health presents an arguable assertion that must be convincingly supported before being accepted.

In many important areas of our lives, widespread factual agreement seldom exists. Is nuclear power generation necessary? Should we take one job or another, live in one location or another, marry one person or another, or marry at all? Should our town increase taxes for schools? Should we risk job security by protesting a policy we feel to be unethical? Is a new building an architectural masterpiece or an eyesore? Is the use of pesticides threatening the lives of farm workers? Such arguable questions are often at the center of our lives, and in most instances they fall into that area where absolute knowledge or truth is simply unavailable. To acknowledge that we can seldom find *absolute* answers to moral, political, and artistic questions, however, is not to say that we cannot move toward agreement on such questions by thinking clearly about them. In fact, this is precisely the way most human knowledge is gained: through the process of moving toward agreement on crucial issues.

In much of your work in college, you will be asked to participate in this process by taking a position and arguing for that position—whether to analyze a trend or explain a historical event or prove a mathematical equation. Such work will usually require you to make an arguable statement, to make a claim based on the statement, and finally to present *good reasons* in support of the claim.

The first step in the process of argument is to make a statement about a topic and then to check that the statement can, in fact, be argued. An arguable statement should have three characteristics:

- It should attempt to convince readers of something, change their minds about something, or urge them to do something.
- It should address a problem for which no easy solution exists or ask a question to which no absolute answers exist.
- It should present a position that readers could disagree with realistically.

EXERCISE 4.1

Using the three guidelines above, decide which of the following statements are arguable and which are not.

1. *Fatal Attraction* was the best movie of the 1980s.
2. The climate of the earth is gradually getting warmer.
3. The United States must drastically reduce military spending in order to balance the budget.
4. Shakespeare died in 1616.
5. Marlowe really wrote the plays of Shakespeare.
6. Water boils at 212 degrees Fahrenheit.
7. Van Gogh's paintings are the work of a madman.
8. The incidence of lung cancer has risen in the last ten years.
9. Abortion denies the fetus's inherent right to life.
10. The national 55-mile-per-hour speed limit was responsible for lower accident rates.

▌ 4b. Formulating an argumentative thesis

Once you have an arguable statement, you need to **make a claim** about the statement, one you will then work to persuade readers to accept. Your claim becomes the working thesis for your argument. For example, look at the following statement:

The use of pesticides endangers the lives of farm workers.

This statement is arguable—it aims to convince, it addresses an issue with no easily identifiable answer, and it can realistically be disagreed with. Although it does make a kind of claim—that pesticides threaten lives—the claim is just a factual statement about *what is*. To develop a claim that can become the working thesis for an argument, you usually need to direct this kind of statement toward some action; that is, your claim needs to move from *what is* to *what ought to be*:

STATEMENT ABOUT WHAT IS

Pesticides endanger the lives of farm workers.

CLAIM ABOUT WHAT OUGHT TO BE

Because pesticides endanger the lives of farm workers, their use should be banned.

This claim becomes your argumentative thesis. Like any working thesis, this one contains two elements, a topic (the statement about what is) and a comment (the claim about what ought to be). See 2f for more discussion of how to formulate a thesis.

TOPIC
Because pesticides endanger the lives of farm workers,
COMMENT
their use should be banned.

In some fields, such as literature or history, you will usually be making a claim that urges readers not to take action, but to interpret something in a certain way. In this case, the claim about what ought to be will usually be implied rather than stated directly. For example, a history essay that makes the claim that moral opposition to slavery was the major underlying cause of the Civil War is in effect arguing that readers should view the Civil War in this light rather than as a constitutional struggle over states' rights or an economic conflict between Northern industrialists and Southern planters. Or if you are asked on an art history examination to argue the claim that Van Gogh's paintings are the works of a madman, you are in effect trying to persuade your instructor that he or she ought to view Van Gogh's works as unconscious products of a disordered mind rather than the result of conscious rational decisions.

EXERCISE 4.2

Using two arguable statements from Exercise 4.1 or two that you create, formulate two working argumentative theses, identifying the topic and the comment for each one.

EXERCISE 4.3

Formulate an arguable statement and create a working argumentative thesis for two of the following general topics.

1. the Arab-Israeli conflict
2. mandatory testing of prison inmates for the AIDS virus
3. free access to computers for all students on campus
4. a new federal student loan program
5. surrogate motherhood

▍ 4c. Formulating good reasons

In his *Rhetoric*, Aristotle discusses the various ways one can argue a point. Torture, he notes, makes for a very convincing argument, but not one that most responsible and reasonable people would resort to. A pointed gun is no substitute for good reasons, and today we still rely on the three types of good reasons named by Aristotle—those that establish credibility, those that appeal to logic, and those that appeal to emotion.

▍ 4d. Establishing credibility

To make your argument convincing, you must first gain the respect and trust of your readers, or **establish your credibility** with them. Your character is embodied in your words, and the way this character is perceived by others largely influences how credible you and your arguments will be. The ancient Greeks called this particular kind of character appeal *ethos* and valued it highly. The little boy who cried "Wolf!" when there really was no wolf approaching was very quickly mistrusted by his townspeople. His was essentially a problem of *ethos*: he lost credibility because he could not be trusted to tell the truth.

In general, writers can establish credibility in three ways: (1) by being knowledgeable about the topic at hand; (2) by establishing common ground with the audience, in the form of respect for their points of view and concern for their welfare; (3) by demonstrating fairness and evenhandedness. Let us now look at each element of credibility more closely.

1. Demonstrating knowledge

A writer can establish credibility first by establishing his or her credentials. You can, for instance, show that you have some personal experience with the subject. In addition, showing that you have studied the subject, done research on it, and thought about it carefully can establish a confident tone. In doing so, your point is not to boast or show off; rather, you are assuring your audience that the position you hold is based on adequate knowledge and is systematically thought out.

To determine whether you can effectively present yourself as one knowledgeable enough to argue an issue, you might consider the following questions:

- Can you provide information from *several* sources to support your claim?
- What are the sources of your information?
- How reliable are your sources?
- Do any sources contradict each other? If so, can you account for or resolve the contradictions?
- If you have personal experience relating to the issue, is this experience directly applicable to your claim?

These questions will help you to probe your own stock of knowledge and assess your own credibility in making a claim, and they may help you to see what other work you need to do to establish your credibility. They may well tell you that you must do more research, check sources, try to resolve contradictions, refocus your working thesis, or even change your topic.

In demonstrating that you are knowledgeable, however, you must be careful not to sound high-handed or self-serving. Not only will you actually lose credibility by seeming to present a one-sided argument, but you will fail to establish common ground between yourself and your readers.

2. Establishing common ground

Many arguments between people or groups are doomed to end without resolution because the two sides occupy no common ground, no starting point of agreement. They are, to use an informal phrase, coming from completely different places. Such has often been the case, for example, in arms-control talks in which the beginning positions of the Soviet Union and the United States were so far apart that no resolution could ever be reached. The lack of common ground also dooms many arguments closer to our everyday lives. If you and your roommate cannot seem to agree on how often to clean the apartment, for instance, your difficulty may well be that your definition of a clean apartment conflicts radically with your roommate's. You may find, in fact, that you will not be able to resolve the issue until you can establish a common definition on which to base the argument. In this way, common ground provides a necessary starting point, one that can turn a futile quarrel into a constructive argument.

Common ground is just as important in written arguments as it is in diplomatic negotiations or personal disputes. Because topics and writers and audiences are so individual and varied, no foolproof or absolute guidelines exist for a writer to establish common ground with an audience. Following are some questions, however, that can help you to find common ground in presenting an argument:

- What are the differing perspectives on this issue?
- What are those aspects of the issue on which all sides agree?
- How can you express such areas of agreement clearly to all sides?
- How can you discover—and consider—opinions on this issue that differ from your own?

If you can establish common ground on an issue, you will have taken a giant step toward demonstrating good will toward your readers. We are inclined, after all, to listen with interest and attention to those we believe to have our best interests at heart. On the other hand, we are naturally suspicious of those who seem to want to further only their *own* interests.

3. Demonstrating fairness

In arguing a position, writers must demonstrate fairness toward opposing arguments. Audiences are more inclined to give credibility to writers they believe to be fairly considering and representing their opponents' views than to those who seem to be ignoring or distorting such views. We have all experienced unfair arguments: a co-worker loses his temper and blames you for a decision that was largely his idea, or a clever politician avoids a tough question at a news conference by giving an answer that ignores the questioner's point and then calling on someone else. Such tactics seem unfair, and to the extent that we recognize them we condemn them. It goes without saying, then, that to be an effective writer, you need to avoid such tactics and establish yourself as open-minded and evenhanded. Doing so often requires a genuine attempt to "walk a mile in the other person's shoes." Following are some questions that can help you discover ways of doing so:

- Can you show that you are taking into account all points of view? How?
- Can you demonstrate that you understand and sympathize with other points of view? How?
- What can you do to show that you have considered evidence carefully, even that which does not support your position?
- How can you demonstrate that you are open to other arguments, that you are not blindly advocating your claim?

4. Recognizing ethical fallacies

Some arguments focus not on establishing the credibility of the writer but on destroying the credibility of an opponent. In some cases such attacks are justified: if a nominee for the Supreme Court has acted in unethical ways in law school, for example, that information is a legitimate argument against the nominee's confirmation. Other times, however, someone may attack a person's character in order to avoid dealing with the issue at hand. Be extremely careful about attacking an opponent's credibility, for doing so without justification can harm your own credibility. Such unjustified attacks are called **ethical fallacies.** They take two main forms: *ad hominem* charges and guilt by association.

Ad hominem (Latin for "to the man") **charges** directly attack someone's character rather than focusing on the issue.

> Senator Kennedy has never fully explained his shameful complicity in the death of Mary Jo Kopechne, so he is not fit to pass judgment on a distinguished jurist like Judge Bork. [The Kopechne tragedy has no connection to Kennedy's judgment about Bork.]

Guilt by association attacks someone's credibility by linking that person with a person or activity the audience considers suspicious or untrustworthy.

> Senator Fleming does not deserve reelection; one of his staff assistants turned out to be involved with the Mafia. [Is there any evidence that the senator knew about the Mafia involvement?]

EXERCISE 4.4

Study the following advertisement for Greenpeace, an environmental group, carefully, and then list the ways in which the copywriters demonstrate knowledge, establish common ground, and demonstrate fairness. Do you think they succeed or fail in establishing credibility?

HELP US MAKE WAVES!

You can help keep the world's most unusual fleet in action...

We go into action without force. Without violence. But we *do* make waves. We're Greenpeace.

From the North Atlantic to the South Pacific, on the Great Lakes or in the near-frozen bays of Antarctica, Greenpeace is fighting for a cleaner environment and a more peaceful earth. You've heard about our campaigns to intercept renegade whalers on the high seas... to confront the nuclear superpowers in their contaminated testing zones... to block the dumping of toxic wastes into our water.

Greenpeace fights to *save* life and preserve our environment. And now *you* can be part of our worldwide campaigns to stop the slaughter of whales, dolphins and other animals... to prevent the spread of toxic pollution... to halt further testing of nuclear weapons and rid the oceans of nuclear-armed warships... to protect wilderness and wildlife from industrial and military exploitation.

Dangerous work? Yes. But we're willing to face the risks.

Over the past 15 years, Greenpeace's nonviolent navy has taken on the U.S. Department of Defense, the Soviet Navy, the Norwegian Coast Guard and the Royal Canadian Mounted Police. Our flagship, the *Rainbow Warrior,* was blown up by French secret service operatives, killing a member of her crew. Our activists have been threatened, arrested and beaten. They've had explosive harpoons shot over their heads and barrels of radioactive waste dropped on their boats.

But tough challenges bring dramatic victories. As a result of just some of Greenpeace's campaigns: the International Whaling Commission voted to end all commercial whaling; 37 years of dumping radioactive waste into the Atlantic Ocean was stopped; the annual slaughter of harp seals in Canada is virtually over; the French ceased atmospheric testing of nuclear weapons.

You can help Greenpeace meet tomorrow's challenges — help win tomorrow's victories.

Greenpeace needs you.

Greenpeace depends on the financial support of thousands of citizens around the world — people like you who care about the future of our planet — to keep our fleet in action. Your tax-deductible contribution today will help pay for the supplies and equipment we must have to take on those who poison our seas and slaughter our marine life.

You benefit as well.

When you support Greenpeace, you'll have the satisfaction of knowing that every Greenpeace victory for the environment is a victory *you* have helped make possible. And, for your contribution of $15 or more, you will receive our colorful, informative magazine, *Greenpeace,* to keep you up to date on our worldwide actions to protect our planet. Make some waves today!

☐ **YES** ... I want to help Greenpeace win more victories for our environment. Here's my contribution of:

☐ $15   ☐ $25   ☐ $35   ☐ $50   ☐ $100   ☐ Other $_____

Name _____

Address _____

City/state/zip _____   G8C

Your contribution to Greenpeace is tax-deductible.

Please make your check payable to Greenpeace, and send it with this coupon today to:
Greenpeace, P.O. Box 3720, Washington, D.C. 20007.

A copy of our annual report is available upon request from Greenpeace or the New York Department of State, Office of Charities Registration, Albany, NY 12231.

EXERCISE 4.5

Using a working argumentative thesis you drafted in Exercise 4.2 or 4.3, write a paragraph or two describing how you would go about establishing your credibility in arguing that thesis.

▌ 4e. Appealing to logic

While the character we present in writing always exerts a strong appeal (or lack of appeal) in an argument, our credibility alone cannot and should not carry the full burden of convincing a reader. Indeed, we are inclined to view the **logic of the argument**—the reasoning behind it—as more important than the character of the person presenting the case. In truth, the two are usually inseparable and thus of equal importance. Nevertheless, strong logical support characterizes most good arguments. This section will examine the most effective means of providing logical support for a written argument: examples and precedents, testimony and authority, and causes and effects.

▌ 1. Providing examples and precedents

Just as a picture can sometimes be worth a thousand words, so can a well-conceived **example** be extremely valuable in arguing a point. No one in recent years has used the example to greater effect than President Ronald Reagan, whose public statements often employed a homespun example from his childhood or even from one of his movies to drive home a point. This paragraph, in fact, has used Reagan as an example in making its point: that examples are one of the staples of everyday argument.

Examples are used most often to support generalizations or to bring abstractions to life. For instance, a *Newsweek* review of the movie *Star Trek IV* made the general statement that the movie contained "nutty throwaway lines that take a minute to sink in" and then illustrated the generalization with this example:

> When the crew, flying the Klingon warship they inherited . . . , land in Golden Gate Park, they fan out to different corners of the city. . . . Kirk's parting command, spoken like a PTA mother at the county fair: "Everybody remember where we parked."

The generalization would have meant little without the example to bring it to life.

Examples can also help us understand abstractions. "Famine," for instance, may be difficult for us to think about in the abstract—but a graphic description of a drought-stricken community, its riverbed cracked dry, its people listless, emaciated, and with stomachs bloated by hunger, speaks directly to our understanding.

Precedents are particular kinds of examples taken from the past. The most common use of precedent occurs in law, where an attorney may argue a case by citing the precedent of past decisions. A judge may be asked to rule that a defendant was negligent, for example, because the Supreme Court upheld a ruling of negligence in an almost identical case ten years earlier.

Precedent appears, however, in everyday arguments as well. If you urge your best friend to work your shift for you on the basis that the last time she needed some time off you worked her shift, you are arguing on the basis of precedent. Or if as part of a report on campus safety, you back up your request for increased lighting in the library parking garage by pointing out that the university has increased lighting in four similar garages in the past year, you are again arguing on the basis of precedent.

In research-based writing, you usually must list your sources for examples and precedents that are not based on your own knowledge (see 40b).

▌2. Citing authority and testimony

Another way to support an argument logically is to cite **authority.** As young children we were easily swayed by authority; it was right to do something simply because our parents (the authorities) said so. In recent years the use of authority has figured prominently in the antismoking movement. Many older Americans will remember, for instance, the dramatic impact of the U.S. surgeon general's 1963 announcement that smoking is hazardous to health. Many people at the time quit smoking, largely convinced by the authority of the person offering the evidence. Authority has been used in a similar way in the more recent effort to control drug use and abuse in the United States.

Citing an authority is thus a time-honored strategy for building support for an argumentative claim. But as with other such strategies, citing authorities demands careful consideration. Following are some questions you might consider to be sure that you are using authorities effectively:

- Is the authority timely? (To argue that the United States should pursue a foreign policy because it is one supported by Thomas Jefferson will probably fail because Jefferson's times were so radically different from ours.)
- Is the authority qualified to judge the topic at hand? (To cite a biologist in an essay on linguistics is not likely to strengthen your argument.)
- Is the authority likely to be known and respected by readers? (To cite an unfamiliar authority without some identification would lessen the impact of the evidence given.)

Authorities are commonly cited in research-based writing (treated in Part Nine), which relies on the findings of other people. In addition, you can cite authorities in answering essay examination questions (treated in Chapter 43) or in an assignment that asks you to review the literature in any field (treated in Chapter 42).

Testimony—the evidence an authority presents in support of a claim—is a feature of much contemporary argument. Most familiar are the testimonials found in advertisements—a television personality giving testimony for dog food, or a star athlete speaking for Wheaties. In fact, we are so inundated with the use of testimonials in television advertising that we may be inclined to think of them only in terms of *mis*use. But if the testimony is timely, accurate, representative, and provided by a respected authority, then it, like authority itself, can add powerful support to an argument. In an essay for a literature class, for example, you might argue that a new edition of a literary work will open up many new areas of interpretation. You could strengthen this argument by adding a quotation from the author's biographer noting that the new edition carries out the author's intentions much more closely than the previous edition did.

In research-based writing you should list your sources for authority and testimony that are not based on your own knowledge (see 40b).

3. Establishing causes and effects

Showing that one event is the cause—or the effect—of another can sometimes help to support an argument. (See Chapters 2 and 5 for a discussion and examples of developing a topic by cause-effect analysis.) To take an everyday example, suppose you are trying to explain, in a petition to change your grade in a course, why you were unable to take the final examination. In such a case you would most naturally try to trace the **causes** of your failure to appear—the death of your grandmother followed by the theft of your car, perhaps—so that the committee reading the petition would change your grade. We tend not to think of such analysis as a form of argument, but in many ways it is: in identifying the causes of a situation, you are implicitly arguing that the **effect**—your not taking the examination—should be given new consideration.

Tracing causes often lays the groundwork for an argument, particularly if the effect of the causes is one we would like to change. Recent figures from the U.S. Department of Education, for example, indicate that the number of high school dropouts is rising. If we can identify and understand the causes of this increased dropout rate—for example, a decline in reading skills—we may be able to make an argument for policies aimed at reversing the trend by affecting the causes in some way—such as hiring more teachers to provide remedial reading instruction.

In college writing, you may often be asked to show causes and effects. In an environmental science class, for example, a student may argue that a national law regulating smokestack emissions from utility plants is needed because (1) acid rain on the East Coast originates from emissions at utility plants in the Midwest, (2) acid rain kills trees and other vegetation, (3) midwestern states have been prevented by utility lobbying from passing strict laws controlling emissions from such plants, and (4) unless checked, acid rain will destroy most eastern forests by 2020. In this case, the first point is that the emissions cause acid rain; the second, that acid rain causes destruction of eastern forests; and the third, that states have not acted to break the cause-effect relationship established by the first two points. The fourth point ties all of the previous points together to provide an overall argument from effect: "unless X, then Y."

In fact, a cause-effect relationship is often extremely difficult to establish. Scientists and politicians continue to disagree, for example, over the extent to which acid rain is responsible for the so-called dieback of many eastern forests. In spite of the difficulty, though, if we can show that X definitely causes Y, we will have a powerful argument at our disposal. That is why so much effort has gone into establishing a definite link between smoking and cancer and between certain dietary habits and heart disease; if the causal link can be established, it will argue most forcefully that we should alter our behavior in certain clear-cut ways.

I 4. Using inductive and deductive reasoning

Traditionally, logical arguments are classified as using either inductive or deductive reasoning, which almost always work together. **Inductive reasoning,** most simply, is the process of making a generalization based on a number of specific instances: if you find you are ill on ten occasions after eating seafood, you will likely draw the inductive generalization that seafood makes you ill. It may not be an absolute certainty that the seafood was the culprit, but the *probability* lies in that direction. We all use such inductive reasoning for simple everyday discussions, but induction can be quite complex, as demonstrated by medical response to the sudden outbreak of an apparently new illness in the mid-1970s. This illness, later named Legionnaires' disease, resulted in many deaths. Medical researchers used a painstaking and time-consuming process of inductive elimination, examining every case in great detail to determine what the patients had in common, before they were able to generalize accurately about the cause of the disease.

Deductive reasoning, most simply, reaches a conclusion by assuming a general principle (known as a **major premise**) and then applying that principle to a specific case (the **minor premise**). In practice, this general principle is usually derived from induction. The inductive generalization "seafood makes me ill," for instance, could serve as the major premise for a deductive argument: "since all seafood makes me ill, the plate of it just put before me is certain to make me ill." The fictional detective Sherlock Holmes was famous for using deductive reasoning to solve his cases. Beginning, for instance, with the major premise "watchdogs always bark at strangers," Holmes applied that premise to the case of a stolen racehorse and reasoned that since the watchdog did not bark when the horse was stolen, the thief was not a stranger but someone the dog knew.

Deductive arguments like these have traditionally been analyzed as **syllogisms,** three-part statements containing a major premise, a minor premise, and a conclusion:

MAJOR PREMISE	All people die.
MINOR PREMISE	I am a person.
CONCLUSION	I will die.

Syllogisms may work for technical logical purposes, but rarely do they prove useful in the kind of arguments you are likely to write. They are simply too rigid and absolute to serve in arguments about questions that have no absolute answers, and they often lack any appeal to an audience. From Aristotle came a less rigid alternative, the **enthymeme,** which calls on the audience to supply the implied major premise. For example:

> This bridge is carrying twice as much traffic as it was built for, so we need to build a new bridge or restrict traffic on this one.

You can analyze this enthymeme by restating it in the form of two premises and a conclusion:

MAJOR PREMISE	Bridges should carry only the amount of traffic they were built for.
MINOR PREMISE	This bridge is carrying twice as much traffic as it was built for.
CONCLUSION	We need to build a new bridge or restrict traffic on this one.

Note that the major premise is one the writer can count on an audience agreeing to, or supplying: safety and common sense demand that bridges carry only the amount of traffic they are built for. By thus inspiring audience "participation," an enthymeme actually gets the audience to *contribute* to the argument.

Whether it is expressed as a syllogism or an enthymeme, however, a deductive conclusion is only as strong as the premises upon which it is based. The citizen who argues that "Edmunds is a crook who shouldn't be elected to public office" is arguing deductively, based on an implied major premise: "No crook should be elected to public office." In this case, most people would agree with this major premise. So the issue in this argument rests on the minor premise—that Edmunds is a crook. Only if that premise can be proven satisfactorily are we likely to accept the deductive conclusion that Edmunds shouldn't be elected to office.

While we may well agree with some unstated major premises (such as that no crook should be elected), at other times the unstated premise may be more problematic. The person who says, "Don't bother to ask for Jack's help with physics—he's a jock" is arguing deductively on the basis of an implied major premise: "jocks don't know anything about physics." In this case, careful listeners would demand proof of the unstated premise. Because bigoted or prejudiced statements often rest on this kind of reasoning, writers should be particularly alert to it.

I **5. Recognizing logical fallacies**

Logical fallacies are errors in reasoning. Though they cannot stand up to analysis, they are commonplace enough that they may be hard to spot as errors. Indeed, such reasoning can often convince uncritical audiences. Sharp readers will detect fallacious appeals, however—and may even reject an otherwise worthy argument that relies on them. Your time will be well spent, therefore, in learning to recognize—and to avoid—these fallacies. Common logical fallacies include begging the question, *post hoc*, non sequitur, either/or, hasty generalizations, and oversimplification.

Begging the question treats a question as if it has already been answered.

> The United States must defend democracy in Nicaragua by supporting the freedom fighters in their struggle with tyranny. [By calling the Nicaraguan rebels freedom fighters and the government a tyranny, this writer begs the question of whether U.S. aid to the rebels will actually help to defend democracy.]

The **post hoc fallacy,** from the Latin *post hoc ergo propter hoc,* which means "after this, therefore caused by this," assumes that just because Event B happened *after* Event A, it must have been *caused* by Event A.

> We should not rebuild the town docks because every time we do a big hurricane comes along and damages them. [Does the reconstruction cause hurricanes?]

A **non sequitur** (Latin for "it does not follow") attempts to tie together two or more logically unrelated ideas as if they *were* related.

> If we can send a spacecraft to Mars, then we can discover a cure for cancer. [These are both scientific goals, but do they have anything else in common? What does achieving one have to do with achieving the other?]

The **either/or fallacy** asserts that a complex situation can have only two possible outcomes, one of which is necessary or preferable.

> If we do not build the new aqueduct system this year, residents of the Tri-Cities area will be forced to move because of lack of water. [What is the evidence for this claim? Do no other alternatives exist?]

A **hasty generalization** bases a conclusion on too little evidence or on bad or misunderstood evidence.

I couldn't understand the lecture today, so I'm sure this course will be impossible. [How can the writer be so sure of this conclusion based on only *one* piece of evidence?]

Oversimplification of the relation between causes and effects is another fallacy based on careless reasoning.

If we prohibit the sale of alcohol, we will get rid of the problem of drunkenness. [This oversimplifies the relation between laws and human behavior.]

EXERCISE 4.6

The following sentences contain deductive arguments based on implied major premises. Identify each of the implied premises.

1. A dream is not an accurate picture of reality since it is heavily influenced by our subjective feelings.
2. In a recent national survey, a majority of Americans said they either smoke marijuana or do not care if others do; therefore, smoking marijuana should be legalized.
3. Active euthanasia is morally acceptable when it promotes the best interests of everyone concerned and violates no one's rights.
4. The law raising the drinking age to twenty-one should not be passed because it would unfairly discriminate against a group of people who are legally considered adults in all other respects.
5. Animals can't talk, so therefore they can't feel pain as humans do.

EXERCISE 4.7

The following brief article from *Newsweek* raises some provocative questions about causes and effects, and in doing so it uses example and authority. Read the article, and assess it in terms of the questions that follow.

Mom always told you chicken noodle soup could cure a cold. But could it prevent a disabling disease like Alzheimer's? That's what researchers are asking about a new chicken soup under development by Thomas J. Lipton Co. Inc. The still-to-be-named soup is enriched with purified lecithin, a nutrient undergoing testing as an Alzheimer's treatment. In accordance with Food and Drug Administration regulations, Lipton stops short of attaching medical claims to its new product. But the company may introduce it simply as "chicken soup with lecithin" sometime next year.

  The soup is the brainchild of MIT Prof. Richard Wurtman and Harvard neurologist John Growden. Wurtman and Growden approached Lipton after discovering that purified lecithin could affect the chemistry of the brain. The purified lecithin, which is more concentrated than that sold in health-food stores, raises blood levels of choline, which, in turn, may aid memory.

Whether the new soup could benefit the general population is still unclear. But Wurtman and Growden are studying the product's effect on memory and fatigue. Says Lipton spokesman Larry Hicks, "The market may be much larger than we now know."

1. What is the cause-effect argument?
2. Is the link between cause and effect fully established?
3. What evidence would be required to establish that link more fully?
4. Does the use of authority or testimony help establish the link? Why, or why not?
5. What example is used in the introduction—and is it effective in illustrating the point?
6. Can you identify any logical fallacies?

EXERCISE 4.8

Analyze the advertisement in Exercise 4.4 for the use of examples and precedents; authority and testimony; causes and effects; induction and deduction; and logical fallacies.

EXERCISE 4.9

Using a working argumentative thesis that you created in Exercise 4.2 or 4.3, write a paragraph describing the logical appeals you would use to support the thesis.

▎ 4f. Appealing to emotion

Most successful arguments appeal to our hearts as well as to our minds. Good writers, therefore, supplement appeals to logic and reason with those designed to **enlist the emotional support** of their readers. This principle was vividly demonstrated a few years ago when Americans began hearing about a famine in Africa. Facts and figures (logical appeals) did indeed convince many Americans that the famine was both real and serious. What brought an outpouring of aid, however, were not the facts and figures but the arresting photographs of children, at once skeletal and bloated, dying of starvation. In this case, the emotional appeal of those photographs spoke more powerfully than did the logical statistics. Writers can gain similarly powerful effects through the use of description, concrete language, and figurative language.

▌1. Using description

Vivid **description** provides one of the most effective means of appealing to emotions. Travel articles and advertisements draw heavily on this principle: think of all the descriptions of sunny beaches that appear in newspapers during the dreary winter months. Description can work just as effectively in your written arguments. Using strong, descriptive details can bring a moving immediacy to any argument.

The student described in Chapter 2 who was at work on a proposal to make the library more accessible to students in wheelchairs had amassed plenty of facts and figures, including diagrams and maps, illustrating the problem. But her first draft seemed dry and lifeless in spite of all her information. She decided, therefore, to ask a friend who used a wheelchair to accompany her to the library—and she revised her proposal to open with a detailed description of that visit and the many frustrations her friend encountered.

▌2. Using concrete language

Concrete language stands at the heart of effective description and hence helps to build emotional appeal. The student urging improved wheelchair access to the library, for instance, could have said simply that her friend "had trouble entering the library." Such a general statement, however, has little impact; it does not appeal to readers' emotions or allow them to imagine themselves in a similar position. The revised version, full of concrete description, does so: *Maria inched her heavy wheelchair up the narrow, steep entrance ramp, her small arms straining to pull up the last twenty feet, her face pinched with the sheer effort of getting into Main Library.* (Concrete language is discussed in greater detail in 25c.)

▌3. Using figurative language

Figurative language, or figures of speech, can also help to paint a detailed and vivid picture. Figurative language does so by making striking comparisons between something you are writing about and something else that is easier for a reader to visualize, identify with, or understand. Figures of speech include metaphors, similes, and analogies (see 26b2). **Metaphors** compare two things directly: *Richard the Lion-Hearted; old age is the evening of life.* **Similes** make comparisons using *like* or *as: Richard is as brave as a lion; old age is like the evening of life.* **Analogies** are extended metaphors or similes that compare an unfamiliar concept or process to a more familiar one to help the reader understand the unfamiliar concept:

> The most instructive way I know to express this cosmic chronology is to imagine the fifteen-billion-year lifetime of the universe (or at least its present incarnation since the Big Bang) compressed into the span of a single year. Then every billion years of Earth history would correspond to about twenty-four days of our cosmic year, and one second of that year to 475 real revolutions of the Earth about the sun.
>
> —CARL SAGAN, "The Cosmic Calendar"

Metaphors, similes, and analogies can all make an abstract or otherwise difficult concept understandable in terms of more concrete, everyday experience. James Watson and Frances Crick, who won the Nobel Prize for their work on the structure of DNA, used the metaphor of a zipper to describe how two strands of molecules could separate during cell division. In the same way, a student arguing for a more streamlined course registration process may find good use for an analogy, saying that the current process makes students feel like laboratory rats in a maze. This analogy, which suggests manipulation, helpless victims, and a clinical coldness, creates a vivid description and hence adds emotional appeal to the argument. For an analogy to work effectively, however, it must be supported by additional evidence: the student would have to show that the current registration process has a number of similarities to a laboratory maze, such as uncaring officials overseeing the process and confused students wandering through complex bureaucratic channels and into dead ends.

▌ 4. Shaping your appeal to your audience

As with appeals to credibility and to logic, appealing to emotions is effective only insofar as it moves your particular audience. Of course, you must always evaluate such appeals, being sensitive to your audience. You can't predict absolutely any audience's emotional response, but you can consider your topic and assess its probable emotional effects.

A student arguing for increased lighting in campus parking garages, for instance, might consider the emotions such a discussion will potentially raise (fear of attackers, anger at being subjected to such danger, pity for victims of such attacks), decide which emotions would be most appropriately appealed to, and then look for descriptive and figurative language to carry out such an appeal.

79

In a leaflet to be distributed on campus, for example, the student might describe the scene in a dimly lighted garage as a student parks her car and then has to walk to an exit alone through shadowy corridors and staircases. Parking in the garage might be compared to running the gauntlet in a fraternity hazing or venturing into a jungle with dangerous animals lurking behind every tree.

In a proposal to the university administration, on the other hand, the student might describe past attacks on students in campus parking garages and the negative publicity and criticism these provoked among students, parents, alumni, and other groups. For the administration, the student might compare the lighting in the garages to gambling, arguing that the university is taking a significant chance with the current lighting conditions and that increased lighting would lower the odds against future attacks.

▌ 5. Recognizing emotional fallacies

Appeals to the emotions of an audience constitute a valid and necessary part of argument. Unfair or overblown emotional appeals, however, attempt to overcome the reasonable judgment of readers. The most common kinds of these **emotional fallacies** include bandwagon appeal, flattery, in-crowd appeal, veiled threats, and false analogies.

Bandwagon appeal suggests that a great movement is under way and that the reader will be a fool or a traitor not to join it.

> Voters are flocking to candidate X by the millions, so you'd better cast your vote the right way. [Why should you jump on this bandwagon? Where is the evidence to support this claim?]

Flattery tries to persuade readers to do something by suggesting that they are thoughtful, intelligent, or perceptive enough to agree with the writer.

> We know you have the taste to recognize that an investment in an ArtForm ring will pay off in the future. [*How* will it pay off?]

In-crowd appeal, a special kind of flattery, invites readers to identify with an admired and select group.

> Thoughtful and progressive listeners find U2 the most consistently interesting band recording today. Join those in the know: subscribe to the *U2 News*. [Who are these listeners? Will subscribing put you "in the know"?]

Veiled threats try to frighten readers into agreement by hinting that otherwise they will suffer adverse consequences.

> If Public Service Electric Company does not get an immediate 15 percent rate increase, its services to you, its customers, will be seriously affected. [What is the evidence for this claim? Is such an effect on services legal or likely?]

False analogies make misleading comparisons between two situations that are *not* alike in most or important respects.

> If the United States gets involved in a land war in the Middle East, it will turn out just like Vietnam. [Is there any point of analogy except that they are both wars?]

EXERCISE 4.10

Make a list of the common human emotions that might be attached to the following topics, and suggest appropriate ways to appeal to those emotions in a specific audience you choose to write for.

1. Prohibiting smoking on campus
2. Capital punishment
3. Nuclear power generation
4. Television evangelism
5. Competency testing for teachers

EXERCISE 4.11

The following brief essay argues that we have to improve our public lives. Read the essay carefully, underlining emotional appeals, including descriptive passages, concrete language, and figurative language.

OK, so the holidays are over. The yuletide fairy has come and gone, dropping 10 pounds of good cheer, five for each hip. The Christmas list is in the wastebasket and the New Year's resolutions are on the refrigerator door.

This year you're going to lower your cholesterol and raise your triceps, burn fat and cool off your credit cards, stop smoking and drink nothing but club soda laced with brewer's yeast. You're going into 1987 lean and mean.

Have you noticed anything funny about this annual passage yet? Have you noticed how the swing season from one year to the next mimics the universe? We go from a warm mood of expansion (and I'm not just talking waistlines) to a grim one of icy contraction. We go from giving to denying.

Most of us start out in December with a list of things to do for others and end up with a list of things to do to ourselves.

I have no beef with self-criticism. I'll give at the office as well as at home to self-improvement. It's the self-centering that gets to me in January. The first month of the new year and we seem to retreat to a personal number one.

Check the national computer printout of New Year's resolutions and I'll wager that more than half of the top 10 have to do with our relationships with our bodies, ourselves. The second tier has to do with family and work. It is a rare list that includes the resolve to change our relationships with strangers. A rare list that mentions improvement in our public lives.

Blame it on the privatization of American life, blame it on the Manhattanization of city living, but increasingly we operate within our own inner concentric circles. We pay our public lives as little attention as we pay the toll-taker on the highway.

It isn't just the infrastructure of bridges and public housing that has deteriorated, it's the human infrastructure. The dozens of daily encounters between strangers who pass each other on the sidewalk, buy from each other in the stores and deal with each other crossing streets have indeed become lean and mean.

Most of us look away when we pass strangers. It is the exceptional person who stops to help the woman maneuvering her kids and groceries up the staircase. We rarely give up our place in line or on the subway. Locked into our automobiles, we prefer gridlock to giving way. Drivers who won't give each other an inch happily give each other the finger.

These daily encounters, when they are angry or alien, diminish our lives enormously. When they are pleasant, we feel buoyed. Yet when we sit at home and make resolutions, we think about what we can accomplish in private spaces: home, work. Too many have given up the belief that they control the public world.

I risk sounding like a greeting card or a bumper sticker—Have You Hugged Your Child Today?—but as individuals, we have enormous control over this human infrastructure. We can change the contour of a day, the mood of a moment, the way people feel.

The demolition and the reconstruction of public life is the result of personal decisions made every day: The decision to give up a seat on the bus. The decision to be patient or pleasant against all odds. The decision to let that jerk take a left-hand turn from the right-hand lane. Without rolling down the window and calling him a jerk.

It's the resolution to be a civil, social creature. Maybe even pick up a few pieces of someone else's litter.

This may be a peak period for the battle against the spread of a waistline and creeping cholesterol. But it is also within our willpower to fight the spread of urban rudeness and creeping hostility. Civility doesn't stop a nuclear holocaust and doesn't put a roof over the head of the homeless. But it makes a difference in the shape of a community, as surely as lifting weights can make a difference in the shape of a human torso.   —ELLEN GOODMAN

EXERCISE 4.12

Read the following paragraph, and then write a paragraph evaluating its use of description and figurative language.

Since 1973, all American women have been legally entitled to have abortions performed in hospitals by licensed physicians. Before they were legal, abortions were frequently performed by persons who bore more resemblance to butchers than they did to doctors. The all too common result was serious complications or death for the woman. If the 1973 Supreme Court decision is reversed, abortion will not end. Instead, women will again resort to illegal abortions, and there will be a return to the slaughterhouse. Since abortions are going to take place no matter what the law says, why not have them done safely and legally in hospitals instead of in basements, alleys, or dirty compartments in some killing shed? The decision to have an abortion is not an easy one to make, and I believe that a woman who makes it deserves to have her wish carried out in the very safest way possible. Critics of abortion stress the importance of the unborn child's life. At the very least, they should also take the woman's life and safety into consideration.

EXERCISE 4.13

Using a working argumentative thesis you formulated in Exercise 4.2 or 4.3, make a list of the emotional appeals most appropriate to your topic and audience. Then spend ten to fifteen minutes brainstorming, looking for descriptive and figurative language to carry out the appeals.

▌ 4g. Organizing an argument

Once you have assembled good reasons in support of an argumentative thesis, you must organize your material in order to present the argument convincingly. While there is no ideal or universally favored organizational framework for an argumentative essay, you may find the classical five-part system useful to try. This five-part pattern was often followed by ancient Greek and Roman orators. The speaker began with an *introduction,* which stated the thesis, then gave the *background* information. Next came the different *lines of argument,* and then the *refutation of opposing arguments.* A *conclusion* both summed up the argument and made an emotional appeal to the audience. You can adapt this format to written arguments as follows:

1. *Introduction*
   gains readers' attention and interest
   establishes your qualifications to write about your topic

establishes common ground with readers
demonstrates fairness
states or implies your thesis
2. *Background*
present any necessary background information
3. *Lines of argument*
present good reasons (including logical and emotional appeals) in
   support of your thesis
generally present reasons in order of importance
demonstrate ways your argument is in readers' best interest
4. *Refutation of opposing arguments*
considers opposing points of view
notes both advantages and disadvantages of opposing views
5. *Conclusion*
summarizes the argument
elaborates on the implication of your thesis
makes clear what you want readers to think or do
makes a strong ethical or emotional appeal

Asked to write an argumentative essay addressed to fellow students about an issue of current interest on her campus, Ohio State University student Tracy Vezdos decided to write about the movement to put warning labels about "explicit lyrics" on record albums. Her thesis: *As a form of censorship, the labeling of record albums has no place in American society.* Following is Tracy's essay, which was written in 1987 and organized according to the five-part classical system. The parts are labeled in the margin. Notice that because the thesis is stated in a negative form, arguing *against* labeling, most of the essay is devoted to refuting the arguments in favor of labeling. Also notice that a source citation is given for a piece of information that Tracy considered specific enough to need it (see 40d).

It's Only Rock 'n' Roll

   Devil worship, premarital sex, drugs,   INTRODUCTION
violence, suicide—can rock music really promote all these detriments to today's youth?
"Yes," says Tipper Gore of the Parents' Music
Resource Center (PMRC). "Absolutely not,"
responds the Musical Majority, a group formed

in opposition to PMRC's campaign to have warning labels placed on rock records. While parents are understandably concerned about rock
songs that seem to glorify promiscuous sex,
drugs, and other vices, this impression is
often misleading. In fact, song lyrics, like
other kinds of language, can invoke many varying interpretations. In recent years, Mark
Twain's most famous novel, <u>The Adventures of
Huckleberry Finn</u>, has been banned from literature courses in many high schools—including yours, perhaps—because of a single
word, <u>nigger</u>. If the persons advocating the
banning of this novel had bothered to read
the book carefully, they would have realized
Twain does not promote racism but denounces
it as ignorant and immoral. People of our age
know only too well how often things that teenagers like or do are misinterpreted by adults
and how any effort to control access to these
things only makes them more attractive. As
a form of censorship, the labeling of record
albums has no place in American society

    The PMRC campaign began in the mid-1980s   BACKGROUND
when Gore, the wife of Senator Albert Gore
of Tennessee, and a number of other wives of
prominent national politicians began lobbying
record companies and performers to label
records that the group considered too "explicit." In September 1985, the Senate Commerce Committee held hearings into the issue,
and soon afterward the twenty-two major record
companies that are members of the Recording
Industry Association of America accepted a

system of voluntary labels. The companies themselves decide which records need labels. If the recording artist agrees, the label <u>Explicit lyrics—parental advisory</u> will be placed on the album cover, or the lyrics will be printed there. (Tapes, which do not have enough room for the lyrics, include a label telling customers to look for the lyrics on the album.) Thus far, the effects of labeling are most obvious in smaller record stores: a decline in sales of labeled records and the refusal of some stores to carry them, for fear of being known as a "pornrock" store.

Do the record companies and artists who permit their albums to be labeled feel their freedom of expression will remain safe despite this first, major step toward censoring their material? Already, PMRC has moved on to the music television channel (MTV), where it wants to have editing done on what it deems explicitly sexual or violent videos. PMRC claims that it does not believe in government censorship. But the group's leaders are wives of prominent political figures who make decisions that affect the recording industry. With this kind of support, PMRC does not need to censor records directly because to avoid offending the politicians, the record companies will censor the artists, or artists will censor themselves. The result will be that no Americans —including those of us of college age—will be able to listen to certain songs that the PMRC considers too explicit for teenagers.

One of the many problems I have with PMRC

LINES OF
ARGUMENT

involves its definition of the word <u>explicit</u>. My dictionary defines <u>explicit</u> as "clearly stated or expressed, with nothing implied; definite." Almost any song could fall under this broad definition. Surprisingly, the main targets of PMRC are not heavy metal bands such as Motley Crue and Black Sabbath, who adorn their album covers with scantily dressed women and sing rebellious, anti—authority songs. Most of the artists with songs on the "Filthy Fifteen," a list compiled by PMRC of the most "harmful" songs of 1986, are mainstream per—formers such as Madonna, Bruce Springsteen, and Cyndi Lauper. Madonna's "Papa, Don't Preach," about a pregnant teenager who wants to get married and keep her baby, had the PMRC in an uproar. If these women would take the time to examine the lyrics carefully, they would realize the pregnant girl attempts to gain her father's acceptance and guidance—not to rebel against his authority. This case of misinterpretation is not an isolated one. At the Senate Commerce Committee hearings, John Denver testified that his song "Rocky Mountain High" had been banned from many radio stations because station managers felt the tune ad—vocated the use of drugs. The lyrics, however, indicate that the "high" Denver feels comes from the Colorado mountains, not marijuana.

The PMRC's concern about lyrics seems unnecessary in any case. A survey of 266 junior high and high school students that was reported in <u>Newsweek</u> showed that the lyrics have very little or no influence on teenagers who listen to them. In fact, 37 percent of the students couldn't even describe what their three favorite songs were about—they just liked them. As for Satanism, sex, drugs, and violence, only 7 percent of the 622 songs that were mentioned contained these elements, according to the students ("So Who Understands").

The PMRC admits that it finds only a small minority of rock lyrics offensive. But it argues that labeling of records with these lyrics is justified in order to give parents information about what their children are listening to and to discourage teenagers from buying—and being influenced by—records that seem to promote harmful and immoral activities. Many people can agree with these goals, and in some cases record labeling may help to accomplish them. But more often, labeling will probably increase teenagers' exposure to the very lyrics the PMRC considers harmful. We all know the thrill of sneaking into an R-rated movie or of looking up the bawdy parts of Chaucer's Canterbury Tales (those not printed in our literature textbooks). In the same way, an Explicit lyrics label will draw teenagers attention and challenge their curiosity. Even if parents can prevent their children from buying a labeled record, the young people will be all the more eager—and likely—to listen to the album at a friend's. Instead of encouraging better communication and understanding between parents and children, labels will only result in more friction.

To find out how those of us who are

arg 4g

slightly older feel about the issue, I took an informal survey of Ohio State students asking whether records should be labeled and why or why not. The majority said "No," on the grounds of freedom of speech. Surprisingly enough, a large minority favored labels as a guide for parents. One answer I received, however, completely dispels the parental guide argument: "We should make our children safe for ideas, not ideas safe for our children. . . . Only naive fools would say 'yes'— a record album should carry a warning about explicit material—and actually believe that the social control that they have imposed on themselves . . . will not grow."

I agree. Parents have an awesome re- **CONCLUSION**
sponsibility in raising their children, and part of that responsibility includes monitoring the material their children are exposed to. Record companies and singers should not have to perform this service for the parents, and a group of politically influential people should not try to make them do so. Americans need to accept responsibility for what is wrong with our society and stop placing the blame on "outside forces" such as record albums. A serious and honest look into ourselves will reveal the true causes of the problems that face teenagers today. After all, as Mick Jagger proclaimed, "It's only rock 'n' roll."

References

So who understands rock lyrics, anyway. (1986, July). Newsweek, p. 71.

EXERCISE 4.14

Using the classical system, draft an argument in support of one of the theses you formulated in Exercises 4.2 or 4.3.

EXERCISE 4.15

Another useful system of argument was developed by the philosopher Stephen Toulmin. Essentially a modern elaboration of the system first put forth by Aristotle, the Toulmin system is presented in 2e as a way of generating material for an argumentative paper but might also be used for organizing such a paper, as follows:

1. State your claim or thesis.
2. Qualify your claim in any way necessary.
3. Present the good reasons you have to support your claim.
4. Discuss any underlying assumptions that support these reasons.
5. Give any evidence that might add support to your claim (facts, statistics, testimony, etc.).
6. Acknowledge and respond to any counterarguments readers might make.

Suppose you were writing an essay about smoking. Your claim might be that smoking should be banned. You could qualify your claim by suggesting that the ban be campuswide. As reasons in support of your claim you might say that smoking causes heart disease and lung cancer, and that nonsmokers are endangered by passive smoke. Your underlying assumptions would be that people are entitled to good health. As evidence you could cite statistics about lung and heart disease and perhaps quote the U.S. Surgeon General as an authority on the subject. One possible counterargument you could anticipate would be that smokers have rights too; you could respond by reminding readers that you are suggesting only a campuswide ban, and that they would be free to smoke *off* campus.

Use the Toulmin system to draft an argument in support of one of the theses you formulated in Exercise 4.2 or 4.3. If you wish, you can write on the same topic you wrote on in Exercise 4.14.

▌ 4h. Analyzing an argument

Guidelines for organizing an argument can also be used to advantage in analyzing an argument to judge how effective it is. Tracy Vezdos used the classical system explained in 4g to analyze her essay

"It's Only Rock 'n' Roll." Here is her analysis, as she entered it in her writing log.

INTRODUCTION

- *What, specifically, have I done to gain the audience's attention and interest?* I've tried to use an eye-catching, controversial opening sentence—and an intriguing title that recalls a familiar phrase—I've tried to show why this argument is important to my readers by making it clear that record labeling is part of a much larger issue that affects all of us—censorship.

- *How have I established my qualifications to write about this topic?* I've used the precedent of *Huckleberry Finn.* I've shown that I am familiar with the arguments of PMRC and Musical Majority.

- *What have I done to establish common ground with readers?* My use of Twain (most people know him)—references to "yours" and "people of our age."

- *How have I shown fairness to opposing viewpoints?* I've said that parents are understandably concerned about the music their children are exposed to.

- *How have I made known my thesis? Is the thesis specific enough?* In the last sentence of the introductory paragraph—censorship is wrong in any form, including warning labels on albums.

BACKGROUND

- *What background have I presented?* I've given history, exact wording of labels, effects of labeling on sales.

LINES OF ARGUMENT

- *What good reasons have I presented to support my thesis?* I've explained how labeling is in fact a form of censorship by political forces.

- *How have I shown that my claim is in readers' best interest?* I've stressed that record labeling threatens their right as Americans to judge for themselves what they want to listen to.

REFUTATION OF OPPOSING ARGUMENTS

- *How have I dealt with opposing points of view and noted their advantages as well as disadvantages?* I've challenged the definition of *explicit,* pointed out the misinterpretation of lyrics, showed that teenagers don't pay attention to lyrics. I've said that labeling may achieve a useful purpose in some cases but is more likely to have the opposite effect.

CONCLUSION

- *How have I summarized my argument?* I've used a striking quotation about censorship from my survey and then begun the concluding paragraph by expressing my agreement with it.

- *How have I elaborated on any implications of my claim?* I've pointed out that parents have a tremendous responsibility for their children that they shouldn't try to delegate to others.

- *What action have I called for from readers? What kind of ethical or emotional appeal have I ended with?* I've called for readers to look within themselves to find the causes of today's problems and to stop blaming record albums.

EXERCISE 4.16

Try analyzing the argument implicit in this advertisement using the six categories in the Toulmin system (described in Exercise 4.15).

DON'T GET WRAPPED UP IN SMUGGLING.

Don't buy exotic leather goods, furs, jewelry, plants or pets unless you're sure they're legal. Help save endangered species from smuggling and extinction. Send for our free Buyer Beware Guide.

World Wildlife Fund

TRAFFIC (U.S.A.)
1255 23rd Street, NW
Washington, DC 20037
800-634-4444

Prepared as a public service by Ogilvy & Mather. Photo by Mistretta.

READING WITH AN EYE FOR ARGUMENT

Return to Colleen Starkey's essay about the Bagelry in Chapter 3. Read it now as an implicit argument that people should eat there frequently. Analyze the essay, using the six Toulmin categories, focusing especially on the assumptions that underlie the claims about the Bagelry. Does the essay succeed as an argument? Why or why not?

FOR EXAMINING YOUR OWN WRITING

Using either the classical or the Toulmin guidelines, analyze the argument in an essay you've recently written or in the draft you wrote in Exercise 4.14. Decide what you need to do to revise your arguments, and write out a brief organizational plan.

5. Constructing Paragraphs

Paragraphs are essential building blocks of writing, ones that every writer can come to understand and use to good effect. Paragraphs have existed for as long as people in the Western world have been writing. Long before the age of the printing press, sections of text were set off from one another by marks in the margin. In Greek, *para graphos* means "mark beside," and these marks looked like this: ¶. With the invention of movable type, printers had to fit lines of type into frames; because they could no longer use the margins easily, they began marking a paragraph by indenting its first line, as we still do today. The old name stuck, however, and so we call these units *paragraphs*.

Most simply, a **paragraph** is a group of sentences or a single sentence set off as a unit. Usually the sentences in a paragraph are related in some way because they all revolve around one main idea. When a new idea comes up, a new paragraph begins. Within this broad general guideline, however, paragraph structure is highly flexible, allowing writers to create many varied individual effects.

The hero of the Rex Stout mysteries, Nero Wolfe, once solved a case by identifying the paragraph structure of a particular writer/murderer. A person's style of paragraphing, Wolfe was later to claim, serves even more reliably than do fingerprints as a stamp of identity. Like Stout's character, you probably already have a characteristic way of paragraphing, although you may never have thought about it.

The following passage comprises a series of paragraphs, run together, from the opening of an essay on friendship by anthropologist
Margaret Mead and Rhoda Metraux. Read this passage carefully, and
decide how you would divide it into paragraphs.

(1) Few Americans stay put for a lifetime. (2) We move from town to
city to suburb, from high school to college in a different state, from a
job in one region to a better job somewhere else, from the home where
we raise our children to the home where we plan to live in retirement.
(3) With each move we are forever making new friends, who become
part of our new life at that time. (4) For many of us the summer is a
special time for forming new friendships. (5) Today millions of Americans vacation abroad, and they go not only to see new sights but also—
in those places where they do not feel too strange—with the hope of
meeting new people. (6) No one really expects a vacation trip to produce
a close friend. (7) But surely the beginning of a friendship is possible?
(8) Surely in every country people value friendship? (9) They do. (10)
The difficulty when strangers from two countries meet is not a lack of
appreciation of friendship, but different expectations about what constitutes friendship and how it comes into being. (11) In those European
countries that Americans are most likely to visit, friendship is quite
sharply distinguished from other more casual relations and is differently
related to family life. (12) For a Frenchman, a German, or an English-
man friendship is usually more particularized and carries a heavier burden of commitment. (13) But as we use the word, *friend* can be applied
to a wide range of relationships—to someone one has known for a few
weeks in a new place, to a close business associate, to a childhood
playmate, to a man or woman, to a trusted confidant. (14) There are
real differences among these relations for Americans—a friendship may
be superficial, casual, situational or deep and enduring. (15) But to a
European, who sees only our surface behavior, the differences are not
clear.

If you compare notes with others in your class, you will most likely
find that you all chose similar paragraph breaks. Your instinctive sense
about the shape and structure of paragraphs led you to that agreement.
In fact, Mead and Metraux divided up their text in a fairly predictable
manner. The first paragraph introduces the theme of the essay, friendship, by opening with a reference to the American tendency to move
frequently and then relating this issue to the need for making friends.
This first paragraph ends after sentence three. Paragraph two shifts the
discussion of making friends to a specific time (summer) and place
(travels abroad), ending with a question about other people's attitudes
toward friendship ("Surely in every country people value friendship?").

The third paragraph opens by answering the question posed at the end of paragraph two, thus moving smoothly into a brief discussion of definitions and expectations for friendship in European countries Americans are likely to visit in their summer travels. The last paragraph in this passage begins with sentence thirteen, which shifts the discussion back from European ideas of friendship to American conceptions.

For special effect, Mead and Metraux might have divided this passage in a less expected way—for instance, by setting sentence nine off as a paragraph by itself. Doing this would have served to emphasize that statement, focusing readers' attention on it in a slightly startling way. But they did not do so. Paragraphs usually develop one main point and contain more than one sentence, and most writers follow these conventions unless they have a reason to do otherwise.

5a. Constructing unified, coherent, and well-developed paragraphs

This introduction should have convinced you that you know more about paragraphs than you may have thought. Let us look now at the specific elements that make up a well-written paragraph—one that makes a point in a way that is easy for readers to understand and follow. Consider the following paragraph by Eudora Welty:

> I never knew anyone who'd grown up in Jackson without being afraid of Mrs. Calloway, our librarian. She ran the Library absolutely by herself, from the desk where she sat with her back to the books and facing the stairs, her dragon eye on the front door, where who knew what kind of person might come in from the public? SILENCE in big black letters was on signs tacked up everywhere. She herself spoke in her normally commanding voice; every word could be heard all over the Library above a steady seething sound coming from her electric fan; it was the only fan in the Library and stood on her desk, turned directly onto her streaming face.   —EUDORA WELTY, *One Writer's Beginnings*

This paragraph begins with a general statement of the main idea: that everyone in Jackson feared Mrs. Calloway. All the other sentences then give specific details about why she inspired such fear. This example demonstrates the three qualities of a successful paragraph: **unity, coherence,** and **development.** It focuses on one main idea (unity); its parts are clearly related (coherence); and its main idea is supported with specifics (development).

5b. Making paragraphs unified: focusing on one main idea

To be readable and effective, paragraphs generally focus on one main idea. One good way to achieve such paragraph **unity** is to state the main idea clearly in one sentence and relate all the other sentences in the paragraph to that idea. The sentence that presents the main idea is called the **topic sentence.** Like the thesis for an entire essay, the topic sentence of a paragraph includes a topic and some comment on that topic (see 2f). In the above paragraph by Eudora Welty, the topic sentence opens the paragraph. Its topic is Mrs. Calloway; its comment is that everyone in Jackson was afraid of her.

1. Positioning a topic sentence

While a topic sentence usually appears at the beginning of a paragraph, it may appear anywhere in the paragraph—or it may not appear at all, but rather be implied.

At the beginning of a paragraph

It is a good idea to open with the topic sentence when you want readers to see your point immediately. Such a strategy can be particularly useful in essay examinations (Chapter 43), in memos (Chapter 44), or in argumentative essays (Chapter 4). The author of the following paragraph opens with a clear topic sentence on which subsequent sentences build:

> *Our friendship was the source of much happiness and many memories.* We danced and popped our fingers simultaneously to the soul tunes of the Jacksons and Stevie Wonder. We sweated together in the sweltering summer sun, trying to win the championship for our softball team. I recall the taste of pepperoni and sausage pizza as we discussed the highlights of our team's victory. Once we even became attracted to the same young man, but luckily we were able to share his friendship.

The topic sentence announces the main topic of the paragraph (friendship) and comments on it (as the source of happiness and memories). The next four sentences elaborate on the topic by giving specific examples and concrete physical description to show the reader how the happiness and memories were created.

At the end of a paragraph

When specific details lead up to a generalization, putting the topic sentence at the end of the paragraph makes good sense. In the following paragraph, the last sentence is a general statement that sums up and accounts for the specifics that have preceded it.

> During the visit, Dee takes the pictures, every one of them, including the one of the house that she used to live in and hate. She takes the churn top and dasher, both whittled out of a tree by one of Mama's uncles. She tries to take Grandma Dee's quilts. Mama and Maggie use these inherited items every day, not only appreciating their heritage but living it too. *Dee, on the other hand, wants these items only for decorative use, thus forsaking and ignoring their* real *heritage.*

In this instance, the concluding topic sentence brings the paragraph to its climax, explaining the significance of the things Dee takes.

At the beginning and end of a paragraph

Sometimes you will want to state a topic sentence at the beginning of the paragraph and then repeat it, usually in a slightly different form, at the end. Such an echo effect adds emphasis, pointing up the importance you attach to the idea. In the following paragraph, the writer begins with a topic sentence announcing a problem:

> *Many of the difficulties we experience in relationships are caused by the unrealistic expectations we have of each other.* Think about it. Women are expected to feel comfortable doing most of the sacrificing. They are supposed to stay fine, firm, and forever twenty-two, while doing double duty in the home and in the workplace. The burden on men is no easier. They should be tall, handsome, and able to wine and dine the woman. Many women go for the glitter and then expect these men to calm down once in a relationship and become faithful, sensitive, supportive, and loving. Let's face it. Both women and men have been unrealistic. *It's time we develop a new sensitivity toward each other and ask ourselves what it is we need from each other that is realistic and fair.*

The last sentence restates the topic sentence as a proposal for a solution to the problem. This repetition of the topic sentence is particularly appropriate, for the essay goes on to specify how the problem can be solved.

Implied but not stated in the paragraph

Occasionally, a topic will be so obvious or so clearly implied that no topic sentence is necessary at all. Here is an example of such a paragraph, from an essay about a car dealership:

> The Reedman newspaper advertisement invites customers to a hundred-and-fifty acre, one-stop car center that has a ten-million-dollar selection of cars—and then, adding the note of exclusivity that is considered necessary in advertising even the world's largest, it says, "Private Sale Now Going On." The premises on which the private sale is held look like the average citizen's vision of the supply depot at Cam Ranh Bay. Behind a series of showrooms on Route 1, just down the road from the Greenwood Dairies, the five thousand cars are lined up on acres and acres of asphalt—the neat rows interrupted by occasional watchtowers and the entire area surrounded by a heavy, iron, electronically monitored fence. On a busy Saturday, attendants direct streams of traffic in and out of the customers' parking lot. Hostesses with the dress and manner of airline stewardesses circulate in the showrooms offering to call a salesman for anybody who feels the need for one. Muzak, which reaches the most remote line of hardtops, is interrupted every two or three bars by calls for salesmen.   —CALVIN TRILLIN, "Working Out a Deal"

Here the implied topic sentence might be stated as *In spite of its pretense of being private and exclusive, Reedman's Car Dealership is huge, overwhelming, and impersonal.* But the writer does not have to state this information explicitly. We can gather it easily from the examples and specific details he provides: any place that brings to mind a "supply depot" with "acres and acres of asphalt," "hostesses" like "airline stewardesses," and "Muzak" can scarcely be regarded as private or exclusive.

EXERCISE 5.1

Choose an essay you have recently written, and identify the topic sentence of each paragraph, noting where in the paragraph each topic sentence appears and whether any is implied rather than stated. Would you now make any revisions in your topic sentences (including moving or adding them), and if so how would you revise, and why?

▌ 2. Relating each sentence to the main idea

Whether the main idea of a paragraph appears in the topic sentence or is only implied, writing unified paragraphs demands that you make sure each sentence relates or contributes to the main idea. Look, for example, at the following paragraph, which opens an essay about black music.

> When I was a teenager, there were two distinct streams of popular music: one was black, and the other was white. The former could only be heard way at the end of the radio dial, while white music dominated everywhere else. This separation was a fact of life, the equivalent of blacks sitting in the back of the bus and "whites only" signs below the Mason-Dixon line. Satchmo might grin for days on "The Ed Sullivan Show" and certain historians hold forth *ad nauseam* on the black contribution to American music, but the truth was that our worlds rarely twined. —MARCIA GILLESPIE,
> "They're Playing My Music, but Burying My Dreams"

The author announces her topic (two streams of popular music: black and white) in sentence one. Sentence two relates the topic to the respective positions of "black" and "white" music on the radio dial, and sentence three expands on this notion of musical separation by comparing it to the separate seats for blacks on buses or their exclusion from certain "public" places. The last sentence of this opening paragraph rephrases the topic sentence in a much more pointed way: though popular black music might appear regularly on television and people might write volumes about how much blacks have contributed to American music, the two worlds of black and white music remained separate. Each sentence clearly relates to the topic, and the paragraph as a whole is unified.

EXERCISE 5.2

Following are some sentences adapted from a newspaper story about the economic prospects of New York City, which came very close to bankruptcy in the mid-1970s. Read the series of sentences carefully. Assuming that you are assigned to write a paragraph for an urban studies course on the economic health of New York City in the late 1970s, (1) compose a topic sentence for the paragraph, (2) decide where to position the topic sentence, and (3) use as many of the sentences as you need to create a unified paragraph. Omit any unnecessary sentences, and change wording if you need to.

1. New York lost 600,000 jobs between 1969 and 1976.
2. In 1975, twenty office buildings in prime Manhattan areas were empty.
3. Between 1970 and 1975, ten major corporations moved their headquarters from New York to the Sunbelt.

4. In 1975, New York was on the brink of bankruptcy.
5. Between February 1977 and February 1978, New York gained 9,000 jobs.
6. Since January 1978, one million square feet of Manhattan office space have been newly rented.
7. AT&T has just built a $110 million headquarters in New York.
8. IBM has just built an $80 million building at 55th Street and Madison Avenue in New York.
9. Rents and prices for cooperative apartments have increased since 1977.
10. Even $1 million luxury penthouses are sold out.
11. There is currently an apartment shortage in Manhattan.
12. The president recently signed a bill authorizing $1.65 billion in federal loan guarantees for New York.

EXERCISE 5.3

The following two paragraphs lack unity. Identify the topic sentence of each one, and revise each paragraph by deleting any sentences unrelated to the topic.

1. Break dancing has produced unity among youngsters, a fact that is often overlooked. As break dancing spread across the United States, nearly every youngster became familiar with it. Many participated in learning the skill, and others just enjoyed watching their friends become "breakers." It is not at all strange to see break dancing groups with people of various races, creeds, and colors all working together in the synchronized steps of the dance routine. This diversity has characterized break dancing from its beginning. Blacks, Puerto Ricans, and other minority groups have played very important roles in the break dance phenomenon. Break dancing has now grown through publicity. Musical videos by top artists, including Lionel Ritchie and Herbie Hancock, feature break dancers. Special television programs have shown break dancing, and interviews have been conducted with those who have mastered the dance. All these factors have made break dancing more popular and exciting.

2. According to advertisers, one side of every woman's personality is sensual, knowing, experienced, worldly, unshockable, well-versed in the art of love: in short, a woman in every sense of the word. The opposing side is shy, sweet, trusting, innocent, untried: a maiden totally immersed in her own purity. Many argue that men possess a split personality, too. This is exactly how I feel as a woman: forever pushed, pulled, jostled, teased, and finally lured into treading a fine thread between blatant maturity and subtle innocence. No wonder so many women begin to feel like a Hugh Lofting "Push-me, Pull-me," the animal with two heads facing in opposite directions, each vying for its own desires and neither budging an inch.

EXERCISE 5.4

Choose one of the following topic sentences, and spend ten or fifteen minutes brainstorming, freewriting, looping, or mapping to gather ideas about the topic (see 2e). Then write a paragraph that includes the topic sentence, making sure that each of the other sentences relates to it. Assume that the paragraph will be part of a letter you are writing to a close friend.

1. I found out quickly that college life was not quite what I had expected.
2. Being part of the "in crowd" used to be of utmost importance to me.
3. My work experience has taught me several important lessons.
4. Until recently, I never appreciated my parents fully.
5. I expect my college education to do more than simply assure me of a job.

EXERCISE 5.5

Choose an essay you have written recently, and examine the second, third, and fourth paragraphs. Does each have a topic sentence or strongly imply one? Do all the other sentences in the paragraph focus on its main idea? Would you now revise any of these paragraphs—and if so, how?

5c. Making paragraphs coherent: fitting details together

A paragraph is **coherent** if its details fit together clearly in a way that readers can easily follow. For a paragraph to be unified, the sentences in it must relate to the same main idea; for it to be coherent, the sentences must relate to one another structurally. You can achieve paragraph coherence by organizing ideas, by repeating key terms or phrases, and by using parallel structures, pronouns, and transitions.

1. Organizing ideas

If you take every fourth sentence of an essay and arrange them together, one after another, in paragraph form, you will *not* end up with a paragraph. Why not? Because the sentences will have only a haphazard relationship to one another. Though they may well be connected to the same topic, the lack of any organizational relationship will result in incoherence. Clear organization of ideas goes a long way toward creating coherence, and the following discussion will review the most often used means of organizing a paragraph—spatial order, chronological order, and logical order. (See 2h for a discussion of organizing an entire essay.)

102

Using spatial order

Paragraphs organized in **spatial order** take a "tour" of an object, person, or place, beginning at one point and moving, say, from near to far, left to right, north to south. Especially useful in **descriptive** paragraphs, spatial order allows a writer to direct readers' attention in an orderly way to various elements of something in physical space. A topic sentence is frequently unnecessary in a paragraph using spatial order, because the way the paragraph is organized will be obvious to the reader. Often, however, a topic sentence is used at the beginning of the paragraph to set the scene or tell the reader what is going to be described. Note the movement from ceiling to walls to floor in the following paragraph.

> The geology professor's voice began to fade into the background as my eyes wandered around the classroom in the old administration building. The water-stained ceiling was cracked and peeling, and the splitting wooden beams played host to a variety of lead pipes and coils. My eyes followed these pipes down the walls and around corners, until eventually I saw the electrical outlets. I thought it was strange that they were exposed, and not built in, until I realized that there was probably no electricity when the building had been built. Below the outlets the sunshine was falling in bright rays across the hardwood floor, and I noticed how smoothly it was worn. Time had certainly taken its toll on this building.

Using chronological order

Paragraphs organized in **chronological order** arrange a series of events according to time, putting earliest events first, followed in sequence by later events, one at a time. Chronological order is used frequently in **narrative** paragraphs, which basically tell a story. Rarely do they require a topic sentence, because the main idea is obvious in the action. The following paragraph uses careful chronology to tell a story and also to build suspense: we want to know what the last event in the sequence will be. The words expressing time help build this suspense: *all of a sudden, three months, a year later,* and so on.

> The experience of Lloyd S., an Oregon businessperson, is one of the most convincing cases for taking vitamins. For his first forty years, Lloyd was healthy and robust. He owned a thriving nursery and loved to hike, fish, and camp. All of a sudden, he started feeling fatigued. A loss of appetite and weight soon followed, and in three months he was

transformed from a ruddy, muscular man into a pallid, emaciated one. Lloyd had cancer of the pancreas. After he was given a prognosis of six months to live, his family and friends were devastated, but Lloyd was a fighter. When the conventional treatments of drugs and chemotherapy did not help, he turned to a holistic approach, which emphasized a change in diet and life style—and large doses of vitamins. After a series of blood tests to discover every possible nutritional deficiency, Lloyd was given concentrated vitamin and mineral supplements to ensure maximum cell efficiency and growth so that his body could attempt to heal itself. At the end of six months, Lloyd not only was alive but also showed improvement. A year later he was free of cancer and began the long battle to regain his original vitality. Coincidence? Perhaps. To Lloyd and me, however, his recovery became a powerful demonstration of how the world's most intricate machine, the human body, performs—if only we supply it with the needed nutrients.

Chronological order is also commonly used in **explaining a process.** Paragraphs that explain how something happens or how something is done proceed in chronological order: first one step, then the next, then the next. You are already very familiar with process as a means of organizing information. After all, every set of directions, every recipe, every user's manual presents a series of steps that make up a process someone wants to learn or to follow. Here is an example.

Before trying to play the flute, figure out how to put it together. The flute is divided into three parts: the mouthpiece, the main body, and the end piece. First remove the main body (the longest part) from the case, and set it down with the keys facing up and the openings away from you. Now, pick up the mouthpiece (the piece with one hole), and attach it to the hole at the far left end of the main body by gently twisting it from side to side, in a manner similar to jiggling a door knob. Repeat the same process in attaching the end piece to the other end of the main body, taking care not to twist or smash the keys. The keys on the end piece should be lined up with those on the main body.

In college writing, you will probably use process paragraphs less often to tell readers how to do something than to explain to them how a process occurs in general—for example, how a bill becomes law in the British Parliament or how aerosol sprays destroy the ozone layer of the atmosphere.

Using logical order

Paragraphs organized in **logical order** arrange details to reflect certain logical relationships. Explanations and examples of some of these relationships—illustration, definition, division/classification, comparison/contrast, cause-effect, and problem-solution—are given in 5d. Two other logical patterns commonly used in paragraphs are *general-to-specific* and *specific-to-general*.

Paragraphs organized in a **general-to-specific** pattern usually open with a topic sentence presenting a general or abstract idea, followed by a number of more specific points designed to substantiate or prove or elaborate on the generalization. The following paragraph uses general-to-specific organization:

> We have surely all cheated at least one time in our lives. People cheat in dozens of ways, ranging from small-scale things like writing notes on their hands for tests to the monumental deception of having an affair. We cheat when we pass the speed limit. Powerful families and corporations cheat their way out of legal binds with the help of highly paid lawyers. Businesspeople record activities, such as dining out, as business-related so they will not have to pay for the expense personally. Dieters are always cheating, and if we really think about it, people cheat when they use makeup or fashion to cover up or disguise features they find unattractive. Even my grandmother cheats by taking short cuts in her prescribed daily walks.

GENERAL TOPIC

SPECIFICS

One common variation on the general-to-specific order moves from a statement of a general topic to a more **restricted topic** and finally to one or more specific details that illustrate the restricted topic. The following paragraph follows such an organizational plan:

> In 1941, war was at hand once again. Since World War I, the U.S. military had enjoyed its role as the symbol of a strong, proud nation. It was a time when "military" and "unity" went hand in hand, a time when soldiers sold products. From Lifesavers to Kodak and from government bonds to mimeograph machines, the soldier was used to give credibility to all kinds of products. One particularly compelling ad I found appeared in the December 15, 1941, issue of *Life* magazine. In it, the American Railroad Association proudly stated that it was "Backing Him Up." The "Him" was presented as a picture of a soldier—a proud soldier dressed for battle with his eyes uplifted, a soldier whose manner lifted him far above the average human. He was a god, or at least a king, and his gun was his scepter, the foxhole his throne. The world of

GENERAL TOPIC

RESTRICTION OF TOPIC

SPECIFIC DETAILS

1941 did not see violence in the gun, but security, and in his eyes it did not see death, but life.

Paragraphs can also follow a **specific-to-general** organization, first providing a series of specific examples or details and then tying them together with a general conclusion. The following paragraph uses a specific-to-general pattern:

Many solutions have been proposed to the problem of nuclear arms. One that has been gaining support calls for a total and immediate freeze on the building, testing, and deployment of all new nuclear weapons by the United States and, if possible, the Soviet Union. A unilateral freeze would be effective only if we could trust the Soviets not to take advantage of the situation and build more and better weapons. History shows we cannot be certain of this outcome. A bilateral freeze cannot be verified by today's surveillance techniques, and even if agreed upon, it would leave the Soviets with a great advantage in nuclear arms. If either plan were implemented at this time, the ability of the nuclear forces of the United States to act as a deterrent would be crippled. The answer is a build-down: an agreement to destroy several existing weapons for every new one that is built. We must first equalize our arsenals through a build-down; only then can a freeze and eventual reduction be possible.

SPECIFIC DETAILS

GENERAL TOPIC

EXERCISE 5.6

Choose one of the following topic sentences or create one of your own, and try writing two different paragraphs on the topic, using a different organizational pattern for each. Then explain, in writing, why you used the organizational patterns you did, which one seems most effective and coherent, and why.

1. I remember very clearly the first time I ever experienced great satisfaction.
2. Explaining _____ to my parents was the hardest thing I've ever done.
3. People who are extremely vain about their looks often go to ridiculous lengths to keep up their appearance.
4. My classes this term can, with understatement, be described as demanding.
5. Many people share one basic fear: public speaking.

▌ 2. Repeating key words and phrases

A major means of building coherence in paragraphs is through **repetition**. Weaving in repeated references to key words and phrases not only links sentences but also alerts readers to the importance the words or phrases hold in the larger piece of writing. Notice how the repetition of the key words *textbooks, tuition, cost, pay,* and *army* helps hold the following paragraph together.

> "Thirty-nine fifty for one *textbook!* You've got to be kidding," I mumbled as I dragged myself slowly toward the checkout stand. I did not know how I was going to *pay* for *tuition,* housing, phone bills, and groceries if all my *textbooks cost* me that much. "I might as well join the *army,*" I thought. At least it would *pay* my *tuition* and give me *army rations.* Right now, *army* chow sounded considerably better than boiled pages from a psychology text. I stood there full of resentment; I had no intention of spending all my hard-earned money on *textbooks.* Yet I had no choice. This was a book I had to have, whatever the *cost.*

Notice also that the cluster of terms related to money helps make the paragraph hang together: *pay, cost, spending, hard-earned money, cost.* Such repetition helps us follow the logic of a paragraph and understand the point the writer is making.

EXERCISE 5.7

Read the following paragraph. Then identify the places where the author repeats key words and phrases, and explain how this strategy brings coherence to the paragraph.

> Nobody knows, of course, how many megatons would be exploded in a real nuclear war. There are some who think that a nuclear war can be "contained," bottled up before it runs away to involve many of the world's arsenals. But a number of detailed analyses, war games run by the U.S. Department of Defense and official Soviet pronouncements, all indicate that this containment may be too much to hope for: Once the bombs begin exploding, communications failures, disorganization, fear, the necessity of making in minutes decisions affecting the fates of millions and the immense psychological burden of knowing that your own loved ones may already have been destroyed are likely to result in a nuclear paroxysm. Many investigations, including a number of studies for the U.S. government, envision the explosion of 5000 to 10,000 megatons—the detonation of tens of thousands of nuclear weapons that now sit quietly, inconspicuously, in missile silos, submarines and long-range bombers, faithful servants, awaiting orders. —CARL SAGAN, "The Nuclear Winter"

3. Using parallel structures

Parallel structures—structures that are grammatically similar—provide another effective way of bringing coherence to a paragraph.

107

Parallel structures emphasize the connection between related ideas or events in different sentences, as in the following paragraph. (See Chapter 19 for further discussion of parallel structures.)

> William Faulkner's "Barn Burning" tells the story of a young boy trapped in a no-win situation. If he betrays his father, he loses his family. If he betrays justice, he becomes a fugitive. In trying to free himself from his trap, he does both.

In this paragraph, the writer skillfully uses the parallel structures *if he X, he Y,* in order to give the effect of a "no-win situation." At the end of the paragraph, we are prepared for the last sentence in the parallel sequence: *In doing X, he Y.* As readers, we feel pulled along by the force of the parallel structures in the paragraph.

EXERCISE 5.8

Read the following paragraph from an essay about wives, and identify every use of repetition and parallel structures. In a brief paragraph of your own, explain how their use helps build coherence in this paragraph.

I would like to go back to school so that I can become economically independent, support myself, and, if need be, support those dependent upon me. I want a wife who will work and send me to school. And while I am going to school I want a wife to take care of my children. I want a wife to keep track of the children's doctor and dentist appointments. And to keep track of mine, too. I want a wife to make sure my children eat properly and are kept clean. I want a wife who will wash the children's clothes and keep them mended. I want a wife who is a good nuturant attendant to my children, who arranges for their schooling, makes sure that they have an adequate social life with their peers, takes them to the park, the zoo, etc. I want a wife who takes care of the children when they are sick, a wife who arranges to be around when the children need special care, because, of course, I cannot miss classes at school. My wife must arrange to lose time at work and not lose the job. It may mean a small cut in my wife's income from time to time, but I guess I can tolerate that. Needless to say, my wife will arrange and pay for the care of the children while my wife is working.   —JUDY SYFERS, "I Want a Wife"

4. Using pronouns

Writers also achieve coherence in a paragraph through the use of **pronouns.** Because pronouns usually refer back to nouns or other pronouns, they act as natural coherence devices, leading readers naturally from sentence to sentence. (See Chapter 11.) The following paragraph, from an essay on old age, uses pronouns effectively in linking sentences to one another. Note how much slower and more awkward the paragraph would be if each pronoun were replaced with the noun it stands for. Also note that the writer uses the name when he first introduces each new artist—and then uses pronouns thereafter to refer to that person. (Italics added for emphasis.)

> For such [old] persons, every new infirmity is an enemy to be outwitted, an obstacle to be overcome by force of will. *They* enjoy each little victory over *themselves*, and sometimes *they* win a major success. Renoir was one of *them*. *He* continued painting, and magnificently, for years after *he* was crippled by arthritis; the brush had to be strapped to *his* arm. "You don't need your hand to paint," *he* said. Goya was another of the unvanquished. At 72 *he* retired as an official painter of the Spanish court and decided to work only for *himself*. *His* later years were those of the famous "black paintings" in which *he* let *his* imagination run (and also of the lithographs, then a new technique). At 78 *he* escaped a reign of terror in Spain by fleeing to Bordeaux. *He* was deaf and *his* eyes were failing; in order to work *he* had to wear several pairs of spectacles, one over another, and then use a magnifying glass; but *he* was producing splendid work in a totally new style. At 80 *he* drew an ancient man propped on two sticks, with a mass of white hair and beard hiding *his* face and with the inscription "*I* am still learning."
>
> —MALCOLM COWLEY, *The View from 80*

EXERCISE 5.9

Choose three paragraphs from an essay you have recently written, and analyze them for pronoun use. How do the pronouns bring coherence to the paragraphs? Is it clear what noun or pronoun each of the pronouns refers back to? Can you see ways of using pronouns to improve the coherence of these paragraphs?

5. Using transitional devices

Transitions are words and phrases that help bring coherence to a paragraph by signaling the exact relationships between sentences. In acting as signposts from one idea to the next, transitional expressions such as *after all, for example, indeed, so,* and *thus* help readers follow the progression of a paragraph. *Finally* indicates that a last point is at hand; *likewise,* that a similar point is about to be made, and so on. To get an idea of how important transitions are in directing readers, look at the following paragraph, from which all transitional devices have been removed:

In "The Fly," Katherine Mansfield tries to show us the "real" personality of "the boss" beneath his exterior. The fly helps her to portray this real self. The boss goes through a range of emotions and feelings. He expresses these feelings on a small but determined fly, whom the reader realizes he unconsciously relates to his son. The author basically splits up the story into three parts, with the boss's emotions and actions changing quite measurably. With old Woodifield, with himself, and with the fly, we see the boss's manipulativeness. Our understanding of him as a hard and cruel man grows.

We can, if we work at it, figure out the relationship of these ideas to one another, for this paragraph is essentially unified by one major idea. But the lack of transitions results in an abrupt, choppy rhythm that lurches from one idea to the next, dragging the confused reader behind. Look how much easier the paragraph is to read and understand when the transitional devices are added:

In "The Fly," Katherine Mansfield tries to show us the "real" personality of "the boss" beneath his exterior. The fly *in the story's title* helps her to portray this real self. *In the course of the story*, the boss goes through a range of emotions and feelings. *At the end*, he *finally* expresses these feelings on a small but determined fly, whom the reader realizes he unconsciously relates to his son. *To accomplish her goal*, the author basically splits up the story into three parts, with the boss's emotions and actions changing quite measurably *throughout*. *First* with old Woodifield, *then* with himself, and *last* with the fly, we see the boss's manipulativeness. *With each part*, our understanding of him as a hard and cruel man grows.

Note how the writer carefully leads us through the points of her paragraph. Most of the transitional devices here point to movement in time, helping us follow the chronology of the story being discussed: *in the course of the story; at the end; finally; throughout; first; then; last.*

It is important to note that transitions can only clarify connections between thoughts; they cannot create connections. As a writer, you must choose transitions that fit your meaning, and not expect a transition to *provide* meaning. If you open a sentence with *therefore*, for example, be sure that the thought expressed by the rest of the sentence really follows logically from the previous sentences.

The following list contains commonly used transitional devices, grouped by the functions they perform.

TO SIGNAL SEQUENCE

again, also, and, and then, besides, finally, first . . . second . . . third, furthermore, last, moreover, next, still, too

TO SIGNAL TIME

after a bit, after a few days, after a while, afterward, as long as, as soon as, at last, at length, at that time, before, earlier, immediately, in the meantime, in the past, lately, later, meanwhile, now, presently, shortly, simultaneously, since, so far, soon, then, thereafter, until, when

TO SIGNAL COMPARISON

again, also, in the same way, likewise, once more, similarly

TO SIGNAL CONTRAST

although, but, despite, even though, however, in contrast, in spite of, instead, nevertheless, nonetheless, notwithstanding, on the contrary, on the one hand . . . on the other hand . . . , regardless, still, though, yet

TO SIGNAL EXAMPLES

after all, even, for example, for instance, indeed, in fact, of course, specifically, such as, the following example . . . , to illustrate

TO SIGNAL CAUSE AND EFFECT

accordingly, as a result, because, consequently, for this purpose, hence, so, then, therefore, thereupon, thus, to this end

TO SIGNAL PLACE

above, adjacent to, below, beyond, closer to, elsewhere, far, farther on, here, near, nearby, opposite to, there, to the left, to the right

TO SIGNAL CONCESSION

although it is true that, granted that, I admit that, it may appear that, naturally, of course

TO SIGNAL SUMMARY, REPETITION, OR CONCLUSION

all in all, as a result, as has been noted, as I have said, as we have seen, in any event, in conclusion, in other words, in short, on the whole, therefore, to conclude, to summarize, to sum up

For a discussion of using transitional devices to link separate paragraphs together, see 5f.

EXERCISE 5.10

Read the following paragraph, and identify all transitional devices. Then read the paragraph with these words or phrases left out, and briefly describe, in writing, the difference the transitional devices make.

The popularity of the various regional styles of American costume, like that of the various national styles, is also related to economic and political factors. Some years ago modes often originated in the Far West and the word "California" on a garment was thought to be an allurement. Today, with power and population growth shifting to the Southwestern oil-producing states, Wild West styles—particularly those of Texas—are in vogue. This fashion, of course, is not new. For many years men who have never been nearer to a cow than the local steakhouse have worn Western costume to signify that they are independent, tough and reliable. In a story by Flannery O'Connor, for instance, the sinister traveling salesman is described as wearing "a broad-brimmed stiff gray hat of the kind used by businessmen who would like to look like cowboys"—but, it is implied, seldom succeed in doing so.

–ALISON LURIE, *The Language of Clothes*

EXERCISE 5.11

The following sentences come from a paragraph of Donna Smith-Yackel's "My Mother Never Worked." They are shown in the following paragraph out of the original order. Rearrange the sentences so that the paragraph is once again coherent.

(1) The sun came out hot and bright, endlessly, day after day. (2) They harvested half the corn, and ground the other half, stalks and all, and fed it to the cattle as fodder. (3) And in the next year the drought hit. (4) They burned it in the furnace for fuel that winter. (5) My mother and father trudged from the well to the chickens, the well to the calf pasture, the well to the barn, and from the well to the garden. (6) The crops shriveled and died. (7) With the price at four cents a bushel for the harvested crop, they couldn't afford to haul it into town.   –DONNA SMITH-YACKEL, "My Mother Never Worked"

EXERCISE 5.12

For the following paragraphs, identify each of the devices—repetition of key words or phrases, parallel structures, pronouns, and transitional expressions—that make the paragraph coherent.

1.   I must make two honest confessions to you, my Christian and Jewish brothers. First, I must confess that over the past few years I have been gravely disappointed with the white moderate. I have almost reached the regrettable conclusion that the Negro's great stumbling block on his stride toward free-

dom is not the White Citizen's Counciler or the Ku Klux Klanner, but the white moderate, who is more devoted to "order" than to justice; who prefers a negative peace which is the absence of tension to a positive peace which is the presence of justice; who constantly says, "I agree with you in the goal you seek, but I cannot agree with your methods of direct action"; who paternalistically believes he can set the timetable for another man's freedom; who lives by a mythical concept of time and who constantly advises the Negro to wait for a "more convenient season." Shallow understanding from people of good will is more frustrating than absolute misunderstanding from people of ill will. Lukewarm acceptance is much more bewildering than outright rejection.

—MARTIN LUTHER KING, JR., "Letter from Birmingham Jail"

2.   Back in 1972, an unknown musician got a much-needed break when *Playboy* magazine featured a brief article picturing a young, long-haired guitar player sporting bell-bottom jeans, a T-shirt, and a cowboy hat. Since that brief debut, Jimmy Buffet has matured and mellowed with age. But his sound, like that of Bruce Springsteen, has remained the same, much to the pleasure of his followers. Since 1972, Buffet has become a true original, and no one has duplicated or even tried to match his unique Caribbean soul music sound. In the last fifteen years, he has branched out into retail business. He owns several shops throughout Florida and the rest of the South that feature an array of goods that any Buffet fan cannot live without. He publishes his own newspaper, *The Coconut Telegraph*, which he sends to his fan club, the Parrot Heads, to keep them up to date on recent events such as releases of his new albums and reviews of his current tour.

▌ 5d. Developing paragraphs fully: providing details

In addition to being unified and coherent, a paragraph must hold readers' interest and explore its topic fully, using whatever details, evidence, and examples are necessary. Without such **development,** a paragraph may seem lifeless and abstract.

Most good essay writing does two things: it presents generalized ideas and explanations, and it backs up these generalities with specifics. This balance, the shifting between general and specific, is especially important at the paragraph level. If a paragraph contains nothing but specific details, with no explanation of how they should be viewed as a whole, readers may have trouble following the writer's meaning. If, on the other hand, a paragraph contains only abstract ideas and general statements, readers will soon become bored or will fail to be convinced by it. General statements or conclusions thus rest on specific, concrete

113

pieces of knowledge and sensory details. Well-developed paragraphs include examples and reasons that demonstrate such knowledge and details. Consider the following poorly developed paragraph:

> No such thing as "human nature" compels people to behave, think, or react in certain ways. Rather, from the time of our infancy to our death, we are constantly being taught by the society that surrounds us the customs, norms, and mores of our distinct culture. Everything in culture is learned, not genetically transmitted.

This paragraph is boring. Although its main idea is clear, and its sentences hold together, it fails to gain our interest, hold our attention, or convince us because it lacks any concrete illustrations. Now look at the paragraph in its original form:

> Imagine a child in Ecuador dancing to salsa music at a warm family gathering, while another child in the United States is decorating a Christmas tree with bright, shiny red ornaments. Both of these children are taking part in their country's cultures. It is not by instinct that one child knows how to dance to salsa music, nor is it by instinct that the other child knows how to decorate the tree. No such thing as "human nature" compels people to behave, think, or react in certain ways. Rather, from the time of our infancy to our death, we are constantly being taught by the society that surrounds us the customs, norms, and mores of our distinct culture. A majority of people feel that the evil in human beings is "human nature." However, the Tasaday, a "Stone Age" tribe who were discovered not long ago in the Philippines, do not even have equivalents in their language for the words *hatred*, *competition*, *acquisitiveness*, *aggression*, and *greed*. Such examples suggest that everything in culture is learned, not genetically transmitted.

Though both paragraphs argue the same point, only the second manages to come to life. It does so by bringing in specific details *from* life. We *want* to read this paragraph, for it appeals to our senses (a child dancing; bright, shiny red ornaments) and our curiosity (who are the Tasaday?).

Almost every paragraph can be improved by making sure that its general ideas rest on enough specific detail. You can, of course, add too many details, pushing examples at the reader when no more are needed. For every writer who has to chop back jungles of detail, however, there are five whose greatest task is to irrigate deserts of generality.

EXERCISE 5.13

Rewrite the following undeveloped paragraphs by adding concrete supporting details, examples, and reasons to them.

1. *The introduction to an essay tentatively titled "A Week on $12.80"*

    Nothing is more frustrating to a college student than being dead broke. Not having money for enough food or for the rent, much less for entertainment, is not much fun. And of course debts for tuition and books keep piling up. No, being broke is not to be recommended.

2. *The introduction to a humorous essay contrasting cats and dogs*

    Have you threatened your cat lately? If not, why not? Why not get a *real* pet—a dog? Dogs, after all, are better pets. Cats, on the other hand, are a menace to the environment.

1. Using logical patterns of development

The **logical patterns** presented in 2h for organizing essays or sections of essays can also serve as a means of developing paragraphs. These patterns include illustrating, defining, classifying and dividing, comparing and contrasting, exploring causes and effects, and considering problems and solutions or questions and answers.

Illustrating a point

Illustrating a point is one of the most useful ways of developing the main idea of a paragraph. You can **illustrate a point** with examples or with reasons.

The following paragraphs use **concrete examples** to illustrate a point. The first offers one extended example, while the second offers a series of examples.

A SINGLE EXAMPLE

The Indians made names for us children in their teasing way. Because our very busy mother kept my hair cut short, like my brothers', they called me Short Furred One, pointing to their hair and making the sign for short, the right hand with fingers pressed close together, held upward, back out, at the height intended. With me this was about two feet tall, the Indians laughing gently at my abashed face. I am told that I was given a pair of small moccasins that first time, to clear up my unhappiness at being picked out from the dusk behind the fire and my two unhappy shortcomings made conspicuous.

                                        —MARI SANDOZ, "The Go-Along Ones"

115

SEVERAL EXAMPLES

There is a lot of energy at the Fair in Des Moines, but it is all peaceful. The double giant Ferris wheel circles, its swaying seats, a thousand men, women, and children walk all day and much of the night across the fairgrounds. Ponies pick up their feet in a slashing trot as if the ground burned them. Hard-rock music backgrounds the soft lowing of a Jersey cow in the cattle barn over her newborn calf, the color of a wild deer. Screaming speeches are made all around the world urging violence; here there are plenty of voices, but they are calling for you to throw baseballs at Kewpie dolls, to pitch nickels at a dish which won't hold them, to buy cotton candy, corn dogs, a paring knife that performs every useful act save mixing a martini.

–PAUL ENGLE, "The Iowa State Fair"

At times illustrating a point involves providing not examples but **good reasons** for believing the main idea of the paragraph to be true (see 4c). The following paragraph opens with a generalization in the topic sentence and then offers reasons to support the generalization:

But I did not want to shoot the elephant. I watched him beating his bunch of grass against his knees, with that preoccupied grandmotherly air that elephants have. It seemed to me that it would be murder to shoot him. At that age I was not squeamish about killing animals, but I had never shot an elephant and never wanted to. (Somehow it always seems worse to kill a large animal.) Besides, there was the beast's owner to be considered. Alive, the elephant was worth at least a hundred pounds; dead, he would only be worth the value of his tusks, five pounds, possibly. But I had got to act quickly. I turned to some experienced-looking Burmans who had been there when we arrived, and asked them how the elephant had been behaving. They all said the same thing: he took no notice of you if you left him alone, but he might charge if you went too close to him.   –GEORGE ORWELL, "Shooting an Elephant"

Defining

You will often have occasion to develop an entire paragraph by **defining** a word or concept. Some college courses, particularly ones that deal with difficult abstractions, require writing that often calls for this strategy. A philosophy exam, for instance, might require you to define words such as *truth* or *validity*. Often, however, you will find it necessary to combine definition with other methods of development. You may need to show examples or draw comparisons or divide a term you are defining into two parts. In the following paragraph, Tom Wolfe defines *pornoviolence*, a word he has coined, by contrasting it first with "accumulated slayings and bone crushings" and then with violence seen from the point of view of "the hero."

It is not the accumulated slayings and bone crushings that make [this TV show into] pornoviolence, however. What makes pornoviolence is that in almost every case the camera angle, therefore the viewer, is with the gun, the fist, the rock. The pornography of violence has no point of view in the old sense that novels do. You do not live the action through the hero's eyes. You live with the aggressor, whoever he may be. One moment you are the hero. The next you are the villain. No matter whose side you may be on consciously, you are in fact with the muscle, and it is you who disintegrate all comers, villains, lawmen, women, anybody. On the rare occasions in which the gun is emptied into the camera—i.e., into your face—the effect is so startling that the pornography of violence all but loses its fantasy charm. There are not nearly so many masochists as sadists among those little devils whispering into one's ears.   —TOM WOLFE, "Pornoviolence"

Dividing and classifying

Dividing breaks a single item into parts. **Classifying,** which is actually a form of dividing, groups many separate items according to their similarities. You could, for instance, develop a paragraph evaluating a history course by dividing the course into several segments— textbooks, lectures, assignments—and examining each one in turn. Or you could use classification in developing a paragraph giving an overview of history courses at your college, grouping the courses in a number of ways—by the time periods or geographic areas covered, by the kinds of assignments demanded, by the numbers of students enrolled, or by some other criterion. In the following paragraph, which introduces the American composer Aaron Copland's essay about how people listen to music, Copland explains the listening process by dividing it into three parts. The rest of the essay goes on to explain each of these parts in greater detail.

We all listen to music according to our separate capacities. But, for the sake of analysis, the whole listening process may become clearer if we break it up into its component parts, so to speak. In a certain sense we all listen to music on three separate planes. For lack of a better terminology, one might name these: (1) the sensuous plane, (2) the expressive plane, (3) the sheerly musical plane. The only advantage to be gained from mechanically splitting up the listening process into these hypothetical planes is the clearer view to be had of the way in which we listen.   —AARON COPLAND, *What to Listen for in Music*

117

The following paragraph discusses dieters by classifying them as two types.

> Two types of people are seduced by fad diets. Those who have always been overweight turn to fad diets out of despair; they have tried everything, and yet nothing seems to work. The second group who succumb are those who appear perfectly healthy but are baited with slogans such as "look good, feel good." These slogans prompt self-questioning and insecurity—do I *really* look good and feel good?—and as a direct result, many of these people also fall prey to fad diets. With both types of people, however, the problems surrounding fad diets are numerous and dangerous. In fact, these diets provide neither intelligent nor effective answers to weight control.

Comparing and contrasting

You can develop some paragraphs easily and effectively by comparing and/or contrasting various aspects of the topic or by comparing and/or contrasting the topic to something else. **Comparing** things highlights their similarities; **contrasting,** their differences. Whether used alone or together, comparing and contrasting both act to bring the topic at hand more clearly into focus (we can better understand an unknown, for example, by comparing it to something we know well) or to help us evaluate the items compared and/or contrasted. You can structure comparison/contrast paragraphs in two basic ways: by first presenting all the information about one item, then presenting all the information about the other item (block method); or by alternating back and forth between the two items, focusing in turn on particular characteristics of each (alternating method). Mary Mebane uses the block method of comparing and contrasting to focus on two groups of job-seekers: the veterans and the rookies:

> You could tell the veterans from the rookies by the way they were dressed. The knowledgeable ones had their heads covered by kerchiefs, so that if they were hired, tobacco dust wouldn't get in their hair; they had on clean dresses that by now were faded and shapeless, so that if they were hired they wouldn't get tobacco dust and grime on their best clothes. Those who were trying for the first time had their hair freshly done and wore attractive dresses; they wanted to make a good impression. But the dresses couldn't be seen at the distance that many were standing from the employment office, and they were crumpled in the crush.
> —MARY MEBANE, "Summer Job"

In the next paragraph, the student writer uses the alternating method of contrasting. Note how transitional expressions like *on the other hand* and *however* are very important in establishing the back and forth pattern and guiding readers from point to point.

> Unlike Martin Luther King, Malcolm X emphasized the use of violence in his movement and employed the biblical principle of "an eye for an eye and a tooth for a tooth." King, on the other hand, felt that blacks should use nonviolent civil disobedience and employed the theme "turning the other cheek," which Malcolm X rejected as "beggarly" and "feeble." The philosophy of Malcolm X was one of revenge, and too often it broke the unity of black Americans. More radical blacks supported him, while more rational and conservative ones supported King. King thought that blacks should transcend their humanity. Malcolm X thought they should embrace it and reserve their love for one another, regarding whites as "devils" and the "enemy." King's politics were those of a rainbow, but Malcolm X's rainbow was insistently one color—black. The distance between Martin Luther King's thinking and Malcolm X's was the distance between growing up in the seminary and growing up on the streets, between the American dream and the American reality of blacks.

EXERCISE 5.14

Outline the paragraph on Martin Luther King and Malcolm X, noting its alternating pattern. Then rewrite the paragraph using block organization: the first part of the paragraph devoted to King, the second to Malcolm X. Finally, write a brief paragraph analyzing which of the two paragraphs seems most coherent and easy to follow and why.

Exploring causes and effects

Certain topics will require you to consider the process of **cause and effect,** and you can often develop paragraphs by detailing the causes of something or the effects that something leads to. A geology study question, for instance, may lead you to write a paragraph describing the major causes of soil erosion in the Midwest—or the effects of such erosion. The following paragraph discusses the effects of television on the American family.

> Television's contribution to family life has been an equivocal one. For while it has, indeed, kept the members of the family from dispersing, it has not served to bring them *together*. By its domination of the time families spend together, it destroys the special quality that distinguishes

119

one family from another, a quality that depends to a great extent on what a family *does*, what special rituals, games, recurrent jokes, familiar songs, and shared activities it accumulates.   —MARIE WINN, *The Plug-in Drug: Television, Children, and the Family*

Considering problems and solutions

As its name implies, paragraphs developed by the **problem-solution pattern** open with a statement of a problem, usually the topic sentence, and then offer a solution in the sentences that follow, as in this paragraph:

All over the nation, textbook choice committees face   PROBLEM
the same challenge: choosing textbooks that are factually accurate, of high intellectual quality, and acceptable to various "watchdog" committees. Such a choice is very difficult for nonspecialists. To aid these committees in   SOLUTION
deciding what textbooks to adopt, I would like to see the formation of an academic journal devoted entirely to reviewing new texts. The most efficient way to accomplish this goal would probably be to have a journal covering each field of study, since it would be inefficient to review English and physics texts in the same journal. The new texts would be scrutinized carefully by scholars in the respective fields and would be judged for their intellectual quality. In this way, the textbook choice committees would have a guide to aid them in selecting texts that are of certified intellectual value.

Considering questions and answers

Like the problem-solution pattern, the **question-answer pattern** of development does just what its name suggests: the first sentence poses a question, and the rest of the paragraph provides the answer. Beginning with a question provides a means of getting readers' attention—and focusing that attention—as it does in the following paragraph from an essay on embarrassing slips of the tongue:

Why then do we hoot at these mistakes? For one thing, it may be that we simply find conventional discourse so predictable and boring that any deviation comes as a delightful relief. In his deeply unfunny "Essay on Laughter" the philosopher Henri Bergson theorized that the act of laughter is caused by any interruption of normal human fluidity or momentum (a pie in the face, a mask, a pun). Slips of the tongue, therefore, are like slips on banana peels; we crave their occurrence if only to break the monotonies. The monotonies run to substance. When that announcer introduced Hoobert Heever, he may also have been saying that the nation had had enough of Herbert Hoover.

—ROGER ROSENBLATT, "Oops! How's That Again?"

Combining patterns

As you might expect, many paragraphs combine these methods of development. In the following paragraph the writer moves from a general topic (her record collection) to one specific part of it (blues) and then develops that topic through the use of classification (blues albums for the morning and for the evening), illustration (Robert Johnson, Ray Charles), and cause-effect (the blues cause a variety of effects on the listener).

My album collection reached the 300 mark, so no matter what mood I'm in, I have a variety of pieces to choose from. In recent years I have found myself buying more and more blues albums. I don't know why, but I've simply been gobbling them up. I can listen to the blues in the morning when my head is still a little foggy, and the voices come through like lighthouses leading the way. Or I can listen to them after a long day and let that simplistic 12-bar rhythm put me to sleep. When I'm feeling bad, I put one of these albums on and sponge up all the raw emotion expressed on that vinyl. From there I can get back in the groove and progress in energy levels, from slow blues (Robert Johnson) to inspired blues (Ray Charles) to faster and upbeat blues (Taj Mahal). In this way the blues actually picks me up; it's like a catharsis of emotion.

EXERCISE 5.15

Identify the specific method of development used in each of the following paragraphs, and explain why you think each paragraph is or is not effectively developed using that method.

1.   Science, which is defined as the body of knowledge derived from observation and experimentation, is usually divided into two main branches. The first is the natural sciences, which study the physical and biological aspects of our world. The second is the social sciences, which study human behavior. The social sciences are further divided into five main fields: psychology, economics, political science, anthropology, and sociology. Psychology is the study of individual behavior. Economics studies the production, distribution, and consumption of goods, and political science concerns itself with principles and methods of government. Anthropology is usually defined as the study of traditional and primitive societies. The study of modern societies is called sociology.

2.   Beyond the alleys and up the road are rows of traditional-style town houses. Many of the town houses have been converted into specialty shops such as clothing boutiques, jewelry shops, hair salons, and gourmet food shops. Crowds browse up and down these shops; some people wear designer clothes. The clothes shops sell fashions that would seem to some people bizarre, and to others high fashion. The jewelry shops have everything from costume bangles to huge diamond rings. The hair salons give designer, punk, or traditional cuts.

3.   Other differences I saw between Florida and Germany were the scenery and the culture. Florida's scenery consisted of one-story houses and green lawns. Palm trees and occasional garbage could be seen along the road. In Germany, houses were weirdly shaped with small lawns, if any. Buildings were very close to the road, and very little garbage could be found on the streets. Driving in Germany could be hazardous as compared with driving in Florida, because in Germany there are not speed limits. Cultural differences, such as the time of day you eat and the food you eat, were apparent between Germany and Florida. Communications were obviously different, with the German language being spoken in Germany.

4.   According to Hollywood, the Indian was always the liar, the thief, the cold-blooded, ruthless killer with no compassion. For example, in many movies a wild band of Indians surround a helpless family and for absolutely no reason at all, slaughter the whole family. The Indians depicted by Hollywood also make sneak attacks on a sleeping town, killing the townspeople, and pillaging every inch of the town. In other films, the Indians rustle cattle and horses from farmers and, of course, slay the farmers. This picture of the "Old West" is one of the greatest fallacies of all time.

EXERCISE 5.16

Choose two of the following topics or two others that interest you, and brainstorm or freewrite about each one for ten minutes (see 2e). Then use the information you have produced to determine what method(s) of development would be most appropriate for each topic.

1. The pleasure a hobby has given you
2. U2's image and Mötley Crüe's image
3. An average Saturday morning
4. Why monopoly is an appropriate metaphor for the values of a capitalistic society
5. The best course you've ever taken

EXERCISE 5.17

Refer to the argument you drafted in Exercise 4.14, and study the ways you have developed each paragraph. For one of those paragraphs, write a brief evaluation of its development, including recommendations for expanding and/ or improving the development.

I 2. Determining paragraph length

While the paragraph has existed as a unit of writing for a long, long time, ideas about and expectations of paragraphs have changed over the years. If you look at Edward Gibbon's *The Decline and Fall of the Roman Empire* (published in the late eighteenth century), for instance, you will see paragraphs longer than the ones you are used to. In general, both paragraphs and sentences have gotten shorter over the last two hundred years. Newspapers and magazines, with their narrow-column formats, are partially responsible for this shift in paragraph length, for they have accustomed readers to short lines and paragraphs. Though paragraph length must be determined to some degree by content, writers must also keep the expectations of readers firmly in mind.

Saying that the average paragraph has so many words or sentences is like saying the average family has 2.3 members and owns 1.8 cars. The information is so general that it means very little. Paragraphs should be long enough to develop an idea, create any particular effect the writer wishes to achieve (such as suspense, humor, or enthusiasm), and advance the piece of writing it is a part of. Fulfilling these aims will sometimes call for short paragraphs, sometimes for long ones.

For example, in an argumentative essay you may want to put all your lines of argument or all the evidence for your claim into one long paragraph to create the impression of a solid, overwhelmingly convincing thesis. In a narrative about an exciting event, on the other hand, a series of short paragraphs may help to create suspense, as the reader keeps reaching the end of a paragraph and rushing to the following one to find out what happened next. An important point to remember is that a new paragraph signals a pause or a break in thought for the reader. Just as timing can make a crucial difference in telling a joke, or a dramatic pause in telling a piece of news or gossip, so the pause signaled by a paragraph can raise readers' anticipation for what is to follow or give them a moment to "digest" mentally the material presented in the previous paragraph.

Notice how the following passage, the last three paragraphs of an essay on women and science, uses a very short paragraph as well as a fairly long one.

Science is undeniably hard. Often, it can seem quite boring. It is unfortunately too often presented as laws to be memorized instead of mysteries to be explored. It is too often kept a secret that science, like art, takes a well developed esthetic sense. Women aren't the only ones who say, "I hate science." That's why everyone who goes into science needs a little help from friends. For the past ten years, I have been getting more than a little help from a friend who is a physicist. But my stepdaughter—who earned the highest grades ever recorded in her California high school on the math Scholastic Aptitude Test—flunked calculus in her first year at Harvard. When my friend the physicist heard about it, he said, "Harvard should be ashamed of itself." What he meant was that she needed that little extra encouragement that makes all the difference. Instead, she got that little extra discouragement that makes all the difference. "In the first place, all the math teachers are men," she explained. "In the second place, when I met a boy I liked and told him I was taking chemistry, he immediately said: 'Oh, you're one of those science types.' In the third place, it's just a kind of social thing. The math clubs are full of boys and you don't feel comfortable joining."

In other words, she was made to feel unnecessary, and out of place.

A few months ago, I accompanied a male colleague from the science museum where I sometimes work to a lunch of the history of science faculty at the University of California. I was the only woman there, and my presence for the most part was obviously and rudely ignored. I was so surprised and hurt by this that I made an extra effort to speak knowledgeably and well. At the end of the lunch, one of the professors turned to me in all seriousness and said: "Well, K. C., what do the women think of Carl Sagan?" I replied that I had no idea what "the women" thought about anything. But now I know what I should have said: I should have told him that his comment was unnecessary, injurious and out of place.   —K. C. COLE, "Women and Physics"

Cole uses the long paragraph to build up our frustrations as we learn about why science is so "hard" for her stepdaughter. The short, one-sentence paragraph then emphasizes the point made by the long paragraph, how out of place the stepdaughter was made to feel. With the final paragraph, the author turns the tables, ending with the assertion that it is really the male comment that is "out of place." As this example illustrates, paragraph length should be determined by the author's purpose, not by a set of hard and fast rules.

EXERCISE 5.18

The following passage introduces an essay describing an interview, and its author has chosen to write a series of very brief paragraphs. Read the passage carefully, considering the paragraph lengths and the effects they create. Then reparagraph the passage, making sure each paragraph is long enough to develop one main idea. Finally, explain your reasons for your changes.

An interview I found very interesting was one with a receptionist, Sharon A. Her job reveals quite a bit about herself and possibly others in her profession.

Sharon A. has developed a negative view of working with people. She does not enjoy her receptionist's job, but a college degree in art history did not seem to get her any further in the working world.

She first reveals that people have no respect for those in her field, especially those who are women. Receptionists are stereotyped as beautiful but dumb. It is not that Sharon does not have any bright ideas, but that others consider her function itself to have little meaning or importance.

Sharon's job deals mainly with the telephone, so the people she talks with at work, whom she cannot see, seem almost nonexistent to her. As a result, her conversations have become very abrupt.

This abruptness has carried over into her personal life, she reveals. Even if she sees the people with whom she is speaking, the conversations are brief. The constant threat of interruption also carries over from her professional to her personal life.

At work, the telephone must be answered the minute it rings, no matter what she is doing. She says this requirement makes her feel like a machine. Sharon seems to have become a little withdrawn, dreaming of a land with no phones, no interruptions.

EXERCISE 5.19

The following passage introduces an essay in which a student attempts to assess the "American dream" after reading an essay by Joan Didion, "Some Dreamers of the Golden Dream." The student uses a very long paragraph for her opening. Read this long paragraph, and decide whether or not it should be broken up into two or more paragraphs and where any new paragraphs should begin. Then explain your reasons for any changes you make and what effects are created by the new paragraphing.

When I think of the "American dream," I visualize a white and blue two-story Colonial house, complete with a two-car garage, white picket fence, happily married husband and wife, two children (one boy, one girl), a dog, and family vacations across the state in the Ford station wagon. I'm not really sure where I received my information on this subject; I have just learned through the years that this is the type of life I should strive for and look forward to. The traditional "American dream" is apparently changing, though. The white and blue two-story house is now a three-story mansion embedded in the cliffs of Malibu overlooking the Pacific Ocean; the happily married husband and wife have usually known the same happiness in three prior marriages; the family vacations are now two weeks in Hawaii with the Mercedes station wagon waiting for them in the Los Angeles airport parking lot. This new and extreme version of the fairy tale is rapidly becoming everyone's new goal, according to Joan Didion's essay "Some Dreamers of the Golden Dream." Didion speaks of Southern California and states that people have derived their new ideal from newspapers and movies, not from reality. I find this statement very true to life, for most people do receive the majority of their ideas about how they should live from newspapers and movies. Therefore, if the movies present an image of gorgeous beachside mansions and expensive imported cars, then that is exactly what most people will strive for. This type of life style may not be right for every individual, though, and many people realize this fact too late. They spend their lives working and striving to become successful in society's eyes. Then, once they have reached their goal, they realize they are not truly happy, for they gained wealth and status for all the wrong reasons.

EXERCISE 5.20

Go through some of your favorite books, looking for two paragraphs—a very long one and a very short one—that impress you as particularly effective. What main idea does each develop? What effects does each create? How does each advance the piece of writing it is a part of?

EXERCISE 5.21

Examine the paragraph breaks in an essay you have written recently. Explain briefly in writing why you decided on each of the breaks. Would you change any of them now? If so, how and why?

▌ 5e. Composing special-purpose paragraphs

In addition to those that make up the main body of an essay, some paragraphs serve more specialized functions. These include opening paragraphs, concluding paragraphs, transitional paragraphs, and dialogue paragraphs.

▌ 1. Introducing an essay

Even a good essay may remain unread if it has a weak opening paragraph. In addition to announcing your topic (usually in a thesis statement), therefore, an introductory paragraph must engage the readers' interest and focus their attention on what is to come next. At their best, introductory paragraphs function as hors d'oeuvres, whetting the appetite for following courses, or as the title sequences in a film, carefully setting the scene and establishing themes the movie will explore. Because of the introduction's importance, writers often leave the *final* drafting of it until last, realizing that the focus of the introduction may change over the process of writing.

The most common kind of opening paragraph follows a general-to-specific pattern, ending with the thesis. In such an introduction, the writer opens with a general statement and then gets more and more specific, concluding with the most specific sentence in the paragraph—the thesis. The following paragraph illustrates such an opening:

> The United States has seen many changes in its **GENERAL STATEMENT** economy during the last hundred years. Among these changes is the organization of workers. Unions were **MOVE TO SPECIFICITY** formed in the late nineteenth and early twentieth centuries to battle against long work hours and bad working conditions. It was not uncommon then for a worker to be required to work twelve or more hours a day, six days a week, in hazardous and often deadly conditions. The workers organized against their employers and won their battles. Today, it is very uncommon to find such oppressive conditions in the workplace. Why, then, do unions still exist today? When we examine many of the labor **THESIS** battles of recent years, we find that unions exist mostly as bargaining units through which workers can gain higher wages—at any cost.

In this paragraph, the opening sentence introduces a general subject, changes in the U.S. economy; subsequent sentences focus more specifically on unionization; and the last sentence presents the thesis, which the rest of the essay will develop. Other ways of opening an essay include quotations, anecdotes, questions, or strong opinions.

Opening with a quotation

"Go back to hell where you came from, you old wart hog," says Mary Grace, an unattractive girl from a Massachusetts college, to Mrs. Ruby Turpin, a hypocritical Southern woman, in Flannery O'Connor's "Revelation." Mary Grace's words sting poor Mrs. Turpin, who is not used to taking criticism from anyone. Mary Grace's message is that Mrs. Turpin is not better than the people she thinks badly of, and her attack causes Mrs. Turpin to stop and scowl, in a moment of uncharacteristic self-doubt.

127

Opening with an anecdote

Imagine awakening to a thunderous roar that sounds like a herd of elephants and banshees, accompanied by an upheaval of your bed that dumps you on the floor. At first you think, "Earthquake!" Then, as you open your eyes and focus on two of the shiniest black boots you have ever seen, you remember where you are. You're in the Army now.

Opening with a question

Why is the American population terrified of turning to nuclear power as a future source of energy? People are misinformed, or not informed at all, about its benefits and safety. If Americans would take time to learn about what nuclear power offers, then their apprehension and fear might be transformed into hope.

Opening with a strong opinion

Exploitation in America is as common as the common cold. Since its beginning, this nation has thrived on economic exploitation, and the problem became especially widespread during the period from 1900 to 1920. During this time many children, as well as adults, were forced to work fourteen to fifteen hours a day for pennies. It did not take long for people to realize they were being exploited, but there was little they could do about it. Some people went on strike, but they accomplished little. Besides being taken advantage of economically, many people were also socially and sexually exploited. Both John Dos Passos's *Nineteen Nineteen* and E. L. Doctorow's *Ragtime* deal with people during this period exploiting one another economically, socially, and sexually. However, Dos Passos's treatment of this theme is pessimistic, while Doctorow's is optimistic.

EXERCISE 5.22

Refer once more to the argument you drafted in Exercise 4.14. Examine your introduction carefully, and then write an alternate introduction. Finally, write a paragraph evaluating which introduction is most effective and why.

▌2. Concluding an essay

A good conclusion wraps up an essay in a meaningful and memorable way. If a strong opening paragraph whets readers' appetite or arouses their curiosity, a strong concluding paragraph satisfies them that the job the essay set out to do is indeed completed, that their expectations have been met. In doing so, a strong conclusion reminds readers of the gist of the essay and leaves them feeling that they know a good deal more than when they began.

One of the most common strategies for concluding an essay makes use of the specific-to-general pattern, often beginning with a restatement of the thesis, and moving to several more general statements, almost in a reverse of the general-to-specific opening. The concluding paragraph of Bruce Catton's essay on Grant and Lee moves in such a way, opening with a final point of contrast, specifying it in several sentences, and then ending with a much more general statement:

> Lastly, and perhaps greatest of all, there was the ability, at the end, to turn quickly from war to peace once the fighting was over. Out of the way these two men behaved at Appomattox came the possibility of a peace of reconciliation. It was a possibility not wholly realized, in the years to come, but which did, in the end, help the two sections to become one nation again . . . after a war whose bitterness might have seemed to make such a reunion wholly impossible. No part of either man's life became him more than the part he played in this brief meeting in the McLean house at Appomattox. Their behavior there put all succeeding generations of Americans in their debt. Two great Americans, Grant and Lee—very different, yet under everything very much alike. Their encounter at Appomattox was one of the great moments of American history.
>
> —BRUCE CATTON, "Grant and Lee: A Study in Contrasts"

Other effective strategies for concluding an essay include questions, quotations, vivid images, calls for action, or warnings.

Concluding with a question

> All so-called "permanent" antifreeze is basically the same. It is made from a liquid known as ethylene glycol, which has two amazing properties: It has a lower freezing point than water, and a higher boiling point than water. It does not break down (lose its properties), nor will it boil away. And every permanent antifreeze starts with it as a base. Also, just about every antifreeze has now got antileak ingredients, as well as antirust and anticorrosion ingredients. Now, let's suppose that, in formulating the product, one of the companies comes up with a solution that is pink in color, as opposed to all the others, which are blue. Presto—an exclusivity claim. "Nothing else looks like it, nothing else performs like it." Or how about, "Look at ours, and look at anyone else's. You can see the difference our exclusive formula makes." Granted, I'm exaggerating. But did I prove a point?
>
> —PAUL STEVENS, "Weasel Words: God's Little Helpers"

Concluding with a quotation

Despite the celebrity that accrued to her and the air of awesomeness with which she was surrounded in her later years, Miss Keller retained an unaffected personality, certain that her optimistic attitude toward life was justified. "I believe that all through these dark and silent years Go l has been using my life for a purpose I do not know," she said. "But one day I shall understand and then I will be satisfied."
–ALDEN WHITMAN, "Helen Keller: June 27, 1880–June 1, 1968"

Concluding with a vivid image

It is, in any case, finally you that I end up having to trust not to laugh, not to snicker. Even as you regard me in these lines, I try to imagine your face as you read. You who read "Aria," especially those of you with your theme-divining yellow felt pen poised in your hand, you for whom this essay is yet another "assignment," please do not forget that it is my life I am handing you in these pages—memories that are as personal for me as family photographs in an old cigar box.
–RICHARD RODRIGUEZ,
from a postscript to "Aria: A Memoir of a Bilingual Childhood"

Concluding with a strong call for action

It is now almost 40 years since the invention of nuclear weapons. We have not yet experienced a global thermonuclear war—although on more than one occasion we have come tremulously close. I do not think our luck can hold forever. Men and machines are fallible, as recent events remind us. Fools and madmen do exist, and sometimes rise to power. Concentrating always on the near future, we have ignored the long-term consequences of our actions. We have placed our civilization and our species in jeopardy.

Fortunately, it is not yet too late. We can safeguard the planetary civilization and the human family if we so choose. There is no more important or more urgent issue. –CARL SAGAN, "The Nuclear Winter"

Concluding with a warning

Because propaganda is so effective, it is important to track it down and understand how it is used. We may eventually agree with what the propagandist says because all propaganda isn't necessarily bad; some advertising, for instance, urges us not to drive drunk, to have regular dental checkups, to contribute to the United Way. Even so, we must be aware that propaganda is being used. Otherwise, we will have consented to handing over our independence, our decision-making ability, and our brains.
–ANN MCCLINTOCK, "Propaganda Techniques in Today's Advertising"

The concluding paragraph provides the last opportunity for you to impress the message of an essay on your readers' minds and to create effects you desire. As such, it is well worth your time and effort.

EXERCISE 5.23

Choose an essay you have recently written, and examine the conclusion carefully. Then write at least one new conclusion for the essay, striving for the maximum effect on readers. Finally, describe and evaluate the techniques you used in your revision.

▌ 3. Using transitional paragraphs

On some occasions, you may need to call your readers' attention very powerfully to a major transition between ideas. To do so, consider using an entire short paragraph to signal that transition, as in the following example from an essay on "television addiction." The opening paragraphs of the essay characterize addiction in general, concluding with the paragraph about its destructive elements. The one-sentence paragraph that follows arrests our attention, announcing that these general characteristics will now be related to television viewing.

> Finally a serious addiction is distinguished from a harmless pursuit of pleasure by its distinctly destructive elements. A heroin addict, for instance, leads a damaged life: his increasing need for heroin in increasing doses prevents him from working, from maintaining relationships, from developing in human ways. Similarly an alcoholic's life is narrowed and dehumanized by his dependence on alcohol.
>
> Let us consider television viewing in the light of the conditions that define serious addictions. —MARIE WINN,
> *The Plug-in Drug: Television, Children, and the Family*

▌ 4. Using paragraphs to signal dialogue

Paragraphs of dialogue can bring added life to almost any sort of writing. The traditional way to set up dialogue in written form is simple: simply start a new paragraph each time the speaker changes, no matter how short each bit of conversation is. Here is an example:

> "Hey Clobberfoot, I bet you can't still ski all the way around the lake!" Chris shouted as I pushed across the overgrown lawn toward her.
> "Are you kidding?" I retorted cheerfully.
> "I'm willing to stake a banana split on it!" Chris added.

"You're on, you fool," I said, taking one last look over my shoulder. As we turned and headed down to the outlying boathouse, I heard a familiar seagull give me a squawk of encouragement as he flew by.

EXERCISE 5.24

Go through some of your favorite books, articles, or essays to find an opening or concluding paragraph that you consider particularly effective. Try to analyze what makes the paragraph so effective. Then, choosing a topic of great interest to you, try to write an opening or concluding paragraph imitating the paragraph you admire—the structure of its sentences, the pattern of its development, its use of particular devices such as quotations, questions, and so on. Then compare the two paragraphs, and decide how effective your own is.

▌ 5f. Linking paragraphs

The same methods that can be used to link sentences and create coherent paragraphs can be used to link paragraphs themselves together so that an essay as a whole flows smoothly and coherently. Some reference to the previous paragraph, either explicitly stated or merely implied, should occur in each paragraph after the introduction of an essay. As in linking sentences, you can create this reference by repeating or paraphrasing key words and terms and by using parallel structures, pronouns, and transitional expressions.

Repeating key words

. . . Thus, I learned that stealing and jealousy are wrong in my culture. Until I began to distinguish *acceptable* from unacceptable *behavior*, constant tension existed between my parents and me.

After I had learned *acceptable behavior*, the second step in my process of maturity was to balance my desires with my conscience in order to become a well-adjusted, acculturated individual. . . .

Using parallel structure

. . . Kennedy made an effort to assure non-Catholics that he would respect the separation of church and state, and most of them did not seem to hold his religion against him in deciding how to vote. Since his election, *the church to which a candidate belongs* has become less important in presidential politics.

The region from which a candidate comes remains an important factor. . . .

Using pronouns

Singer's tale is of a pathetic Polish Jew, Gimpel, who because of *his* strong faith believes everything *he* is told. At the beginning of the tale, we learn that Gimpel has had a gruesomely cruel life. *He* is an orphan, and all *his* life *he* has been teased and tormented for believing everything *he* hears.

Even the most ridiculous and far-fetched tales take *him* in. For example, when *he* is told that the messiah has come and *his* parents have risen from the dead, *he* goes out to search for *them!* In *his* seemingly foolish search, *he* is berated by the townsfolk.

Using other transitional devices

. . . While the Indian, in the character of Tonto, was more positively portrayed in "The Lone Ranger," such a portrayal was more the exception than the norm.

Moreover, despite this brief glimpse of an Indian as an ever-loyal sidekick, Tonto was never accorded the same stature as the man with the white horse and silver bullets. . . .

EXERCISE 5.25

Look at the essay you drafted in Exercise 2.11 or the argument you drafted in Exercise 4.14, and identify the ways your paragraphs are linked together. Identify each use of repetition, parallel structures, pronouns, and transitional expressions, and then evaluate how effectively you have joined paragraphs.

▌ 5g. Checking paragraphs

Here is a checklist you can use to evaluate—and to improve—your paragraphing:

1. What is the topic sentence of each paragraph, and is it stated or implied? Where in the paragraph does it fall? Should it come at some other point? Would any paragraph be improved by deleting or adding a topic sentence?
2. Which sentences, if any, do not relate in some way to the topic sentence? Is there any way to justify their inclusion?
3. What is the most general sentence in each paragraph? If not the topic sentence, should it remain or be omitted?
4. Is each paragraph organized in a way that is easy for readers to follow? By what means are sentences linked in each paragraph? Do any more

links need to be added? Do any of the transitional expressions try to create links that do not really exist between ideas?

5. How completely does each paragraph develop its topic sentence? What methods of development are used, and are they effective? What other methods might be used? Does the paragraph need more material?

6. How long is each paragraph? Are paragraphs varied in length? Does any paragraph seem too long or too short? Is there anything that might be given strong emphasis by a one-sentence paragraph?

7. By what means are the paragraphs linked together? Do any more links need to be added? Do any of the transitional expressions try to create links that do not really exist between ideas?

8. How does the introductory paragraph catch the interest of readers? How exactly does it open—with a quotation? an anecdote? a question? a strong statement? How else might it open?

9. How does the last paragraph draw the essay to a conclusion? What lasting impression will it leave with readers? How exactly does it close—with a question? a quotation? a vivid image? a warning or call for action? How else might this essay conclude?

READING WITH AN EYE FOR PARAGRAPHS

Think of a writer you admire, and read something she or he has written. Find one or two paragraphs that impress you in some way, and analyze them using the above questions. Try to decide what makes them effective as paragraphs.

FOR EXAMINING YOUR OWN PARAGRAPHS

Examine one or two paragraphs you have written, using the questions in 5g to evaluate their unity, coherence, and development. Identify the topic of each paragraph, the topic sentence (if one is explicitly stated), any methods of development, and any means used to create coherence. Decide whether or not each paragraph is successful as a paragraph, and explain your reasons. Finally, choose one paragraph and revise it.

PART TWO

Sentences: Making Grammatical Choices

6. Constructing Grammatical Sentences

When you hear the word *grammar*, the main subject of this chapter, you may think of any number of definitions: a way words are arranged into meaningful patterns ("Every language has a *grammar*"), the formal study of such patterns ("She is a well-known *grammarian*"); or a kind of linguistic good manners ("Oops—I'd better watch my *grammar!*"). In this chapter you will be concentrating on understanding the first of these definitions—grammar as the patterns into which words can be arranged to convey meanings.

Outside of school, you may not have thought very much about grammar. Indeed, you may agree in principle with the fifteenth-century Holy Roman Emperor Sigismund, who answered a question about his Latin grammar by saying, "I am the Roman emperor and am above grammar." In one sense, all native speakers of a language are, like Sigismund, "above" grammar. All speakers, that is, learn the grammar of their language naturally as they learn to speak. This intuitive grasp of grammar allows us to say, "The bright red cardinal surprised me," rather than "Cardinal bright the surprised me red"—without even thinking about it. This ability to make meaningful sentences comes, in fact, very early to each of us and accounts for the fact that young children often produce sophisticated sentences out of the blue, without having to study or "learn" a system by which to produce them.

But in another sense, none of us, including an emperor, is above grammar. As the sample sentence about the cardinal indicates, we are bound by certain patterns or "rules" in producing sentences. And breaking those "rules" moves a speaker from sense to nonsense, from being easily understood to being completely misunderstood.

If we learn the basic grammar of language as we learn to speak, then why bother to study it? In the first place, though all speakers know the *basic* grammatical "rules," these rules can generate a very broad range of sentences, some of which will be much more skillful and effective than others. As someone who uses written language, you want not simply to write, but to write skillfully and effectively, and understanding grammatical structures can help you do so.

Furthermore, within the basic "rules" of English grammar, wide latitude exists. Not everyone, for instance, grows up speaking with precisely the same set of grammatical principles. Knowledge of the differences can help you produce sentences that are not only grammatical but appropriate to a particular situation. The "rules" that allow you to say "Hey, man, this be one *fine* set of wheels" in one situation, for example, are not quite the same as those that lead you to say "Yes, sir, this car is completely acceptable" in another. If you understand grammar, you will not only understand both statements but know when and why to use one and when the other. Finally, because language is so closely related to thought, studying our language patterns, our grammar, can give us insight into our own ways of thinking. If in some important sense we *are* what we say (and write), then examining the principles through which we express our meanings can help us understand ourselves as well as others.

This chapter takes a look at what makes our language tick—those elements that allow us to produce meaningful sentences.

❚ 6a. Understanding the basic grammar of sentences

Put most simply, a **sentence** is a grammatically complete group of words that expresses a thought. To be grammatically complete, a group of words must contain two major structural components—a subject and a predicate. The **subject** identifies what the sentence is about, and the **predicate** asserts or asks something about the subject, or it tells the subject to do something.

SUBJECT	PREDICATE
We	shall overcome.
I	could have danced all night.
Life	is just a bowl of cherries.
(You)	Whistle a happy tune.
The rain in Spain	stays mainly on the plain.
Puff, the magic dragon,	lived by the sea.

Some very brief sentences have one-word subjects and predicates (for example, *Time passes*) or even a one-word predicate with an implied or "understood" subject (for example, *Stop!*). Most sentences, however, contain additional words that expand the basic subject and predicate. In the last of the examples above, for instance, the subject might have been simply *Puff*; the words *the magic dragon* merely say more about the subject. Similarly, the predicate of that sentence could grammatically be *lived*; the words *by the sea* expand the predicate by telling us where Puff lived. No matter how many words a sentence contains, however, it can always be divided into two basic parts—a subject and a predicate.

EXERCISE 6.1

The following sentences are taken from "A Hanging," an essay by George Orwell. Identify the subject and predicate in each sentence, underlining the subject once and the predicate twice.

> *Example*
> One prisoner had been brought out of his cell.

1. We set out for the gallows.
2. He was an army doctor, with a gray toothbrush moustache and a gruff voice.
3. The rest of us, magistrates and the like, followed behind.
4. The dog answered the sound with a whine.
5. The hangman, a gray-haired convict in the white uniform of the prison, was waiting beside his machine.

❚ 6b. Recognizing the parts of speech

If the basic parts of sentences are subjects and predicates, the central elements of subjects and predicates are nouns and verbs. For example:

```
┌───SUBJECT───┐┌──────PREDICATE──────┐
    NOUN   VERB
```
The little train rumbled over the tracks.*

Nouns and verbs are two of the eight **parts of speech,** one set of grammatical categories into which words may be classified. The other six parts of speech are pronouns, adjectives, adverbs, prepositions, con-

---

* From *The Little Engine That Could,* by Watty Piper, Platt & Munk (NY: Putnam, 1984).

junctions, and interjections. Many English words can function as more than one part of speech. Take the word *book*, for instance: when you *book a plane flight*, it is a verb; when you *take a good book to the beach*, it is a noun; and when you *have book knowledge*, it is an adjective.

The system of categorizing words by part of speech comes to English from Latin, where it was first set forth by the Roman grammarian Donatus in the fourth century A.D. The differences between Latin and English are many, of course, and the parts of speech system is in certain ways not as precise for English as it is for Latin. Many grammarians argue that students of English grammar should focus less on the parts of speech and more on the parts of a sentence. Even so, the parts of speech remain an important part of our grammatical vocabulary, and all dictionaries use them to label their entries. In this chapter we will see how the various parts of speech are used in sentences.

1. Recognizing verbs

The word *verb* comes from the Latin *verbum*, which simply means "word." As this history indicates, **verbs** are among the most important words, for they move the meaning of sentences along by showing action (*glance, jump*), occurrence (*become, happen*), or a state of being (*be, live*).

Verbs change form to show *time, person*, and *number*.

TIME	we *work*, we *worked*
PERSON	I *work*, she *works*
NUMBER	one person *works*, two people *work*

See 9a for a discussion of how verbs change form to show person and number. **Auxiliary verbs** (also known as **helping verbs**) combine with other verbs (often called **main verbs**) to create *verb phrases*. Auxiliaries include the forms of *be, do*, and *have*, which are also used as main verbs, and the words *can, could, may, might, must, shall, should, will*, and *would*.

I *must get* some sleep tonight!

You *can find* Professor Kinder during his office hours.

Chapter 8 provides a complete discussion of the forms and functions of verbs.

EXERCISE 6.2

Identify and underline the verbs in each of the following sentences.

Example

Charlie <u>should do</u> fine in Saturday's tennis match.

1. His future does look bright.
2. The ice cream ran all over the table and the floor.
3. Over the next few days, I tapped about seventy maple trees.
4. One person can collect sap, a second might run the evaporator, and a third should finish the syrup.
5. A trip to Florida would be great.
6. On a crisp morning in early spring, a man walked alone through the forest.
7. The deer population rose drastically in the early twentieth century, after the disappearance of the cougar and the wolf.
8. The bookcase will extend from floor to ceiling.
9. One Saturday morning my mother, an orthopedic surgeon, took my brother and me to the hospital.
10. The dormitory kitchen smelled like old fish.

▌ 2. Recognizing nouns

The word *noun* comes from the Latin *nomen*, which means "name." That is what **nouns** do: they name things. Nouns can name persons (*aviator, chef*), places (*lake, library*), things (*truck, suitcase*), or concepts (*happiness, balance*). **Proper nouns** name specific persons, places, things, or concepts: *Tom, Iowa, General Mills, Buddhism*. Proper nouns are capitalized. (See 33b for an explanation of which nouns are considered proper nouns.) **Collective nouns** name groups: *team, flock, navy*. (See 9d for more information about collective nouns.)

Most nouns can be changed from **singular** (one) to **plural** (more than one) by adding *-s* or *-es: horse, horses; box, boxes*. Some nouns, however, have irregular plural forms: *woman, women: alumnus, alumni; mouse, mice*. (See 22e for more information about forming plurals.) **Mass nouns** cannot be made plural because they name something that cannot easily be counted: *dust, peace, tranquility*.

Nouns can also take a **possessive** form to show ownership. You form the possessive by adding *-'s* to a singular noun and just an apostrophe to a plural noun: *the horse's owner, the boys' department*. (See 30a for more information about forming possessives.)

Nouns are often preceded by one of the **articles** *a, an,* or *the: a rocket, an astronaut, the launch.* Articles are also known as **noun markers** or **determiners.**

EXERCISE 6.3

Identify the nouns, including possessive forms, and the articles in each of the following sentences. Underline the nouns once and the articles twice.

Example

The Puritans' hopes were dashed when Charles II was restored to the throne.

1. Nightlife begins in Georgetown even before the sun goes down.
2. Although plagiarism is dishonest and illegal, it does occur.
3. All I want for Christmas is my two front teeth.
4. Henderson's story is a tale of theft and violation.
5. In the front row sat two people, a man with slightly graying hair and a young woman in jeans.

▌ 3. Recognizing pronouns

Pronouns function as nouns in sentences and often take the place of specific nouns, serving as short forms so that we do not have to repeat a noun that has already been mentioned. A specific noun that a pronoun replaces or refers to is called the **antecedent** of the pronoun. (See Chapters 9 and 11 for more about pronouns and antecedents.) In the following example, the antecedent of the pronoun *it* is *bus.*

The *bus* was already late, but *it* stopped for Charlotte.

You are already familiar with pronouns; we could scarcely speak or write without them. (The preceding sentence, for instance, includes the pronouns *you, we,* and *them.*) You may not, however, be familiar with all the categories of pronouns, which include the following:

Personal pronouns refer to specific persons or things.

PERSONAL   I, you, he, she, it, we, they
PRONOUNS

After the scouts made camp, *they* ran along the beach.

Each personal pronoun has several different forms (for example, *I, me, my, mine*) depending on how it functions in a sentence. (See Chapter 7 for a discussion of these forms and how to use them.)

Reflexive pronouns refer back to the subject of the sentence or clause in which they appear. They end in *-self* or *-selves*.

| REFLEXIVE PRONOUNS | myself, yourself, himself, herself, itself, oneself, ourselves, yourselves, themselves |

The seals sunned *themselves* on the warm rocks.

Intensive pronouns have the same form as reflexive pronouns. They are used to emphasize their antecedents.

He decided to paint the apartment *himself.*

Indefinite pronouns do not refer to specific nouns, although they may refer to identifiable persons or things. They express the idea of "all," "some," "any," or "none." Indefinite pronouns are one of the largest categories of pronouns; the following list does not include all of them.

| INDEFINITE PRONOUNS | all, anybody, both, each, everything, few, most, none, one, some, somebody |

Somebody screamed when the lights went out.

Demonstrative pronouns identify or point to specific nouns.

| DEMONSTRATIVE PRONOUNS | this, that, these, those |

These are Peter's books.

Interrogative pronouns are used to ask questions.

| INTERROGATIVE PRONOUNS | who, which, what |

Who is teaching composition this term?

Relative pronouns introduce dependent clauses and "relate" the dependent clause to the rest of the sentence (see 6c4).

| RELATIVE PRONOUNS | who, which, that, what, whoever, whichever, whatever |

Margaret owns the car *that* is parked by the corner.

The interrogative pronoun *who* and the relative pronouns *who* and *whoever* have different forms depending on how they are used in a sentence. (See Chapter 7.)

Demonstrative pronouns, the possessive forms of personal pronouns, and some indefinite, interrogative, and relative pronouns can be used as adjectives. (See 6b4 for further discussion of pronouns used as adjectives.)

Reciprocal pronouns refer to the individual parts of a plural antecedent.

RECIPROCAL PRONOUNS   each other, one another

The pirates began to quarrel with *one another* over their booty.

EXERCISE 6.4

Identify the pronouns and any antecedents in each of the following sentences, underlining the pronouns once and the antecedents twice.

Example

As identical <u>twins</u>, <u>they</u> really do understand <u>each other</u>.

1. She thanked everyone for helping.
2. The crowd that greeted the pope was the largest one I have ever seen.
3. Who knows better than Mark himself what he should do?
4. Celia chose to move from Bahia to New York, but still she considers herself more Brazilian than American.
5. People who are extremely fastidious often annoy those who are not.

4. Recognizing adjectives

Adjectives modify (limit the meaning of) nouns or pronouns, usually by describing, identifying, or quantifying those words.

The *red* Corvette ran off the road. [describes]

It was *red*. [describes]

That Corvette needs to be repaired. [identifies]

We saw *several* Corvettes race by. [quantifies]

Most adjectives, like *red* in the examples above, are used to describe. In addition to their basic form, most descriptive adjectives have other forms that are used to make comparisons: *small, smaller, smallest; foolish, more foolish, most foolish, less foolish, least foolish.*

This year's attendance was *smaller* than last year's.

This year's attendance was the *smallest* in ten years.

Many of the pronouns introduced in 6b3 can also be used as adjectives to identify or quantify.

144

Those are my favorite dogs. [pronoun]

Those dogs should be on a leash. [adjective]

Kinds of pronouns that can be used as adjectives include personal (*her* idea), interrogative (*which* model should we buy?), relative (we're not sure *which* model we should buy), demonstrative (*this* book), and indefinite (*many* moons). Other kinds of adjectives that identify or quantify are articles (*a, an, the*) and numbers (*three, sixty-fifth, five thousand*).

Proper adjectives are adjectives that are formed from or related to proper nouns (*French, Emersonian*). Proper adjectives are capitalized. (See 33b for more information about proper adjectives.)

Chapter 10 provides a complete discussion of the forms and functions of adjectives.

▌ 5. Recognizing adverbs

Adverbs modify verbs, adjectives, other adverbs, or entire clauses. You can recognize many adverbs by their *-ly* ending, though some adverbs do not have such an ending (*always, never, very, well*) and some words that end in *-ly* are not adverbs but adjectives (*friendly, lovely*). Among the most common adverbs is *not*.

Virginia and Kim *recently* visited Santa Fe. [modifies the verb *visited*]

They had an *unexpectedly* exciting trip. [modifies the adjective *exciting*]

They *very* soon fell under the spell of New Mexico. [modifies the adverb *soon*]

Frankly, they would have liked to stay another month. [modifies the independent clause that makes up the rest of the sentence]

Adverbs often answer one of the following questions: *how? when? where? why? to what extent?* In the first example sentence above, for instance, *recently* answers the question *when?* In the third sentence, *very* answers the question *to what extent?*

Many adverbs, like many adjectives, have different forms that are used in making comparisons: *forcefully, more forcefully, most forcefully, less forcefully, least forcefully.*

The senator spoke *more forcefully* than her opponent.

Of all the candidates, she speaks the *most forcefully.*

Conjunctive adverbs modify an entire clause and express the connection in meaning between that clause and the preceding clause (or sentence). Examples of conjunctive adverbs include *however, furthermore, therefore,* and *likewise.* (See 6b7 for more information about conjunctive adverbs.)

The most movable of all parts of speech, adverbs can often be placed in different positions in a sentence without changing or disrupting the meaning of the sentence. Notice in the following examples how placement creates only slight differences in emphasis:

Quickly Charles ran for the door.

Charles *quickly* ran for the door.

Charles ran for the door *quickly.*

Chapter 10 provides a complete discussion of the forms and functions of adverbs.

EXERCISE 6.5

Identify the adjectives and adverbs in each of the following sentences, underlining the adjectives once and the adverbs twice. Remember that articles and some pronouns are used as adjectives.

Example
Luckily, each day brought new challenges.

1. You are lucky that your roommate rarely becomes extremely angry.
2. Anxiously, I took my place in the long line to register for classes.
3. The aromas from the pantry were rather mysterious, and our stomachs grumbled hungrily.
4. Twenty Italian flags snapped in the strong breeze.
5. Ms. Peters was the most inspirational of the three instructors.
6. Those people adjusted quite happily to their new situation.
7. Never did I expect to move to a small town in Texas.
8. After the election the president spoke more pessimistically about the future of the country.
9. The biggest factor in homelessness is a drop in federal aid for housing.
10. Some say that the personal life of a political candidate is not relevant.

EXERCISE 6.6

Expand each of the following sentences by adding appropriate adjectives and adverbs. Delete *the* if you need to.

Example

The veterinarians examined the patient.

Eventually, the *three young* veterinarians *thoroughly* examined the *nervous* patient.

1. A corporation can fire workers.
2. The heroine marries the prince.
3. In the painting a road curves between hills.
4. Students are using the library for research.
5. Feminists have staged demonstrations against the movie.

❙ 6. Recognizing prepositions

Prepositions are important structural words that express relationships—in space, time, or other senses—between nouns or pronouns and other words in a sentence.

> We did not want to leave *during* the game.

> Careful writers read their own pages *with* infinite care.

> Drive *across* the bridge, go *down* the avenue *past* three stoplights, and then turn left *before* the Gulf station.

Here is a list of some common prepositions:

about	before	from	over
above	behind	in	past
across	beneath	inside	regarding
after	beside	into	since
against	between	like	through
along	beyond	near	toward
among	by	of	under
around	down	off	until
as	during	on	up
at	except	onto	with
below	for	out	without

In addition to the words on this list, some prepositions, called **compound prepositions,** are made up of more than one word: *according to, because of, by way of, due to, except for, in addition to, in front of, in place of, in spite of, instead of, next to, out of, with regard to.*

If you are ever in doubt about which preposition to use (for example, whether to write *agree to* or *agree with*), consult your dictionary. Your library may also have Frederich Wood's *English Prepositional Idioms,* a dictionary devoted entirely to prepositions.

A *prepositional phrase* is made of a preposition together with the noun or pronoun it connects to the rest of the sentence. For more information about prepositional phrases, see 6c3.

EXERCISE 6.7

Identify and underline the prepositions in each of the following sentences.

Example
In the dim interior of the hut crouched an old man.

1. A gust of wind blew through the window, upsetting the vase on the table.
2. He ran swiftly through the brush, across the beach, and into the sea.
3. A few minutes past noon the police arrived at the scene.
4. Far from sight, beyond the horizon, our ship heads toward the open sea.
5. The book, by Anne Morrow Lindbergh, describes the flight the Lindberghs made to the Orient by way of the Great Circle Route.

▌ 7. Recognizing conjunctions

Conjunctions connect other words or groups of words to one another. There are four kinds of conjunctions: coordinating conjunctions, correlative conjunctions, subordinating conjunctions, and conjunctive adverbs.

Coordinating conjunctions (*and, but, or, nor, for, so, yet*) join equivalent structures—two or more nouns, pronouns, verbs, adjectives, adverbs, prepositions, conjunctions, phrases, or clauses.

T. S. Eliot wrote poems *and* plays.

A strong *but* warm breeze blew across the desert.

Please print *or* type the information on the application form.

Her work demanded much time, *yet* she was able to join the team.

Nor, for, and *so* can connect independent clauses only.

He did not have much money, *nor* did he know how to get any.

The student glanced anxiously at the clock, *for* only twenty minutes remained in the exam period.

Ellen worked two shifts on Thursday, *so* she can take Friday off.

Correlative conjunctions (*both . . . and, either . . . or, just as . . . so, neither . . . nor, not only . . . but (also), whether . . . or*) also join equivalent words or word groups.

Both W. H. Auden *and* William Carlos Williams wrote poems about Bruegel's *Fall of Icarus.*

Jeff *not only* applied for a summer job *but also* volunteered to work at the community center.

Subordinating conjunctions introduce dependent clauses and signal the relationship between that clause and another clause, usually an independent clause. For instance, in the following sentence the subordinating conjunction *while* signals a time relationship, letting us know that the two events in the sentence happen simultaneously.

Sweat ran down my face *while* I frantically searched for my child.

Following are some of the most common subordinating conjunctions:

after	before	since	unless
although	even though	so that	until
as	if	than	when
as if	in order that	that	where
because	once	though	while

Unless sales improve dramatically, the company will soon be bankrupt.

My grandmother began traveling *after* she sold her house.

Conjunctive adverbs connect one independent clause (or sentence) to another. As their name suggests, conjunctive adverbs can be considered both adverbs and conjunctions because they modify the second clause in addition to expressing the connection in meaning between it and the preceding clause. Like many other adverbs and unlike other conjunctions, they can be moved to different positions in a clause without changing or disrupting the meaning of the clause. Look at the following sentences:

The cider tasted bitter; *however,* each of us drank a tall glass of it.

The cider tasted bitter; each of us, *however,* drank a tall glass of it.

The cider tasted bitter. Each of us drank a tall glass of it, *however.*

Commonly used conjunctive adverbs include the following:

also	furthermore	likewise
anyway	however	meanwhile
besides	incidentally	moreover
certainly	indeed	namely
finally	instead	nevertheless

next	similarly	therefore
now	still	thus
otherwise	then	undoubtedly

Independent clauses connected by a conjunctive adverb must be separated by a semicolon or a period, not just a comma (see 13c1).

Carmen grabbed the ball and ran down the street; *consequently*, the stickball game came to an abrupt end.

Some of these problems could occur at any company; many, *though*, could happen only here.

EXERCISE 6.8

Identify and underline the coordinating, correlative, and subordinating conjunctions and the conjunctive adverbs in each of the following sentences.

Example
David used his sleeping bag <u>even though</u> the cabin was furnished with sheets <u>and</u> blankets.

1. When we arrived at the pond, we saw many children playing there.
2. Pokey is an outside cat; nevertheless, she greets me at the front door each night as I arrive home.
3. The colt walked calmly, for he seemed to know he would win the race.
4. The shops along the waterfront were open, but business was slow.
5. The Environmental Protection Agency was once forced to buy an entire town because dioxins had rendered it uninhabitable.
6. The office manager found imperfections not only in everything I did but also in the work every other employee did.
7. I did not know whether to laugh or to cry after I realized my mistake.
8. Exhausted men worked the pumps until their arms ached.
9. Although I live in a big city, my neighborhood has enough trees and raccoons to make me feel as if I live in the suburbs.
10. Neither Henry nor Rachel could understand the invitation; therefore, they did not respond to it.

▌ 8. Recognizing interjections

Interjections are words that express surprise or emotion: *oh, ouch, ah, hey*. Interjections often stand alone, as fragments, and even when they are included in a sentence, they are not related grammatically to the rest of the sentence. They are used mostly in speaking; in writing they are used mostly in dialogue.

"Yeah! All right!" The watching crowd hurled hats in the air and jumped up in joy.

We tiptoed cautiously through the dark basement until—*oh, no!*—we saw what lay under the pile of discarded clothing in the corner.

▌ 6c. Recognizing the parts of a sentence

While the parts of speech system helps us to understand the grammar of sentences, a sentence is not just made up of individual words. Every sentence has a grammatical pattern or structure, and the parts of speech are simply the categories of words used to create this structure.

Look again at the word *book*. In 6b we saw that *book* can function as various parts of speech—as a noun, an adjective, and a verb.

NOUN
A book is always a welcome gift.

ADJECTIVE
Henry has more book knowledge than wisdom.

VERB
May I book a flight to Fort Worth?

Notice that *book* has exactly the same form for each part of speech; it would be impossible to recognize its meaning outside the context of a particular sentence. In fact, even in a sentence a word that can be categorized as a certain part of speech can function in more than one way.

SUBJECT
This book looks great!

DIRECT OBJECT
I need a certain book.

Book acts as a noun in both of these sentences, yet in the first it serves as the subject of the verb *looks*, and in the second it serves as the direct object of the verb *need*. Knowing the word's part of speech tells only part of the story; we have to recognize the part it plays in the pattern or structure of the sentence.

Most English sentences follow one of five basic patterns: (1) subject/verb, (2) subject/verb/subject complement, (3) subject/verb/direct object, (4) subject/verb/indirect object/direct object, and (5) subject/verb/direct object/object complement. For example:

     S   V
1. Babies cry.

     S   V   SC
2. Babies seem fragile.

     S   V   DO
3. Babies drink milk.

     S   V   IO   DO
4. Babies give grandparents pleasure.

     S   V   DO   OC
5. Parents consider babysitters essential.

This section examines the essential parts of a sentence—subjects, predicates, objects, complements, phrases, and clauses—and provides practice in using them to construct sentences of various kinds.

1. Recognizing subjects

As explained in 6a, almost every sentence has a stated subject, which identifies whom or what the sentence is about. The **simple subject** consists of one or more nouns or pronouns; the **complete subject** consists of the simple subject with all its modifiers. Depending on the kinds of modifiers, subjects can be as plain as one word or far more complex. The following examples show the complete subjects in italics, with the simple subjects labeled *ss*:

   ss
Baseball is a summer game.

             ss
Sailing over the fence, the ball crashed through Mr. Wilson's window.

   ss
Stadiums with real grass are hard to find these days.

   ss
Those who sit in the bleachers have the most fun.

A **compound subject** contains two or more nouns or pronouns joined with a coordinating conjunction (*and, but, or*) or a correlative conjunction (*both . . . and, either . . . or, neither . . . nor, not only . . . but also*).

Mays and Mantle destroyed pitchers.

Both he and Mantle destroyed pitchers.

In imperative sentences, which express requests or commands, the subject *you* is implied but not stated.

(*You*) Keep your eye on the ball.

In English sentences the simple subject usually comes before the predicate, or verb, but not always. Sometimes writers reverse this order for effect.

Up to the plate stepped *Casey*.

High were the *hopes* of Mudville fans.

In questions, the subject usually appears between the auxiliary verb and the main verb.

Did *Casey* save the game?

In sentences beginning with *there* or *here* followed by a form of the verb *be* (*is, are, was, were, have been, will be*, and so on), the subject always follows the verb. *There* and *here* are never the subject.

Here is the sad *ending* of the poem.

There was no *joy* in Mudville.

EXERCISE 6.9

Identify the complete subject and the simple subject in each of the following sentences. Underline the complete subject once and the simple subject twice.

Example

A fresh, moist <u>breeze</u> kicked up at just the right time.

1. The novels of F. Scott Fitzgerald depict the Jazz Age.
2. A two-foot snowfall on April 13 was most unexpected.
3. Decisions about courses and majors should be the students'.
4. Anyone who lives in a glass house should never throw stones.
5. Some women worried about osteoporosis take calcium supplements.

2. Recognizing predicates

In addition to a subject, every sentence has a predicate which asserts or asks something about the subject or tells the subject to do something (as explained in 6a). The "hinge" or key word of most predicates is a verb. As we saw in 6b1, a verb can include auxiliary verbs (as in this sentence, where *can* is an auxiliary and *include* is the main verb). The **simple predicate** of a sentence is the main verb and any auxiliaries; the **complete predicate** also includes any modifiers of the verb and any objects or complements and their modifiers. In the following examples, the complete predicates are italicized and the simple predicates are labeled *sp:*

┌─SP─┐
My roommate *seems wonderful.*

┌─SP─┐
She *originally comes from St. Paul, Minnesota.*

┌───SP───┐
Both of us *are planning to major in history.*

A **compound predicate** contains two or more verbs that have the same subject and are usually joined by a coordinating or correlative conjunction.

> The student *shut the book, put it back on the shelf, and sighed.*

> The Amish *neither drive cars nor use electricity.*

On the basis of how they function in predicates, verbs can be divided into three categories: linking, transitive, and intransitive.

Linking verbs

A **linking verb** links, or joins, the subject with a **subject complement,** a word or word group that identifies or describes the subject. If it identifies the subject, the complement is a noun or pronoun (and is sometimes called a **predicate noun**). If it describes the subject, the complement is an adjective (and is sometimes called a **predicate adjective**). In the following two sentences, for example, *an investment banker* is a predicate noun and *rich* is a predicate adjective:

┌──S──┐ V ┌────SC────┐
Christine is an investment banker.

S V SC
She is rich.

The forms of *be,* when used as main verbs rather than as auxiliary verbs, are linking verbs (like *are* in this sentence). Other verbs, such as *appear, become, feel, grow, look, make, seem, smell,* and *sound,* can also function as linking verbs, depending on the sense of the sentence.

┌──────────S──────────┐┌──V──┐┌─SC─┐
Our mayor's famed contentiousness has become tedious.

┌────────S────────┐┌─V─┐┌─SC─┐
His political rivals seem pleased.

Transitive and intransitive verbs

If a verb is not a linking verb, it is either transitive or intransitive. A **transitive verb** expresses action that is directed toward a noun or pronoun, called the **direct object** of the verb.

> S ——V—— ——DO——
> I will analyze three poems.

A direct object answers the question *what?* or *whom?* about the transitive verb. In the preceding example sentence, the subject and verb alone do not express a complete thought: *what* will I analyze? The direct object completes the thought.

A direct object may be followed by an **object complement,** a word or words that identifies or describes the direct object.

> S ——V—— ——————DO—————— ——OC——
> I consider Marianne Moore's poetry exquisite.
> ——————————S—————————— —V——DO—— ——OC——
> Her poems and personality made Moore a celebrity.

A transitive verb may also be followed by an **indirect object,** which tells to whom or to what, or for whom or for what, the verb's action is done. You might say that the indirect object is the recipient of the direct object.

> ——————————S—————————— —V——IO——————DO——————
> Moore's poems about the Dodgers give me considerable pleasure.
> ——S—— —V—— ——————IO—————— ——DO——
> Brooklyn owes Marianne Moore something.

An **intransitive verb** expresses action that is not directed toward an object or is directed toward an object that is not mentioned. Therefore, an intransitive verb does not have a direct object.

> ——————S—————— ——V——
> The Red Sox persevered.
> ——S—— ——V——
> Their fans watched helplessly.

In the preceding sentences, the action of the verb *persevered* has no object (it makes no sense to ask *persevered what?* or *persevered whom?*), and the action of the verb *watched* is directed toward an object that is implied but not expressed.

Some verbs that express action can be only transitive or intransitive, but most such verbs can be used both ways, with or without a direct object.

```
      ┌──────────S──────────┐ ┌─V─┐ ┌──DO──┐
      The senator from Wyoming opened the hearings.

      ┌──S──┐ ┌─V─┐
      The door opened silently.
```

EXERCISE 6.10

Identify and underline the predicate in each of the following sentences. Then identify each verb as linking, transitive, or intransitive. Finally, identify all subject and object complements and all direct and indirect objects.

Example

```
   ┌──V──┐ ┌─DO─┐ ┌──OC──┐
We considered city life unbearable.
```

1. California is dry in the summer.
2. The U.S. Constitution made us a nation.
3. The real victims become the taxpayers.
4. Hollywood shall rise again.
5. Advertisers promise uncritical consumers the world.

▌ 3. Recognizing and using phrases

A **phrase** is a group of words that lacks either a subject or a predicate or both. Phrases function in useful ways to add information to a sentence or shape it effectively. Look at the following sentence:

The new law will restrict smoking *in most public places.*

The basic subject and predicate of this sentence is simply *the new law will restrict smoking;* additional information is provided by the prepositional phrase *in most public places.* The phrase functions in the sentence as an adverb, telling *where* smoking will be restricted. This section will discuss the various kinds of phrases: noun, verb, prepositional, verbal, appositive, and absolute.

Noun phrases

Made up of a noun and all its modifiers, a **noun phrase** can function in a sentence as a subject, object, or complement.

```
      ┌──────────SUBJECT──────────┐
*Delicious, gooey peanut butter* is surprisingly healthful.
```

┌─OBJECT─┐
Dieters prefer *green salad.*

┌─COMPLEMENT─┐
A tuna sandwich is *a popular lunch.*

Verb phrases

A main verb and its auxiliary verbs make up a **verb phrase,** which functions in a sentence in only one way: as a predicate.

Frank *had been depressed* for some time.

His problem *might have been caused* by tension between his parents.

Prepositional phrases

A **prepositional phrase** includes a preposition, a noun or pronoun called the **object of the preposition,** and any modifiers of the object. Prepositional phrases function as either adjectives or adverbs.

ADJECTIVE   Our house *in Maine* was a cabin.

ADVERB   *From Cadillac Mountain* you can clearly see the northern lights.

EXERCISE 6.11

Following are some sentences written by the sports columnist Red Smith. Identify and underline all the prepositional phrases. Then choose two of the sentences, and write sentences that imitate their structures.

Example
He glanced <u>about the room with a cocky, crooked grin</u>.
The cat stalked around the yard in her quiet, arrogant way.

1. In those days the Yankees always won the pennant.
2. Fear wasn't in his vocabulary and pain had no meaning.
3. Coaching in Columbus is not quite like coaching in New Haven.
4. He stepped out of the dugout and faced the multitude, two fists and one cap uplifted.
5. The old champ looked fit, square of shoulder and springy of tread, his skin clear, his eyes bright behind the glittering glasses.

EXERCISE 6.12

Combine each of the following pairs of sentences into one sentence by making the second sentence into one or more prepositional phrases.

157

Example

The Greeks won a tremendous victory. They were fighting the Persians.
The Greeks won a tremendous victory *over the Persians*.

1. Socrates was condemned. His fellow citizens made up the jury that condemned him.
2. Socrates faced death. He had no fear.
3. The playwright Aristophanes wrote a comedy. Its subject was Socrates.
4. Everyone thought Socrates was crazy. Only a few followers disagreed.
5. Today Socrates is honored. He founded Western philosophy.

Verbal phrases

Verbals are verb forms that do not function as verbs in sentences. Instead, they function as nouns, adjectives, and adverbs. There are three kinds of verbals: participles, gerunds, and infinitives.

The **present participle** is the *-ing* form of a verb: *dreaming, being, seeing*. The **past participle** of most verbs ends in *-ed: dreamed, watched*. But some verbs have an irregular past participle: *been, seen, hidden, gone*. (See 8b for a list of irregular past participles.) Participles function as adjectives in sentences.

His kiss awakened the *dreaming* princess.

The cryptographers deciphered the *hidden* meaning in the message.

The **gerund** has the same form as the present participle but functions in sentences as a noun.

SUBJECT	*Writing* takes practice.
OBJECT	More than anything, Woody Hayes loved *winning*.

The **infinitive** is the *to* form of a verb: *to dream, to be, to see*. An infinitive can function in a sentence as a noun, adjective, or adverb.

NOUN	She wanted *to write*.
ADJECTIVE	They had no more time *to waste*.
ADVERB	The corporation was ready *to expand*.

A verbal can never stand alone as the verb of a sentence because it is a **nonfinite,** or "unfinished," **verb.** Take the present participle *barking*, for instance. *The terrier barking* is not a sentence; to make it a sentence you need to add one or more auxiliary verbs: *The terrier is barking* or

158

The terrier had been barking. The verb phrases *is barking* and *had been barking* are **finite verbs,** which do not need any other auxiliary to function as verbs in a sentence.

Verbal phrases are made up of a verbal and any modifiers, objects, or complements. Let us turn now to examine the forms and functions of the various kinds of verbal phrases.

Participial phrases

Participial phrases consist of a present participle or past participle with any modifiers, objects, or complements. Participial phrases always function as adjectives in sentences.

Thrilled with her performance, Mary Lou awaited the scores.

The old woman *standing self-righteously in the corner* is Mrs. Turpin.

Notice that many participial phrases may appear in different places in a sentence, as long as it is clear which word they modify (see Chapter 15). Decisions about where to place participial phrases must usually be made within the larger context of a piece of writing; the choice often depends on the rhythm or emphasis the writer wants to achieve.

Fearing that I would be left alone, I quickly followed the group.

I followed the group, *fearing that I would be left alone.*

Gerund phrases

Gerund phrases consist of a gerund with any modifiers, objects, or complements: *hoping for a victory, critical thinking.* In sentences, gerund phrases function as nouns—as a subject, a subject complement, a direct object, an indirect object, or an object of a preposition.

Opening my eyes to the problem [S] was not easy.

His downfall was *relying too much on his computer.* [SC]

They suddenly heard *a loud wailing from the sandbox.* [DO]

The critics gave *Pavarotti's singing* [IO] their enthusiastic approval.

In addition to *being confused,* [OBJ OF PREP] she was alone.

Infinitive phrases

Infinitive phrases consist of an infinitive with any modifiers, objects, or complements: *to be happy, to see a show tonight.* They can function as nouns, adjectives, or adverbs.

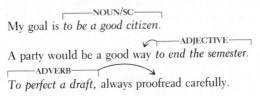

My goal is *to be a good citizen.*

A party would be a good way *to end the semester.*

To perfect a draft, always proofread carefully.

Notice that infinitive phrases used as adverbs, like the last example above, may appear in different places in a sentence as long as it is clear which word they modify (see Chapter 15). For example, *To perfect a draft* could be moved to the end of its sentence. As with participial phrases, the placement should depend on the effect it creates within the larger context of the piece of writing.

EXERCISE 6.13

Identify each participial phrase, gerund phrase, and infinitive phrase in the following sentences, and specify which part of speech it functions as in the sentence.

Example

┌────────PARTICIPIAL-ADJ────────┐
Pacing the hall with impatience, I wished my friends would arrive.

1. Buying his first Corvette was the happiest moment in Ron's life.
2. After four years of careful saving, he got his car.
3. The solution was to warn Georgina: unless she worked to improve her behavior, she could not continue to attend our school.
4. Raised in Idaho, I spent plenty of time exploring nature.
5. Sitting by the window and listening to the wind blowing through the trees, I feel happy and lucky to be alive.

Absolute phrases

An **absolute phrase** consists of a noun or pronoun and a participle, together with any objects or modifiers. It modifies an entire sentence rather than a particular word. Absolutes may appear almost anywhere in a sentence and are always set off from the rest of the sentence with punctuation, usually commas. (See Chapter 27.)

I jumped into the car and took off, *tires screeching in protest.*

My fears laid to rest, I climbed into the plane for my first solo flight.

Appositive phrases

A noun phrase that renames the noun or pronoun that immediately precedes it is called an **appositive phrase.**

Maya Angelou, *the celebrated writer,* will appear on campus tonight.

That's my sister, *the skinny kid in tights.*

EXERCISE 6.14

Read the following sentences, and identify and label all of the prepositional, verbal, absolute, and appositive phrases. Notice that one kind of phrase may appear within another kind.

Example

┌────ABSOLUTE────┐
His voice breaking, Ed thanked us for the award.

1. Approaching the rope, I suddenly fell into the icy pond.
2. To listen to Bruce Springsteen is sheer delight.
3. The figure outlined against the sky seemed unable to move.
4. Floating on my back, I ignored my practice requirements.
5. Jane stood still, her fingers clutching the fence.
6. Bobby, a sensitive child, was filled with a mixture of awe and excitement.
7. Shocked into silence, they kept their gaze fixed on the odd creature.
8. Basking in the sunlight, I had been lost somewhere in a reminiscence of golden birch trees.
9. Susan, the leader of the group, was reluctant to give up any authority.
10. His favorite form of recreation was taking a nap.

Using phrases to shape and expand sentences

Phrases provide valuable tools for shaping or expanding sentences. Not only do they bring in additional information, but they can help you to emphasize certain parts of a sentence and deemphasize others. In this way they help to distinguish the main idea of the sentence from the extra details. Look, for instance, at the following sentence:

Jupiter crashed through the tomato vines with the remains of a felt hat in his mouth.   —JOHN CHEEVER, "The Country Husband"

161

Cheever might have expressed the ideas in this sentence in many other ways. For instance:

> Jupiter crashed through the tomato vines. He had the remains of a felt hat in his mouth.

> Crashing through the tomato vines, Jupiter held the remains of a felt hat in his mouth.

In the first possibility, turning some of the prepositional phrases into a second sentence separates the statement into two parts and thus weakens or at least changes the impact it has on readers—perhaps because we see the crash and the torn hat at a greater chronological distance from each other. In the second possibility, turning the verb of the original sentence into a participle puts greater emphasis on what was in the dog's mouth than on his crash through the vines and thus describes a slightly different scene.

As you write sentences, you should be alert to how you can use phrases to present your ideas and bits of information in particular ways. This consideration is especially important when you are revising. As you read over a draft, consider each sentence individually to see if phrases could help you add necessary detail, make your point clearer, or emphasize one idea instead of another.

Following are some examples of how some student writers used various kinds of phrases to shape and expand particular sentences.

NOUN PHRASE

That car will never win the race.

That battered, valveless, bent-up bone-shaker will never win the race.

PARTICIPIAL PHRASE

The subway was anything but inviting. It was covered with graffiti and packed with commuters.

Covered with graffiti and packed with commuters, the subway was anything but inviting.

ABSOLUTE PHRASE

The dictator's long period of absolute rule was over, and he stepped into his limousine.

His long period of absolute rule over, the dictator stepped into his limousine.

Positioning phrases

As noted earlier, many phrases can be placed either at the beginning, in the middle, or at the end of a sentence, as the following examples illustrate:

Calling on every ounce of energy, Jo sprinted toward the finish line.

Jo, *calling on every ounce of energy,* sprinted toward the finish line.

Jo sprinted toward the finish line, *calling on every ounce of energy.*

The phrase in these examples is a participial phrase that modifies *Jo.* While changing the placement of the phrase does not alter the basic meaning of the sentence, it does affect rhythm and emphasis, most notably in the third example by changing the important concluding words of the sentence.

Prepositional, infinitive, and absolute phrases can also occupy more than one sentence position. There are no absolute guidelines for placement, but always (1) check to see that the phrase clearly modifies any word it should modify (see Chapter 15), and (2) read the sentence in the context of the surrounding sentences to see which placement seems most effective (see 20b).

EXERCISE 6.15

Use prepositional, participial, infinitive, gerund, absolute, or appositive phrases to expand each of the following sentences.

Example

The apples dropped from the limb.

In response to my vigorous shake, the apples dropped from the limb.

1. Nancy jogged down Willow Street.
2. She looked healthy when he saw her the second time.
3. Richard had lost almost all of his hair.
4. The Sunday afternoon dragged.
5. The smell of burning leaves filled the air.
6. The candidates shook hands with the voters.
7. We were uncertain what to do.
8. Ben often thought regretfully about the past.
9. The sunshine made the day crystal clear.
10. They lived in a trailer.

EXERCISE 6.16

Use a participial, infinitive, gerund, absolute, or appositive phrase to combine each of the following pairs of sentences into one sentence.

Example

He complained constantly. This habit irritated his co-workers.

His constant complaining irritated his co-workers.

1. David Klein performed a monologue at the club. He is an actor and comedian.
2. We waited to go through customs. Our passports were clutched in our hands.
3. She bought a new dress. This purchase lifted her spirits.
4. Michael had his ear pierced. He did this because it annoyed his parents.
5. The protesters were carrying their banners. They headed down the street.

▌ 4. Recognizing and using clauses

A **clause** is a group of words containing a subject and a predicate. There are two kinds of clauses: independent and dependent. **Independent clauses** (also known as **main clauses**) can stand alone as complete sentences.

The window is open.

The batter swung at the ball.

Independent clauses may be joined with a coordinating conjunction and a comma. For more on joining independent clauses, see 6b7.

The window is open, *so* we'd better be quiet.

The batter swung at the ball, *and* the umpire called her out.

Like independent clauses, **dependent clauses** (also known as **subordinate clauses**) contain a subject and a predicate. They cannot stand alone as complete sentences, however, for they begin with a subordinating word—a subordinating conjunction (see 6b7) or a relative pronoun (see 6b3). The subordinating word connects the dependent clause to an independent clause. Each of the following sentences, for instance, consists of one brief independent clause.

The window is open.

The room feels cool.

You might choose to combine these two independent clauses with a comma and coordinating conjunction: *The window is open, and the room feels cool.* But you could also combine the two clauses by turning one into a dependent clause.

164

Because the window is open, the room feels cool.

In this combination the subordinating conjunction *because* transforms the independent clause *the window is open* into a dependent clause. In doing so, it indicates a causal relationship between the two clauses.

Dependent clauses function in sentences as nouns, adjectives, or adverbs.

Noun clauses

Noun clauses can function as subjects, direct objects, subject complements, or objects of prepositions. Thus they are always contained within another clause rather than simply attached to it, as adjective and adverb clauses are. They usually begin with a relative pronoun (*that, which, what, who, whom, whose, whatever, whoever, whomever, whichever*) or with *when, where, whether, why,* or *how.*

```
              ┌────────────S────────────┐
That he had a college degree was important to her.
                  ┌──────────DO──────────┐
She asked where he went to college.
                      ┌──────────SC──────────┐
The real question was why she wanted to know.
                          ┌──────────OBJ OF PREP──────────┐
She was looking for whatever information she could get.
```

Notice that in each of these sentences the noun clause is an integral part of the independent clause that makes up the sentence; for example, in the second sentence the independent clause is not just *She asked* but *She asked where he went to college.*

Adjective clauses

Adjective clauses modify nouns and pronouns in another clause. Usually, they follow immediately after the words they modify. Most adjective clauses begin with the relative pronouns *who, whom, whose, that,* or *which.* Some begin with *when, where,* or *why.*

Zoe's decision, *which astonished everyone,* was to have a baby.

Aren't babies devious little creatures *who cry a great deal?*

All parents experience moments *when they feel that way.*

Sometimes the relative pronoun introducing an adjective clause may be deleted, as in the following example:

That is one book [that] I intend to read.

Adverb clauses

Adverb clauses modify verbs, adjectives, or other adverbs. They always begin with a subordinating conjunction (see 6b7). Like adverbs, they usually tell why, when, where, how, under what conditions, or to what extent.

We hiked *where there were few other hikers.*

My backpack felt heavier *than it ever had.*

I climbed as swiftly *as I could under the weight of my backpack.*

Like adverbs, adverb clauses can usually be placed in different positions in a sentence without affecting the meaning.

If you look up from the valley, you will see Half Dome.

You will see Half Dome *if you look up from the valley.*

EXERCISE 6.17

Identify the independent and dependent clauses and any subordinating conjunctions and relative pronouns in each of the following sentences.

Example

┌────────DEPENDENT CLAUSE────────┐
If I were going on a really long hike, I would carry a lightweight stove.
[*If* is a subordinating conjunction.]

1. The driver who won the race was driving a tan Pontiac.
2. As a potential customer entered the store, Tony nervously attempted to retreat to the safety of the back room.
3. The names they called my grandmother still haunt me.
4. When she was deemed old enough to understand, she was told the truth, and she finally knew why her father had left home.
5. Though most of my grandfather's farm was wooded, there were also great expanses of green lawns and quiet, trickling streams.
6. Mary and John decided to bake a chocolate cream pie, which was Timothy's favorite.

7. When they asked him to accompany them, he became very excited, but he also felt some trepidation.
8. It was easier than she had expected.
9. After she finished the painting, Linda cleaned the brushes.
10. I could see that he was very tired, but I had to ask him a few questions.

Using clauses to shape and expand sentences

Like phrases, clauses are an important means of shaping sentences in particular ways or expanding sentences into more varied or interesting ones. For example, look at the following sentences, each of which consists of one independent clause expressing one idea:

Sarah's parents disliked her boyfriend. She was determined to marry him.

Now look at how clauses can be used to combine these ideas in one sentence.

1. Although her parents disliked her boyfriend, Sarah was determined to marry him.
2. Sarah's parents disliked her boyfriend, whom she was determined to marry.
3. Sarah's parents disliked her boyfriend, but she was determined to marry him.

In sentence 1, putting the information about the parents' dislike of the boyfriend into a dependent adverb clause gives less emphasis to that idea and more emphasis to the idea expressed in the subject and predicate—Sarah's determination to marry him. In sentence 2, on the other hand, the idea of Sarah's determination is deemphasized by being placed in a dependent adjective clause. Finally, in sentence 3, the two ideas are given equal emphasis by being expressed in two independent clauses connected by the coordinating conjunction *but*.

As you write sentences, and especially when you are revising a draft, pay attention to how you can use clauses to add details or emphasis to your ideas and information. Following are some examples of how student writers used various kinds of clauses to shape and expand particular sentences.

NOUN CLAUSE

Charles later learned the truth.

Charles later learned *what Vinnie had known for years.*

ADJECTIVE CLAUSE

Everything was swept away.

Everything *that he valued most in life* was swept away.

My childhood seemed entirely happy. I grew up on a large farm.

My childhood, *which was spent on a large farm*, seemed entirely happy.

ADVERB CLAUSE

Many young men opposed the war, and they burned their draft cards.

Because they opposed the war, many young men burned their draft cards.

For more information about using clauses to shape and expand sentences, see Chapters 17–20.

Positioning clauses

Like many phrases, most *adverb* clauses can be placed at the beginning, in the middle, or at the end of a sentence.

If nothing goes wrong, the furniture will be delivered tomorrow.

The furniture, *if nothing goes wrong*, will be delivered tomorrow.

The furniture will be delivered tomorrow *if nothing goes wrong*.

Changing the position of the adverb clause *if nothing goes wrong* does not affect the basic meaning of the sentence, but it affects the rhythm and the emphasis by highlighting or downplaying the possibility that something could go wrong. For more information about positioning clauses within sentences, see 15a and 20b.

EXERCISE 6.18

Expand each sentence below by adding at least one dependent clause.

Example

The books tumbled from the shelves.

As the earth continued to shake, the books tumbled from the shelves.

1. The Angolan army was exhausted.
2. George was worried about his real estate investments.
3. The new computer made a strange noise.
4. Rob always borrowed money from friends.
5. The streets were ringing with loud music.
6. We stood outside for an hour.
7. The history seminar begins tomorrow.
8. Erin won the translation contest.

9. A river flowed through the forest.
10. A man was killed in that mill in 1867.

EXERCISE 6.19

Following are some sentences from the letters of E. B. White. Read each one carefully, focusing on the phrases and clauses. Underline any dependent clauses once and any phrases twice. Finally, choose two sentences, and use them as a model to write sentences of your own, imitating White's structure phrase for phrase and clause for clause.

> *Example*
> I was born in 1899 and expect to live forever, searching for beauty and raising hell in general.
> Sarah was hired in May and plans to work all summer, living at home and saving money for law school.

1. You can see at a glance that Professor Strunk omitted needless words.
2. Either Macmillan takes Strunk and me in our bare skins, or I want out.
3. I regard the word *hopefully* as beyond recall.
4. Life in a zoo is just the ticket for some animals and birds.
5. I recall the pleasures and satisfactions of encountering a Perelman piece in a magazine.
6. The way to read Thoreau is to enjoy him—his enthusiasms, his acute perception.
7. When I start a book, I never know what my characters are going to do, and I accept no responsibility for their eccentric behavior.
8. No sensible writer sets out deliberately to develop a style, but all writers do have distinguishing qualities, and they become very evident when you read the words.
9. When I wrote "Death of a Pig," I was simply rendering an account of what actually happened on my place—to my pig, who died, and to me, who tended him in his last hours.
10. A good many of Charlotte's descendants still live in the barn, and when the warm days of spring arrive there will be lots of tiny spiders emerging into the world.

▮ 6d. Classifying sentences

Like words, sentences can be classified in several different ways: grammatically, functionally, or rhetorically. Grammatical classification groups sentences according to how many and what types of clauses they contain. Functional classification groups them according to whether they make a statement, ask a question, issue a command, or express an exclamation. Rhetorical classification groups them according to where in the sentence the main idea is located. Understanding these methods of classification can help you analyze and assess your sentences as you write and revise.

▌ 1. Classifying sentences grammatically

Grammatically, sentences fall into one of the following types: *simple sentences, compound sentences, complex sentences,* and *compound-complex sentences.* You have already seen most of these types in the section on clauses.

Simple sentences

A **simple sentence** consists of one independent clause and no dependent clause. The subject or the predicate of the independent clause, or both, may be compound.

The trailer is surrounded by a wooden deck.

Both my roommate and I had left our keys in the room.

At the country club, the head pro and his assistant give lessons, run the golf shop, and try to keep the members content.

Compound sentences

A **compound sentence** consists of two or more independent clauses and no dependent clause. The clauses may be joined by a comma and a coordinating conjunction, by a comma and a correlative conjunction, or by a semicolon. (See Chapters 13, 18, 27, and 28).

Occasionally, a car goes up the dirt trail, and dust flies everywhere.

Not only are the adults unable to relax there, but their conflicting interests create even more tension among them.

George is obsessed with soccer; he eats, breathes, and lives the game.

Complex sentences

A **complex sentence** consists of one independent clause with at least one dependent clause.

┌─────DEPENDENT CLAUSE─────┐
Many people believe that anyone can earn a living.

┌─────DEPENDENT CLAUSE─────┐
Those who do not like to get dirty should not go camping.

┌─────DEPENDENT CLAUSE─────┐
As I awaited my interview, I sat with other nervous candidates.

170

Notice that when a dependent clause comes before the independent clause, as in the last example above, it is usually set off with a comma (see 27a).

Compound-complex sentences

A **compound-complex sentence** consists of two or more independent clauses and at least one dependent clause.

```
 ┌───IND CL───┐   ┌─────IND CL─────┐ ┌───────DEP CL───────┐
```
We liked Joe, for he was a kind man who was nice to everyone.

Sister Lucy tried her best to help Martin, but he was an undisciplined boy who drove many teachers to despair.

▌ 2. Classifying sentences functionally

In terms of function, sentences can be classified as **declarative** (making a statement), **interrogative** (asking a question), **imperative** (giving a command), or **exclamatory** (expressing strong feeling).

DECLARATIVE	Julian plays oboe for the Cleveland Orchestra.
INTERROGATIVE	Has he also performed with other orchestras?
IMPERATIVE	Get me a ticket for his next performance.
EXCLAMATORY	What a talented musician he is!

▌ 3. Classifying sentences rhetorically

In addition to permitting functional and grammatical classifications, some sentences can be classified rhetorically as either cumulative or periodic sentences. Such a classification is important because the two patterns create very different rhythms and emphases. Learning to identify them takes you well on the way toward incorporating such sentences in your own writing.

Cumulative sentences begin with the subject and predicate containing the main thought and then build on this foundation with a series of phrases or clauses. When they are constructed skillfully, cumulative sentences create a strong rhythm and make for easy, often exciting, reading. Look at the following examples (the second example includes two cumulative sentences):

The old man sat, waiting, watching, never tiring of his self-appointed task of keeping track of all who passed, his hat pulled tightly over his forehead, hiding eyes that missed nothing.

I could still feel the way I'd moved with the horse, the ripple of muscle through both the striving bodies, uniting as one. I could still feel the irons round my feet, the calves of my legs gripping, the balance, the nearness to my head of the stretching brown neck, the mane blowing in my mouth, my hands on the reins.   –DICK FRANCIS

In contrast, **periodic sentences** save the subject and verb of the independent clause until the end, building toward them and making the reader wait for the full meaning or significance to emerge.

Pulling my tie off and flinging it haphazardly onto the sofa, stretching and sighing with the ease of homecoming, listening to the familiar silences of the place, I felt—as usual—the welcoming peace unlock the gritting tensions of my outside world.

Though we long for the easy answer, the simple solution, the quick rationalization, only the harsh truth shall set us free.

Although cumulative sentences are more common in most modern prose than are periodic sentences, the ability to construct both will give you stylistic options that will strengthen your writing. For more information on such sentence types, see 20c.

EXERCISE 6.20

Classify each of the following sentences as simple, compound, complex, or compound-complex. In addition, note any sentences that could be classified as cumulative or periodic or as imperative, interrogative, or exclamatory.

1. Should he admit his mistake, or should he keep quiet and hope to avoid discovery?
2. The screen door creaked and banged when she ran into the house.
3. Solve your problems yourself.
4. People go on safari to watch wild animals in their natural habitat.
5. What a risk they took, but what a prize they won!
6. Although I used to believe that love was all that I needed to make my marriage work, I now realize that my marriage failed not from a lack of love but rather from a lack of communication, honesty, and trust.
7. Keeping in mind the terrain, the weather, and the length of the hike, decide what you need to take.
8. Dreams are necessary, but they can be frustrating unless you have the means to attain them.

9. Anticipation grew as the band played, and the crowd went wild when the team ran onto the field.

10. Wandering in the stockroom, searching futilely for pairs of shoes that I would swear were not there and finally meekly asking my coworkers to help me find them, I wasted countless hours during my first week on the job.

EXERCISE 6.21

The following paragraph is adapted from "The Hard Kind of Patriotism," a speech once given by Adlai Stevenson. The sentences in the paragraph have been simplified greatly. Try revising the paragraph by using phrases and clauses to combine some of the sentences. You might find it necessary to add or drop words. There is no one "correct" way to revise the paragraph; the object of the exercise is simply to practice using the various structures presented in this chapter.

America is much more than an economic fact. It is much more than a geographical fact. It is a political fact. It is a moral fact. It is the first community in which men set out in principle to institutionalize freedom. It is the first community in which men set out to institutionalize responsible government. It is the first community in which they set out to institutionalize human equality. And we love it for this audacity! Jefferson and Lincoln saw in this vision "the last, best hope of man." How easy it is, contemplating this vision, to see in it "the last, best hope of man." To be a nation founded on an ideal in one sense makes our love of country a vital force. It is a more vital force than any instinctive pieties of blood. It is a more vital force than any instinctive pieties of soil.

READING WITH AN EYE FOR SENTENCES

The following sentences come from the openings of well-known works. Read each sentence carefully, and be prepared to identify the independent clauses and dependent clauses. Then choose one of the sentences, and write a sentence that imitates its structure clause for clause and phrase for phrase.

Example

She is an open and trusting child, unprepared for and unaccustomed to the ambushes of family life, and perhaps it is just as well that I can offer her little of that life.   —JOAN DIDION, "On Going Home"

Those were long and desperate years, filled with and burdened by the pain of multiple loss, yet now it is clear to me that they gave me strength for the future.

1. Most people who bother with the matter at all would admit that the English language is in a bad way, but it is generally assumed that we cannot by conscious action do anything about it.
—GEORGE ORWELL, "Politics and the English Language"
2. We observe today not a victory of party but a celebration of freedom, symbolizing an end as well as a beginning, signifying renewal as well as change.
—JOHN F. KENNEDY, Inaugural Address
3. Once in a long while, four times so far for me, my mother brings out the metal tube that holds her medical diploma.
—MAXINE HONG KINGSTON, "Photographs of My Parents"
4. Moths that fly by day are not properly to be called moths; they do not excite that pleasant sense of dark autumn nights and ivy blossom which the commonest yellow underwing asleep in the shadow of the curtain never fails to rouse in us.   —VIRGINIA WOOLF, "The Death of the Moth"
5. When Ulysses S. Grant and Robert E. Lee met in the parlor of a modest house at Appomattox Court House, Virginia, on April 9, 1865, to work out the terms for the surrender of Lee's Army of Northern Virginia, a great chapter in American life came to a close, and a great new chapter began.
—BRUCE CATTON, "Grant and Lee: A Study in Contrasts"

FOR EXAMINING YOUR OWN SENTENCES

Look at one or two paragraphs of an essay you have written recently, and classify the sentences grammatically (6d1) and rhetorically (6d3). Does your classification reveal that you vary the types of sentences you use, or do you tend to write primarily one type of sentence? If you find that you depend primarily on one type, revise the paragraphs to include other types—for example, if you write mainly simple sentences, try combining some of them to make compound or complex sentences. If you keep a writing log, you might record this work there.

7. Understanding Pronoun Case

The grammatical term *case* may be unfamiliar to you (since it comes, like many such terms, from Latin), but the concept it represents is one you will recognize immediately. Take a look, for example, at the first-person pronouns in the following excerpt from Judy Syfers's well-known essay about the advantages of having a wife.

> *I* want a wife who will care for *me* when *I* am sick and sympathize with *my* pain. . . . *I* want a wife who will keep *my* clothes clean, ironed, mended, replaced when need be, and who will see to it that *my* personal things are kept in their proper place. . . .
> —JUDY SYFERS, "I Want a Wife"

Most of us know intuitively when to use *I*, when to use *me*, and when to use *my*. Our choices reflect differences in **case,** the form a noun or pronoun takes to indicate its function in a sentence. The italicized words in the excerpt show the singular first-person pronoun in three different cases: the subjective case (*I*), the objective case (*me*), and the possessive case (*my*). As the example sentences demonstrate, pronouns functioning as subjects are in the subjective case; those functioning as objects are in the objective case; and those functioning as possessives are in the possessive case.

Nouns and indefinite pronouns have the same form whether they function as subjects or objects, but they have a separate possessive case. It is usually formed by adding 's to a singular noun or an indefinite pronoun (*the cat's meow, nobody's fool*) or an apostrophe to a plural noun (*the players' strike*). See Chapter 30 for additional discussion and examples of the possessive case of nouns and indefinite pronouns.

175

This chapter focuses on the following pronoun case forms:

SUBJECTIVE

I/we	you	he/she/it	they	who/whoever

OBJECTIVE

me/us	you	him/her/it	them	whom/whomever

POSSESSIVE

my	your	his/her/its	their	whose
mine	yours	his/hers/its	theirs	

▌ 7a. Using the subjective case

A pronoun should be in the **subjective case** when it is a subject of a clause, a subject complement, or an appositive renaming a subject or subject complement. (See 6b and 6c.)

SUBJECT OF AN INDEPENDENT CLAUSE

They could either fight or face certain death with the lions.

We felt that Betty was enthusiastic and wanted to learn the material.

My brother and *I* adored our grandparents.

Who wrote "Araby"?

SUBJECT OF A DEPENDENT CLAUSE

Before *they* could get to the front, the war ended.

Jason did not seem like the type of person *who* would plagiarize.

Our group appealed to *whoever* was willing to listen.

SUBJECT COMPLEMENT

Even though pronouns used as subject complements should, grammatically, be in the subjective case, Americans often use the objective case, especially in conversation: "Who's there? It's *me*." To many speakers of English, "it's me" sounds not only acceptable but preferable to "it's I." Nevertheless, you should use the subjective case for all formal writing.

The first person to see Monty after the awards was *she*.

The players invited for a second audition were Cheryl and *I*.

It is *he* who brings life and spirit to the class.

If you find the subjective case for a subject complement stilted or awkward, try rewriting the sentence using the pronoun as the subject.

She was the first person to see Monty after the awards.

APPOSITIVE RENAMING A SUBJECT
Three students—Peter, Richard, and *she*—worked on the report.

APPOSITIVE RENAMING A SUBJECT COMPLEMENT
The finalists were two dark horses, Michael and *I*.

▌ 7b. Using the objective case

A pronoun should be in the **objective case** when it functions as a direct or indirect object (of a verb or verbal), a subject of an infinitive, an object of a preposition, or an appositive renaming an object. (See 6b3 and 6c3.)

OBJECT OF A VERB

The professor surprised *them* with a quiz. [direct object of *surprised*]

Martin Luther King, Jr., gave *us* hope. [indirect object of *gave*]

Reagan was a president *whom* conservative Americans adored. [direct object of *adored*]

OBJECT OF A VERBAL

The Parisians were wonderful about helping *me*, and I ended the year speaking fluently. [object of gerund]

Wishing *her* luck, the coach stepped back to watch the performance. [object of participle]

Leonard offered to show *him* around town. [object of infinitive]

SUBJECT OF AN INFINITIVE

The objective case is also used in sentences like the following, where the pronoun is preceded by a verb and followed by an infinitive. Even though the pronoun in such constructions is called the subject of the infinitive, it is in the objective case.

Writing helps *me* to know myself better.

The student campaigners convinced his wife and *him* to vote in favor of the school bond.

The trip led *us* to appreciate how much California owes to Mexico.

OBJECT OF A PREPOSITION

As Paul entered the room, a strange feeling came over *me*.

Alice planned a surprise party for *them*.

APPOSITIVE RENAMING AN OBJECT

We selected two managers, Joan and *her*, to attend the seminar.

■ 7c. Using the possessive case

A pronoun should be in the **possessive case** when it shows possession or ownership. Notice that there are two forms of possessive pronouns: adjective forms, which are used before nouns or gerunds (*my, your, his, her, its, our, their, whose*), and noun forms, which take the place of a noun (*mine, yours, his, hers, its, ours, theirs, whose*). (See Chapter 30.)

ADJECTIVE FORMS

Many of Hitchcock's movies put viewers on the edge of *their* seats.

Whose life is it, anyway?

The sound of *his* hammering echoed through the corridor.

When a pronoun precedes a verb form ending in *-ing*, as in the preceding example, you need to decide whether the verb form is a gerund or a present participle to determine whether to use the possessive or the objective case of the pronoun. Gerunds always function as nouns, and if the verb form is a gerund, the pronoun modifies it and must be in the possessive case. Present participles function as adjectives, and if the verb form is a participle, it modifies the pronoun, which should be in the objective case.

Usually you can tell from the context of the sentence whether an *-ing* verb form is a gerund or a participle. In the example sentence, for instance, you can tell that *hammering* is a gerund and the pronoun should be *his* because it was the sound of *hammering*, not the sound of *him*, that was echoing through the corridor. In some sentences like this, however, you could use either an objective or a possessive pronoun, depending on the exact meaning you intend. Look at these two sentences:

I remember *his* singing.

I remember *him* singing.

In the first example, the memory is of *singing*, which is a gerund, modified by the possessive pronoun *his*. In the second example, the memory is of *him*, which functions as a direct object of *remember* and thus is in the objective case; *singing* is a present participle modifying *him*.

NOUN FORMS

The responsibility is *hers*.

"It's *mine!*" declared the child, clutching the golf club.

Whose did she borrow?

EXERCISE 7.1

The following passage comes from "University Days," James Thurber's classic essay about his years as a student at Ohio State University. Most of its pronouns have been removed. Put a correct pronoun in each blank, labeling each one as subjective, objective, or possessive case.

Another course that <u>I</u> didn't like, but somehow managed to pass, was economics. _____ went to that class straight from the botany class, which didn't help _____ to understand either subject. _____ used to get them mixed up. But not as mixed up as another student in _____ economics class who came there direct from a physics laboratory. _____ was a tackle on the football team, named Bolenciecwcz. At that time Ohio State University had one of the best football teams in the country, and Bolenciecwcz was one of _____ outstanding stars. In order to be eligible to play it was necessary for _____ to keep up in _____ studies, a very difficult matter, for while _____ was not dumber than an ox _____ was not any smarter. Most of _____ professors were lenient and helped _____ along. None gave _____ more hints in answering questions or asked _____ simpler ones than the economics professor, a thin, timid man named Bassum. One day when _____ were on the subject of transportation and distribution, it came Bolenciecwcz's turn to answer a question. "Name one means of transportation," the professor said to _____. No light came into the big tackle's eyes. "Just any means of transportation" said the professor. Bolenciecwcz sat staring at _____. "That is," pursued the professor, "any medium, agency, or method of going from one place to another." Bolenciecwcz had the look of a man _____ is being led into a trap. "You may choose among steam, horse-drawn, or electrically propelled vehicles," said the instructor. "I might suggest the one which _____ commonly take in making long journeys across land." There was a profound silence in which everybody stirred uneasily, including Bolenciecwcz and Mr. Bassum. Mr. Bassum abruptly broke this silence in an amazing manner. "Choo-choo-choo," _____ said, in a low voice, and turned instantly scarlet.

_____ glanced appealingly around the room. All of _____, of course, shared Mr. Bassum's desire that Bolenciecwcz should stay abreast of the class in economics, for the Illinois game, one of the hardest and most important of the season, was only a week off. "Toot, toot, too-tooooooot!" some student with a deep voice moaned, and _____ all looked encouragingly at Bolenciecwcz. Somebody else gave a fine imitation of a locomotive letting off steam. Mr. Bassum himself rounded off the little show. "Ding, dong, ding, dong," _____ said, hopefully. Bolenciecwcz was staring at the floor now, trying to think, _____ great brow furrowed, _____ huge hands rubbing together, _____ face red.   —JAMES THURBER, "University Days"

EXERCISE 7.2

Insert a correct possessive pronoun in the blank in each sentence.

Example
<u>My</u> eyes ached after studying for ten hours.

1. Your parents must be pleased about _____ going back to college.
2. Kevin's dinner arrived after a thirty-minute wait, but she waited an hour for _____.
3. We all agreed to pool _____ knowledge in studying for the European history examination.
4. Even many supporters of Lincoln opposed _____ freeing the slaves.
5. _____ responsibility should it be to teach moral values?

▌ 7d. Using *who, whoever, whom,* and *whomever*

One of the most common problems with pronoun case is deciding whether to use *who* or *whom.* In speech and even in some informal writing, *whom* has become a rarely used word. Even when traditional grammar requires *whom,* many Americans use *who* instead. Nevertheless, in formal written English, which includes most of the writing you do at college, the case of the pronoun should properly reflect its grammatical function. *Who* and *whoever* are the subjective case forms and should be used when the pronoun is a subject or subject complement. *Whom* and *whomever* are the objective case forms and should be used when the pronoun is a direct or indirect object or the object of a preposition.

Most writers find that two particular situations can lead to confusion with *who* and *whom:* when they begin a question and when they introduce a dependent clause. In a dependent clause, you may also have to choose between *whoever* and *whomever.* (See 6c4.)

| 1. Beginning a question with *who* or *whom*

You can determine whether to use *who* or *whom* at the beginning of a question by answering the question using a personal pronoun. If the answer is in the subjective case, use *who;* if the answer is in the objective case, use *whom.*

> *Who* could best narrate such a story? *She* could best narrate such a story. [*She* is subjective; thus *who* is correct.]
>
> *Whom* did you visit? [I visited *them. Them* is objective; thus *whom* is correct.]
>
> *Whom* are you voting for? [I am voting for *her. Her* is objective; thus *whom* is correct.]

Notice that even if the *who/whom* clause is interrupted by the main subject and verb of the sentence—for example, *did you say* or *does she think*—answering the question using a personal pronoun will still tell you the right case to use.

> *Who* does he think can best narrate such a story? [He thinks *she* can best narrate such a story. *She* is subjective; thus *who* is correct.]

| 2. Beginning a dependent clause with *who, whoever, whom,* or *whomever*

The case of a pronoun in a dependent clause is determined by its function in the clause, no matter how that clause functions in the sentence. If the pronoun acts as a subject in the clause, use *who* or *whoever.* If the pronoun acts as an object, use *whom* or *whomever.* (See 6c4.)

> The new president was not *whom* she had expected. [*Whom* is the object of the verb *had expected* in the clause *whom she had expected.* Though the clause as a whole is the complement of the subject *president,* the pronoun should be in the objective case.]
>
> The waitress's work schedule changed from week to week, depending on *whoever* needed time off. [*Whoever* is the subject of the clause *whoever needed time off.* Though the clause as a whole is the object of the preposition *on,* the pronoun should be in the subjective case.]
>
> Richard feels like a knight *who* is headed for great adventure. [*Who* is the subject of the clause *who is headed for great adventure.*]
>
> *Whomever* the party suspected of disloyalty was executed. [*Whomever* is the object of the verb *suspected* in the clause *Whomever the party sus-*

181

pected of disloyalty. Though the clause as a whole is the subject of the sentence, the pronoun should be in the objective case.]

If you are not sure which case to use, try separating out the dependent clause from the rest of the sentence and looking at it in isolation. Rewrite the clause as a new sentence with a personal pronoun instead of *who(ever)* or *whom(ever)*. If the pronoun is in the subjective case, use *who* or *whoever* in the original clause; if it is in the objective case, use *whom* or *whomever*.

> Anyone can hypnotize a person (*who/whom*) wants to be hypnotized. [Separate out the clause *who/whom wants to be hypnotized.* Substituting a personal pronoun gives you *he wants to be hypnotized. He* is subjective case; therefore: Anyone can hypnotize a person *who* wants to be hypnotized.]

> The minister grimaced at (*whoever/whomever*) made any noise. [Separate out the clause *whoever/whomever made any noise.* Substituting a personal pronoun gives you *they made any noise. They* is subjective case; therefore: The minister grimaced at *whoever* made any noise.]

> The minister smiled at (*whoever/whomever*) she greeted. [Separate out the clause *she greeted whoever/whomever.* Substituting a personal pronoun gives you *she greeted them. Them* is objective case; therefore: The minister smiled at *whomever* she greeted.]

If the dependent clause is interrupted by an expression such as *he thinks* or *she says*, delete the expression when you separate out the clause.

> The minister grimaced at (whoever/whomever) she thought made any noise. [Separate out the clause *whoever/whomever made any noise,* deleting the interrupting expression *she thought.* Substituting a personal pronoun gives you *they made any noise. They* is subjective case; therefore: The minister grimaced at *whoever* she thought made any noise.]

EXERCISE 7.3

Insert *who, whoever, whom,* or *whomever* correctly in the blank in each of the following sentences.

Example

She is someone <u>who</u> will go far.

1. _____ shall I say is calling?
2. _____ the voters choose faces an almost impossible challenge.
3. The manager promised to reward _____ sold the most cars.

4. Professor Quiñones asked _____ we wanted to collaborate with.
5. _____ will the new tax law benefit most?

■ 7e. Using the correct case in compound structures

Most problems with case of personal pronouns occur when the pronoun is part of a compound subject, complement, or object. Each part of a compound structure should be in the same case as it would if used alone: pronouns in compound subjects and subject complements should be in the subjective case; pronouns in compound objects should be in the objective case.

SUBJECTS

Mrs. Wentzel and *I* simply could not exist in the same classroom.

When *Zelda* and *he* were first married, they lived in New York.

SUBJECT COMPLEMENTS

The winners of the competition were *Renata* and *he*.

The next two speakers will be *Philip* and *she*.

OBJECTS OF VERBS

Smith College accepted *Andrea* and *me*. [direct object]

Rutgers University offered *Bob* and *her* a scholarship. [indirect object]

OBJECTS OF PREPOSITIONS

This morning saw yet another conflict between *my sister* and *me*.

My aunt put me in the room once shared by *my uncle* and *her*.

If you are unsure whether to use the subjective or the objective case in a compound structure, make each part of the compound into a separate sentence.

Come to the park with my roommate and (*I/me*). [Separating the compound structure gives you *come to the park with my roommate* and *come to the park with me*; thus: Come to the park with my roommate and *me*.]

■ 7f. Using the correct case in appositives

The case of a pronoun that is part of an appositive is determined by the word that the appositive renames. If the word functions as a subject or subject complement, the pronoun should be in the subjective case; if it functions as an object, the pronoun should be in the objective case.

> Three students—Victor, Sally, and *he*—were named Rhodes scholars. [*Students* is the subject of the sentence, so the pronoun in the appositive *Victor, Sally, and he* should be in the subjective case.]

> The poker game that night produced two big winners, my mother and *me*. [*Winners* is the direct object of the verb *produced,* so the pronoun in the appositive *my mother and me* should be in the objective case].

7g. Using the correct case in elliptical constructions

Elliptical constructions are those in which some words are understood but left out. In comparisons with *than* or *as,* we often leave words unsaid: *I see Elizabeth more often than* [*I see*] *her sister.* When sentences with such constructions end in a pronoun, the pronoun should be in the case it would be in if the construction were complete.

> His brother has always been more athletic than *he* [is].

In some constructions like this, the case of the pronoun depends on the meaning intended.

ELLIPTICAL	Willie likes Lily more than *she.*
COMPLETE	Willie likes Lily more than *she* [likes Lily].
ELLIPTICAL	Willie likes Lily more than *her.*
COMPLETE	Willie likes Lily more than [he likes] *her.*

As these examples demonstrate, use the subjective case if the pronoun is actually the subject of an omitted verb; use the objective case if it is an object of an omitted verb.

7h. Using *we* and *us* correctly before a noun

When the first-person plural pronoun is used with a noun, the case of the pronoun depends on the way the noun functions in the sentence. If the noun functions as a subject, the pronoun should be in the subjective case (*we*); if the noun functions as an object, the pronoun should be in the objective case (*us*).

> *We* fans never give up hope. [*Fans* is the subject.]

> The Orioles depend on *us* fans. [*Fans* is the object of a preposition.]

184

If you are unsure about which case to use, recasting the sentence without the noun will give you the answer. Use whichever pronoun would be correct if the noun were omitted: *We never give up hope. The Orioles depend on us.*

EXERCISE 7.4

Choose the appropriate pronoun from the pair in parentheses in each of the following sentences.

> *Example*
> The fear of (*them*/*their*) taking advantage of him never entered his mind.

1. The relationship between (*they*/*them*) and their brother was often strained.
2. When I was young, I had a friend (*who*/*whom*) I idolized.
3. This love for children probably began because there were three children younger than (*I*/*me*) in my family.
4. The only candidates left in the race were (*he*/*him*) and Dukakis.
5. I am getting more and more interested in (*him*/*his*) accompanying me on the trip.
6. When Carol and (*she*/*her*) first met, they despised each other.
7. The two people closest to me, (*he*/*him*) and my mother, expected me to return home after graduation.
8. Soap operas appeal to (*whoever*/*whomever*) is interested in intrigue, suspense, joy, pain, grief, romance, infidelity, sex, or violence.
9. Later (*we*/*us*) "rejects" were taken to watch the taping of the show.
10. The only mother and father (*who*/*whom*) they know are the people (*who*/*whom*) raised them and took care of them.

EXERCISE 7.5

Edit each of the following sentences to correct errors in pronoun case. (Not all sentences contain errors.)

> *Example*
> Of the group, only her and I finished the race.
> Of the group, only *she* and I finished the race.

1. The readers, her and me, agreed that the story was very suspenseful.
2. Just between you and I, this course is a disaster!
3. The people who Jay worked with were very cold and unsociable.
4. Who would have thought that twenty years later there would be a black presidential candidate.
5. Roderigo becomes involved in the plot without him knowing it.
6. Only him, a few cabinet members, and several military leaders were aware of the steady advance Japan was making toward Pearl Harbor.

7. All of the job candidates were far more experienced than I.
8. As out-of-towners, my buddy and me did not know too many people.
9. I never got to play that role in front of an audience, but I am one of the few performers who really did "break a leg."
10. Constance always lent money to whomever asked her for it.

READING WITH ATTENTION TO CASE

The poet E. E. Cummings often broke the standard rules of grammar and word order to create particular effects in his poetry. Read the following poem by Cummings, and note the function of each pronoun. Then rearrange the words of the poem so that they follow as closely as possible the normal order they would take in an ordinary sentence. How does pronoun case give you a clue to this arrangement?

> Me up at does
>
> out of the floor
> quietly stare
>
> a poisoned mouse
>
> still who alive
>
> is asking What
> have i done that
>
> you wouldn't have

FOR EXAMINING CASE IN YOUR OWN WRITING

Research shows that one of the most overused words in any language is the word for *I*. Whenever you write anything that includes your own opinions, you probably rely to some degree on first-person pronouns, singular and plural. Read over the excerpt from James Thurber's "University Days," in Exercise 7.1, and then write a paragraph or two about your own least favorite class. When you are finished, underline all the personal pronouns you used, and label each one for case. Do you find any patterns? If you find that you rely heavily on any one case—that half your sentences begin with *I*, for example— decide whether your writing seems at all monotonous as a result. If so, try revising, paying attention to pronoun case. See, in other words, whether revising some sentences to change *I* to *me* (or vice versa) brings greater variety to your writing. If you keep a writing log, you might enter your work into it, noting what you have learned about your use of pronoun case.

8. Using Verbs

When used skillfully, verbs can be called the heartbeat of prose, moving it along, enlivening it, carrying its action. Verbs are extremely flexible and can change form to mark grammatical agreement with the subject (see Chapter 9) or to indicate *tense, voice,* or *mood.*

CHANGE IN TENSE	The runner *skims* around the track. [present tense]
	The runner *skimmed* around the track. [past tense]
CHANGE IN VOICE	She *savors* every step. [active voice]
	Every step *is savored.* [passive voice]
CHANGE IN MOOD	She *is* completely content. [indicative]
	If she *were* not content, she *would* not *be* smiling. [subjunctive]

This chapter explores in detail the way verbs work, with attention to form, tense, voice, and mood.

VERB FORMS

Except for *be,* all English verbs have five forms.

BASE FORM	PAST TENSE	PAST PARTICIPLE	PRESENT PARTICIPLE	-S FORM
talk	talked	talked	talking	talks
adore	adored	adored	adoring	adores
jog	jogged	jogged	jogging	jogs

The **base form** is the one listed in the dictionary. For all verbs except *be*, it is the form used to indicate action that takes place (or a condition that exists) in the present when the subject is a plural noun or the pronoun *I, you, we,* or *they.*

> In the ritual the women *go* into trances.
>
> The men *take* knives and *point* them at their chests.

The **past tense** indicates action that took place (or a condition that existed) in the past. The past tense of most verbs is formed by adding *-ed* or *-d* to the base form. Some verbs, however, have an irregular past tense form, as is explained in 8b. *Be* has two past-tense forms, *was* and *were.*

> The Globe *served* as the playhouse for many of Shakespeare's works.
>
> In 1613 it *caught* fire and *burned* to the ground.

The **past participle** usually has the same form as the past tense. As with the past tense, some verbs have irregular forms for the past participle (see 8b). The past participle cannot function alone as the predicate of a clause or sentence. To function as a predicate, it must be used with a form of the auxiliary verb *have* or *be*. In addition, the past participle can function as an adjective, modifying a noun or pronoun. (See 8e).

> She *had accomplished* the impossible.
>
> The doctors *have asked* for my cooperation.
>
> No one *was injured* in the explosion.
>
> *Standardized* tests usually require *sharpened* pencils.

The **present participle** is constructed by adding *-ing* to the base form. Like the past participle, it cannot function alone as a predicate but must be used with one or more auxiliary verbs. A present participle used with the auxiliary *be* is called the progressive form of a verb and indicates continuing action. The present participle can also function as an adjective, like the past participle, or as a noun, called a gerund. (See 6c.)

> Several hundred students *are competing* in the race.
>
> He tried to comfort the *crying* child.
>
> Philosophy emphasizes the value of *thinking.*

Except for *be* and *have,* the **-s form** consists of the base form plus *-s* or *-es.* This form indicates the present tense when the subject is third-person singular. All singular nouns, the pronouns *he, she,* and *it,* and many indefinite pronouns (such as *everyone,* or *someone*) are third-person singular.

> Life *demands* our participation.
>
> She usually *takes* the shortcut across campus.
>
> No one *believes* his story.

It is very important to note that the *-s* form occurs *only* in the third-person singular.

	SINGULAR	PLURAL
FIRST PERSON	I wish	we wish
SECOND PERSON	you wish	you wish
THIRD PERSON	he/she/it wishes	they wish
	Joe wishes	children wish
	someone wishes	

Some dialects of English use the base form instead of the *-s* form with a third-person singular subject. In addition, some people skip carelessly over the *-s* form in speech and then, as a result, often tend to forget the *-s* or *-es* in writing.

DIALECT	She *live* in a high-rise apartment.
ACADEMIC WRITING	She *lives* in a high-rise apartment.

The forms of *be* and *have* corresponding to the *-s* form of other verbs are *is* and *has.*

> The second stage of the ritual *is* the so-called liminal stage.
>
> A whale *has* lungs instead of gills.

➤ Checking for *-s* and *-es* endings

If you tend to leave off the *-s* and *-es* verb endings, you should check for them systematically when proofreading. Underline every verb, and then circle all those in the present tense. Find the subject for every verb you circle. If the subject is third-person singular (a singular noun; *he, she,* or *it;* or most indefinite pronouns), be sure the verb ends in *-s* or *-es.* If it is not third-person singular, the verb should not have an *-s* or *-es* ending.

Forms of be

Be has three different forms in the present tense and, as mentioned earlier, two forms in the past tense.

Present tense

	SINGULAR	PLURAL
FIRST PERSON	I *am*	we *are*
SECOND PERSON	you *are*	you *are*
THIRD PERSON	he/she/it *is*	they *are*
	Jane *is*	children *are*
	somebody *is*	some *are*

Past tense

	SINGULAR	PLURAL
FIRST PERSON	I *was*	we *were*
SECOND PERSON	you *were*	you *were*
THIRD PERSON	he/she/it *was*	they *were*
	Jane *was*	children *were*
	somebody *was*	some *were*

Although some dialects of English use the base form *be* in place of *am*, *is*, and *are* and the base form *have* in place of *has*, you should always use *am*, *is*, *are*, or *has* in college and other formal writing.

DIALECT	She *be* the oldest member of the family.
ACADEMIC WRITING	She *is* the oldest member of the family
DIALECT	She *have* ten great-grandchildren.
ACADEMIC WRITING	She *has* ten great-grandchildren.

▌ 8a. Using auxiliary verbs

Sometimes called helping verbs, **auxiliary verbs** are used with a base form, present participle, or past participle to create verb phrases. The base form or participle in a verb phrase is called the main verb. The most commonly used auxiliaries include forms of *have*, *be*, and *do*, which are used to indicate a completed action or condition (see 8c and 8d), to indicate the passive voice, to indicate a continuing action or condition, to add emphasis, to ask questions, and to make negative statements. *Will* and *shall* are auxiliaries used to show future time; unlike most auxiliaries, they never change form.

190

Dennis *has worked* late all month.

I *am working* hard.

She *has been warned* several times.

We *do respect* your viewpoint.

Do you *know* the answer?

He *does* not *like* wearing a tie.

They *will explain* the procedure.

Modal auxiliaries—*can, could, might, may, must, ought to, should, would*—show possibility, necessity, obligation, and so on.

You *can see* three states from the top of the mountain. [possibility]

I *must try* harder. [necessity]

She *should visit* her parents more often. [obligation]

Although some dialects of English use the base form *be* as an auxiliary instead of *am, is,* or *are,* always use the standard forms in college and other formal writing.

DIALECT	They *be* working to earn money for tuition.
ACADEMIC WRITING	They *are* working to earn money for tuition.
DIALECT	I *be* scheduled to take biology next semester.
ACADEMIC WRITING	I *am* scheduled to take biology next semester.

In making a negative statement, some dialects use *don't* with a third-person singular subject. In formal writing, always use *doesn't* in such constructions.

DIALECT	The character *don't* seem true to life.
ACADEMIC WRITING	The character *doesn't* seem true to life.

Some dialects use the past participle or the present participle of a verb without an auxiliary verb as the predicate of a sentence. Many writers also leave out the auxiliary accidentally. In formal writing, a participle must have an auxiliary verb attached to it in order to function as a predicate. (See Chapter 14.)

DIALECT	They *working* to earn money for tuition.
ACADEMIC WRITING	They *are working* to earn money for tuition.
DIALECT	My roommate *gone* to her seminar.
ACADEMIC WRITING	My roommate *has gone* to her seminar.

| DIALECT | The porch needs fixed. |
| ACADEMIC WRITING | The porch needs to be fixed. |

EXERCISE 8.1

Edit the following sentences so that all verb forms are acceptable in formal written English. (Some of the sentences do not require any change.)

Example
Although Joe seem in control, his actions making me wonder.
Although Joe *seems* in control, his actions *make* me wonder.

1. When the dance begin, a man in costume appears.
2. The man have long fingernails and a mask.
3. All of the people in the village participate in the ceremony.
4. The doctor works two nights a week at a clinic.
5. A hot shower always relax me.
6. The thought of nuclear war be terrifying to most people.
7. New mothers often suffers from depression.
8. He don't know whether to try again or to give up.
9. The deposit refunded if the customer doesn't buy the equipment.
10. Mayor Burns running for reelection this fall.

▌ 8b. Using regular and irregular verbs

A verb is **regular** when its past tense and past participle are formed by adding *-ed* or *-d* to the base form:

BASE FORM	PAST TENSE	PAST PARTICIPLE
love	loved	loved
honor	honored	honored
obey	obeyed	obeyed

The past tense and past participle of regular verbs sometimes cause difficulty for writers in spelling, because some of them double the final consonant or change final *y* to *i* before adding *-ed*. (See 22d.)

➤ Checking for *-ed* or *-d* endings

Some people skip over the *-ed* or *-d* endings in conversation and thus forget to include them in writing. If you tend to make this mistake, you should make a point of systematically checking for it when proofreading. Underline all the verbs, and then underline a second time any that are past tense or past participles. Check each of these for an *-ed* or *-d* ending. Unless the verb is irregular (see below), it should end in *-ed* or *-d*.

Irregular verbs

A verb is **irregular** when it does not follow the *-ed* or *-d* pattern. The past tense and past participle of irregular verbs are most often formed by changing an internal vowel: *begin, began, begun.* In some verbs like this, *-en* or *-n* is also added to the past participle: *break, broke, broken.* Other verbs change form more radically: *go, went, gone.* Still others do not change at all: *hurt, hurt, hurt.* If you are uncertain about the correct verb form, consult your dictionary, which lists any irregular past tense and past participle forms under the entry for the base form.

You probably know most irregular verb forms intuitively, but you may want to take the time now to memorize any that cause you difficulty. Here are some of the most common irregular verbs.

BASE FORM	PAST TENSE	PAST PARTICIPLE
arise	arose	arisen
be	was/were	been
bear	bore	borne/born
beat	beat	beaten
become	became	become
begin	began	begun
bite	bit	bitten
blow	blew	blown
break	broke	broken
bring	brought	brought
build	built	built
burn	burned/burnt	burned/burnt
burst	burst	burst
buy	bought	bought
catch	caught	caught
choose	chose	chosen
come	came	come
cost	cost	cost
cut	cut	cut
dig	dug	dug
dive	dived/dove	dived
do	did	done
draw	drew	drawn
drink	drank	drunk

drive	drove	driven
eat	ate	eaten
fall	fell	fallen
feel	felt	felt
fight	fought	fought
find	found	found
fly	flew	flown
forget	forgot	forgotten/forgot
freeze	froze	frozen
get	got	gotten/got
give	gave	given
go	went	gone
grow	grew	grown
hang[1]	hung	hung
have	had	had
hear	heard	heard
hide	hid	hidden
hit	hit	hit
keep	kept	kept
know	knew	known
lay	laid	laid
lead	led	led
leave	left	left
lend	lent	lent
let	let	let
lie (recline)[2]	lay	lain
lose	lost	lost
make	made	made
mean	meant	meant
meet	met	met
pay	paid	paid
prove	proved	proved/proven
put	put	put
read	read	read
ride	rode	ridden
ring	rang	rung
rise	rose	risen
run	ran	run
say	said	said
see	saw	seen

---

[1] *Hang* meaning "execute by hanging" is regular: *hang, hanged, hanged.*
[2] *Lie* meaning "tell a falsehood" is regular: *lie, lied, lied.*

vb 8b

send	sent	sent
set	set	set
shake	shook	shaken
shine (give light)³	shone	shone
shoot	shot	shot
show	showed	showed/shown
shrink	shrank	shrunk
sing	sang	sung
sink	sank	sunk
sit	sat	sat
sleep	slept	slept
speak	spoke	spoken
spend	spent	spent
spread	spread	spread
spring	sprang/sprung	sprung
stand	stood	stood
steal	stole	stolen
strike	struck	struck/stricken
swim	swam	swum
swing	swung	swung
take	took	taken
teach	taught	taught
tear	tore	torn
tell	told	told
think	thought	thought
throw	threw	thrown
wake	woke/waked	waked/woken/woke
wear	wore	worn
win	won	won
wind	wound	wound
write	wrote	written

³ *Shine* meaning "polish" is regular: *shine, shined, shined.*

EXERCISE 8.2

Complete each of the following sentences by filling in each blank with the past tense or past participle of the verb listed in parentheses. Remember that a past participle cannot function by itself as a verb; for a past participle to fit in a blank, one or more auxiliary verbs must precede it.

Example

We had not <u>eaten</u> (eat) since lunch, yet we <u>felt</u> (feel) no hunger.

195

1. Clearly, this short story would not have _____(be) as effective if it had been _____(write) in the third-person.
2. Once she had _____(come) to this realization, she _____(find) that she was no longer afraid of change.
3. The process of hazing _____(begin) soon after fraternities were formed.
4. Hearnes _____(lose) control of the fight, and Hagler _____(take) advantage of this loss.
5. On the Saturdays before Geiberger and Langer _____(win) their respective tournaments, each had _____(shoot) a sixty-eight.
6. People think that we _____(grow) up together because we are practically inseparable.
7. I painfully _____(draw) ninety-five dollars from my wallet and _____(set) the money on the counter.
8. It would have been helpful if someone had _____(meet) me at the airport and had _____(take) me to the hotel.
9. As the boat _____(sink), the passengers _____(put) on their life preservers and _____(say) their prayers.
10. When I first _____(meet) her, I _____(think) that she was the most unpleasant person I had ever _____(know).

EXERCISE 8.3

Edit the following sentences to eliminate any inappropriate verb forms. (One of the sentences does not require any change.)

Example
She begin the examination on time.
She *began* the examination on time.

1. Socrates drank the hemlock calmly and died a few hours later.
2. The band had sang its last song before the fight had begun.
3. When the battle was over, the rebels had been beat badly.
4. By the mid-1970s New York had almost went bankrupt.
5. The lake freezed early this year.

▌ 8c. Using *lie* and *lay, sit* and *set, rise* and *raise*

Three pairs of verbs—*lie* and *lay, sit* and *set,* and *rise* and *raise*—cause problems for many writers because the two verbs in each pair have similar-sounding forms and somewhat related meanings. In each pair one of the verbs is transitive, meaning that it takes a direct object; the other is intransitive, meaning that it does not take an object. The best way to avoid confusing the two is to memorize their forms and meanings. All of these verbs except *raise* are irregular. Their forms are as follows:

BASE FORM	PAST TENSE	PAST PARTICIPLE	PRESENT PARTICIPLE	-S FORM
lie	lay	lain	lying	lies
lay	laid	laid	laying	lays
sit	sat	sat	sitting	sits
set	set	set	setting	sets
rise	rose	risen	rising	rises
raise	raised	raised	raising	raises

Lie is intransitive and means "recline" or "be situated." *Lay* is transitive and means "put" or "place." This pair is especially confusing because *lay* is also the past-tense form of *lie*.

INTRANSITIVE	He *lay* on the floor unable to move.
TRANSITIVE	I *laid* the package on the counter.

Sit is intransitive and means "be seated." *Set* is transitive and usually means "put" or "place."

INTRANSITIVE	She *sat* in the rocking chair daydreaming.
TRANSITIVE	She *set* the package on the counter.

Rise is intransitive and means "get up" or "go up." *Raise* is transitive and means "lift" or "cause to go up."

INTRANSITIVE	He *rose* from the bed and left the room.
TRANSITIVE	He *raised* himself to a sitting position.
INTRANSITIVE	The price of coffee is *rising*.
TRANSITIVE	The store is *raising* the price of coffee.

EXERCISE 8.4

Choose the appropriate verb form from the pair in parentheses in each of the following sentences.

1. Sometimes she just (*lies/lays*) and stares at the ceiling.
2. I (*lay/laid*) my books down just as the telephone rang.
3. The doctor asked the patient to (*lie/lay*) on his side for an injection.
4. He used whatever was (*lying/laying*) around the house.
5. Doctors urge us to (*sit/set*) aside fad diets once and for all.
6. I (*sat/set*) back, closed my eyes, and began to meditate.
7. (*Sitting/Setting*) in the sun too long can lead to skin cancer.
8. The Federal Reserve Bank is planning to (*rise/raise*) interest rates.
9. When the temperature (*rises/raises*), the relative humidity usually declines.
10. We (*rose/raised*) every morning at six and went jogging.

197

VERB TENSES

Tenses are the forms of a verb that show when the action or condition expressed by the verb takes place or exists. We characteristically think of time in terms of present, past, and future, and the three *simple tenses* are the present tense, the past tense, and the future tense.

PRESENT TENSE	I jump
PAST TENSE	I jumped
FUTURE TENSE	I will jump

More complex aspects of time relationships, such as ongoing or completed actions or conditions, are expressed through *progressive, perfect,* and *perfect progressive forms* of the simple tenses. Such terminology sounds complicated in the abstract, but, in fact, you use all these forms in everyday speech. Here are all the tense forms of one verb, *ask.*

SIMPLE PRESENT	she *asks*
SIMPLE PAST	she *asked*
SIMPLE FUTURE	she *will ask*
PRESENT PERFECT	she *has asked*
PAST PERFECT	she *had asked*
FUTURE PERFECT	she *will have asked*
PRESENT PROGRESSIVE	she *is asking*
PAST PROGRESSIVE	she *was asking*
FUTURE PROGRESSIVE	she *will be asking*
PRESENT PERFECT PROGRESSIVE	she *has been asking*
PAST PERFECT PROGRESSIVE	she *had been asking*
FUTURE PERFECT PROGRESSIVE	she *will have been asking*

The simple tenses locate an action or condition only within the three basic time frames of present, past, and future. The perfect form of each tense expresses the idea of a *completed* action or condition in the present, past, or future, and the progressive form expresses the idea of a *continuing* action or condition. Finally, the perfect progressive form expresses the idea of an action or condition continuing up to a point of completion. The next section describes in greater detail how each of the forms of each tense is used.

▌ 8d. Using the present tense forms

The **simple present** indicates actions or conditions occurring at the time of speaking or writing, as well as those occurring habitually and those considered to be general truths or scientific facts. In addition, with appropriate expressions of time, the simple present can be used to indicate a scheduled event in the future.

> He now *lives* in San Diego.
>
> They *are* very angry about the decision.
>
> I *eat* breakfast every day at 8:00 A.M.
>
> Love *conquers* all.
>
> Water *freezes* at 0 degrees Celsius.
>
> The United States Constitution *guarantees* certain rights to all citizens.
>
> Residents of Greenland *endure* bitter cold for most of the year.
>
> Grandpa *arrives* tomorrow.

The simple present is also used in discussing literary and artistic works created in the past that exist in our experience as timeless. For example, a literary character such as Ishmael in *Moby Dick*, created by Herman Melville over a century ago, exists in our present time as well.

> Ishmael slowly *comes* to realize all that *is* at stake in the search for the white whale.

The **present progressive** indicates actions or conditions that are ongoing or continuous in the present.

> The children *are playing* in the back yard this afternoon.
>
> The defense attorney *is asking* for a retrial.

The present progressive is typically used to describe an action that is happening at the moment of speaking, in contrast to the simple present, which more often indicates habitual actions.

PRESENT PROGRESSIVE	You *are driving* too fast.
SIMPLE PRESENT	I always *drive* carefully.

With an appropriate expression of time, the present progressive can also be used to indicate a scheduled event in the future.

> We *are having* friends over for dinner tomorrow night.

The **present perfect** indicates actions or conditions begun in the past and either completed at some unspecified time in the past or continuing into the present.

> My father *has told* me many stories of his childhood.
>
> Uncontrolled logging *has destroyed* many tropical forests.
>
> Anti-abortion activists *have tried* to reverse the decision.

The **present perfect progressive** indicates that an ongoing action or condition begun in the past is very likely to continue into the present.

> For many years the United States and the Soviet Union *have been trying* to negotiate treaties to control nuclear arms.
>
> Since I *have been taking* vitamins regularly, I have had no colds.
>
> The company's management *has been fighting* an attempted takeover.

8e. Using the past tense forms

The **simple past** indicates actions or conditions that occurred at a specific time and do not extend into the present.

> She *felt* better as soon as her exams were over.
>
> Germany *invaded* Poland on September 1, 1939.
>
> We *moved* to this city only last year.

The **past progressive** indicates continuing actions or conditions in the past, often with specified limits.

> Lenin *was living* in exile in Zurich when the tsar was overthrown.
>
> By the 1970s many Americans *were buying* smaller cars.
>
> I *was visiting* a pecan orchard when I got a craving for a piece of pie.

The **past perfect** indicates actions or conditions that were completed by a specific time in the past or before some other past action or condition occurred.

> By the fourth century Christianity *had become* the state religion.
>
> She *had asked* the instructor for help before she turned to me.
>
> Homesteaders found that speculators *had* already *taken* the best land.

The **past perfect progressive** indicates continuous actions or conditions in the past that began before a specific time in the past or before some other past action or condition began.

They *had been living* beyond their means for years before they went bankrupt.

When they returned to Venice, the Polos *had been traveling* for almost twenty-five years.

Carter *had been planning* a naval career, but he returned to Plains to run the family business.

▌ 8f. Using the future tense forms

The **simple future** indicates actions or conditions that have yet to begin.

The exhibition *will come* to Washington in September.

I *shall graduate* the year after next.

Mortgage rates *will rise* if the money supply is restricted.

The **future progressive** indicates continuing actions or conditions in the future.

The loans *will be coming* due in the next two years.

A team of international observers *will be monitoring* the elections.

The **future perfect** indicates actions or conditions that will be completed by or before some specified time in the future.

They *will have exhausted* all their resources before the new year arrives.

In ten years the original investment *will have doubled*.

Finally, the **future perfect progressive** indicates continuing actions or conditions that will be completed by some specified time in the future.

By the time the session ends, the negotiators *will have been working* for ten hours without a break.

Hannah *will have been playing* the piano for five years this June.

➤ Checking verb tenses

Errors in verb tenses take several forms. Some are errors in verb form: writing *seen* for *saw*, for example, which is an instance of mixing up the participle and past tense forms. Others are errors in time: using the simple past (*Uncle Charlie arrived*) when meaning requires the present perfect (*Uncle Charlie has arrived*). Still others result from using

201

dialect (*we be going*) in situations requiring standard edited English (*we are going*).

If you have trouble with verb tenses, the best thing you can do is to keep a log of your errors and then to look for patterns. Once you can identify specific problems, you can make a point of routinely proofreading for them.

EXERCISE 8.5

Complete each of the following sentences by filling in the blank with an appropriate form of the verb listed in parentheses. Since more than one form will sometimes be possible, be prepared to explain reasons for your choices.

1. In spite of the poor turnout in today's referendum, local officials _____(expect) the bond issue to pass.
2. Ever since the first nuclear power plants were built, opponents _____ (predict) disaster.
3. Thousands of Irish peasants _____(emigrate) to America after the potato famine of the 1840s.
4. The newspaper _____(arrive) late every day this week.
5. The committee _____(meet) again next week.
6. President Kennedy was shot while he _____(ride) in a limousine.
7. By eleven o'clock this morning, stock prices _____(fall) fifteen points.
8. By the time a child born today enters first grade, he or she _____ (watch) thousands of television commercials.
9. In "The Road Not Taken" the man _____(come) to a fork in the road.
10. The supply of a product _____(rise) when the demand is great.

EXERCISE 8.6

Verb tenses are essential for creating a sense of time. Read the following passage from an essay by Alice Walker, paying attention to the italicized verbs. Then reread the passage substituting forms of the simple past or past progressive for these verbs, and write a brief paragraph describing the difference in immediacy—and in emphasis—the substitutions make.

I *am* eight years old and a tomboy. I *have* a cowboy hat, cowboy boots, checkered shirt and pants, all red. My playmates *are* my brothers, two and four years older than I. Their colors *are* black and green, the only difference in the way we *are* dressed. On Saturday nights we all *go* to the picture show, even my mother; westerns *are* her favorite kind of movie. Back home, "on the ranch," we *pretend* we *are* Tom Mix, Hopalong Cassidy, Lash LaRue . . . ; we *chase* each other for hours rustling cattle, being outlaws, delivering damsels from distress. Then my parents *decide* to buy my brothers guns. These *are* not "real" guns. They *shoot* "BBs." . . . Because I *am* a girl, I *do* not *get* a gun. Instantly, I *am relegated* to the position of Indian. Now there *appears* a great distance between us. They *shoot* and *shoot* at everything with their new guns. I *try* to keep up with my bow and arrows.

One day while I *am standing* on top of our makeshift "garage"—pieces of tin nailed across some poles—holding my bow and arrow and looking out toward the fields, I *feel* an incredible blow in my right eye. I *look* down just in time to see my brother lower his gun.

—ALICE WALKER, "Beauty: When the Other Dancer Is the Self"

▌ 8g. Using verb tenses in sequences

Because tense is crucial to our understanding of when actions or conditions occur and because time relationships can be very complex, careful and accurate use of tenses is important to clear writing. Even the simplest narrative describes actions that take place at different times; using particular tenses for particular actions allows readers to follow such time changes readily.

The relationship between the tense of the verb in the independent clause of a sentence and the tense of a verb in a dependent clause or a verbal is called the **sequence of tenses.** In general, the verb in a dependent clause may be in any tense form required for your meaning. The only limitation is that the relationship between the forms in the independent and dependent clauses make sense. For example, all of the following make sense and are acceptable grammatically:

> He *lent* her the money because he *is* a generous man. [past/present]
>
> He *lent* her the money because he *loved* her. [past/past]
>
> He *lent* her the money because she *will invest* it wisely. [past/future]

Even though in general you can use almost any sequence of tenses, in a particular sentence the tense of the verb in the dependent clause may be limited by the meaning. For example, it makes no sense to say *He lent her the money because he will love her* or *He lent her the money because she had invested it wisely.*

Different forms of an infinitive are used to indicate the time relationship between the action expressed by the infinitive and that expressed by the verb in the predicate. The **present infinitive**, consisting of *to* plus the base form, indicates action occurring at the same time as or later than the action of the predicate verb.

I *wanted to swim* in the ocean last summer. [The wanting and the swimming occurred at the same time in the past.]

I *expect to swim* in the ocean next summer. [The expecting is present; the swimming is in the future.]

The **perfect infinitive**, consisting of *to have* plus the past participle, indicates action occurring *before* the action of the predicate verb.

She *seems to have lost* her self-confidence. [The loss of self-confidence took place before the "seeming."]

He *was reported to have left* his fortune to his cat. [The leaving of the fortune took place before the reporting.]

Similarly, different kinds of participles are used to indicate the time relationship between the action expressed by the participle and that expressed by the verb in the predicate. The **present participle** indicates action occurring at the same time as that of the verb.

Seeking to relieve unemployment, Roosevelt *established* several public works programs. [Both the seeking and the establishment of the programs occurred simultaneously in the past.]

The **present perfect participle** indicates action occurring before that of the predicate verb. The present perfect participle consists of *having* plus the past participle: *having sent, having walked*.

Having won the election, he *is planning* his inauguration. [He began planning after he won the election.]

The **past participle** can indicate action occurring either before or at the same time as that of the predicate verb.

Flown by an expert pilot, the passengers *felt* completely secure. [The flying and the feeling were simultaneous.]

Flown to the front, the troops *joined* their hard-pressed comrades. [The flying occurred before the joining.]

EXERCISE 8.7

Edit each of the following sentences to create the appropriate sequence of tenses between the verb in the predicate and the participle or infinitive.

Example
He needs to send in his application before today.
He needs to *have sent* in his application before today.

1. When he was twenty-one, he wanted to have become a millionaire by the age of thirty.
2. Leaving England in December, the settlers arrived in Virginia in May.
3. They hoped to plant their garden by now.
4. Cutting off all contact with her parents, she did not know whom to ask for help.
5. Having sung in the shower, he did not hear the doorbell.

VOICE

Voice is the feature of transitive verbs that tells whether the subject is acting (*he questions us*) or being acted upon (*he is questioned*). When the subject is acting, the verb is in the **active voice;** when the subject is being acted upon, the verb is in the **passive voice.** The passive voice is formed, as in this sentence, by using the appropriate form of the auxiliary verb *be* followed by the past participle of the main verb.

	ACTIVE VOICE	PASSIVE VOICE
PRESENT	He *questions* us.	He *is questioned.*
PAST	He *questioned* us.	He *was questioned.*
FUTURE	He *will question* us.	He *will be questioned.*
PRESENT PERFECT	He *has questioned* us.	He *has been questioned.*
PAST PERFECT	He *had questioned* us.	He *had been questioned.*
FUTURE PERFECT	He *will have questioned* us.	He *will have been questioned.*

Most contemporary writers use the active voice as much as possible because it makes prose more *active*, more lively. To say that "the mail was opened" (passive voice) does not give the sense of action or immediacy that "Cheryl opened the mail" (active voice) does. In the passive construction, the mail is just there—being opened, by no one or nothing in particular. Even adding "by Cheryl" does not do much to enliven the passive version. When passive-voice verbs pile up in a writing passage, that passage will generally be harder to understand and remember. For instance, readers indicate they *remember* passages as being in the active voice even if the version they read used the passive voice.

The most problematic use of the passive voice occurs when writers seek to avoid taking responsibility for what they have written. A university president who announces that "it is recommended that fees be raised substantially" skirts a number of pressing questions: recommended by whom? raised by whom?

In spite of such questionable uses, however, the passive voice can work to good advantage in some situations. Much scientific writing uses the passive voice effectively to highlight the object or phenomenon being studied rather than the person or persons doing the studying. Look at the following example, from an essay describing brain surgery:

> A curved incision was made behind the hairline so it would be concealed when the hair grew back. It extended almost from ear to ear. Plastic clips were applied to the cut edges of the scalp to arrest bleeding. The scalp was folded back to the level of the eyebrows. Incisions were made in the muscle of the right temple, and three sets of holes were drilled near the temple and the top of the head because the tumor had to be approached from directly in front. The drill, powered by nitrogen, was replaced with a fluted steel blade, and the holes were connected. The incised piece of skull was pried loose and held out of the way by a large sponge.   –ROY C. SELBY, JR., "A Delicate Operation"

Reporters often use the passive voice when they want to protect the confidentiality of their sources, as in the familiar phrase "It is reported that . . . ," or when the performer of an action is unknown or less important than the recipient of the action. When Tom Wicker submitted his article on the assassination of President Kennedy to the *New York Times*, he began this way:

> DALLAS, Nov. 22—President John Fitzgerald Kennedy was shot and killed by an assassin today.
>
> He died of a wound in the brain caused by a rifle bullet that was fired at him as he was riding through downtown Dallas in a motorcade.
>
> Vice President Lyndon Baines Johnson, who was riding in the third car behind Mr. Kennedy's, was sworn in as the 36th President of the United States 99 minutes after Mr. Kennedy's death.
>
> –TOM WICKER, *New York Times*

Wicker's article uses the passive voice with good reason: he wants the focus of the sentences on Kennedy, not on who killed him, and on Johnson, not on who swore him in.

Writers, then, must decide for themselves when the passive voice is appropriate and when it is not. If you find that you overuse the passive, you may want to practice shifting your sentences to active voice. To do so, convert the subject of the verb into a direct or indirect object, and make the performer of the action into the subject.

PASSIVE	The test administrator *was told* to give the student an electric shock each time a wrong answer *was given*.
ACTIVE	Researchers *told* the test administrator to give the student an electric shock each time he or she *gave* a wrong answer.
PASSIVE	I *was awakened* promptly at seven by the huge brown alarm clock.
ACTIVE	The huge brown alarm clock *awakened* me promptly at seven.

See 12c and 21b for further discussion of voice.

EXERCISE 8.8

Convert each of the following sentences from active to passive voice or from passive to active, and note the differences in emphasis and rhythm these changes make.

Example
Machiavelli advises the prince to gain the friendship of the people.
The prince *is advised* by Machiavelli to gain the friendship of the people.

1. Flannery O'Connor employs the images of both a boxcar and a swinging bridge to show the inconsistencies between Mrs. Turpin's classification of people and God's classification of people.
2. Huge pine trees were uprooted by the storm.
3. Marianne avoided such things as elevators, subways, and closets.
4. For months the baby kangaroo is protected, fed, and taught how to survive by its mother.
5. The lawns and rooftops of the neighborhood were covered with the first snow of winter.

EXERCISE 8.9

Look at several essays you have written recently or pieces of writing by others that you particularly like, and find five examples each of the active voice and the passive voice. Convert each of the examples to the other voice, and note the difference in emphasis and rhythm the changes make.

MOOD

The **mood** of a verb indicates the attitude of the speaker or writer toward what he or she is saying or writing. Different moods are used to express a fact or inquiry (indicative mood), a command or request (imperative mood), or a wish, requirement, or condition contrary to fact (subjunctive mood).

INDICATIVE   I *ate* the plums

IMPERATIVE   *Eat* the plums.

SUBJUNCTIVE   If I *were to eat* the plums, I would be sick.

The most frequently used mood is the **indicative mood**, the one used for stating facts or opinions or asking questions.

The Frisbees *soar* through the air.

Carter *lost* the 1980 election.

Where *are* you *going*?

The **imperative mood** is used for giving commands or making requests. It always uses the base form of the verb and almost always omits the subject, (*you*).

Look at the girl with the orange spiked hair.

Take the appropriate wrench, and *loosen* the plug counterclockwise.

You *sit* down at once!

Help!

The **subjunctive mood** expresses wishes, conditions that are contrary to fact, requests, or demands. It is used primarily in dependent clauses beginning with *that* or *if*.

▌ 8h. Using the subjunctive

The present tense of the subjunctive uses the base form of the verb. The past tense of the subjunctive is the same as the past tense of the indicative mood except for the verb *be*, which uses *were* for all subjects.

PRESENT

The professor demanded that she *arrive* as early as possible.

It is important that children *be* psychologically ready for a new sibling.

PAST

He spent money as if he *had* infinite credit.

If the store *were* better located, it would attract more customers.

Because the subjunctive can create a rather formal tone, many speakers today have a tendency to substitute the indicative in informal situations. Nevertheless, formal writing still requires the use of the subjunctive in the following kinds of dependent clauses:

INDICATIVE   If I *was* a better typist, I would type my own papers.
SUBJUNCTIVE   If I *were* a better typist, I would type my own papers.

1. Those expressing a wish

I wish I *were* with you right now.

He wished that his mother *were* not reluctant to quit smoking.

2. Those beginning with *if* and expressing a condition that does not exist

If the federal government *were* to ban the sale of tobacco, tobacco companies and distributors would suffer a great loss.

If no one *were allowed* to ignore the rules, language would cease to develop.

3. Those beginning with *as if* and *as though*

He cautiously started down the trail as if he *were walking* on thin ice.

During the 1920s Americans speculated in Florida real estate as though it *were* a risk-free investment.

4. Those beginning with *that* and expressing a demand, request, requirement, or suggestion

It is required that each fraternity *sponsor* three community service projects each semester.

Dad advised that neither of us *do* anything too hastily.

The job demands that the employee *be* in good physical condition.

EXERCISE 8.10

Revise any of the following sentences that do not use the appropriate subjunctive verb forms required in formal writing.

Example
I saw how carefully he moved, as if he was caring for an infant.
I saw how carefully he moved, as if he *were* caring for an infant.

1. Her stepsisters treated Cinderella as though she was a servant.
2. Hamlet wishes that he was not responsible for avenging his murdered father.
3. Freud recommended that an analyst use dreams as a means of studying the human personality.
4. If more money was available, the university would be able to offer more scholarships.
5. It is necessary that the manager knows how to do any job in the store.

EXERCISE 8.11

The poem below is a famous example of nonsense verse, one that plays games with words—and freely *invents* words. Read the poem out loud, and then underline all the verbs, whether actual English words (like *bite*) or made-up ones (like *outgrabe*).

'Twas brillig, and the slithy toves
    Did gyre and gimble in the wabe;
All mimsy were the borogoves,
    And the mome raths outgrabe.

"Beware the Jabberwock, my son!
    The jaws that bite, the claws that catch!
Beware the Jubjub bird, and shun
    The frumious Bandersnatch!"

He took his vorpal sword in hand;
    Long time for manxome foe he sought—
So rested he by the Tumtum tree,
    And stood awhile in thought.

And, as in uffish thought he stood,
    The Jabberwock, with eyes of flame,
Came whiffling through the tulgey wood,
    And burbled as it came!

One, two! One, two! And through and through
    The vorpal blade went snicker-snack!
He left it dead, and with its head
    He went galumphing back.

"And hast thou slain the Jabberwock?
    Come to my arms, my beamish boy!
O frabjous day! Callooh! Callay!"
    He chortled in his joy.

210

'Twas brillig, and the slithy toves
    Did gyre and gimble in the wabe;
And mimsy were the borogoves,
    And the mome raths outgrabe.
      –LEWIS CARROLL, "Jabberwocky"

READING WITH AN EYE FOR VERBS

Read the following paragraph carefully, noting the way the author uses verbs to create a scene from his past. Especially note his one use of the present tense, which emphasizes the fact that he is recollecting a past experience. What different effects might this passage have if it were written all in the present tense?

    I came to suspect that I was setting about life in reverse: drawing the conclusions before experiencing the data. My eyes were opened by Bernard Berenson, whom my family knew quite well, and with whom I was staying at Vallombrosa. One day we took a tiny walk. I use that term because B.B., rug over immaculately tailored forearm, would creep along a few steps, halt, seize your elbow, swinging you around in front, and then say something. We were tottering along in this way when B.B. asked me, "What will you be doing next year?" "I may work on a doctorate in comp. lit.," I replied. His face clouded slightly. "What do you think of comp. lit.?" I inquired anxiously. He stopped, seized my elbow, swinging me around in front, and bayed hoarsely, *"Comp. lit. is as dead as cold mutton!"* Since he always said he had gone astray in his own life in becoming an art "expert," he was glad to set young men straight.
      —JOHN TRAIN, from a postscript to
      "For the Adventurous Few: How to Get Rich"

FOR EXAMINING VERBS IN YOUR OWN WRITING

Write a few paragraphs about a past event in your life—a visit, a ceremony, a job, anything you remember that you wish to write about. Describe it as a past event, using past-tense verbs. Then rewrite your description in the present tense, as if the event were taking place right now. Study the two versions, and write down any observations you can make about the effectiveness of each approach.

| 9. Maintaining Agreement

In ordinary language, **agreement** refers to an accord or a correspondence between ideas or actions: you reach an *agreement* with your boss about salary; the United States and the Soviet Union negotiate an *agreement* about nuclear arms. This ordinary meaning of *agreement* covers its grammatical use as well. When subjects and verbs or pronouns and antecedents match each other in person, in number, and in gender, we say that they "agree." This chapter explores the conventions governing such agreement.

SUBJECT-VERB AGREEMENT

A verb must agree with its subject in number (singular or plural) and in person (first, second, or third).

Annie Dillard comes from Pittsburgh. [third-person singular]

We always *wear* rubber gloves in the lab. [first-person plural]

Whales are mammals. [third-person plural]

In practice, only a very few subject-verb constructions cause confusion, so we will look at those constructions in greater detail.

| 9a. Making verbs agree with third-person singular subjects

English once used a complex system of word endings to reflect the person, number, and gender of the subject. Over the centuries, however, most such endings have disappeared from use. Today the

212

main kinds of subjects requiring a special verb form are third-person singular subjects: singular nouns and third-person singular pronouns. To make a present-tense verb agree with a third-person singular subject, we normally add -*s* or -*es* to the base form.

> A vegetarian diet *lowers* the risk of heart disease.
>
> He *wishes* to go to Europe next summer.

The only two verbs that do not follow this -*s* or -*es* pattern for third-person singular subjects in the present tense are *have* and *be*. *Have* changes to *has*; *be* has different forms for both the first and third persons and for both the present and past tense. (See 8b.)

Notice that although an -*s* or -*es* ending indicates a plural noun, the same kind of ending indicates a "singular" verb form. If the subject is a *plural* noun, the verb form does *not* take the -*s* or -*es*.

> A car *needs* regular maintenance.
>
> Cars *need* regular maintenance.

Some dialects of English do not use the -*s* or -*es* ending with a third-person singular subject, and many people forget to use it in writing because it is often not stressed or pronounced clearly in speech. Always use the ending, however, in any writing you do for college or a job. If you have trouble with this particular pattern of subject-verb agreement, you should proofread especially for it; see page 189.

9b. Making the subject and verb agree when separated by other words

When the simple subject of a sentence or clause is separated from the verb by other words, such as a prepositional phrase, be careful to make the verb agree with the subject and not with another noun that is closer to the verb.

> A *vase* of flowers *makes* a room attractive.
>
> Many *books* on the best-seller list *have* little literary value.

Many writers forget to maintain agreement when a plural noun falls between a singular subject and the verb, as in the first example above, or when a singular noun falls between a plural subject and the verb, as in the second example. In the first sentence, notice that the single subject is *vase*, not *flowers*, which is the object of the preposition *of*.

In the second sentence, the simple subject is *books*, not *list*, which is the object of the preposition *on*.

Also be careful when a simple subject is followed by a phrase beginning with *as well as, along with, together with, in addition to*, or a similar expression. Make the verb agree with the simple subject, not with a noun in the intervening phrase.

> The *president*, along with many senators, *opposes* the bill.

> A *passenger*, as well as the driver, *was injured* in the accident.

Some writers think it awkward to use a singular verb form when the complete subject, including the intervening phrase, expresses a plural idea. If a sentence like this strikes you as awkward, revise it by making the subject plural and using a plural verb form (see 9c).

> The president and many senators *oppose* the bill.

> The driver and a passenger *were injured* in the accident.

If you know that you have problems with subject-verb agreement when the simple subject and the verb are separated by other words, proofread each of your sentences to identify the simple subject and the verb. Then mentally delete the intervening words, if any, to make sure that the subject and verb agree in number and person.

EXERCISE 9.1

Underline the appropriate verb form in each of the following sentences

> *Example*
> The benefits of family planning (*is*/*are*) not apparent to many peasants.

1. It (*pains*/*pain*) me to see so much misery in the world.
2. I, together with my sister, (*am*/*is*/*are*) planning a surprise party for him.
3. Walls of glass (*characterizes*/*characterize*) much modern architecture.
4. The system of sororities and fraternities (*supplies*/*supply*) much of the social life on college campuses.
5. The buck (*stops*/*stop*) here.
6. The soldiers, along with their commanding officer, (*was*/*were*) cited for bravery beyond the call of duty.
7. In many species the male, as well as the female, (*cares*/*care*) for the off-spring
8. He (*holds*/*hold*) a controlling interest in the company.
9. The author of those stories (*writes*/*write*) beautifully.
10. Current research on AIDS, in spite of the best efforts of hundreds of scientists, (*leaves*/*leave*) serious questions unanswered.

▌ 9c. Making verbs agree with compound subjects

Two or more subjects joined by *and* generally require a plural verb form.

> Tony and his friends *commute* every day from Louisville.
>
> Faith, hope, and charity *represent* virtues to most of us.

When subjects joined by *and* are considered a single unit or refer to a single person or thing, they take a singular verb form.

> Drinking and driving *remains* a major cause of highway fatalities.
>
> Bagels and cream cheese *is* Colleen's idea of a great breakfast.
>
> His closest friend and political ally *was* his brother.

If the word *each* or *every* precedes singular subjects joined by *and*, the verb form is singular.

> Each boy and girl *chooses* one gift to take home.
>
> Every city, town, and hamlet *has* a Main Street.

For compound subjects whose parts are joined by *or* or *nor*, the verb agrees in number and person with the part of the subject closest to the verb.

> Laws or convention *governs* most of our everyday decisions.
>
> Neither my roommate nor my parents *plan* to vote.
>
> Either Jean or you *were* at fault.
>
> Either you or I *am* wrong.

To avoid awkwardness with compound subjects made up of both singular and plural parts, place a plural part closest to the verb.

> AWKWARD   Either the pigs or the cow *tramples* down my rhubarb every year.
>
> REVISED   Either the cow or the pigs *trample* down my rhubarb every year.

▌ 9d. Making verbs agree with collective-noun subjects

Collective nouns, such as *family, team, audience, group, jury, crowd, band, class, flock,* and *committee,* are singular in form but refer to a group of individual persons or things. When used as subjects,

215

collective nouns can take either singular or plural verb forms, depending on the context. When they refer to a group as a single unit, they take a singular verb form.

> The team wearing red and black *controls* the ball.
>
> Waving banners frenetically, the crowd *screams* its support.

When they refer to the individual members of a collective, however, they take a plural verb form.

> The family of ducklings *scatter* when the cat approaches.
>
> The committee *have* not agreed on many points.

The meaning of a sentence as a whole is your guide to whether the collective noun refers to a unit or to the separate parts of a unit.

> After deliberating, the jury *reports* its verdict. [as a single unit]
>
> The jury still *disagree* on a number of counts. [as separate individuals]

9e. Making verbs agree with indefinite-pronoun subjects

Indefinite pronouns can pose difficulties with subject-verb agreement because they do not refer to specific persons or things, because some of them can be either singular or plural, and because some of them (*everybody, everyone, everything*) sound plural but are grammatically singular.

The following indefinite pronouns are singular in meaning and thus take singular verb forms:

another	everyone	nothing
anybody	everything	one
anyone	much	other
anything	neither	somebody
each	nobody	someone
either	no one	something

> Of the two jobs, neither *holds* much appeal.
>
> Each of the plays *depicts* a hero undone by a tragic flaw.

Indefinite pronouns that take plural verb forms include *both, few, many, others,* and *several.*

Though many *apply*, few *are* chosen.

Both *require* careful attention.

Several indefinite pronouns—*all, any, enough, more, most, none, some*—can be singular or plural, depending on the noun they refer to.

SINGULAR   All of the cake *was* eaten.

PLURAL   All of the candidates *promise* to improve the schools.

9f. Making verbs agree with relative-pronoun subjects

When the relative pronouns *who, which,* or *that* act as the subject of a dependent clause, the verb in the clause should agree in number with the antecedent of the pronoun.

Fear is an ingredient that *goes* into creating stereotypes. [*That* refers to *ingredient*; hence the singular verb form *goes*.]

Guilt, jealousy, and fear are ingredients that *go* into creating stereotypes. [*That* refers to *ingredients*; hence the plural verb form *go*.]

When the phrase *one of the* precedes the relative pronoun, you have to be especially careful to determine whether the pronoun refers to the word *one* or to another word. Look at the following sentence:

Alex is one of the *employees* who always *work* overtime.

In this sentence a number of employees always work overtime, and Alex is among them. Thus *who* refers to *employees*, and the verb form is plural. Now look at the following sentence:

Alex is the only *one* of the employees who always *works* overtime.

In this sentence only one employee always works overtime, and that employee is Alex. Thus *one* and not *employees* is the antecedent of *who*, and the verb form is singular.

9g. Making linking verbs agree with their subjects, not complements

A linking verb should agree with its subject, which precedes it, not with the subject complement, which follows it (see 6c2).

217

The signings of three key treaties *are* the topic of my talk. [The subject is *signings*.]

Nero Wolfe's passion *was* orchids. [The subject is *passion*.]

9h. Making verbs agree with subjects that are plural in form but singular in meaning

Some nouns that seem plural in form (such as *athletics, mathematics, measles, politics, statistics*) are usually singular in meaning and take singular verb forms.

Mathematics *is* not always an exact science.

Measles still *strikes* many Americans.

Some of these nouns may be either singular or plural.

Statistics *is* a course I really dread.

The statistics in that study *are* highly questionable.

In the first sentence above, *statistics* refers to a single course of study; hence it takes a singular verb form. In the second sentence, *statistics* refers to a number of individual figures; hence it takes a plural verb form.

When the subject is the title of a book, film, or other work of art, the verb form is singular even if the title is plural in form.

Sons and Lovers was left to the mercy of critics, many of whom did not fully comprehend it.

Similarly, a word referred to as a word requires a singular verb form even if the word itself is plural.

Scruples has always sounded funny to me.

Steroids is a little word that packs a big punch in the world of sports.

9i. Making verbs agree with subjects that follow them

In English, the subject usually precedes the verb, so check carefully for subject-verb agreement when this order is inverted, or reversed. Make the verb agree with the subject, not with a noun that happens to precede it. Writers often invert word order to ask questions or to emphasize the subject.

Is a shark a vertebrate? [The subject is *shark.*]

Beside the tracks *stand* silos filled with grain. [The subject is *silos.*]

Another common inversion of subject-verb order occurs in sentences beginning with *there* followed by a form of *be* (*is, are, was, were*). *There* is never the subject in such constructions; usually it has no meaning and serves only as an introductory word, or expletive (see 21a1).

There *are* five basic positions in classical ballet. [The subject is *positions.*]

➤ Checking for subject-verb agreement

Underline each finite verb. Then identify the subject that corresponds to the verb. Read the two together to see if they sound right. For example, the sentence *The players on our side is sure to win* can be stripped down to a simple subject-verb *players is.* Bringing together the subject and verb in this way helps some writers to recognize agreement problems; here the verb should be *are: players are.* If, however, you find that you cannot trust your ear, you need to check each verb to see that it agrees with its subject.

EXERCISE 9.2

Revise any of the following sentences as necessary to establish subject-verb agreement. (Some of the sentences do not require any change.)

Example

Into the shadows dart the frightened raccoon.

Into the shadows *darts* the frightened raccoon.

1. Every check and money order cost 50 cents.
2. Talking and getting up from my seat was my crime.
3. If rhythm and blues is your kind of music, drive down Green Springs Highway to Mary Lou's.
4. His merry disposition and his recognized success in business make him popular in the community.
5. *The vapors* were a Victorian term for hypochondria.
6. Neither the lighting on the painting nor the wall it is hanging on display it well.
7. Child abuse is far more commonplace than anyone care to admit.
8. Most of the voters support a reduction in nuclear weapons.
9. Each of the players are dealt five cards to start the game.
10. Either his phony smile or his bragging seem to fool many people.

11. The team needs time to learn to cooperate with one another.
12. Her grandmother is the only one of her relatives who still goes to church.
13. The situation is not entirely hopeless, for some do see the light.
14. *Our Tapes* were one of Fitzgerald's earlier titles for *Tender Is the Night*.
15. Sweden was one of the few European countries that was neutral in 1943.
16. Politics have been defined as the art of the possible.
17. The short-term effect of the company's expansion were lower dividends.
18. Mumps cause swelling of the salivary glands.
19. In the foreground is two women playing musical instruments and singing.
20. Dr. Pangloss believes that everything that happen is for the best.

PRONOUN-ANTECEDENT AGREEMENT

Most pronouns function in sentences as replacements for nouns or other pronouns, known as their antecedents. Like a verb with its subject, a pronoun must agree with its antecedent in person and number. In addition, a third-person singular pronoun must agree with its antecedent in *gender*—masculine, feminine, or neuter. (See 6b3.)

Angry, *Mr. Blanchard* called in to say *he* was sick. [third-person singular, masculine]

The *workers* elected a representative to voice *their* common complaints. [third-person plural]

As with subject-verb agreement, only a few kinds of pronoun-antecedent constructions cause problems in practice, so we will look at those constructions in greater detail.

9j. Making pronouns agree with compound antecedents

A compound antecedent whose parts are joined by *and* requires a plural pronoun.

With great excitement, the children and I began *our* search for the perfect house.

Keith, Molly, and Jane hid behind Dad's chair, and nobody saw *them*.

When a compound antecedent is preceded by *each* or *every*, however, it takes a singular pronoun.

Every plant and animal has *its* own ecological niche.

A compound antecedent that refers to a single person or thing also takes a singular pronoun.

> The producer and director invested all of *her* savings in the film.

With a compound antecedent whose parts are joined by *or* or *nor*, the pronoun agrees with the nearest antecedent.

> Neither the players nor the owners will change *their* tactics.

> For us to win the meet, Marianne or Charlyce must win *her* next dive.

This kind of sentence, however, may be awkward if the parts of the antecedent are of different genders. Consider, for example, the following sentence:

> AWKWARD   For us to win the meet, Jim or Charlyce must win *her* next dive.

Such a sentence can be revised in a number of ways to eliminate the awkwardness.

> REVISED   For us to win the meet, Jim or Charlyce must win *his or her* next dive.

> REVISED   For us to win the meet, Jim must win *his* next dive, or Charlyce must win *hers*.

With compound antecedents containing both singular and plural parts, the sentence may sound awkward unless a plural part comes last.

> AWKWARD   Neither the Pointer Sisters nor Wayne Newton would disclose *his* income for 1985.

> REVISED   Neither Wayne Newton nor the Pointer Sisters would disclose *their* incomes for 1985.

9k. Making pronouns agree with collective-noun antecedents

When a collective-noun antecedent (*herd, team, committee, audience,* for example) refers to a single unit, it requires a singular pronoun.

> The audience fixed *its* attention on center stage.

> Finally, our team scored *its* first victory.

When such an antecedent refers to the individual parts of the unit, however, it requires a plural pronoun.

> The crew divided the loot among *themselves*.
>
> The director chose this cast because *they* had experience in the roles.

Remember that collective nouns referring to single units require not only singular pronouns but also singular verb forms. Collective nouns referring to separate individuals in a unit, on the other hand, require plural pronouns and plural verb forms.

> Each generation *has its* own slang. [*generation* as single unit]
>
> My generation *have* sold *their* souls for money. [*generation* as separate individuals]

9l. Making pronouns agree with indefinite-pronoun antecedents

A pronoun whose antecedent is an indefinite pronoun should agree with it in number. Indefinite pronouns may be always singular (as with *one*) or plural (as with *many*), or their number may depend on their context. (See 9e for a list.)

> One of the ballerinas lost *her* balance. [singular]
>
> Many in the audience jumped to *their* feet. [plural]
>
> All of the music was familiar to *its* listeners. [singular meaning for *all*]
>
> All of the principal dancers took *their* bows. [plural meaning for *all*]

9m. Avoiding sexism with pronouns

One somewhat complicated problem in pronoun-antecedent agreement involves a pronoun referring to a singular antecedent that may be either male or female. Look at the following passage:

> . . . the Country Club pool was small. One diving board, no spinning top. But its size only seemed to me to be a measure of its exclusiveness. *Whoever* had laid out plans for the Country Club was an entrepreneur with an eye for the one beautiful, rolling and wooded piece of land outside Ames. *He* must have known immediately that such an acreage had to be saved; *he* had a true aristocrat's instinct and converted it into a private preserve.   —SUSAN ALLEN TOTH, "Swimming Pools"

Notice that although the author apparently does not know who laid out the plans for the Country Club, she uses the pronoun *he* to refer to this person. In traditional English grammar, writers used masculine pronouns, known as the **generic he**, in such cases. In recent decades, however, many people have pointed out that such wording ignores or even excludes females—and thus should be avoided. There are several ways of avoiding the generic *he*. Consider, for example, the following sentence:

> Every citizen should know *his* rights under the law.

Now look at three ways to express the same idea without the *he*.

1. Every citizen should know *his or her* rights under the law.
2. All citizens should know *their* rights under the law.
3. Everyone should have some knowledge of basic legal rights.

As these examples show, you have three basic options: (1) using both masculine and feminine pronouns—*he or she, his or her,* and so forth; (2) revising into the plural; and (3) revising the sentence altogether. Keep in mind that overuse of *he or she* can be awkward.

When the antecedent is an indefinite pronoun (*anybody, both, each, few, neither, none, somebody,* see 6b3 for a more complete list), some people avoid the generic *he* by using a plural pronoun. For example:

> Everyone had *their* own theory about Marcia's resignation.

You will probably hear—and perhaps use—such sentences in conversation, but you should be careful about using them in writing. Although this usage is now gaining some acceptance, it is probably a good idea to talk to your instructor to see what he or she advises before using it in academic work. See 11c5 and 26b1 for more discussion of how to avoid sexist language.

> ## Checking for pronoun-antecedent agreement

Circle all pronouns, and then identify the antecedent of each one. Check to see that the pronoun agrees in person and number with its antecedent; if it does not, revise the pronoun accordingly. Look especially carefully at any compound antecedents (9j), indefinite-pronoun antecedents (9e and 9l), and collective-noun antecedents (9h) to see that the pronouns agree in both person and number.

EXERCISE 9.3

Revise the following sentences as necessary to create pronoun-antecedent agreement and to eliminate the generic *he* and any awkward pronoun references. Some of the sentences can be revised in more than one way, and some of them do not require any change.

> *Example*
> Every graduate submitted his diploma card.
> Every graduate submitted *his or her* diploma card.

1. With tuition on the rise, a student has to save money wherever they can.
2. Everyone does not get along with his roommate, but the two can usually manage to tolerate each other temporarily.
3. Congress usually resists presidential attempts to encroach on what they consider their authority.
4. Either Tom or Teresa would be willing to lend us her car.
5. If his own knowledge is all the reader has to go by, how can he identify one source as more reliable than another?
6. Every house and apartment has their advantages and their drawbacks.
7. Neither the scouts nor their leader knew their way out of the forest.
8. Our team no longer wears their red and white uniforms.
9. To create a positive impression, a candidate attempts to flood the media with favorable publicity about themselves.
10. Sometimes she turns on the bathroom fan and the infrared light and neglects to turn it off.

EXERCISE 9.4

Revise the following paragraph to create subject-verb and pronoun-antecedent agreement and to eliminate the generic *he*.

> By this time, most of us has heard from one source or another that an excess of salt in our diets are damaging to our health. Why, then, does recent statistics indicate that Americans are consuming as much salt as ever? First of all, few of us is aware of how much salt the average person consumes unnecessarily each day. Second, once we acquire a taste for salt, food begin to taste bland without it. Third, and perhaps most important, almost nobody realize what salt does to their bodies and why they should cut down on the excess. The American has to shake his salt habit.

READING WITH AN EYE FOR PRONOUNS

Following is the opening paragraph from *Democracy in America*, Alexis de Tocqueville's classic critique of American institutions and culture, which was first published in 1835. Read the paragraph with an eye for pronouns. Does the use of the masculine pronoun to refer to both men and women seem odd to you? Revise the paragraph to eliminate the use of masculine pronouns to refer to both men and women.

> After the birth of a human being, his early years are obscurely spent in the toils or pleasures of childhood. As he grows up, the world receives him, when his manhood begins, and he enters into contact with his fellows. He is then studied for the first time, and it is imagined that the germ of the vices and the virtues of his maturer years is then formed. This, if I am not mistaken, is a great error. We must begin higher up; we must watch the infant in his mother's arms; we must see the first images which the external world casts upon the dark mirror of his mind, the first occurrences which he witnesses; we must hear the first words which awaken the sleeping powers of thought, and stand by his earliest efforts,—if we would understand the prejudices, the habits, and the passions which will rule his life. The entire man is, so to speak, to be seen in the cradle of the child.
>
> —ALEXIS DE TOCQUEVILLE, *Democracy in America*

FOR EXAMINING YOUR OWN WRITING

In a paragraph or two, describe some "typical" person—a typical student at your school, a typical citizen in your hometown, a typical new parent, whatever. You might begin with the sentence "The typical _____ is. . . ." Then analyze your description for agreement—between subjects and verbs, of course, but especially between pronouns and their antecedents.

10. Using Adjectives and Adverbs

As words that describe other words, adjectives and adverbs add liveliness and color to the flat gray surface of writing, helping writers to *show* rather than just tell. Adjectives and adverbs allow us to show readers what we want them to see—to help them visualize objects, scenes, or even abstractions. See, for instance, how much Gretel Ehrlich relies on adjectives and adverbs in the following description of the cowboy.

> In our *hellbent* earnestness to romanticize the cowboy we've *ironically* disesteemed his *true* character. . . . Instead of the *macho, trigger-happy* man our culture has *perversely* wanted him to be, the cowboy is *more apt* to be *convivial, quirky,* and *softhearted.* . . .
> —GRETEL EHRLICH, "About Men"

Ehrlich could have said simply, "We have misrepresented the cowboy. He is not really so macho." But we would not be able to picture the cowboy and understand his image as we do in the passage above. Adjectives such as *convivial* and *soft-hearted* and adverbs such as *ironically* and *perversely* create a vivid image of the cowboy and evoke a definite impression of Ehrlich's own attitude about her subject.

Adjectives are particularly useful for conveying concrete and sensory details in physical descriptions. Look, for example, at the sensory adjectives Annie Dillard uses in describing a young copperhead snake.

> Although it lay in a *loose* sprawl, all I saw at first was a *camouflage* pattern of *particolored* splotches confused by the *rushing* speckles of light

in the weeds between us, and by the *deep twilight* dark of the quarry pond beyond the rock. Then suddenly the form of its head emerged from the confusion: *burnished brown, triangular, blunt* as a *stone* ax.

—ANNIE DILLARD, "The Copperhead and the Mosquito"

Adverbs can also make writing vivid or add emphasis to a point. In the following sentence, the qualifications provided by the adverbs carry the central idea:

After three years of torture, the man was found guilty—*legally, officially,* but *unjustly* found guilty.

The three adverbs build up to culminate in an accusation: the verdict is not a just one.

But if adjectives and adverbs can create many dramatic effects in writing, they can also "betray" a writer who uses them inappropriately. Like any other part of a sentence, they must follow certain rules and conventions. This chapter discusses some of these rules and conventions and common problems that writers have with adjectives and adverbs.

▌10a. Distinguishing adjectives from adverbs

Although adjectives and adverbs both modify other words, they each modify different parts of speech. **Adjectives** modify nouns and pronouns, answering the questions *which?, how many?,* and *what kind?* Many adjectives are formed by adding the suffixes *-able, -ful, -ish, -less* or *-y* to nouns and verbs.

Many customers wrote *angry* letters to *the* company.

His one comfortable chair is covered in *a colorful Spanish* fabric.

Participles and infinitives can also function as adjectives. (See 6c3.)

The *perplexed* clerk looked at me with a *questioning* expression.

Sandra could not decide which job *to take.*

Although adjectives usually precede the noun or pronoun they modify, they sometimes follow it instead. An adjective can also appear after a linking verb, as a subject complement that modifies the subject of the sentence or clause (see 6c2 and 10b).

227

Butler found the Victorian family *stifling*.

Chocolate is *irresistible* to Lee.

For information about when to capitalize adjectives, see 33b. For information about when to use commas between adjectives preceding a noun, see 27d.

Adverbs modify verbs, adjectives, and other adverbs; they answer the questions *how?*, *when?*, *where?*, or *to what extent?* Many adverbs are formed by adding *-ly* to adjectives.

The bride smiled *nervously*. [modifies the verb *smiled*]

She was *almost* ready. [modifies the adjective *ready*]

The guests had arrived *rather* early. [modifies the adverb *early*]

Adverbs can also modify an entire clause.

Fortunately, the rain had ended before the wedding.

Infinitives can function as adverbs. (See 6c3.)

Her sister hoped *to catch* the bouquet. [modifies the verb *hoped*]

While adjectives usually are closely tied to the words they modify, adverbs that modify verbs or clauses can often move easily from one position in a sentence to another.

Connor *gleefully* tore open his presents.

Connor tore open his presents *gleefully*.

Gleefully, Connor tore open his presents.

Since adjectives and adverbs both act as modifiers, often have similar forms, and can sometimes occupy the same positions in sentences, sometimes the only way of recognizing an adjective or an adverb is to identify its function in the sentence. Remember: adjectives modify *nouns* and *pronouns*, adverbs modify *verbs*, *adjectives*, and other *adverbs*.

EXERCISE 10.1

Read the following paragraph with an eye for the adjectives and adverbs. Identify each one, and determine which word each modifies.

The peacock does most of his serious strutting in the spring and summer when he has a full tail to do it with. Usually he begins shortly after breakfast, struts for several hours, desists in the heat of the day, and begins again in the late afternoon. Each cock has a favorite station where he performs every day in the hope of attracting some passing hen; but if I have found anyone indifferent to the peacock's display, besides the telephone lineman, it is the peahen. She seldom casts an eye at it. The cock, his tail raised in a shimmering arch around him, will turn this way and that, and with his clay-colored wing feathers touching the ground, will dance forward and backward, his neck curved, his beak parted, his eyes glittering. Meanwhile the hen goes about her business, diligently searching the ground as if any bug in the grass were of more importance than the unfurled map of the universe which floats nearby.

—FLANNERY O'CONNOR, "The King of the Birds"

▌ 10b. Using adjectives after linking verbs

Be careful to use adjectives, not the corresponding *-ly* adverbs, after linking verbs. The most frequently used linking verbs are forms of *be*, but they also include sensory verbs such as *look, appear, seem, sound, feel, smell,* and *taste* and verbs of becoming such as *become, grow, prove,* and *turn.* (See 6c2). When they function as linking verbs, they are always followed by adjectives (or nouns). Most of these verbs, however, can also be used to express action. When they express action, they can be followed by adverbs.

> The dog looked *hungry.* [linking verb with adjective]
>
> The dog looked *hungrily* at the steak. [action verb with adverb]

▌ 10c. Using adverbs to modify verbs, adjectives, and adverbs

Be careful to use adverbs, not adjectives, to modify verbs, adjectives, and other adverbs.

NOT	His writing style is *excessive* formal.
BUT	His writing style is *excessively formal.*

Good *and* well, bad *and* badly

The modifiers *good, well, bad,* and *badly* cause problems for many writers because the distinctions between *good* and *well* and between *bad* and *badly* are often not observed in conversation and because *well* can function as either an adjective or an adverb. Be careful to use the appropriate word in formal writing.

Good and *bad* are adjectives, and can be used after a linking verb.

Do not use them to modify a verb, an adjective, or an adverb; use *well* or *badly* instead.

> Amanda looks *good* in black.

> He felt *bad* about missing his father's retirement party.

NOT	He plays the trumpet *good* and the trombone not *bad*.
BUT	He plays the trumpet *well* and the trombone not *badly*.

Badly is an adverb and can be used to modify a verb, an adjective, or another adverb. Do not use it after a linking verb; use *bad* instead.

> In her first recital, the soprano sang *badly*.

NOT	The clams tasted *badly*.
BUT	The clams tasted *bad*.

Well can be either an adjective (meaning "in good health") or an adverb.

ADJECTIVE	After a week of rest Julio felt *well* again.
ADVERB	He cooks *well* enough to be a chef.

Real *and* really

Be careful also to observe the distinction between *real* and *really*. In conversation and informal writing, the adjective *real* is often used in place of the adverb *really*, but in formal and academic writing, use the adverb form.

INFORMAL	Most Americans were *real* shocked by the attack.
FORMAL	Most Americans were *really* shocked by the attack.

EXERCISE 10.2

Revise each of the following sentences to maintain correct adverb and adjective use. Then identify each adjective or adverb that you have revised, and point out the word each modifies.

> *Example*
> Their shocking bad behavior annoyed us.
> Their *shockingly* bad behavior annoyed us.

1. Honest lawyers are not complete obsessed with status or money.
2. Although the hero reacts negative to her in this episode, in the next he proposes marriage!

3. Hypochondriacs call a doctor whenever they feel badly.
4. Christmas Day was real cold, and it was raining heavy.
5. A politician's wardrobe is often careful chosen.
6. When fully grown, the silkworm stops eating good and spins its cocoon.
7. One soldier was wounded bad in the chest.
8. Computers have sure made a difference in Americans' lives.
9. On the new stereo, many of the records sounded differently.
10. They brought up their children very strict.

▌ 10d. Using comparatives and superlatives

In addition to their simple or positive form, many adjectives and adverbs have two other forms, the **comparative** and **superlative**, that are used for making comparisons.

POSITIVE	COMPARATIVE	SUPERLATIVE
large	larger	largest
early	earlier	earliest
careful	more careful	most careful
happily	more happily	most happily

Canada is *larger* than the United States

He promised to be *more careful* with his money.

They are the *most happily* married couple I know.

As these examples suggest, the comparative and superlative of most short (one-syllable and some two-syllable) adjectives are usually formed by adding the endings *-er* and *-est*. *More* and *most* are also used with short adjectives, however, and can sometimes create a more formal tone. The only ways to form the comparative and superlative of longer adjectives—three syllables or more—and of most adverbs is with *more* and *most*. If you are not sure whether an adjective or adverb has *-er* and *-est* forms, consult the dictionary entry for the simple form, where the *-er* and *-est* forms are usually listed if they exist.

▌ 1. Recognizing irregular forms

Some adjectives and adverbs have irregular comparative and superlative forms. Here is a list of them.

POSITIVE	COMPARATIVE	SUPERLATIVE
Adjectives		
good	better	best
well	better	best
bad	worse	worst
ill	worse	worst
little (quantity)	less	least
many	more	most
some	more	most
much	more	most
Adverbs		
well	better	best
ill	worse	worst
badly	worse	worst

▌ 2. Distinguishing between comparatives and superlatives

The comparative form of an adjective or adverb is used to compare two things. The superlative form is used to compare three or more things.

Rome is a much *older* city than New York.

Damascus is one of the *oldest* cities in the world.

In conversation, you will often hear the superlative form used even when only two things are being compared: *Of those two suits, the black one is the most becoming.* In academic or professional writing, however, be sure to use the comparative form: *Of those two suits, the black one is the more becoming.*

▌ 3. Checking for double comparatives and superlatives

Double comparatives and superlatives unnecessarily use both the *-er* or *-est* ending and *more* or *most*. When you edit an essay, check to make sure you have not used *more* or *most* before an adjective or adverb ending in *-er* or *-est*.

INCORRECT	Paris is the *most loveliest* city in the world.
REVISED	Paris is the *loveliest* city in the world.
INCORRECT	Rome lasted *more longer* than Carthage.
REVISED	Rome lasted *longer* than Carthage.

4. Checking for incomplete comparisons

In speaking, we sometimes use incomplete comparisons—ones that specify only one of the things being compared—because the context makes the rest of the comparison clear. If, after comparing an essay of yours to a classmate's essay, you say "Yours is better," the context makes it clear that you mean "Yours is better *than mine.*" In writing, that context may not exist. So take time when editing to check for incomplete comparisons—and to complete them if they are unclear.

INCOMPLETE	The patients taking the drug appeared *healthier.*
COMPLETE	The patients taking the drug appeared *healthier than those receiving a placebo.*
INCOMPLETE	Many musicians consider Mozart *the greatest.*
COMPLETE	Many musicians consider Mozart *the greatest of all composers.*

EXERCISE 10.3

Choose three of the following numbered words, and write a brief passage that uses the simple, comparative, and superlative forms of each one.

Example
frisky   friskier   friskiest

George adopted a small, *frisky* puppy named Brutus. Quickly, Brutus became even *friskier,* chasing neighbors and jumping on children. He was at his *friskiest* the day Aunt Victoria came to visit.

1. loudly 2. well (adverb) 3. wholesome 4. some 5. little
6. rare 7. good 8. thirsty 9. heavily 10. sarcastically

10e. Using nouns as modifiers

Sometimes a noun can function as an adjective by modifying another noun, as in the following examples:

chicken soup	control center	atom bomb	law school
money supply	space station	day care	rye bread

In familiar terms such as those listed above, we have no trouble understanding the meaning. In fact, a phrase like *chicken soup* is the most succinct and direct way of expressing the idea of soup made from chicken. If noun modifiers pile up, however, they can obscure meaning and should thus be revised.

> AWKWARD   The 1964 New York Kitty Genovese murder story prompted a number of articles and television specials.
>
> REVISED   The 1964 story of Kitty Genovese's murder in New York prompted a number of articles and television specials.

Here the string of nouns is broken up by turning one (*Kitty Genovese*) into a possessive and two (*murder* and *New York*) into objects of prepositions.

EXERCISE 10.4

Revise each of the following sentences to use modifiers correctly, clearly, and effectively. Many of the sentences can be revised in more than one way.

> *Example*
> The mayor is sponsoring a housing project finance plan approval bill.
> The mayor is sponsoring a bill to approve a financial plan for the housing project.

1. In the Macbeths' marriage, Lady Macbeth is presented as the most ambitious of the two.
2. The article argued that walking is more healthier than jogging.
3. St. Francis made Assisi one of the famousest towns in Italy.
4. Most of the elderly are women because women tend to live longer.
5. Minneapolis is the largest of the Twin Cities.
6. A University of Arizona Lunar and Planetary Laboratory research scientist agrees that mining asteroids may well prove economically important.
7. My graduation day will be the most happiest day of my life.
8. The student cafeteria is operated by a college food service system chain.
9. Japanese cars captured much of the American market because American consumers found they were more reliable.
10. I think *Oedipus Rex* is a successfuler play than *The Sandbox*.

EXERCISE 10.5

Read the following passage, from which most adjectives and adverbs have been removed. Fill the blanks with adjectives or adverbs that seem effective and appropriate to you. Then compare your version with those of other students and with the original version printed in your instructor's copy of this text.

What Elvis demanded for his travels was a flying hotel suite. The forward cabin is a very plushy, _____ _____ club room, furnished with

_____ _____ _____ _____ sofas covered with
_____ cushions of _____ velour, one _____, the other
_____ _____. The _____ _____ carpet catches
the light from the _____ ceiling, which is padded with
_____ _____ vinyl.   —ALBERT GOLDMAN, "Graceland".

READING WITH AN EYE FOR ADJECTIVES AND ADVERBS

Find some examples of adjectives and adverbs that you consider noteworthy.
You might look anywhere—in essays, short stories, newspaper editorials, your
own journal. Copy down five examples, and comment in writing on why they
impress you as so effective. What do they add to the larger piece of writing?
What would be lost if they were removed?

FOR EXAMINING THE ADJECTIVES AND
ADVERBS IN YOUR OWN WRITING

Think of something you can observe or examine closely, and take a few minutes
to study it. In a paragraph or two, describe your subject for someone who has
never seen it. Identify all the adjectives and adverbs in your description, and
list two possible synonyms for each one. Would changing any of these modifiers
strengthen your description? Are there any places where you could make it
more specific or vivid by adding an adjective or adverb? Do you see any adjectives or adverbs that are not really necessary or that do not create exactly
the image you intend? Revise the description with such considerations in mind.

PART THREE

Sentences: Making Conventional Choices

11. Maintaining Clear Pronoun Reference

In writing, one of your key responsibilities to your readers is making sure that any pronouns refer clearly to their antecedents. Clear pronoun reference oils the wheels of good prose, helping avoid unnecessary repetition and moving a passage along easily, as in the following paragraph:

> *He* was crude, certainly, my Uncle Jake; *he* was coarse, of course; gross, it goes without saying; uncouth, beyond question. But was *he* vulgar? I don't think *he* was. For one thing, *he* was good-hearted, and it somehow seems wrong to call anyone vulgar who is good-hearted. But more to the point, I don't think that if you had accused *him* of being vulgar, *he* would have known what the devil you were talking about. To be vulgar requires at least a modicum of pretension, and this Uncle Jake sorely lacked.   —JOSEPH EPSTEIN, "What Is Vulgar?"

If you read the paragraph again, repeating *Uncle Jake* in place of every *he* and *him,* you can see for yourself how useful these pronouns can be. Now look what happens if another uncle is added to the story:

> *He* was crude, certainly, my Uncle Jake, and my Uncle Alfred was sloppy; *he* was coarse, of course. . . .

In this instance, the reference for the first *he* is clear, because it is followed by *Uncle Jake.* But what about the second *he*—does it refer to Uncle Jake, or to Uncle Alfred?

This chapter will alert you to ways of avoiding such problems in your own writing by maintaining clear pronoun reference.

11a. Matching pronouns to their appropriate antecedents

If more than one possible antecedent for a personal pronoun appears in a sentence or passage, a pronoun must refer unambiguously to only *one* of them.

> AMBIGUOUS   The meeting between Bowman and Sonny makes *him* compare *his* own unsatisfying domestic life with one that is emotionally secure and involved.

> CLEAR   The meeting between Bowman and Sonny makes *Bowman* compare *his* own unsatisfying domestic life with one that is emotionally secure and involved.

> CLEAR   Meeting Sonny makes *Bowman* compare *his* own unsatisfying domestic life with one that is emotionally secure and involved.

> CLEAR   After meeting Sonny, whose domestic life is emotionally secure and involved, *Bowman* finds *his* own domestic life unsatisfying.

In the ambiguous sentence, readers cannot tell whether Bowman or Sonny is the antecedent of *him* and *his*. All three revisions make the reference clear. The first does so by replacing a pronoun (*him*) with a noun (*Bowman*), but it requires repeating the noun. The second alternative eliminates one of the pronouns, and the third recasts the sentence altogether.

If you are reporting what someone else said, check carefully for clear pronoun reference. In the sentence *Karen told Ellen she should be ready soon*, readers cannot be sure which of the two people should be ready because *she* does not clearly relate to one or the other. Such a sentence can be revised by quoting directly to make clear who is saying what, or it can be reworded to eliminate the ambiguity.

> Karen told Ellen to be ready soon.

> Karen told Ellen, "I should be ready soon."

> Karen told Ellen, "You should be ready soon."

11b. Keeping pronouns and antecedents close together

If a pronoun is too far from its antecedent, readers will have trouble making the connection between the two. Maintaining clear reference calls for keeping pronouns and their antecedents in close proximity.

CONFUSING   The right-to-life coalition believes that a zygote, an egg at the moment of fertilization, is as deserving of protection as is the born human being, and thus that abortion is as much murder as is the killing of a child. The coalition's focus is on what *it* will become, a conscious being with reasoning power, a sense of self, and the capacity to communicate, as much as on what *it* is now.

CLEAR   The right-to-life coalition believes that a *zygote*, an egg at the moment of fertilization, is as deserving of protection as is the born human being, and thus that abortion is as much murder as is the killing of a child. The coalition's focus is on what *the zygote* will become, a conscious being with reasoning power, a sense of self, and the capacity to communicate, as much as on what *it* is now.

EXERCISE 11.1

Revise each of the following items to clarify pronoun reference. All of the items can be revised in more than one way. If a pronoun refers ambiguously to more than one possible antecedent, revise the sentence in at least two different ways, reflecting each possible meaning.

Example
While Melinda was away, Sheila found the ring she had lost.
While Melinda was away, the ring she had lost was found by Sheila.
Sheila found Melinda's lost ring while Melinda was away.
Sheila found her lost ring while Melinda was away.

1. Anna smiled at her mother as she opened the birthday package.
2. Lear divides his kingdom between the two older daughters, Goneril and Regan, whose extravagant professions of love are more flattering than the simple affection of the youngest daughter, Cordelia. The consequences of this error in judgment soon become apparent, as they prove neither grateful nor kind to him.
3. In many cases of child abuse, especially when the parents totally ignore their children, they eventually become criminals.
4. New England helped to shape many aspects of American culture, including education, religion, and government. As New Englanders moved west, they carried its institutions with them.
5. Leroy went to the races with George because he was feeling lonely.

6. Jimmie told Allen that his mother was ill.
7. After Ms. Callahan hired Patricia for the job, she felt relieved.
8. When drug therapy is combined with psychotherapy, the patients relate better to their therapists, are less vulnerable to what disturbs them, and are more responsive to them.
9. Not long after the company set up the subsidiary, it went bankrupt.
10. If guns cause crimes, outlaw them.

▮ 11c. Recognizing troublesome pronoun references

Matching a pronoun to one specific antecedent and keeping pronouns and antecedents close together will take you a long way toward establishing clear pronoun reference. A few pronouns, however, cause particular problems for writers. The sections that follow provide practice in checking to see that these pronouns are used clearly and properly.

▮ 1. Checking for vague and ambiguous use of *it, this, that,* and *which*

Writers are often tempted to use *it, this, that,* or *which* as a kind of shortcut, a quick and easy way of referring to something mentioned earlier. But such shortcuts can often cause confusion. Make sure that these pronouns refer clearly to a specific antecedent.

VAGUE — The Engineering Society sponsored a charity drive last week, and students responded enthusiastically. *It* really surprised us. [What does *it* refer to—the fact that the Engineering Society sponsored a charity drive, that students responded enthusiastically, or perhaps both?]

CLEAR — The Engineering Society sponsored a charity drive last week, and students responded enthusiastically. *The response* really surprised us.

VAGUE — The art of rhetoric was created in the ancient world in response to the economic and political need for a fair method of property redistribution. Corax devised the first known system for *this*. [For what, exactly—creating rhetoric? redistributing property?]

CLEAR — Rhetoric was created in the ancient world out of the economic and political need for a fair method of property redistribution. Corax devised the first *such method* known.

AMBIGUOUS   I am taking a course in Romantic poetry, *which* has been the bane of my existence. [What does *which* refer to—the course or the poetry?]

CLEAR   I am taking a course in Romantic poetry, *a kind of literature* that has been the bane of my existence.

CLEAR   I am taking a course in Romantic poetry, *a class* that has been the bane of my existence.

If *that* or *which* opens a clause that refers to a specific noun, put *that* or *which* directly after the noun, if possible.

AMBIGUOUS   We worked all night on the float for the Rose Parade *that* our club was going to sponsor. [Does *that* refer to the float or the Rose Parade?]

CLEAR   We worked all night on the float *that* our club was going to sponsor for the Rose Parade.

2. Checking for appropriate use of *who, which,* and *that*

Be careful to use the relative pronouns *who, which,* and *that* appropriately. *Who* refers primarily to people or to animals with names. *Which* refers to animals or to things, and *that* refers to animals, things, and anonymous persons or people treated collectively. (See 27c for information about the use of commas with clauses beginning with *who, which,* and *that.*)

Stephen Jay Gould, *who* has won many awards for his writing about science, teaches at Harvard.

The whale, *which* has only one baby a year, is subject to extinction because it does not reproduce quickly.

People *that* support animal rights oppose laboratory experimentation with animals.

People *who* support animal rights oppose laboratory experimentation with animals.

3. Checking for indefinite use of *you* and *they*

In conversation, we frequently use *you* and *they* in an indefinite sense, as in such expressions as *you never know* and *on television they said*. In college and professional writing, however, such constructions are inappropriately informal and often unnecessarily wordy. Be careful to use *you* only to mean "you, the reader," and *they* only to refer to a clear antecedent.

INAPPROPRIATE	Television commercials try to make *you* buy without thinking.
REVISED	Television commercials try to make *viewers* buy without thinking.
INAPPROPRIATE	In France *they* allow dogs in most restaurants.
REVISED	Most restaurants in France allow dogs.

4. Checking to see that antecedents are nouns or pronouns, not adjectives or possessives

In conversation, a pronoun often refers to an antecedent that is an adjective or the possessive form of a noun. In writing, an antecedent must always be a noun or pronoun in the subjective case.

INAPPROPRIATE	In Welty's story, *she* characterizes Bowman as a man unaware of his own isolation.
REVISED	In her story, Welty characterizes Bowman as a man unaware of his own isolation.
REVISED	In Welty's story, Bowman is characterized as a man unaware of his own isolation.

5. Checking for sexist pronoun usage

Remember to avoid using masculine pronouns to refer to antecedents that include or may include both males and females. For example, the sentence *Every attorney values his client's testimony* implies that only men are attorneys. Such a sentence can be revised in several ways: by eliminating the pronoun, by using both masculine and feminine pronouns, or by shifting to the plural. A more complete discussion of nonsexist pronoun usage can be found in 9m.

Every attorney values *a* client's testimony.

Every attorney values *his or her* client's testimony.

All attorneys value *their* clients' testimonies.

➤ Checking for vague pronoun reference

Circle all pronouns, and draw an arrow from each one to its antecedent. Look especially at *this, that, which,* and *it* to be sure you can relate them to a specific word in the same sentence. If you cannot find an antecedent in the sentence, revise by replacing the pronoun with a noun or by supplying an antecedent to which the pronoun clearly refers. Next look to see if the pronoun could relate to more than one antecedent. If so, revise by replacing the pronoun with the appropriate noun or by rewriting the sentence so that the pronoun can refer to only one possible antecedent.

EXERCISE 11.2

Revise the following sentences to establish clear and appropriate pronoun reference, and to eliminate any sexist pronoun usage. Most of the sentences can be revised in more than one way.

> ### Example
> It says in the newspaper to expect rain today.
> The newspaper says to expect rain today.

1. On the turnpike they charge very high prices for gasoline.
2. In Texas, you often hear about the influence of big oil corporations on political candidates.
3. They said on the radio that somebody had won the lottery.
4. A friend of mine recently had a conversation with a Vietnam veteran that changed his view of the war.
5. She dropped off a friend which had gone to the party with her.
6. Not only was the chair delivered three weeks late, but the store told me this was normal.
7. I take care not to get too bundled up in the winter because it will be too hot when you are indoors.
8. The company had a policy prohibiting smoking, which many employees resented.
9. I called as soon as the catalog arrived, but they were already sold out of the leather moccasins.
10. Every doctor can count on making his fortune within ten years of graduation.

READING WITH ATTENTION TO PRONOUN REFERENCE

The following poem depends on its title to supply the antecedent for the pronouns that follow and that knit the poem together. Read the poem out loud, and then provide its one-word title. How did you know what the title should be? Then try writing a poem of your own (perhaps three or four verses) like this one, using pronouns and other words to give "clues" to your title.

His art is eccentricity, his aim
How not to hit the mark he seems to aim at,

His passion how to avoid the obvious,
His technique how to vary the avoidance.

The others throw to be comprehended. He
Throws to be a moment misunderstood.

Yet not too much. Not too errant, arrant, wild,
But every seeming aberration willed.

Not to, yet still, still to communicate
Making the batter understand too late.

                                    —ROBERT FRANCIS

FOR EXAMINING PRONOUN REFERENCE
IN YOUR OWN WRITING

Write a paragraph or two describing two favorite aunts—or two people or animals of the same sex. Then analyze your use of pronouns. Have you used any pronouns that do not refer clearly and directly to the correct antecedent? Any whose antecedents could be ambiguous? Using the guidelines shown in this chapter, revise as necessary.

12. Recognizing Shifts

A **shift** in writing is, most simply, an abrupt change of some sort that results in inconsistency. Consider, for example, the very famous opening lines of *The Adventures of Huckleberry Finn:*

> You don't know about me without you have read a book by the name of *The Adventures of Tom Sawyer;* but that ain't no matter. That book was made by Mr. Mark Twain, and he told the truth, mainly. There was things which he stretched, but mainly he told the truth.

Now replace the last sentence with this one: *On occasion Mr. Twain has been known to utter falsehoods; nevertheless, he did in this instance show proper respect for factuality.* As readers, we would be jolted and no doubt confused by such a shift in tone, from exaggerated informality to almost straightlaced formality.

Such a shift, because it is so blatant, is hard to miss. This chapter will help you to recognize shifts that are a bit more subtle and will offer strategies for revising to eliminate them. These include shifts in the tense, mood, and voice of verbs; in the person and number of pronouns; from direct to indirect discourse; and in tone and diction. If you have had such shifts pointed out in your writing, take the time to make checking for and revising shifts a regular part of your writing process.

▮ 12a. Recognizing shifts in tense

If the verbs in a sentence or passage refer to actions occurring at different times, they may require different tenses: *Mac <u>started</u> the kennel because he <u>had</u> always <u>loved</u> dogs.* Be careful, however, not to change tenses unnecessarily or in a way that does not make sense. Look, for instance, at this sentence: *Clarissa* yowled *until her owner* looks up. The shift in tenses from past to present confuses readers, who are left to guess which tense is the correct one.

INCONSISTENT	A very few countries *produce* most of the world's illegal drugs, but drug addiction *affected* many more countries.
REVISED	A very few countries *produce* most of the world's illegal drugs, but drug addiction *affects* many more countries.
INCONSISTENT	Some people never really *settle* down to a profession. In fact, such people *have found* jobs only when they *needed* food or shelter.
REVISED	Some people never really *settle* down to a profession. In fact, such people *find* jobs only when they *need* food or shelter.

See Chapter 8 for a complete discussion of verb tense.

> ## Checking for unnecessary shifts in tense

Because we deliberately—and necessarily— shift back and forth among tenses all the time, it can be difficult to spot tense shifts that are not logically consistent. If you have problems with shifts, try circling all the verbs in a draft and then checking carefully any shifts from one tense to another, *both within a sentence and between sentences.* Any time a shift occurs, check to be sure that it is logically consistent. You might even find it helpful to chart out verbs in timeline fashion.

EXERCISE 12.1

Revise any of the following sentences in which you find unnecessary shifts in verb tense. Most of the sentences can be revised in more than one way.

Example
The local newspaper covers campus events, but it did not appeal to many student readers.

The local newspaper *covers* campus events, but it *does not appeal* to many student readers.

1. The day is hot, stifling, and typical of July, a day when no one willingly ventured out onto the burning asphalt.

2. Then, suddenly, the big day arrives. The children were still a bit sleepy, for their anticipation had kept them awake.
3. The importance of music to society is evident throughout the entire magazine. A good example was the first advertisement.
4. A cloud of snow powder rose as skis and poles fly in every direction.
5. After fitness became popular in the 1970s, all of a sudden there are fewer and fewer fleshy Americans parked in front of their television sets.

▌ 12b. Recognizing shifts in mood

Be careful not to shift from one mood to another without reason. The mood of a verb can be indicative (*He* _closes_ *the door*), imperative (_Close_ *the door*), or subjunctive (*If the door* _were closed_, . . .). (See Chapter 8 for a discussion of mood.)

INCONSISTENT	*Keep* your eye on the ball, and you *should bend* your knees. [shift from imperative to indicative]
REVISED	*Keep* your eye on the ball, and *bend* your knees.
INCONSISTENT	The counselor asked that Rhonda *tutor* the Laotian children in English and that she *teaches* them some American games as well. [shift from subjunctive to indicative]
REVISED	The counselor asked that Rhonda *tutor* the Laotian children in English and that she *teach* them some American games as well.

EXERCISE 12.2

Revise the following sentences to eliminate any unnecessary shifts in mood.

Example

Walk over to the field house, and then you should get in line.

Walk over to the field house, and then get in line.

1. Place a test strip on the subject area; you should expose the test strip to light and develop it for two and a half minutes.
2. I think it is better that Grandfather die painlessly, bravely, and with dignity than that he continues to live in terrible physical pain.
3. Whether women be homemakers or are business executives, they deserve respect.
4. The consultant recommended that the candidates tell more jokes and that they should smile more during their speeches.
5. Say no to drugs, and you should consider alcohol a drug, too!

■ 12c. Recognizing shifts in voice

Do not shift unnecessarily between the active voice (*She sold the furniture*) and the passive voice (*The furniture was sold*). Sometimes a shift in voice is perfectly justified. In the sentence *I am known for being unpredictable and adventurous, but I consider myself a practical person,* the shift from passive (*am known*) to active (*consider*) allows the writer to keep the emphasis on the subject *I*. Making both verbs active (*People know me as an unpredictable and adventurous person, but I consider myself a practical person*) changes the focus of the sentence. Often, however, shifts in voice merely confuse readers. (See Chapter 8.)

INCONSISTENT	After we finished decorating the house, it was photographed by us.
REVISED	After we finished decorating the house, we photographed it.
INCONSISTENT	Four youngsters approached him, and he was asked to buy a raffle ticket.
REVISED	Four youngsters approached him and asked him to buy a raffle ticket.

EXERCISE 12.3

Revise each of the following sentences that contains an unnecessary shift in voice. One of the sentences does not require any change.

Example

Although she enjoys rock music, jazz is preferred by her.

Although she enjoys rock music, she prefers jazz.

1. I call it smooth, but it is seen as sneaky and devious by my parents.
2. Once these shells housed creatures; now they are crushed by the waves.
3. When someone says "roommate" to a high school senior bound for college, thoughts of no privacy and potential fights are conjured up.
4. The first thing that is seen as we start down the slope is a large green banner.
5. The physician moves the knee around to observe the connections of the cartilage and ligaments, and a fluid is injected into the joint.

■ 12d. Recognizing shifts in person and number

Do not shift unnecessarily between first person (*I, we*), second person (*you*), and third person (*he, she, it, one,* or *they*) or between singular and plural. Such shifts in person and number create confusion.

INCONSISTENT	One can do well in college if *you* budget *your* time carefully.
REVISED	One can do well in college if *one* budgets *one's* time carefully.
REVISED	You can do well in college if *you* budget *your* time carefully.
INCONSISTENT	*Nurses* are paid much less than doctors, even though *a nurse* has the primary responsibility for daily care of patients.
REVISED	*Nurses* are paid much less than doctors, even though *nurses* have the primary responsibility for daily care of patients.

Many shifts in number are actually problems with pronoun-antecedent agreement (see 9j–9m).

INCONSISTENT	I have difficulty seeing another *person's* position, especially if *their* opinion contradicts mine.
REVISED	I have difficulty seeing another *person's* position, especially if *his or her* opinion contradicts mine.
REVISED	I have difficulty seeing other *people's* positions, especially if *their* opinions contradict mine.

➤ Checking for unnecessary shifts in pronoun

To check a draft for illogical pronoun shifts, try circling all the pronouns and then drawing a line from pronoun to pronoun watching for shifts. Look especially at the pronouns *I, you,* and *one* to see that you don't shift among them interchangeably. If you do have problems with pronoun shifts, keep a list of your mistakes, see if they fall into any predictable patterns, and then proofread especially for them.

EXERCISE 12.4

Revise each of the following sentences to eliminate any unnecessary shifts in person or number. Some of the sentences can be revised in more than one way. Be prepared to explain your answers.

Example

When a person goes to college, you face many new situations.

When a person goes to college, he or she faces many new situations.

When you go to college, you face many new situations.

When people go to college, they face many new situations.

1. Suddenly we heard an explosion of wings off to our right, and you could see a hundred or more ducks lifting off the water.
2. Workers with computer skills were in great demand, and a programmer could almost name their salary.
3. I liked the sense of individualism, the crowd yelling for you, and the feeling that I was in command.
4. New parents often find it hard to adjust to having a baby around; you can't just get up and go someplace.
5. A person needs to feel that they are respected by others to perform well in a leadership position.

12e. Recognizing shifts between direct and indirect discourse

When you quote someone's exact words, setting them off in quotation marks, you are using **direct discourse.** On the other hand, when you summarize or report what someone has said (rather than quote the exact words), you are using **indirect discourse.**

DIRECT   Ambrose Bierce defined *love* as "a temporary insanity curable by marriage."

INDIRECT   Ambrose Bierce said that love is a temporary form of madness that can be cured by marriage.

Do not shift between direct and indirect discourse in the same sentence. Use *either* direct or indirect discourse throughout.

INCONSISTENT   Chief Seattle *said* that one nation *followed* another like the waves of the sea and therefore "regret is useless."

REVISED   Chief Seattle said that "nation follows nation, like the waves of the sea" and that therefore "regret is useless."

REVISED   Chief Seattle said that one nation followed another like the waves of the sea and that therefore feeling sad was useless.

EXERCISE 12.5

Revise each of the following sentences to eliminate the shifts between direct and indirect discourse by putting the direct discourse into indirect form.

Example

Nathaniel Hawthorne once stated that there was nothing he preferred to "my own solitude."

Nathaniel Hawthorne once stated that there was nothing he preferred to his own solitude.

1. Loren Eiseley feels an urge to join the birds in their soundless flight, but in the end he knows that he cannot, and "I was, after all, only a man."
2. According to the article, the ozone layer is rapidly dwindling, and "we are endangering the lives of future generations."
3. The instructor told us, "Please read the next two stories before the next class" and that she might give us a quiz on them.
4. Oscar Wilde wrote that books cannot be divided into moral and immoral categories, and "books are either well-written or badly written."
5. Richard Rodriguez acknowledged that intimacy was not created by a language; "it is created by intimates."

■ 12f. Recognizing shifts in tone and diction

Tone in writing refers to the way the writer's attitude toward the topic and/or audience comes across to the audience. (See 3g4.) Tone is closely related to **diction,** or word choice—not only the choice of individual words, but the overall level of formality, technicality, or other effects created by the individual words. Within a sentence, a paragraph, or an entire piece of writing, be careful not to change your tone or level of diction unless you have a reason for doing so. (See Chapters 25 and 26 for a complete discussion of diction and tone.)

Tone

When they are used for emphasis or humor, shifts in tone can be effective. Mark Twain was a master of such shifts. In the following passage, he presents a mock graduation address, "Advice to Youth," beginning with a serious tone and then shifting at the beginning of the second paragraph to characteristic humor:

> Being told I would be expected to talk here, I inquired what sort of a talk I ought to make. They said it should be something suitable to youth—something didactic, instructive, or something in the nature of good advice. Very well. I have a few things in my mind which I have often longed to say for the instruction of the young; for it is in one's tender early years that such things will best take root and be most enduring and most valuable. First, then, I will say to you, my young friends—and I say it beseechingly, urgingly—

> Always obey your parents, when they are present. This is the best policy in the long run, because if you don't they will make you. Most parents think they know better than you do, and you can generally make more by humoring that superstition than you can by acting on your own better judgment.   —MARK TWAIN, "Advice to Youth"

Twain opens with a flowery, slightly pompous tone with references to the "instruction of the young" and "one's tender early years." With the adverbs *beseechingly, urgingly,* he seems about to launch into a stereo-typically high-flown "leaders of tomorrow" commencement speech. Abruptly, however, he overturns readers' expectations in the second paragraph, to deliver his subversive advice in brisk, plain language. The only "formal" phrase in this paragraph, *humoring that superstition,* only highlights and contributes to the informal comic tone.

Unintended shifts in tone, on the other hand, confuse readers and leave them wondering what the writer's real attitude is. In the following passage, notice how the tone shifts in the last sentence:

> The question of child care forces a society to make profound decisions about its economic values. Can most families with young children actually live adequately on only one salary? If some conservatives had their way, June Cleaver would still be stuck in the kitchen baking cookies for the Beaver and waiting for Ward to bring home the bacon, except that with only one income the Cleavers would be lucky to afford hot dogs.

The first two sentences of this passage set a serious, formal tone, discussing child care in fairly general, abstract terms, but in the third sentence the writer shifts suddenly to a sarcastic attack based on references to television characters. Readers cannot tell whether the writer is presenting a serious analysis of the child-care issue or a passionate argument about a hotly debated topic. See how the passage was revised to make the tone consistent.

> The question of child care forces a society to make profound decisions about its economic values. Can most families with young children actually live adequately on only one salary? Some conservatives believe that women with young children should not work outside the home, but many are forced to do so for financial reasons.

Diction

Like shifts in tone, inappropriate shifts in level of diction can confuse readers. In general, diction may be classified as technical (*Araucaria araucama* instead of *monkey puzzle tree*), informal or colloquial (*Give me a ring if there's anything I can do*), formal, (*Please inform me if I can be of further assistance*), or slang (*He used to be a real jock, but now he's a couch potato*). In the following sentences, the diction shifts from formal to highly informal, giving an odd, disjointed feeling to the passage:

INCONSISTENT   The law enabled illegal aliens who had entered the United States before 1982 and resided there continuously to obtain legal status and citizenship. But folks who'd hopped a plane for home since the beginning of 1982 were up the creek.

REVISED   The law enabled illegal aliens who had entered the United States before 1982 and resided there continuously to obtain legal status and citizenship. But aliens who had left the United States since the beginning of 1982 were not eligible.

READING WITH AN EYE FOR SHIFTS

Read the following passages carefully, noting any shifts in tone and diction. Then revise them for consistency.

1. Lately, I have been bugged because there are not enough cashiers on each shift. We cashiers attempt to ring the customer's orders through quickly and efficiently, but sometimes we make a few mistakes, and the customers get mad that we are messing up their bills. Some people are very mean and sarcastic toward us, and, of course, we cannot protest. Repressing my feelings is the most frustrating thing about this job. The customers complain about high prices, too, something over which we have no control. In short, it is difficult to work in such a high-pressure atmosphere. Cashiering is a hard job; we deserve more respect than we normally get.

2. In *The Great Gatsby*, the rich and poor alike can harbor malevolence. For instance, Myrtle Wilson is unkind to her husband primarily because he is poor. To Myrtle, the rich are better people, so she becomes a rich man's mistress. Her lover, Tom Buchanan, is filthy rich, but he smacks the living daylights out of Myrtle. Hey, there must be a message here!

FOR EXAMINING YOUR OWN WRITING FOR SHIFTS

Think of a well-known person you admire and find an article about that person. Then write a paragraph or two about him or her, making a point of using direct quotations and of reporting in your own words statements made by that person. Using the guidelines in 12e, check your writing for any inappropriate shifts between direct and indirect discourse, and revise as necessary.

13. Identifying Comma Splices and Fused Sentences

The terms *comma splice* and *fused sentence* grow out of metaphors based on the words *splice* and *fuse*. In grammatical terms, a **comma splice** occurs when two independent clauses are joined with only a comma; a **fused sentence,** when two independent clauses are joined with no punctuation or connecting word between them.

SPLICE   It was already spring, the tulips were in bloom.

FUSED   It was already spring the tulips were in bloom.

Comma splices and fused sentences can be problematical, for though both are considered "errors," we see them frequently in literary and journalistic writing. Like many other structures we commonly identify as "errors," each can be used to powerful effect.

E. M. Forster, for instance, is known as a careful and correct stylist, yet he often deviates from the "correct" to create special effects. Look, for example, at the following passage from his essay about the 1937 Paris Exhibition:

> . . . For the Soviet Pavilion . . . is trying . . . to dodge money and to wipe away the film of coins and notes which keeps forming on the human retina. One of the evils of money is that it tempts us to look at it rather than at the things that it buys. They are dimmed because of the metal and the paper through which we receive them. That is the fundamental deceitfulness of riches, which kept worrying Christ. That is the treachery of the purse, the wallet and the bank-balance, even from the capitalist point of view. *They were invented as a convenience to the flesh, they have become a chain for the spirit.*
>
> —E. M. FORSTER, "The Last Parade"

Forster uses a comma splice in the last sentence to emphasize parallel ideas; any conjunction, even *and*, would change the causal relationship he wishes to show. The effect is to stop us in our tracks as readers—because the grammar is unexpected, it attracts just the attention that Forster wants for his statement.

In your college writing, you will seldom if ever wish to focus attention on sentences in this particular way. In fact, doing so will almost always be identified not as a means of creating emphasis or special effect but as an error. This chapter aims to help you learn to recognize comma splices and fused sentences in your own writing and provides five methods of revising to eliminate them.

➤ Checking for comma splices
   and fused sentences

Go through your draft, underlining every independent clause. Then go through again looking for places where independent clauses fall one after the other. Look at what comes between any two independent clauses. If you find only a comma (without any other word), you have identified a comma splice. If you find nothing at all between the two clauses, you have identified a fused sentence. In either case, you can revise according to any one of the five methods described in this chapter.

Five methods of eliminating comma splices
and fused sentences

13a. Revise by separating the clauses into two sentences
13b. Revise by linking the clauses with a semicolon
13c. Revise by linking the clauses with a comma and a coordinating conjunction
13d. Revise by recasting the two clauses as *one* independent clause
13e. Revise by recasting one of the independent clauses as a dependent clause

As a writer, you must decide which method to use in revising—or avoiding—comma splices and fused sentences. The choice requires looking at the sentences before and after the ones you are revising, to see how a particular method will affect the rhythm of the passage, and perhaps reading the passage aloud to see how the revision will sound. You will have an opportunity to practice such decision-making in exercises in this chapter.

▌ 13a. Separating the clauses into two sentences

The simplest way to revise comma splices or fused sentences is to separate them into two sentences.

COMMA SPLICE	Emma encourages Harriet to reject a proposal from a young farmer and to expect one from Mr. Elton, her interference soon leads to embarrassment.
FUSED SENTENCE	Emma encourages Harriet to reject a proposal from a young farmer and to expect one from Mr. Elton her interference soon leads to embarrassment.
REVISED	Emma encourages Harriet to reject a proposal from a young farmer and to expect one from Mr. Elton. Her interference soon leads to embarrassment.

Although this method may be the simplest, it is not always the most appropriate. In the preceding example, choosing to divide the two independent clauses into two separate sentences makes good sentence sense: the combined sentences contain twenty-four words, and dividing them into two sentences of eighteen and six words adds emphasis to the last six words by putting them in a sentence of their own. If the two spliced or fused clauses are very short, however, dividing them into two separate sentences may not succeed so well.

COMMA SPLICE	Emma gives Harriet advice about marriage proposals, she soon regrets having done so.
FUSED SENTENCE	Emma gives Harriet advice about marriage proposals she soon regrets having done so.
REVISED	Emma gives Harriet advice about marriage proposals. She soon regrets having done so.

Here the two short sentences in a row, both opening with the subject, sound abrupt and overly terse, and some other method of revision would probably be preferable. (See Chapter 20.)

▌ 13b. Linking the clauses with a semicolon

If the ideas in the two independent clauses in a comma splice or fused sentence are closely related and you want to give them equal emphasis, link them with a semicolon.

COMMA SPLICE	This photograph is not at all realistic, it uses dreamlike images to convey its message.

FUSED SENTENCE	This photograph is not at all realistic it uses dreamlike images to convey its message.
REVISED	This photograph is not at all realistic; it uses dreamlike images to convey its message.

In the preceding example, the second independent clause elaborates on and gives a reason for the statement in the first independent clause: it offers evidence that the photograph is not at all realistic. Because the two independent clauses are closely related and of equal importance, linking them with a semicolon represents a sound choice.

13c. Linking the clauses with a comma and a coordinating conjunction

For comma splices and fused sentences in which the two clauses are fairly closely related and equally important, another alternative for revision is to use a comma and a coordinating conjunction: *and, but, or, nor, for, so,* or *yet.* Using a coordinating conjunction helps to indicate what kind of link exists between the ideas in the two clauses. For instance, *but* and *yet* signal opposition or contrast (*I am strong, but she is stronger*); *for* and *so* signal cause-effect relationships (*The cabin was bitterly cold, so we built a fire*).

COMMA SPLICE	Windows were opened to the warm night air, furnaces were turned off for the season.
FUSED SENTENCE	Windows were opened to the warm night air furnaces were turned off for the season.
REVISED	Windows were opened to the warm night air, *and* furnaces were turned off for the season.

In the preceding example, two acts simply occur in conjunction with each other; thus *and* is an appropriate conjunction to link the two clauses.

See 18a for more information about using coordinating conjunctions to write more varied and interesting sentences.

1. Distinguishing between coordinating conjunctions and conjunctive adverbs or transitional phrases

The seven coordinating conjunctions can be used with a comma alone to link independent clauses. Do not confuse them with conjunctive adverbs (words like *however, therefore, moreover, then, also*) or with transitional phrases (*in fact, in contrast, in addition*). (See 6b7.) Such words and phrases, even if preceded by a comma, are not enough to link independent clauses grammatically; they must be used with a semicolon, a period, or a coordinating conjunction. In fact, the inappropriate use of conjunctive adverbs and transitional phrases is responsible for many comma splices and fused sentences.

COMMA SPLICE	Most Third World countries have very high birthrates, therefore most of their citizens are young.
FUSED SENTENCE	Most Third World countries have very high birthrates therefore most of their citizens are young.
REVISED	Most Third World countries have very high birthrates. Therefore, most of their citizens are young.
REVISED	Most Third World countries have very high birthrates; therefore, most of their citizens are young.
REVISED	Most Third World countries have very high birthrates; most of their citizens, therefore, are young.
REVISED	Most Third World countries have very high birthrates, and therefore most of their citizens are young.

As you can see from the preceding example, any of the three methods discussed thus far in this chapter can be used to revise a comma splice or fused sentence that uses a conjunctive adverb or transitional phrase inappropriately. The context of the passage can help you decide which method to choose. Notice that conjunctive adverbs and transitional phrases, unlike coordinating conjunctions, can appear in positions other than between independent clauses. These words and expressions are usually set off from the rest of the clause by commas (see 27a).

13d. Recasting the two clauses as a single independent clause

Sometimes two independent clauses that are spliced or fused together can be reduced to a single independent clause that gets the point across in fewer words.

COMMA SPLICE	High school and college prepare students for later life, they do so in slightly different ways.
FUSED SENTENCE	High school and college prepare students for later life they do so in slightly different ways.
REVISED	High school and college prepare students for later life in slightly different ways.

The revision deletes *they do so*, three words that simply repeat what has been said in the first independent clause. Deleting these three words reduces the sentence to a single independent clause that is more direct and succinct than the original version. (See 17b for more information about ways to avoid needless repetition.)

13e. Recasting one of the independent clauses as a dependent clause

Another option for revising two spliced or fused independent clauses is to convert one of them to a dependent clause. This method is most appropriate when the meaning or effect of one clause is dependent on the other or when one is less important than the other.

COMMA SPLICE	Herman Melville is regarded as one of America's foremost novelists, he died in obscurity.
FUSED SENTENCE	Herman Melville is regarded as one of America's foremost novelists he died in obscurity.
REVISED	*Although* Herman Melville is regarded as one of America's foremost novelists, he died in obscurity.

In the preceding example, the first clause stands in contrast to the second one: in contrast to Melville's importance today (he is held in high esteem) are the circumstances of his death (obscurity and poverty). In the revision, the writer chose to emphasize the second clause and to make the first one into a dependent clause by adding the subordinating conjunction *although*. (For a review of subordinating conjunctions, see 6b7.)

COMMA SPLICE	The Arts and Crafts movement called for simplicity, it reacted against Victorian clutter.
FUSED SENTENCE	The Arts and Crafts movement called for simplicity it reacted against Victorian clutter.
REVISED	The Arts and Crafts movement, *which reacted against Victorian clutter*, called for simplicity.

In this example, both clauses discuss related aspects of the Arts and Crafts movement. In the revision, the writer chose to emphasize the first clause, the one describing what the movement advocated, and to make the second clause, the one describing what it reacted against, into a dependent clause by adding the relative pronoun *which*. (For a review of relative pronouns, see 6b3.)

Notice that dependent clauses must often be set off from the rest of the sentence with commas. For information about the use of commas with dependent clauses, see Chapter 27.

See 18a2 and 18b2 for more information about using dependent clauses to write more varied and effective sentences.

EXERCISE 13.1

Revise each of the following sentences to correct any comma splices or fused sentences in *two* of the five methods presented in this chapter. Use each of the methods at least once.

> *Example*
> I had misgivings about the marriage, I did not attend the ceremony.
> I had misgivings about the marriage, *so* I did not attend the ceremony.
> *Because* I had misgivings about the marriage, I did not attend the ceremony.

1. I was sitting on a log bridge, the sun sank lower in the sky.
2. Film-makers today have no choice they must use complicated electronic equipment.
3. I cannot find answers to certain questions, these are the ones that stick in my mind.
4. My mother taught me to read my grandmother taught me to *love* to read.
5. *David Copperfield* was originally written as a serial it is ideally constructed for television adaptation.

EXERCISE 13.2

Combine each of the following pairs of sentences into one sentence, using one of the five methods presented in this chapter for revising comma splices and fused sentences. Use each method at least once. In some sentences, you may have to add, delete, or change words.

> *Example*
> The rain subsided.
> The players returned to the field.
> The rain subsided, *and* the players returned to the field.
> *As soon as* the rain subsided, the players returned to the field.

1. Lincoln called for troops to fight the Confederacy.
   Four more southern states seceded as a result.
2. The mother eagle called twice.
   The young eagle finally answered.

3. Jim grew beautiful tulips.
   He had less success with strawberries.
4. The Soviet Union expelled Solzhenitsyn in 1974.
   He eventually settled in Vermont.
5. The music lifted her spirits.
   She stopped sighing and began singing.

EXERCISE 13.3

Revise the following paragraph, eliminating all comma splices by using a period or a semicolon. Then revise the paragraph again, this time using any of the other methods presented in this chapter. Comment on the two paragraphs you have written. What differences in rhythm do you detect? Which version do you prefer, and why?

My sister Mary decided to paint her house last summer, consequently, she had to buy some paint. She wanted inexpensive paint, at the same time, it had to go on easily and cover well, that combination was unrealistic to start with. She was sure that she would have no trouble doing the work all herself, however, she had never done exterior painting before, she did not even own a ladder. She was a complete beginner, on the other hand, she was a hard worker and was willing to learn. She got her husband, Dan, to take a week off from work, likewise she let her two teenage sons take three days off from school to help. Mary went out and bought the "dark green" paint for $6.99 a gallon, it must have been mostly water, in fact, you could almost see through it when it was opened. Mary and Dan and the boys put one coat of this paint on the house, as a result, their white house turned a streaky light green. Dan and the boys rebelled, declaring they would not work any more with this cheap paint. Mary was forced to go out and buy all new good-quality paint, even so, the house did not really get painted until September.

EXERCISE 13.4

Revise the following paragraph, eliminating the comma splices and fused sentences by using any of the methods discussed in this chapter. Then revise the paragraph again, this time eliminating each comma splice and fused sentence by a *different* method. Decide which paragraph is most effective and why. Finally, compare the revision you prefer with the revisions of several other students, and discuss the ways in which the versions differ in meaning.

Gardening can be very satisfying, it is also hard work people who just see the pretty flowers may not realize this. My mother spends long hours every spring tilling up the soil, she moves many wheelbarrow-loads of disgusting cow manure and chicken droppings, in fact, the whole early part of gardening is nauseating. The whole garden area has to be rototilled every year, this process is not much like the advertisements showing people walking quietly behind the Rototiller, on the contrary, my father has to fight that machine every inch of the way, sweating so much he looks like Hulk Hogan after a hard bout. Then the planting all must be done by hand, my back aches, my hands get raw, my skin gets sunburned. All my clothes get filthy whenever I go near that garden my mother always asks me to help, though. When harvest time comes the effort is *almost* worth it, however, there are always all those extra zucchinis I have to try to give away at school everybody else is trying to give away zucchinis, too. We also have tomatoes, squash, beans, and lettuce, there is always more than we need and we feel bad wasting it wouldn't you like this nice five-pound bag of cucumbers?

READING WITH AN EYE FOR PROSE STYLE

Comma splices and fused sentences are sometimes used to create special effects. In the following passage, see how Anne Cameron uses comma splices to create momentum and build to a climax:

> Golden eagles sit in every tree and watch us watch them watch us, although there are bird experts who will tell you in all seriousness that there are NO golden eagles here. Bald eagles are common, ospreys abound, we have herons and mergansers and kingfishers, we have logging with percherons and belgians, we have park land and nature trails, we have enough oddballs, weirdos, and loons to satisfy anybody.

In the second sentence, six independent clauses are spliced together with commas. The effect: a rush of details, from the rather oddball birds to the oddball people, and finally to the *loons*, a word that can apply to either birds or people.

Look through some stories or essays to find some comma splices and fused sentences. Copy down one or two, including enough of the surrounding text to show context, and comment in writing on the effect they create.

FOR EXAMINING YOUR OWN WRITING
FOR COMMA SPLICES AND FUSED SENTENCES

Go through the last two or three essays you have written, checking for comma splices and fused sentences. If you find any, revise them using one of the methods discussed in this chapter. Comment in writing on your chosen methods.

14. Recognizing Sentence Fragments

Sentence fragments are groups of words punctuated as sentences but lacking some element grammatically necessary to a sentence, usually either a subject or a finite verb. We see them sometimes in literary works, used to add dramatic emphasis, to speed up rhythm, or to create realistic dialogue. Notice the effect that is achieved with a sentence fragment in the following example:

> The history of England is the history of the male line, not of the female. Of our fathers we know always some fact, some distinction. They were soldiers or they were sailors; they filled that office or they made that law. But of our mothers, our grandmothers, our great-grandmothers, what remains? *Nothing but a tradition.* One was beautiful; one was red-haired; one was kissed by a Queen. We know nothing of them except their names and the dates of their marriages and the number of children they bore.   —Virginia Woolf, "Women and Literature"

Nothing but a tradition. This fragment brings drama to Woolf's statement, arresting readers' attention in a way that a complete sentence would not. Notice how it gives added emphasis to the word *nothing*, and thus to Woolf's point.

Sentence fragments pose potential problems for you as a student writer, however, for although you will read them in literature, hear them in conversation, and see them everywhere in advertising, they are usually considered "errors" in most academic prose. This chapter will provide you with practice at recognizing and revising sentence fragments.

➤ Checking for sentence fragments

If you have a tendency to write fragments, you should check for them in every piece of writing that you do. A group of words must meet the following three criteria to be a complete sentence. If it does not meet all three, it is a fragment and must be revised.

1. It must have a subject.
2. It must have a finite verb, not just a verbal (see 6c3).
3. Unless it is a question, it must have at least one clause that does *not* begin with a subordinating word (see 6b3 and 6b7).

Two methods of eliminating fragments

In general, a fragment can be revised by combining it with an independent clause or by turning it into an independent clause.

FRAGMENT	The beaver dam holding back the shallow pond.
REVISED	I was startled at the sight of the beaver dam holding back the shallow pond. [combined with independent clause *I was startled*]
REVISED	The beaver dam was holding back the shallow pond. [turned into independent clause by adding *was* to participle *holding*, making verb finite]
FRAGMENT	Barely seven inches long, with nothing but a barrel, a handle, and a trigger.
REVISED	He was holding a gun barely seven inches long, with nothing but a barrel, a handle, and a trigger.
REVISED	It was barely seven inches long, with nothing but a barrel, a handle, and a trigger.

▌14a. Revising phrase fragments

Phrases, groups of words lacking either a subject, a finite verb, or both, appear frequently as fragments. Most common are verbal phrases, prepositional phrases, noun phrases, and appositive phrases.

Verbal-phrase fragments

A verbal phrase includes a gerund, an infinitive, a present participle, or a past participle, together with any objects or modifiers (see 6c3). To revise, combine them with an independent clause or turn them into two separate sentences.

FRAGMENT	Vivian stayed out of school for three months after Julia was born. *To recuperate and to take care of her.*
REVISED	Vivian stayed out of school for three months after Julia was born to recuperate and to take care of her. [combined with independent clause]
REVISED	Vivian stayed out of school for three months after Julia was born. She did so to recuperate and to take care of her. [turned into complete sentence]

Prepositional-phrase fragments

A prepositional phrase consists of a preposition, its object, and any modifiers of the object (see 6c3). Like verbal-phrase fragments, prepositional-phrase fragments contain neither subjects nor finite verbs. Usually you can best revise them by simply joining them to the independent clause containing the word they modify.

FRAGMENT	Several civic groups are sponsoring public debates. *With discussions afterward.*
REVISED	Several civic groups are sponsoring public debates with discussions afterward.

Noun-phrase fragments

A noun phrase consists of a noun together with any adjectives, phrases, or clauses that modify it (see 6c3). Noun-phrase fragments contain a subject but no finite verb, and they frequently appear before fragments containing a verb but no subject. You can best revise such fragments by combining them into one sentence containing both a subject *and* a verb.

FRAGMENTS	*His editorial making a plea for better facilities for severely handicapped children. Pointed out that these facilities are always located in poor areas.*
REVISED	In his editorial making a plea for better facilities for severely handicapped children, he pointed out that these facilities are always located in poor areas.
REVISED	His editorial making a plea for better facilities for severely handicapped children pointed out that these facilities are always located in poor areas.

Appositive-phrase fragments

An appositive phrase is a noun phrase that renames or describes another noun (see 6c3). You can revise appositive-phrase fragments by joining them to the independent clause containing the noun to which the appositive phrase refers.

FRAGMENT One of our nation's most cherished dreams seems to be in danger. *The dream of a good education for every child.*

REVISED One of our nation's most cherished dreams, the dream of a good education for every child, seems to be in danger.

REVISED One of our nation's dreams seems to be in danger: the dream of a good education for every child. [In this revision, the use of the colon creates greater emphasis.]

▌ 14b. Revising compound-predicate fragments

A compound predicate consists of two or more verbs, along with their modifiers and objects, that have the same subject (see 6c2). Compound-predicate fragments occur when one of these verbs is punctuated as a separate sentence without a subject. These fragments usually begin with the conjunction that connects the parts of the compound. You can revise them by attaching them to the independent clause that contains the rest of the predicate.

FRAGMENT The miser put some of the money in the bank. *But hid most of it under his mattress.*

REVISED The miser put some of the money in the bank but hid most of it under his mattress.

EXERCISE 14.1

Revise each of the following items to eliminate any sentence fragments, either by combining fragments with independent clauses or by rewriting them as separate sentences.

Example
Zoe looked close to tears. Standing in the door with her head bowed.
Standing in the door with her head bowed, Zoe looked close to tears.
Zoe, standing in the door with her head bowed, looked close to tears.
Zoe looked close to tears. She was standing in the door with her head bowed.

1. Small, long-veined, fuzzy green leaves. Add to the appeal of this newly developed variety of carrot.

2. Living with gusto. That is what many Americans yearn for.
3. The region has dry, sandy soil. Blown into strange formations by the ever-present wind.
4. The climbers had two choices. To go over a four-hundred-foot cliff or to turn back. They decided to make the attempt.
5. Connie picked up the cat and started playing with it. It scratched her neck. With its sharp little claws.
6. Westerners objected to one law in particular. The law that limited traffic speed to fifty-five miles an hour.
7. Trying to carry a portfolio, art box, illustration boards, and drawing pads. I must have looked ridiculous.
8. Organized crime has been able to attract graduates just as big business has. With good pay, good working conditions, and the best equipment money can buy.
9. The captain sent some crew members up onto the remaining rigging. And ordered the rest to arm themselves.
10. Wollstonecraft believed in universal public education. Also, in education that forms the heart and strengthens the body.

■ 14c. Revising dependent-clause fragments

Unlike phrases, dependent clauses contain both a subject and a finite verb. Because they *depend* upon an independent clause to complete their meaning, however, they cannot stand alone as grammatically complete sentences (see 6c4). Such clauses usually begin with a subordinating conjunction—such as *after, even though, if*—or a relative pronoun—such as *who, which, that.* (See 6b3 and 6b7 for lists of relative pronouns and subordinating conjunctions.) You can usually revise dependent clause fragments by either combining the dependent clause with the independent clause that precedes or follows it, or by deleting the subordinating word to create an independent clause.

FRAGMENT	*If a woman chooses the traditional role of mother and homemaker.* She may fear the loss of her own identity.
REVISED	If a woman chooses the traditional role of mother and homemaker, she may fear the loss of her own identity.
FRAGMENT	The plane landed at Heathrow. *Which is one of the world's largest airports.*
REVISED	The plane landed at Heathrow, which is one of the world's largest airports.

FRAGMENT Injuries in automobile accidents occur in two ways. *When an occupant is hurt by something inside the car, or when an occupant is thrown from the car.*

REVISED Injuries in automobile accidents occur in two ways: when an occupant is hurt by something inside the car, or an occupant is thrown from the car.

REVISED Injuries in automobile accidents occur in two ways. An occupant is hurt by something inside the car, or an occupant is thrown from the car.

EXERCISE 14.2

Revise each of the following items to eliminate any fragments, either by combining them with independent clauses or by making them into separate complete sentences.

Example

Miss Marple heard doors slamming and angry voices shouting. Before she heard the shot.

Miss Marple heard doors slamming and angry voices shouting before she heard the shot.

1. Almost all of my former colleagues have quit. Because they were bored.
2. The researchers saw few, if any, teachers threaten students with bodily harm. Though occasionally they saw a teacher *resist* striking a student.
3. Although my friend fell in and got his jeans wet. The canoe trip was a success.
4. She scooped up the fur jacket. Which had been thrown into a heap on the dirt floor.
5. Many people take offense at Joe. Whose remarks are often thoughtless.

EXERCISE 14.3

Identify all of the sentence fragments in the following items, and explain why each is grammatically incomplete. Then revise each one in at least two ways.

Example

Controlling my temper. That has been one of my goals this year.

Controlling my temper has been one of my goals this year.

One of my goals this year has been controlling my temper.

1. When Rick was in the fifth grade. His parents often left him with his sister.
2. The protagonist comes to a decision. To leave his family and go to London.

3. Fear, one of the basic emotions people have experienced throughout time.
4. Many senators from the West opposed the bill. Because of its restrictions on mining and oil drilling.
5. I plan to buy a computer. Which will help me organize my finances and my calendar.
6. Forster stopped writing novels after *A Passage to India*. One of the greatest novels of the twentieth century.
7. This battery never runs out of water. Eliminating the possibility of ruined clothing from battery acid.
8. I loved Toni Morrison's *Beloved*. And thought she deserved the Pulitzer Prize.
9. The president appointed five members. Who drew up a set of bylaws.
10. One might say that rebellion is normal. Because the younger generation often rejects the ways of its elders.

READING WITH AN EYE FOR FRAGMENTS

Each of the following paragraphs includes a sentence fragment. Read each paragraph, identify the fragment, and then decide what effect each writer wished to achieve by using a fragment rather than a complete sentence.

I was looking through binoculars at a pair of whistling swans. Whistling swans! It is impossible to say how excited I was to see whistling swans in Daleville, Virginia. The two were a pair, mated for life, migrating north and west from the Atlantic coast to the high arctic. They had paused to feed at Daleville Pond. I had flushed them, and now they were flying and circling the pond. I crouched in the reeds so they would not be afraid to come back to the water.   —ANNIE DILLARD, "Lenses"

Now one can hear the warning rumble begin: if everyone is allowed to take drugs everyone will and the GNP will decrease, the Commies will stop us from making everyone free, and we shall end up a race of zombies, passively murmuring "groovy" to one another. Alarming thought. Yet it seems most unlikely that any reasonably sane person will become a drug addict if he knows in advance what addiction is going to be like.   —GORE VIDAL, "Drugs"

FOR EXAMINING YOUR OWN WRITING FOR FRAGMENTS

Read through several essays you have written to see whether they include any sentence fragments. Check each group of words punctuated as a sentence to be sure that it contains the three elements listed at the beginning of this chapter: (1) a subject, (2) a finite verb, and (3) unless the sentence is a question, at least one clause that does not begin with a subordinating word. If you find any groups of words that lack any of these elements, revise them to form complete sentences.

15. Recognizing Misplaced, Disruptive, and Dangling Modifiers

Adjectives, adverbs, and the various kinds of phrases and clauses used as adjectives and adverbs enrich writing by making it more concrete, vivid, and memorable. As a writer, you want to take full advantage of them. To be effective, however, these **modifiers** must be carefully placed and must refer clearly to another word or words in the sentence. If modifiers seem to modify words they are not meant to, if they disrupt the continuity of a grammatical structure or of the sentence as a whole, or if they are not clearly attached to any other word in the sentence, the results can be ambiguous, confusing, or even nonsensical.

We see examples of modifiers with these problems even in the work of many professional writers, for they are among the most difficult things to spot when editing. James Thurber was perhaps being somewhat defensive in poking fun at one of the most common problems of this kind:

> Where to use *only* in a sentence is a moot question, one of the mootest questions in all rhetoric. The purist will say the expression "He only died last week" is incorrect, and that it should be "He died only last week." The purist's contention is that the first sentence, if carried out to a natural conclusion, would give us something like this: "He only died last week; he didn't do anything else; that's all he did." It isn't a natural conclusion, however, because nobody would say that. . . . The best way is often to omit *only* and use some other expression. Thus . . . one could say: "It was no longer ago than last Thursday that George L. Wodolgoffing became an angel."
>
> –JAMES THURBER, "Ladies and Gentlemen's Guide to Modern English Usage"

272

Unfortunately, modifiers often cause greater confusion than in Thurber's example, nor is his revision the kind a writer can often use. This chapter will examine three types of problem modifiers—misplaced, disruptive, and dangling—and ways of revising them that do not depend on the assistance of angels.

▌ 15a. Revising misplaced modifiers

Misplaced modifiers are words, phrases, and clauses that cause ambiguity or confusion because they are not placed close enough to the words they modify or because they could modify the words either before or after them.

▌ 1. Misplaced words and phrases

In the sentence *Softly I could hear the tumbleweeds rustling in the wind*, the adverb *softly* seems to modify *could hear*. Yet the writer obviously meant it to modify *rustling*. Such confusion can be avoided by placing a modifier close to the word or words it really refers to.

I could hear the tumbleweeds *softly* rustling in the wind.

I could hear the tumbleweeds rustling *softly* in the wind.

Be especially careful with the placement of **limiting modifiers** like *almost, even, hardly, just, merely, nearly, only, scarcely,* and *simply*. In general, these modifiers should be placed right before the words they modify, because putting them in other positions may produce not just ambiguity but a completely different meaning. Consider the following set of sentences:

AMBIGUOUS	The court only hears civil cases on Tuesday.
CLEAR	The court hears *only* civil cases on Tuesday.
CLEAR	The court hears civil cases *only* on Tuesday.

In the first sentence, placing *only* before the verb makes the meaning ambiguous. Does the writer mean that civil cases are the only kind of cases heard on Tuesdays, or that those are the only days on which civil cases are heard? The second and third sentences each express one of these meanings clearly.

Phrases also should ordinarily be placed close to the words they modify. The most common type of phrase modifier, the prepositional phrase, usually appears right after the word it modifies. In the following sentences, note how misplaced prepositional phrases cause confusion.

MISPLACED   The runners stood ignoring the crowd in their lanes. [This sentence implies that the crowd were in the lanes.]

REVISED   The runners *stood in their lanes* ignoring the crowd.

MISPLACED   She will be teaching a seminar this term on voodoo at Skyline College. [Surely the voodoo was not at the college.]

REVISED   She will be teaching *a seminar on voodoo* this term at Skyline College.

Participial phrases usually appear right before or right after the words they modify. In the following sentences, notice how misplacing these phrases can lead to confusion.

MISPLACED   The host pointed out the moose head to the guests mounted on the wall. [This sentence implies that the guests were mounted on the wall.]

REVISED   The host pointed out the *moose head mounted on the wall* to the guests.

REVISED   The host pointed out to the guests the *moose head mounted on the wall.*

MISPLACED   Billowing from every window, we saw clouds of smoke. [People cannot billow from windows.]

REVISED   We saw *clouds of smoke billowing from every window.*

EXERCISE 15.1

Revise each of the following sentences by moving any misplaced modifying words and phrases so that they clearly modify the words they are intended to.

Example
The blue law only allowed food and medicine to be sold on Sundays.
The blue law allowed *only food and medicine* to be sold on Sundays.

1. Slick and professional, the audience applauded the comedian's routine.
2. Enthusiastically, I heard my friends talk about their great weekends while I tried to finish my assignment.
3. The city almost spent $2 million on the new stadium that opened last year.
4. On the day in question, the patient was not normally able to breathe.
5. The reporter barely submitted his story ahead of deadline.
6. He sat very quietly rolling his eyes in his chair.
7. I went through the process of taxiing and taking off in my mind.

8. Vernon made an agreement to pay back the loan with his father.
9. The bank offered flood insurance to the homeowners underwritten by the federal government.
10. Revolving out of control, the maintenance worker shut down the turbine.

▌2. Misplaced clauses

While you have more flexibility in the placement of dependent clauses than of modifying words and phrases, you should still try whenever possible to place them close to whatever you wish them to modify. If you do not, unintended meanings can result.

MISPLACED	The man carrying a baby *who was quoting Cicero* startled us. [Surely the baby wasn't quoting Cicero.]
REVISED	The *man who was quoting Cicero* and carrying a baby startled us.
MISPLACED	Nixon told reporters that he planned to get out of politics after he lost the 1962 gubernatorial race. [The sentence implies that Nixon planned to lose the race.]
REVISED	*After he lost the 1962 gubernatorial race*, Nixon told reporters that he planned to get out of politics.

EXERCISE 15.2

Revise each of the following sentences by moving any misplaced modifying clauses so that they clearly modify the words they are intended to.

Example

The book was missing from the library that we needed to finish our research.

The *book that we needed to finish our research* was missing from the library.

1. Illegal aliens are often exploited by employers who are afraid of being deported.
2. I was glad to know that the money would stay in my pocket that I had made for the night.
3. Elderly people and students live in the neighborhood surrounding the university, which is full of identical tract houses.
4. His doctor recommended a new examination for heart disease, which is painless.
5. She knew that the investment would pay off in a dramatic way before she decided to buy the stock.

3. Squinting modifiers

If a modifier could refer to *either* the word(s) before it *or* the word(s) after it, it is called a **squinting modifier**. For example:

SQUINTING Students who practice writing *often* will improve their grades.

The modifier *often* might describe either *practice* or *will improve*. That is, the sentence might have either of the following meanings:

REVISED Students who *often practice* writing will improve their grades.

REVISED Students who practice writing will *often improve* their grades.

If a sentence could be read more than one way because of your placement of a modifying word, phrase, or clause, move the modifier to a position where it clearly relates to only a single term.

EXERCISE 15.3

Revise each of the following sentences in at least two ways by moving the squinting modifier so that it unambiguously modifies either the word(s) before it or the word(s) after it.

Example
The course we hoped would challenge us severely depressed us.
The course we hoped would *severely challenge us* depressed us.
The course we hoped would challenge us *depressed us severely*.

1. He remembered vividly enjoying the sound of Mrs. McIntosh singing while cleaning her house.
2. The mayor promised during her first term she would not raise taxes.
3. People who can hear normally have trouble imagining what life is like for a deaf person.
4. Doctors can now restore limbs that have been severed partially to functioning condition.
5. The speaker said when he finished his talk he would answer questions.

15b. Revising disruptive modifiers

Whereas misplaced modifiers confuse readers by appearing to modify the wrong word(s), **disruptive modifiers** cause problems because they interrupt the connections between parts of a grammatical structure or a sentence, making it hard for readers to follow the progress of the thought. Be careful not to place modifiers in such a way that they disrupt the normal grammatical flow of a sentence.

▌1. Modifiers splitting an infinitive

In general, do not split an infinitive by placing a modifier between the *to* and the verb. Doing so makes it hard for readers to recognize that the two go together.

DISRUPTIVE	Hitler expected the British to fairly quickly surrender.
REVISED	Hitler expected the British *to surrender* fairly quickly.

In some cases, however, a modifier sounds awkward in any position other than between the parts of the infinitive.

She hopes this year *to* almost exactly *equal* her last year's income.

To avoid a split infinitive, it may be best to reword the sentence to eliminate the infinitive altogether.

She hopes that this year she will earn almost exactly as much as she did last year.

▌2. Modifiers between the parts of a verb phrase

A verb phrase consists of a main verb together with one or more auxiliary verbs: *had studied, will be moving* (see 6c3). Modifiers consisting of one or even two or three adverbs can often appear between parts of a verb phrase without causing awkwardness: *He <u>had</u> very seldom actually <u>fired</u> a gun in the line of duty.* In general, however, do not interrupt a verb phrase with modifiers that are phrases or clauses.

DISRUPTIVE	Vegetables will, if they are cooked too long, lose most of their nutritional value.
REVISED	Vegetables *will lose* most of their nutritional value if they are cooked too long.
REVISED	If they are cooked too long, vegetables *will lose* most of their nutritional value.

▌3. Modifiers between a subject and verb

Adjective phrases and clauses often appear between a subject and verb: *The <u>books</u> that the librarians had decided were no longer useful <u>were discarded</u>.* In general, however, do not use an adverb clause or phrase in this position, because it disrupts the natural progression from subject to verb that readers expect.

DISRUPTIVE	The books, because the librarians had decided they were no longer useful, were discarded.
REVISED	The *books were discarded* because the librarians had decided they were no longer useful.
REVISED	Because the librarians had decided the books were no longer useful, *they were discarded.*

4. Modifiers between a verb and an object or subject complement

In general, do not place an adverb phrase or clause between a verb and a direct object or subject complement, because readers expect the object or complement to follow directly after the verb.

DISRUPTIVE	He bought with his first paycheck a secondhand car.
REVISED	He *bought a secondhand car* with his first paycheck.
REVISED	With his first paycheck he *bought a secondhand car.*

EXERCISE 15.4

Revise each of the following sentences by moving the disruptive modifier so that the sentence reads smoothly.

Example

Rock festivals became during the 1960s a form of political protest.

During the 1960s, rock festivals became a form of political protest.

1. Eastern North America was, when the first Europeans arrived, covered in forest.
2. The exhibit, because it had been heavily publicized, attracted large audiences.
3. The Soviet skaters were expected to easily take the gold medal.
4. Bookstores sold, in the first week after publication, fifty thousand copies.
5. The singer had because of illness canceled her concert.

15c. Revising dangling modifiers

Dangling modifiers are words (usually adverbs), phrases (prepositional or participial), and elliptical clauses (clauses from which a word or words have been left out) that modify nothing in particular in the rest of a sentence. They often seem to modify something that is suggested or implied but does not exist grammatically in the sentence.

Such modifiers are called dangling because they hang loosely from the rest of the sentence, attached to no specific element. They frequently appear at the beginnings or ends of sentences.

To revise dangling modifiers, you can change the subject of the main clause so that the modifier clearly refers to it, or you can change the dangling modifier itself into a phrase or a nonelliptical clause that clearly modifies an existing part of the sentence.

▮ 1. Dangling words and phrases

DANGLING	Satisfactorily, Martin was confined to the dugout for a week. [There is no indication of who found the confinement satisfactory.]
REVISED	*To the umpires' satisfaction,* Martin was confined to the dugout for a week.
DANGLING	Raised in the suburbs, a built-in swimming pool and a two-car garage seem rather basic. [*Raised in the suburbs* does not refer specifically to anything in the sentence, though it seems to refer to a person or persons who are not mentioned.]
REVISED	*Raised in the suburbs,* I consider a built-in swimming pool and a two-car garage rather basic.
REVISED	*Because I was raised in the suburbs,* a built-in swimming pool and a two-car garage seem rather basic.
REVISED	*To those raised in the suburbs,* a built-in swimming pool and a two-car garage seem rather basic.
DANGLING	As a young boy, his grandmother told stories of her years as a country schoolteacher. [His grandmother was never a young boy.]
REVISED	*As a young boy, he* heard his grandmother tell stories of her years as a country schoolteacher.
REVISED	*When he was a young boy,* his grandmother told stories of her years as a country schoolteacher.
DANGLING	In thumbing through the magazine, my eyes automatically noticed the perfume ads. [Eyes cannot thumb through magazines.]
REVISED	*In thumbing through the magazine, I* automatically noticed the perfume ads.
REVISED	*As I was thumbing through the magazine,* my eyes automatically noticed the perfume ads.

279

EXERCISE 15.5

Revise each of the following sentences to correct the dangling words or phrases.

Example

Having spent the last six summers on my grandparents' farm, my return was expected this summer.

Having spent the last six summers on my grandparents' farm, *I was expected* to return this summer.

1. Looking at the statistics on gun ownership, more American women are taking up arms.
2. Given the sharp increase in the crime rate, their safety seems threatened.
3. To protect themselves, twelve million guns are owned.
4. Training in the use of weapons is achieved by going to shooting ranges and gun clubs.
5. Based on surveys, the vast majority of women buying guns are not doing so for sporting reasons.

▎ 2. Dangling elliptical clauses

DANGLING	Where still seen, tourists find these aging flower children a picturesque spectacle. [Is it the tourists who are still seen?]
REVISED	*Where these aging flower children are still seen*, tourists find them a picturesque spectacle.
REVISED	Tourists find *these aging flower children, where still seen*, a picturesque spectacle.
DANGLING	Although a reserved and private man, everyone who met him seemed to like him. [The elliptical clause cannot refer to *everyone*.]
REVISED	*Although he was a reserved and private man*, everyone who met him seemed to like him.
REVISED	*Although a reserved and private man, he* seemed to be liked by everyone who met him.

EXERCISE 15.6

Revise each of the following sentences to correct any dangling elliptical clauses.

Example

While cycling through southern France, the music on my Sony Walkman entertained me.

While cycling through southern France, I was entertained by the music on my Sony Walkman.

1. However unhappy, my part-time job is something I have to put up with.
2. While attending a performance at Ford's Theater, Booth shot Lincoln.
3. A waiter's job can become very stressful when faced with a busy restaurant full of hungry people.
4. Dreams are somewhat like a jigsaw puzzle; if put together in the correct order, organization and coherence become obvious.
5. No matter how costly, my family insists on a college education.

➤ Checking for misplaced or dangling modifiers

Check each sentence for modifiers. Draw an arrow from each modifier to the word it modifies. If they are far removed from each other, try to move them closer together. Then check again, to see if the modifier could possibly refer to any other words in the sentence. If so, move the modifier so that it clearly refers to only one word. If you cannot find a word to which the modifier relates, you have a dangling modifier. Revise the sentence so that it has a clear referent for the modifier, or revise the modifier itself as a complete cause.

EXERCISE 15.7

Revise the following passage to eliminate any misplaced, disruptive, or dangling modifiers.

One day last December, before going to class, a blizzard forced the administration to, for the first time anyone could remember, announce that all classes would be until further notice suspended. After leaving the dorm, the first thing that we noticed was the silence. The snow that had been falling all night steadily covered the ground. Being the last day of the semester, we weren't very worried about classes, so we "arranged," with another dormitory, a snowball fight. While building up a stock of good snowballs near Lord Hall, our jackets began to get oppressively warm. Eventually, we peeled down to shirt sleeves, ready for a fight. The central lawn became the battleground for the great Stoke-Lord Snowball Fight, where the Stoke Hall people finally set up their forts. Our piles of snowballs almost reached the tops of our forts, which were well-packed and handy to be picked up and thrown. At last both sides were ready, and the first snowball flew through the air from the "Stoke stack." The bombardment was for a while fierce and deadly. I learned that when throwing a snowball, the standing position is very risky, getting a hard one in the mouth. Finally, having almost thrown all of our snowballs, the Stoke charge was met and resisted. The timing was measured with great accuracy, being sure not to countercharge until we saw that Stoke was low on snowballs. Then we all ran toward the enemy carrying three or four snowballs each and routed them.

READING WITH ATTENTION TO LIMITING MODIFIERS

E. B. White was a master of precise wording, choosing—and positioning—his words with great care. Read the following sentences by White, paying attention to the limiting modifiers italicized in each one. Identify which word or words each one modifies, and then consider what would happen if the modifier were placed somewhere else in the sentence.

1. When we got back for a swim before lunch, the lake was exactly where we had left it, the same number of inches from the dock, and there was *only* the merest suggestion of a breeze.   —"Once More to the Lake"
2. Most of the time she *simply* rode in a standing position, well aft on the beast, her hands hanging easily at her sides, her head erect, her straw-colored ponytail lightly brushing her shoulders, the blood of exertion showing faintly through the tan of her skin.   —"The Ring of Time"
3. *Even* our new shoes seemed to be working out all right and weren't hurting much.   —"Twins"
4. It was, among other things, the sort of railroad you would occasionally ride *just* for the hell of it, a higher existence into which you would escape unconsciously and without hesitation.   —"Progress and Change"

FOR EXAMINING MODIFIERS IN YOUR OWN WRITING

Choose two pages of a draft you have written recently, and examine them for clear and effective modification. Can you identify any misplaced, disruptive, or dangling modifiers? Using the guidelines in this chapter, revise as need be.

16. Maintaining Consistent and Complete Grammatical Structures

About fifteen years ago, a writing instructor who had studied thousands of student essays came to a simple but profound conclusion about many of the sentences in them: though at first glance the sentences seemed incoherent or nonsensical, they actually fell into certain patterns. They could be better characterized, the instructor decided, either as (1) unsuccessful attempts to combine sentence structures that did not fit together grammatically or sensibly or as (2) sentences missing some element necessary to complete meaning. In fact, many writers who produce garbled sentences do so in an attempt to use and master complex and sophisticated structures. What look like "errors," then, may be stepping stones on a writer's way to greater stylistic maturity. This chapter will provide practice in recognizing such mixed or incomplete structures and, more important, in revising or building on them.

▌ 16a. Making grammatical patterns consistent

Mixed construction results from beginning a sentence with one grammatical pattern and then switching to another one. In informal speech, we are all familiar with the kind of "sentence" that starts out one way and ends another, as in the following example:

MIXED   The fact that I get up at 5 A.M. every day, which explains why I'm always tired in the evenings.

The speaker starts out with a subject (*fact*) followed by a dependent clause (*that I get up at 5 A.M. every day*). This structure should lead into a predicate to complete the independent clause begun by *The fact,* but instead the speaker shifts to another dependent clause (*which explains why I'm always tired in the evenings*). Thus the independent clause is never completed, and what results is a fragment. In writing, this fragment could be revised into a complete sentence in at least two ways:

REVISED	The fact that I get up at 5 A.M. every day explains why I'm always tired in the evenings. [Deleting *which* changes the second dependent clause into a predicate.]
REVISED	I get up at 5 A.M. every day, which explains why I'm always so tired in the evenings. [Deleting *The fact that* makes the first dependent clause into an independent clause.]

Although most listeners would have little difficulty in following the speaker's intended meaning, failure to maintain consistent grammatical patterns often leads to confusion, especially in writing. Recognizing and revising mixed sentences call for very careful proofreading, and especially for noting the relationship between subject and predicate or between clauses. Here are some other examples of mixed sentences:

MIXED	Before the world as we know it was created, the universe was only chaos existed—a mass of nothing. [*Only chaos* must function in two different ways: as the subject complement of *universe* and as the subject of *existed*.]
REVISED	Before the world as we know it was created, the universe was only chaos—a mass of nothing. [Deleting *existed* leaves *only chaos* as a subject complement only.]
REVISED	Before the world as we know it was created, only chaos existed—a mass of nothing. [Deleting *was* leaves *only chaos* as a subject only.]
MIXED	Because hope was the only thing left when Pandora finally closed up the mythical box explains why we never lose hope no matter how bad life gets. [The adverb clause beginning with *Because* is followed not by an independent clause but by a predicate beginning with *explains*, which lacks a subject.]
REVISED	Because hope was the only thing left when Pandora finally closed up the mythical box, we never lose hope no matter how bad life gets. [Deleting *explains why* changes the original predicate into an independent clause to which the adverb clause can be attached.]

▌ 16b. Matching subjects and predicates

Another kind of mixed sentence occurs when a subject and predicate do not fit together grammatically or do not make sense together. Such a mismatch, sometimes called **faulty predication**, often appears in sentences with the verb *be*, in which the subject complement that follows the verb does not grammatically or sensibly rename the subject. In many cases, faulty predication results from using forms of *be* in sentences in which another verb would be stronger and more appropriate.

FAULTY   A characteristic that I admire is a person who is generous.

This sentence says that a person is a kind of characteristic. To make its subject and predicate consistent, you could change either the subject or the complement to make them both refer to either persons or characteristics, or you could rewrite the sentence to change the verb.

REVISED   A *characteristic* that I admire is *generosity*.

REVISED   A *kind of person* that I admire is *one who is generous*.

REVISED   I *admire* a person who is generous.

The verb *be* also leads to faulty predication when it is used before an adverb clause opening with *when* or *where*.

FAULTY   A stereotype is when someone characterizes a group unfairly.

Although you will often hear constructions like this in conversation, an adverb clause cannot function as a subject complement in academic or other formal writing. To revise this sentence, you can change the complement to a noun that will grammatically match the subject *stereotype*, or you can rewrite the sentence to change the verb.

REVISED   A *stereotype* is an unfair *characterization* of a group.

REVISED   A stereotype characterizes a group unfairly.

REVISED   *When someone characterizes a group unfairly*, he or she *creates* a stereotype.

Using *the reason (that)* . . . *is because* construction, which causes inconsistency between the subject and the subject complement, is another form of faulty predication.

FAULTY   The reason I like to play soccer is because it provides aerobic exercise.

REVISED   I like to play soccer *because* it provides aerobic exercise. [Deleting *the reason (that)* leaves an independent clause to which the *because* clause can be attached.]

REVISED   *The reason* I like to play soccer *is that* it provides aerobic exercise. [Changing *because* to *that* makes the adverb clause into a noun clause that can function as a subject complement.]

Faulty predication also occurs with verbs other than *be*, as the following examples illustrate:

FAULTY   The rules of the corporation expect employees to be properly dressed. [*Rules* cannot expect anything.]

REVISED   As its rules state, the corporation expects employees to be properly dressed.

REVISED   The rules of the corporation require that employees be properly dressed.

FAULTY   The popularity of underground comics began to appear in many stores throughout the country. [*Popularity* cannot appear in stores.]

REVISED   The popularity of underground comics began to be obvious to owners of many stores throughout the country.

REVISED   Increasing numbers of underground comics began to appear in many stores throughout the country.

EXERCISE 16.1

Revise each of the following sentences in two ways to make its structures consistent in grammar and meaning.

Example
The fact that our room was cold that night we put an electric space heater between our beds.
Because our room was cold that night, we put an electric space heater between our beds.
The fact that our room was cold that night led us to put an electric space heater between our beds.

1. My interest in a political career would satisfy my desire for public service.
2. To find out if you need braces, your dentist will usually tell you.
3. The reason air pollution standards should not be relaxed is because many people would suffer.

4. By not prosecuting white-collar crime as vigorously as violent crime encourages white-collar criminals to think they can ignore the law.
5. Her age is a bit deceiving, with looks of a twenty-one-year-old but a true age of only eighteen.
6. Love is when two people want to make each other happy.
7. Hawthorne's short stories are experiences drawn from his own life.
8. When Oedipus suddenly realizes he has killed his father and married his mother causes a "shock of recognition."
9. One controversial element of the curriculum has been colleges with a required course in Western culture.
10. The European discovery of Australia became a penal colony for Britain.

▌ 16c. Using elliptical structures carefully

Sometimes writers can avoid repetition and gain emphasis by using **elliptical structures**, in which they omit certain words or phrases in compound structures, as the following sentences demonstrate (omitted words are in brackets):

> We are wise in mind but [we are] weak in body.

> A person without an education, or [without] the desire for one, is an unlucky person indeed.

> His hair was red, his skin [was] fair, and his body [was] underweight.

These sentences are clear and effective because the omitted words match those in the other part of the compound.

In the following sentence, however, the omitted verb does not match the one that occurs in the first part of the compound, and so the sentence is incomplete. Therefore, the sentence must be revised to include both verbs.

INCOMPLETE	His skills are underdeveloped, and his performance only average.
REVISED	His skills *are* underdeveloped, and his performance *is* only average.

▌ 16d. Checking for missing or misused words

In the rush of composing, when the brain almost always runs ahead of the hand, writers sometimes accidentally leave out words, especially short ones like articles, pronouns, and prepositions. The best way to catch such inadvertent omissions is to proofread carefully, reading each sentence slowly—and aloud. If a word or phrase is missing, you are very likely to hear its omission.

INCOMPLETE	A good transportation system makes easier for people move from one place to another.
REVISED	A good transportation system makes *it* easier for people *to* move from one place to another.
INCOMPLETE	Finally, it is impossible to ignore fact that women were not able to participate fully political activities.
REVISED	Finally, it is impossible to ignore *the* fact that women were not able to participate fully *in* political activities.

Especially in speaking, we often omit *that* when it introduces a noun clause following a verb: *Yesterday, I realized* [*that*] *I was hopelessly behind in my work.* In this instance, omitting *that* does not obscure meaning. If any possible confusion could arise, however, be sure to include the *that* in writing.

UNCLEAR	I noticed many motorcycles from the 1940s had become classics. [Readers at first assume *many motorcycles* is the object of *noticed* rather than the subject of the subordinate clause.]
REVISED	I noticed *that* many motorcycles from the 1940s had become classics.

> ### Checking for wrong prepositions

Circle the prepositions in a draft, and then read aloud any sentences in which they appear. Are you unsure about any of them? If so, check a dictionary to see that you've used them properly. (The *Oxford Advanced Learners* dictionary has especially good coverage of prepositions.) Keep a list of any that you misuse, with the sentences in which you used them incorrectly. Check carefully for them in your drafts.

16e. Checking comparisons for completeness, consistency, and clarity

As you revise and proofread your writing, check comparative structures closely, remembering that when you compare two or more things, the comparison must be *complete, logically consistent,* and *clear.* (See Chapter 10 for further discussion of comparative and superlative forms of adjectives and adverbs.)

Complete comparisons

INCOMPLETE	A person who drives drunk is more dangerous. [More dangerous than what?]
REVISED	A person who drives drunk is more dangerous *than one who drives carelessly.*
INCOMPLETE	My two sisters are so different. [So different than what?]
REVISED	My two sisters are so different *that they can hardly communicate with each other.*

Logically consistent comparisons

ILLOGICAL	Woodberry's biography is better researched than Fields. [This sentence compares *biography*, a book, to *Fields*, a person.]
REVISED	Woodberry's biography is better researched than *the one by* Fields.
REVISED	Woodberry's biography is better researched than *Fields's is.*

Clear comparisons

UNCLEAR	Ted always felt more affection for his brother than his sister. [Did Ted feel more affection for his brother than his sister did or more affection for his brother than he felt for his sister?]
REVISED	Ted always felt more affection for his brother than *he did for* his sister.
REVISED	Ted always felt more affection for his brother than his sister *did.*

EXERCISE 16.2

Revise each of the following sentences to eliminate any inappropriate elliptical constructions; to make comparisons complete, logically consistent, and clear; and to supply any other omitted words that are necessary for meaning.

Example

Most of the candidates are bright, and one brilliant.

Most of the candidates are bright, and one is brilliant.

1. My new stepmother makes my father happier.
2. Argentina and Uruguay were originally colonized by Spain, and Brazil by Portugal.
3. Jasmine and Donna get along together better on a double date.
4. During the strike, fans were angrier at the players than the owners.
5. Most young people think their parents are so old and out of touch.
6. The picture made me think about whether Baby M's life would be more difficult than many other children.
7. Taking a driving test was the most nerve-wracking experience.
8. The personalities of marijuana smokers are very different from nonsmokers.
9. The driver never saw the light had turned red.
10. One way to develop a topic for essay is to jot down on a sheet paper whatever comes to mind.

FOR EXAMINING YOUR OWN WRITING
FOR MIXED OR INCOMPLETE STRUCTURES

Read over three or four paragraphs from a draft or completed essay you have written recently, checking for any mixed sentences, and incomplete or missing structures. Revise the paragraphs to correct any problems you find.

PART FOUR

Sentences: Making Stylistic Choices

17. Constructing Effective Sentences

The philosopher, critic, and poet Kenneth Burke defines *form* in writing as "the arousal and fulfillment of desire." Odd as this definition may seem at first, it suggests an excellent test for effective prose. Substituting the more mundane *expectations* for Burke's deliberately provocative *desire* illustrates the test more clearly. An **effective sentence** is one that creates or appeals to certain expectations and then either fulfills those expectations or—as is sometimes the case—startles or amuses or alarms readers by *not* fulfilling them. Look at the following sentence:

> I sometimes think of the reader as a cat, endlessly fastidious, capable, by turns, of mordant indifference and riveted attention, luxurious, recumbent, and ever poised.
>
> —Patricia Hampl, "Memory and Imagination"

This sentence fulfills expectations by following up on the image of the reader as cat with cat imagery ("endlessly fastidious," "luxurious"), thus linking the picture of the reader with one of a cat. In addition, the sentence is structured so as to pull its readers along, saving its most powerful image for the end, closing with the image of the catlike reader, "ever poised."

The writer of the following sentence, on the other hand, surprises readers by *breaking* expectations:

> He was a tall, dark, and handsome creep.

In this sentence, the writer plays on readers' expectations with the loaded words *tall*, *dark*, and *handsome*—only to undercut those expectations with the final *creep*.

You may want to try using such an element of surprise as one way to create effective sentences. The rest of this chapter, however, will focus on two basic devices writers use to create effective sentences by fulfilling rather than breaking expectations: *emphasis* and *conciseness*.

▌ 17a. Emphasizing main ideas

Effective sentences put the spotlight on main ideas, thus letting readers know which elements of the sentence are most important. We call this spotlighting of significant words and ideas **emphasis**. Careful control of the emphasis in each sentence will make your writing both easier and more enjoyable to read. This section focuses on the ways you can emphasize main ideas by putting them in opening and closing positions and by arranging them in climactic order.

▌ 1. Using opening and closing positions for emphasis

When you read a sentence, what are you most likely to remember? Other things being equal, you remember the end. This is the part of the sentence that should move the writing forward by providing new information, as it does in the following example:

To protect her skin, *she took plenty of sun-block lotion.*

A less emphatic but still important position in a sentence is the opening, which hooks up the new sentence with what has come before.

When Rosita went to the beach, she was anxious not to get a sunburn. *To protect her skin*, she took plenty of sun-block lotion.

In this example, *to protect her skin* connects the new sentence to *anxious not to get a sunburn* in the sentence before. The second sentence would lose emphasis if the key words, *plenty of sun-block lotion*, were buried in the middle, as in the following version:

To protect her skin, *she took plenty of sun-block lotion*, and she also planned to stay under a beach umbrella most of the time.

Placing relatively unimportant information in the memorable closing position of a sentence undercuts proper emphasis or gives more emphasis to the closing words than you may intend:

> She contributed $500,000 to the campaign last month.

Revised to gain emphasis, the sentence reads:

> Last month she contributed $500,000 to the campaign.

To emphasize the amount of the contribution even more, the sentence could be reworded this way:

> Last month she gave the campaign committee $500,000.

2. Using climactic order

Presenting ideas in **climactic order** means sequencing them in order of increasing importance, power, or drama: building to climax. The following sentences show climactic order at work:

> Dissidents risk social rejection, forced relocation, long imprisonment, and almost certain death.

> The primary danger of the television screen lies not so much in the behavior it produces—although there is danger there—as in the behavior it prevents: the talks, the games, the family festivities and arguments through which much of the child's learning takes place and through which his character is formed. —MARIE WINN,
> *The Plug-in Drug: Television, Children, and the Family*

Each of the preceding examples derives much of its power from the sequencing of its details. If the first sentence concluded with "long imprisonment" rather than "almost certain death," it would not make such an emphatic statement; similarly, the second example saves its most dramatic item for last, making its point forcefully. The following sentence includes a series that fails to achieve strong emphasis by not sequencing verbs in order of increasing power:

UNEMPHATIC	Soap operas assault our eyes, damage our brain cells, and offend our ears.
REVISED	Soap operas offend our ears, assault our eyes, and damage our brain cells.

3. Checking for emphatic sentences

As you revise a draft, make sure that each sentence emphasizes the ideas you *want* emphasized. First, identify the word or words you want to receive special emphasis, and underline them. If those words are buried in the middle of the sentence or blurred in some way, revise the sentence to change their position, remembering that the end position is generally most emphatic.

Next, note any sentences that include a series of three or more words, phrases, or clauses. Check to see whether the items in the series could be arranged in climactic order and, if so, whether they are. If they could be but are not, decide whether the sentence would be stronger with climactic order, and rearrange if necessary.

Notice how the sentence below can be revised using these two steps:

> For a whole complex of claimed "reasons," we in the Student Senate have for years been saddled with the burdens, which we're tired of, of low budgets, no real legislative power, and a depressing room to meet in.

The main point the writer wants to emphasize, that the Student Senate is tired of being saddled with poor conditions and no power, is obscured by unemphatic placement in the middle of the sentence. A revision of it might look like this:

> We in the Student Senate are tired of being saddled, whatever the claimed "reasons," with low budgets, no real legislative power, and a depressing room to meet in.

Next, we have to look for climactic order. The items in the series at the end of the sentence do not seem to be arranged in any particular order, even though they could be. In climactic order, the meeting room is least important and the lack of power most important. So the final revision might read:

> We in the Student Senate are tired of being saddled, whatever the claimed "reasons," with a depressing room to meet in, low budgets, and no real legislative power.

EXERCISE 17.1

Revise each of the following sentences to highlight what you take to be the main or most important ideas.

Example
Tobacco companies continue to fight the antismoking campaign—through the highest courts of the land, through congressional lobbying, through local advertising.

Tobacco companies continue to fight the antismoking campaign—
through local advertising, through congressional lobbying, through the
highest courts of the land.

1. All seagoing vessels, whether outrigger canoes, giant aircraft carriers, or run-
of-the-mill cargo ships, must be designed according to certain specifications.
2. Also notable is the image of chrysanthemums throughout the story.
3. I feel that living in the dorm was easier to adjust to than living in my
condominium.
4. The presence of the Indian in these movies always conjures up destructive
stereotypes of bloodthirsty war parties, horse thieves, and drunkenness.
5. Victorian women were warned that if they smoked, they would become
sterile, grow a moustache, die young, contract tuberculosis, or have trouble
breathing.

▌ 17b. Being concise

In general, effective sentences are as **concise** as possible. There
are exceptions: on some occasions, writers want—or need—to hammer
home a point or create a certain effect by using what in other situations
might look like unnecessary redundancy, or repetition. In *The Elements
of Style*, E. B. White uses such repetition to good effect when he says,
"There is no satisfactory explanation of style, no infallible guide to
good writing, . . . no key that unlocks the door, no inflexible rule by
which the young writer may shape his [or her] course." So as White's
advice both suggests and illustrates, every writer must decide individually when "redundancy" is worthwhile and when it is not. More often
than not, however, making a point in the fewest possible words is a
hallmark of effective prose. Look at the following sentence:

It is not a mistake—nor is it incorrect—to say that the characteristics of
repetition, redundancy, and saying the same thing over and over again
that typify most or much or at least a great deal of writing in the modern
world of today should be eliminated or done away with by every means
available to the person or persons who teach these writers.

Why write that when you could instead write the following?

Instructors should use all means of decreasing redundancy in their students' writing.

This example demonstrates how radical a change can be wrought by
snipping away at the underbrush of *unnecessary* words and phrases in
a sentence. Doing so involves several kinds of changes: deleting un-

necessarily redundant words, deleting or replacing "buzzwords," replacing wordy phrases with one-word equivalents, and simplifying grammatical structures.

1. Deleting unnecessarily redundant words

Some of the most common unnecessary words are parts of redundant phrases, in which only one word of the phrase is necessary to the meaning. Such phrases include *few in number, large in size, combine together, continue on, continue to remain, repeat again, red in color,* and *free gift.* Redundancy can also result from unnecessary repetition of information that can be found elsewhere in the sentence.

REDUNDANT	*Physical aerobic exercise* is her hobby.
REVISED	*Aerobic exercise* is her hobby.
REDUNDANT	Delia sold houses at a *large 600-home* development.
REVISED	Delia sold houses at a *600-home* development.
REDUNDANT	"*Contemporary* antiques" *made recently* have been showing up more and more at auctions.
REVISED	"*Contemporary* antiques" have been showing up more and more at auctions.
REVISED	"Antiques" *made recently* have been showing up more and more at auctions.

2. Deleting or replacing buzzwords

In addition to unnecessarily redundant words, you should note another class of unnecessary words, called **buzzwords** because, while they *sound* as if they mean something, they are only "vibrating" or "buzzing" without contributing any real meaning. Common buzzword nouns include the following: *angle, area, point, aspect, case, nature, character, element, factor, field, sort, kind, situation, scope, type, thing,* and so on. The other important class of buzzwords consists of adjectives and adverbs used as all-purpose modifiers: *absolutely, definitely, really, very, quite, literally, great, awfully, fine, weird, major, central, important,* and so on. Taken together, buzzwords can build up whole sentences that say almost nothing at all:

> The scope of this thing, the importance of this field, is so absolutely vital that I get really overwhelmed at the significance of the situation.

Because buzzwords tend to make your writing dull as well as wordy, use them very sparingly. When you cannot simply delete them, take the time to think of a more specific term that says exactly what you mean.

WORDY	I found that *the area of encyclopedia sales* did not offer the *sort of thing* I was looking for *in the marketing field.*
REVISED	I found that *encyclopedia sales* did not offer the *varied marketing experience* I was looking for.
WORDY	She found the apartment *quite nice in most ways,* and although she was nervous about *the situation of living alone* the friendly neighbors were *the major factor in her decision* to stay.
REVISED	She found the apartment *bright and spacious,* and although she was nervous about *living alone,* the friendly neighbors *made her decide* to stay.

3. Replacing wordy phrases

Writers sometimes fall back on wordy, stereotyped phrases, as they do on buzzwords, rather than taking time to think of a single word that will convey meaning more forcefully. Usually, such roundabout "filler" expressions only clutter up a page and put up barriers to comprehension. Here are some of the most common filler phrases and their more concise counterparts.

at the present time	now/today
at that point in time	then
in the event that	if
it is believed by many	many believe
form a consensus of opinion	agree
exhibit a tendency to	tend to
inform as to the fact that	tell

WORDY	I see no reason at this point in time why we should not rely, as has often been the case in the past, on the good offices of the mayor.
REVISED	We should rely now, as we have in the past, on the help of the mayor.

Sometimes writers resort to this kind of wordiness because they think it sounds more formal, more official. Such might have been the case in what has come to be a classic story about the dangers of wordiness.

A plumber wrote to the Federal Bureau of Standards that he had found hydrochloric acid did a fine job of clearing out his clogged drains.

The Bureau answered: "The effectiveness and efficiency of hydrochloric acid is indisputable, but the corrosive or detrimental residue is incompatible with metallic permanence."

The plumber replied he was delighted the Bureau agreed with him.

Then the Bureau wrote: "We cannot and must not assume responsibility or admit to culpability in event of the production of toxic and noxious residue with hydrochloric acid and, therefore, recommend you use an alternate or secondary procedure."

Again the plumber responded that he was delighted that the Bureau agreed.

At last the Bureau wrote, with admirable unity, emphasis, and concision, a reply that spoke volumes to the plumber: "Don't use hydrochloric acid. It eats the hell out of the pipes."

Jargon, including corporate, bureaucratic, academic, and scientific jargon, is often the cause of wordiness. Examples of jargon include: *facilitate, viable, ambulate.*

I 4. Simplifying grammatical structures

Using the simplest grammatical structures possible to express your meaning will tighten and strengthen your sentences considerably. In the following sentence, for example, notice how conciseness results from reducing an adjective clause to an appositive phrase, deleting a grammatically unnecessary *to be,* and reducing an adverb phrase to a one-word adverb.

WORDY   Kennedy, *who was only the second Roman Catholic to be nominated for the presidency by a major party,* had to handle the religion issue *in a delicate manner.*

REVISED   Kennedy, *only the second Roman Catholic nominated for the presidency by a major party,* had to handle the religion issue *delicately.*

In the following example, reducing an adverb clause to an elliptical form and combining two sentences by using a compound predicate produces one concise sentence.

WORDY   When she was questioned about her previous job, she seemed nervous. She also tried to change the subject.

REVISED   When questioned about her previous job, she seemed nervous and tried to change the subject.

Other ways to achieve conciseness by simplifying grammatical structures include using strong verbs and nouns, avoiding expletive constructions (those beginning with *there* or *it* followed by a form of *be*), and using the active rather than the passive voice. All of these methods are discussed in detail in Chapter 21.

5. Checking for conciseness

When you revise a draft, work on making each sentence as concise and powerful as possible. To do so, underline any unnecessarily redundant words or buzzwords that you can find. Then go back over each sentence, seeking out stereotyped phrases and other official-sounding but unnecessarily wordy language. Finally, look for grammatical structures that could be simplified. When you have identified the words and phrases that do not add directly to your meaning, rephrase or delete them until you have tightened up each sentence. In the following sentence, note how the writer has trimmed unnecessary words and phrases to produce a much shorter but a much more pithy and effective sentence:

> Her constant and continual use of the vulgar expressions with obscene meanings indicated to her pre-elementary supervisory group that she was rather deficient in terms of her ability to interact in an efficient manner with peers in her potential interaction group.

> Her constant use of "four-letter words" told the day-care workers that she might have trouble getting along with other four-year-olds.

EXERCISE 17.2

Revise each of the following sentences to make it clear and concise by eliminating unnecessary words and phrases.

Example
Let me fill you in on the main points of the overall picture here.
Let me summarize.

1. At the present time, many different forms of hazing occur, such as various forms of physical abuse and also mental abuse.
2. A prime example, it seems to me, was the seizure of American hostages by Iranian radicals, which resulted in the death of eight Marines who died as a result of a disastrous rescue attempt.
3. One of the major problems that is faced at this point in time is that there is world hunger.

4. After I stopped the practice of exercising regularly, I became ten pounds heavier in weight in a relatively short amount of time.
5. It frequently happens that a child can be scolded a numerous amount of times for doing something wrong, and he or she will persist in performing the forbidden act.
6. The way in which one goes about checking the engine is to listen for rattling or pinging noises.
7. A situation of quality, deep-powder snow symbolizes a goal that is not easily attainable by skiers and that they can achieve only in rare cases.
8. It is Randall's approach that exposes the injustices with which the black American is confronted.
9. Humans are very socially oriented beings; this statement is substantiated by the fact that a person left completely alone in a room with adequate food and water would eventually die from the lack of social interaction. However, the opposite end of the social interaction concept relates to the idea that the case of two people forced to be together all of the time is not healthy either.
10. Sweeping and mopping half a restaurant after running around waitressing for five or six hours is enough to give occasion for an exhaustive collapse.

EXERCISE 17.3

Read over Colleen Starkey's essay in 3i, paying attention to the sentences. Then choose a paragraph, and evaluate its sentences in terms of emphasis and conciseness. Try to find a paragraph that you think might be made more emphatic or more concise, and revise accordingly.

READING WITH AN EYE FOR SENTENCE STYLE

Here are some sentences from "Memory and Imagination," Patricia Hampl's essay about memoir writing. (You will recognize the example sentence from the opening of this chapter.) Each sentence makes a powerfully emphatic statement. Read each one, and decide how Hampl achieves such uncommonly strong emphasis. Then choose one to use as a model for writing a sentence of your own.

Example

I sometimes think of the reader as a cat, endlessly fastidious, capable, by turns, of mordant indifference and riveted attention, luxurious, recumbent, and ever poised.

I sometimes think of television as a shrew, incessantly noisy, demanding attention at all times to its advertising and mindless programming, insistently shrill, forever heckling.

1. We wish to talk to each other about life and death, about love, despair, loss, and innocence.
2. The heart, the guardian of intuition with its secret, often fearful intentions, is the boss.
3. I am forced to admit that memoir is not a matter of transcription, that memory itself is not a warehouse of finished stories, not a static gallery of framed pictures.

FOR EXAMINING SENTENCE EFFECTIVENESS IN YOUR OWN WRITING

Study two or three paragraphs you have written recently to determine how emphatic and effectively concise each sentence is. Using the suggestions in this chapter, revise your paragraphs, making each sentence as emphatic and concise as possible.

18. Creating Coordinate and Subordinate Structures

Creating effective sentences calls on a writer to act as a conductor, directing the arrangement and flow of verbal passages just as the conductor of an orchestra does with musical passages. Such effective orchestration very often involves creating sentences that use *coordinate* and *subordinate* structures. **Coordinate structures** give essentially equal importance to two or more words, phrases, or clauses, often linking them together with coordinating conjunctions like *and* or *but*. In the following sentence, linking the two clauses with *but* gives them equal significance:

> Freud's theories cannot be proved by laboratory experiment, but their "rightness" can be sensed in myths and legends.

Subordinate structures create different levels of significance, stressing some ideas by expressing them in independent clauses or in key nouns or verbs and subordinating others by putting them into dependent clauses, phrases, or single words. In the following sentence, beginning the first clause with *although* subordinates the idea in that clause to the one in the second clause.

> Although Freud's theories cannot be proved by laboratory experiment, their "rightness" can be sensed in myths and legends.

Learning to use different kinds of coordinate and subordinate structures will increase your sentence repertoire and allow you to write varied, interesting, and effective sentences. Look, for instance, at the following sentences:

> Kit went through the new part of the library to the old.
> He walked around for a while.

Then he went to the periodical section.
He started looking at the *Times* on microfilm.

We could choose to combine these sentences in several ways:

Using coordination

Kit went through the new part of the library to the old, and he walked
around for a while; then he went to the periodical section and started
looking at the *Times* on microfilm.

Using subordination

After going through the new part of the library to the old and walking
around for a while, Kit went to the periodical section, where he started
looking at the *Times* on microfilm.

Of course, these sentences could be combined in a number of other
ways as well, but these two will serve to illustrate how coordinate structures differ from subordinate structures. In the example that uses coordination, the four actions of going through the new part of the library
to the old, walking around, going to the periodical section, and looking
at the *Times* are all given the same emphasis or importance by being
placed in three independent clauses, the last of which has a compound
predicate. The second combination gives a different emphasis to the
sentence, suggesting that Kit's destination, the periodical section, is
most important. The action of his going there is expressed in an independent clause, whereas the other three actions are given less emphasis by being placed in a prepositional phrase (with compound
gerund-phrase objects) and a dependent clause.

In addition to indicating emphasis, coordination and subordination
can be used to create special, sometimes dramatic effects in writing. As a
writer, you must often decide whether to use coordination, subordination,
both, or neither, depending on which structure provides the emphasis
and effect you want to achieve. This chapter will furnish you with some
guidelines for using these structures appropriately.

▌ 18a. Using coordination to relate equal ideas

What can you say about the following passage?

It was my birthday today, and I took cupcakes to school, and I wore a
birthday crown, and we ate cupcakes, and we sang "Happy Birthday,"
and I sat in the middle, and I'm six years old.

We realize early on that the writer is a child—or someone writing from a child's point of view. Because the passage mentions cupcakes and school and a crown, we make this assumption even before we find out, in the last clause, that the writer is six years old. But the *style* of this passage, as well as its content, helps identify the writer. We get a clue from the seven short independent clauses strung together like beads with the coordinating conjunction *and*, a style typical of young writers who are learning to sequence events in a story. Note that aside from the clue "I'm six years old" at the very end of the sentence (generally an emphatic spot), we are given no grammatical signals to tell us how these clauses rank in importance. Were the cupcakes most significant to the writer? the birthday crown? We cannot tell, because the coordinate structure makes all the clauses grammatical equals.

Not all coordination must sound like "Run, Spot, run," however. When used well, coordinate structures relate separate but equal elements, making clear the emphasis given to different ideas. The precise relationship is stated in the element that links the ideas, usually a coordinating conjunction (*and, but, for, nor, or, so, yet*) or a semicolon. The following sentences by N. Scott Momaday all use coordination, but note that the precise relationship between clauses differs in each sentence as expressed in the connecting element:

> They acquired horses, *and* their ancient nomadic spirit was suddenly free of the ground.

> There is perfect freedom in the mountains, *but* it belongs to the eagle and the elk, the badger and the bear.

> No longer were they slaves to the simple necessity of survival; they were a lordly and dangerous society of fighters and thieves, hunters and priests of the sun.   –N. SCOTT MOMADAY, "The Way to Rainy Mountain"

I 1. Using coordination for special effect

Coordination can also be used to create special effects. Note the way in which coordination creates a particular effect in a passage by Carl Sandburg describing the reaction of the American people to Abraham Lincoln's assassination:

> Men tried to talk about it and the words failed and they came back to silence.
> To say nothing was best.
> Lincoln was dead.
> Was there anything more to say?

Yes, they would go through the motions of grief and they would take part in a national funeral and a ceremony of humilation and abasement and tears.

But words were no help.

Lincoln was dead.   –CARL SANDBURG, *The War Years*

Together with the other short simple sentences, the coordinate clauses, phrases, and words in sentences 1 and 5 create a very definite effect: everything in the passage is grammatically equal, flattened out by the pain and shock of the death. In this way, the sentence structure and grammar mirror the dazed state of the populace. The short sentences and clauses are almost like sobs and illustrate the thought of sentence 1, that "the words failed." Here coordination is used to create a very powerful effect.

The formal name for the conspicuous use of conjunctions to join words, phrases, or clauses is **polysyndeton**, from Greek *poly* ("many") *syndeton* ("connectives.") Following are some additional examples:

Satan pursues his way. And swims, or sinks, or wades, or creeps, or flies.   –JOHN MILTON, *Paradise Lost*

Here the use of coordination piles up images of movement, giving the impression that Satan can use *any* kind of movement and cannot be stopped.

He [the writer] must teach himself that the basest of all things is to be afraid; and, teaching himself that, forget it forever, leaving no room in his workshop for anything but the old verities and truths of the heart, the old universal truths lacking which any story is ephemeral and doomed—*love and honor and pity and pride and compassion and sacrifice.*   –WILLIAM FAULKNER, Nobel Prize Acceptance Speech

Here the repetition of the coordinating conjunction *and* creates a solemn rhythm, almost like the tolling of a bell.

Are you familiar with Motel 8? It's a chain of cheesy cheap motels across the South—twenty dollars a night gets you peeling beaverboard walls *and* thin pink blankets. There's no phone in the room, *but* a TV set that's always tuned to the Nashville Channel, *and* an air conditioner that's always got a screw or three loose *and* vibrates like a 747 on takeoff. You see piles of emptied cigarette butts in the parking lot, *and* always cigarette burns on the table, *and* more cigarette burns on the carpet, *and* a poorly repaired hole in the wall where some redneck put his fist through it in anger at his pregnant sixteen-year-old wife who didn't wanna go out to the Ponderosa.

Here the use of *and* and *but* results in a catalogue of colorful, if somewhat unsavory, detail. By stringing together images in this way, the author presents them in a kind of heap, which contributes to the overall impression of the Motel 8.

2. Revising for more effective coordination

As you revise, consider the relative importance of the different ideas within each sentence. How many coordinate structures can you identify in the draft? If you find few, see whether any ideas or elements should be linked in some way. If you find that you depend primarily on coordination rather than subordination to link ideas, does the draft sound jerky or unnatural? Should any of the coordinate structures be deleted or changed to subordinate ones?

You can answer this last question by taking the following steps. Underline all of the coordinating conjunctions (*and, but, for, nor, or, so, yet*) or semicolons. Now look on either side of each conjunction, and ask yourself two questions. First, does the conjunction link words, phrases, or clauses that really need to be related? Second, are the words, phrases, or clauses linked by the conjunction *equally important* ideas? If the answer to either of these questions is no, revise the sentence to eliminate the coordinate structure or to substitute a subordinate one. Notice how the following passage can be analyzed and revised.

> Part of the problem is that spring semester is a heavy semester for me, <u>and</u> I have five courses, <u>but</u> part of the problem is that I just promised too much to too many people, <u>so</u> I have to do a lot of other library work too. In addition, I had to begin wearing that back brace, <u>and</u> it's making my skin sore, <u>and</u> each night I have to come home <u>and</u> take it off, <u>and</u> that takes time, <u>or</u> I have to go out to the library.

This passage depends too heavily on coordination, which obscures the ways in which the ideas in the sentences relate to one another. Rewritten, with more subordinate structures and with the first sentence separated into two sentences with the coordinating conjunction *but* replaced by the conjunctive adverb *though*, the passage reads more clearly.

> Part of the problem is that spring semester is a heavy semester for me, with five courses. Part of the problem, though, is that I just promised too much to too many people, so I have to do a lot of other work, especially in the library at night. In addition, I had to begin wearing that back brace, which makes my skin sore, and when I come home each night, I have to spend time taking it off.

If you think you are using too many coordinating conjunctions in your own writing, turn to 18b for advice about using subordination.

In addition to checking for excessive and insufficient coordination, check to see that the relationship between coordinated elements of a sentence is clear and makes sense. Look at the following sentence:

> Watching television is a good way to spend some leisure time and makes viewers apathetic.

The relationship of the ideas here is confusing. What does being a good way to spend leisure time have to do with making viewers apathetic? This sentence might be revised in either of the following ways:

> Watching television is a good way to spend some leisure time, but excessive watching makes viewers apathetic and indifferent to their real lives.

> Although watching television is a good way to spend some leisure time, excessive watching makes viewers apathetic and indifferent to their real lives.

Notice that the revisions not only signal a contrast by using *but* or *although* but also add information to explain *apathetic*.

EXERCISE 18.1

Many of the ideas in the following passage are related in ways that are not made clear. Revise the passage by using coordinate structures, where appropriate, to clarify the relationships between equally important ideas.

We came to the Friday Candlelight Dinner. We had a wonderful meal. We got a tour from Bud that we both found quite moving. We came away with very good memories of Quaker Village. We came away with very good memories of the people we had met there, all of whom seemed to go out of their way to be pleasant. On Monday, a Visa slip came for me in the mail. It indicated that I would be charged $48.00 despite my cancellation of two of the reservations. I called to ask if this bill was a mistake. I engaged in a conversation with Sophie that was deeply disturbing. She told me then that the Candlelight Dinner had a 48-hour cancellation policy. She told me that both Dori and I had been charged the full $48.00 for the dinner. She refused to consider any argument. I argued that I had never been told about the policy. I said that if I had known about it, I could have brought two other friends on Friday. That way the meals would not have been wasted. I was told repeatedly that this was the policy. I was told that I should have known the policy. I was told that she had been too busy to tell me the policy when I called Thursday to cancel the reservations. It was, to tell the truth, like a scene from Kafka.

EXERCISE 18.2

Using the principles of coordination to signal equal importance or to create special emphasis, combine and revise the following twelve short sentences into several longer and more effective ones. Add or delete words if you need to.

The bull-riding arena was fairly crowded.
The crowd made no impression on me.
I had made a decision.
It was now time to prove myself.
I was scared.
I walked to the entry window.
I laid my money on the counter.
The clerk held up a Stetson hat filled with slips of paper.
I reached in.
I picked one.
The slip held the number of the bull I was to ride.
I headed toward the stock corral.

18b. Using subordination to distinguish main ideas

Subordination provides the means of distinguishing major points from minor points or bringing in supporting context or details. If, for instance, you put your main idea in an independent clause, you might then put any lesser ideas in dependent clauses, phrases, or even single words. Look, for instance, at the following sentence by Maya Angelou, which shows the subordinated point in italics:

> Mrs. Viola Cullinan was a plump woman *who lived in a three-bedroom house somewhere behind the post office.*
>
> —MAYA ANGELOU, "My Name Is Margaret"

In this sentence, the dependent clause adds information about Mrs. Cullinan. While the information is important, it is grammatically subordinate to the independent clause, which carries the main idea: *Mrs. Viola Cullinan was a plump woman.*

Notice that the choice of what to subordinate rests with the writer and depends on the intended meaning. Angelou might have given the same basic information differently: *Mrs. Viola Cullinan, a plump woman, lived in a three-bedroom house somewhere behind the post office.* Subordinating the information about Mrs. Cullinan's size to that about her house would have resulted in a slightly different meaning, of course. As a writer, you must think carefully about where you want your emphasis to be and subordinate accordingly.

Besides adding information, subordination also helps establish logical relationships among the facts in a sentence. These relationships are often specified by the subordinating conjunctions introducing many dependent clauses—words such as *after, because,* or *so* (see 6b7 for a complete list). Look, for example, at two more sentences from Maya Angelou, shown with the subordinate clauses italicized and the subordinating conjunctions underlined.

> I left the front door wide open <u>so</u> *all the neighbors could hear.* She usually rested her smile until late afternoon <u>when</u> *her women friends dropped in and Miss Glory, the cook, served them cold drinks on the closed-in porch.*
> —MAYA ANGELOU, "My Name Is Margaret"

Subordination can be used to combine short sentences in ways that signal logical relationships. For example:

SEPARATE SENTENCES

Todd tried to explain the frying process.

I was mesmerized by the blast of heat.

The heat billowed from the vat of grease.

COMBINED SENTENCE

While Todd tried to explain the frying process, I was mesmerized by the blast of heat *that* billowed from the vat of grease.

Depending on what grammatical structures you use to subordinate, you can call attention to a less important element of a sentence in various ways, as the following series demonstrates:

The Parks Council report was persuasively written. It contained five typed pages. [no subordination]

The Parks Council report, *which contained five typed pages,* was persuasively written. [clause]

The Parks Council report, *containing five typed pages,* was persuasively written. [participial phrase]

The *five-page* Parks Council report was persuasively written. [single-word modifier]

The Parks Council report, *five typed pages,* was persuasively written. [appositive]

311

EXERCISE 18.3

Combine each of the following sets of sentences into one sentence that uses subordination to signal the relationships among ideas.

> ### Example
> I was looking over my books.
> I noticed that *Burr* was missing.
> This book is a favorite of my roommate's.
>
> While I was looking over my books, I noticed that *Burr*, one of my roommate's favorite books, was missing.

1. I entered the hospital room.
   I was shocked.
   Tubes and life-support machines filled the room.
2. Entwistle and Townshend met Roger Daltrey.
   Roger Daltrey played guitar and sang.
   They formed a group called the High Numbers.
3. We had dug a seventy-foot ditch.
   My boss would pour gravel into the ditch.
   I would level the gravel with a shovel.
4. *Working* was written by Studs Terkel.
   It is an important book.
   It examines the situation of the American worker.
5. The scenery there is beautiful.
   The mountains have caps of snow.
   The lakes are deep and full of fish.
   The pastures are green.
   It is an ideal spot to spend spring break.

EXERCISE 18.4

Revise the following paragraph, subordinating the less important ideas to the more important where appropriate.

I stayed with my friend Louise. She owns a huge mangy wolf. It is actually a seven-eighths wolf cross. The poor creature is allergic to everything. It looks like a shabby, moth-eaten exhibit of a stuffed wolf in a third-rate museum. Louise and Bill feed it rice and raw potatoes. It slavers all over everything. It snaps up the pieces of potato. It never goes out of the house. It sleeps on the beds. They are covered with animal hair. It makes no sounds. It just looks at you with those sunken, wild eyes. It is not dangerous or ferocious. It is just completely miserable. This animal should never have been born. It's trying to tell you that with every twitch.

▌1. Using subordination for special effect

Carefully used subordination can create powerful effects. Some particularly fine examples come from Martin Luther King, Jr. In the following passage he piles up dependent clauses to gain emphasis for his main statement, given in the independent clause. This emphasis is heightened by the repetition of the subordinating conjunction *when* to suggest forcefully, "why we find it difficult to wait."

Perhaps it is easy for those who have never felt the stinging darts of segregation to say, "Wait." But *when* you have seen vicious mobs lynch your mothers and fathers at will and drown your sisters and brothers at whim; *when* you have seen hate-filled policemen curse, kick, and even kill your black brothers and sisters; . . . *when* you have to concoct an answer for a five-year-old son who is asking: "Daddy, why do white people treat colored people so mean?"; *when* you take a cross-country drive and find it necessary to sleep night after night in the uncomfortable corners of your automobile because no motel will accept you; . . . *when* your first name becomes "nigger," your middle name becomes "boy" (however old you are) and your last name becomes "John," and your wife and mother are never given the respected title "Mrs."; . . . *when* you are forever fighting a degenerating sense of "nobodiness"—then you will understand why we find it difficult to wait.

–Martin Luther King, Jr., "Letter from Birmingham Jail"

Look now at a student example that uses subordination in a similar way:

Though dogs are messy and hard to train, *though* they chew up my shoes and give me the blues, *though* they howl like wolves but jump at their own shadows, *though* they eat me out of house and home—still, I love them all.

A dependent clause can also be used to create an ironic effect if it somehow undercuts the independent clause. Probably no American writer was better at using this technique than Mark Twain. In a tongue-in-cheek commencement address, Twain once opened a paragraph with this sentence (which you can see in context in 12f as an example of a shift in tone):

Always obey your parents, *when they are present.*

–Mark Twain, "Advice to Youth"

In undercutting the parental authority asserted in the independent clause, this dependent clause creates irony—and makes us laugh. Now look at a student writer's use of the same technique:

Never eat fattening foods—*unless you are hungry.*

2. Revising for more effective subordination

When you are revising a draft, it is a good idea to give some attention to the way you use subordination, especially if you tend to use too many short sentences or coordinate structures. Begin by figuring out which of your ideas are most important. Take a page of your draft, and underline the main ideas. You may find it useful to underline major ideas twice, lesser ones once. If the ideas marked as *most* important do not appear in independent clauses, revise the page so that they do. Subordinate the less important ideas by putting them in dependent clauses or phrases. If ideas are of equal importance, turn back to 18a2 for advice.

Study the following passage from an essay about Edgar Allan Poe's "William Wilson," a strange tale about a young man who meets his double. Notice how the paragraph can be revised in order to connect and order its ideas more effectively.

In the following years at the academy, <u>the two William Wilsons shared a bizarre relationship.</u> <u>The second Wilson established himself as equal to the first.</u> He was equal both in the classroom and on the playground. The first Wilson was used to feeling superior to his schoolmates, so <u>he was quite disturbed at the thought of having an equal.</u> He was especially disturbed that this equal had the same name and birthdate.

This passage depends heavily on simple sentences and use of simple coordination. Underlining the most important ideas gives the writer an idea of what might be subordinated to them, and the revision changes three of the less important ideas into prepositional phrases, an adjective clause, and an appositive phrase (shown here in italics).

In the following years at the academy, the two William Wilsons shared a bizarre relationship. The second Wilson established himself as equal to the first, *both in the classroom and on the playground.* The first Wilson, *who was used to feeling superior to his schoolmates,* was quite disturbed at the thought of having an equal, *especially one with the same name and birthdate.*

In addition to checking for places where subordination might be more effective than coordination or separate sentences, you need to

314

make sure that you have not used subordination inappropriately. **Excessive subordination** occurs when too many subordinating structures, usually dependent clauses, are strung together, so that readers have trouble keeping track of the main idea expressed in the independent clause. Look, for example, at the following sentence:

> Philip II sent the Spanish Armada to conquer England, which was ruled by Elizabeth, who had executed Mary because she was plotting to overthrow Elizabeth, who was a Protestant, whereas Mary and Philip were Roman Catholics.

The long string of subordinate clauses at the end of this sentence makes the relationship of the ideas very hard to follow and also makes it hard for readers to remember the idea in the independent clause at the beginning. Notice how changing one of the dependent clauses to the independent clause of a new sentence and reducing two others to appositive phrases makes the relationship of ideas clearer:

> Philip II sent the Spanish Armada to conquer England, which was ruled by Elizabeth. She had executed Mary, a Roman Catholic like Philip, because Mary was plotting to overthrow Elizabeth, a Protestant.

READING WITH AN EYE FOR COORDINATION AND SUBORDINATION

Turn to the first draft of "The Bagelry," in 2j. Read it over with special attention to the use of coordination and subordination. Do you notice any patterns—is there some of each? more of one than the other? Analyze one paragraph, identifying the coordinate and subordinate phrases and clauses. Do they make their points with clear emphasis? If not, revise the paragraphs following the advice given in 18a2 and 18b2.

FOR EXAMINING SUBORDINATION IN YOUR OWN WRITING

Choose two paragraphs from one of your current drafts, and analyze them for use of subordination. How many dependent clauses do you find? How do they function in the sentences—as nouns, adjectives, or adverbs? Are the ideas in the dependent clauses those that *should* be subordinate to the ones in the independent clauses? On the basis of this analysis, revise the passage to use subordination effectively.

19. Creating and Maintaining Parallel Structures

Parallel grammatical structures form many of our most familiar phrases: *sink or swim, live and let live, shape up or ship out.* These clichés demonstrate **parallelism,** expressing parallel elements in the same grammatical form. But parallelism goes far beyond such clichés, and, in fact, characterizes some of the most elegant passages in our language. Look, for example, at how E. B. White uses parallel structures to describe the enchantment of watching a bareback circus rider practicing her act:

> The enchantment grew *not out of something that happened* or was performed *but out of something that seemed* to go round and around and around with the girl, attending her, a steady gleam in the shape of a circle—a ring *of ambition, of happiness, of youth.*
>
> —E. B. WHITE, "The Ring of Time"

This description uses the power of parallelism to create its special rhythms. Just as the young woman goes "round and around and around," balanced easily on her horse, so the sentence circles rhythmically too, balanced by a series of parallel phrases and clauses. Read the sentence aloud, and you will hear the effect of those parallel structures, rocking gently back and forth much as does the horse in the ring.

This chapter will provide you the opportunity to practice parallelism and help you to create pleasing rhythmic effects in your own writing.

316

▎ 19a. Using parallel structures in a series

All items in a series should be in parallel form—all nouns, all prepositional phrases, all adverb clauses, and so on. Parallel structure makes the series clear and easy to follow, bringing both grace and coherence.

> The quarterhorse *skipped, pranced,* and absolutely *sashayed* onto the track. [verbs]

> Three subjects guaranteed to cause a fight are *politics, religion,* and *money.* [nouns]

> A cloud *of critics, of compilers, of commentators,* darkened the face of learning, and the decline *of genius* was soon followed by the corruption *of taste.* [prepositional phrases]
> —EDWARD GIBBON, *The Decline and Fall of the Roman Empire*

> As more and more antismoking laws are passed, we see legions of potential nonsmokers *munching Nicorette, gnawing peppermints, chewing pencils, knitting sweaters,* or *practicing self-hypnotism.* [participial phrases]

> *Pushing a pen or pencil, pounding a typewriter,* or *manipulating a word processor* just does not appeal to me. [gerund phrases]

When parallel elements are *not* presented in parallel grammatical form, the result can be awkward and even difficult to follow.

> NONPARALLEL   The duties of the job included baby-sitting, house-cleaning, and the preparation of the meals.

> PARALLEL   The duties of the job included *baby-sitting, house-cleaning,* and *preparing the meals.*

Lists

Items in a list should also be parallel in structure. Note the lack of parallelism in the following list:

> Please observe the following regulations when using the library coffee service:
>
> 1. Coffee *to be made* only by library staff.
> 2. Coffee service *to be closed* at 4 P.M.
> 3. Doughnuts *to be kept* in cabinet.
> 4. No faculty members *should handle* coffee materials.

The fourth item on the list is not parallel with the others because it contains a finite verb rather than an infinitive, and thus is a full sentence, not a phrase. Rewritten to maintain parallelism, this item could read:

    4. Coffee materials *not to be handled* by faculty members.

A formal outline should also be parallel in form (see 40b3.)

EXERCISE 19.1

Using two of the example sentences above as models to imitate, write two sentences of your own that include a series of parallel phrases.

▌ 19b. Using parallel structures with pairs

One common use of parallel structures occurs in the pairing of two ideas. If the ideas in a pair are parallel in thought, they should be parallel in grammatical structure. Parallel structures are especially appropriate when two ideas are being compared or contrasted.

> History became popular, and historians became alarmed.
> > —WILL DURANT

> It's easier to drive a new pickup truck than an old luxury car.

When two clauses in a sentence express compared or contrasted ideas in exactly or almost exactly parallel structures, they produce a **balanced sentence,** one with two parts that "mirror" each other. Balanced sentences create an especially forceful impression.

> Mankind must put an end to war, or war will put an end to mankind.
> > —JOHN F. KENNEDY

> There is much in your book that is original and valuable—but what is original is not valuable, and what is valuable is not original.
> > —SAMUEL JOHNSON

With coordinating conjunctions

In general, use the same grammatical structure on both sides of any of the coordinating conjunctions—*and, but, or, nor, for, so.* (See 6b7 for more information about coordinating conjunctions). The more nearly parallel the two structures are, the stronger the connection of ideas will be.

> The group performed *whenever anyone would listen* and *wherever anyone would pay.*

When elements connected by a coordinating conjunction are not parallel in form, the relationship of the elements can be hard to see.

NONPARALLEL	Medical surveys suggest that Americans *are dieting more* but *still consume too much fat.*
REVISED	Medical surveys suggest that Americans *are dieting more* but *are still consuming too much fat.*

With correlative conjunctions

Use the same structure after both parts of a *correlative conjunction—either . . . or; both . . . and; neither . . . nor; not only . . . but also.* (See 6b7 for more information about correlative conjunctions.)

Native Son depicts a world where blacks have neither *decent housing* nor *secure family lives.*

NONPARALLEL	I wanted not only *to go away to school* but also *to New England.*
REVISED	I wanted not only *to go away to school* but also *to live in New England.*

EXERCISE 19.2

Complete the following sentences, using parallel words or phrases in each case.

Example

The best teacher is one who <u>loves learning</u>, <u>respects students</u>, and <u>demands the best</u>.

1. _____, _____, and _____, for tomorrow we die.
2. My favorite pastimes include _____, _____, and _____.
3. We must either _____ or _____.
4. I want not only _____ but also _____.
5. The ideal parent will be _____, _____, and _____.

EXERCISE 19.3

Revise the following sentences to eliminate any errors in parallel structure.

Example

Roger has studied archery, forestry, and how to treat wild animals.

Roger has studied *archery, forestry,* and the *treatment of wild animals.*

1. I remember the sticky, humid afternoons with the air as heavy as a mother's suitcase, my body dripping with sweat, how my sandy mouth yearned for an ice-cold glass of water.

319

2. Most readers begin reading with an implicit faith in the coherence of the text and that the writer will convey meaning clearly.
3. It was a question of either reducing their staff, or they had to somehow find new customers for their baked potatoes.
4. To need a new pair of shoes and not being able to afford them is enough to make anybody sensitive.
5. I'll never forget the good times we had—skiing, the swims, and especially that you taught me how to handle a windsurfer.
6. Too many students come to college only for fun, to find a husband or wife, or for putting off having to go to work.
7. We can improve the cafeteria by doing several things: less noise, not leaving trays around, and we should leave the tables clean.
8. Her job was to show new products, help Mr. Greer with sales, and an opportunity was given to be part of advertising.
9. The Greek system not only provides the individual with an incentive for striving toward academic success but also it contributes to the development of leadership skills.
10. Stress can result in low self-esteem, total frustration, inability to sleep, nervous breakdown, or eventually resulting in suicide.

19c. Including all necessary words in parallel constructions

In addition to making parallel elements grammatically similar, be careful to include any other necessary words—prepositions, relative pronouns, and so on.

NONPARALLEL   We considered moving to a small town in the Southwest or a suburb of San Francisco.

PARALLEL   We considered moving *to a small town in the Southwest* or *to a suburb of San Francisco.*

NONPARALLEL   High on our list was Mill Valley, located in Marin County and which is only a half-hour from San Francisco.

PARALLEL   High on our list was Mill Valley, *which is located in Marin County* and *which is only a half-hour from San Francisco.*

19d. Using parallel structures for emphasis and special effect

Parallel structures can help a writer emphasize the most important ideas in a sentence. Look at the following sentence:

> The dancers wore costumes that were exquisitely perfect in every detail, and they filed onto the stage with their arms akimbo and their toes pointed.

The meaning of this sentence is clear, but what seems to be the most important idea, the exquisitely perfect costumes, is buried in a dependent clause in the middle of the sentence. This idea can be emphasized by making it the last in a series of parallel absolute phrases arranged in climactic order:

> The dancers filed onto the stage, arms akimbo, toes pointed, costumes exquisitely perfect in every detail.

See 17a for more information about emphasis within a sentence.

Besides emphasizing main ideas, parallel structures can create a number of different stylistic effects. One of these is orderliness, a sense of steady or building rhythm, as in the following sentence:

> Most police work is concerned with scared people who have been bitten by dogs, frantic people whose children have run away from home, old people who have no one to talk to, and impatient people whose first response to any situation is to "call the cops."

Note here how the repetition of the parallel phrases *scared people* . . . , *frantic people* . . . , *old people* . . . , *impatient people* builds a rhythm or beat that leads us to expect more of the same. Parallel elements thus work to create and fulfill reader expectations.

> At work, he may have time to gulp down a cup of coffee if the dining halls are running smoothly, if all the workers show up, and if the boss is not asking questions.

This sentence creates an impression of somewhat desperate activity as it piles up the three parallel *if* clauses.

EXERCISE 19.4

Underline the parallel structures in the following passage. Then use the passage as a model to imitate in creating a passage that uses parallelism in a similar way. You might begin such a passage with "But love is not all . . ." or "But youth is not all . . ." or even "But getting a degree is not all. . . ."

> But life is not all eloquence and adulation: life is wiping the baby's bum; it is a bad case of croup; it is quarrels with one's spouse; it is disappointment, distraction, indignities by the dozen; it is the death of friends, wife, son, and

brothers, carried off like fluff in the wind; it is alien evenings, cold stairwells, frosty sheets, lack of love; for what does the great spirit need that touches the body but the touch of the body, as oratory needs silence, and revolution peace? We are nourished by our absences and opposites; contraries quench our thirst.

—WILLIAM GASS, "Emerson and the Essay"

EXERCISE 19.5

Revise the following sentences to make effective use of parallel clauses. Change or add words if need be.

Example

Where we eat, how we eat, what we eat, and what are our reasons for eating—these are major questions for many yuppies.

Where we eat, how we eat, what we eat, and *why we eat*—these are major questions for many yuppies.

1. I will always remember how the girls dressed in green plaid skirts and the boys wearing green plaid ties.
2. There are three ways to apply Ninhydrin to the area to be examined: it may be applied with a brush; it may be sprayed on with a spray gun; or you can dip the object in the solution.
3. No longer are women required to play supporting roles behind their male leads; they do not have to play empty-headed debutantes whose only attributes are superficial, either.
4. There are two types of wallflowers: the male wallflower is known as the nerd, and the female, who is known as the skeeve.
5. Kris was off to the big university and sorority life; Stacy, on the other hand, was remaining at home and attending the local community college.

READING WITH AN EYE FOR PARALLELISM

The following paragraph about a bareback rider practicing her circus act is laden with parallelism. (You will recognize the second sentence as the example used to open this chapter.) Read the paragraph, and identify all the parallel structures. Consider what effect they create on you as a reader, and try to decide why the author chose to put his ideas in such overtly parallel form. Try imitating the penultimate sentence, the one beginning *In a week or two.*

The richness of the scene was in its plainness, its natural condition—of horse, of ring, of girl, even to the girl's bare feet that gripped the bare back of her proud and ridiculous mount. The enchantment grew not out of anything that happened or was performed but out of something that seemed to go round and around and around with the girl, attending her, a steady gleam in the shape of a circle—a ring of ambition, of happiness, of youth. (And the positive pleasures of equilibrium under difficulties.) In a week or two, all would be changed, all (or almost all) lost: the girl would wear makeup, the horse would wear gold, the ring would be painted, the bark would be clean for the feet of the horse, the girl's feet would be clean for the slippers that she'd wear. All, all would be lost.   –E. B. WHITE, "The Ring of Time"

FOR EXAMINING PARALLELISM IN YOUR OWN WRITING

Choose four or five paragraphs from a draft you have recently written. Read through them carefully, noting any series of words, phrases, or clauses. Determine whether these series are in parallel form, and if not, revise them for parallelism. Then reread the paragraphs, looking for places where parallel structures would add emphasis or clarity to your writing, and revise those places to use such structures.

20. Varying Sentence Structures

Row upon row of trees identical in size and shape may appeal at some level to our sense of orderliness, but in spite of that appeal they soon become very boring. Constant unanimity in anything, in fact, soon gets tiresome; perhaps variety *is* the spice of life. Certainly that is true in sentence structures, where sameness can result in dull, listless prose. The truth of this maxim was illustrated anew not long ago in a college classroom discussion of one student's essay. The group had worked on the essay for most of an hour, correcting errors, reorganizing paragraphs, clarifying the major points. Finally, one person said, "Okay, okay—but it's still BORING." All of the others, including the author, agreed. But they were stuck. The group could not come up with any new ideas and was about ready to give up when one student exclaimed, "I've got it! Look at these sentences. They all look about the same length!"

And they were. In fact, impossible as it may sound, every sentence in the essay was between twenty-two and twenty-five words long. Once the group realized this fact, they could begin to work again, carving some of the sentences into very short ones and combining others to create new rhythms. Through this revision, the essay took on new life as its boring sameness faded away.

This chapter will examine how to use the traditional foes of boring sentences—variety in lengths, in openings, and in grammatical, functional, and rhetorical patterns.

▌ 20a. Varying sentence lengths

The situation described in the introduction above illustrates perfectly the need for varying sentence length. Doing so not only makes prose more readable and interesting but also creates a pleasing rhythmic effect, what some students have called "flow." Once you begin to pay attention to sentence length, varying it for specific effects can be very satisfying.

Deciding how and when to vary and balance sentence length is not always easy, however. How short is too short? How long is too long? Is there a "just right" length for a particular sentence or idea? These questions are difficult to answer because the answers depend on, among other things, the writer's purpose, intended audience, and topic. A children's story, for instance, may call for mostly short sentences, while an article on nuclear disarmament in *The Atlantic* may call for considerably longer ones. In other words, in different situations, either very long or very short sentences can be effective.

▌ 1. Using short sentences

Very short sentences can often pack a powerful punch. Study the following famous short sentences, and see if you agree that each owes much of its power to its brevity; more words would detract.

Nice guys finish last.

Crime doesn't pay.

Let them eat cake.

War is hell.

The following passage from a speech by Chief Sitting Bull illustrates how effective a series of short sentences and other short structures can be:

What treaty that the whites have kept has the red man broken? Not one. What treaty that the white men ever made with us have they kept? Not one. When I was a boy the Sioux owned the world; the sun rose and set on their land; they sent ten thousand men to battle. Where are the warriors today? Who slew them? Where are our lands? Who owns them?
—SITTING BULL, *Touch the Earth*

Notice how Sitting Bull's short questions, clauses, and fragments build a rhythm that gives power to his indictment of the white world. Repeated short sentences, if used with awareness of their effect, can go far beyond "See Spot run" into rhythmic beat and cadenced dignity.

▌ 2. Using long sentences

In contrast to short sentences, long sentences are particularly useful for presenting a set of complex, interlocking ideas or for building up momentum. The following paragraph shows how a series of long sentences can be used effectively in this way:

> Femininity pleases men because it makes them appear more masculine by contrast; and, in truth, conferring an extra portion of unearned gender distinction on men, an unchallenged space in which to breathe freely and feel stronger, wiser, more competent, is femininity's special gift. One could say that masculinity is often an effort to please women, but masculinity is known to please by displays of mastery and competence while femininity pleases by suggesting that these concerns, except in small matters, are beyond its intent. Whimsy, unpredictability and patterns of thinking and behavior that are dominated by emotion, such as tearful expressions of sentiment and fear, are thought to be feminine precisely because they lie outside the established route to success.
> —SUSAN BROWNMILLER, *Femininity*

Notice that each of the three long sentences encapsulates the complex relationships between femininity and masculinity, and between women and men, that Brownmiller is seeking to explore. Short sentences would not work as effectively here because they would not adequately reflect the complexity of the ideas being presented.

▌ 3. Alternating short and long sentences

Although series of short and long sentences can both be effective in individual situations, frequent alternation in sentence length characterizes much memorable writing. After one or more long sentences that express complex ideas or images, the pith of a short sentence can be refreshing and arresting. Similarly, a long sentence that follows a series of short ones can serve as a climax or summation that relaxes the tension or fulfills the expectation created by the series, giving readers a sense of completion. Notice the difference between these two passages, one of which contains sentences of fairly uniform length and the other of which varies sentence length.

326

UNIFORM LENGTHS

The house is a fixer-upper, of course. For the past two days, I've been fixing things. It seems like the past two decades. I've been crawling about in the basement, which is dirt-floored, trying to learn to fix copper plumbing. The people renting the house last winter froze and burst the pipes. As a result, I have to put in all new stuff, learning as I go. With five-foot headroom, it's a real joy to be playing with torch and hot solder down there. I climb around oozing soilpipes from another era. I crouch Quasimodo-like, measuring, cutting, crouching, slouching, until my back is permanently bent. I have been picking spiders out of my beard, and my clothes are indescribable.

VARIED LENGTHS

The house is a fixer-upper, of course, and so for the past two days (it seems like the past two decades), I've been fixing things, crawling about in the basement—dirt-floored, naturally—trying to learn to fix copper plumbing. What a nightmare! The people renting the house last winter froze and burst the pipes, and so I have to put in all new stuff. I'm learning as I go. With five-foot headroom, it's a real joy to be playing with torch and hot solder down there, climbing around oozing soilpipes from another era, crouching Quasimodo-like, measuring, cutting, crouching, slouching. My back is permanently bent. My beard is full of spiders. My clothes are indescribable.

See the next section (20a4) for an analysis of this passage.

4. Checking for varied sentence lengths

As you revise a draft, begin by looking at the lengths of your sentences. If they do not seem to vary enough in length, begin revising them so that they do. Do not, however, change sentence lengths arbitrarily. Rather, balance them so they most effectively convey your meaning. Think about the ideas you want to emphasize, and try to arrange your sentence lengths in a way that emphasizes them. For example, if two or more short sentences in a row express closely related ideas, ask yourself if you could make the relationship between these ideas clearer or more precise by using coordination or subordination to combine them into a single, longer sentence. (See Chapter 18 for more information about coordination and subordination.) You may discover, on the other hand, that a long sentence contains two or three important ideas that would be more emphatic if each was expressed in a short sentence of its own.

Look back at the passage in 20a3 to see how this kind of revision can bring life to prose that suffers from overly uniform sentence lengths. In the second version, the writer uses coordination and subordination to combine the first four sentences of the first version into one long sentence that connects the main ideas of *a fixer-upper*, doing the fixing, and crawling about the basement. After this long sentence, he then adds a very short exclamatory sentence that both sums up the ideas in the first sentence and points ahead to the rest of the passage. Next, he combines two closely related ideas, about burst pipes and the installation of new ones, into one sentence of medium length, changing the participial phrase *learning as I go* into a separate short sentence. The next three sentences of the original version, all dealing with the ordeal of working in the basement, are combined into one long sentence. Finally, a dependent clause and the two short clauses of a compound sentence are separated into three short, parallel sentences (see Chapter 19), which give a blunt, hammering effect to the writer's expression of his complaints.

EXERCISE 20.1

Following is a paragraph that can be improved by varying sentence length. Read the paragraph aloud to get a sense of how it sounds. Then revise it, creating some short emphatic sentences and combining other sentences to create more effective long sentences. Add words or change punctuation as you need to.

Before beginning to play bridge, it is necessary to have the proper materials, the correct number of people, and a knowledge of the rank of suits and cards. The necessary materials include a full deck of playing cards (minus the jokers) and a score pad, along with a pen or pencil. Bridge is played by four people divided into two partnerships, which are usually decided by drawing cards from a shuffled deck. The two players who draw the highest cards and the two who draw the lowest are partners, and the partners sit across from each other. The person who draws the highest card during partnership is the first dealer. Starting with the person on his or her left and going clockwise, the dealer deals each person one card at a time, face down. The deal continues until all four players have thirteen cards apiece. After the deal, the players sort their cards by suit, usually alternating black and red suits. The players then arrange the cards in ranking order from the highest, the ace, to the lowest, the deuce. The five highest cards, the ace, king, queen, jack, and ten, are referred to as honors. There is one suit that has great power and outranks every other one, the trump suit, which is designated at the start of the game.

▌ 20b. Varying sentence openings

In making prose readable and interesting, beginning sentences in different ways is just as important as making them of different lengths. For instance, when each sentence begins with the subject of an independent clause, a passage may seem to lurch or jerk along:

> *The way* football and basketball are played is as interesting as the players. *Football* is a game of precision. *Each play* is diagrammed to accomplish a certain goal. *A coach* designs the plays like an engineer would design a bridge. *Basketball* is a game of availability. *A basketball game* looks like a track meet. *The team* that drops of exhaustion first loses. *Basketball players* are also often compared to artists. *The players' moves and slam dunks* are their masterpieces.

Varying sentence openings can prevent this jerky effect. This section will focus on three ways of varying openings—transitional expressions; prepositional, verbal, and absolute phrases; and dependent clauses.

▌ 1. Using transitional expressions

Note the ways in which opening transitions bring variety and clarity to this passage:

> In order to be alert Friday morning in New York, I planned to take the shuttle from Washington Thursday night. *On Thursday morning* it began to snow in Washington and to snow even harder in New York. *By mid-afternoon* I decided not to risk the shuttle and caught a train to New York. *Seven hours later* the train completed its three-hour trip. I arrived at Penn Station to find a city shut down by the worst blizzard since 1947.   —LINDA ELLERBEE, *"And So It Goes"*

Here the transitional words establish chronology and help carry us along smoothly through the paragraph. Other groups of transitional expressions that establish a sequence include *on the one hand . . . on the other hand* and *on the left . . . straight ahead . . . on the right.*

Single-word transitional expressions that can be used to vary sentence openings include these:

ADVERBS	suddenly, fortunately, surprisingly
COORDINATING CONJUNCTIONS	and, but, or, nor, for, so, yet
CONJUNCTIVE ADVERBS	however, nevertheless, therefore, hence

Be careful to check that any such sentence opening suits the occasion and signals the appropriate chronological, spatial, or logical relationship with the preceding sentence. (See 5c5 for a discussion and list of transitional expressions.)

▌ 2. Using phrases

Prepositional, verbal, and absolute phrases can also provide variety in sentence openers.

Prepositional phrases

At each desk, a computer printout gives the necessary data.

From a few scraps of wood in the Middle Ages to a precisely carved, electrified instrument in the 1980s, the guitar has gone through uncounted changes.

Verbal phrases

Dressed in denim jeans and a dark-blue chamois shirt, a young woman appeared at the door.

To qualify for flight training, one must be in good physical condition and pass a written test.

Absolute phrases

Our hopes for snow shattered, we started home.

Baton raised in a salute, the maestro readied the orchestra.

▌ 3. Using dependent clauses

Dependent clauses are another way to open a sentence.

While the boss sat on his tractor, I was down in a ditch pounding in stakes and leveling out the bottom.

Who she is is difficult to explain.

▌ 4. Checking for varied sentence openings

As you revise, especially if you think your writing may be choppy, look carefully at your sentence openings. Underline the subject of each sentence. If most of your sentences begin with the subject, revise some of them by opening with transitional expressions, phrases, or dependent clauses.

Look at the following passage, which uses only subject openings, and then see how varying the sentence openings makes the passage easier to read.

FIRST DRAFT

<u>Most marathon runners</u> find that running with another person is helpful. <u>They</u> must not be afraid to pass this person, though, in order to run as well as possible. <u>Runners</u> must realize furthermore that even if they do not win the race, they achieve a victory by pushing their bodies to finish.

REVISED

Most marathon runners find that running with another person is helpful. In order to run as well as possible, though, *they* must not be afraid to pass this person. Furthermore, *runners* must realize that even if they do not win the race, they achieve victory by pushing their bodies to finish.

EXERCISE 20.2

Go back to the paragraph comparing football and basketball in 20b. Using transitional expressions, phrases, and/or dependent clauses, revise the paragraph to vary its sentence openings and thus to make the passage smoother and more coherent.

▌ 20c. Varying sentence types

In addition to using different lengths and openings, you can help to vary your sentence structures by using different *types* of sentences. Sentences can be classified in three different ways: grammatically, functionally, and rhetorically (see 6d).

Grammatical types

Grammatically, sentences fall into four categories—**simple, compound, complex,** and **compound-complex**—based on the number of independent and dependent clauses they contain. Varying your sentences among these grammatical types will go a long way toward creating readable, effective prose. (See 6d1 for an explanation and examples of each type.)

Functional types

Functional types of sentences include **declarative** (making a statement), **interrogative** (asking a question), **imperative** (giving a command), and **exclamatory** (expressing strong feeling). (See 6d2.) Most sentences in essays are declarative, but occasionally you may want to include a command, a question, or even an exclamation of some kind if such sentence types are appropriate for your purpose. Note how they are used in these examples:

> Coal-burning plants undoubtedly harm the environment in various ways; among others, they contribute to acid rain. *But consider the alternatives.*

> We kept pressing on into the park. *And why? Why would sixteen middle-aged people try to backpack thirty-seven miles?* At this point, I was not at all sure.

> *Divorcés! They were everywhere!* Sometimes he felt like a new member of an enormous club, the Divorcés of America, that he had never before even heard of.

Rhetorical types

Two rhetorical sentence types, periodic and cumulative, spotlight sentence endings and beginnings and can be especially helpful in achieving sentence variety. Although not all sentences can be classified as cumulative or periodic, they can create strong effects when used in appropriate situations.

Periodic sentences postpone the main idea (usually in an independent clause) until the very end of the sentence. Effectively written periodic sentences are especially useful for building tension or building toward a climactic or surprise ending. At their best, they keep us alert by forcing us to hold information in a kind of "suspended animation" until the end. (See 6d3 for more discussion.)

> Early one morning, under the arc of a lamp, carefully, silently, in smock and leather gloves, old Doctor Manza grafted a cat's head onto a chicken's trunk.   —DYLAN THOMAS

> Few more obvious, natural, apparent, ostensible, plain, intelligent, literal, and downright objects exist on this earth than a boiled potato.
> —MARY ELLEN CHASE

> Even though large tracts of Europe and many old and famous states have fallen or may fall into the grasp of the Gestapo and all the odious apparatus of Nazi rule, we shall not flag or fail.   —WINSTON CHURCHILL

Note in each example how the writer holds back the main idea, thus using the end of the sentence to shock, surprise, or inspire.

Look at the following sentence and its revision to see how periodic order can provide emphasis.

The nations of the world have no alternative but coexistence because another world war would be unwinnable and because total destruction would certainly occur.

PERIODIC

Because another world war would be unwinnable and because total destruction would certainly occur, the nations of the world have no alternative but coexistence.

Nothing is wrong with the first sentence, which conveys the information clearly. But to put greater emphasis on the idea in the independent clause of the sentence—no alternative but coexistence—the writer chose to revise using the periodic pattern.

Cumulative sentences, which begin with an independent clause and then add details in phrases and other clauses, are the dominant rhetorical pattern today, far more common than periodic sentences. They are useful when you want to provide both immediate understanding of the main idea and a great deal of supporting detail. Note how the writers of the following sentences use the cumulative pattern not only to add important detail to the independent clause but also to end with a strong word or image:

> From boyhood to manhood, I have remembered him in a single image— seated, asleep on the sofa, his head thrown back in a hideous corpselike grin, the evening newspaper spread out before him.
>
> —RICHARD RODRIGUEZ, "My Parents"

> Four steps past the turnstiles everybody is already backed up haunch to paunch for the climb up the ramp and the stairs to the surface, a great funnel of flesh, wool, felt, leather, rubber and steaming alumicrom, with the blood squeezing through everybody's old sclerotic arteries in hopped-up spurts from too much coffee and the effort of surfacing from the subway at the rush hour.   —TOM WOLFE

EXERCISE 20.3

Revise the following sentences into periodic form.

1. The members of the crew team entered the shell house one by one, tired and weary, at four o'clock on a cold, damp morning in Seattle, Washington.
2. I became the best salesperson in our store once I mastered the problems that I had encountered at the beginning and once I had become thoroughly familiar with the stock.

▌1. Checking for varied sentence types

As you revise, check to see that you have varied your sentence types sufficiently. Begin by noting the grammatical types you have used, marking each of your sentences as simple, compound, complex, or compound-complex. If any one or two patterns overwhelmingly predominate, combine, divide, and otherwise revise sentences until you have a wide range of types in your draft.

Next, note any sentences that are commands, questions, or exclamations. Decide whether these sentences are appropriate in context, and if not, delete or revise them.

To check for rhetorical sentence types, underline the independent clause(s) in each sentence. If a sentence opens with an independent clause and then builds with a series of modifying details, label it cumulative. If a sentence opens with a series of subordinating clauses or phrases and holds the independent clause "in suspense" until the end, label it periodic. (Many sentences will be neither.) Now consider whether each type is being used as effectively as possible. For each periodic sentence, see if you have used suspense to best advantage and built up to a climax. For each cumulative sentence, see if you have established your main point at the beginning and if the information in the rest of the sentence develops this point clearly and grammatically.

Finally, look at the balance of all sentence types. If your writing is like most people's, you will have few periodic sentences; few imperative, interrogative, or exclamatory sentences; and few compound-complex sentences. Be aware of this information as you revise, but do not revise arbitrarily to include more of a specific type. Revise only when the content calls for it—if, for instance, a sentence contains a surprise, a periodic structure will help emphasize that surprise.

Study how the sentences in the following passage are identified and then revised:

FIRST DRAFT

The purpose of speech is most often to persuade. [simple] It is seldom to generate understanding or to stimulate thoughtful response. [simple] Speeches on television take advantage of this fact. [simple] A televised speech gives viewers the time only to receive information, to respond emotionally to it, to "feel" it. [simple/cumulative] Viewers can simply enjoy or deplore its impact. [simple] Unlike a televised speech, a written speech can be read, reread, and analyzed. [simple] The reader can thoroughly process and analyze it. [simple] For this reason, I prefer to read and study a speech, not watch and instantly swallow it. [simple] This preference is limited to speeches that may be of great importance to me. [simple]

REVISED

The purpose of speech is most often not to generate understanding or to stimulate thoughtful response; rather, its purpose is merely to persuade. [compound] A televised speech takes advantage of this merely persuasive purpose by giving viewers time only to receive information, to respond emotionally to it, to "feel" or simply enjoy or deplore it. [simple/cumulative] Unlike a televised speech, a written speech can be read and reread, thoroughly analyzed and processed. [simple/periodic] For this reason, I prefer to read and study, not watch and instantly "swallow," any speech that may be of great importance to me. [complex]

EXERCISE 20.4

Following is an introductory paragraph from an essay. Analyze the paragraph carefully, noting for each sentence, the length, the kind of opening, and the grammatical and rhetorical type. Then revise the paragraph to add variety in sentence lengths, sentence openings, and sentence types.

When we arrived at the accident scene, I could tell that the injuries were not minor. I walked up to the car nearest me to check the injuries of the people inside. I looked through the driver's window and saw the woman's body entangled in the steering wheel. I told dispatch, via two-way radio, to send medics "code red, lights and siren." I then went to see how the passenger in the car was. The passenger appeared to be in shock and had a broken leg. The officer walked over and checked the other vehicle. The driver of the other vehicle was drunk and had received no injuries at all.

READING WITH AN EYE FOR SENTENCE VARIETY

Read the following paragraph, paying careful attention to the way the author varies its sentences—in length, opening, and types (grammatical, functional, and rhetorical).

I was never much of an athlete, but I was once a member of a team. Indeed, I was its star, and we were champions. I belonged to a squad of speed readers, although I was never awarded a letter for it. Still, we took on the top teams in our territory, and read as rapidly as possible every time we were challenged to a match, hoping to finish in front of our opponents: that tow-headed punk from Canton, the tomato-cheeked girl from Marietta, or that silent pair of sisters, all spectacles and squints, who looked tough as German script, and who hailed from Shaker Heights, Ohio, a region noted for its swift,

mean raveners of text. We called ourselves "The Speeders." Of course. Everybody did. There were the Sharon Speeders, the Steubenville Speeders, the
Sperryville Speeders, and the Niles Nouns. The Niles Nouns never won. How
could they—with that name. Nouns are always at rest.

–WILLIAM GASS, "On Reading to Oneself"

FOR EXAMINING SENTENCE VARIETY IN YOUR OWN WRITING

Choose several paragraphs of an essay you have recently written, and examine
them very carefully for variety of sentence structure. For each sentence, note
the length, the kind of opening, and the grammatical, functional, and rhetorical type. Then revise the paragraphs to achieve as wide a range of variation
as possible in these qualities. Read the original and revised versions aloud,
noting the differences in rhythm and impact.

21. Creating Memorable Prose

How many times have you read something so striking that you wanted immediately to share it with a friend? And how many times have you remembered the exact words of something you have read or heard? All of us recognize, and can even quote, certain passages from literature or history—the opening of *A Tale of Two Cities*, perhaps, or passages from "I Have a Dream." As students of writing, we would profit by taking the time to examine some of the elements that make pieces such as these so memorable. Consider, for instance, some lines from one of the most quoted speeches of recent times, John F. Kennedy's Inaugural Address:

> Let every nation know, whether it wishes us well or ill, that we shall 1
> pay any price, bear any burden, meet any hardship, support any friend,
> oppose any foe to assure the survival and the success of liberty.
>
> In your hands, my fellow citizens, more than mine, will rest the final 2
> success or failure of our course.
>
> And so, my fellow Americans, ask not what your country can do for 3
> you; ask what you can do for your country.
>
> —JOHN F. KENNEDY, Inaugural Address

What strategies did Kennedy use to make these lines so very memorable? First would be his use of *repetition*: in sentence 1, the repetition of short verb phrases, each with the word *any*, creates a powerful, hammerlike rhythm. Second might be his use of *inverted word order*: saving the subject until the end of sentence 2 adds dramatic emphasis to his statement. Third would be his use of *antithesis*, seen in sentence 3 in the two parallel clauses that accentuate the contrast of self and country. Finally, Kennedy's reliance on *strong verbs* and the *active voice* results in prose that is lively and thus memorable.

Each of these strategies and devices can be used to good effect by all writers. This chapter will examine each one and offer practice to help you use them in your work, to make your writing not only worth reading—but worth remembering.

▌ 21a. Choosing strong verbs

The greatest writers in any language are those with a genius for choosing the precise words that will arrest and hold a reader's attention. In your own writing, you can help to gain this attention by using precise nouns and adjectives instead of vague, catchall "buzzwords" (see 17b2). Perhaps even more important, however, you can use strong, precise verbs instead of weak, catchall verbs and instead of nouns.

▌ 1. Using strong, precise verbs

Verbs serve as the real workhorses of our language. Take a look, for instance, at the strong, precise verbs in the following passage:

> A fire engine, out for a trial spin, *roared* past Emerson's house, hot with readiness for public duty. Over the barn roofs the martens *dipped* and *chittered*. A swarthy daughter of an asparagus grower, in culottes, shirt, and bandanna, *pedalled* past on her bicycle.
>
> –E. B. WHITE, "Walden"

Instead of the italicized verbs, White could have used more general verbs such as *drove, flew, called,* and *rode*. But the more precise verbs are stronger because they give readers vivid sensory impressions of the actions they express. In White's verbs, readers can hear the roar of the fire engine, see the martens swooping downward and hear them chirping shrilly, and feel the girl pushing on the pedals of her bicycle.

Some of the most common verbs in English—especially *be, do,* and *have*—carry little or no sense of specific action, and many writers tend to overuse them in a situation where a more precise verb would be clearer and more effective. Look at how the following sentences are strengthened by replacing forms of *be, do,* and *have* with more precise verbs:

WEAK	Constant viewing of rock videos *is* harmful to children's emotional development.
REVISED	Constant viewing of rock videos *stunts* and *distorts* children's emotional development.
WEAK	In front of the hotel, an artist would *do* your portrait on a framed sheet of glass.
REVISED	In front of the hotel, an artist would *etch* your portrait on a framed sheet of glass.
WEAK	We *had* basic training at Fort Ord.
REVISED	We *sweated* through basic training at Fort Ord.

The verb *be* is essential to writing; indeed, it appears in some of the most memorable English prose, such as the opening of the Gospel According to St. John:

In the beginning was the Word, and the Word was with God, and the Word was God.

As the three examples above illustrate, however, forms of *be* can often be replaced by verbs that express action. As a general rule of thumb, if forms of *be* (*is, are, was, were, has been,* and so on) account for more than about a third of the verbs in a piece of writing, the writing may well seem static and flat.

Expletives

One potentially weak verb construction to watch out for is the **expletive,** which begins with *there* or *it* followed by a form of *be.* Expletives can be effective ways of introducing something with extra emphasis, but too many writers tend to overuse them, resulting in sentences that needlessly bury action in a noun, verbal, or dependent clause. Notice how the following sentences are strengthened by deleting the expletive:

WEAK	*There are* many people who fear success because they believe they do not deserve it.
REVISED	Many people *fear* success because they believe they do not deserve it.
WEAK	*It is* necessary for a presidential candidate today to perform well on television.
REVISED	A presidential candidate today *must perform* well on television.

339

EXERCISE 21.1

Revise the following sentences, replacing any weak verbs—especially forms of *be*, *do*, and *have*—with stronger and more specific verbs.

> *Example*
> It is argued by many that doctors do unnecessary tests to make more money.
> Many argue that doctors *order* unnecessary tests to collect more money.

1. Fanatic groups are a threat to the American people.
2. I have a job with two brothers who have a hardware store.
3. There is an opportunity for two hundred students to be extras in a movie to be shot on our campus.
4. The sweater is soft and warm.
5. In some places, children have tests to get into kindergarten.

EXERCISE 21.2

Revise the sentences in the following paragraph, replacing weak verbs (and particularly forms of *be*) with stronger and more specific verbs.

Dating is a socially acceptable form of getting to know members of the opposite sex. On a date, a couple is supposed to have fun. This outcome has not been the case with me lately. My last two dates were fiascos. Steve was one extreme, and Dave was another. As far as personalities were concerned, they were both duds.

2. Changing nouns to verbs

Much modern writing tends to express action by using nouns that are formed from verbs, a process called **nominalization.** Although nominalization can help make prose clearer and more concise—for example, using *abolition* instead of *the process of abolishing*—it can also produce the opposite effect, making a sentence unnecessarily wordy and hard to read. Nominalization reduces the *active* quality of a sentence, burying the action in an abstract noun and forcing the writer to use weak, generalized verbs and too many prepositional phrases. Too often, writers use nominalizations not to make a complex process easier to talk about but to make an idea *sound* more complex and abstract than it really is. Bureaucratic writing especially tends to use excessive nominalization in this way.

You can decide when to use a nominalized form and when to use the verb from which it derives by asking one question: which is most readily understandable? Take a look at the following sentence, for example:

> The firm is now engaged in an assessment of its procedures for the development of new products.

This sentence scarcely impresses itself on our memories, and it sounds pretentious and stuffy as well. In contrast, note the more easily understood and forceful version:

> The firm is now assessing its procedures for developing new products.

3. Checking your verbs and nouns

To revise a draft for stronger verbs, first circle all the verbs, and look to see whether you are relying too much on *be, do,* and *have.* If so, try to substitute more specific verbs whenever possible. Next, circle every noun whose meaning could be expressed by a verb. Try rewriting the sentence using the verb instead of the noun, adjusting any words necessary to keep the meaning you intended. Finally, underline all expletives, omitting any that are not used to create special emphasis. Study how the following passage is revised:

WEAK

Last February, when I made the determination to buy a house, I opened a separate checking (and savings) account in order to give attention more easily to my household expenses. (There is a credit union policy that for every checking account there must be a matching savings account: thus the dormant savings account.) This new checking account was where the deposit of the inheritance from my grandmother occurred along with any other accumulation of money from outside sources.

REVISED

Last February, when I determined to buy a house, I opened a separate checking (and savings) account to deal more easily with household expenses. (Credit union policy demands a matching savings account for every checking account; thus the dormant savings account.) Into this new checking account I deposited the inheritance from my grandmother, along with any other money I accumulated from outside sources.

EXERCISE 21.3

Revise the following paragraph to eliminate weak verbs and unnecessary nominalizations and expletives.

There has long been resistance to the proposition that the effectiveness of methods and teachers must be measured in terms of the results secured. Those responsible for evaluating teachers have exalted procedures in teaching and have seldom examined the products, that is, the efficiency of the teacher as indicated by what his or her pupils can do following instruction. However, we are beginning to see an increasing number of bold proposals founded on the assumption that the American public has expectations of results from schooling. As public support of education increases, there will be greater insistence on judging a teacher in the light of his or her ability to enhance the learning of pupils.

▌ 21b. Choosing between active and passive voice

In addition to choosing strong, precise verbs, you can help to make your prose memorable by varying those verbs appropriately between active and passive voice. Look at the following paragraph:

> A young man might go into military flight training believing that he was entering some sort of technical school in which he was simply going to acquire a certain set of skills. Instead, he found himself all at once enclosed in a fraternity. And in this fraternity, even though it was military, men were not rated by their outward rank as ensigns, lieutenants, commanders, or whatever. No, herein the world was divided into those who had it and those who did not. This quality, this *it*, was never named, however, nor was it talked about in any way.
>
> –Tom Wolfe, *The Right Stuff*

In this paragraph, Wolfe introduces the indefinable quality that he has made the title of his book. Notice that in the first sentence, the focus is on someone, a hypothetical young man, *doing* things: going into flight training, entering a school, acquiring skills. All of the verbs are in the active voice.

In the second sentence, the verb is still active. But notice that because the subject and object are the same person, because the subject of the verb *found* also receives the action of the verb, the sentence almost has the *feel* of being in the passive voice, as if the verb were *was enclosed*. And in the independent clauses of the last three sentences, the focus clearly shifts to things *being done* (or not done): men not being rated, the world being divided, and a quality never being named or talked about. The persons doing these things are unimportant or unknown; in fact, like the quality itself, they are never named, and the verbs are in the passive voice. Notice, however, that Wolfe returns to the active voice when he again wants to emphasize the persons doing something: *those who had it and those who did not.*

To make your writing memorable, try to use the active voice whenever possible. Because the passive focuses attention away from the performer of an action and because it is usually wordier than the active, excessive use of it makes for dull and difficult reading.

But as the Wolfe paragraph indicates, the passive can be used very effectively in certain situations: when the performer is unknown, unwilling to be identified, or less important than the recipient of the action. In the last sentence, for example, Wolfe could have written *No one ever named this quality, this it, however, nor did anyone talk about it in any way.* By using the passive voice, however, he focuses attention on the quality itself rather than on the persons who do not name or talk about it; in fact, by not mentioning them, he heightens the sense of a mysterious quality that cannot be defined.

See Chapter 8 for further discussion of voice.

EXERCISE 21.4

Look at the following sentences, in which some of the verbs are active and some passive. Then rewrite each sentence in the other voice, and decide which version you find preferable and why.

> *Example*
> You are hereby relieved of your duties by me.
> I hereby relieve you of your duties.

1. In Gower's research, it was found that pythons often dwell in trees and live near rivers.
2. They started shooting pool, and before Marie knew it, she owed the kid ten dollars.
3. When I was eight, my father's crazy dreams uprooted our family from Florida to California.
4. For me, living in a dorm was more easily adjusted to than living in an apartment.
5. The image of native Americans has been totally distorted by Hollywood in most of its films about the West.

▌ 21c. Creating special effects

Contemporary movies often live or die, succeed or fail, on the basis of their special effects. In the same way, special effects, like repetition, antithesis, and inversion can animate your prose and often make it much more memorable.

▌ 1. Using repetition

Carefully used, repetition of sounds, words, phrases, or other grammatical constructions serves as a powerful stylistic device. Orators in particular have long known its power. Here is a famous use of repetition, from one of Sir Winston Churchill's addresses to the British people during World War II:

> We shall not flag or fail, we shall go on to the end. We shall fight in France, we shall fight on the seas and oceans, we shall fight with growing confidence and growing strength in the air, we shall defend our island, whatever the cost may be; we shall fight on the beaches, . . . we shall fight in the fields and in the streets, . . . we shall never surrender.
>
> —WINSTON CHURCHILL

In this passage, the constant hammering *we shall*, accompanied by the repetition of *f* sounds (*flag, fail, fight, France, confidence, defend, fields*) had the effect of strengthening British resolve.

Though we may not be prime ministers, we can use repetition to equally good effect. Here are some examples by students.

> So my dream date turned into a nightmare. Where was the quiet, considerate, caring guy I thought I had met? In his place appeared this jerk. He strutted, he postured, he preened—and then he bragged, he bellowed, he practically brayed—just like the donkey he so much reminded me of.

> Pepperoni and sausage, mushrooms and olives, onions and anchovies, peppers and tomatoes, and cheese and cheese and cheese: we ate it all. We ate, and ate, and ate, and ate. And when we couldn't possibly eat another bite, . . . then we ate some more.

Be careful, however, to use repetition only for a deliberate purpose. See 17b for a discussion of how unnecessary repetition can lead to wordiness.

EXERCISE 21.5

Go through the examples above, identifying all of the uses of repetition. Then, using one example as a model, write a passage of your own that uses repetition effectively.

2. Using antithesis

Another special effect that can contribute to memorable writing is **antithesis,** the use of parallel structures to highlight contrast or opposition. Like other uses of parallelism (see Chapter 19), antithesis provides a pleasing rhythm that calls readers' attention to the contrast, often in a startling or amusing way. For example:

> Love is an ideal thing, marriage a real thing.

> The congregation didn't think much of the new preacher, and what the new preacher thought of the congregation she didn't wish to say.

> It is a sin to believe evil of others—but it is not a mistake.
> –H. L. MENCKEN

You can often use antithesis effectively when you are developing a paragraph by the alternating method of comparison and contrast (see 2h3 and 5d). By using parallel form to express the differences between two things or ideas or between two aspects of the same thing or idea, antithesis helps to clarify the points of contrast in a way that is easy for readers to follow and remember. Look at the following sentences from a paragraph contrasting the situation of ROTC on American campuses during the Vietnam War and in the late 1980s; each sentence is an example of antithesis:

> Yesterday's officers admired and emulated Pershing and Patton; today's cadets admire and emulate Lee Iacocca or Bunker Hunt. The management of money and materials, not the command of combat troops, is of the most interest to many of them.

EXERCISE 21.6

Using one of the examples of antithesis above, create a sentence of your own that uses antithesis. Then consider whether the antithesis makes the sentence more memorable or effective. You might begin by thinking of pairs of opposites you could build on: hope-despair, good-evil, spring-fall, fire-ice. Or you might begin with a *topic* you want to write an antithesis about: success, greed, generosity, pet peeves, and so on.

3. Using inverted word order

Inversion, or altering the usual word order of a sentence, can make for memorable writing by creating surprise or putting emphasis on a particular word or phrase. The word order in English is usually subject–verb–object/complement (if any). Inversion refers to any change in that order, such as putting the verb before the subject or putting the object or complement before the subject and verb. Look at the following example:

NORMAL   Two dead birds plummeted out of the tree.

INVERTED   Out of the tree plummeted two dead birds.

The inverted word order of the second version makes for a more dramatic sentence by putting the emphasis on *two dead birds* at the end of the sentence.

As with any unusual sentence pattern, inverted word order should be used sparingly. But as the following examples illustrate, inversion can indeed create special effects:

Into this grey lake plopped the thought, I know this man, don't I?
                                        –DORIS LESSING

In a hole in the ground there lived a hobbit.   –J. R. R. TOLKIEN

The bulk of her estate she left to the SPCA.

Good-looking he was not; wealthy he was not; but brilliant—he was.

Vietnam passed and with its passing came a new era for ROTC.

EXERCISE 21.7

After studying the examples of inversion above, look at an essay you have recently written, and find a sentence that might be more effective with inverted word order. Experiment with the word order, reading the results aloud and comparing differences in effect.

READING WITH AN EYE FOR MEMORABLE PROSE

Think of something in either your past or your current reading that sticks in your mind as particularly memorable. Then find that piece of writing, and reread it to identify what structures, techniques, and special effects make the passage so memorable.

FOR CREATING MEMORABLE PROSE OF YOUR OWN

The last five chapters have presented many elements that mark effective prose. One excellent—and amusing—way to practice these elements lies in a special kind of imitation. Choose a writer you very much admire—Virginia Woolf, Chaucer, Shakespeare, Alice Walker, Stephen King, Erma Bombeck—or any writer whose style you find unique. Then reread this writer's work, getting a "feel" for the rhythms, the structures, the special effects of the prose. Make a list of the elements that contribute to his or her distinctive style. Then choose a well-known story, and retell it in the style of your chosen author.

Following is the opening of a version of "The Three Little Pigs" written by one freshman as he imagined Edgar Allan Poe might have done. You can, if you wish, read one or two of Poe's stories and try finishing this version of "The Three Little Pigs."

It began as a mere infatuation. I admired them from afar, with a longing which only a wolf may know. Soon, these feelings turned to torment. Were I even to set eyes upon their porcine forms, the bowels of my soul raged, as if goaded by some festering poison. As the chilling winds of November howled, my gullet yearned for them. I soon feasted only upon an earnest and consuming desire for the moment of their decease.

FOR CREATING WRETCHED PROSE

Prose can be memorable for reasons quite different from those presented in this chapter. The Bulwer-Lytton Competition, known less formally as the "Wretched Writing" contest, challenges writers to produce an opening sentence to a novel, one that will celebrate the possibilities of "deliberate wretchedness" without hurting anyone's feelings. Writing strikingly bad opening sentences is great fun—and can be a true challenge. Here are a few finalists in a recent competition:

1. It was the eve of the yearly whale-slaughtering festival, thought Mamook as her horny fingers relentlessly pushed the whalebone needle through the sole of the mukluk; and suddenly, unaccountably, uncontrollably, she began to blubber.
2. Shirley doubted that her alien escort, composed as he was of vegetable matter, seaweed, and a thick coating of swampy muck, would be a suitable date for the Intergalactic kegger, but he turned out to be a real fungi.
3. When the last of the afterglow faded and the air was still, Josh liked to sit in the porch swing, in the dark, and test his night vision by spitting through the banisters.

Think of an idea for a story, and then write an opening sentence. Try to make it a "wonderfully bad" sentence. And why not enter it in the contest? Just send it to The Bulwer-Lytton Competition, c/o Professor Scott Rice, San Jose State University, San Jose, CA 95192.

PART FIVE

Selecting Effective Words

22. Mastering Spelling

The historical evolution of the English language from the tongue of Germanic tribes to a hybrid of Germanic, Scandinavian, and Norman French, with a multitude of other languages represented as well, makes English spelling a complex system. For example, English includes at least twelve different ways of representing the *sh* sound: *shoe, sugar, ocean, issue, nation, schist, pshaw, suspicion, conscious, nauseous, mansion,* and *fuchsia.* As everyone who has ever struggled to remember—or to find—a correct spelling knows, this complexity can lead to much frustration, and in fact, some have called for "spelling liberation." When a judge in Dickens's *Pickwick Papers* asks Sam Weller how to spell a particular word, for instance, Weller insists, "That depends entirely upon the taste and fancy of the speller, my Lord." Closer to home, President Andrew Jackson once exclaimed in exasperation. "It's a damn poor mind that can think of only one way to spell a word!"

In spite of this tradition of complaint, modern linguists have demonstrated that English spelling is much more regular than is commonly thought and that this regularity relates not only to sound-letter connections but also to our stored visual memory of related words. We know that *president* is not spelled "presadent," for example, because we recognize its relation to *preside.*

The good news, then, is simply this: careful attention to your own spelling patterns and attention to some fairly straightforward guidelines of English spelling can lead you to master spelling. This chapter will introduce you to these guidelines and help you begin your analysis.

22a. Mastering the most commonly misspelled words

A study of the spelling errors in the three thousand freshman essays that were used in the research for this book revealed a fairly small number of persistently misspelled words. A list of the fifty most common misspellings appears below. You may want to look over it carefully and compare it with words you have trouble spelling correctly (see 22f for ways to establish your own spelling inventory).

1. their/there/they're	18. through	35. business/es
2. too/to	19. until	36. dependent
3. a lot	20. where	37. every day
4. noticeable	21. successful/ly	38. may be
5. received/e/es	22. truly	39. occasion/s
6. lose	23. argument/s	40. occurrences
7. you're/your	24. experience/s	41. woman
8. an/and	25. environment	42. all right
9. develop/s	26. exercise/s/ing	43. apparent/ly
10. definitely	27. necessary	44. categories
11. than/then	28. sense	45. final/ly
12. believe/d/s	29. therefore	46. immediate/ely
13. occurred	30. accept/ed	47. roommate/s
14. affect/s	31. heroes	48. against
15. cannot	32. professor	49. before
16. separate	33. whether	50. beginning
17. success	34. without	

EXERCISE 22.1

Choose the correct spelling from the pair of words in the parentheses in each of the sentences below. After checking your answers, compare your misspellings with the list of fifty words most frequently misspelled. Enter the words you misspelled in your spelling log.

1. (*Their/There/They're*) going to put (*their/there/they're*) new stereo system over (*their/there/they're*) in the corner.
2. My little brother wants (*to/too*) go swimming (*to/too*).
3. The (*begining/beginning*) of spring term is (*a lot/alot*) earlier this year than last.
4. The rise in temperature isn't (*noticable/noticeable*) (*until/untill*) the humidity rises.

5. The accident (*occured/occurred*) (*before/befour*) I could step aside.
6. We couldn't (*beleive/believe*) the national champions were expected to (*loose/lose*) the playoffs.
7. In making your major life decisions, (*your/you're*) (*definately/definitely*) on (*your/you're*) own.
8. Nothing (*affects/effects*) (*success/sucess*) more (*than/then*) self-confidence or (*its/it's*) absence.
9. We (*received/recieved*) our notice (*threw/through*) the mail.
10. The group hopes to (*develop/develope*) a (*trully/truly*) (*succesful/successful*) fast-food franchise.
11. We (*can not/cannot*) easily (*separate/seperate*) fact and opinion.
12. Please tell me (*wear/where*) (*an/and*) when we should meet.
13. Our (*argumants/arguments*) (*against/aginst*) continuing to pollute the (*enviroment/environment*) fell on deaf ears.
14. Local (*businesses/businesses*) are (*dependant/dependent*) on a strong tourist trade.
15. (*Heroes/Heros*) are (*necesary/necessary*) to every culture's mythology.
16. Our first (*experiance/experience*) with aerobic (*exercise/exercize*) left us tired.
17. The (*professor/profesor*) agreed to (*accept/except*) our essays on Friday.
18. Our top speaker qualified for three (*catagories/categories*) in the (*final/finel*) competition.
19. The two (*roomates/roommates*) would be lost (*without/witout*) each other.
20. We intend to celebrate the (*ocasion/occasion*) (*weather/whether*) or not the (*weather/whether*) cooperates.
21. The plane to Chicago (*may be/maybe*) late; (*therefore/therfore*), we don't need to leave for the airport (*imediately/immediately*).
22. A (*woman's/women's*) place is now wherever she wants it to be.
23. Police report (*occurences/ocurrences*) of more and more burglaries (*every day/everyday*).
24. (*Its/It's*) not (*all right/alright*) to forego common (*since/sense*).
25. (*Aparently/Apparently*), the shipment of books never arrived.

▌ 22b. Recognizing homonyms

Of the words most often misspelled by college students, the largest number are **homonyms**—words that sound alike but have different spellings and meanings. English has many homonyms, but a relatively small number of them—eight pairs or trios—cause student writers frequent trouble. If you tend to confuse any of these words, now is a good time to stop and study them, looking for some twist of memory to help you remember the differences.

their [possessive form of *they*]
there [in that place]
they're [contraction of *they are*]

to [in the direction of]
too [in addition; excessive]
two [number between one and three]

your [possessive form of *you*]
you're [contraction of *you are*]

affect [to have an influence]
effect [noun: result]
      [verb: to cause to happen]

weather [climatic conditions]
whether [if]

accept [to take or receive]
except [to leave out]

who's [contraction of *who is* or *who has*]
whose [possessive form of *who*]

its [possessive form of *it*]
it's [contraction of *it is* or *it has*]

For your easy reference, here is a list of other homonyms and of other words that are frequently confused because they sound *nearly* alike:

Homonyms and frequently confused words

advice [suggestion]
advise [to suggest (to)]

allude [to refer]
elude [to avoid or escape]

allusion [reference]
illusion [false idea or appearance]

altar [sacred platform or table]
alter [to change]

are [form of *be*]
our [belonging to us]

bare [uncovered]
bear [animal; to carry or endure]

board [piece of lumber]
bored [uninterested]

brake [device for stopping]
break [to fragment]

buy [to purchase]
by [near; beside; through],

capital [principal city]
capitol [legislative building]

cite [to refer to]
sight [seeing; something seen]
site [location]

coarse [rough or crude]
course [plan of study; path]

complement [something that completes; to make complete]
compliment [praise; to praise]

conscience [feeling of right and wrong]
conscious [mentally aware]

council [leadership group]
counsel [advice; to advise]

dairy [source of milk]
diary [journal]

desert [dry area; to abandon]
dessert [sweet course of a meal]

device [something planned or invented]
devise [to plan or invent]

die [to expire]
dye [color; to color]

elicit [to draw forth]
illicit [illegal]

eminent [distinguished]
immanent [inherent]
imminent [expected in the immediate future]

fair [just or right; light in complexion; exposition]
fare [price of transportation; to go through an experience]

forth [forward; out into view]
fourth [between third and fifth]

gorilla [ape]
guerrilla [irregular soldier]

hear [to perceive with the ears]
here [in this place]

heard [past tense of *hear*]
herd [group of animals]

hoarse [sounding rough or harsh]
horse [animal]

know [to understand]
no [opposite of *yes*]

lead [a metal; to go before]
led [past tense of *lead*]

loose [not tight; not confined]
lose [to misplace; to fail to win]

meat [flesh used as food]
meet [to encounter]

passed [went by; received a passing grade]
past [beyond; events that have already occurred]

patience [quality of being patient]
patients [persons under medical care]

peace [absence of war]
piece [part]

personal [private or individual]
personnel [employees]

plain [simple, not fancy; flat land]
plane [airplane; tool; flat surface]

presence [condition of being]
presents [gifts; gives]

principal [most important; head of a school]
principle [fundamental truth]

rain [precipitation]
rein [strap to control a horse]
reign [period of rule]

right [correct; opposite of left]
rite [ceremony]
write [to produce words on a surface]

road [street or highway]
rode [past tense of *ride*]

scene [setting; view]
seen [past participle of *see*]

sense [feeling; intelligence]
since [from the time that; because]

stationary [unmoving]
stationery [writing paper]

than [as compared with]
then [at that time; therefore]

threw [past tense of *throw*]
thorough [complete]
through [in one side of and out
  the other; by means of]

waist [part of the body]
waste [to squander]

weak [feeble]
week [seven days]

wear [to put onto the body]
were [past tense of *be*]
where [in what place]

which [what; that]
witch [woman with supernatural
  power]

EXERCISE 22.2

Choose the appropriate word in parentheses to fill each blank in the following paragraph.

If _____ (*your/you're*) looking for summer fun, _____ (*accept/except*) the friendly _____ (*advice/advise*) of thousands of happy adventurers: spend three _____ (*weaks/weeks*) kayaking _____ (*threw/thorough/through*) the inside passage _____ (*to/too/two*) Alaska. For ten years, Outings, Inc., has _____ (*lead/led*) groups of novice kayakers _____ (*passed/past*) some of the most breathtaking scenery in North America. _____ (*Their/There/They're*) goal is simple: to give participants the time of _____ (*their/there/they're*) lives. As one of last year's adventurers said, " _____ (*Its/It's*) a trip I will remember vividly, one that _____ (*affected/effected*) me powerfully."

1. Recognizing words with more than one form

One special group of homonyms appearing in the list of words most often misspelled by college writers are words written sometimes as one word and other times as two words. The correct spelling depends on the meaning. Note the differences illustrated here:

Of course, they did not wear *everyday* clothes *every day* of the year.

Ideally, children *always* love their parents—in *all ways*.

By the time we were *all ready* for the game to begin, the coach's patience was *already* exhausted.

We *may be* on time for the meeting, or *maybe* we won't!

Nobody was surprised when the police announced that they had found *no body* at the scene of the crime.

The study of three thousand freshman essays mentioned in the introduction to this chapter revealed three particularly troublesome words that are often written in the wrong form. Two of them are always written as two words: *a lot* and *all right*. The third is written as one word: *cannot*. If you tend to misspell these words, take time now to commit the correct spelling to memory.

2. Recognizing American, British, and Canadian spellings

Spelling varies slightly among English-speaking countries. What is considered "correct" in Britain or Canada may be considered "incorrect" in the United States, and vice versa. Following is a list of some words that are spelled differently in American and British English. If you have trouble remembering the American spellings of words like these—whether, for example, a verb ends in -*ise* or -*ize*—always consult a dictionary.

AMERICAN	BRITISH AND CANADIAN
center	centre
check	cheque
color	colour
criticize	criticise
judgment	judgement

22c. Linking spelling and pronunciation

Even for words without homonyms, pronunciation often leads spellers astray. Pronunciation can vary considerably from one region of the United States to another, many words have letters that are not pronounced in any region, and the informality of spoken English allows us to slur or blur other letters or syllables. The best way to link spelling and pronunciation is to learn to "pronounce" words mentally as they look, every letter and syllable included (so that, for example, you hear the *b* at the end of *crumb*) and to enunciate them slowly and clearly when you are trying to spell them.

1. Noting unpronounced letters or syllables

Learning to "see" words with unpronounced letters or syllables will help you remember to spell them correctly. Here are some of the most frequently misspelled words of this kind, with their unpronounced letters or syllables italicized:

can*di*date	fore*i*gn	pro*b*ably
condem*n*	govern*m*ent	quan*ti*ty
diffe*r*ent	int*e*rest	resta*u*rant
drastica*ll*y	lib*ra*ry	sep*a*rate (adjective)
environ*m*ent	ma*rri*age	su*r*prise
Feb*r*uary	mus*c*le	We*d*nesday

▌ 2. Noting unstressed vowels

In English words, *a*, *i*, and *e* can often sound alike if they are in syllables that are not stressed. Hearing the word *definite*, for instance, gives us few clues as to whether the vowels in the second and third syllables should be *i*'s or *a*'s. In this case, remembering how the related word *finite* looks or sounds helps us know that the *i*'s are correct. If you are puzzled about how to spell a word containing unstressed vowels, first try to think of a related word that would give you a clue to the correct spelling. Then check your dictionary.

▌ 22d. Taking advantage of spelling rules

Fortunately, English spelling does follow some general rules that can be of enormous help to writers. This section focuses on those rules closely related to commonly misspelled words.

▌ 1. Remembering "i before e"

Most of you probably memorized the "*i* before *e*" rule long ago. Here is a slightly expanded version:

> *I* before *e* except after *c*
> or when pronounced *ay*
> as in *neighbor* or *weigh*
> or in *weird* exceptions like *either*
> and *species*.

i BEFORE *e*

ach*ie*ve	exper*ie*nce	p*ie*ce
bel*ie*ve	fr*ie*nd	rel*ie*ve
br*ie*f	f*ie*ld	th*ie*f
ch*ie*f		

EXCEPT AFTER *c*

c*ei*ling	dec*ei*ve	perc*ei*ve
conc*ei*ve	rec*ei*ve	

OR WHEN PRONOUNCED "AY"

neighbor   weigh   eighth

OR IN WEIRD EXCEPTIONS

either	seize	species
weird	foreign	ancient
neither	height	conscience
leisure	caffeine	science

EXERCISE 22.3

Insert either *ei* or *ie* in the blank in each of the following words.

1. sl—gh
2. consc—nce
3. anc—nt
4. l—sure
5. p—rce
6. caff—ne
7. ch—f
8. rec—ve
9. ach—ve
10. h—ress

2. Adding prefixes

Prefixes are verbal elements placed at the beginnings of words to add to or qualify their meaning. The prefix *re-*, for example, adds repetition to the meaning of a word: *reappear* means "appear again." (See 24c for more information about prefixes.) Prefixes do not change the spelling of the words they are added to, even when the last letter of the prefix and the first letter of the word it is added to are the same. In such cases, keep both letters:

    dis- + service = disservice
    over- + rate = overrate

Some prefixes require the use of hyphens. For a discussion of such usage, see 36b. If you are in doubt about whether to hyphenate a word beginning with a prefix, always check your dictionary.

3. Adding suffixes

Suffixes are verbal elements placed at the *ends* of words in order to form related words. For example, we can build on the basic word *short* to get the following words:

short*age*   short*en*   short*er*   short*ly*   short*ness*

This section will provide guidance to spelling words with suffixes.

Dropping the final e

For words ending in an unpronounced e (*receive, lose, definite*), you must decide whether or not to drop the e when adding a suffix. In general, if the suffix starts with a vowel, *drop* the e.

explore + -ation = exploration
imagine + -able = imaginable
future + -ism = futurism
exercise + -ing = exercising
continue + -ous = continuous
productive + -ity = productivity

EXCEPTIONS

■ To distinguish homonyms or potentially confusing words
dye + -ing = dyeing (not *dying*)
singe + -ing = singeing (not *singing*)

■ To clarify pronunciation
be + -ing = being (not *bing*)
shoe + -ing = shoeing (not *shoing*)

■ To keep the sound of c or g soft
notice + -able = noticeable
marriage + -able = marriageable
salvage + -able = salvageable
courage + -ous = courageous
peace + -able = peaceable

Keeping the final e

If the suffix starts with a consonant, *keep* the e.

force + -ful = forceful
excite + -ment = excitement
state + -ly = stately
same + -ness = sameness

EXCEPTIONS

acknowledge + -ment = acknowledgment
argue + -ment = argument
judge + -ment = judgment
true + ly = truly
whole + -ly = wholly
nine + -th = ninth

EXERCISE 22.4

Combine each of the following words and suffixes, dropping the unpronounced *e* when necessary.

1. future + -ism
2. whole + -ly
3. argue + -ment
4. lone + -ly
5. malice + -ious

6. dye + -ing
7. hope + -ful
8. continue + -ous
9. exercise + -ing
10. outrage + -ous

Using -ally

Use *-ally* if the base word ends in *ic*.

drastic + -ally = drastically
basic + -ally = basically
characteristic + -ally = characteristically
dramatic + -ally = dramatically

Using -ly

Use *-ly* if the base word does not end in *ic*.

apparent + -ly = apparently
certain + -ly = certainly
conscious + -ly = consciously
quick + -ly = quickly
supposed + -ly = supposedly

EXCEPTION
public + -ly = publicly

EXERCISE 22.5

Insert either *-ally* or *-ly* in the blank in each of the following words.

1. tragic _____
2. fatal _____
3. realistic _____
4. final _____
5. apparent _____

Using -cede, -ceed, and -sede

The suffixes *-cede*, *-ceed*, and *-sede* are especially easy to master because almost all words ending in the sound pronounced "seed" use the spelling *-cede*. Use *-sede* with only one word: supersede. Use *-ceed* with only three words: exceed, proceed, succeed. Use *-cede* with all other words ending in the "seed" sound:

accede   intercede   recede
concede   precede   secede

Words ending in consonant and y

For words ending in y, you must sometimes change the y to *i* when you add a suffix. In general, if the y is preceded by a consonant, *change* the y.

bounty + -ful = bountiful
try + -ed = tried
silly + -er = sillier
breezy + -ness = breeziness
busy + -ily = busily

EXCEPTIONS

■ Keep the y before the suffix *-ing.*

dry + -ing = drying
liquefy + -ing = liquefying
carry + -ing = carrying

■ Keep the y in some one-syllable base words.

shy + -er = shyer
dry + -ly = dryly
wry + -ness = wryness

■ Keep the y if the base word is a proper name.

Kennedy + -esque = Kennedyesque

Words ending in vowel and y

If the y is preceded by a vowel, keep the y.

joy + -ous = joyous
play + -ful = playful
employ + -ment = employment
buoy + -ed = buoyed

EXCEPTIONS

day + ly = daily
gay + ly = gaily

EXERCISE 22.6

Combine each of the following words and suffixes, changing the final *y* to *i* when necessary.

1. lonely + -er
2. carry + -ing
3. defy + -ance
4. study + -s
5. supply + -ed
6. duty + -ful
7. likely + -hood
8. obey + -ed
9. rainy + -est
10. coy + -ly

Doubling the final consonant

When a word ends in a consonant, the consonant is sometimes doubled when a suffix is added. If the word ends in consonant-vowel-consonant, the suffix begins with a vowel, and the word contains only one syllable or ends in an accented syllable, double the final consonant.

stop + -ing = stopping
slap + -ed = slapped
hot + -est = hottest
run + -er = runner
begin + -ing = beginning
occur + -ence = occurrence
refer + -ing = referring

DO NOT DOUBLE THE CONSONANT

- If it is preceded by more than one vowel or by another consonant
  bait + -ing = baiting
  sleep + -ing = sleeping
  fight + -er = fighter
  start + -ed = started

- If the suffix begins with a consonant
  ship + -ment = shipment
  fit + -ness = fitness

- If the word is not accented on the last syllable
  benefit + -ing = benefiting
  fasten + -er = fastener

- If the accent shifts from the last to the first syllable when the suffix is added.
  infer + -ence = inference
  prefer + -ence = preference

If the last letter of the word and the first letter of the suffix are the same, keep both letters:

> mortal + -ly = mortally
> room + -mate = roommate
> rotten + -ness = rottenness
> usual + -ly = usually

EXERCISE 22.7

Combine each of the following words and suffixes, doubling the final consonant when necessary.

1. occur + -ed
2. fast + -est
3. skip + -er
4. refer + -ence
5. commit + -ment

6. regret + -able
7. submit + -ed
8. drastic + -ally
9. benefit + -ed
10. weep + -ing

▌ 22e. Making words plural

Making singular nouns into plurals calls for using several different spelling guidelines.

Adding -s

For most words, add -*s*.

pencil, pencils   computer, computers

Adding -es

For words ending in *s*, *ch*, *sh*, *x*, or *z*, add -*es*.

Jones, Joneses   church, churches
bus, buses   flash, flashes
fox, foxes   buzz, buzzes

For words ending in *o*, add -*es* if the *o* is preceded by a consonant.

potato, potatoes   hero, heroes   veto, vetoes

EXCEPTIONS

memo, memos   piano, pianos
pro, pros   solo, solos

■ Add -*s* if the *o* is preceded by a vowel.

rodeo, rodeos   patio, patios
zoo, zoos   curio, curios

Words ending in f or fe

For some words ending in *f* or *fe*, change *f* to *v* and add *-s* or *-es*.

calf, calves	shelf, shelves
half, halves	elf, elves
self, selves	leaf, leaves
life, lives	hoof, hooves
wife, wives	knife, knives

Words ending in y

For words ending in *y*, change *y* to *i* and add *-es* if the *y* is preceded by a consonant.

theory, theories	huckleberry, huckleberries
eighty, eighties	sky, skies

EXCEPTIONS

- Proper names
  Henry, Henrys

- Keep the *y* and add *-s* if the *y* is preceded by a vowel.

guy, guys	attorney, attorneys
delay, delays	alloy, alloys

Irregular plurals

For irregular plurals and nouns that have the same form in the singular and plural, memorize those you do not already know.

man, men	bacterium, bacteria	deer, deer
woman, women	locus, loci	sheep, sheep
child, children	alga, algae	moose, moose
foot, feet	basis, bases	series, series
tooth, teeth	phenomenon, phenomena	species, species

Compound words

For compound nouns written as one word, make the last part of the compound plural.

briefcase, briefcases	bookshelf, bookshelves
mailbox, mailboxes	grandchild, grandchildren

For compound nouns written as separate words or hyphenated, make the most important part of the compound plural.

brother-in-law, brothers-in-law
lieutenant governor, lieutenant
   governors

sergeant major, sergeants major
leap year, leap years
bus stop, bus stops

EXERCISE 22.8

Form the plural of each of the following words.

1. tomato
2. hoof
3. volunteer
4. baby
5. dish

6. stepchild
7. turkey
8. mile per hour
9. radio
10. phenomenon

11. spoof
12. beach
13. yourself
14. golf club
15. rose

▌ 22f. Taking a personal spelling inventory

This chapter has surveyed general spelling rules and guidelines. You need now to tailor this advice to your own spelling patterns and problems. Doing so means becoming a detective of your own writing, looking for clues in as large and varied a sample of your prose as you have time to examine.

▌ 1. Identifying troublesome words and patterns

You can begin your inventory by looking through several essays you have written and making a list of every word misspelled. Whenever possible, identify the guideline in this chapter that deals with the misspellings. Here is the beginning of one student's personal spelling inventory:

WORD	MISSPELLING	GUIDELINE
their	there	homonyms
receiving	recieving	"*i* before *e*"
hastiest	hastyest	suffix with final *y*
beginning	begining	double consonants
affect	effect	homonyms
sharing	shareing	unpronounced final *e*
environment	enviroment	unpronounced letters
theories	theorys	plural for words ending in *y*
successful	succesful	double consonants
dissatisfied	disatisfied	prefix

2. Using a spell checker

If you write on a word processor and have some essays in draft or if you have some of your writing that has not been marked for spelling, you can use the *spell checker* on most word processing programs to identify misspelled words and add them to your personal spelling inventory. Those who use this feature frequently, however, know that it provides only limited help. It will not, for instance, pick up homonym problems—*you're* may be the wrong spelling in the context of the essay, but the spell checker will recognize it only as a correct possible spelling. (See Chapter 45 for more information on using spell checkers when revising and editing a draft.)

3. Annotating your dictionary

For mastering particularly troublesome words, author John Irving recommends making a mark and listing the date whenever you look up a word in the dictionary. If you follow this advice, you will be able to identify words you are looking up frequently—and take steps to learn the correct spelling once and for all. You may also find that some or most of these words follow a similar pattern. This discovery can then become part of your personal spelling inventory.

4. Building on memory cues

Before the advent of printing, not to mention photocopying machines, people learned to train their memories extensively. You can learn to use memory cues, or **mnemonic devices** (named for the Greek goddess of memory, Mnemosyne), in mastering words whose spelling tends to trip you up. Here are some memory cues one student devised to go along with her personal spelling inventory:

WORD	MISSPELLING	CUE
environment	enviroment	There's *iron* in our environment.
all right	alright	I wouldn't write *alwrong*, would I?
a lot	alot	I wouldn't write *alittle*, would I?
government	goverment	Government should serve those it *governs*.
separate	seperate	*Separate* rates two *a*'s.
definitely	definately	There are a *finite* number of ways to spell *definitely*.

EXERCISE 22.9

Read the following passage from a brief student essay, noting and correcting each misspelling. Whenever possible, classify the misspelling under one of the guidelines presented in this chapter. Then draw up three or four tips you could give this particular student on how to improve spelling.

For me, the ideel ocupation would be an arangement in which I could play with a band for six months and tour the other six months of the year. I wouldn't want to teach music because I would probly have to teach in a school, where many students are forced to take music by there parrents. When children are forced to do something, its likly that they won't enjoy it. If I were able to both tour an teach, however, I would be happy.

I'm realy glad that I've gotten involved in music; it looks as if I'm destined to be a profesional musician. Surly I don't know what else I could do; I dout I'd be a good administrater or bussiness executive or lawyer. And the idea of being a doctor or denist and probing around people's bodys or looking at teeth that have huge, roting cavities isn't appealing to me. The more I think about it, the happyer I am with my music. I definately plan to pursue that career.

READING FOR SPELLING

Readers store the visual memory of words in their minds and can often spell them correctly by "seeing" them. You can make use of this fact by attending to the spelling of new or unfamiliar words as you read, making a conscious mental "note" of how the word looks correctly spelled. Many writers, in fact, jot down new words as they read and later concentrate on learning the meaning—and spelling—of them.

Once you start paying attention to spelling as you read, you will probably marvel at how well you generally spell. That is the whole point of the following humorous poem, entitled "Spelling and Pronunciation—Hints for Foreigners."

> I take it you already know
> Of tough and bough and cough and dough?
> Others may stumble but not you,
> On hiccough, thorough, laugh and through
> Well done! And now you wish, perhaps,
> To learn of less familiar traps?
>
> Beware of heard, a dreadful word
> That looks like beard and sounds like bird,
> And dead: it's said like bed, not bead—
> For goodness' sake don't call it "deed"!
> Watch out for meat and great and threat
> (They rhyme with suite and straight and debt.)

A moth is not a moth in mother
Nor both in bother, broth in brother,
And here is not a match for there
Nor dear and fear for bear and pear,
And then there's does and rose and lose—
Just look them up—and goose and choose,
And cork and work and card and ward,
And font and front and word and sword,
And do and go and thwart and cart—
Come, come, I've hardly made a start!
A dreadful language? Man alive,
I'd mastered it when I was five.

FOR EXAMINING YOUR OWN SPELLING

If you are keeping a writing log, devote a section of it to a personal spelling inventory. Choose a sample of your recent writing, and identify every misspelling. If you have any drafts in a word processor, use a spell checker, and ask an instructor or several friends who are good spellers to help you. Then, following the format presented in 22f1, enter the word, your misspelling, and the guideline or pattern that relates to it. For persistent misspellings, create a memory cue (see 22f4), and enter it in the log along with the correct spelling of the word.

| 23. Using Dictionaries

In the opening scene of Rex Stout's *Gambit*, master sleuth Nero Wolfe is "in the middle of a fit," solemnly tearing the pages out of a large volume and dropping them into a fire. What is the book that Wolfe finds "subversive and intolerably offensive"? It is a dictionary—specifically, the third edition of *Webster's New International Dictionary*. Guilty of thousands of "crimes" and threatening the very "integrity of the English language," this dictionary must be destroyed, Wolfe declares, down to its very fine binding.

You may not have thought of dictionaries as the cause of violent controversy, but very often they have been. Such controversy usually relates to a tension between two basic and competing aims for dictionaries. One aim is to fix a standard of the language, so that users of it can know once and for all what is "right" and what is "wrong." Before the advent of the printing press, English spelling in particular was far from fixed, and with good reason; few people had occasion to write words down. Even later, the author we designate as Shakespeare is known to have spelled his own name in several different ways. By the eighteenth century, however, writers such as Alexander Pope urged a codification of the language, which they felt had reached perfection. Enter Samuel Johnson, whose *English Dictionary* (1755) established an authoritative right and wrong for a long time.

The second and competing aim of an English dictionary was articulated forcefully about one hundred years after Johnson: to record a full inventory of the language as it is used, without trying to prescribe "right" and "wrong." What enraged Wolfe was its focus on this second aim rather than the first. These dual aims persist in our dictionaries today and may in fact influence your choice of which dictionary to use on which occasion. This chapter will map the territory covered by dictionaries and provide you with a means of choosing the dictionaries you want to work with.

▌ 23a. Exploring the dictionary

A good dictionary packs a surprising amount of information into a relatively small space, including much more than the correct spelling. Take a look, for instance, at this entry in *Webster's New World Dictionary,* Third College Edition:

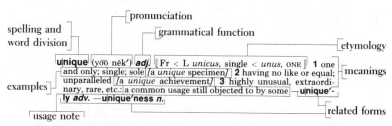

In fact, a dictionary entry may contain a dozen or more kinds of information about a word, the most common of which are listed below. The first six normally appear in all entries, the others only where they are necessary or relevant.

1. *Spelling,* including alternate spellings if they exist
2. *Word division,* with bars and/or dots separating syllables and showing where a word may be divided at the end of a line
3. *Pronunciation,* including alternate pronunciations
4. *Grammatical functions and irregular forms,* including plurals of nouns, principal parts of verbs, and comparative and superlative forms of adjectives and adverbs
5. *Etymology,* the languages and words that the word comes from
6. *Meanings,* in order of either development or frequency of use
7. *Examples* of the word in the context of a phrase or sentence
8. *Usage labels and notes* (see explanation below)
9. *Field labels,* indicating that a word has a specialized meaning in a particular field of knowledge or activity
10. *Synonyms* and *antonyms*

11. *Related words* and their grammatical functions
12. *Idioms*, phrases in which the word appears and their meanings

Usage labeling and notes

For some words, many dictionaries include a kind of usage labeling, intended to let readers know that some or all meanings of the word are not considered appropriate in certain contexts. You can generally find such labels identified at the beginning of the dictionary. Here are some of the labels the *Webster's New World* uses.

1. *Archaic:* rarely used today except in specialized contexts
2. *Obsolete:* no longer used
3. *Colloquial:* characteristic of conversation and informal writing
4. *Slang:* extremely informal
5. *Dialect:* used mostly in a particular geographical or linguistic area, often one that is specified, such as Scotland and New England

In addition to labels, dictionaries sometimes include notes discussing usage in greater detail. In the *Webster's New World* entry for *unique*, notice that the third meaning includes a note that using the word with this meaning is "common" but is "still objected to by some."

EXERCISE 23.1

Look up the spelling, syllable division, and pronunciation of the following words in your dictionary. Note any variants in spelling and/or pronunciation.

1. process (noun)   5. whippet   8. hurrah
2. heinous   6. crayfish   9. greasy
3. exigency   7. macabre   10. theater
4. schedule

EXERCISE 23.2

Look up the etymology of the following words in your dictionary.

1. rhetoric   5. apple   8. tortilla
2. student   6. sex   9. cinema
3. curry (noun)   7. okra   10. video
4. whine

EXERCISE 23.3

Use your dictionary to find synonyms (and antonyms) for the following words.

1. coerce   4. odious
2. prevaricate   5. awesome
3. parameter

▎ 23b. Distinguishing among dictionaries

Since the time of Samuel Johnson's 1755 dictionary and Noah Webster's *American Dictionary of the English Language* (1828), the number and kinds of English-language dictionaries have multiplied many times over. You may in fact own several dictionaries and have easy access to many more. While they all share the name *dictionary*, these numerous volumes differ considerably from one another. You may most often use an easily portable paperback dictionary, but you should be familiar with larger abridged and unabridged dictionaries as well.

▎ 1. Abridged dictionaries

Abridged or "abbreviated" **dictionaries** are the type most often used by college writers. Though they are not as complete as unabridged dictionaries, they are more affordable and more portable than their larger cousins. Among the most helpful abridged dictionaries are *Webster's New World Dictionary* and *The American Heritage Dictionary*.

Webster's New World Dictionary of the American Language, 3rd College Edition. New York: Simon, 1988. This abridged dictionary lists all of its more than 170,000 entries in alphabetical order; within individual entries, meanings are listed chronologically as they entered the language. Geographical and biographical names are included among the regular entries, and more than 800 drawings are provided.

The American Heritage Dictionary. 2nd College Edition. Boston: Houghton, 1982. The more than 200,000 listings in this dictionary are augmented by 5,000 new scientific and technical terms and 3,000 new photographs supplementing the many photographs, drawings, and maps in the first edition. The *American Heritage* lists meanings in the order of most to least common. Notes on usage are extensive. Introductory essays provide a context for the usage notes in the form of a debate on the issue. Sections on biographical and geographical names, also liberally illustrated, follow the dictionary of general vocabulary, as does a section on abbreviations and a list of the addresses for four-year colleges and universities.

Here is the *American Heritage* entry for *unique*. Notice that instead of the third meaning listed in the *Webster's New World* entry, it provides a note discussing the Usage Panel's opinion of this usage.

> **u·nique** (yoo-nēk′) *adj.* **1.** Being the only one of its kind; sole. **2.** Being without an equal or equivalent; unparalleled. [Fr. < Lat. *unicus*, sole < *unus*, one.] **—u·nique′ly** *adv.* **—u·nique′ness** *n.*
>   ***Usage:*** Traditional grammarians are uncompromising in the insistence that *unique* is an "absolute" term—either something is unique or it isn't—so that it does not allow qualification of degree. The vast majority of the Usage Panel finds unacceptable such uses as are found in the advertising claim *"Omaha's most unique restaurant is now even more unique,"* whose author might have avoided the scorn of the grammarians if he had used instead a word like *unusual* or *remarkable.* Like other absolute words such as *chief* and *unanimous,* however, *unique* can be modified by words like *almost* and *nearly.*

2. Unabridged dictionaries

Unabridged, or "unabbreviated," **dictionaries** are the royalty of their species—the most complete, richly detailed, and thoroughly presented dictionaries of English. Whereas good abridged dictionaries may include 200,000 items, unabridged dictionaries far more than double that figure. Because they are large and often multivolume—and hence expensive, you may not own an unabridged dictionary, but you will want and need to consult one on occasion in your library. Among the leading unabridged dictionaries are the *Oxford English Dictionary* and *Webster's Third New International Dictionary of the English Language.*

The Oxford English Dictionary. 13 volumes and 4 supplements. New York: Oxford UP, 1933, 1972, 1976. The grandparent of unabridged dictionaries in English, *The Oxford English Dictionary* (known as the *OED*) began in Britain in the nineteenth century as an attempt to give a full history of each English word, recording its entry into the language and illustrating the development of its various meanings with dated quotations in chronological order. Volunteers all over the world contributed quotations to the editors at Oxford University, and the dictionary was published piecemeal over a period of more than forty years. The *OED* lists more than half a million words and is unparalleled in its historical account of changes in word meanings and spellings. The *OED* is also available now at an affordable price in a large two-volume version, featuring photographically reduced pages that can be read with the magnifying glass that accompanies this edition.

Here is the *OED*'s entry for *unique*. Notice that in addition to the meanings given in the two abridged dictionaries, it lists several obsolete and specialized meanings for *unique* as an adjective; it also includes meanings and examples for *unique* as a noun, a use that is apparently too rare to find space in the abridged dictionaries. Compared with these, the *OED* also provides more detailed etymological information and uses a different system of phonetic symbols for pronunciation. Finally, notice that the related forms *uniquely* and *uniqueness* are not included because they have their own entries.

Unique (yūnī·k), *a.* and *sb.* Also 7 **unick(e**, 7–8 unio. [a. F. *unique* (+ *unic* masc.), ad. L. *ūnic-us* (whence also Sp., Pg., It. *unico*) single, sole, alone of its kind, f. *ūnus* one. In early use also directly ad. L. *ūnicus*, and stressed on the first syllable.]

Regarded by Todd (1818) as 'an affected and useless term of modern times'.

A. *adj.* **1.** Of which there is only one; one and no other; single, sole, solitary.

1602 DOLMAN *La Primaud. Fr. Acad.* (1618) III. 639 Engendring one eternitie, and by an alone vnique action never disturbed, his linage full of understanding. *c* 1645 HOWELL *Lett.* II. xliv, He hath lost..his unic Son in the very flower of his age. 1677 GALE *Crt. Gentiles* IV. I. ii. 53 Divines, who make..right Reason the unic Criterion or Rule of moral Virtue. 1818 TODD, *Unique,* adj.,..sole ;..without another of the same kind known to exist. 1861 PALEY *Æschylus, Prometh.* (ed. 2) 39 The student will notice the unique example of στιχομυθία. 1873 HAMERTON *Intell. Life* III. iii. 87 A man ..who made Latin scholarship his unique intellectual purpose. 1882 FARRAR *Early Chr.* II. 476 St. John instantly leaves the subject..to which he has made this unique and passing allusion.

2. That is or forms the only one of its kind; having no like or equal; standing alone in comparison with others, freq. by reason of superior excellence; unequalled, unparalleled, unrivalled.

In this sense readopted from French at the end of the 18th c. and regarded as a foreign word down to the middle of the 19th, from which date it has been in very common use, with a tendency to take the wider meaning of 'uncommon, unusual, remarkable'.

The usage in the comparative and superlative, and with advs. as *absolutely, most, quite, thoroughly, totally,* etc., has been objected to as tautological.

1618 W. BARCLAY *Well at King-horne* A vij, This is a soueraigne and vnicke remedie for that disease in Women. 1794 R. J. SULIVAN *View Nat.* I. 3 A concentrated, and an unique aggregation of almost all the wonders of the natural world. 1809 R. K. PORTER *Trav. Sk. Russia & Sweden* (1813) I. xxv. 285 As it was thoroughly *unique*, I cannot forbear presenting you with so singular a curiosity. 1842 J. P. COLLIER *Armin's Nest Ninn.* Introd., A relic.. not only *unique* in itself, but unprecedented in its kind. 1866 LIDDON *Bamp. Lect.* v. (1867) 368 [Christ's] relationship to the Father..is absolutely unique. 1871 B. TAYLOR *Faust* (1875) II. II. i. 84 A thing so totally unique The great collectors would go far to seek. 1885 *Harper's Mag.* April 703/1 When these summer guests found themselves defrauded of their uniquest recreations.

b. Of persons.

1808 FOSTER *Contrib. Eclectic Rev.* (1844) I. 233 [Sir T. More] is a person so *unique* in the records of statesmen, that [etc.]. 1871 BLACKIE *Four Phases* 15 Such a unique mortal.. no man can describe. 1885 MABEL COLLINS *Prettiest Woman* xi, He believed this woman whom he loved to be unique.

c. *absol.* with *the*: (see quots.).

1767 *Phil. Trans.* LVIII. 26 All these are examples of the *unique*; that is, of quantities in a state that is..exclusive of all others. 1849 C. BRONTE *Shirley* xxiii, She felt that Rose Yorke was a peculiar child—one of the unique.

† **3.** Formed or consisting of one or a single thing. *Obs.*⁻¹

a 1631 DONNE *Lett.* (1651) 163 A Mathematique point, which is the most indivisible and unique thing which art can present.

B. *sb.* **1.** A thing of which there is only one example, copy, or specimen ; esp., in early use, a coin or medal of this class.

1714 R. THORESBY *Diary* 23 June, My Lord showed me some unics and other valuable curiosities. 1730 A. GORDON *Maffei's Amphith.* 47 It .may be an Unic, for what we know as yet. 1774 *Gentl. Mag.* XLIV. 8 A coin, which I have reason to think is a Unic. 1826 DISRAELI *V. Grey* II. viii, Mr. Vivian Grey had promised his Lordship, who was a collector of medals, an unique which had never yet been heard of. 1872 O. W. HOLMES *Poet Breakf.-t.* iii. 89 A unique, sir, and there is a pleasure in exclusive possession.

† **b.** Something of which only one is possessed by a person or persons. *Obs. rare.*

1783 H. WALPOLE *Let. to C'tess Upper Ossory* 20 June, Lady Pembroke having lent them a servant besides their own unique. 1806 SURR *Winter in Lond.* III. 170 This Belcher girdle was not old; but being an *unique*, it had been..constantly in use.

2. A thing, fact, or circumstance which by reason of exceptional or special qualities stands alone and is without equal or parallel in its kind.

1768 *Phil. Trans.* LVIII. 215 When I presented this map to the Academy..it was looked upon as an Unique. 1781 *Gentl. Mag.* LI. 280/2 The dedication [of a volume of Sermons] being an *unique* in its kind. 1794 PALEY *Evid.* II. ix. iii. ad fin., The propagation of Christianity..is an unique in the history of the species. 1835 *Tait's Mag* II. 651 It is.. an *unique* in English biography. 1838 DE QUINCEY *Lamb* Wks. 1858 IX. 156 Of Lamb's writings..some were so memorably beautiful as to be uniques in their class. 1844 N. Brit. *Rev.* I. 124 A conflict, that stands out from all shadow of parallelism—a wild originality—a terrible unique.

b. A person of this class.

1758 *Case of Authors Stated* 14 He presumes, that he, this *Unic*, must therefore appear in the same stupendous Magnitude to every body else. 1782 COWPER *Let.* Nov., Wks. (1876) 121 He is a man much to my taste, and quite an unique in this country. 1802 MRS. E. PARSONS *Myst. Visit* IV. 145, I trust that he though very good, is not an unique. 1813 *Examiner* 22 Feb. 122/2 Those..charms of manner, which constitute an *unique*. 1866 ALGER *Solit. Nat. & Man* II. 65 The peculiar endowment in which he so far surpasses others as to be an insulated unique.

Webster's Third New International Dictionary of the English Language. Springfield, MA: Merriam, 1986. Containing more entries than any dictionary besides the *OED*—more than 450,000 in all, this one-volume work stirred considerable controversy at its publication because of its tendency, as mentioned in the introduction to this chapter, to *describe* rather than to *prescribe* usage. In all, the editors collected 6,165,000 examples of recorded usage, on which they drew for their Usage Notes. *Webster's Third* lists meanings in order of their entry into the language and quotes from over 14,000 different authors to provide illustrations of words in context.

Here are the *Webster's Third* entries for *unique* as an adjective and as a noun. Notice that the adjective entry simply lists the meaning "unusual, notable" and examples of the use of *most unique*, without discussing the controversy over this usage. In addition, notice that at the end of the entry, the notation **syn** refers the reader to the entries for *single* and *strange*, where the shades of meaning that distinguish *unique* from its synonyms are explained. The phonetic symbols differ slightly from those in either the *OED* or the abridged dictionaries.

¹**unique** \yü'nēk, '≠,≠\ *adj, sometimes* -ER/-EST [F, fr. L *unicus* sole, single, unique, fr. *unus* one + -*icus* -ic — more at ONE] **1 a :** being the only one **:** SOLE ⟨earning money whose ∼ object could be nothing but Cyril's welfare —Arnold Bennett⟩ ⟨has thus preserved the original and often ∼ records —G.B. Parks⟩ ⟨you are a miracle, a wonder, a mystery . . . one single ∼ and inimitable living thing —J.C.Powys⟩ **b** *of a book* **:** known to exist in no other copy **2 :** being without a like or equal **:** single in kind or excellence **:** UNEQUALED ⟨they stand alone, ∼, objects of supreme interest —A.B.Osborne⟩ ⟨as historian he knows that events, like persons, are ∼ —J.M. Barzun⟩ ⟨remains singularly himself, a ∼ lyrist of the first water —I.L.Salomon⟩ ⟨an almost ∼ experience —Havelock Ellis⟩ ⟨tendencies present in our contemporary world which make our own times somewhat ∼ —M.B.Smith⟩ ⟨story of his life is considerably more ∼ than most autobiographies —Dorothy C. Fisher⟩ ⟨the more we study him, the less ∼ he seems —Harry Levin⟩ — sometimes used with *to* ⟨the problem of what to do with surplus women is by no means ∼ to our own society — Ralph Linton⟩ or *with* ⟨by no means ∼ with the song sparrow —*Nature Mag.*⟩ **3 :** UNUSUAL, NOTABLE ⟨possessed ∼ ability in the raising of funds —C.F.Thwing⟩ ⟨the wife of a career diplomat has a ∼ opportunity to observe the world political scene —Ray Pierre⟩ ⟨a frankness ∼ in literature —David Daiches⟩ ⟨∼ peace and privacy —R.W.Hatch⟩ ⟨cheap, nourishing, and a ∼ dining experience —T.H.Fielding⟩ ⟨the most ∼ characteristic of that environment —R.A.Billington⟩ ⟨she's the most ∼ person I ever met —Arthur Miller⟩ ⟨the most ∼ theater in town —*advt*⟩ **4 :** capable of being performed in only one way ⟨the factorization of a number into its prime factors is ∼⟩ **syn** see SINGLE, STRANGE

²**unique** \"\ *n* -s **:** something (as a specimen, thing, circumstance, or person) that is unique **:** the only one of its kind ⟨mistaking the ∼ for the typical —W.J.Reilly⟩ ⟨the zest of the collector for possession of a ∼ —Roy Bedichek⟩ ⟨a display of glass, including undercoated ∼s —*Danish Foreign Office Jour.*⟩ ⟨the phoenix, the ∼ of birds —Thomas De Quincey⟩

EXERCISE 23.4

Compare two of the entries on *unique* in this chapter for their advice on how to use the word correctly. Then write a paragraph in which you summarize their major differences of opinion.

EXERCISE 23.5

Look up the following words in at least one abridged and one unabridged dictionary, and compare the entries. Record any differences or disagreements you find, and bring this record to class for discussion.

1. dogmatism
2. alienate
3. discriminate
4. hopefully
5. humanism

EXERCISE 23.6

Look up one of the following words in the *OED*, and write a paragraph describing any changes in meaning it has undergone since its entry into English.

1. lie (verb)
2. cheerful
3. machine
4. ornament (noun)
5. vulgar
6. humor (noun)
7. quaint
8. honest
9. testify
10. romance

▌ 23c. Consulting specialized dictionaries

The dictionaries you have just surveyed will provide you with an enormous amount of information. Sometimes, however, you will need to turn to additional sources for more specialized information. Such sources are available in dictionaries of usage, of synonyms, of slang, and of particular subjects (such as philosophy, mathematics, and biography).

▌ 1. Dictionaries of usage

As the entries for *unique* in 23a and 23b demonstrate, dictionaries sometimes are unable to provide agreed-upon answers to questions of usage. More often than not, questions of usage are not reducible to any simple, easy right or wrong; most of them are very complex and relate not only to linguistic concerns but to social, educational, economic, and regional matters as well. In cases where usage is disputed or where you feel unsure of your own usage, you may wish to consult a specialized dictionary of usage. The most widely used such work, although it is much more about British than about American usage, is H. W. Fowler's *Dictionary of Modern English Usage*, which was published in 1926 and revised by Sir Ernest Gowers in 1965. Here is Fowler's discussion of *unique*.

unique. A watertight definition or paraphrase of the word, securing it against confusion with all synonyms that might be suggested, is difficult to frame. In the first place, it is applicable only to what is in some respect the sole existing specimen, the precise like of which may be sought in vain. That gives a clean line of division between it and the many adjectives for which it is often ignorantly substituted—*remarkable, exceptional, fabulous, rare, marvellous,* and the like. In the qualities represented by those epithets there are degrees; but uniqueness is a matter of yes or no only; no unique thing is more or less unique than another unique thing, as a rare thing may be rarer or less rare than another rare thing. The adverbs that *u.* can tolerate are e.g. *quite, almost, nearly, really, surely, perhaps, absolutely,* or *in some respects;* and it is nonsense to call anything *more, most, very, somewhat, rather,* or *comparatively u.* Such nonsense, however, is often written:

What made Laker's achievement all the more unique was. . . . / *I am now at one of* the most unique *writers' colonies imaginable.* / *I have just come across the production of a boy aged seven which is, in my experience,* somewhat unique. / *Sir, I venture to send you a copy of* a rather unique *inscription on a tombstone.* / *A* very unique *child, thought I.*

But, secondly, there is another set of synonyms—*sole, single, peculiar to,* etc.—from which *u.* is divided not by a clear difference of meaning, but by an idiomatic limitation (in English though not in French) of the contexts to which it is suited. It will be admitted that we improve the two following sentences if we change *u.* in the first into *sole,* and in the second into *peculiar: In the always delicate and difficult domain of diplomatic relations the Foreign Minister must be* the unique *medium of communication with foreign Powers.* / *He relates Christianity to other religions, and notes what is* unique *to the former and what is common to all of them. Unique* so used is a GALLICISM.

EXERCISE 23.7

Look up *unique* in Bergen Evans and Cornelia Evans's *A Dictionary of Contemporary American Usage* and in Margaret M. Bryant's *Current American Usage*. Compare their entries with the one printed above from Fowler. Then write a brief description of how these three works agree and disagree on the usage of *unique*.

❙ 2. Dictionaries of synonyms

All writers are sometimes stuck for just the right word, and at such times, a dictionary of synonyms or a thesaurus is a friend indeed. These works follow each entry with a list of words whose meanings are similar to the meaning of the entry. A useful source for students is *Webster's Dictionary of Synonyms*, which includes the following entry for *unique:*

unique 1 *single, sole, lone, solitary, separate, particular
Ana *only, alone
2 singular, *strange, peculiar, eccentric, erratic, odd,
queer, quaint, outlandish, curious
Ana *exceptional: uncommon, rare, *infrequent

The entry indicates, by way of asterisks, that further information on synonyms for *unique* may be found by looking up several other words (the abbreviation *Ana.* marks analogous words). Checking these entries carefully should help you decide which, if any, of these synonyms would be appropriate in a particular sentence.

A **thesaurus,** which comes from a word meaning "treasure" or "storehouse," provides lists of antonyms as well as synonyms for many words. Two are particularly helpful: *Webster's Collegiate Thesaurus* and *The New Roget's Thesaurus of the English Language in Dictionary Form.*

Remember, however, to use dictionaries of synonyms and thesauruses very carefully, because very rarely in English are two words so close in meaning that they can be used interchangeably in radically different contexts. As Mark Twain put it, the difference between the right word and the almost-right word is the difference between lightning and the lightning bug.

EXERCISE 23.8

Look up the entry *strange* in *Webster's New Dictionary of Synonyms.* Read it carefully, and then write a brief summary of what the entry has to say about the relationship of *unique* to *strange.* Then look up *strange* in *The New Roget's Thesaurus,* and compare that entry with the one in *Webster's.*

3. Dictionaries of etymology, regional English, and slang

On some occasions, you may want or need to find out all you can about the origins of a word, to find out about a term used only in one area of the country, or to see whether a term is considered to be slang or not. The following specialized dictionaries can help out:

The Oxford Dictionary of English Etymology, ed. C. T. Onions. New York: Oxford UP, 1966.

Dictionary of American Regional English, ed. Frederic G. Cassidy. Cambridge, MA: The Belknap Press of Harvard UP, 1985.

Dictionary of American Slang, 2nd supplemented edition, ed. Harold Wentworth and Stuart Berg Flexner. New York: Crowell, 1978.

EXERCISE 23.9

Look up the following words in several specialized dictionaries, and find out as much as you can about their meanings, origins, and uses.

1. wazoo
2. tip
3. scam
4. jazz
5. whammy

| 4. Subject dictionaries

Special subject dictionaries can help us understand specialized or technical vocabulary and provide a rough map of any field. Such dictionaries exist for music, classical literature, biography, mathematics, philosophy, geography, religion, and many other fields. Suppose, for instance, that you find the word *unique* used in a math textbook in a way that puzzles you. Check a source such as the *Mathematics Dictionary*, 4th edition (eds. Glen James and Robert C. James. New York: Van Nostrand Reinhold Co., 1976). There you will find the following entry:

> **U-NIQUE′**, *adj.* Leading to one and only one result; consisting of one, and only one. The product of two integers is unique; the square root of an integer is not unless the integer is 0.
>
> **unique factorization.** See DOMAIN—integral domain, FUNDAMENTAL—fundamental theorem of arithmetic, IRREDUCIBLE—irreducible polynomial.

You will find more on special subject dictionaries in Chapter 39.

READING WITH ATTENTION TO WORDS

In his autobiography, Malcolm X says that he taught himself to write by reading and copying the dictionary. Certainly you can teach yourself to be a better writer by reading with very careful attention to the way other writers use words you are not very familiar with. Choose a writer whose work you admire, and read that author's work for at least thirty minutes, noting down six or seven words that you would not ordinarily have thought to use in such a situation. Do a little dictionary investigative work on these words, and bring your results to class for discussion.

FOR EXAMINING SOME WORDS IN YOUR OWN WRITING

Look back through the last several essays or drafts of essays you have written, looking for two or three words you have used that interest you but that you know very little about. Then look up those words in at least one abridged and one unabridged dictionary and in any specialized dictionary that might give you further information. On the basis of what you have learned, check the way you have used these words in your essays. How accurately and appropriately have you used them? What synonyms could you have appropriately substituted?

24. Enriching Vocabulary

In one of the great heroic tales in English literature, Beowulf faces a series of difficult challenges. In the face of them, he calls not for weapons or for superhuman strength. Instead he says, quite simply, "I will unlock my word-hoard." Beowulf regards his "word-hoard," his vocabulary or language, as his greatest strength. Indeed, throughout the history of the West, the connection between language and creative power has been very close. In the Bible, for instance, how does God create the world? By calling it into existence through *naming* it.

Vocabulary comes from a Latin term for "name" (*vocabulum*), which in turn comes from the Latin verb for "call." Thus, our vocabulary "calls forth" or names things in our worlds. This connection between vocabulary and calling into being is what led a famous philosopher to declare that "the limits of my language are the limits of my world." You can recognize what the philosopher means easily enough by remembering a time in your life when you learned the name of something new. Before that time, this thing did not exist for you; yet curiously enough, once you know its name, you begin to recognize it all around you. Such is the power of vocabulary in enriching not only your personal language but our lives as well.

▌ 24a. Extending your vocabulary

If you grew up speaking English, your English vocabulary is already extensive. At its largest, it includes all those words whose meanings you either recognize or can deduce from context. This, your

processing vocabulary, allows you to interpret the meanings of many passages whose words you might not actively use yourself. Your **producing vocabulary** is more limited, comprising those words you actually use in writing and/or speaking.

Part of what it means to mature intellectually is to broaden your mental horizons by learning how to name more things more accurately, to increase your own word-hoard. Doing so involves consciously strengthening the bridges between your processing vocabulary and your producing vocabulary by beginning to use in your own speaking and writing more of the words you recognize and can interpret in context. To accomplish this goal, you must become an investigative reporter of your own language and the language of others.

▌ 24b. Charting the history of English

Try to imagine a world without language. In fact, you probably cannot do so, for language is perhaps the most ancient heritage of the human race. Because language brings us together and indeed allows us to name and structure our experience of the world, it is well worth understanding how this heritage originated and has changed over the centuries. Knowing at least a little about the relationship of English to German, Norse, Latin, Greek, and French can guide you as you seek to learn more about any particular modern English word.

English has always been a hybrid language, what Daniel Defoe called "your Roman-Saxon-Danish-Norman English." Where did this hybrid come from, and how did it evolve? English, like one-third of all languages in the world, descends from Indo-European, a language spoken by a group of seminomadic peoples who almost certainly had domestic animals, worked leather, wove wool, and planted some crops. Where they lived is the subject of great controversy, though their home must have been in some part of north-central Europe. Scholars began to argue for Indo-European, the language of these people, as a "common source" and to try to identify its features when they noted more and more striking resemblances between words in a number of languages:

English	Latin	French	Greek	German	Dutch	Swedish	Danish
three	*tres*	*trois*	*treis*	*drei*	*drie*	*tre*	*tre*

Eventually, a version of Indo-European was brought to Britain by the Germanic invasions following 449. This early language, called Anglo-

Saxon or Old English, was further influenced by Latin and Greek when Christianity was reintroduced into England beginning in 597, was later shaped by the Viking invasions beginning in the late 700s (the Danes feature prominently in *Beowulf*), and was transformed after the Norman Conquest (1066) by French.

While the English vernacular continued to evolve in the centuries after the Conquest, however, Latin and French remained the languages of the learned—of the church and court. (Indeed, lectures at Oxford University were delivered in Latin well into the nineteenth century.) It was Chaucer, through his decision in the late 1300s to write *The Canterbury Tales* not in Latin or French but in the earthy language of the people, who helped establish English as the political, legal, and literary language of Britain. And with the advent of printing in the mid-1400s, that language became more accessible and more standardized.

One brief example will give you an idea of how much English had evolved up to this time. Here are three versions of a Biblical passage:

ANGLO-SAXON GOSPELS, AROUND 1000 A.D.

And eft hē ongan hī æt þǣre sǣ lǣran. And him wæs mycel męnegu tō gegaderod, swā þæt hē on scip ēode, and on bǣre sǣ wæs; and eall sēo męnegu ymbe þē sǣ wæs on lande.

WYCLIFFE BIBLE, ABOUT 1380

And eft Jhesus bigan to teche at the see; and myche puple was gaderid to hym, so that he wente in to a boot, and sat in the see, and al the puple was aboute the see on the loond.

KING JAMES VERSION, 1611

And he began again to teach by the seaside: and there was gathered unto him a great multitude, so that he entered into a ship, and sat in the sea; and the whole multitude was by the sea on the land.

Note that in the Old English text, only a few words—*and, he, him, waes, lande, sae*—look familiar. By the time of Chaucer, however, many words are recognizable. And by the time of the Renaissance, the language is easily readable by us.

In the last four hundred years, as the extension of British, and later American, political and cultural influence has made English the second most widely spoken language in the world, continued borrowings from many languages have given it the world's largest vocabulary. Modern English, then, is a composite language, a plant growing luxuriously in the soil of multiple sources.

■ 24c. Recognizing word roots

As its name suggests, a **root** is a word from which other words grow, usually through the addition of prefixes or suffixes. From the Latin roots -*dic*- or -*dict*- ("speak"), for instance, grows a whole range of words in English: *contradict, dictate, dictator, diction, edict, predict, dictaphone,* and others. From the Greek root -*chrono*- ("time") come our words *chronology, chronometer, synchronize,* and so on.

Here are some other Latin (marked L) and Greek (marked G) roots. Recognizing them will help you recognize networks of words in the language.

ROOT	MEANING	EXAMPLES
-audi- (L)	to hear	audience, audio, auditorium
-bene- (L)	good, well	benevolent, benefit, benefactor
-bio- (G)	life	biography, biosphere, biopsy
-duc(t)- (L)	to lead or to make	ductile, reduce, reproduce
-gen- (G)	race, kind	genealogy, gene
-geo- (G)	earth	geography, geometry
-graph- (G)	to write	graphic, photography, pictograph
-jur-, -jus- (L)	law	justice, jurisdiction
-log(o)- (G)	word, thought	biology, logical, logocentric
-luc- (L)	light	lucid, translucent
-manu- (L)	hand	manufacture, manual, manipulate
-mit-, -mis- (L)	to send	permit, transmission, intermittent
-path- (G)	feel, suffer	empathy, pathetic
-phil- (G)	love	philosopher, bibliophile
-photo- (G)	light	photography, telephoto
-port- (L)	to carry	transport, portable
-psych- (G)	soul	psychology, psychopath
-scrib-, -script- (L)	to write	inscribe, manuscript, descriptive
-sent-, -sens- (L)	to feel	sensation, resent

-tele- (G)	far away	telegraph, telepathy
-tend- (L)	to stretch	extend, tendency
-terr- (L)	earth	inter, territorial
-therm- (G)	heat	thermonuclear, thermostat
-vac- (L)	empty	vacuole, evacuation
-vid-, -vis- (L)	to see	video, envision, visit

EXERCISE 24.1

Using the list of roots above, try to figure out the meaning of each of the following words. Write a potential definition for each one, and then compare your dictionary's definition to yours.

1. terrestrial
2. scriptorium
3. geothermal
4. lucent
5. beneficent
6. audiology
7. vacuous
8. pathogenic
9. juridical
10. graphology

▌ 24d. Recognizing prefixes and suffixes

Originally individual words themselves, prefixes and suffixes are groups of letters added to words or to word roots to create new words. These word additions account for much of the flexibility of English, often allowing dozens of words to be built on one root.

▌ 1. Prefixes

Prefix appropriately demonstrates its own meaning: it is made up of a prefix (*-pre-*) and a root (*-fix-*) and means literally "fasten before." Fastened to the beginnings of words or roots, prefixes modify and extend meanings. Recognizing common prefixes can often help you decipher the meaning of otherwise unfamiliar words.

Prefixes of negation or opposition

PREFIX	MEANING	EXAMPLES
a-, an-	without, not	ahistorical, anemia
anti-	against	antibody, antiphonal
contra-	against	contravene, contramand
de-	from, take away from	demerit, declaw
dis-	apart, away	disappear, discharge
il-, im-, in-, ir-	not	illegal, immature, indistinct, irreverent

mal-	wrong	malevolent, malpractice
mis-	wrong, bad	misapply, misanthrope
non-	not	nonentity, nonsense
un-	not	unbreakable, unable

Prefixes of quantity

PREFIX	MEANING	EXAMPLES
bi-	two	bipolar, bilateral
milli-	thousand	millimeter, milligram
mono-	one, single	monotone, monologue
omni-	all	omniscient, omnipotent
semi-	half	semicolon, semiconductor
tri-	three	tripod, trimester
uni-	one	unitary, univocal

Prefixes of time and space

PREFIX	MEANING	EXAMPLES
ante-	before	antedate, antebellum
circum-	around	circumlocution, circumnavigate
co-, col-, com-, con-, cor-	with	coequal, collaborate, commiserate, contact, correspond
e-, ex-	out of	emit, extort, expunge
hyper-	over, more than	hypersonic, hypersensitive
hypo-	under, less than	hypodermic, hypoglycemia
inter-	between	intervene, international
mega-	enlarge, large	megalomania, megaphone
micro-	tiny	micrometer, microscopic
neo-	recent	neologism, neophyte
post-	after	postwar, postscript
pre-	before	previous, prepublication
pro-	before, onward	project, propel
re-	again, back	review, recreate
sub-	under, beneath	subhuman, submarine
super-	over, above	supercargo, superimpose
syn-	at the same time	synonym, synchronize
trans-	across, over	transport, transition

EXERCISE 24.2

Using the list of prefixes above and the list of roots in 24c, try to figure out the meaning of each of the following words. Write a potential definition for each one, and then compare your dictionary's definition to yours.

1. remit
2. subterranean
3. translucent
4. monograph
5. distend
6. superscript
7. deport
8. neologism
9. inaudible
10. apathetic

2. Suffixes

Attached to the ends of words and word roots, **suffixes** modify and extend meanings, many times by altering the grammatical function or part of speech of the original word. Suffixes can, for example, turn the verb *create* into a noun, an adjective, or an adverb.

VERB	create
NOUNS	crea*tor*/crea*tion*/creati*vity*/crea*ture*
ADJECTIVE	creat*ive*
ADVERB	creative*ly*

Noun suffixes

SUFFIX	MEANING	EXAMPLES
-acy	state or quality	democracy, privacy
-al	act of	rebuttal, refusal
-ance, -ence	state or quality of	maintenance, eminence
-dom	place or state of being	freedom, thralldom
-er, -or	one who	trainer, investor
-ism	doctrine or belief characteristic of	liberalism, Taoism
-ist	one who	organist, physicist
-ity	quality of	veracity, opacity
-ment	condition of	payment, argument
-ness	state of being	watchfulness, cleanliness
-ship	position held	professorship, fellowship
-sion, -tion	state of being or action	digression, transition

Verb suffixes

SUFFIX	MEANING	EXAMPLES
-ate	cause to be	concentrate, regulate
-en	cause to be or become	enliven, blacken

| -ify, -fy | make or cause to be | unify, terrify, amplify |
| -ize | cause to become | magnetize, civilize |

Adjective suffixes

SUFFIX	MEANING	EXAMPLES
-able, -ible	capable of being	assumable, edible
-al	pertaining to	regional, political
-esque	reminiscent of	picturesque, statuesque
-ful	having a notable quality	colorful, sorrowful
-ic	pertaining to	poetic, mythic
-ish	having the quality of	prudish, clownish
-ious, -ous	of or characterized by	famous, nutritious
-ive	having the nature of	festive, creative, massive
-less	without	endless, senseless

EXERCISE 24.3

Using the list of suffixes above, figure out the meaning of each of the following words. (Use your dictionary if necessary.) Then choose two of the words, and use each one in a sentence.

1. contemplative
2. fanciful
3. impairment
4. liquefy
5. barrenness
6. defiance
7. defiantly
8. redden
9. standardize
10. satirist

▌ 24e. Building a word-hoard

Making good use of prefixes or suffixes will increase the power of your vocabulary, but other methods will be even more helpful in creating a word-hoard that is a match for Beowulf's. These methods include analyzing word contexts, becoming an active reader, and becoming a collector of words.

▌ 1. Analyzing word contexts

If you have ever run into a person you knew but simply could not place—until you remembered the place where you normally saw the person (at the grocery store, say, or the bank), you know firsthand the importance of context in helping you identify people and things. The same principle holds true for words. So if a word is at first unfamiliar to you, look carefully at its context, paying attention to all the clues that context can give; often you will be able to deduce the meaning.

For instance, if the word *accouterments* is unfamiliar in the sentence *We stopped at a camping supply store to pick up last-minute accouterments*, you can figure out its meaning from its context: *the camping supply store* and *last-minute* suggest strongly that *equipment* or some similar word fits the bill. And that is what *accouterments* means.

Sometimes, as in the following sentences, the context will include examples or definitions of unfamiliar words:

> In grammars of the late medieval period, figures of speech were organized into *schemes*—figures having to do with word choice—and *tropes*—figures having to do with sentence construction.

> The troop leader quickly removed all *incendiary* materials—matches, gas lanterns, and firecrackers.

Sometimes, however, deciphering the meaning of a word calls on your greatest detective powers. The following example, for instance, demands very careful attention to context:

> Interpretive frameworks at their most radical become reflexive, arguing that the observer's own understanding of any phenomenon must arise through a complex interaction between the process of observing and the characteristics of the thing being observed.

This is not an easy sentence to read, because much of the diction is general and abstract. *Interpretive frameworks* suggests structures that interpret information or data. *Radical* interpretive frameworks is more problematic. Although *radical* refers back to Latin *radix* ("root"), the usual meaning of *radical* today is "extreme." So the most extreme forms of interpretive frameworks become reflexive. What might that mean? A reflex is a response, like the knee-jerk reflex, so *reflexive* probably has to do with response. The sentence structure tells us that *become reflexive* here means that an observer's understanding arises through an interaction between observing and what is observed. Perhaps that interaction is the response that *reflexive* seems to refer to. Our provisional understanding of this sentence, then, might be paraphrased as "extreme forms of interpretation depend on an interaction of observer and observed." When you encounter such passages, your best strategy is to continue reading, looking for additional contextual clues to meaning.

EXERCISE 24.4

Identify the contextual clues that help you understand any unfamiliar words in the following sentences. Then write paraphrases of three of the sentences.

1. Before Prohibition, the criminal fringe in the United States had been a self-effacing, scattered class with little popular support.
2. I felt ambivalent. I was angry with Sylvia, but I understood why she behaved so audaciously in asking for a raise after three days on the job.
3. The community's reaction to the preternatural creature in Mary Shelley's *Frankenstein* shows that people are often more monstrous than a monster.
4. My fifth-grade teacher was the epitome of what I wanted to be, and I began to imitate him scrupulously.
5. Aristarchus showed that the sun is larger than the earth and proposed a heliocentric model of the solar system. During the second century A.D., however, Ptolemy challenged this theory with his geocentric model, which came to dominate astronomical thought for the next 1,400 years.

2. Becoming an active reader

As processors of information, we can read words alone, or we can read meanings. To read meanings means filling in blanks, making connections, leaping ahead, asking questions, taking mental notes. Active readers flex their mental muscles while reading; they exercise their own understanding and thereby stretch to greater knowledge. Out of such activity great word-hoards are born. Here are some tips for building your vocabulary through active reading:

- Make a habit of paraphrasing or summarizing unfamiliar words or phrases. Then check the dictionary to see how accurate your paraphrase is.
- Practice naming the opposites of words. If you see *abbreviation*, for instance, try supplying its opposite—*enlargement, elaboration,* etc.
- Challenge authors by trying to come up with a better word or words than the ones they used.
- Read aloud to yourself from time to time, noting any words whose pronunciation you are unsure of. Check them out in the dictionary.

3. Becoming a collector of words

Collecting words is an important part of reading actively. Pay close attention to words, choosing those you like best and taking them home as part of your producing vocabulary. You are already a collector of words in one sense: you probably add words to your vocabulary on a fairly regular basis. All you need to do now is make that activity more conscientious and systematic. Begin by choosing a writer you admire and reading for as long as it takes to identify several words you like but would not use in speaking or writing. Your collection has started. Now analyze these words for what you like about them—for pronunciation, meaning, and usage. Next, try the words out on your friends and instructors. And then just continue to build your collection.

READING WITH ATTENTION TO VOCABULARY

Read each of the following passages, paying particular attention to the italicized words. See if you can determine the meaning of any words that are not part of your processing vocabulary by using the clues suggested in this chapter—context, prefixes, roots, suffixes. Check your understanding by then looking up each word in the dictionary.

1. Now, I doubt that the imagination can be suppressed. If you truly *eradicated* it in a child, he would grow up to be an eggplant. Like all our evil *propensities*, the imagination will win out.
   —URSULA LEGUIN, "Why Are Americans Afraid of Dragons?"
2. I am enjoying a *reprieve* of warm sun in a season of rain and *impending* frost. Around me today is the wine of the garden's final ripening.
   —LIANE ELLISON NORMAN,
   "Pedestrian Students and High-Flying Squirrels"
3. But this is the *hiatus* between harvests; the oppressive lull before the bust of monsoon rains; the season of flies and dust, heat and disease, *querulous* voices and frayed tempers—and the season of want.
   —PEGGY AND PIERRE STREIT, "A Well in India"
4. I now firmly believe that when it comes to *instilling* in others—and in myself—the virtues of the Christmas spirit, there is no better way than as Santa Claus. How else could I so easily set aside my *inhibitions* . . . and become a *mirthful*, winking, ho-ho-ho-ing, joking, hugging, *exuberant* man?   —MARK L. DEMBERT, "Being Santa"
5. I think it is agreed by all parties, that this *prodigious* number of children in the arms, or on the backs, or at the heels of their mothers . . . is in the present *deplorable* state of the kingdom, a very great additional *grievance.* . . .   —JONATHAN SWIFT, "A Modest Proposal"

FOR EXAMINING VOCABULARY IN YOUR OWN WRITING

Read over a piece of writing you are working on or have recently completed. Underline any words you think could be improved on, and then come up with several possible substitutes. Bring them and your piece of writing to class for discussion.

25. Analyzing and Using Diction

In writing of someone you work with, you might choose one or more of the following words: *accomplice, ally, associate, buddy, cohort, collaborator, colleague, comrade, co-worker, mate, partner, sidekick.* The choice you make is a matter of **diction,** which derives from the Latin word for "say" and means literally how you say or express something. Good diction, or choosing words well, involves many issues discussed elsewhere in this book, such as being concise (see 17b), using parallel structures (see Chapter 19), choosing strong, precise verbs (see 21a), using dictionaries (see Chapter 23), strengthening vocabulary (see Chapter 24), and establishing tone (see Chapter 26). This chapter will give you some guidance about three other aspects of good diction: using language appropriate to the writer's purpose, topic, and audience; choosing words with the right denotations and connotations; and balancing general and abstract words with specific and concrete ones.

■ 25a. Choosing appropriate language

Musing on the many possible ways to describe a face, Ford Maddox Ford says,

> That a face resembles a Dutch clock has been said too often; to say that it resembles a ham is inexact and conveys nothing; to say that it has the mournfulness of an old smashed-in meat tin, cast away on a waste building lot, would be smart—but too much of that sort of thing would become a nuisance. —FORD MADDOX FORD, *Joseph Conrad*

Ford here implies a major point about diction: effective word choice can be made only on the basis of what is appropriate to the writer's purpose, to the topic, and to the audience. Specifically, he is saying that making appropriate word choices requires a writer to take into account a number of considerations. For instance, many terms vary from one region to another: the hard round object in the center of a cherry might be described as a stone, a pit, a pip, or a seed, depending on where the writer comes from. *Cherry pip* and *cherry stone* are examples of **regionalisms,** words or expressions peculiar to only one region or part of the country. Regionalisms form one aspect of **dialects,** forms of a language that are distinctive to a particular region or social or ethnic group. In addition to distinctive words and expressions, dialects usually include distinctive pronunciations and grammatical constructions.

If you have never heard the phrase *cherry pip* used before, that particular choice of words will sound odd and perhaps puzzling to you. In other cases, especially in writing, a phrase or construction perfectly understandable and acceptable to users of one dialect will sound not only odd or puzzling but wrong to others. The verb constructions in *the car needs washed* or *the grass be dried up,* for example, would look wrong to most Americans who read them in a book or magazine, even though in certain American dialects these are standard ways of speaking. Knowing what features of your dialect do not "match" those of many other Americans can help you decide how to make appropriate diction choices.

In addition to considerations of region or dialect, a writer must also be alert to the level of formality, or register, that is appropriate for a particular topic and audience. Doing so requires that the writer recognize slang and colloquial language.

Slang is extremely informal language that is often confined to a relatively small group of people and usually becomes obsolete rather quickly. In the 1980s, examples of slang that gained fairly wide use included *yuppie, sleaze,* and *number-crunching.*

Colloquial language, such as *a lot, in a bind,* or *snooze,* is less informal, more widely used, and longer-lasting. Like regional and dialectical words and constructions, slang and colloquial language can expose a writer to the risk of not being understood or of sounding wrong. If you are writing for a general audience about arms-control negotiations, for example, and you use the term *nukes* to refer to nuclear missiles, some readers may not know what you mean, and others may be distracted or irritated by what they see as a frivolous reference to a deadly serious subject.

For most of the college writing you do, meeting the challenge of appropriateness means choosing words that will be most clear and most understandable to a wide range of educated readers. Edited American English (sometimes referred to as EAE) ordinarily fulfills this goal because it is *shared* by most writers throughout the country. In general, edited American English does not use regionalisms, dialect, slang, or colloquial language except deliberately for a special purpose. So if you find instances of these in your writing, examine them very closely. Most often, they will be *inappropriate* for college writing; in Ford Maddox Ford's words, "too much of that sort of thing" is not "smart."

▌ 25b. Denotation and connotation

Think of a stone tossed into a pool, and imagine the ripples spreading out from it, circle by circle. Or think of a note struck clear and clean, and the multiple vibrations that echo from it. In such images you can capture the distinction between **denotation,** the general meaning of a word, and **connotation,** the ripples, vibrations, associations that accompany the word. As a writer, you want to choose words that are both denotatively and connotatively appropriate.

Words with similar denotations may have connotations that vary widely. The words *maxim, epigram, proverb, saw, saying,* and *motto,* for instance, all carry roughly the same denotation. Because of their different connotations, however, *proverb* would be the appropriate word to use in reference to a saying from the Bible; *saw* in reference to the kind of wisdom handed down to us anonymously; *epigram* in reference to something written by Oscar Wilde. *Dirt* and *soil* have roughly the same denotative meaning, and their connotations are close enough to allow us to use them interchangeably in most cases. *Pushy* and *assertive* also have much the same denotative meaning, but in this case their connotations suggest different attitudes on the part of the speaker or writer, one neutral or positive, the other negative.

Mistakes in denotation are bound to occur as we try out new words. A person who writes "The party managed to diverge my thoughts from the hard work ahead" is confusing *divert* and *diverge* but is on the way to learning to use both. To avoid mistakes in denotation, pay careful attention to the way words are used in context, and check your dictionary whenever you are unsure of meaning.

395

Although words with the wrong connotations for your intended meaning may not be as obvious as those with wrong denotations, take equal care to avoid them. Good writers and readers are sensitive to the power of connotation for a number of reasons. In the first place, we do not want to be misunderstood: calling someone *skinny* rather than *slender*, for instance, might be taken as an insult or joke when such a meaning was unintended. And because connotation plays an important part in the language of politics and advertising (to name only the two most obvious fields), being alert to connotation and its power can help us read and listen more critically. Look, for instance, at the differences in connotation among the following three statements:

> Antiapartheid activists built a symbolic shanty on the green this morning to protest the university's refusal to sell its investments in companies doing business in South Africa.

> A gang of left-wing agitators threw up an eyesore right on the green this morning to try to stampede the university into politicizing its investment policy.

> Supporters of human rights in South Africa challenged the university's investment in racism by erecting a protest shanty in the heart of the campus this morning.

As this example demonstrates, positive and negative connotations can shift meaning significantly. Take note of such powerful uses of connotation in the writing of others; even more important, examine the connotative power of your own writing, and try to use connotation to help make your meanings clear and effective.

Many words carry fairly general connotations, evoking similar associational responses in most listeners or readers. But connotations can be personal or distinctive to a particular audience as well. If you ever got violently ill right after eating some particular dish as a child, you know the power of personal connotation. The mere mention of, say, peanut butter cookies carries powerful negative connotations.

The power of connotations to a particular audience was well illustrated by the meeting between Michael Dukakis and Jesse Jackson at the 1988 Democratic National Convention. Jackson was offended that Dukakis, who had clinched the party's presidential nomination, had asserted his leadership by describing himself as "the quarterback on this team," a phrase that reminded blacks of the stereotype that they were not intelligent enough to play quarterback on football teams. For his part, Dukakis was upset by Jackson's having told the new voters he had brought into the party that they were being used to "carry bales of cotton" up to "the big house," because the connotations of this language suggested to blacks that Dukakis was like a white plantation owner profiting from the labor of black slaves. Whenever you write for a particular audience, try to be aware of the connotations your language will hold for that group of people.

> Checking for wrong words

"Wrong word" errors take so many different forms that it is very difficult to name any foolproof methods of checking for them. If you often find yourself using the "wrong word," however, it will probably be well worth your time to go through each draft looking carefully at every word you are not absolutely sure of. Check each one in a dictionary to see that you're using it properly. Next, look for homonyms, words that sound like other words (such as *to, too,* and *two*). Using the information in 22b, make sure you are using the correct form. If you have persistent problems with wrong words, ask someone to read your drafts. Keep a list of any words you use incorrectly, including example sentences showing the way you've misused them. Make a point of proofreading carefully for them.

EXERCISE 25.1

For each of the following sentences, choose the word in parentheses whose denotative meaning makes sense in the context of the sentence. Use a dictionary if necessary.

1. She always listened *(apprehensively/attentively)* to the lecture and took excellent notes.
2. Going swimming on a hot day can be a *(rapturous/ravenous)* experience.
3. Please take good care of this antique photo album; it's very *(fractious/fragile)*.
4. The instructor congratulated Bev for improving her backhand *(dramatically/ drastically)* since the last lesson.
5. Benjamin Franklin advised readers of *Poor Richard's Almanac* to be *(feudal/ frugal)* and industrious.

EXERCISE 25.2

The contractor who advertises "We don't build *houses*, we build *homes*" counts on the positive connotations of *home* to boost sales. *New* and *improved* apparently have such powerful connotations that advertisers rely on them regularly.

397

Look through a magazine you read frequently, and find three or four especially effective uses of connotation—either negative or positive—in advertisements. Bring these advertisements to class for discussion.

EXERCISE 25.3

Study the italicized words in each of the following passages, and decide what each word's connotations contribute to your understanding of the passage. Think of a synonym for each word, and see if you can decide what difference your word would make to the effect of the passage.

1. The Burmans were already *racing* past me across the mud. It was obvious that the elephant would never *rise* again, but he was not dead. He was breathing very rhythmically with long *rattling gasps*, his great *mound* of a side painfully rising and falling.
   –GEORGE ORWELL, "Shooting an Elephant"
2. If boxing is a sport, it is the most *tragic* of all sports because, more than any human activity, it *consumes* the very excellence it *displays:* Its very *drama* is this consumption.   –JOYCE CAROL OATES, "On Boxing"
3. We caught two bass, *hauling* them in *briskly* as though they were mackerel, pulling them over the side of the boat in a *businesslike* manner without any landing net, and stunning them with a *blow* on the back of the head.
   –E. B. WHITE, "Once More to the Lake"
4. The air *held* a *keenness* that made her nose *twitch*. The harvesting of the corn and cotton, peanuts and squash, made each day a golden *surprise* that caused excited little *tremors* to *run* up her jaw.
   –ALICE WALKER, "The Flowers"
5. The Kiowas are a summer people; they *abide* the cold and keep to themselves; but when the *season turns* and the land becomes warm and *vital*, they cannot *hold still*; . . .
   –N. SCOTT MOMADAY, "The Way to Rainy Mountain"

25c. Balancing general and specific diction

Good writers move their prose along and help readers follow the meaning by balancing **general words**—those that refer to groups or classes of things—with **specific words**—those that refer to individual things. One kind of general words, **abstractions,** are words or phrases that refer to qualities or ideas, things we cannot perceive through our five senses. Specific words are often **concrete words;** they name things we can see, hear, touch, taste, or smell. Most often, we cannot draw a clear-cut line between general or abstract words on the one hand and specific or concrete ones on the other. Instead, most words and phrases fall somewhere on a continuum between these two extremes:

GENERAL	LESS GENERAL	SPECIFIC	MORE SPECIFIC
book	dictionary	unabridged dictionary	my 1988 edition of *Webster's Dictionary*
furniture	bed	antique bed	1840 curly maple bedstead of my grandmother's

ABSTRACT	LESS ABSTRACT	CONCRETE	MORE CONCRETE
culture	art	painting	Van Gogh's *Starry Night*
winter	cold weather	icicles	fifteen-inch icicle hanging from the eaves of the dormitory

Because passages that contain mostly general terms or abstractions demand that readers supply most of the specific examples or concrete details, such writing is often hard to read. Taken to extremes, it is dull or boring. But writing that is full of specifics can also be tedious and hard to follow if the main point is not made clearly or is lost amid a flood of extraneous details. Strong writing must usually both provide readers with a general idea or "big picture" and tie that idea down with specific examples or concrete details.

In the following passage, for instance, the author might have simply made a main general statement—*their breakfast was always liberal and good*—or simply described the breakfast in detail. Instead, he does both.

> There would be a brisk fire crackling in the hearth, the old smoke-gold of morning and the smell of fog, the crisp cheerful voices of the people and their ruddy competent morning look, and the cheerful smells of breakfast, which was always liberal and good, the best meal that they had: kidneys and ham and eggs and sausages and toast and marmalade and tea.   —THOMAS WOLFE, *Of Time and the River*

Here are two student writers balancing general statements with illustrative specific details.

GENERAL   My neighbor is a nuisance.

SPECIFIC   My next-door neighbor is a nuisance, poking and prying into my life, constantly watching me as I enter and leave my house, complaining about the noise when I am having a good time, and telling my parents whenever she sees me kissing my date.

GENERAL   Central Texas has an unusual climate.

SPECIFIC   Few places in the United States display the wild climatic
               variations of central Texas: at one moment, the sky may
               be clear blue and the air balmy; at another, a racing flash
               flood may drown the landscape and threaten people's
               lives.

EXERCISE 25.4

Choose two of the following abstract terms, and write a sentence for each one
that provides concrete illustration of the term: *fear, joy, inspiration, boredom,
contentment, exhaustion.*

EXERCISE 25.5

Rewrite each of the following sentences to make them more specific and concrete.

1. The entryway of the building was dirty.
2. The sounds at dawn are memorable.
3. Sunday dinner was good.
4. The attendant came toward my car.
5. The child played on the beach.

READING WITH AN EYE FOR DICTION

The following passage is from Joan Didion's essay "In Bed." Read it carefully,
and identify the balance of abstract and concrete and of general and specific
diction.

Migraine is something more than the fancy of a neurotic imagination. It is an
essentially hereditary complex of symptoms, the most frequently noted but by
no means the most unpleasant of which is a vascular headache of blinding
severity, suffered by a surprising number of women, a fair number of men
(Thomas Jefferson had migraine, and so did Ulysses S. Grant, the day he
accepted Lee's surrender), and by some unfortunate children as young as two
years old. (I had my first when I was eight. It came on during a fire drill at
the Columbia School in Colorado Springs, Colorado. I was taken first home
and then to the infirmary at Peterson Field, where my father was stationed.
The Air Corps doctor prescribed an enema.) Almost anything can trigger a
specific attack of migraine: stress, allergy, fatigue, an abrupt change in baro-
metric pressure, a contretemps over a parking ticket. A flashing light. A fire
drill. One inherits, of course, only the predisposition. In other words I spent

yesterday in bed with a headache not merely because of my bad attitudes, unpleasant tempers and wrongthink, but because both my grandmothers had migraine, my father has migraine and my mother has migraine.

—JOAN DIDION, "In Bed"

FOR EXAMINING DICTION IN YOUR OWN WRITING

Write a paragraph or two describing one of your friends. Then analyze what you have written, and identify the concrete and abstract language you used. Decide whether you have achieved the proper balance between the two, and if not, revise accordingly.

26. Establishing Tone

Anyone who has spent any time with a child knows firsthand the truth of what linguists tell us: regardless of the words actually used, children sense immediately whether a parent is sad, angry, delighted, or alarmed. They get this important information from the tone of voice with which the words are spoken, a tone that creates a strong overall impression. So it is with the **tone** of a piece of writing: it creates an overall or **dominant impression**—perhaps humorous, outraged, friendly, skeptical. Tone, then, is the atmosphere of a piece of writing. Just as you can distinguish the atmosphere created by "The Star-Spangled Banner," "I've Been Working on the Railroad," and a heavy-metal rock song, so can you distinguish among tones in writing. And like the blend of musical notes and lyrics in a song, the tone of any piece of writing results from a blend of several factors: the writer's purpose, the writer's relationship to the audience, and the writer's relationship to the topic. This chapter explores each of these factors.

26a. Considering purpose and audience

The key to establishing an *effective* tone, to creating the impression that you *want* to create, is to consider carefully what tone is most appropriate to your purpose, audience, and topic. Your choice of tone should always reflect the reason that you are writing and the particular readers you want to address: you say something one way to entertain or inform close friends, another way to explain to parents, and yet another way to persuade an audience you do not know well. For instance, you might say the following to friends:

> I had to pull an incomplete in psych because I was barfing with that stomach flu all finals week and couldn't book it at all.

That same thought might be expressed to parents as:

> I had to take an incomplete in psychology because I had the stomach flu that was going around and couldn't study because I was throwing up all night before the final exam.

And to a committee that is evaluating you for a scholarship, you might explain (probably in writing):

> I was forced to request an incomplete in my Psychology 102 course because I had been violently ill with an intestinal virus for three days before the final examination (doctor's letter is enclosed) and was therefore unable to study.

What are the differences between these versions? Diction is the most obvious difference, but if you look more closely, you will see that each version reveals definite judgments about purpose, audience, and context, or how much the audience already knows. Consider how strange your friends would think you if you spoke to them in the language you might use to the scholarship committee. Your distant, formal tone, created by giving such full background, would confuse them. Similarly, if you wrote to the scholarship committee in the words you would use with friends, the committee would be equally confused. They would probably think either that you were trying to be funny at a serious time or that you did not know how to address people outside your personal circle. In either case, you would be less likely to achieve your purpose in writing—to persuade the committee to give you the scholarship.

As this example indicates, the better you know the audience, the less context or background information you must specify. (Note that the three examples get progressively longer as the speaker must supply more and more context.) Your friends know you well, know about incompletes, know about finals week, know about the flu. They know your context, and thus you can use slang and informal terms that are short and telegraphic. Your parents do not know as much of your context. You must be slightly more formal with them (they have always hated the word *barf*) in addition to explaining more of the situation. For the committee, you must be even more formal, supplying a detailed explanation that will show them your seriousness. This implicit knowledge about your purpose and audience leads you to create a different tone for each version.

▍26b. Appealing to your audience

Like a pair of shoes, tone needs to "fit" an audience, striking just the right note, creating just the right impression, making just the right appeal. To make judgments about tone and audience, ask yourself these questions:

1. Of all the people whom I want to read this piece of writing, who is least well known to me?
2. What is my relationship with that person? What attitudes and word choices does that person expect from me?
3. What attitudes or word choices might offend or disturb that person?
4. What kind of response do I want to evoke from that person? What dominant impression do I want to create?

The answers to these questions can guide word choice as you seek the proper tone for any piece of writing. The reason for considering the potential reader *least* well known to you is that you must shape your tone to appeal to this person, who is least likely to identify with you or accept what you say just because you are the one saying it. For this person, you must make more arguments, supply more context, and use more formal language than would be necessary for people who knew you better.

Philosopher of language Kenneth Burke notes that we use language as a primary means of identifying with other people. The example in 26a, for instance, showed how you could use different language to appeal to friends, parents, and a scholarship committee and lead each of these groups to identify with you and your situation. Tone is crucial to such identification. Audiences are less likely, for instance, to identify with a writer whose tone is abusive or malicious, and much more likely to identify with and respond to the appeal of a writer whose tone is friendly and respectful. How can you make sure that your tone wins your audience's empathy? Because audiences, purposes, and topics for writing vary so widely, few absolute guidelines exist. Two rules of thumb, however, should serve you well: (1) use language that is respectful and courteous to your audience, and (2) use figurative language, to help the audience understand your message as clearly and dramatically as possible. (See 4d and 4f.)

1. Remembering the "golden rule"

As young children, most of us learned to "do to others what you would have done to you." To that lesson, we could add "say to others what you would have said to you." Language has power. It can praise, delight, inspire. It can also hurt, maim, destroy. Language that insults or offends any group of readers—such as racial, religious, ethnic, sexual, or age-related stereotyping—breaks the golden rule of language use, destroying identification and harming the writer's credibility. By avoiding such language, you can help establish the appropriate tone of respect for and courtesy toward your audience.

In many instances, doing so is simple enough: we can safely assume, for instance, that no readers respond well to a slur on their race or to a form of address like "you complacent slobs," and that such language use will reflect not on the audience but on the writer or speaker. But other cases are more subtle and may well call for some investigation. One student found, for example, that a group he had been referring to as *senior citizens* were irritated by that label. In another instance, a writer discovered that the native people of Alaska wished to be referred to as Eskimos, while those in British Columbia preferred to be called Inuit. Before using a term referring to a group of people, be sure that members of that group approve of it.

Using nonsexist language

Growing awareness of and sensitivity to sexism have done much to demonstrate how powerfully and often invisibly elements of language affect the ways we think and behave. We now know, for instance, that many young women at one time failed to consider careers in medicine or engineering at least partially because our language always referred to a hypothetical doctor or engineer as *he*. Sexist language, those words and phrases that stereotype members of one sex, can be corrected readily enough. We can substitute terms such as *mail carrier* and *police officer* for *mailman* and *policeman*, we can avoid using phrases that call unnecessary attention to gender (such as *coed, woman engineer,* or *male secretary*), and we can use personal and professional titles on an equal basis for both men and women (Mr. Hinojosa and Ms. Walker or Hinojosa and Walker instead of Hinojosa and Ms. Walker).

405

By far the most problematic of sexist terms for writers is the traditional use of *man, mankind,* and the masculine pronouns to refer to all humanity or to people who could be either male or female, as in "all men are mortal" or "a lawyer must pass his bar exam before he can begin to practice." Because such usage ignores half the human race, it does not help build identification between the writer and those this usage excludes. Here are some alternatives to such usage:

1. Use plural forms:

   Lawyers must pass *their* bar exams before beginning to practice.

2. Use *he or she, him or her,* and so on:

   A lawyer must pass *his or her* bar exam before beginning to practice.

3. Eliminate the pronouns:

   A lawyer must pass the bar exam before beginning to practice.

4. Use *humanity, humans, people,* and *humankind*:

   All people are mortal.

For further discussion of nonsexist pronoun use, see 9m and 11c5.

EXERCISE 26.1

The following paragraph is from Mark Twain's *Old Times on the Mississippi.* Read it carefully, noting any language we today might consider sexist. Then do your best to substitute nonsexist words or phrases.

My father was a justice of the peace, and I suppose he possessed the power of life and death over all men and could hang anybody that offended him. This was distinction enough for me as a general thing; but the desire to be a steamboatman kept intruding, nevertheless. I first wanted to be a cabin-boy, so that I could come out with a white apron on and shake a table-cloth over the side, where all my old comrades could see me; later I thought I would rather be the deck-hand who stood on the end of the state-plank with the coil of rope in his hand, because he was particularly conspicuous. But these were only daydreams—they were too heavenly to be contemplated as real possibilities.   —MARK TWAIN, *Old Times on the Mississippi*

❙ 2. Using figurative language

A second good way to create a tone that will appeal to an audience and allow them to "identify" with the writer is by using figurative language, or figures of speech. Such language paints pictures in our minds, allows us to "see" a point and hence understand more readily and clearly. Economists trying to explain the magnitude of the federal deficit use figurative language when they tell us how many times hundred-thousand-dollar bills would have to circle the globe to equal it; scientists describing the way genetic data are transmitted use figurative language when they liken the data to a messenger that carries bits of information from one generation of cells to another. Far from being a mere "decoration" of writing, figurative language plays a crucial role in helping us follow the writer's meaning, quickly and easily. Particularly helpful in building an appealing tone are figures that compare one thing to another—similes, metaphors, and analogies. Other figures include personification, hyperbole, litotes, irony, and allusion.

Similes

Similes make explicit the comparison between two things by using the terms *like, as,* or *as if:*

> Buttresses flew like angels' wings against the exteriors.
> —BARBARA TUCHMAN, "Mankind's Better Moments"

> The comb felt as if it was raking my skin off.
> —MALCOLM X, "My First Conk"

> The migraine acted as a circuit breaker, and the fuses have emerged intact. —JOAN DIDION, "In Bed"

Metaphors

Metaphors are *implicit comparisons*, omitting the *like, as,* or *as if* of similes.

> Black women are called, in the folklore that so aptly identifies one's status in society, "the mule of the world," because we have been handed the burdens that everyone else—everyone else—refused to carry.
> —ALICE WALKER, *In Search of Our Mothers' Gardens*

> Lee was tidewater Virginia, and in his backyard were family, culture, and tradition.
> —BRUCE CATTON, "Grant and Lee: A Study in Contrasts"

Analogies

Analogies compare similar features of two dissimilar things and are often extended to several sentences or paragraphs in length. The following sentence, for example, uses an analogy to help us understand the rapid growth of the computer industry:

> If the aircraft industry had evolved as spectacularly as the computer industry over the past twenty-five years, a Boeing 767 would cost five hundred dollars today, and it would circle the globe in twenty minutes on five gallons of fuel.

The analogy in the next passage helps us "see" an abstract point.

> Our lives are plays, and we are the actors playing the parts. The scenes are set, and each of us takes on a role—followers, leaders, manipulators. Manipulators, who coax and coerce people into doing what the manipulators want, are often the playwrights in our lives.

Before you use an analogy, though, make sure that the two things you are comparing have enough points of similarity so that the comparison is justified and will convince readers. For further discussion of analogies, see 4f3.

Clichés and mixed metaphors

Just as effective use of figurative language can create the tone or impression that the writer wants to create, so *ineffective* figures of speech can create the *wrong* impression by boring, irritating, or unintentionally amusing readers. Among the most common kinds of ineffective figurative language are clichés and mixed metaphors.

Cliché comes from the French word for "stereotype," a metal plate cast from a page of type and used, before photographic printing processes, to produce multiple copies of a book or page without having to reset the type. So a **cliché** in language is an expression stamped out in duplicate to avoid the trouble of "resetting" the thought. Many clichés, like *busy as a bee* or *youth is the springtime of life*, are similes or metaphors.

By definition, we use clichés all the time, especially in speech, and many serve us quite usefully as familiar shorthand for familiar ideas. But as a writer you should use them with caution, for good reason: if your audience recognizes that you are using stereotyped, paint-by-the-numbers language, they are likely to conclude that what you are saying is not very new or interesting—or perhaps even true. The person who tells you that you look "pretty as a picture" uses a clichéd simile that may well sound false or insincere. Compare it with a more original compliment a grandmother once paid to her grandchildren: "You all look as pretty as brand-new red shoes."

How can you check for clichés? While one person's trite phrase may be completely new to another, one rule of thumb will serve you well: if you can predict exactly what the upcoming word(s) in a phrase will be, it stands a very good chance of being a cliché.

Mixed metaphors are comparisons that are not consistent. Instead of creating a clear and dominant impression, they confuse the reader by pulling against one another, often in unintentionally funny ways, as in the announcement by a government official that "we must not drag our dirty linen through the eye of the public."

Here is a mixed metaphor revised for consistency.

MIXED   The lectures were like brilliant comets streaking through the night sky, drenching the listeners with a blizzard of insight

REVISED   The lectures were like brilliant comets streaking through the night sky, dazzling listeners with flashes of insight.

Personification

Personification gives human qualities to animals, inanimate objects, or ideas, making them more vivid or understandable.

[Television] . . . stays in one corner of the room like a horrible electronic gossip.   —JONATHAN MILLER

In the meanwhile there came along a single red ant on the hillside of this valley, evidently full of excitement, who had either dispatched his foe, or had not yet taken part in the battle; . . . whose mother had charged him to return with his shield or upon it.
—HENRY DAVID THOREAU, "The Battle of the Ants"

Hyperbole

Hyperbole, or **overstatement**, deliberately exaggerates to create special emphasis or a humorous tone.

Under certain emotional circumstances, I can stand the spasms of a rich violin, but the concert piece and all wind instruments bore me in small doses and flay me in large doses.   —VLADIMIR NABOKOV

What a travesty of truth are those TV commercials in which we watch a family falling over themselves to reach the fast-food restaurant before they drown in their own drool!   —MAX WYMAN

Litotes

Like hyperbole, **litotes** (or **understatement**) depends on a gap between statement and fact. But while hyperbole is loud and noisy, litotes turns the volume down to a whisper. Understatement can help create a very solemn tone, as it does when one of the characters in Stephen Crane's *The Open Boat*, faced with imminent death, remarks that if he drowns, it "will be a shame"—or when the hero of Ernest Hemingway's *A Farewell to Arms*, having lost his wife and baby in childbirth, quietly "left the hospital and walked back to the hotel in the rain." It can also create humor and other tones. In their first article on DNA, Watson and Crick were reporting that they had discovered what they felt was the secret of life. Yet they carefully closed the article with understatement, creating a tone of quiet confidence: "It has not escaped our notice that the specific pairing we have postulated immediately suggests a possible copying mechanism for the genetic material."

Irony

Irony, language that suggests a meaning that contrasts with or undercuts the literal meaning of the words, can result in a lighthearted, spoofing tone or a serious and bitter one. In probably the most famous piece of sustained irony in English literature, Jonathan Swift's "A Modest Proposal," Swift solemnly recommends the sale and consumption of children, a proposal intended to reveal the poverty and inhuman conditions in Ireland that were condoned by its British rulers at the time. The following "definition" of *writing principles* provides an example of more lighthearted irony.

> Write hurriedly, preferably when tired. Have no plans; write down items as they occur to you. . . . Hand in your manuscript the moment it is finished.   —AMBROSE BIERCE

Irony can work well to gain an audience's attention and set a definite tone, but only if the audience can be expected to recognize and appreciate the irony. (See 3ld for a discussion of ways you can use quotation marks to convey irony.)

Allusion

Allusions, indirect references to cultural works, people, or events, can bring an entire world of associations to the minds of readers who recognize them. If, for instance, you tell a friend in a letter that you have to return to your herculean task of writing a research essay, you are expecting that your reader will understand, by your allusion to the

Labors of Hercules in classical mythology, how big a job you think the essay is. If you choose to title an essay on the antiapartheid movement in the 1980s "A Terrible Beauty Is Born," your allusion to William Butler Yeats's poem about the Irish Rebellion of 1916 will give readers the idea that you see important parallels between the two struggles.

You can draw allusions from history, from literature, from the Bible, from common wisdom, or from current events. Many current popular songs are full of allusions. Remember, however, that allusions work to create effective tone only if your audience recognizes them.

EXERCISE 26.2

Evaluate the effectiveness of similes, metaphors, and analogies in the following sentences, and revise any that are mixed or clichés.

1. These children were brought up to eat, drink, and sleep tennis.
2. In presenting his alibi, the defendant chose the alley he was going to bowl on—and the jury wouldn't swallow it.
3. The president's economic plan is about as useful as rearranging the deck chairs on the *Titanic*.
4. The narrative was heavy as lead—it just flowed on and on and on.
5. For as long as I can remember, my mother has been the backbone for my father's convictions.

EXERCISE 26.3

Here are some metaphorical definitions of slang. Decide which one you like best—and why, and then create your own metaphorical definition of slang or of some other abstraction.

> [Slang] is always strong. . . . Cut these words and they would bleed; they are vascular and alive; they walk and run.
>
> —RALPH WALDO EMERSON

> Slang is the speech of him who rolls the literary garbage carts on their way to the dump.   —AMBROSE BIERCE

> Slang is language that takes off its coat, spits on its hands, and gets to work.   —CARL SANDBURG

> Slang: words with their shoes off.   —PATRICK HARTWELL

EXERCISE 26.4

Identify the similes and metaphors in the following passages, and decide how each contributes to your understanding of the passage it appears in.

1. Most often we walked on the banks of the Cuyahoga River to see the drawbridge come apart and rise up, like giant black jaws taking a bite of sky.   —SALLY CARRIGHAR, "The Blast Furnace"
2. Where a satirist like Pope destroys his victims with flashes of lightning, . . . Jane Austen often roasted her victims over a fire so slow and nicely judged that the thick-skinned feel no discomfort on their behalf but only a gentle tickling.   —WILLIAM GOLDING, *A Moving Target*
3. At the very beginning, when my father's old touring car . . . still remained in our garage, Myers had certain seedy cronies whom he took riding in it or who simply sat in it in our driveway, as if anchored in a houseboat. . . .
    —MARY McCARTHY "Uncle Myers"
4. I was watching everyone else and didn't see the waitress standing quietly by. Her voice was deep and soft like water moving in a cavern.
    —WILLIAM LEAST HEAT MOON, "In the Land of 'Coke-Cola' "
5. My horse, when he is in his stall or lounging about the pasture, has the same relationship to pain that I have when cuddling up with a good murder mystery—comfort and convenience have top priority.
    —VICKI HEARNE, "Horses in Partnership with Time"

EXERCISE 26.5

Read through a magazine, an essay, a story, or some reading you have been assigned and find some examples of personification, hyperbole, litotes, irony, and allusion. Bring these examples to class for discussion.

▌ 26c. Using the appropriate register

On the basis of the writer's relationship to the topic and the audience, we can distinguish four general levels of diction, or **registers**, that constitute one of the major elements of tone. In order of increasing distance from the writer, these levels are *familiar, informal, formal,* and *ceremonial.* While the formal register is the one most often appropriate and useful for college writing, you should be able to recognize and use other registers as well.

▌ 1. Familiar register

Familiar register represents a very close relationship between writer and topic and between writer and audience—it is the language you probably use to talk to yourself or to those you are closest to. It is the register found in diaries, journals, and personal letters; writers sometimes use it in essays, stories, plays, and novels to create a sense of intimacy between themselves and readers or between characters.

Among the characteristics of familiar register are the frequent use of the first person (*I*) and first names, a lack of explicitly stated context (because the audience does not need it), and the use of sentence fragments, contractions, slang, colloquial language, regionalisms, dialect, and other grammatical constructions that disregard the "rules."

You will seldom, if ever, be called on to write in familiar register in college writing. You should, however, learn to recognize it as a reader. The following example is a letter from the English writer Virginia Stephen responding to a marriage proposal from her future husband, Leonard Woolf:

> My dear Leonard,
>
> I am rushing for a train so I can only send a line in answer. There isn't anything really for me to say, except that I should like to go on as before; and that you should leave me free, and that I should be honest. As to faults, I expect mine are just as bad—less noble perhaps. But of course they are not really the question. I have decided to keep this completely secret, except for Vanessa; and I have made her promise not to tell Clive. I told Adrian that you had come up about a job which was promised you. So keep this up if he asks.
>
> I am very sorry to be the cause of so much rush and worry. I am just off to Firle.
>
> Yrs.
> VS

Notice that Stephen assumes Woolf will know what her "line" is "in answer" to, what "this" is, and who Vanessa, Clive, and Adrian are. She uses a contraction (*isn't*) and abbreviations (*Yrs.*, her initials), as well as the colloquial expression *keep this up* to mean "pretend that this story is true." Because she was a professional writer living in a different time and a different culture, your familiar register is probably less formal than hers, but you can see that she is writing to a very intimate audience (of one) on a very intimate topic.

2. Informal register

Informal register assumes a fairly close but not extremely close relationship or familiarity between the writer and the audience and topic. It may use colloquial language, slang, and regionalisms or dialect (see 25a), as well as contractions and other grammatical constructions that are not considered appropriate in more formal writing. The language of most conversation and of much popular media, it is often

found in short stories and novels as well, especially in dialogue. Some
of your college classes, particularly if you take journalism, communications, or creative writing, may call on you to use informal register.
Here is an example.

> If I went through anguish in botany and economics—for different
> reasons—gymnasium work was even worse. I don't even like to think
> about it. They wouldn't let you play games or join the exercises with
> your glasses on and I couldn't see with mine off. I bumped into profes-
> sors, horizontal bars, agricultural students, and swinging iron rings. Not
> being able to see, I could take it but I couldn't dish it out.
>
> —JAMES THURBER, "University Days"

Thurber is obviously closely involved with his topic, although the involvement is not as close as that of Virginia Stephen with Leonard
Woolf's marriage proposal; Thurber is looking back at his college gym-
nasium work from the distance of years. Nor is he as intimately related
to his audience, but his use of contractions (*don't, wouldn't, couldn't*)
and the indefinite *They* and *you* create an informal tone of easy fa
miliarity. Notice that in the last sentence he amuses the audience—a
purpose for which informal register is often used—by coming up with
a twist on a clichéd slang expression.

▌ 3. Formal register

Formal register is the language found in most academic, business, and professional writing and in serious nonfiction books and
magazine articles. Because most of the writing you will do in college
and probably throughout your life should be in formal register, study
carefully the following list of its characteristics:

1. Emotional distance between the writer and the audience: your stance
   should be friendly and courteous but not chummy or intimate.
2. Emotional distance between the writer and the topic: though you may
   know the topic very well and have strong feelings about it, your stance
   toward it should be as objective as possible.
3. No colloquial language, slang, regionalisms, and dialects.
4. Careful attention to the conventions of edited American English, the
   grammatical "rules" like those presented in this book.
5. Attention to the logical relationships among words and ideas: phrases
   and sentences should be carefully structured, not just tossed out.

Here is an example of formal register.

"A people who mean to be their own governors," James Madison wrote, "must arm themselves with the power knowledge gives. A popular government without popular information or the means of acquiring it, is but a prologue to a farce or a tragedy, or perhaps both."

Tragedy looms larger than farce in the United States today. Illiterate citizens seldom vote. Those who do are forced to cast a vote of questionable worth. They cannot make informed decisions based on serious print information. Sometimes they can be alerted to their interests by aggressive voter education. More frequently, they vote for a face, a smile, or a style, not for a mind or character or body of beliefs.

–JONATHAN KOZOL, "The Human Cost of an Illiterate Society"

Notice that Kozol opens with an appeal to authority, citing the fourth United States president who, in very strong and serious terms, warns against the effect of a populace without knowledge. Kozol repeats the key terms of Madison's warning, *tragedy* and *farce*, in the next sentence, and goes on to develop one tragic aspect of illiteracy. His brief, straightforward sentences state the facts objectively, building up to the parallel structures of the last sentence, which contrasts voting for "a smile" with voting for "character." Though Kozol knows a great deal about his subject and feels strongly that illiteracy is a national tragedy, his tone throughout is restrained.

4. Ceremonial register

For some solemn occasions, speakers or writers move beyond formal language to **ceremonial register**, the language of ceremony or ritual. You can recognize ceremonial register by its very careful attention to rhythm or cadence, to the sound of words, and to building toward a climax, a powerful dominant impression. If you are ever asked to make a statement at a funeral, to present a very important award, or to address a group on a very important occasion, you may want to use ceremonial register. Here is a famous example.

With malice toward none, with charity for all, with firmness in the right as God gives us to see the right, let us finish the work we are in, to bind up the nation's wounds, to care for him who shall have borne the battle, and for his widow and his orphans, to do all which may achieve and cherish a just and lasting peace among ourselves and with all nations.

–ABRAHAM LINCOLN, Second Inaugural Address

Notice how this conclusion to a speech delivered just before the end of the Civil War uses antithesis (in the opening phrases), parallelism

415

(*to bind . . . to care . . . to do*), alliteration, and a lofty metaphor (*bind up the nation's wounds*) to build to a stirring climax.

5. Register in technical writing

One special kind of language frequently found in formal register is the technical discourse used in particular fields that have created special vocabularies or given common words special meaning. Business people talk about *greenmail* and *upside movement*, biologists about *nucleotides* and *immunodestruction*, and baseball fans about *fielder's choices* and *suicide bunts*. Such terms are understood by other specialists, but they can be very confusing to those outside the field. You need, then, to judge any use of technical language very carefully, making sure that your intended audience will understand your terms and replacing or defining those that they will not. Technical language can be divided into two overlapping categories: jargon and neologisms.

Neologisms

New words that have not yet found their way into dictionaries, **neologisms** can be very helpful to writers, especially in the sciences and applied disciplines, where new things and concepts appear every day and need names. Terms like *byte, thermosiphon, deconstruct,* and *neutrino,* for example, could not be easily replaced except by a much longer and more complex explanation. Some neologisms, however, do not meet a real need. Words like *deaccess* and *prioritization* could be easily replaced by existing words or phrases that general readers would understand.

Jargon

Jargon is the special vocabulary of a trade or profession, enabling members to speak and write concisely to one another. Thus, jargon should be reserved as much as possible for a specific technical audience. Here is an example of jargon used inappropriately in writing addressed to general readers:

JARGON   The VDT's were down at the newspaper office last week, so we had to do the page makeup on dummies and use a wheel to crop the pictures.

Notice that the following revision eliminates some of the jargon terms and defines others:

REVISED   The video display terminals were not working at the
           newspaper office last week, so we had to arrange the type
           for each page on a large cardboard sheet and use a wheel,
           a kind of circular slide rule, to figure out the size and
           shape of the pictures.

▌ 6. Pompous language, euphemisms, and doublespeak

In addition to avoiding inappropriate use of technical language,
be alert to three other kinds of language sometimes found in formal
register that can make for ineffective tone: pompous language, euphemisms, and doublespeak.

Pompous language is unnecessarily formal for the purpose, audience, or topic. Hence it often gives writing an insincere or unintentionally humorous tone, making the writer's idea seem less significant
or believable rather than more so.

POMPOUS   Pursuant to the recent memorandum issued August 9,
           1979, because of petroleum supply exigencies, it is in-
           cumbent upon us all to endeavor to make maximal utili-
           zation of telephonic communication in lieu of personal
           visitation.

REVISED   As of August 9, 1979, shortages of petroleum require us
           to try to use the telephone as much as possible rather
           than make personal visits.

Euphemisms are terms designed to make an unpleasant idea more
attractive or acceptable. *Your position is being eliminated* seeks to soften
the blow of being fired or laid off; the British call this *being declared
redundant*, while Canadians refer to *being made surplus*. Other euphemisms include *pass on* for *die* and *sanitation engineer* for *garbage
collector*.

While euphemisms can appeal to an audience by showing that
the writer is considering their feelings, they can also sound pompous
or suggest a wishy-washy, timid, or evasive attitude. Moreover, when
they are used to protect the speaker or writer rather than the audience,
they cross the line into doublespeak. Therefore, use euphemisms with
great care.

The name given by George Orwell to the language of Big Brother
in his novel *1984*, **doublespeak** is the use of language to hide or distort
the truth in the interest of the speaker or writer. The extensive use of
such language by public officials led the National Council of Teachers

of English to form a committee to alert citizens to such verbal sleight of hand and to promote honesty and clarity in public language use. The committee publishes a *Doublespeak Newsletter* and each year presents an award for the best example of honesty in public discourse and a series of awards for the worst doublespeakers. One year such an award went to a military official who said to reporters: "You always write it's bombing, bombing, bombing. It's not bombing! It's air support!"

As you read and listen to public discourse, watch especially for doublespeak. And why not "nominate" the worst example you find for a Doublespeak Award? To do so, send your example, including the place and date of its publication or broadcast, to the Committee on Public Doublespeak, NCTE, Urbana, Illinois 61801.

EXERCISE 26.6

Revise each of the following sentences to use formal register consistently.

> *Example*
> I can be all enthused about writing, but as soon as I sit down to write, my mind immediately goes out to lunch.
>
> I can be excited about writing, but as soon as I sit down to write, my mind immediately goes blank.

1. Desdemona's attitude is that of a wimp; she just lies down and dies, accepting her death as inevitable.
2. All candidates strive for the same results: you try to make the other guy look gross and to persuade the majority of voters that you're okay for the job.
3. Sometimes, instead of firing an incompetent teacher, school officials will transfer the person to another school in order to avoid the hassles involved in a dismissal.
4. The more she flipped out about his actions, the more he rebelled and continued doing what he pleased.
5. My family lived in Trinidad for the first ten years of my life, and we went through a lot, but when we came to America, we thought we had it made.

EXERCISE 26.7

Try to identify the meanings of the following doublespeak terms.

> *Example*
> therapeutic misadventure
> doctor's mistake

1. radiation enhancement device
2. mutual assured destruction
3. incomplete success
4. pacification
5. arbitrary deprivation of life

READING WITH AWARENESS OF TONE

Read the following brief poem, and then identify its tone. Then identify the specific words and phrases that help create that tone.

> What happens to a dream deferred?
>
> Does it dry up
> Like a raisin in the sun?
> Or fester like a sore—
> And then run?
> Does it stink like rotten meat?
> Or crust and sugar over—
> Like a syrupy sweet?
>
> Maybe it just sags
> Like a heavy load.
>
> Or does it explode?
> —LANGSTON HUGHES, "Harlem"

FOR EXAMINING THE TONE OF YOUR OWN WRITING

Write a paragraph about something you might want to do at school—change your major, spend your junior year abroad, take a semester off, or something else. Use familiar register, assuming your audience to be someone close— parents, spouse, good friend. Then rewrite your paragraph to address your academic adviser, using formal register. Finally, analyze each paragraph to identify the elements that create familiar or formal register.

PART SIX

Understanding
Punctuation Conventions

27. Using Commas

The word *comma* comes from the Greek *komma*, meaning "cut" or "segment." A clause, for example, is a segment of a sentence, and it is often set off with a comma. In English, the comma is the most frequently used punctuation mark, serving to separate words and word groups.

While the familiar comma appears everywhere in modern writing, reducing this particular punctuation mark to hard and fast rules is very difficult, for several reasons. First, the comma can play a number of different roles in a sentence, making general rules hard to come by. More important, many decisions about commas relate to matters of purpose, rhythm, and style. As a result, comma conventions can and do differ from one English-speaking country to another, even from one professional writer to another.

In the essay "In Praise of the Humble Comma," Pico Iyer likens a comma to a flashing yellow light that asks the reader to slow down.* You can see what he means by reading through the following sentences, first with the commas and then without.

> The hangman, a gray-haired convict in the white uniform of the prison, was waiting beside his machine.
>
> And then, when the noose was fixed, the prisoner began crying out to his god.
>
> The prisoner had vanished, and the rope was twisting on itself.
>
> "Well, that's all for this morning, thank God."
>
> —GEORGE ORWELL, "A Hanging"

---

* *Time*, 13 June 1988.

You can, no doubt, *hear* the need for the commas in each of these sentences. In fact, however, each comma is governed not just by sound, but by *sentence structure*. For this reason, commas count in your writing. In fact, the study of student writing undertaken as part of the research for this book reveals that five of the twenty most common errors involve the comma. Getting full control of comma usage in your own writing thus presents a special challenge to you, one that involves not only learning some rules but practicing the use of commas in writing and concentrating on the stylistic decisions you must learn to make as a writer. This chapter presents an opportunity for you to accomplish both these goals.

▌ 27a. Using commas after introductory elements

A comma usually follows an introductory word, expression, phrase, or clause. Introductory elements that are followed by commas include adverbs (see 6b5); conjunctive adverbs (see 6b7); transitional expressions (see 5c5); participles, infinitives, and prepositional, participial, infinitive, and absolute phrases (see 6c3); and adverb clauses (see 6c4).

Slowly, she became conscious of her predicament. [adverb]

Nevertheless, the hours of a typist are flexible. [conjunctive adverb]

In fact, only you can decide. [transitional expression]

Frustrated, he wondered whether he should change careers. [participle]

In Fitzgerald's novel, the color green takes on great symbolic qualities. [prepositional phrase]

Sporting a pair of specially made running shoes, Jamie prepared for the race. [participial phrase]

To win the contest, Paul needed luck. [infinitive phrase]

Pens poised in anticipation, the students waited for the test to be distributed. [absolute phrase]

Since her mind was not receiving enough stimulation, she had to resort to her imagination. [adverb clause]

For certain kinds of introductory elements—adverbs, infinitives, prepositional and infinitive phrases, and adverb clauses—some writers omit the comma if the element is short and does not seem to require a pause after it. Try to use your ear to decide if a comma is needed in such cases; if in doubt, put in the comma.

At the racetrack Henry lost nearly his entire paycheck.

If the introductory element is followed by inverted word order, with the verb preceding the subject, do not use a comma.

From directly behind my seat came huge clouds of cigar smoke.

➤ Checking for commas after introductory elements

To check for commas after introductory elements, place a check mark next to every sentence that opens directly with the subject, with no introductory word, phrase, or clause. Then look carefully at each sentence not checked to decide if it needs a comma after the opening element.

First, look for sentences that open with adverbs, conjunctive adverbs like *however* or *therefore*, or transitional expressions like *in fact*, *for example*, or *in the first place*. Read the sentence aloud to see if a pause after the opening word or phrase indicates a need for a comma. Conjunctive adverbs and transitional expressions almost always need a comma after them; for other adverbs, listen carefully to see whether a comma sounds right or would break up the rhythm of the sentence unnecessarily.

Next, look for sentences that begin with participial phrases or absolute phrases. Use a comma after these phrases.

Then look for sentences beginning with participles, infinitives, infinitive phrases, and prepositional phrases. Read the sentence aloud to judge the need for a comma after these elements. In general, use a comma if the sentence opens with a sequence of two or more prepositional phrases.

At this point, look at all the sentences you have revised so far. In any of them, is the introductory element immediately followed by the verb? If so, do not use a comma after the element.

Finally, look for sentences opening with adverb clauses, those beginning with subordinating conjunctions like *although, because, unless*, and *when*. (See 6b7 for a list of subordinating conjunctions.) Read the sentence aloud to judge the need for a comma; in general, use one unless the adverb clause is very short.

EXERCISE 27.1

Place a comma after the introductory element in any of the following sentences where the comma is needed. Some of the sentences do not require a comma.

1. In one of his most famous poems Frost asks why people need walls.
2. Unfortunately the door to the kennel had been left open.
3. Unable to make such a decision alone I asked my brother for help.
4. If you follow instructions carefully you will be able to install your radio.
5. Therefore answering the seemingly simple question is very difficult.
6. With the fifth century came the fall of the Roman Empire.
7. Their bags packed they waited for the taxi to the airport.
8. To become an Olympic competitor an athlete must train for years.
9. Like all other disciplines psychology draws general principles from specific observations.
10. Founded by Alexander the Great Alexandria became a great center of learning.

▌ 27b. Using commas in compound sentences

A comma usually precedes a coordinating conjunction (*and, but, or, for, nor, so,* or *yet*) that joins two independent clauses in a compound sentence.

> The title may sound important, but *administrative clerk* is only a euphemism for *photocopier.*
>
> The climbers will reach the summit today, or they must turn back.
>
> The show started at last, and the crowd grew quiet.
>
> I was often bullied in grade school, for I was the smallest in my class.

You may want to use a semicolon rather than a comma when the clauses are long and complex or contain other punctuation.

> Since baseball time is measured only in outs, all you have to do is succeed utterly; keep hitting, keep the rally alive, and you have defeated time.   —ROGER ANGELL, *The Summer Game*

If the clauses are very brief, on the other hand, you can often omit the comma before *and* or *or.*

> She saw her chance and she took it.

Always use the comma if there is any chance the sentence will be misread without it.

> CONFUSING   The game ended in victory and pandemonium erupted on the court.
>
> REVISED   The game ended in victory, and pandemonium erupted on the court.

Be careful not to use *only* a comma between independent clauses; doing so is considered a serious grammatical error, called a comma splice. Either use a coordinating conjunction after the comma, or use a semicolon. (See Chapter 13 for further discussion of comma splices.)

COMMA SPLICE	Do not thank "luck" for your new job, give yourself the credit you deserve.
REVISED	Do not thank "luck" for your new job, *but* give yourself the credit you deserve.
REVISED	Do not thank "luck" for your new job; give yourself the credit you deserve.

➤ Checking for commas in compound sentences

To check a draft for commas in compound sentences, first circle every coordinating conjunction: *and, but, or, nor, for, so, yet.* Then look at each sentence in which you found such a conjunction, and examine the words before it. Could they function as a complete sentence, with a subject and predicate? Now look at the words following the conjunction. Could they function as a sentence? If the answer to both of these questions is yes, the two groups of words are two independent clauses joined with a coordinating conjunction: a compound sentence. Check to see that the conjunction is preceded (*not* followed) by a comma.

EXERCISE 27.2

Use a comma and a coordinating conjunction (*and, but, or, for, nor, so,* or *yet*) to combine each of the following pairs of sentences into one sentence. Delete or rearrange words if necessary.

Example
I had finished studying for the test. I went to bed.
I had finished studying for the test, so I went to bed.

1. Max Weber was not in favor of a classless society. It would lead to the expansion of the power of the state over the individual.
2. Immigrants came to the United States with high hopes. Their illusions were often shattered.
3. It felt good to be home. I had the odd feeling of being an outsider.
4. A basic quality of leather is stretchability. It takes on the shape of a foot.
5. Babies never have to feed themselves. They are not punished for misbehaving, either.

27c. Using commas to set off nonrestrictive elements

Nonrestrictive elements of a sentence—clauses, phrases, and appositives that do not limit or "restrict" the meaning of the words they modify or refer to—are set off from the rest of the sentence with commas. **Restrictive** elements *do* limit meaning and are *not* set off with commas. Look at the following examples:

RESTRICTIVE   Drivers *who have been convicted of drunken driving* should lose their licenses.

NONRESTRICTIVE   The two drivers involved in the accident, *who have been convicted of drunken driving*, should lose their licenses.

In the first sentence, the clause *who have been convicted of drunken driving* is essential to the meaning of the sentence because it limits the word it modifies, *Drivers*, to only those drivers who have been convicted of drunken driving. Therefore, it is not set off by commas. In the second sentence, the same clause is not essential to the meaning because it does not limit what it modifies, *The two drivers involved in the accident*, but merely provides additional information about these drivers. Therefore, it *is* set off with commas.

Notice how using or not using commas to set off such an element can change the meaning of a sentence:

The bus drivers *rejecting the management offer* remained on strike.

The bus drivers, *rejecting the management offer*, remained on strike.

In the first sentence, not using commas to set off the participial phrase *rejecting the management offer* makes the phrase restrictive, limiting the meaning of *The bus drivers*. This sentence says that only some of the total group of bus drivers, the ones who rejected the offer, remained on strike, implying that other drivers went back to work. In the second sentence, using the commas around the participial phrase makes it nonrestrictive, implying that *The bus drivers* refers to all of the drivers and that all of them remained on strike.

To decide whether a sentence element is restrictive or nonrestrictive, mentally delete the element, and then decide whether the deletion changes the meaning of the rest of the sentence or makes it unclear. If it does, the element is probably restrictive and should not be set off with commas; if it does not, the element is probably nonrestrictive and requires commas.

Sentence elements that may be nonrestrictive and require commas to set them off include adjective and adverb clauses; participial, infinitive, and prepositional phrases; and appositive phrases.

▌ 1. Using commas with adjective and adverb clauses

Adjective clauses begin with *who, whom, whose, which, that, when, where,* or *why.* (See 6c4.) Adverb clauses begin with subordinating conjunctions like *because, although,* or *before.* (See 6b7 and 6c4.) Adverb clauses are usually essential to the meaning of the sentence; do not set them off with commas unless they precede the independent clause (see 27a) or begin with *although, even though, while, whereas,* or another conjunction expressing the idea of contrast.

NONRESTRICTIVE CLAUSES

The Indians, *who range in color from mocha to Dentyne,* are generally under five feet tall. [The central statement of this sentence is that the Indians are under five feet tall; the information about their color simply provides additional information and therefore should be set off with commas.]   —JOHN UPDIKE, "Venezuela for Visitors"

I borrowed books from the rental library of Shakespeare and Company, *which was the library and bookstore of Sylvia Beach at 12 rue de l'Odeon.* [The adjective clause gives additional information not necessary to complete the meaning of the independent clause and therefore is set off with a comma.]   —ERNEST HEMINGWAY, *A Movable Feast*

The park soon became a popular gathering place, *although some nearby residents complained about the noise.* [The adverb clause expresses the idea of contrast; therefore it is set off with a comma.]

RESTRICTIVE CLAUSES

I grew up in a house *where the only regular guests were my relations.* [The information in the adjective clause is essential to the meaning of the sentence and therefore should not be set off with commas.]
   —RICHARD RODRIGUEZ, "Aria: A Memoir of a Bilingual Childhood"

The claim *that men like seriously to battle one another to some sort of finish* is a myth. [The adjective clause beginning with *that* is necessary to the meaning of the sentence because it explains *which* claim is a myth.]   —JOHN MCMURTRY, "Kill 'Em! Crush 'Em! Eat 'Em Raw!"

An adjective clause that begins with *that* is always restrictive and is not set off with commas. An adjective clause beginning with *which* may be either restrictive or nonrestrictive; however, some writers prefer to use *which* only for nonrestrictive clauses.

2. Using commas with participial, infinitive, and prepositional phrases

Participial phrases may be either restrictive or nonrestrictive. Infinitive and prepositional phrases are usually restrictive but sometimes are not essential to the meaning of a sentence and are therefore set off with commas.

NONRESTRICTIVE PHRASES

Stephanie, amazed, stared at the strange vehicle. [The participle does not limit the meaning of *Stephanie.*]

The "synfuels" program, *launched at the height of the energy crisis,* languished with the drop in fuel prices. [The participial phrase does not limit the meaning of the *"synfuels" program* or change the central meaning of the sentence.]

Her long-term goal, *to become a child psychologist,* would require great financial discipline. [The infinitive phrase does not limit the meaning of *Her long-term goal.*]

Howard Hughes, *despite his billions,* lived a tortured life. [The prepositional phrase does not limit the meaning of *Howard Hughes.*]

RESTRICTIVE PHRASES

A penny *saved* is a penny *earned.* [Without the participles, the sentence has a very different meaning.]

Wood *cut from living trees* does not burn as well as dead wood. [The participial phrase is essential to the meaning.]

His ability *to make decisions quickly* made him a valuable employee. [The infinitive phrase restricts the meaning of *ability.*]

The wire *for the antenna* is the last one to be connected. [The prepositional phrase restricts the meaning of *wire.*]

3. Using commas with appositive phrases

An appositive phrase is a noun or noun substitute, together with its modifiers, that renames the noun immediately preceding it. When the appositive phrase is not essential to identify the noun it follows, it is set off with commas.

NONRESTRICTIVE APPOSITIVES

Ms. Baker, *my high school chemistry teacher,* inspired my love of science. [Ms. Baker's name identifies her; the appositive simply provides extra information.]

Beethoven's opera, *Fidelio,* includes the famous "Prisoners' Chorus." [*Fidelio* is nonrestrictive because Beethoven wrote only one opera, so the name is not essential.]

RESTRICTIVE APPOSITIVES

The editorial cartoonist *Thomas Nast* helped to bring about the downfall of the Tweed Ring in New York City. [The appositive identifies *The editorial cartoonist* as a specific cartoonist.]

Mozart's opera *The Marriage of Figaro* was considered revolutionary in the eighteenth century. [The appositive is restrictive because Mozart wrote more than one opera.]

➤ Checking for commas with nonrestrictive elements

To check a draft for commas with nonrestrictive elements, first find and underline all the dependent clauses. Then put a check mark beside each adjective clause beginning with *which, who, whom, whose, when,* or *where.* For each clause, ask yourself if the clause *identifies* the noun or pronoun it modifies by answering the question "which?" or "what kind of?" about it. If it does not answer one of these questions but merely provides "extra" information about the noun or pronoun, it is nonrestrictive. Check to see that there is a comma before it (if it falls at the end of the sentence) or before and after it (if it falls in the middle of a sentence).

Now look at the underlined clauses that are not checked to see if any of them begin with *although, while, whereas,* or another conjunction expressing the idea of contrast. If such clauses are not set off with commas, add them.

Next, find and put parentheses around all the participial phrases and around all the infinitive and prepositional phrases that follow a noun or pronoun. Draw an arrow from each phrase to the word it modifies. If a participial or infinitive phrase modifies a noun or pronoun other than the one just before it, it is nonrestrictive; make sure it is set off with commas. If a participial, infinitive, or prepositional phrase does modify the noun or pronoun immediately preceding it, ask yourself if the phrase *identifies* the noun or pronoun by answering the question "which?" or "what kind of?" If it does not answer one of these

431

questions but merely provides "extra" information about the noun or pronoun, it is nonrestrictive; make sure it is set off with commas. (Most of the infinitive and prepositional phrases will be restrictive and should not be set off.)

Finally, find and circle all the appositives and appositive phrases. Ask yourself if each appositive or phrase is essential to identify the noun or pronoun it refers to. If it is not, if it merely provides "extra" information about the noun or pronoun, it is nonrestrictive; make sure it is set off with commas.

EXERCISE 27.3

Identify the restrictive and the nonrestrictive elements in these sentences.

1. One of the great mystery writers, John D. MacDonald, died in 1987.
2. She who laughs last laughs best.
3. Neil Armstrong, who first walked on the moon, is a national hero.
4. Salmon smoked over an alder wood fire has a unique flavor.
5. Bill Reid, a highly respected practitioner of Haida Indian art, is creating a sculpture for the Mall in Washington, D.C.

EXERCISE 27.4

Use commas to set off nonrestrictive clauses, phrases, and appositives in any of the following sentences that contain such elements. Some of the sentences do not contain nonrestrictive elements.

1. Anyone who is fourteen years old faces strong peer pressure every day.
2. Embalming is a technique that preserves a cadaver for viewing.
3. I would feel right at home in the city dump which bears a striking resemblance to my bedroom.
4. The first one is the power wire which is usually red; the second is the ground wire which is usually black.
5. Most noteworthy is Aristarchus who showed that the sun is larger than the earth and proposed a heliocentric model for the solar system.
6. The Zunis an ancient tribe dwelling in New Mexico have a highly integrated culture.
7. Sociology which encompasses most of the other social sciences is the study of human social behavior.
8. An important nineteenth-century sociologist was Karl Marx who believed that his role as a social thinker was to change the world.
9. About two-thirds of the Swiss speak a German dialect while most of the rest speak French.
10. Britain and France agreed to come to each other's aid if one of them was attacked.

27d. Using commas to separate items in a series

A comma is used after each item in a series of three or more words, phrases, or clauses.

> I bumped into professors, horizontal bars, agricultural students, and swinging iron rings. —JAMES THURBER, "University Days"

> He has plundered our seas, ravaged our coasts, burnt our towns, and destroyed the lives of our people.
> —THOMAS JEFFERSON, Declaration of Independence

You may often see a series with no comma after the next-to-last item, particularly in newspaper writing, as in *The day was cold, dark and dreary*. Occasionally, however, omitting the comma can cause confusion, and you will never be wrong to include it.

When the items in a series are long and complex or when they contain commas of their own, use semicolons rather than commas to separate them (see 28b).

Coordinate adjectives, those that relate equally to the noun they modify, should be separated by commas. In the sentence *They are sincere, inquisitive, talented researchers*, the three adjectives are coordinate: they each modify *researchers* and are therefore separated by commas. Here are some other examples of coordinate adjectives.

> The *long, twisting, muddy* road led to a shack in the woods.

> His *bizarre, outrageous* sense of humor endeared him to his friends.

In a sentence like *The cracked bathroom mirror reflected his face*, however, *cracked* and *bathroom* are not coordinate because *bathroom mirror* is the equivalent of a single word, which is modified by *cracked*. Hence they are *not* separated by commas.

> Byron carried an *elegant pocket* watch.

> *Outdated black nylon furniture* sat in dusty silence on the porch.

You can determine whether adjectives are coordinate by inserting the conjunction *and* between them. If the sentence makes sense with the *and*, the adjectives are coordinate and should be separated by commas.

> They are sincere *and* talented *and* inquisitive researchers. [The sentence makes sense with the inserted *and*'s, so the adjectives *sincere, talented,* and *inquisitive* should be separated by commas.]

> Byron carried an elegant *and* pocket watch. [In this instance, the sentence does not make sense with the *and*, so, the adjectives *elegant* and *pocket* should not be separated by a comma.]

433

> Checking for commas in a series

To check a draft for commas in a series, circle every *and* and *or* in the draft. Then look at each one to see if it joins only two words, phrases, or clauses, or if it comes at the end of a series of three or more. Next, look through the draft for any series that do not use an *and* or *or*. If you find any series, check to see that each item except the last is followed by a comma; if not, add the necessary commas. Do *not* add a comma before the first item in the series or after the last item.

EXERCISE 27.5

Revise each of the following sentences that require commas to set off words, phrases, or clauses in a series. Some of the sentences do not require commas.

1. They found employment in truck driving farming and mining.
2. The social sciences include economics psychology political science anthropology and sociology.
3. Members plant tend and harvest corn.
4. The daddy-long-legs's orange body resembled a colored dot amidst eight black legs.
5. A prestigious car a large house and membership in an exclusive club are taken as signs of success.
6. Superficial observation does not provide accurate insight into people's lives—how they feel what they believe in how they respond to others.
7. What is impossible today may soon become reality: traveling to other planets colonizing the moon maybe even reaching out to distant galaxies.
8. I timidly offered to help a loud overbearing lavishly dressed customer.
9. Ellen is an accomplished free-lance writer.
10. These Cosell clones insist on calling every play judging every move and telling everyone within earshot exactly what is wrong with the team.

27e. Using commas to set off parenthetical and transitional expressions, contrasting elements, interjections, direct address, and tag questions

Use commas to set off parenthetical and transitional expressions, elements expressing a contrast with what precedes them, mild interjections, words directly addressing readers, and tag questions.

Parenthetical and transitional expressions

Parenthetical expressions are relatively unimportant comments by the writer or pieces of supplementary information. Transitional expressions include conjunctive adverbs like *however* and *furthermore* (see 6b7) and other words and phrases used to express connections between clauses, sentences, or paragraphs. (For a full list, see 5c5.)

Some studies, *incidentally*, have shown that chocolate, *of all things*, helps to prevent tooth decay.

Ceiling fans are, *moreover*, less expensive than air conditioners.

Many people do not realize that ozone is produced by dry cleaning, *for example*.

Contrasting elements

On official business it was she, *not my father*, one would usually hear on the phone or in stores. . . .
  —RICHARD RODRIGUEZ, "Aria: A Memoir of a Bilingual Childhood"

The story is narrated objectively at first, *subjectively toward the end*.

Interjections

My God, who wouldn't want a wife?
                                —JUDY SYFERS, "I Want a Wife"

We had hiked for, *say*, seven miles before stopping to rest.

Stronger interjections are followed by exclamation points (see 29c).

Direct address

Ah, *swinging generation*, what new delights await?
                                —TOM WOLFE, "Pornoviolence"

My friends, I must say to you that we have not made a single gain in civil rights without determined legal and nonviolent pressure.
    —MARTIN LUTHER KING, JR., "Letter from Birmingham Jail"

Tag questions

Tag questions "echo" the statement preceding them.

The homeless are our fellow citizens, *are they not?*

Seattle is not the capital of Washington, *is it?*

EXERCISE 27.6

Revise each of the following sentences, using commas to set off parenthetical and transitional expressions, contrasting elements, interjections, words used in direct address, and tag questions.

435

1. One must consider the society as a whole not its individual components to understand a particular culture.
2. The West in fact has become solidly Republican in presidental elections.
3. Her friends did not know about her illness did they?
4. Fictions about race not the facts influence human relations.
5. We found therefore that we had more tomatoes than we could use.
6. We must act quickly to stop this threat to our health and safety.
7. Oh I do not know how to do anything but farm.
8. And now customers follow along as I demonstrate the latest in video discs.
9. Regional accents have shown few signs of weakening surprisingly enough.
10. This is imported pâté not chopped liver.

27f. Using commas in dates, addresses, titles, and numbers

Commas are used according to established rules within dates, addresses and place names, and numbers. Commas are also used to separate personal and professional titles from the name preceding them.

Dates

For dates, use a comma between the day of the week and the month, between the day of the month and the year, and between the year and the rest of the sentence, if any.

Reagan was elected president on *Tuesday, November 7, 1980,* and was inaugurated on *January 20, 1981.*

Do not use a comma with dates in inverted order or with dates consisting only of the month and the year.

16 January 1987

Thousands of Cubans stormed the American embassy in Havana in *May 1980* and asked for asylum in the United States.

Addresses and place names

In addresses and place names, use a comma after each part, including the state if no ZIP code is given. In addresses that include the ZIP code, do not use a comma either before or after it.

Forward my mail to The Department of English, Ohio State University, Columbus, Ohio 43210 until further notice.

Miami, Florida, is now a bilingual city because about half its population is Cuban.

Titles

Use commas to set off a title such as *Jr.*, *M.D.*, and so on from the name preceding it and from the rest of the sentence.

> James Siddens, *Ph.D.*, recently joined the faculty as the new dean of the School of Arts and Sciences.

> Martin Luther King, *Jr.*, was one of this century's greatest orators.

Numbers

In numbers of five digits or more, use a comma between each group of three digits, starting from the right.

> Give me *10,000* reasons, and then I'll change my mind.

Do not use a comma within street numbers or ZIP codes.

> My parents live at *11311* Wimberly Drive, Richmond, Virginia 23233.

The comma is optional within numbers of four digits, except for years, where it is never used.

> The college has an enrollment of *1,789* (or *1789*) this semester.

> The French Revolution began in 1789.

EXERCISE 27.7

Revise each of the following sentences, using commas appropriately with dates, addresses and place names, titles, and numbers.

1. People were cultivating crops before 10000 B.C.
2. Ithaca New York has a population of about 20000.
3. The ship was hit by two torpedoes on May 7 1915 and sank in less than half an hour.
4. The Modern Language Association headquarters recently moved to 10 Astor Place New York New York 10003.
5. The nameplate on the office door read *Donald Good R.N.* and looked quite impressive.

▮ 27g. Using commas with quotations

Commas are used to set off quotations from words used to introduce or explain the quotations. A comma following a quotation goes *inside* the closing quotation mark.

> "No one becomes depraved all at once," wrote Juvenal.

A German proverb warns, "Go to law for a sheep, and lose your cow."

"Nothing has really happened," said Virginia Woolf, "until it has been recorded."

When a quotation followed by explanatory words is a question or an exclamation, do not use a comma after the question mark or exclamation point.

"What's a thousand dollars?" asks Groucho Marx in *Coconuts*. "Mere chicken feed. A poultry matter."

"Out, damned spot!" cries Lady Macbeth.

Do not use a comma when a quotation is introduced by *that* or when the rest of the sentence includes more than the words used to introduce or explain the quotation.

The writer of Ecclesiastes concludes that "all is vanity."

People who say "Have a nice day" irritate me.

Do not use a comma before an indirect quotation, one that does not use the speaker's exact words.

Patrick Henry declared that he wanted either liberty or death.

Virginia Woolf said that a woman needs money and her own room in order to write fiction.

EXERCISE 27.8

Insert a comma in each of the following sentences that requires one. Some of the sentences do not need an additional comma.

1. "The public be damned!" William Henry Vanderbilt was reported to have said. "I'm working for my stockholders."
2. Joseph Epstein admits, "I prefer not to be thought vulgar in any wise."
3. Paul Fussell argues that "if the dirty little secret used to be sex, now it's the facts about social class."
4. "Neat people are lazier and meaner than sloppy people" according to Suzanne Britt.
5. "Who shall decide when doctors disagree?" asked Alexander Pope.

▌ 27h. Using commas to facilitate understanding

Sometimes a comma, though not required, can make a sentence much easier to read or understand.

CONFUSING	The members of the dance troupe strutted in in matching tuxedos and top hats.
REVISED	The members of the dance troupe strutted in, in matching tuxedos and top hats.
CONFUSING	Still liquids are necessary to sustain life.
REVISED	Still, liquids are necessary to sustain life.

EXERCISE 27.9

Revise the following paragraph by inserting commas where necessary. Be prepared to explain why you added each comma.

As the most recent show confirmed the audience at a Jimmy Buffet concert compares to no other. Dressed from head to toe in outlandish tropical prints and sunglasses the Parrot Heads danced rocked rolled juked and jived through the duration of the concert. At one point a fan pitched a giant blow-up Godzilla onto the stage and Buffet gently took the monster in his arms and danced the two-step. Beach balls flew around the amphitheater as people called for margaritas margaritas and more margaritas to the sounds of "Margaritaville." Never ceasing were the dancing and conga lines that wove serpent-like through the crowd of 20000. Even when the band had cleared the stage and the dust had settled the greedy crowd wanted more. After two hours of prime performance they would not be denied an encore. Buffet rising to the occasion returned for one last number. The audience had come to hear a Buffet connoisseur's extravaganza which was exactly what they got.

EXERCISE 27.10

In the following passage, Richard Wright tells about his discovery of books and his subsequent self-education. Read the passage aloud, listening for Wright's use of commas. Then read it again, mentally deleting the commas and noting how their absence affects meaning and rhythm. Finally, choose two of the sentences to use as a model for imitation, creating a similar pair of sentences of your own.

I ran across many words whose meanings I did not know, and I either looked them up in a dictionary or, before I had a chance to do that, encountered the word in a context that made its meaning clear. But what strange world was this? I concluded the book with the conviction that I had somehow overlooked something terribly important in life. I had once tried to write, had once reveled in feeling, had let my crude imagination roam, but the impulse to dream had been slowly beaten out of me by experience. Now it surged up again and I hungered for books, new ways of looking and seeing. It was not a matter of believing or disbelieving what I read, but of feeling something new, of being affected by something that made the look of the world different.

         –RICHARD WRIGHT, "The Library Card"

▌ 27i. Checking for unnecessary commas

Just like insufficient use, excessive use of commas can spoil what may otherwise be a fine sentence or passage. This section will help you avoid using commas unnecessarily.

▌ 1. Omitting commas around restrictive phrases and clauses

Do not use commas to set off restrictive elements, which limit or restrict the meaning of the words they modify or refer to (see 27c).

UNNECESSARY	I don't let my children watch TV shows, that are violent.
REVISED	I don't let my children watch TV shows that are violent. [restrictive adjective clause]
UNNECESSARY	The decision, to stop the flow of irrigation water, is long overdue.
REVISED	The decision to stop the flow of irrigation water is long overdue. [restrictive infinitive phrase]
UNNECESSARY	My only defense, against my allergies, is to stay indoors.
REVISED	My only defense against my allergies is to stay indoors. [restrictive prepositional phrase]
UNNECESSARY	The actor, James Earl Jones, will speak on campus this fall.
REVISED	The actor James Earl Jones will speak on campus this fall. [restrictive appositive phrase]

➤ Checking for unnecessary commas with restrictive elements

To check a draft for unnecessary commas with restrictive elements, first underline all the dependent clauses. Then put a check mark beside each adjective clause, and look to see what word introduces it. If a clause is introduced by *that*, it is restrictive; if you have set it off with commas, remove them. If it is introduced by another word, such as *which*, *who*, or *when*, ask yourself if the clause *identifies* the noun or pronoun it modifies by answering the question "which?" or "what kind of?" If so, it is restrictive and should not be set off with commas.

Now look at the underlined clauses that are not checked. Put an X beside each adverb clause, and look to see what subordinating conjunction introduces it. Unless the clause is introduced by *although*, *while, whereas*, or another conjunction expressing the idea of contrast, it is probably restrictive and should not be set off with commas.

Next, find and put parentheses around all the participial, infinitive, and prepositional phrases that immediately follow a noun or pronoun. Draw an arrow from each phrase to the word it modifies. If a phrase modifies the noun or pronoun immediately preceding it, decide if it *identifies* the noun or pronoun by answering the question "which?" or "what kind of?" If so, it is restrictive and should not be set off with commas. (Most prepositional phrases are restrictive.)

Finally, circle all the appositives and appositive phrases. Decide if each appositive or phrase is essential to identify the noun or pronoun it refers to. If so, it is restrictive and should not be set off with commas.

2. Omitting commas between subjects and verbs, verbs and objects or complements, and prepositions and objects

Do not use a comma between a subject and its verb, a verb and its object or complement, or a preposition and its object. This general rule holds true even if the subject, object, or complement is a long phrase or clause.

UNNECESSARY	*Watching movies on my VCR late at night,* has become an important way for me to relax. [comma between subject and verb]
REVISED	Watching movies on my VCR late at night has become an important way for me to relax.
UNNECESSARY	Parents *must decide, how much TV their children may watch.* [comma between verb and object]
REVISED	Parents must decide how much TV their children may watch.
UNNECESSARY	The winner *of, the trophy* stepped forward. [comma between preposition and object]
REVISED	The winner of the trophy stepped forward.

❙ 3. Omitting commas in compound constructions

Do not use a comma before or after coordinating conjunctions joining the two parts of a compound construction.

UNNECESSARY	*Defense spending, and economic deregulation* were the Reagan administration's goals. [compound subject]
REVISED	Defense spending and economic deregulation were the Reagan administration's goals.
UNNECESSARY	Mark Twain *trained as a printer and, worked as a steamboat pilot.* [compound predicate]
REVISED	Mark Twain trained as a printer and worked as a steamboat pilot.

❙ 4. Omitting commas before the first item or after the last item in a series

Do not use a comma before the first item or after the last item in a series, unless another rule requires a comma.

UNNECESSARY	Our government's first priority is to ensure, *freedom of speech and press, the right to assemble peacefully, and the right to petition the government for redress of grievances.*
REVISED	Our government's first priority is to ensure freedom of speech and press, the right to assemble peacefully, and the right to petition the government for redress of grievances.
UNNECESSARY	The swimmer took slow, powerful, strokes.
REVISED	The swimmer took slow, powerful strokes.

EXERCISE 27.11

Revise each of the following sentences that contains unnecessary commas.

1. There are four types of nonverbal communication: kinesic, haptic, proxemic, and dormant, communication.
2. Observers watch, and interpret facial expressions and gestures.
3. There was nothing to do, after we ate, but go to bed, so we all crawled into our sleeping bags.
4. Our supper that evening, consisted of, stale bologna sandwiches, soggy cookies, and leftover trail mix.

5. The ability to use language, to express ourselves, is a unique human trait.
6. As we sat around the campfire, we felt boredom, and disappointment.
7. Movies, such as *Jaws* and *E.T.*, depend heavily on special effects.
8. The photographer, Edward Curtis, is known for his depiction of the West.
9. We all took panicked, hasty, looks at our notebooks.
10. Driving a car, and talking on the car phone at the same time demand care.

READING WITH AN EYE FOR COMMAS

The following poem by Robert Frost uses commas to create rhythm and guide readers. Read the poem aloud, listening especially to the effect of the commas at the end of lines one and five. Then read it again as if those commas were omitted, noting the difference. What is the effect of Frost's decision *not* to use a comma at the end of line three?

Some say the world will end in fire,
Some say in ice.
From what I've tasted of desire
I hold with those who favor fire.
But if it had to perish twice,
I think I know enough of hate
To say that for destruction ice
Is also great
And would suffice.
        —ROBERT FROST, "Fire and Ice"

FOR EXAMINING COMMAS IN YOUR OWN WRITING

Study the way Alice Walker uses commas in the following description of a scene from her childhood. Write a paragraph about some scene from your life, perhaps beginning as she has: "It is a _____ day in _____." Try imitating the structure of her second sentence, using commas as she does. Then examine your own use of commas: read your paragraph aloud, listening for the rhythm of your description.

It is a bright summer day in 1947. My father, a fat, funny man with beautiful eyes and a subversive wit, is trying to decide which of his eight children he will take with him to the county fair. My mother, of course, will not go. She is knocked out from getting most of us ready: I hold my neck stiff against the pressure of her knuckles as she hastily completes the braiding and then beribboning of my hair. . . . Whirling happily in my starchy frock, showing off my biscuit-polished patent-leather shoes and lavender socks, tossing my head in a way that makes my ribbons bounce, I stand, hands on hips, before my father. "Take me, Daddy," I say with assurance; "I'm the prettiest!"
        —ALICE WALKER, *In Search of Our Mothers' Gardens*

28. Using Semicolons

In classical Greek, groups of words comparable to what we call sentences were set off and called *colons*. A semicolon, therefore, is literally half of a colon, or half of a sentence divided by the punctuation mark we call a **semicolon**. Lewis Thomas demonstrates effective use of the semicolon as he defines it, noting that

> The semicolon tells you that there is still some question about the preceding full sentence; something needs to be added. . . . It is almost always a greater pleasure to come across a semicolon than a period. The period tells you that is that; if you didn't get all the meaning you wanted or expected, you got all the writer intended to parcel out and now you have to move along. But with a semicolon there you get a pleasant little feeling of expectancy; there is more to come; read on; it will get clearer.
> —LEWIS THOMAS, "Notes on Punctuation"

As Thomas suggests, semicolons have the effect of creating a pause stronger than that of a comma but not as strong as the full pause of a period. Their primary uses are to link coordinate independent clauses and to separate items in a series.

28a. Using semicolons to link independent clauses

You can join independent clauses in several ways: with a comma and a coordinating conjunction (see 27b), with a colon (see 32d), with a dash (see 32c), or with a semicolon. Semicolons provide writers with subtle ways of signaling closely related clauses: the second clause often restates an idea expressed in the first, as it does in the first sentence of the Lewis Thomas passage above, or it sometimes exemplifies or presents a contrast to the first. As a writer, you must choose when and where to use semicolons to signal such relationships. Note, for instance, the way semicolons are used in the following examples:

> Shakespeare wrote for the Medium of his day; if Shakespeare were alive now, he'd be writing *My Fair Lady.*
> —RANDALL JARRELL, "A Sad Heart at the Supermarket"

> The power of science for good and evil has troubled other minds than ours. We are not fumbling here with a new dilemma; our subject and our fears are as old as the tool-making civilizations.
> —JACOB BRONOWSKI, "The Creative Mind"

In the first sentence, Jarrell uses a semicolon to lead to a clause that exemplifies the statement made in the first clause. He might have joined the two clauses with the coordinating conjunction *and,* but such a link would be somewhat misleading, for *and* tells readers to expect more information, not an example. He might also have used a period to separate the two clauses into two sentences, but then the two ideas would not be so clearly linked. In the second example, the semicolon links two contrasting clauses; the logical connection between the two clauses is far more subtle and more immediate than it would be had Bronowski instead used the coordinating conjunction *for.*

The sentences above are compound sentences containing only two independent clauses, but semicolons can also join independent clauses in compound-complex sentences and in compound sentences containing more than two independent clauses.

> The Good Souls will, doubtless, gain their reward in Heaven; on this earth, certainly, theirs is what is technically known as a rough deal.
> On Mother's Day, Good Souls conscientiously wear carnations; on St. Patrick's Day, they faithfully don boutonnieres of shamrocks; on Columbus Day, they carefully pin on miniature Italian flags.
> —DOROTHY PARKER, "Good Souls"

A semicolon can also be used to link independent clauses joined by conjunctive adverbs like *therefore, however,* and *indeed* or transitional expressions like *in fact, in addition,* or *for example.* (See 6b7 and 5c5 for lists of conjunctive adverbs and transitional expressions.)

> The West German economy recovered quickly from the devastation of World War II; indeed, the recovery was labeled the "economic miracle."

Note that conjunctive adverbs can change position in a sentence:

> Fine diamonds are colorless; some, however, have a yellowish color.
>
> Fine diamonds are colorless; some have a yellowish color, however.

If two independent clauses joined by a coordinating conjunction contain commas, use a semicolon instead of a comma before the conjunction. The semicolon makes such a sentence easier to read.

> Every year, whether the Republican or the Democratic Party is in office, more and more power drains away from the individual to feed vast reservoirs in far-off places; and we have less and less say about the shape of events which shape our future.
> —WILLIAM F. BUCKLEY, JR., "Why Don't We Complain?"

EXERCISE 28.1

Revise each of the following sentences by adding a semicolon to link independent clauses.

Example

The exam begins in two hours please be on time.

The exam begins in two hours; please be on time.

1. If you are preoccupied, your game will suffer an opportunity for a relaxing afternoon will turn into a frustrating experience.
2. City life offers many advantages, however, in many ways, life in a small town is much more pleasant.
3. *Newspeak* greatly reduced people's vocabulary they could no longer understand philosophical and scientific works.
4. Physical education forms an important part of a university's program nevertheless, few students and professors clearly recognize its value.
5. Physical education provides students with exercise moreover, games and sports provide a chance for them to mingle outside of the classroom.
6. Voltaire was concerned about the political implications of his skepticism he warned his friends not to discuss atheism in front of the servants.
7. Kerosene, solar power, and electricity are popular sources of energy for heating homes in New England the most popular, however, is wood.
8. My high school was excessively competitive virtually everyone went on to college, many to the top schools in the nation.
9. Pittsburgh was once notorious for its smoke and grime today its skies and streets are cleaner than those of many other American cities.
10. Propaganda is defined as the spread of ideas to further a cause therefore, propaganda and advertisement are synonymous terms.

▌ 28b. Using semicolons to separate items in a series

Ordinarily, commas separate items in a series (see 27d). But when the items themselves contain commas or other punctuation, using semicolons will make the sentence clearer and easier to read.

> Anthropology encompasses archaeology, the study of ancient civilizations through artifacts; linguistics, the study of the structure and development of language; and cultural anthropology, which examines the life styles of various peoples, especially those in small, nonindustrialized societies.

> I recognized the film as a political document, expressing the worst sentiments of America in the cold war: its hero, a tough military man who wants only to destroy the enemy utterly; its villain, a naively liberal scientist who wants to learn more about it; the carrot and its flying saucer, a certain surrogate for the red menace; the film's famous last words—a newsman's impassioned plea to "watch the skies"—an invitation to extended fear and jingoism.
>
> —STEPHEN JAY GOULD, *Ever Since Darwin*

Note that a semicolon never introduces a series (see 28d).

EXERCISE 28.2

Using one of the example sentences in 28a or 28b as a model, write a sentence of your own that uses semicolons to separate items in a complex series.

▌ 28c. Checking for overused semicolons

If semicolons are used too often, they distract readers in the same way unnecessary repetition does, by calling attention to themselves instead of to what the writer is saying. In addition, sentence upon sentence punctuated with semicolons will sound monotonous and jerky.

OVERUSED	Like many people in public life, he spoke with confidence; perhaps he even spoke with arrogance; yet I noted a certain anxiety; it touched and puzzled me; he seemed too eager to demonstrate his control of a situation and his command of the necessary data.
REVISED	Like many people in public life, he spoke with confidence, perhaps even with arrogance; yet I noted a certain anxiety that touched and puzzled me. He seemed too eager to demonstrate his control of a situation and his command of the necessary data.

EXERCISE 28.3

Revise the following passage, substituting other punctuation for some of the semicolons. Add or delete words if necessary.

Remember when the neighborhood kids played football out in the vacant lot; they were there every Saturday, having a good time. Whatever happened to just playing for a good time? Now, uniformed coaches yell at young players to win; they put more and more pressure on them; and parents join in the chant of win, win, win; in fact, if the child is not a winner, he or she must be—that's right—a loser. The young athlete is constantly told that winning is everything; what used to be fun is now just like a job; play to win, the adults say, or do not play at all.

▌ 28d. Checking for misused semicolons

A comma, not a semicolon, should separate an independent clause from a dependent clause or a phrase.

MISUSED	For centuries, the Plains Indians maintained their way of life; which included hunting, fishing, and gathering wild berries.
REVISED	For centuries, the Plains Indians maintained their way of life, which included hunting, fishing, and gathering wild berries.

A colon, not a semicolon, should introduce a series.

MISUSED	The tour includes visits to the following art museums; the Prado, in Madrid; the Louvre, in Paris; and the Rijksmuseum, in Amsterdam.
REVISED	The tour includes visits to the following art museums: the Prado, in Madrid; the Louvre, in Paris; and the Rijksmuseum, in Amsterdam.

EXERCISE 28.4

Revise each of the following sentences to correct the misuse of semicolons.

Example
The new system would encourage high school students to take more academic courses; thus strengthening college preparation.
The new system would encourage high school students to take more academic courses, thus strengthening college preparation.

448

1. The comparison Osborne makes between the two wages is based primarily on three factors; the amount of time dedicated to work, the degree of responsibility, and the traditions attached to the jobs.
2. If the North had followed up its victory at Gettysburg more vigorously; the Civil War might have ended sooner.
3. The time seemed to fly; which was surprising because I was not having any fun whatsoever.
4. Our uniforms were unbelievably dingy; stained from being splattered with food and often torn here and there.
5. Verbal scores have decreased more than fifty-four points; while math scores have decreased more than thirty-six.

▌ 28e. Using semicolons with quotation marks

Ordinarily, a semicolon goes *outside* closing quotation marks.

Jackson's most famous story is "The Lottery"; it is a horrifying allegory about the power of tradition and the search for scapegoats.

EXERCISE 28.5

In the reading you are currently doing, find two passages that use semicolons particularly effectively. Then choose those two passages or two of the following ones, and use them as models for sentences of your own.

1. An evening with [composer Richard Wagner] was an evening spent in listening to a monologue. Sometimes he was brilliant; sometimes he was maddeningly tiresome. But whether he was brilliant or dull, he had one topic of conversation: himself.   —DEEMS TAYLOR, "The Monster"
2. The real question, however, it appears to me, is not whether poor people will adopt the middle-class mentality once they are well fed; rather, it is whether they will ever be well fed enough to be able to choose whatever mentality they think will suit them.
   —ALICE WALKER, "The Civil Rights Movement: What Good Was It?"
3. Baseball, football, basketball—these quintessentially American pastimes are recognizably sports because they involve play: They are games. One *plays* football; one doesn't *play* boxing.   —JOYCE CAROL OATES, "On Boxing"

READING WITH AN EYE FOR SEMICOLONS

In the following paragraph, Annie Dillard describes a solar eclipse in elaborate detail, using semicolons to separate each part of her description. Read the paragraph with attention to the use of semicolons. What different effect would

449

the paragraph have if Dillard had used periods instead of semicolons? Imagine also if she had used commas and coordinating conjunctions. What is the effect of all the semicolons?

You see the wide world swaddled in darkness; you see a vast breadth of hilly land, and an enormous, distant, blackened valley; you see towns' lights, a river's path, and blurred portions of your hat and scarf; you see your husband's face looking like an early black-and-white film; and you see a sprawl of black sky and blue sky together, with unfamiliar stars in it, some barely visible bands of cloud, and over there, a small white ring. The ring is as small as one goose in a flock of migrating geese—if you happen to notice a flock of migrating geese. It is one 360th part of the visible sky. The sun we see is less than half the diameter of a dime held at arm's length.

— Annie Dillard, "Solar Eclipse"

FOR EXAMINING SEMICOLONS IN YOUR OWN WRITING

Think of something you might take five or ten minutes to observe—a football game, a brewing storm, an ant awkwardly carrying a crumb—and write a paragraph describing your observations point by point and using semicolons to separate each point, as Annie Dillard does in the paragraph above. When you have finished, look at the way you used semicolons. Are there places where a period or a comma and a coordinating conjunction would better serve your meaning? Revise appropriately.

29. Using End Punctuation

Ending a sentence with a well-chosen period, question mark, or exclamation point allows your readers a certain satisfaction: they have reached the end of one unit of thought and can pause and take a mental breath before moving on to the next one. As a writer, you are most often guided by meaning in your choice of end punctuation. Sometimes, however, you can use end punctuation for special effect. Look, for instance, at the way end punctuation guides readers in the following three sentences:

> Am I tired.
>
> Am I tired?
>
> Am I tired!

In these brief examples, the end punctuation tells us how to read each sentence: the first one as a dry, matter-of-fact statement; the second as a puzzled or perhaps ironic query; the last as a note of exasperation. This chapter will explain how you can use these three kinds of end punctuation.

▮ 29a. Using periods

Use a period to close sentences that make statements or give mild commands.

> All I know about grammar is its infinite power.
> —JOAN DIDION, "Why I Write"

> Never use a foreign phrase, a scientific word or a jargon word if you can think of an everyday English equivalent.
> —GEORGE ORWELL, "Politics and the English Language"

A period also closes indirect questions, which report rather than ask questions.

> I asked how old the child was.
>
> We all wonder who will win the election.
>
> Many parents ask if autism is an inherited disorder.

Periods are also used with most abbreviations:

Mr.	A.M./a.m.	B.C.	Dr.	D.D.S.
Ms.	P.M./p.m.	A.D.	Ph.D.	R.N.
Mrs.	Jr.	ibid.	M.D.	M. Ed.

Some abbreviations do not require periods. Among them are the two-capital-letter abbreviations of state names used with ZIP codes, such as *FL* and *TN* (though note that the traditional abbreviations of state names such as *Fla.* or *Tenn.* do call for periods); abbreviations of familiar businesses, organizations, and government agencies (*NBC, YWCA, CIA*); and groups of initials that are pronounced as words (*NASA, MADD, UNICEF*).

If you are not sure whether a particular abbreviation should include periods, check the term in a dictionary. (See Chapter 34 for more information about abbreviations.)

EXERCISE 29.1

Revise each of the following sentences, inserting periods in appropriate places.

Example
Ms Maria Jordan received both a PhD in chemistry and an MEd
Ms. Maria Jordan received both a Ph.D. in chemistry and an M.Ed.

1. Please attend the meeting on Tuesday at 10 AM in the Board Room
2. Cicero was murdered in 43 BC
3. "What's the matter, Darryl?" I asked
4. In April 1981, NBC interviewed Dr Spock
5. A national voluntary effort by the AMA could help contain hospital costs

▌ 29b. Using question marks

A question mark closes sentences that ask direct questions.

> If women's professional sports can thrive in Europe, why not in the United States?

> How can we admit that the agreeable past, which we thought was permanent and inviolable, has slipped away like a Mississippi steamboat?
> —EVAN CONNELL, "The Palace of Moorish Kings"

Question marks do not close *indirect* questions, which report rather than ask questions. Indirect questions close with a period (see 29a).

Do not use a comma or a period after a question mark that ends a direct quotation.

> "What do I do now?" my mind kept repeating.

> My mind kept repeating, "What do I do now?"

Polite requests phrased as questions can be followed by periods rather than question marks.

> Would you please close the door.

Question marks appear between questions in a series even when the questions do not form separate sentences:

> I often confronted a dilemma: should I go to practice? finish my homework? spend time with my friends?

A question mark in parentheses can be used to indicate that a writer is unsure about a date, figure, or word.

> The house has a total of 5,000 square feet (?).

> Quintilian died in A.D. 95 (?).

> The meeting is on Oleonga (?) Street.

EXERCISE 29.2

Revise each of the following sentences, adding question marks and substituting them for other punctuation where appropriate. One of the sentences does not require any question marks.

> *Example*
> She asked the travel agent, "What is the air fare to Greece."
> She asked the travel agent, "What is the air fare to Greece?"

1. Social scientists face difficult questions: should they use their knowledge to shape and guide society, merely describe human behavior, try to do both.
2. Are people with so many possessions really happy.
3. "Can I play this" asked Manuel.
4. I looked at him and asked what his point was.
5. "Were you lying about our friendship" I yelled at her.

▌ 29c. Using exclamation points

Exclamation points close sentences that show surprise or strong emotion: emphatic statements, interjections, and emphatic commands.

Look out!

Help!

In those few moments of geologic time will be the story of all that has happened since we became a nation. And what a story it will be!
—JAMES RETTIE, "But a Watch in the Night"

Use exclamation points very sparingly because they can distract your readers by suggesting an exaggerated sense of urgency. Do not, for instance, use exclamation points with mild interjections or to suggest sarcasm or criticism. In general, try to create emphasis through diction (see Chapter 25) and sentence structure (see 17a) rather than exclamation points.

Do not use a comma or a period after an exclamation mark that ends a direct quotation.

"We shall next be told," exclaims Seneca, "that the first shoemaker was a philosopher!"   —THOMAS BABINGTON MACAULAY, "Francis Bacon"

EXERCISE 29.3

Revise each of the following sentences, adding exclamation points and substituting them for other punctuation where appropriate and removing any unnecessary exclamation points and other punctuation.

Example

Look out. The tide is coming in fast.

Look out! The tide is coming in fast!

1. This university is so large, so varied, that attempting to tell someone everything about it would take three years!
2. I screamed at Jamie, "You rat. You tricked me."
3. "This time we're starting early!," she shouted.
4. Get away from that window right now.
5. Oh, no. A flash flood warning.

EXERCISE 29.4

Turn to the passage by Tom Wolfe that opens Chapter 32. Read it over, and you will see that Wolfe has punctuated it as one very long sentence. Revise the sentence by breaking it into several shorter sentences. Try using periods, question marks, and exclamation points to achieve the same rhythm that Wolfe has. Change the wording as you need to (probably, you will not need to change much).

READING WITH AN EYE FOR END PUNCTUATION

Read the following passage and consider the author's use of end punctuation. Then read it again, and experiment with changing some of the end punctuation. What would be the effect of deleting the exclamation point from the quote by Cicero? What would be the effect of changing Cicero's question to a statement?

To be admired and praised, especially by the young, is an autumnal pleasure enjoyed by the lucky ones (who are not always the most deserving). "What is more charming," Cicero observes in his famous essay *De Senectute,* "than an old age surrounded by the enthusiasm of youth! . . . Attentions which seem trivial and conventional are marks of honor—the morning call, being sought after, precedence, having people rise for you, being escorted to and from the forum. . . . What pleasures of the body can be compared to the prerogatives of influence?" But there are also pleasures of the body, or the mind, that are enjoyed by a greater number of older persons.

—MALCOLM COWLEY, *The View from 80*

FOR EXAMINING END PUNCTUATION IN YOUR OWN WRITING

Look through an essay you have written recently, noting end punctuation carefully. How many of your sentences end with periods? How many with question marks? Have you used any exclamation points, and if so, are they actually called for? Then read through the essay again, seeing if you can find any sentences that might be better phrased as questions. If you find that all or almost all of your sentences end with periods, see if changing one or more to questions or exclamations proves effective. If you keep a writing log, you might copy some of this work into it for future study.

| 30. Using Apostrophes

As a mark of the possessive case, the punctuation mark we call the apostrophe has an unusual history. In Old English, the endings of nouns changed depending on their grammatical function—a noun used as a subject, for example, had a different ending from the same noun used as a direct object. By the fourteenth century, Middle English had dropped most of this complicated system except for possessive and plural endings: *Haroldes* (or *Haroldis* or *Haroldys*) *sword* was still used to mean "the sword of Harold." Then, in the sixteenth century, scholars concluded that the ending *-es* and its variant forms were actually contractions of *his*. Believing that *Haroldes sword* meant "Harold his sword," they began using an apostrophe instead of the *e: Harold's sword*.

Even though this theory was later discredited, the possessive ending retained the apostrophe because it was a useful way to distinguish between possessive and plural forms in writing. Today, we use the apostrophe primarily to signal possessive case, contractions and other omissions of words and letters, and certain plural forms. This chapter presents the conventions governing its use.

▌ 30a. Using apostrophes to signal possessive case

The possessive case denotes ownership or possession of one thing by another (see Chapter 7). The apostrophe is used to form the possessive case of nouns and indefinite pronouns—*Francine's mink coat, nobody's fault*.

1. Forming the possessive case of singular nouns and indefinite pronouns

Add an apostrophe and -*s* to form the possessive of most singular nouns and indefinite pronouns, including those singular nouns that end in -*s*.

His *coach's* advice helped Sydney win the class.

John Wayne's first westerns are considered classics.

The reading list included *Keats's* poem.

Anyone's guess is as good as mine.

Apostrophes are *not* used with the possessive forms of *personal* pronouns: *yours, his, hers, its, ours, theirs.*

2. Forming the possessive case of plural nouns

For plural nouns not ending in -*s*, add an apostrophe and -*s* as with singular nouns.

The *women's* caucus will include representatives from thirty cities.

The *children's* first Christmas was spent in Wales.

For plural nouns ending in -*s*, add only the apostrophe.

The *clowns'* costumes were bright green and orange.

Fifty dollars' worth of groceries filled only two shopping bags.

3. Forming the possessive case of compound words

For compound words, make the last word in the group possessive.

The *secretary of state's* speech was televised.

Her *daughters-in-law's* birthdays both fall in July.

His *in-laws'* disapproval dampened his enthusiasm for the new house.

4. Forming the possessive case with two or more nouns

To signal individual possession by two or more owners, make each noun possessive.

There are great differences between *John Wayne's* and *Henry Fonda's* westerns. [Wayne and Fonda appeared in different westerns.]

To signal joint possession, make only the last noun possessive.

> *Rogers and Astaire's* first film together was *Flying Down to Rio.*

➤ Checking for possessive apostrophes

To check for possessive apostrophes, circle all the nouns that end in -*s*. Then look at the circled nouns, and put a check mark beside each one that shows ownership or possession. Make sure that each of these nouns has an apostrophe in the right place, either before or after the -*s*. Next underline all the indefinite pronouns (someone, nobody— see 6b3 for a more complete list); any that end in -*s* should have an apostrophe before the -*s*.

EXERCISE 30.1

Complete each of the following sentences by inserting '*s* or an apostrophe alone to form the possessive case of the italicized words.

1. Grammar is *everybody* favorite subject.
2. *CBS* acquisition of the guitar company disappointed some musicians.
3. I was having a good time at *P.J.*, but my friends wanted to go to *Sunny.*
4. *Carol and Jim* income dropped drastically after Jim quit his job.
5. Parents often question their *children* choice of friends.
6. Many smokers disregard the *surgeon general* warnings.
7. The restaurant management took a percentage of *everyone* tips.
8. The *governors* attitudes changed after the convention.
9. This is the strangest dog I've ever seen; she has a *beagle* ears, and a *St. Bernard* nose and feet.
10. *My friend and my brother* cars have the same kind of stereo system.

30b. Using apostrophes to signal contractions and other omissions

Contractions are combinations of two words that are formed by leaving out certain letters, which are indicated by apostrophes. Note the use of the apostrophe in the following commonly contracted forms:

it is	it's	would not	wouldn't
was not	wasn't	do not	don't
I am	I'm	does not	doesn't
he is, he has	he's	will not	won't
you will	you'll	let us	let's
I would	I'd	who is, who has	who's
he would	he'd	cannot	can't

Contractions are common in conversation and informal writing. Most academic work, however, calls for greater formality. Check with your instructor about the appropriateness of contractions in your college writing.

Do not confuse the possessive pronoun *its* with the contraction *it's*. *Its* is the possessive form of *it*. *It's* is a contraction for *it is*.

This disease is unusual; *its* symptoms vary from person to person.

It's a difficult disease to diagnose.

(See 22b for other commonly confused pairs of possessive pronouns and contractions—*their/they're, whose/who's*, and *your/you're*.)

An apostrophe is also used to signal omission of letters or numbers in other common phrases:

ten of the clock	rock and roll	class of 1989
ten o'clock	rock 'n' roll	class of '89

In addition, writers can use an apostrophe to signal omitted letters in approximating the sound of spoken English or some specific dialect of spoken English. Note the way Mark Twain uses the apostrophe to form contractions in the following passage, in which Huckleberry Finn tells Jim about King Henry the Eighth:

> S'pose people left money laying around where he was—what did he do? He collared it. S'pose he contracted to do a thing, and you paid him, and didn't set down there and see that he done it—what did he do? He always done the other thing. S'pose he opened his mouth—what then? If he didn't shut it up powerful quick he'd lose a lie every time. That's the king of a bug Henry was; and if we'd 'a' had him along 'stead of our Kings he'd 'a' fooled that town a heap worse than ours done.
> —MARK TWAIN, *The Adventures of Huckleberry Finn*

➤ Checking for misuse of *its* and *it's*

To check a draft for misuse of *its* and *it's*, first circle each *its* in the draft. Check to see that it shows possession; if not, add an apostrophe before the -s. Then underline each *it's*. Check to see that it means "it is"; if not, remove the apostrophe.

EXERCISE 30.2

Go through the Twain passage in 30b, writing out the full form in place of each contraction. Then read the two versions aloud, and note how much more the one with contractions sounds like spoken English.

30c. Using apostrophes to form the plural of numbers, letters, symbols, and words used as terms

An apostrophe and -s are used to form the plural of numbers, letters, symbols, and words referred to as terms.

Several Cessna *150*'s sat on the ground.

The gymnasts need marks of *8*'s and *9*'s to qualify for the finals.

Ideally, all swimmers should know the *ABC*'s of lifesaving.

The computer prints *e*'s whenever there is an error in the program.

I marked special passages with a series of three ***'s.

The five *Shakespeare*'s in the essay were spelled five different ways.

Note that numbers, letters, and words referred to as terms are usually italicized; but the plural ending is not, as in the examples above.

The plural of years can be written with or without the apostrophe (*1990*'s or *1990s*). Whichever style you follow, be consistent.

EXERCISE 30.3

The following sentences, from which all apostrophes have been deleted, appear in Langston Hughes's "Salvation." Insert apostrophes where appropriate in each sentence.

Example

"Sister Reed, what is this childs name?"

"Sister Reed, what is this child's name?"

1. There was a big revival at my Auntie Reeds church.
2. That night I was escorted to the front row and placed on the mourners bench with all the other young sinners. . . .
3. Finally Westly said to me: . . ."Lets get up and be saved."
4. Then I was left all alone on the mourners bench.
5. That night, . . . I cried, in bed alone, and couldnt stop.

READING WITH AN EYE FOR APOSTROPHES

In "Danny Deever," Rudyard Kipling uses apostrophes to mark contractions and omitted letters. Both help create a sense of informal spoken English in late nineteenth century Britain. Read the following stanza aloud, listening for the rhythm of the language. To get a sense of how apostrophes help to create this rhythm, you might try reading the poem with the missing letters filled in.

> "What's that so black agin the sun?" said Files-on-Parade.
> "It's Danny fightin' 'ard for life," the Color-Sergeant said.
> "What's that that whimpers over'ead?" said Files-on-Parade.
> "It's Danny's soul that's passin' now," the Color-Sergeant said.
>   For they're done with Danny Deever, you can 'ear the quickstep play,
> The Regiment's in column, an' they're marchin' us away;
> Ho! the young recruits are shakin', an' they'll want their beer today,
> After hangin' Danny Deever in the mornin'!
>   –RUDYARD KIPLING, "Danny Deever"

FOR EXAMINING YOUR OWN USE OF APOSTROPHES

As a tool for presenting contractions and omitted letters, apostrophes play a larger role in informal writing than in formal writing. One thing that many students need to learn is to write with few or no contractions, a task that requires some effort because we all use contractions in conversation. To get an idea of the difference between spoken and written language, try transcribing a "paragraph" or so of your own spoken words. Make a point of using apostrophes whenever you use a contraction or otherwise omit a letter. Look over your paragraph to see how many apostrophes you used, and then revise the piece to make it more formal, eliminating all or most apostrophes.

31. Using Quotation Marks

"By necessity, by proclivity,—and by delight, we all quote," wrote Ralph Waldo Emerson. Quotation marks, which tell readers that certain words were spoken or written by someone other than the writer, have been a convention of written English since before the time of the printing press. As printing techniques evolved and became standardized, quotation marks came to signal not only direct quotations but also certain titles, definitions, and words used ironically or invented by the writer. This chapter presents the conventions governing their use.

31a. Using quotation marks to signal direct quotation

In written American English, double quotation marks signal a direct quotation.

> "Imagery," Laurence Perrine states, "may be defined as the representation through language of sense experience."

> He smiled and said, "Son, this is one incident that I will never forget."

Single quotation marks enclose a quotation within a quotation. Open and close the passage you are quoting with double quotation marks, and change any quotation marks that appear *within* the quotation to single quotation marks.

> In "The Uses of the Blues," James Baldwin says that "The title 'The Uses of the Blues' does not refer to music; I don't know anything about music."

Do not use quotation marks for *indirect* discourse, which does not quote the speaker's or writer's exact words.

The father smiled and said that he would never forget the incident.

1. Quoting longer passages

If the passage you wish to quote exceeds four typewritten or hand-written lines, set it off from the rest of the text by starting it on a new line and indenting it ten spaces from the left margin. Double-space above and below the quotation, and double-space the quotation itself. This format, known as **block quotation,** does not require quotation marks.

Jean Shepherd identifies the Van People, who he says

> tend to be heavily bearded, dedicated lifetime subscribers to *Rolling Stone*, compulsive consumers of granola. . . . The Van People are fond of plastering their equipment with such goodies as: Danger—I Brake for Animals (apparently on the assumption that the mean old Others are endlessly and maliciously bashing their cars into goats, pigs, elderly St. Bernards, draft horses, mud turtles, and other lowly creatures with which we share this planet). . . .
>
> –JEAN SHEPHERD, "The Van Culture and the Camper Crowd"

2. Quoting poetry

The same general rules apply to quoting poetry as to quoting prose. If the quotation is brief (fewer than four lines), include it within your text, enclosed in double quotation marks. Separate the lines of the poem with slashes, each preceded and followed by a space.

> In one of his best-known poems, Robert Frost remarks, "Two roads diverged in a yellow wood, and I— / I took the one less traveled by / And that has made all the difference."

If the poetic quotation is longer, set it off from the text with double spacing, and indent each line ten spaces from the left margin.

> The duke in Robert Browning's "My Last Duchess" is clearly a jealous, vain person, whose arrogance is illustrated through his statement:
>
> > She thanked men—good! but thanked
> > Somehow—I know not how—as if she ranked
> > My gift of a nine-hundred-years-old name
> > With anybody's gift.

When you quote poetry, take care to follow the indentation, spacing, capitalization, punctuation, and other features of the original passage.

EXERCISE 31.1

Use quotation marks to enclose direct quotations in the following passage:

> After the speaker of the sonnet becomes so depressed that he despises himself, he happens to think of his lover, and his mood suddenly changes. In this transitional section, Shakespeare's main device is the imagery in lines 11 and 12: Like to the lark at break of day arising / From sullen earth, sings hymns at heaven's gate. The image of a lark rising from the earth suggests freedom, joy, and rapture. In addition, the phrase at break of day arising / From sullen earth suggests rebirth or a new beginning.

▌ 31b. Using quotation marks to signal dialogue

When you write dialogue or quote a conversation, enclose the words of each speaker in quotation marks, and mark each shift in speaker by beginning a new paragraph, no matter how brief the quoted remark may be.

> "But I can see you're bound to come," said his father. "Only we ain't going to catch us no fish, because there ain't no water left to catch 'em in."
> "The river!"
> "All but dry."
> "You been many times already?"
> "Son, this is my first time this year."
> —EUDORA WELTY, "Ladies in Spring"

Beginning a new paragraph with each change in speaker helps readers follow the dialogue. In the example above, we know when the father is speaking and when the son is speaking without the author's having to repeat "said his father" and so on.

▌ 31c. Using quotation marks to signal titles and definitions

Quotation marks are used to enclose the titles of short poems, short stories, articles, essays, songs, sections of books, and episodes of television and radio programs.

Matthew Arnold moves from calmness to sadness in "Dover Beach."
[poem]

Woodberry uses "The Devil in Manuscript" to show that Hawthorne's
writing reflects his life. [short story]

In "Don't Pay the Language No Mind, Honey," William Grieder uses
informal language effectively. [essay]

A recent *Newsweek* article on Pablo Picasso is entitled "Portrait of a
Raging Bull." [article]

To distract the children, we began singing "She'll Be Coming 'Round
the Mountain" and "The Green Grass Grows All Around." [songs]

Throughout the chapter "Chamber Under the Eaves," Turner implies
that Hawthorne's life during this period was one of complete dedication
and solitude. [section of book]

In tonight's episode, "Murder Most Foul," Jessica matches wits with a
psychopath. [television episode]

Use italics rather than quotation marks for the titles of longer works,
such as books and magazines (see 35a).

Definitions of words or phrases are sometimes set off with quotation marks:

The French phrase *idée fixe* means literally "fixed idea."

Oxymoronic means "self-contradictory."

31d. Using quotation marks to signal irony and coinages

One way of showing readers that you are using a word or a phrase
ironically is to enclose it in quotation marks.

During that rehearsal, I really was "lucky" enough to break a leg. [The
quotation marks around the word *lucky* suggest ironically that the narrator was anything but lucky.]

Quotation marks are also used to enclose words or phrases coined by
the writer.

Your whole first paragraph or first page may have to be guillotined in
any case after your piece is finished: it is a kind of "forebirth." [The
word *forebirth* was coined by the writer.]

–JACQUES BARZUN, "A Writer's Discipline"

465

EXERCISE 31.2

Revise each of the following sentences, using quotation marks appropriately to signal titles, definitions, irony, or coinages.

1. Daddy, a poem by Sylvia Plath, describes a young woman's attitude toward her father.
2. In Flannery O'Connor's short story Revelation, colors symbolize passion, violence, sadness, and even God.
3. The little that is known about gorillas certainly makes you want to know a great deal more, writes Alan Moorehead in an essay called A Most Forgiving Ape.
4. The fun of surgery begins before the operation ever takes place.
5. I will evaluate an article entitled The Graying of the Campuses.
6. Big Bill, the first section of Dos Passos's U.S.A., opens with a birth.
7. Tolkien refers to this sudden, joyous turn as a eucatastrophe, a word he invented to mean the consolation of the happy ending.
8. Pink Floyd's song Time depicts the impact of technology on society.
9. My dictionary defines *isolation* as the quality or state of being alone.
10. This review will examine a TV episode entitled 48 Hours on Gang Street.

▌ 31e. Checking for misused quotation marks

Use quotation marks only when there is a reason for them; do not use them just to emphasize particular words or phrases, as in the following sentence:

MISUSED   "Some of the boys," not including Travis, of course, would take "stingers" off wasps and bees and then put the insects "down" others' shirts.

REVISED   Some of the boys, not including Travis, of course, would take stingers off wasps and bees and then put the insects down others' shirts.

Do not use quotation marks around slang or colloquial language that you think is inappropriate for formal register (see 26c3); they create the impression that you are apologizing for using such language. In general, try to express your idea in formal language. If you have a good reason to use a slang or colloquial term, use it without quotation marks.

MISUSED   After their twenty-mile hike, the campers were "wiped out" and ready to "hit the sack."

REVISED   After their twenty-mile hike, the campers were exhausted and ready to go to bed.

Even though you enclose many titles in quotation marks to refer to them in writing, do not use them with the titles of your own essays.

EXERCISE 31.3

According to Lewis Thomas, "The most objectionable misuse of quotation marks, but one which illustrates the dangers of misuse in ordinary prose, is seen in advertising." What is the effect of the quotation marks in the following advertisements?

On a movie marquee: Coming "Attractions"

At a supermarket: "Fresh" Asparagus

31f. Using quotation marks with other punctuation

1. Periods and commas go inside quotation marks.

"Marriage has many pains," wrote Samuel Johnson, "but celibacy has no pleasures."

2. Colons and semicolons go outside quotation marks.

Everything is dark, and "a visionary light settles in her eyes"; this vision, this light, is her salvation.

I felt only one emotion after finishing "Eveline": pity.

3. Question marks, exclamation points, and dashes go inside quotation marks if they are part of the quotation.

PART OF QUOTATION

Gently shake the injured person while asking, "Are you all right?"

"Jump!" one of the firefighters shouted.

"Watch out—watch out for—" Jessica began nervously.

NOT PART OF QUOTATION

Is Hawthorne expressing his subconscious thoughts in "My Kinsman, Major Molineaux"?

What a shame that Scott Joplin did not live to see the popularity of his "Maple Leaf Rag"!

"Break a leg"—that phrase is supposed to bring good luck to a performer.

‖ 4. Footnote numbers go outside quotation marks.

Tragedy is defined by Aristotle as "an imitation of an action that is serious and of a certain magnitude."[1]

For more information on footnotes and for examples of quotation marks used with bibliographical references, see Chapter 41.

EXERCISE 31.4

Revise each of the following sentences, deleting quotation marks used inappropriately, moving those placed incorrectly, and using more formal language in place of slang expressions in quotation marks.

Example
> In Herman Melville's "Bartleby, the Scrivener", Bartleby states time and again, "I would prefer not to".
> In Herman Melville's "Bartleby, the Scrivener," Bartleby states time and again, "I would prefer not to."

1. The grandmother in O'Connor's story shows she is still misguided when she says, "You've got good blood! I know you wouldn't shoot a lady"!
2. What is Hawthorne telling the readers in "Rappaccini's Daughter?"
3. You could hear the elation in her voice when she said, "We did it".
4. This "typical American" is Ruby Turpin, who in the course of the story receives a "message" that brings about a "change" in her life.
5. Being overweight is a "big" problem because "excess" weight is hard to lose and can be dangerous to a person's health.
6. One of Jackson's least-known stories is "Janice;" this story, like many of her others, leaves the reader shocked.
7. Macbeth "bumps off" Duncan to gain the throne for himself.
8. In his article "How the Freeze Movement Was Born", Michael Kazin states that a freeze's "bilateral nature nullifies fears of a Soviet advantage[1]."
9. "Know thyself—" this is the quest of the main characters in both Ibsen's *Peer Gynt* and Lewis's *Till We Have Faces.*
10. One thought flashed through my mind as I finished "*In Search of Our Mothers' Gardens:*" I want to read more of this writer's work.

READING WITH AN EYE FOR QUOTATION MARKS

Read the following passage from an essay by Joan Didion about the painter Georgia O'Keeffe, paying particular attention to the use of quotation marks. What effect is created by Didion's use of quotation marks around the words *Hardness, crustiness,* and *crusty?* How do the quotations by O'Keeffe help to support Didion's description of her?

"Hardness" has not been in our century a quality much admired in women, nor in the past twenty years has it even been in official favor for men. When hardness surfaces in the very old we tend to transform it into "crustiness" or eccentricity, some tonic pepperiness to be indulged at a distance. On the evidence of her work and what she has said about it, Georgia O'Keeffe is neither "crusty" nor eccentric. She is simply hard, a straight shooter, a woman clean of received wisdom and open to what she sees. This is a woman who could early on dismiss most of her contemporaries as "dreamy," and would later single out one she liked as "a very poor painter." (And then add, apparently by way of softening the judgment: "I guess he wasn't a painter at all. He had no courage and I believe that to create one's own world in any of the arts takes courage.") This is a woman who in 1939 could advise her admirers that they were missing her point, that their appreciation of her famous flowers was merely sentimental. "When I paint a red hill," she observed coolly in the catalogue for an exhibition that year, "you say it is too bad that I don't always paint flowers. A flower touches almost everyone's heart. A red hill doesn't touch everyone's heart."   –JOAN DIDION, "Georgia O'Keeffe"

FOR USING QUOTATION MARKS IN YOUR OWN WRITING

Choose a topic that is currently of interest to students on your campus, and interview one of your friends about it for ten or fifteen minutes. On the basis of your notes from the interview, write two or three paragraphs about your friend's views on the topic, using as many direct quotations as possible. Then look at what you have written to see how closely you followed the conventions for quotation marks that have been explained in this chapter.

32. Using Other Punctuation Marks

Parentheses, brackets, dashes, colons, slashes, and ellipses are marks that allow writers to punctuate sentences so that readers can best understand their meaning. Following is a sentence that demonstrates the use of all these punctuation marks.

> Likewise, "hassling"—mock dogfighting—was strictly forbidden, and so naturally young fighter jocks could hardly wait to go up in, say, a pair of F-100s and start the duel by making a pass at each other at 800 miles an hour, the winner being the pilot who could slip in behind the other one and get locked in on his [never *her* or *his or her!*] tail ("wax his tail"), and it was not uncommon for some eager jock to try too tight an outside turn and have his engine flame out, whereupon, unable to restart it, he has to eject . . . and he shakes his fist at the victor as he floats down by parachute and his million-dollar aircraft goes *kaboom!* on the palmetto grass or the desert floor, and he starts thinking about how he can get together with the other guy back at the base in time for the two of them to get their stories straight before the investigation: "I don't know what happened, sir. I was pulling up after a target run, and it just flamed out on me."   –Tom Wolfe, *The Right Stuff*

Here Wolfe uses dashes, parentheses, ellipses, slashes, and colons to create rhythm and build momentum in a very long (178-word) sentence that starts with a definition of *hassling* set off by dashes and builds to the pilot's less-than-truthful "story" after the colon: "I don't know what happened, sir." The editorial comment inserted in brackets calls attention to the fact that the "right stuff" is, in the world Wolfe describes, always male. This chapter will guide you in deciding when you can use these marks of punctuation to signal relationships among sentence parts, to create particular rhythms, and to help readers follow your thoughts.

▍ 32a. Using parentheses

Parentheses can be used to add information that is of minor or secondary importance—information that clarifies, comments on, or illustrates what precedes it. Parentheses are also used around numbers or letters that precede items in a list.

Adding information

Once a star of the Green Bay Packers, Jerry Kramer is an oil and energy executive whose transition from sports to business was made smoother by several best-selling books (*Instant Replay* and more recently *Distant Replay*) about his old team.

Normal children do not confuse reality and fantasy—they confuse them much less often than we adults do (as a certain great fantasist pointed out in a story called "The Emperor's New Clothes").
—URSULA LEGUIN, "Why Are Americans Afraid of Dragons?"

Boxing is a purely masculine world. (Though there are female boxers— the most famous is the black champion Lady Tyger Trimiar with her shaved head and tiger-striped attire—women's role in the sport is extremely marginal.) —JOYCE CAROL OATES, "On Boxing"

As the second and third examples above demonstrate, a period may be placed either inside or outside a closing parenthesis, depending on whether the material inside the parentheses is a complete sentence. A comma, on the other hand, is always placed *outside* a closing parenthesis (and never before an opening one).

Gene Tunney's single defeat in an eleven-year career was to a flamboyant and dangerous fighter named Harry Greb ("The Human Windmill"), who seems to have been, judging from boxing literature, the dirtiest fighter in history. —JOYCE CAROL OATES, "On Boxing"

If the material in parentheses is a question or an exclamation, use a question mark or exclamation mark inside the closing parenthesis.

Our laughing (so deep was the pleasure!) became screaming.
—RICHARD RODRIGUEZ, "Aria: A Memoir of a Bilingual Childhood"

As a writer, you can punctuate supplemental information in three ways: with commas, with parentheses, or with dashes. The distinction is partially one of how interruptive the information is and partially one of personal style. In general, use commas when the material is least interruptive (see 27c and f), parentheses when it is more interruptive, and dashes when it is the most interruptive (see 32c). One other consideration is whether the material to be added ends in an exclamation point or question mark (as does the preceding Rodriguez example); if so, you can use *only* parentheses or dashes.

Use parentheses judiciously, because they break up the flow of a sentence or passage, forcing readers to hold the original train of thought in their minds while considering a secondary one. To decide whether to use parentheses, read the sentence or passage aloud, or have someone read it aloud to you. Decide whether the parentheses make it harder to follow; if so, try to revise to eliminate them.

Enclosing numbers or letters in a list

Five distinct styles can be distinguished: (1) Old New England, (2) Deep South, (3) Middle American, (4) Wild West and (5) Far West or Californian.   –ALISON LURIE, *The Language of Clothes*

We then settled down, coming to rest on the presumption that: (a) someone connected with the management of the theatre must soon notice the blur and make the connection; or (b) that someone seated near the rear of the house would make the complaint in behalf of those of us up front; or (c) that—any minute now—the entire house would explode into catcalls and foot stamping, calling dramatic attention to the irksome distortion.
–WILLIAM F. BUCKLEY, JR., "Why Don't We Complain?"

▌ 32b. Using brackets

Brackets are used to set off parenthetical elements in material within parentheses and to set off explanatory words or comments inserted into a quotation. If your typewriter does not include keys for brackets, draw them in by hand.

Setting off material within parentheses

Eventually the investigation had to examine the major agencies (including the previously sacrosanct National Security Agency [NSA]) that were conducting covert operations.

472

Adding material to quotations

In the following sentence, the bracketed word replaces the word *he* in the original quotation.

> Turner writes, "[Hawthorne] is known as Oberon and has shown himself closely akin to the Oberon in 'The Devil in Manuscript.' "

In the following sentence, the bracketed material explains what the *that* in the quotation refers to.

> In defending his station's inferior children's programs, a network executive states, "If we were to do that [supply quality programs in the afternoon, one of the demands of ACT], a lot of people might say: 'How dare they lock the kids up for another two and a half hours.' "
> –MARIE WINN, *The Plug-In Drug: Television, Children, and the Family*

In the quotation in the following sentence, the artist Gauguin's name is misspelled. The bracketed word *sic*, which means "thus," tells readers that the person being quoted made the mistake—not the writer.

> One admirer wrote, "She was the most striking woman I'd ever seen— a sort of wonderful combination of Mia Farrow and one of Gaugin's [sic] Polynesian nymphs."

EXERCISE 32.1

Revise the following sentences, using parentheses and brackets correctly.

Example

She was in fourth grade or was it third? when she decided to become a writer.

She was in fourth grade (or was it third?) when she decided to become a writer.

1. One incident of cruelty was brought to public attention by the Animal Liberation Front ALF.
2. During my research, I found that a flat-rate income tax a single-rate tax with no deductions has its problems.
3. Nixon mentions his family early in the speech, saying he "would have preferred to carry it the presidency through to the finish whatever the personal agony it would have involved."
4. Many researchers used the Massachusetts Multiphasic Personal Inventory the MMPI for hypnotizability studies.
5. Some of the alternatives suggested include 1 tissue cultures, 2 mechanical models, 3 *in vitro* techniques, and 4 mathematical and electrical models.

▋ 32c. Using dashes

Pairs of dashes allow you to interrupt the normal word order of a sentence to insert additional explanation or information. Compared with parentheses or commas, dashes bring special emphasis to the added material.

Interrupting the normal word order

The pleasures of reading itself—who doesn't remember?—were like those of Christmas cake, a sweet devouring.

–EUDORA WELTY, "A Sweet Devouring"

Emphasizing parenthetical or explanatory elements

Mr. Angell is addicted to dashes and parentheses—small pauses or digressions in a narrative like those moments when the umpire dusts off home plate or a pitcher rubs up a new ball—that serve to slow an already deliberate movement almost to a standstill.

–JOEL CONARROE, *New York Times Book Review*

Single dashes are used to mark a sudden shift in tone, to introduce a summary or explanation of what has come before, or to indicate hesitation in speech.

Emphasizing a sudden change in tone

Under democracy, one party always devotes its chief efforts to trying to prove that the other is unfit to rule—and both commonly succeed and are right.   –H. L. MENCKEN, "Minority Report"

If you are truly serious about preparing your child for the future, don't teach him to subtract—teach him to deduct.

–FRAN LEBOWITZ, "Parental Guidance"

Introducing a summary or explanation

In walking, the average adult person employs a motor mechanism that weighs about eighty pounds—sixty pounds of muscle and twenty pounds of bone.   –EDWARD WAY TEALE

Indicating hesitation or awkwardness in speech

As the officer approached his car, the driver stammered, "What—what have I done?"

The difference between a single dash and a colon is a subtle one. In general, dashes are much less formal than colons. In fact, you should use dashes sparingly, if at all, in most of your college writing.

EXERCISE 32.2

Punctuate the following sentences with dashes where appropriate.

Example

He is quick, violent, and mean they don't call him "Dirty Harry" for nothing but appealing nonetheless.

He is quick, violent, and mean—they don't call him "Dirty Harry" for nothing—but appealing nonetheless.

1. Union Carbide's plant in Bhopal, India, sprang a leak a leak that killed over 2,500 people and injured 150,000 more.
2. Even if smoking is harmful and there is no real proof of this assertion it is unjust to outlaw smoking while other harmful substances remain legal.
3. I recall thinking to myself, "I'm going I'm going to oh, I don't know!"
4. Many people would have ignored the children's taunts but not Ace.
5. On the morning of April 30, 1975, the remaining American military personnel in South Vietnam the eleven Marines who guarded the American embassy were finally evacuated.

█ 32d. Using colons

Colons are used to introduce a sentence that is an explanation, example, or appositive of what precedes it; to introduce a series, list, or quotation; and to separate elements such as hours, minutes, and seconds; biblical chapter numbers; titles and subtitles; and parts of bibliographical references.

Introducing an explanation, example, or appositive

And we are all on our own when it comes to keeping those lines open to ourselves: your notebook will never help me, nor mine you.

—JOAN DIDION, "On Keeping a Notebook"

The men may also wear the getup known as Sun Belt Cool: a pale beige suit, open collared shirt (often in a darker shade than the suit), cream-colored loafers and aviator sunglasses.

—ALISON LURIE, *The Language of Clothes*

Introducing a series, list, or quotation

As the name implies, this stretch of the river was in fact so easy and gentle that the trip could be and was made by all sorts of amateurs: by Boy Scouts, Camp Fire Girls, stenographers, school teachers, students, little old ladies in inner tubes.

—EDWARD ABBEY, "The Damnation of a Canyon"

We began a series of workshops on nonviolence, and we repeatedly asked ourselves: "Are you able to accept blows without retaliation?"
–MARTIN LUTHER KING, JR., "Letter from Birmingham Jail"

Separating elements according to standard use

HOURS, MINUTES, AND SECONDS

4:59 P.M.

2:15:06

BIBLICAL CHAPTERS AND VERSES

Deuteronomy 17:2–7

I Chronicles 3:3–5

TITLES AND SUBTITLES

"Grant and Lee: A Study in Contrasts"

Nuclear War: The Facts of Our Survival

PARTS OF BIBLIOGRAPHICAL REFERENCES

New York: St. Martin's Press [The colon separates the place of publication from the publisher.]

Newsweek, November 5, 1978: 53 [The colon separates the year from the page number.]

Checking for incorrect colons

Except when it is used to separate the standard elements discussed in the preceding section, a colon should be used only at the end of an independent clause.

Do not put a colon between verb and object or complement, or between preposition and object. Avoid putting colons after such expressions as *such as, especially,* or *including.*

MISUSED   Some of these effects include: reddening of the eyes, an increase in heartbeat, dryness of the mouth, and irritation of the throat.

REVISED   Some of these effects include reddening of the eyes, an increase in heartbeat, dryness of the mouth, and irritation of the throat.

MISUSED   The artificial heart can cause complications, especially: blood clots, brain seizures, and strokes.

REVISED   The artificial heart can cause complications, especially blood clots, brain seizures, and strokes.

MISUSED	Every year, in the name of science, thousands of animals are exposed to: severe pain, physical and behavioral stress, extreme heat and cold, electric shock, starvation, and mutilation.
REVISED	Every year, in the name of science, thousands of animals are exposed to severe pain, physical and behavioral stress, extreme heat and cold, electric shock, starvation, and mutilation.
MISUSED	In poetry, additional power may come from devices such as: simile, metaphor, and alliteration.
REVISED	In poetry, additional power may come from devices such as simile, metaphor, and alliteration.

EXERCISE 32.3

Insert a colon in each of the following items that needs one. Some of the items do not require a colon, and one requires two colons.

Example
Canada A Story of Challenge is required reading for the course.
Canada: A Story of Challenge is required reading for the course.

1. The sonnet's structure is effective in revealing the speaker's message love has changed his life and ended his depression.
2. Another example is taken from Psalm 139 16.
3. Nixon claims that throughout the Watergate investigation he believed it was his duty to stay on as president "to make every possible effort to complete the term of office to which you elected me."
4. Layton, Ed. *Martin Luther King The Peaceful Warrior.* 3rd ed. Englewood Cliffs, NJ Prentice-Hall, 1968.
5. Education can alleviate problems such as poverty, poor health, and the energy shortage.
6. Gandhi urged four things tell the truth even in business, adopt more sanitary habits, abolish caste and religious divisions, and learn English.
7. Some of the improvements included the establishment of after-school recreation programs and a consumer cooperative, the opening or expansion of health clinics, and changes in the content of school curricula.
8. *Signs of Trouble and Erosion A Report on Education in America* was submitted to Congress and the president in January 1984.
9. Even more important was what money represented success and prestige.
10. The article in *Time* reported that at 418 p.m. the surgeon, Dr. William DeVries, leaned over the heavily sedated man and said, "Everything went well—perfectly."

■ 32e. Using slashes

Slashes are used to mark line divisions in poetry quoted within text (see 31a2), to separate two alternative terms, and to separate the parts of fractions. When used to separate lines of poetry, the slash should be surrounded by space.

Marking line divisions in poetry

In "Sonnet 29," the persona states, "For thy sweet love rememb'red such wealth brings, / That then I scorn to change my state with kings."

Separating alternatives

"I'm not the typical wife/girlfriend of a baseball player—those women you see on TV with their hair done up and their Rose Bowl Parade wave to the crowds."   –ROGER ANGELL, "In the Country"

Separating parts of fractions

Over the last thirty years, the average yield of American farms increased by only 2½ percent.

■ 32f. Using ellipses

Ellipses are three equally spaced dots used to indicate that something has been omitted from a quoted passage. They can also be used to signal hesitation, in the same way that a dash can (see 32c).

Indicating omissions

Just as you should be very careful to use quotation marks around any material that you quote directly from a source, so you should use an ellipsis to indicate that you have left out part of a quotation that appears to be a complete sentence. Look at the following example:

ORIGINAL TEXT

The quasi-official division of the population into three economic classes called high-, middle-, and low-income groups rather misses the point, because as a class indicator the amount of money is not as important as the source.   –PAUL FUSSELL, "Notes on Class"

WITH ELLIPSES

As Paul Fussell argues, "The quasi-official division of the population into three economic classes . . . rather misses the point. . . ."

In this example, the ellipses are used to indicate two different omissions—one in the middle of the sentence and one at the end of the sentence. When you omit the last part of a quoted sentence, add a period before the ellipsis—for a total of four dots. Be sure a complete sentence comes before and after the four points. If your quotation ends with a source documentation (such as a page number, a name, or a title), follow these steps:

1. Use three ellipsis points but no period after the quotation.
2. Add the closing quotation mark, closed up to the third ellipsis point.
3. Add the source documentation in parentheses.
4. Use a period to indicate the end of the sentence.

Hawthorne writes, "My friend, whom I shall call Oberon—it was a name of fancy and friendship between him and me . . ." (575).

Indicating a pause or hesitation

What you get is . . . the view from Oswald's rifle.
                                        —TOM WOLFE, "Pornoviolence"

Because of her creativity with her flowers, even my memories of poverty are seen through a screen of blooms—sunflowers, petunias, roses, dahlias, forsythia, spirea, delphiniums, verbena . . . and on and on.
                        —ALICE WALKER, *In Search of Our Mothers' Gardens*

EXERCISE 32.4

Complete the following sentence, incorporating only those *parts* of the passage below it that you need to make a complete grammatical sentence. Use ellipsis points to indicate what you have omitted.

In Mortimer Adler's *How to Read a Book*, he says that . . .

If we consider men and women generally, and apart from their professions or occupations, there is only one situation I can think of in which they almost pull themselves up by their bootstraps, making an effort to read better than they usually do. When they are in love and are reading a love letter, they read for all they are worth. They read every word three ways; they read between the lines and in the margins; they read the whole in terms of the parts, and each part in terms of the whole; they grow sensitive to context and ambiguity, to insinuation and implication; they perceive the color of words, the odor of phrases, and the weight of sentences. They may even take the punctuation into account. Then, if never before or after, they read.
                            —MORTIMER ADLER, *How to Read a Book*

EXERCISE 32.5

The following sentences use the punctuation marks presented in this chapter very effectively. Read the sentences carefully; then choose one, and use it as a model for writing a sentence of your own, making sure to use the punctuation marks in the same way in your sentence.

1. The dad was—how can you put this gracefully?—a real blimp, a wide load, and the white polyester stretch-pants only emphasized the cargo.
   —GARRISON KEILLOR, "Happy to Be Here"

2. I took exercise daily (as I still do), did not smoke (and still don't), and though excessively fond of wine, seldom drank spirits, not much liking the taste of them.   —JAN MORRIS, "To Everest"

3. Not only are the distinctions we draw between male nature and female nature largely arbitrary and often pure superstition: they are completely beside the point.   —BRIGID BROPHY, "Women"

4. One day a man would be ascending the pyramid at a terrific clip, and the next—bingo!—he would reach his own limits in the most unexpected way.
   —TOM WOLFE, The Right Stuff

5. A few traditions, thank heaven, remain fixed in the summer state of things—the June collapse of the Giants, Gaylord Perry throwing (or not throwing) spitballs, Hank Aaron hitting homers, and the commissioner . . . well, commissioning.   —ROGER ANGELL, Five Seasons

READING WITH AN EYE FOR PUNCTUATION

Although Emily Dickinson's poems are characteristically punctuated with dashes, the first editor of her work systematically eliminated them. Here is a brief Dickinson poem—with her original dashes restored. Read it twice, first ignoring the dashes and then using them to guide your reading. What effect does the final dash have? Finally, try composing a four-line poem that uses dashes to guide reading and meaning.

> Much Madness is divinest Sense—
> To a discerning Eye—
> Much Sense—the starkest Madness—
> 'Tis the Majority
> In this, as All, prevail—
> Assent—and you are sane—
> Demur—you're straightway dangerous—
> And handled with a Chain—
>
>   —EMILY DICKINSON

FOR EXAMINING PUNCTUATION IN YOUR OWN WRITING

Look through a draft you have recently written or are working on, and check your use of parentheses, brackets, dashes, colons, slashes, and ellipses. Have you followed the conventions presented in this chapter? If not, revise accordingly. Then read through the draft again, looking especially at all the parentheses and dashes. Are there too many? Check the material in parentheses to see if it could use more emphasis and thus be set off instead with dashes. Then check any material in dashes to see if it could do with less emphasis and thus be punctuated with commas or parentheses. If you keep a writing log, enter some examples of this work in your log.

PART SEVEN

Understanding Mechanical Conventions

33. Using Capitals

AT ONE TIME, ALL LETTERS WERE WRITTEN AS CAPITALS, LIKE THIS. By the time that movable type was invented, a new system had evolved, and printers used a capital letter only for the first letter of any word they felt was particularly important. Today, the conventions of capitalization are fairly well standardized. This chapter presents those conventions.

33a. Using capitals for the first word of a sentence or of a line of poetry

Capitalize the first word of a sentence.

Family photos bring great pleasure.

May I take your picture?

Smile, and say cheese!

If you are quoting a full sentence, set off that sentence, too, with an initial capital letter.

Everyone was asking the question, "What will I do after I graduate?"

Capitalization of a sentence following a colon is optional.

Gould cites the work of Darwin: The [or the] theory of natural selection incorporates the principle of evolutionary ties between all animals.

A sentence that is set off within another sentence by dashes or parentheses should not be capitalized. Note, however, that a sentence within parentheses that stands by itself *is* capitalized.

Those assigned to transports were not humiliated like washouts—*somebody* had to fly those planes—nevertheless, they, too, had been *left behind* for lack of the right stuff.

It *heaved*, it moved up and down underneath his feet, it pitched up, it pitched down, it rolled to port (this great beast *rolled!*) and it rolled to starboard, as the ship moved into the wind and, therefore, into the waves, and the wind kept sweeping across, sixty feet up in the air out in the open sea, and there were no railings whatsoever.

Or a man could go for a routine physical one fine day, feeling like a million dollars, and be grounded for *fallen arches*. It happened!—just like that! (And try raising them.)

—Tom Wolfe, *The Right Stuff*

The first word of each line in a poem is also usually capitalized.

> Loveliest of trees, the cherry now
> Is hung with bloom along the bough,
> And stands about the woodland ride
> Wearing white for Eastertide.
> —A. E. Housman, "Loveliest of Trees"

Some poets do *not* capitalize each line, however. When citing lines from a poem that has unconventional capitalization, copy them exactly as they appear in their original form.

> What was our hurry? Sunday afternoon
> beckoned with radioed ballgames, soft ice cream,
> furtive trips into the country, naps
> for the elderly, daydreams for the young,
> while blind growth steamed to the horizon of hills,
> the Lord ignoring His own injunction to rest.
> —John Updike, "Leaving Church Early"

33b. Using capitals for proper nouns and proper adjectives

Capitalize **proper nouns** (those naming specific persons, places, and things) and **proper adjectives** formed from them. In general, do not capitalize **common nouns** (those naming general classes of people, places, and things) unless they start a sentence. When used as part of a proper noun, however, many common nouns are capitalized.

PROPER	COMMON
Alfred Hitchcock, Hitchcockian	a director, directorial
Brazil, Brazilian	a nation
Golden Gate Bridge	a bridge

Following are some categories of words that are commonly capitalized:

NAMES OF INDIVIDUALS

Martin Luther King, Jr.	Eleanor Roosevelt
Bette Davis	Willie Mays
X. J. Kennedy	Toni Morrison
Aristotelian logic	Petrarchan sonnet form

NAMES OF GEOGRAPHICAL AREAS

Asia	Pacific Ocean
Nepal	Painted Desert
St. Louis	Sugarloaf Mountain
the Dead Sea	Michigan Avenue

STRUCTURES AND MONUMENTS

Flatiron Building	Lincoln Memorial
Golden Gate Bridge	Coit Tower

SHIPS, TRAINS, AIRCRAFT, AND SPACECRAFT

S.S. *Titanic*	Broadway Limited
Spirit of St. Louis	*Pioneer II*

INSTITUTIONS AND ORGANIZATIONS

Library of Congress	Kiwanis Club
University of Oklahoma	United Auto Workers
Skyline High School	Democratic Party

HISTORICAL EVENTS, ERAS, AND CALENDAR ITEMS

Shays' Rebellion	Saturday
the Great Depression	July
Reformation	Memorial Day

RELIGIONS AND RELIGIOUS SUBJECTS

Buddhism, Buddhists	Allah
Catholicism, Catholics	Jesus Christ
Hinduism, Hindus	God
Islam, Moslems or Muslims	the Bible
Judaism, Jews	the Koran

RACES, NATIONALITIES, AND LANGUAGES

Afro-American	Portuguese
Chicano	Chinese
Slavic	Japanese
Arab	Latin

TRADE NAMES

Reeboks	Huggies
Xerox	Levi's
Chanel	Land's End

▌1. Using capitals for titles of individuals

Capitalize titles used before a proper name, but not those used alone or following a proper name.

Justice O'Connor	Sandra Day O'Connor, the justice
Senator Paul Simon	Paul Simon, the senator
Professor Lisa Ede	Lisa Ede, the professor
Doctor Edward Davies	Edward Davies, the doctor

When they are used without a name attached, most titles are not capitalized. The only exceptions are titles of some very powerful officials—for example, many writers capitalize the word *President* when it refers to the President of the United States.

▌2. Using capitals for specific academic institutions and courses

Capitalize specific schools, departments, or courses, but not the common nouns or names of general subject areas.

University of California (*but* a California university)
History Department (*but* a history major)
Political Science 10 (*but* political science for nonmajors)

33c. Using capitals for titles of works

Capitalize most words in titles of books, articles, stories, essays, plays, poems, documents, films, paintings, and musical compositions. Articles *(a, an, the)*, prepositions, conjunctions, and the *to* of an infinitive are not capitalized unless they are the first or last words in a title or subtitle.

Gone with the Wind	"Fire and Ice"
"Revelation"	Magna Carta
"Shooting an Elephant"	*Dirty Harry*
Our Town	*The Magic Flute*

Remember to capitalize the titles of your own compositions.

33d. Using capitals for the pronoun *I* and the interjection *O*

Always capitalize the pronoun *I* and the interjection *O*. Be careful, however, to distinguish between the interjection *O* and *oh*. *O* is an older form that is usually used for direct address in ceremonial register (see 26c4). It is always capitalized, whereas *oh* is not unless it begins a sentence.

I took her advice, and oh, how I regretted it!

Grant us peace, O Lord.

33e. Checking for unnecessary capitals

1. With compass directions, unless the word designates a specific geographic place

John Muir headed west, filled with the need to explore. The nation was at that time divided into three competing economic sections: the Northeast, the South, and the West.

2. With family relationships, unless the word is used as part of the name or as a substitute for the name

My nieces, Jamie and Marianne, both live in blue jeans.

We all agreed that Father had every right to be grumpy.

The train on which Uncle Charlie arrived spewed out thick black smoke, foreshadowing a disastrous visit.

3. With medical and scientific terms, except for proper nouns that are part of the term

scarlet fever
Kaposi's sarcoma
insectivore

deoxyribonucleic acid
Wassermann test
homo sapiens

EXERCISE 33.1

Capitalize words as needed in the following sentences.

Example

t. s. eliot, who wrote *the waste land,* worked as an editor at faber and faber.

T. S. Eliot, who wrote *The Waste Land,* worked as an editor at Faber and Faber.

1. the town in the south where i was raised had a civil war monument in the center of main street.
2. eating at a restaurant, whether it be a fast-food, chinese, or italian place, is always a treat.
3. his car skidded right into the rear end of a plymouth van.
4. the council of trent was convened to draw up the catholic response to the protestant reformation.
5. in the *odyssey,* three members of odysseus's crew go ashore and lose their memories by eating the lotus plant.
6. i wondered if my new lee jeans were faded enough and if i could possibly scuff up my new nikes just a little more before i arrived for spring term.
7. in a speech accepting an award for the musical score for the film the high and the mighty, dimitri tiomkin began by thanking beethoven, brahms, wagner, and strauss.
8. in this essay i will be citing the works of vladimir nabokov, in particular his novels *pnin* and *lolita* and his story "the vane sisters."
9. the battle of lexington and concord was fought in april 1775.
10. few music lovers can resist the music of george gershwin. (*rhapsody in blue* and *porgy and bess* are two personal favorites.)

EXERCISE 33.2

Turn to page 186, and read the poem by E. E. Cummings. Pay particular attention to his use of capitalization: how does it help you to understand the poem?

CHECKING FOR UNNECESSARY CAPITALS

READING WITH AN EYE FOR CAPITALIZATION

The following poem uses capitalization in an unconventional way. Read it
over a few times, at least once aloud. What effect does the capitalization have
on your understanding and recitation of the poem? Why do you think the poet
chose to use capitals as she did?

> A little Madness in the Spring
> Is wholesome even for the King,
> But God be with the Clown—
> Who ponders this tremendous scene—
> This whole Experiment of Green—
> As if it were his own!
> —EMILY DICKINSON

FOR EXAMINING YOUR OWN USE OF CAPITAL LETTERS

Read over something you have written recently with an eye for capitalization.
Have you capitalized all proper nouns and adjectives? Have you used capitals
properly with dashes and parentheses? Have you capitalized sentences following
colons, and if so, have you done so consistently? If you keep a writing log,
enter notes and examples of any problems you have with capital letters.

34. Using Abbreviations and Numbers

In his essays and by the example of his life, Henry David Thoreau urged us to "simplify, simplify." Two of the tools that help us as writers to reach that goal are abbreviations and numerals. Both serve to speed up prose and thus to allow readers to process information most efficiently. As with other elements, there are certain conventions for using abbreviations and numerals, especially in formal or academic work. This chapter will explain these conventions to help you as a writer use abbreviations and numbers appropriately and correctly.*

ABBREVIATIONS

▌ 34a. Abbreviating personal and professional titles

When they are used before or after a name, most personal and professional titles and academic degrees are regularly abbreviated, even in academic writing.

Ms. Gloria Steinem   St. Matthew
Mr. Richard Guenette   Paul Irvin, M.D.
Dr. Nancy Carlman   Jamie Barlow Kayes, Ph.D.

---

*For rules on using abbreviations and numbers in a particular discipline, you might ask your instructor what style manual you should consult. In general, the *MLA Handbook for Writers of Research Papers* is usually followed in the humanities; the *Publication Manual of the American Psychological Association*, in the social sciences; and the *CBE Style Manual*, in the natural sciences.

Less common titles, including religious, military, academic, and government titles, may be abbreviated when they appear before a full name. If they appear before only a surname, the title should be spelled out. In academic writing, such titles should always be spelled out.

Rev. Jesse Jackson	the Reverend Jesse Jackson
Col. Oliver Wickham	Colonel Wickham
Prof. Linda Johnson	Professor Johnson
Sen. Nancy Kassebaum	Senator Kassebaum

Never abbreviate personal or professional titles used alone.

MISUSED   She was a rigorous *prof.*, and we worked hard.

REVISED   She was a rigorous *professor*, and we worked hard.

Use either a title or an academic degree, but not both.

MISUSED   Dr. James Dillon, Ph.D.

REVISED   Dr. James Dillon

REVISED   James Dillon, Ph.D.

▮ 34b. Using abbreviations with numerals

The following abbreviations are always acceptable, as long as they are used with numerals.

399 B.C. ("before Christ"; follows the date)

A.D. 49 (*anno Domini*, Latin for "year of our Lord"; precedes the date)

11:15 A.M. (*ante meridiem*, Latin for "before noon")

9:00 P.M. (*post meridiem*, Latin for "after noon")

2700 r.p.m. (revolutions per minute)

212°F (Fahrenheit scale)

24°C (Centigrade or Celsius scale)

Abbreviations for some units of measurement *(km, cc, lb., qts.)* are frequently used in scientific and technical writing—but again, only with a numeral (see 34d).

▮ 34c. Using acronyms and initial abbreviations

Abbreviations that can be pronounced as words are called **acronyms:** NOW, for example, is the acronym for the National Organization of Women. **Initial abbreviations** are those which are pronounced, quite literally, as separate initials: ETS for Educational Testing Service, for instance. Many of the most common abbreviations of these types come from business, government, and science: NASA, PBS, DNA, GE, UNICEF, AIDS, SAT.

As long as you can be sure your readers will understand them, you can use such abbreviations in much of your college writing. You have to use them carefully and according to convention, however. If you are using a term only once or twice in a paper, you should spell it out, but when you need to use a term repeatedly, abbreviating it will serve as a convenience for you and your readers alike.

If you need to use an abbreviation your readers may not know, you can do so as long as you first "define" it for them. Spell out the full term at the first use, and give the abbreviation in parentheses. After that, you can use the abbreviation by itself.

> The Comprehensive Test Ban (CTB) Treaty was first proposed in the 1950s. For those nations signing it, the CTB would bring to a halt all nuclear weapons testing.

∎ 34d. Checking for inappropriate abbreviations

Abbreviations exist to facilitate reading and writing, but they are not appropriate in all writing contexts. The following guidelines will help you to use some common abbreviations in the writing you do for your college courses.

Company names

It is acceptable to use such abbreviations as *Inc.*, *Co.*, and *Corp.* and the ampersand symbol (&) if they are part of a company's official name. You should not, however, use these abbreviated forms in most other contexts.

> One company—Sears, Roebuck & Co.—had sales of over $27 billion and a net income of just over $650 million in 1981 alone.

Reference information

Though it is conventional to abbreviate such words as *chapter* (ch.) or *page* (p.) in endnotes or source citations, it is not acceptable to do so in the body of your essay.

| INAPPROPRIATE | In his preface to the 1851 *ed.* of *Twice-Told Tales,* Hawthorne states that the stories are not autobiographical. |
| REVISED | In his preface to the 1851 *edition* of *Twice-Told Tales,* Hawthorne states that the stories are not autobiographical. |

Latin abbreviations

In general, avoid the following abbreviations except when citing sources or making parenthetical remarks.

c.f.	compare *(confer)*
e.g.	for example *(exempli gratia)*
et al.	and others *(et alii)*
etc.	and so forth *(et cetera)*
i.e.	that is *(id est)*
N.B.	note well *(nota bene)*

| INAPPROPRIATE | Many firms now have policies to help working parents—e.g., flexible hours, maternity leave, day care. |
| REVISED | Many firms now have policies to help working parents—*for example,* flexible hours, maternity leave, day care. |

Geographical places

Place names can be abbreviated in informal correspondence or in reference notes, but they should always be written out within sentences.

| INAPPROPRIATE | Tired of life in the East, we set off for Cloverdale, *Calif.* |
| REVISED | Tired of life in the East, we set off for Cloverdale, *California.* |

One common exception is *U.S.,* which is acceptable used as an adjective, though not as a noun.

| UNACCEPTABLE | As an exchange student, I spent a summer in the *U.S.* |
| ACCEPTABLE | The *U.S. delegation* negotiated the treaty with success. |

495

Symbols

Symbols such as ¢ @ # % + and = should not be used in the body of a paper, though they are commonly used in graphs and tables. One common exception is the dollar sign ($), which is acceptable to use with figures.

INAPPROPRIATE	Less than 50% of those who applied were accepted.
REVISED	Less than 50 *percent* of those who applied were accepted.

Units of measurement

Except for scientific and technical writing, most units of measurement should not be abbreviated in the body of a paper.

INAPPROPRIATE	The ball sailed 400 *ft.* over the leftfield fence.
REVISED	The ball sailed 400 *feet* over the leftfield fence.

EXERCISE 34.1

Revise each of the following sentences to eliminate any abbreviations that would be inappropriate in academic writing.

Example

Ishi's story began in Oroville, Calif., in the early 1900s.

Ishi's story began in Oroville, California, in the early 1900s.

1. We breathed a sigh of relief when we met the dr., a young woman with a very confident manner.
2. An MX missile is 71 ft. long, 92 in. around, and weighs 190,000 lbs.
3. Even AT&T has lowered its long-distance rates by 6% this year.
4. In 1955 the Rev. Martin Luther King, Jr., was elected president of the Montgomery Improvement Assoc.
5. Levi Strauss is one co. that has long offered childcare to its workers.
6. Like black-and-white TV, the 5¢ candy bar is a relic of the past.
7. Founded in 1966, NOW fights discrimination against women.
8. PBS is promoting more and better programs in the arts throughout the country, not just in L.A. and N.Y.C.
9. After less than a yr. of attendance, Edgar Allan Poe withdrew from the U. of VA and joined the U.S. army.
10. Dostoevsky was influenced by many European writers—e.g., Dickens, Stendhal, and Balzac.

NUMBERS

▌ 34e. Spelling out numbers of one or two words

If a number can be written as one or two words, spell it out.

The victim's screams were heard by *thirty-eight* people, none of whom called the police.

Six days later, police arrested the assailant.

▌ 34f. Using figures for numbers longer than two words

Numbers that cannot be written in one or two words should be stated in figures.

Did you know that a baseball is wrapped in 174 yards of blue-gray wool yarn and is held together by 216 red stitches?

If one of several numbers in the same sentence needs to be expressed in figures, they all should be expressed that way.

INCONSISTENT	A complete audio system can range in cost from one hundred dollars to $2,500; however, a reliable system can be purchased for approximately five hundred dollars.
CONSISTENT	A complete audio system can range in cost from $100 to $2,500; however, a reliable system can be purchased for approximately $500.

▌ 34g. Spelling out numbers that begin sentences

When a sentence begins with a number, spell out the number or rewrite the sentence.

INAPPROPRIATE	277,000 hours, or 119 years, of CIA labor cost taxpayers $16 million.
HARD TO READ	Two hundred seventy-seven thousand hours, or one hundred nineteen years of CIA labor, cost taxpayers $16 million.
REVISED	Taxpayers spend $16 million for 277,000 hours, or 119 years, of CIA labor.

▌ 34h. Using figures according to convention

ADDRESSES

23 Main Street; 175 Fifth Avenue, New York, NY 10010

DATES

September 17, 1951, 411 B.C., 1865
Spell out dates that do not include the year: *June sixth.*
Spell out decades and centuries: *the fifties, the twentieth century.*

DECIMALS, FRACTIONS, AND PERCENTAGES

65.34, 8½, 77% (or 77 percent)

DIVISIONS OF BOOKS AND PLAYS

Volume 5, Pages 81–85 (*not* 81–5)
Act III, Scene ii (or Act 3, Scene 2), lines 3–9

SPECIFIC AMOUNTS OF MONEY

$7,348, $1.46 trillion
Spell out dollars or cents of two or three words: *fifty cents.*

SCORES AND STATISTICS

an 8–3 Red Sox victory, a verbal score of 650
average age of 22, a mean of 53, a ratio of 3 to 1

TIME OF DAY

6:00 A.M., 5:45 P.M., eight o'clock
Without A.M. or P.M., spell out time: *five in the morning.*
With the word *o'clock*, spell out time: *four o'clock*, not *4 o'clock.*

EXERCISE 34.2

Revise the numbers in the following sentences as necessary for correctness and consistency. If a sentence is correct, circle its number.

Example
The art of rhetoric began, in Sicily, in the 5th century B.C.
The art of rhetoric began, in Sicily, in the *fifth century* B.C.

1. 307 miles long and eighty-two miles wide, the island offered little.
2. Some call it the handbook for the 90s.
3. You can travel around the city for only 65 cents.

4. I am writing in response to a letter submitted to the *Times-Picayune* on December ninth, 1984 by George F. Lundy.
5. The Department of Health and Human Services has received 1,633 calls and has investigated forty-three incidents.
6. Educational broadcasting is at present available to seventy-two percent of the population.
7. Walker signed a three-year, $4.5 million contract.
8. In the thirty-five through 44 age group, the risk is estimated to be about 1 in 2,500.
9. Frankly, we consider 25 cents enough for a five-year-old.
10. The ancient amulet measured one and one-eighth by two and two-fifths inches.

EXERCISE 34.3

Revise the following passage adapted from an essay by Jean Shepherd ("Hairy Gertz and the Forty-Seven Crappies") to make its treatment of abbreviations and numbers correct and consistent.

> And in the middle of the lake, several yds. away, are over 17,000 fishermen, in wooden rowboats rented at a buck and a ½ an hr. It is 2 A.M. The temp is 175, with humidity to match. And the smell of decayed toads, the dumps at the far end of the lake, and an occasional soupçon of Std. Oil, whose refinery is a couple of mi. away, is enough to put hair on the back of a mud turtle. 17 thousand guys clumped together in the middle fishing for the known 64 crappies in that lake. . . . Each boat contains a minimum of 9 guys and 14 cases of beer. And once in a while, in the darkness, is heard the sound of a guy falling over backward into the slime: SSSSGLUNK!

FOR EXAMINING YOUR OWN USE OF ABBREVIATIONS AND NUMBERS

Look over an essay or two that you have written, noting all the places where you use abbreviations and numbers. Check your usage for both correctness and consistency. If you discover anything you have done wrong, make a note of it (in your writing log, if you are keeping one) so that you will do it correctly the next time.

35. Using Italics

After the invention of printing, most type-carvers produced type that printed letters with the vertical strokes straight up and down, as in this sentence; today such type is called *roman*. Early Italian type designers, however, came to specialize in a slanted type, *like this*, known today as *italic*. Italics are used to set off words and phrases for special consideration or emphasis. As with other formal devices in writing, italic usage is governed by conventions, which this chapter presents.

If you have a fairly sophisticated word processor and printer, you may be able to print italic type. Otherwise, you can indicate italics by underlining the words you wish to treat in that way.

35a. Using italics for titles

In general, italics are used to signal the titles of long or complete works; shorter works or sections of works are set off with quotation marks. Use italics for the following kinds of works:

BOOKS

A *Tale of Two Cities*
Personal Memoirs of U. S. Grant

CHOREOGRAPHIC WORKS

Martha Graham's *Frontier*
Agnes De Mille's *Rodeo*

FILMS

Psycho
Black Orpheus

JOURNALS

New England Journal of Medicine
Daedalus

LONG MUSICAL WORKS

Bach's *The Well-Tempered Clavier*
The Grateful Dead's *American Beauty*

LONG POEMS

The Odyssey
Hiawatha

MAGAZINES

Newsweek
the *New Yorker*

NEWSPAPERS

the *New York Times*
the *Cleveland Plain Dealer*

PAMPHLETS

Thomas Paine's *Common Sense*

PAINTINGS AND SCULPTURE

Picasso's *Three Musicians*
O'Keeffe's *Black Iris*

PLAYS

Long Day's Journey into Night
She Stoops to Conquer

TELEVISION AND RADIO PROGRAMS

The David Letterman Show
All Things Considered

A couple of exceptions are worth noting. Sacred books, such as the
Bible or the Koran; and public documents, such as the Constitution
or the Magna Carta, should *not* be italicized. Notice also with magazines and newspapers that an initial *the* is neither italicized nor capitalized, even if it is part of the official name.

35b. Using italics for words, letters, and numbers referred to as words

Italicize words, letters, or numbers referred to as words.

> Words like *romantic, plastic, values, human, dead, sentimental, natural, vitality,* as used in art criticism, are strictly meaningless, in the sense that they not only do not point to any discoverable object, but are hardly ever expected to do so by the reader.
>
> —GEORGE ORWELL, "Politics and the English Language"

> The first four orbitals are represented by the letters *s, p, d,* and *f,* in lieu of numerical values.

> On the back of his jersey was the famous *24.*

Italics are also sometimes used to signal a word that is being defined.

> Learning to play the flute depends mostly on *embouchure*—the way in which the lips are positioned over the mouthpiece.

35c. Using italics for foreign words and phrases

Italicize words and phrases from other languages unless they are so frequently used by English speakers that they have come to be considered a part of English. The French word "bourgeois" or the Italian "pasta," for instance, do not need to be italicized. If you are in doubt about whether or not to italicize a particular word, most dictionaries offer guidelines.

> At last one of the phantom sleighs gliding along the street would come to a stop, and with gawky haste Mr. Burness in his fox-furred *shapka* would make for our door.
>
> —VLADIMIR NABOKOV, *Speak, Memory*

> One cannot overestimate the usefulness of *Schlag* and *Zug.*
>
> —MARK TWAIN, "The Awful German Language"

Note, in addition, that Latin genus and species names are always signaled by italics.

> The caterpillars of *Hapalia,* when attacked by the wasp *Apanteles machaeralis,* drop suddenly from their leaves and suspend themselves in air by a silken thread.
>
> —STEPHEN JAY GOULD, "Nonmoral Nature"

35d. Using italics for the names of vehicles

Italicize names of specific aircraft, spacecraft, ships, and trains. Do not italicize types and classes, such as "Learjet," "space shuttle," "airbus," or "Bonanza."

AIRCRAFT AND SPACECRAFT

Spirit of St. Louis
Pioneer VII

SHIPS

the *Santa Maria*
U.S.S. *Missouri*

TRAINS

The *Orient Express*
The *Montrealer*

35e. Using italics for special emphasis

Just as vocal stress can add emphasis in spoken language, so italics can help create emphasis in writing.

> *Now* is the time to make real the promises of democracy.
> —MARTIN LUTHER KING, JR., "I Have a Dream"

> Gil's homer pulled the cork, and now there arose from all over the park a full, furious, happy shout of "Let's go, *Mets!* Let's go, *Mets!*" There were wild cries of encouragement before every pitch, boos for every called strike. . . . The fans' hopes, of course, *were* insane.
> —ROGER ANGELL, *The Summer Game*

> I am one of those unambitious lawyers who never address a jury, or in any way draw down public applause; but, in the cool tranquillity of a snug retreat, do a snug business among rich men's bonds, and mortgages, and title-deeds. All who know me, consider me an eminently *safe* man.
> —HERMAN MELVILLE, "Bartleby, the Scrivener"

Although italic emphasis is useful on occasion, especially in informal writing, it is best to use it sparingly. It is usually better to create emphasis with sentence structure and word choice.

EXERCISE 35.1

In each of the following sentences, underline any words that should be italicized and circle any italicized words that should not be.

> *Example*
> Those who can take it consider Dirty Harry a first-rate film.
> Those who can take it consider *Dirty Harry* a first-rate film.

1. Hawthorne's story *My Kinsman, Major Molineux* bears a striking resemblance to Shakespeare's play A Midsummer Night's Dream.
2. When people think about the word business, they may associate it with people and companies that care about nothing but making money.
3. Georgetown offers a great blend of cultures and styles, a *potpourri* of people.
4. The word *veterinary* comes from the Latin *veterinarius,* meaning *of beasts of burden.*
5. Niko Tinbergen's essay *The Bee-Hunters of Hulshorst* is a diary of the experiments performed by the author on *Philanthus triangulum Fabr,* the *bee-killer wasp.*
6. Flying the Glamorous Glennis, a plane named for his wife, Chuck Yeager was the first pilot to fly faster than the speed of sound.
7. The Washington Post provides extensive coverage of Congress.
8. The Waste Land is a long and difficult but ultimately rewarding poem.
9. If you have seen only a reproduction of Picasso's Guernica, you can scarcely imagine the impact the original painting makes.
10. My grandparents remember the sinking of the Titanic.

READING WITH AN EYE FOR ITALICS

The following passage about a graduate English seminar uses italics in several different ways—for emphasis, for a foreign phrase, and for a title. Read the passage carefully, particularly noting the effects created by the italics. How would it differ without any italic emphasis? What other words or phrases might Ozick have chosen to emphasize?

> To get into this seminar, you had to submit to a grilling wherein you renounced all former allegiance to the then-current literary religion, New Criticism, which considered that only the text existed, not the world. I passed the interview by lying—cunningly, and against my real convictions. I said that probably the world *did* exist—and walked triumphantly into the seminar room.
> There were four big tables arranged in a square, with everyone's feet sticking out into the open middle of the square. You could tell who was nervous, and how much, by watching the pairs of feet twist around each other.

The Great Man presided awesomely from the high bar of the square. His head was a majestic granite-gray, like a centurion in command; he *looked* famous. His clean shoes twitched only slightly, and only when he was angry.

It turned out he was angry at me a lot of the time. He was angry because he thought me a disrupter, a rioter, a provocateur, and a fool; also crazy. And this was twenty years ago, before these things were *de rigueur* in the universities. Everything was very quiet in those days: there were only the Cold War and Korea and Joe McCarthy and the Old Old Nixon, and the only revolutionaries around were in Henry James's *The Princess Casamassima*.

–CYNTHIA OZICK, "We Are the Crazy Lady"

FOR EXAMINING ITALICS IN YOUR OWN WRITING

Write a paragraph or two describing the most eccentric person you know. Make a point to italicize some words for special emphasis. Read your passage aloud to see what effect the italics bring. Consider italicizing any other words you wish to emphasize. Now explain each use of italics, stating in words the reason for the special attention. If you find yourself unable to give a reason, ask yourself whether the word should in fact be italicized at all. Then revise the passage to eliminate *all but one* use of italics. Try revising sentences and choosing more precise words to convey emphasis without italics. Compare the various versions, and decide which one is the most effective. Can you make any conclusions about using italics for emphasis? If you keep a writing log, add to it any thoughts, with examples from this exercise. In addition, you might keep your eye open for italics in your reading and copy down in your log any examples that impress you.

36. Using Hyphens

the lady whose odd smile is the merest hyphen
—KARL SHAPIRO

The "merest" hyphen is a small horizontal line used to divide words at the end of a line and to link words or word parts (such as *hand-me-down* or *bye-bye*). As such, it serves purposes both mechanical and rhetorical. Its mechanical ones are fairly straightforward, with simple rules that tell us when and where to divide a word at the end of a line. The rhetorical ones, however, are somewhat more complicated, for though they are governed in some cases by rules, they are, in other cases, defined by the needs of readers. Stewart Beach points out the rhetorical usefulness of a hyphen nicely in his comments about one experience he recalled having as a reader:

> I came across a word I thought was a series of typos for *collaborators*. Reading it again, I realized the word was *colaborers*. But a hyphen would have [prevented] all the confusion.   —STEWART BEACH

Indeed, had the word included a hyphen—*co-laborers*—its meaning would have been instantly clear. Sometimes the dictionary will tell you when to hyphenate a word. Other times, you will be putting together words in ways not listed in a dictionary, and you will have to decide whether or not to add a hyphen. This chapter will help you with the decisions and the rules that go along with using hyphens.

36a. Using hyphens to divide words at the end of a line

Hyphens are used at the end of a line to break a word that will be completed on the next line. It is best not to have to divide words in this way, but sometimes you must. When you do, the main thing to remember is to break words between syllables. The word *metaphor*, for instance, is made up of three syllables (*met-a-phor*), and you could break it after either the *t* or the *a*. All dictionaries show syllable breaks, and so the best advice for dividing words correctly is simply to look them up. In addition, you should follow certain other conventions, including the following:

- *Never divide one-syllable words*, even relatively long words such as *draught* or *through*.
- *Divide compound words only between the parts.* Words such as *head-ache* or *mother-in-law* should be broken between their parts (*head-ache*) or at their hyphens (*mother-in-law*).
- *Divide words with prefixes or suffixes between the parts.* The word *disappearance*, then, might be broken after its prefix (*dis-appearance*) or before its suffix (*disappear-ance*). Prefixed words that include hyphens, such as *self-righteous*, should be divided at the hyphen.
- *Never divide abbreviations, contractions, or figures.* Though such "words" as *NASA*, *didn't*, and *250* do have audible syllables, it is not permissible to divide them in writing.
- *Leave at least two letters when dividing a word.* Words such as *acorn* (*a-corn*) or *scratchy* (*scratch-y*), therefore, cannot be divided at all, and a word such as *Americana* (*A-mer-i-can-a*) can be broken only after the *r* or the *i*.

EXERCISE 36.1

Divide each of the following words into syllables, first referring to your dictionary. Then indicate with a hyphen the places where you might break each word at the end of a line. Indicate any words that cannot be divided into syllables or broken at the end of a line.

1. passable
2. retract
3. scoffed
4. military
5. antechamber

6. other-centered
7. haven't
8. dimming
9. anonymous
10. attitude

■ 36b. Using hyphens with compound words

Compound words are words such as *rowboat* or *up-to-date* that are made up of more than one word. Compound words are written as one word, as separate words, or with hyphens.

ONE WORD	*grandmother, textbook, extraterrestrial*
SEPARATE WORDS	*high school, parking meter, floppy disk*
WITH HYPHENS	*city-state, great-grandmother, ex-husband*

It is difficult, maybe even impossible, to know when a particular compound word is one word, separate words, or hyphenated. Even compounds that begin with the same word are even treated every which way—*blueberry, blue-collar,* and *blue cheese,* for instance. In general, then, you should always consult the dictionary to know how to spell compounds. There are, in addition, some conventions that can guide you in using hyphens with compound words.

1. Hyphenating compound modifiers

Often you will use compound modifiers that are not listed in a dictionary. The guiding principle then is to hyphenate most compound adjectives that precede a noun but not to hyphenate ones that follow a noun.

> a *hard-nosed* boss, a *two-to-one* decision
>
> My boss is extremely *hard nosed.*
>
> The decision against the plan was *two to one.*

In general, the reason for hyphenating such compound modifiers is to facilitate reading. Notice, for example, how the hyphen affects your understanding of the following two sentences.

> The designers used potted palms as *living room* dividers.
>
> The designers used potted palms as *living-room* dividers.

In the first sentence, the word *living* seems to modify *room dividers*; in the second, the hyphen makes clear that it is part of a compound adjective. Compound adjectives that are commonly used and thus likely to be easily understood by your readers, however, do not always need to be hyphenated—*income tax reform* or *first class mail* would never be misunderstood, for example.

Two more instances of compound modifiers that are never hyphenated include those with an adverb ending in *-ly* and those with comparative or superlative forms.

> a *radically different* approach
>
> *more extensive* coverage, the *most stimulating* group

A series of compound words in a sentence that share the same base word can be shortened by the use of suspended hyphens.

> I taught *two-, three-,* and *four-year-olds.*

I 2. Hyphenating specially coined compounds

You may sometimes coin your own original compounds, usually for descriptive reasons. Such **coined compounds** should always be hyphenated.

> Unfortunately, nature is very much a *now-you-see-it, now-you-don't* affair.   —ANNIE DILLARD, "Sight into Insight"
>
> The . . . problem with a *no-first-use* policy is that it might paradoxically increase the chances of nuclear war.
> —CHARLES KRAUTHAMMER, "In Defense of Deterrence"

I 3. Hyphenating fractions and compound numbers

To write out fractions, use a hyphen to join the numerator and denominator.

> one-seventh
> seven-sixteenths

Use hyphens to spell out whole numbers from twenty-one to ninety-nine, both when they stand alone and when they are part of larger numbers. (Note that such larger numbers can usually be written as numerals.)

> thirty-seven
> three hundred fifty-four thousand

I 36c. Using hyphens with prefixes and suffixes

Most words with prefixes or suffixes are written as one word, without hyphens: *antiwar, misinform, understated.* Only in the following cases do you need a hyphen with prefixed or suffixed words:

CAPITALIZED BASE WORDS

post-Civil War, pro-Democrat, un-American

FIGURES

pre-1960, post-1945

509

WITH ALL-, EX-, SELF-, AND -ELECT

all-state, ex-husband, self-possessed, mayor-elect

Note, however, that *selfish* is written without a hyphen because *self* acts as a root, not a prefix.

BEFORE COMPOUND WORDS

pre-high school, pro-civil rights

TO AVOID CONFUSION WITH HOMONYMS

Re-cover means to "cover again"; the hyphen distinguishes it from *recover* meaning "get well."

EXERCISE 36.2

Using the dictionary and this chapter, insert hyphens as needed in the following items. Circle the number of any item that is correct as it stands.

1. deionization
2. pre World War II
3. two and four-cylinder motorcycles
4. happily married couple
5. a come up and see me sometime gaze
6. self important
7. president elect
8. seven hundred thirty three
9. a hard working farmer
10. a politician who is quick witted

EXERCISE 36.3

Insert any necessary hyphens, delete any unnecessary ones, and correct any incorrect word divisions in the following sentences. Use your dictionary if necessary. Some of the sentences do not require any change.

1. Stress can lead to hypertension and ulcers.
2. McKuen began to write as an escape from his on the move life, which included various odd jobs ranging from ditchdigging to cookiecutting.
3. The carpenter asked for a two pound bag of three quarter inch nails.
4. Suicide among teen-agers has tripled in the past thirty five years, making it the third leading cause of death among fifteen to twentyfour year olds.
5. We encouraged him to be more open minded and to temper his dogmatic views.
6. Since the use of PCB's has been out-lawed, environmentalists feel somewhat encouraged.

7. One of Mikhail Baryshnikov's favorite dancers is none other than Fred A-staire.
8. The government declared an all-out war on poverty and homelessness.
9. The antiAmerican rally attracted large crowds.
10. The beautifully-written essay earned high praise.

READING WITH AN EYE FOR HYPHENATION

The following paragraph about semi-professional baseball uses many hyphens. Read it carefully, and note how the hyphens make the paragraph easier to read. Why is it necessary to hyphenate *junior-college* in the last sentence?

All semi-pro leagues, it should be understood, are self-sustaining, and have no farm affiliation or other connection with the twenty-six major-league clubs, or with the seventeen leagues and hundred and fifty-two teams (ranging from Rookie League at the lowest level, to Class A and Summer Class A, up to the AAA designation at the highest) that make up the National Association— the minors, that is. There is no central body of semi-pro teams, and semi-pro players are not included among the six hundred and fifty major-leaguers, the twenty-five hundred-odd minor-leaguers, plus all the managers, coaches, presidents, commissioners, front-office people, and scouts, who, taken together, constitute the great tent called organized ball. (A much diminished tent, at that; back in 1949, the minors included fifty-nine leagues, about four hundred and forty-eight teams, and perhaps ten thousand players.) Also outside the tent, but perhaps within its shade, are five college leagues, ranging across the country from Cape Cod to Alaska, where the most promising freshman, sophomore, and junior-college ballplayers may compete against each other in the summertime without losing their amateur status. . . .

–ROGER ANGELL, "In the Country"

FOR EXAMINING HYPHENATION IN YOUR OWN WRITING

Look carefully at an essay or assignment you are working on, particularly noting your use of hyphens. Have you broken words at the ends of lines correctly? Have you followed the conventions governing use of hyphens in compound words, with prefixes and suffixes, with fractions and numbers? If you find you are misusing hyphens or are unclear about how to use them in certain situations, check those instances against the advice in this chapter. If you are keeping a writing log, make an entry in it about anything with hyphens that confused you.

PART EIGHT

Doing Research and Using Sources

37. Becoming a Researcher

The English word *research* derives not only from the French *chercher*, which means to "search," but from the Late Latin *circare*, which means to "circle around, explore." **Research,** then, is a means of critical inquiry, of circling carefully around and around a subject, a process that the editors of the famous eleventh edition of the *Encyclopaedia Britannica* identify as all "investigations . . . based on sources of knowledge." Without research, they go on, "no authoritative words could have been written, no scientific discoveries or inventions made, no theories of any value propounded." Nor could many personal or work-related decisions be made. Consider the following situations:

> Your employer tells you that the company needs a new intercom system and asks you to recommend the best system for the money.
>
> You have an opportunity to visit Tokyo, but you can stay only one week. You want to plan that week.
>
> Some friends tell you that a song you admire is dedicated to the "disappeared." You determine to find out all you can about the song and the dedication.
>
> Your introduction to sociology professor asks you to write an essay on the clothing styles characteristic of young teenagers. You decide to visit a local junior high school.
>
> You are part of a task force charged with charting the responses of consumers to a product's new packaging.

As these situations illustrate, much, if not most, work relies on research: we find something out, and then we report on it. Some professions rely heavily on research—news reporting, police detection, and law, for example. In fact, this process of investigating sources and drawing conclusions based on what we find pervades our personal lives as well as our work. This chapter rests on that assumption. From this basic assumption come five important premises:

1. *You already know how to do research.* It is impossible to live in our consumer-oriented culture without knowing how to find out about things *and* how to act on such information. You act as a researcher whenever you investigate a product—whether a videotape, a cosmetic, a computer, or a car—by reading up on its reliability, discussing its features with your friends, or checking several stores to see what is in stock, how much it costs, and what it can do. You conducted research when you chose a college—and then when you studied the catalog, consulted your adviser, and talked with other students to plan your academic program.

You may not be able to name all the procedures of conducting research and presenting it in writing, but you do already possess many essential research skills. You know how to combine experience, observation, and new information when you try to solve a problem, answer a question, make a decision, or analyze a situation. You know how to seek out pieces of information, evaluate their usefulness, fit them all together, and then use them to make an "educated guess." Such basic research methods are not just academic requirements but important skills for working and living. You do—and will—use these skills whenever you make reasoned choices or whenever you discover and share knowledge with others. And these are the very skills you will build on as you become more familiar with academic research.

2. *Presenting your research in writing draws you into the conversation surrounding any area of inquiry.* Good research, in fact, makes you into a genuine expert. If you approach your research with serious intent, you may gradually become someone who knows more than anyone else on campus about Joseph McCarthy's political affiliations, or Wordsworth's "Lucy poems," or new uses of metal hybrids, or Jackie Robinson's place in sports history. You will be truly knowledgeable, and you will be able to add your knowledge to the conversation of educated people that goes on all about you, not only in college but in the media, in community groups, and in the workplace.

3. *Research is always driven by a purpose.* Whether for common everyday needs or for formal academic inquiry, researchers seek out facts and opinions for a reason—wanting to make a discovery; hoping to answer a question, solve a problem, or prove something; wishing to

teach or to correct an error or to advocate a position. Research is not an end in itself. Instead it is a process or method, used in many situations and fields, for systematically discovering, testing, and sharing new ideas.

4. *Your purpose influences the research you do, which in turn refines your purpose.* When you begin any research, it is impossible to know exactly what you will find out. You begin with a question you want to answer or a general idea that you want to probe or illustrate or prove. As research discovery leads to discovery, your initial idea may come into sharper focus and become stronger and more detailed—or it could fail to take useful shape and even be replaced by some other idea. Only after you have done a fair amount of searching, re-searching, and writing will you know whether your initial idea should remain the focus of your research.

5. *Although research typically begins with a problem or question and moves toward a solution or answer, it is almost always a recursive rather than a linear process.* In other words, research rarely progresses in a neat line from start to finish. Doing research might be likened to following an upward spiral, winding round and round but steadily progressing toward the top. You begin with an idea that may or may not be concrete, explorable, or supportable. Then you follow the spiral through some background research and perhaps some writing. Your initial investigation may lead you to start all over again—or to modify your idea and then to spiral further upward to more specific sources. This additional research sharpens your idea even more, leading you to more and more specific sources. As you read and investigate the topic, your initial ideas get focused and modified (and occasionally completely disproved) by what you find. The spiral sometimes causes you to circle past familiar materials; occasionally seeing them from a different perspective helps you to ask different and more sophisticated questions. Writing is an important part of this investigative spiral, for it forces you to sharpen your ideas and perhaps to turn back to your sources for more information. Wherever the spiral of research takes you, however, your overriding goal remains the same: to develop a strong critical understanding of the information you are gathering.

One student's experience illustrates how ideas can change and develop during the research process. Assigned to write an essay on a topic of current interest to him, this student began by puzzling over whether modern rock guitar styles could be traced to the electric guitar styles developed in Chicago in the 1940s by urban blues groups. This beginning was a good one; the student liked the subject and already knew something about it. Starting with background sources about modern rock guitarists like Eric Clapton and Pete Townshend, he found repeated references to Muddy Waters, B. B. King, Albert King, and other Chicago blues singers. He listened to a number of records and found repeated riffs (musical phrases) and clear derivations. So far, so good. Based on the information he found about his subject and his understanding of the records themselves, he began to make notes toward an essay.

This student's research might have ended at the point of drafting, but it did not. In several sources on the Chicago electric blues tradition, he found references to "country blues" and Southern "race records" as influences on the Chicago artists. He was not sure what these terms meant but wanted to find out. As he continued his research, the writer learned of a more complex and far older blues tradition than he had known existed. He discovered that blues music harks back to nineteenth-century slave songs and chants, that the country blues was nearly always played on a single acoustic guitar, and that the well-documented history of country blues guitar styles was easily traced back to the 1920s.

This new information called out for investigation. He felt that his early conjecture about the influence of the Chicago blues singers still held true, but clearly the story was older and the traditions much deeper than he had imagined. He decided to get more books about Southern and country blues musicians of the 1920s and 1930s in order to learn all he could about the guitar styles of musicians like Robert Johnson, Leadbelly, John Hurt, and Lightnin' Hopkins. In addition, he began to consider the differences between electric and acoustic instruments. Finally, he looked for records still available by some of the very early country blues musicians. To his amazement, the writer heard on these very early records some of the exact guitar riffs and techniques he so admired by contemporary guitarists. Thus, this writer arrived at this point of his research with a stronger and deeper idea for development, a far better grasp of musical history, and more and better research sources. And he had accumulated enough information and evidence to begin crafting a fine essay.

Research for writing

For college work, much of the research you will do will be for writing projects—to find evidence for a proposal, to discover anecdotes for an autobiographical essay, to investigate a subject for a term paper. The results of your research—your discoveries, your evidence, your conclusions, your new ideas—may be only one small part of an essay. You might, for example, need to do minimal research to supply background details about a topic or evidence for an argument. On the other hand, your research may be reported in a full-scale "research essay," devoted entirely to the results of your investigation. Chapters 37–41 provide guidelines to help you with any research done for the purpose of writing—from defining a topic to discovering and evaluating evidence to arguing a thesis and documenting your sources.

▌ 37a. Using both primary and secondary sources

Samuel Johnson once remarked that "knowledge is of two kinds: we know a subject ourselves, or we know where we can find information upon it." Johnson has summed up, in this sentence, the distinction between primary sources—firsthand knowledge—and secondary sources—knowledge available from the work of others.

Primary sources represent the basic sources of raw information. Primary sources you produce include laboratory experiments you conduct, notes you take in the field, and surveys or interviews you conduct. Also considered primary sources are objects or art works you examine, literary works you read, and performances you attend. Other primary sources include diaries, letters, firsthand accounts of events by eyewitnesses, contemporary news reports, historical documents, or raw data from experiments conducted by others.

Secondary sources consist of oral and written accounts of phenomena produced by others. Secondary sources include reports and analyses by scholars, experts, and researchers of other people's laboratory work, field experiences, surveys, and so forth. Secondary sources also include various sorts of critical writing.

Sometimes, what constitutes a primary or secondary source depends on your purpose or your field of study. A critic's evaluation of a painting, for instance, serves as a secondary work if you are writing an essay on that painting, but as a primary work if you are conducting a study of that critic's writings.

Most research writing depends on both primary and secondary sources. The primary sources ground the project in facts from firsthand accounts and your own discoveries, while the secondary sources provide background for your investigation and support for your conclusions.

Literary research, for instance, is very likely to combine primary and secondary sources: your major primary source is the text of the work you are examining, and secondary sources are biographies, analyses of the text, and other works of criticism.

Some projects may require no primary sources at all, such as a background survey or a review of the literature on a given topic. Secondary sources, on the other hand, are necessary for most research projects; even a report of a laboratory experiment is ordinarily prefaced by a discussion of what other researchers have done previously. Research very often builds on secondary sources in this way: you read to find out what is known or not known about a problem; you formulate a question based on what needs to be found out; then you devise a research method to answer that question. The research process, in fact, calls for active reading and writing throughout. As you read sources, you write out questions, summaries, notes, and so on. These in turn lead you back to more reading.

▎ 37b. Understanding and choosing a research topic

Sometimes a research topic may choose you: it so fascinates or compels you that you simply *must* explore it, or an assignment you are working on—a proposal for a business class or a personal essay for a journalism class—may call for some research. Other times, a specific research topic is assigned. Even in these cases, however, you will probably have some leeway in tailoring the assigned topic to your interests. In doing so, you want to follow your own curiosity, to conduct research that will enlighten you or answer a question that intrigues or puzzles you. Accomplishing this goal, however, calls for careful thinking on your part: you want to end up pursuing a topic that is not only interesting and challenging to you but manageable as well.

▎ 1. Analyzing an assigned topic

In college writing, most research responds to a writing assignment. You can begin your research, then, by paying very close attention to the exact wording of that assignment. If the assignment is handed out to you, study it, and keep it for future reference. If it is written on the chalkboard or if your instructor reads it aloud, copy it carefully, word for word. Consider any requirements for the essay's essential purpose, research scope, audience, length, and deadline.

Identifying the purpose

Read through the assignment for **cue words,** those like *describe, survey, analyze, explain, classify, compare,* or *contrast,* that describe the logical pattern the instructor expects the essay to follow. What do words like these mean in the context of this particular research assignment? For instance, in a biology class, *analyze* means "to break down into parts"; in a literature class, *analyze* means "to interpret." What do these meanings suggest about the purpose(s) of the assignment?

Gauging the scope

Next consider any information about the kind of research you will need to do. Does the assignment specify anything about the use of library sources, about how many sources you can or should use? Does the instructor require that you use a minimum number of sources of different sorts? (For example, your instructor may require that you consult a mix of books, periodicals, and interviews so that you gain experience with each kind of source.) If your assignment includes such requirements, plan your research accordingly.

Identifying the audience

Find out if your assignment specifies an audience other than the instructor. Then spend some time considering what this audience and your instructor will expect you to provide in a discussion of your topic. Make some preliminary notes based on these considerations, answering the following questions:

- Who will be interested in the information you gather, and why?
- What will they want to know?
- What will they already know?
- What response do you want to elicit from them?
- What assumptions might they hold about your topic?
- What information will you need to present in order to convince them?
- What will your instructor expect in a strong essay on this topic?

Noting the length

Does your assignment specify or limit the number of pages in the final essay? The amount of research and writing time you must budget for a five- to seven-page essay differs markedly from that needed for one of fifteen to twenty pages.

Working toward the deadline

What is your deadline for the completed project? Are any preliminary materials—a working bibliography, a research thesis, an outline, or a first draft—due before this date? Answering these questions will help you to construct a reasonable timetable for completing your work.

❙ 2. Choosing your own topic

If your assignment does not specify a topic, you can best begin articulating one by considering what subjects puzzle you, challenge you, engage your curiosity in some way. Ask yourself the following questions:

- What subjects do you know something about?
- What subjects might you like to become an "expert" on?
- What subjects evoke a strong reaction from you—intense curiosity, puzzlement, or skepticism?
- Are there any subjects others have investigated and written about that you would like to look into?

In addition, skim through your textbooks or class notes, looking for subjects that catch your interest. Or browse through current magazines, journals, or standard reference works, again looking for some topic or question that intrigues you. You may find the techniques presented in 2e for exploring a topic—brainstorming, freewriting, looping, mapping, or questioning—useful for discovering one.

Getting response to your topic

As soon as you can, draft several sentences that describe the topic (or topics) you have come up with; then try to get some response—from your instructor and perhaps from friends or classmates. Ask them to consider the following questions:

- What do you think of this approach to the topic?
- Is the topic manageable?
- Can you suggest any other angles?
- Can you suggest any good sources of information on this topic?
- Would you be interested in reading about this topic?
- Can you suggest any approach that might be more provocative?

Make sure you understand any specifications about purpose, scope, audience, length, and deadline (see 37b1).

▋ 37c. Narrowing and focusing a topic

Any topic you choose to research must be manageable—must suit the purpose, scope, audience, length, and time limits for your final writing purpose. Making a topic manageable often requires "narrowing" it, but narrowing is not always sufficient in itself. "World War II" may be too general a topic, but the "Battle of Midway" will probably not be any easier to manage. Rather than simply narrowing a broad subject to a smaller one, then, it may be more useful to *focus* on a specific aspect, on a particular slant, looking for a governing question to guide your research.

Asking a research question and developing a hypothesis

The result of this focusing process is a **research question,** a query or problem or issue that can be answered or solved or considered through research data. The research question may be tentatively answered by a **hypothesis,** a statement of what you anticipate your research might show. Thus you can begin your research by trying to answer this question, eventually trying to prove, disprove, or illustrate your hypothesis. (If the research question you pose has an obvious answer or if it requires technical knowledge beyond your grasp, go back to the drawing board to refocus your question.)

Like a working thesis (see 2f), a hypothesis must be not only manageable, but interesting and specific. In addition, it must be argumentative, a debatable proposition that can be proved or disproved by research evidence (see 4b). For example, a statement like this one cannot be disproved: "Roy Cohn was an assistant to Senator Joseph McCarthy during the 1950s." No one would argue against this fact, and its statement is not a hypothesis. On the other hand, this statement is debatable: "Roy Cohn's political views and assiduous but biased research while he was an assistant to Senator Joseph McCarthy during the 1950s were responsible for the larger part of McCarthy's anti-Communist witch hunts." Such a statement would have to be proved or disproved; thus, it is a hypothesis.

In most cases, you will want to explore your topic by doing background reading and making notes before you can formulate a research question or develop a hypothesis. In moving from a general topic of interest to a useful hypothesis, you progress from subject to issue to research question and eventually to hypothesis. In other words, from a large field of knowledge or interest, you narrow down to one single manageable issue within the field. You then raise a question about that issue and put forward a possible answer, your hypothesis. Throughout this process, you will profit by *writing*, by trying to articulate your thoughts as clearly as possible. The following examples outline two students' movement from general subject to hypothesis:

SUBJECT	World War II
ISSUE	technological innovations in World War II
RESEARCH QUESTION	Did technological innovations in World War II make a significant difference to the Allies?
HYPOTHESIS	Superior technological innovations in a number of areas allowed the Allies to gain a decisive advantage in World War II.

SUBJECT	Shelley's poetry
ISSUE	my responses to the poem "The Sensitive Plant"
RESEARCH QUESTION	What accounts for the fact that I seem to read this poem in two conflicting ways?
HYPOTHESIS	Shelley's "The Sensitive Plant" resists easy reading or set interpretation in surprising ways.

Each of these student writers focuses on an issue about which a research question can be asked. The hypothesis that tentatively answers each question is precise enough to be supported or challenged by a manageable amount of research.

37d. Investigating what you know about your topic

Once you have narrowed and focused a topic, you need to marshal everything you already know about it. In practice, this step calls for what computer scientists call a "data dump": you try to "dump" all your immediate thoughts about the topic onto paper. Here are some useful methods for getting all your knowledge down on paper.

Brainstorming

Take five minutes to list everything you can think of concerning your hypothesis. Put down everything you know or wonder about your topic. You may find it helpful to work with one or two other students, using one another as sounding boards.

Freewriting in favor of your hypothesis

For five minutes, write without stopping about every reason that you believe your hypothesis is true. Put down everything you can think of. As in any freewriting (see 2e2), do not stop writing for any reason; simply go on writing for the full five minutes. No one will see this writing; its purpose is simply to provoke you to recall and write down what you already know and think about a topic.

Freewriting against your hypothesis

For five minutes, write down every argument you can think of that someone opposed to your hypothesis would make. Simply attack your hypothesis in every way you can, even in ways that might seem improbable.

Freewriting on your audience

Write for five minutes about your audience, including your instructor. Write about what they need or want to know in order to accept your hypothesis. What do they currently believe about your topic? What sorts of evidence will convince them to believe your hypothesis? What sorts of sources will they respect?

Tapping your memory for sources

List, in the form of short notes, everything you can remember about *where* you learned about the topic you are writing on: books, magazines, courses, conversations, television. Much of what you know may seem to you "common knowledge," but remember that common knowledge comes from somewhere. The places where you learned things can serve as starting points for investigation.

▌ 37e. Moving from hypothesis to working thesis

If you begin research with a research question and a hypothesis, your next goal is a working thesis. In between, as your research proceeds, your question is likely to be refined and your hypothesis is likely to go through some significant changes. Only after you have tested it, sharpened it, supported it, and explored it through your reading and writing does the hypothesis become a working thesis.

The hypotheses illustrated in 37c, for instance, might be focused further, or even completely changed, once research begins. The first writer might be able to discover very little on air force innovations but so much on naval technology and innovation during World War II that she decides to stick to that focus. The second writer might find in his research a critical reading of the Shelley poem that resolves his conflicting readings. In consequence, he would have to change the whole thrust of his discussion.

In doing research, you may find that a whole line of inquiry is unproductive, that a journal you need to complete an argument is not available, or that your hypothesis is simply wrong and must be discarded completely. In each case, the process of research pushes you to know more and more about your hypothesis, to make it more focused and precise. Such learning is what research is all about: in pursuing a research question and refining it into a hypothesis and eventually into a working thesis, you are teaching yourself how to become an expert. You are, in short, becoming a researcher.

READING ABOUT RESEARCH

In the following passage, astronomer Carl Sagan describes the excitement of the kind of research in which he is engaged, research that makes you *"really think"* and consequently *"experience a kind of exhilaration."* Read Sagan's description carefully. Have you done any research that fits his description? Try to think of one or two topics that you would really like to know more about or questions to which you have always wanted to know the answers. What kind of research would allow you to experience "exhilaration?"

. . . the main trick of [doing research in] science is to *really* think of something: the shape of clouds and their occasional sharp bottom edges at the same altitude everywhere in the sky; the formation of a dewdrop on a leaf; the origin of a name or a word—Shakespeare, say, or "philanthropic"; the reason for human social customs—the incest taboo, for example; how it is that a lens in sunlight can make paper burn; how a "walking stick" got to look so much like a twig; why the Moon seems to follow us as we walk; what prevents us from digging a hole down to the center of the Earth; what the definition is of "down" on a spherical Earth; how it is possible for the body to convert yesterday's lunch into today's muscle and sinew; or how far is up—does the universe go on forever, or if it does not, is there any meaning to the question of what lies on the other side? Some of these questions are pretty easy. Others, especially the last, are mysteries to which no one even today knows the answer. They are natural questions to ask. Every culture has posed such questions in one way or another. Almost always the proposed answers are in the nature of "Just So Stories," attempted explanations divorced from experiment, or even from careful comparative observations.

But the scientific cast of mind examines the world critically as if many alternative worlds might exist, as if other things might be here which are not. Then we are forced to ask why what we see is present and not something else. Why are the Sun and the Moon and the planets spheres? Why not pyramids, or cubes, or dodecahedra? Why not irregular, jumbly shapes? Why so symmetrical, worlds? If you spend any time spinning hypotheses, checking to see whether they make sense, whether they conform to what else we know, thinking of tests you can pose to substantiate or deflate your hypotheses, you will find yourself doing science. And as you come to practice this habit of thought more and more you will get better and better at it. To penetrate into the heart of the thing—even a little thing, a blade of grass, as Walt Whitman said—is to experience a kind of exhilaration that, it may be, only human beings of all the beings on this planet can feel. We are an intelligent species and the use of our intelligence quite properly gives us pleasure. In this respect the brain is like a muscle. When we think well, we feel good. Understanding is a kind of ecstasy.

–CARL SAGAN, *Broca's Brain*

FOR EXAMINING YOUR OWN WRITING

If you have done research for an essay before, now is a good time to go back and evaluate the work you did both as a researcher and as a writer in light of the principles developed in this chapter. What was the purpose of that research? What kinds of sources did you use? Did you have any audience other than your instructor? How was your topic focused? What were you most pleased with about your research, and about your essay? What were you least pleased with? What advice would you give yourself if you were to revise that essay?

527

38. Conducting Research

Once you have a topic or research question or hypothesis, how do you go about conducting research on it? That question was recently faced by an enterprising pair of writers with a passion for ice cream, who wanted to write an article for a local magazine on the best ice cream in Pittsburgh. Their guiding research questions (who has the best ice cream, and what makes it the best?) led them first to the library, where they did background reading on the history of ice cream and on how it is made. Then they went into the field, systematically tasting ice cream all over the city and interviewing ice cream makers. In preparing their article, these writers carried out the two basic kinds of research—*field* and *library* research.

38a. Collecting data in the field

For many research projects, you will need to collect data "in the field"—whether that field is an ice cream parlor, your own home, a laboratory, or the corner grocery store. When you gather information in the field, you are the primary reporter. You must discover where you can find relevant information, decide on the best ways to gather it, and find the best people to inform you about it. As a field researcher, you will become a detective not only of books and journals, but of the world. Three useful techniques for field research include observing, interviewing, and surveying.

1. Observing

Much professional writing depends on careful direct observation: a doctor's diagnostic notes, a reporter's news article, a social worker's case study. Observing can also provide rich information for your research writing. Sometimes called naturalistic research, **observation** calls on you to look at phenomena without trying to alter them in any way, keeping yourself out of the picture as much as possible. You can observe anything in this way, from the use of bicycle paths on campus to the kinds of products advertised during Saturday morning television shows to the growth of chicks in an agriculture lab.

Careful observation can supply support for a hypothesis or working thesis. For example, one student decided to write a proposal to try to persuade the traffic and parking division of his college to provide more motorcycle parking space in his dormitory parking lot. Because he wanted to show the need for such space, he set aside an eight-hour period to sit in the lot, recording the number of cars and motorcycles unable to find space. When he found that the ratio of motorcycles to cars was roughly three to one, direct observation paved the way for his request by helping to demonstrate a need.

Observation is also useful for finding out what people are actually doing as opposed to what they think or say they are doing. A reference librarian may believe he answers ten questions every five minutes and may report that to you in an interview, but observation may show you that he actually averages only seven questions every five minutes. The head of the dining commons may believe that most students eat two eggs for breakfast, but observation of people eating may reveal that most of them throw away at least one egg.

Preparing for observation

Before you go out into the field to observe, decide exactly what you are trying to find out and try to anticipate what you are likely to see. Are you going to observe an action repeated by many people (such as pedestrians crossing a street) or a sequence of actions (such as a medical procedure)? Are you observing a situation that might produce many different reactions—a child crying in a grocery store, for example? Try to decide exactly what you want to record and how to do so. In the grocery store, for instance, decide whether to observe the crying child, his or her parents, other shoppers, or store employees, and what you want to note—what they say, or what they do.

A checklist for conducting observation

- Determine the purpose of the observation, and review your research question and hypothesis to see that they relate.
- Set a definite period of time for the observation.
- If necessary, make an appointment.

- Develop a system for recording information. (The student studying motorcycle parking, for instance, used lined paper with three vertical columns to tabulate cars, motorcycles, and times.)
- Take materials for keeping notes.
- Consider using a camera, tape recorder, or videocassette recorder.
- Assume the role of reporter, using the questions in 2e5 (*who, what, when, where, why,* and *how*) to note down what you see and hear.

2. Interviewing

Sometimes you will need information that is best sought by **interviewing,** or asking direct questions, of other people. If you can talk with an expert, in person or on the telephone, you might get information you could not get through any other kind of research. In addition to getting "expert opinion," you might ask for first-hand accounts, for biographical information, or for suggestions of other places to look or people to consult.

Finding people to interview

How do you go about identifying people to interview? Check first to see whether your research thus far names any people you might contact directly. Next, try to think of people who might be helpful— take a few minutes to brainstorm for names. In addition to authorities on your topic, consider people in your community who might be knowledgeable—lawyers, librarians, local government officials, alumni of your college.

Once you identify people you would like to talk with, either write or telephone to see whether an interview might be arranged. (See 44b for a discussion of letters of inquiry.)

Composing questions

To prepare useful questions, you need to know your topic well and to know a fair amount about your interviewee. Try to learn as much as you can about his or her experience and opinions. You will probably want to ask several kinds of questions. **Factual questions** ask for specific answers, ones that do not invite expansion or opinion.

How many firebases was your unit posted to during your tour of duty in Vietnam?

What flavors of ice cream does your company produce?

How many people contributed to this year's United Way campaign?

530

In contrast, **open-ended questions** ask the interviewee to think out loud, to go in directions that interest him or her, and to give additional details or anecdotes.

How would you characterize the atmosphere of the Watergate hearings?

How does public acceptance of modern art today compare with the situation forty years ago? How would you account for the change?

How do you feel now about your decision to go to Canada in 1968 rather than be drafted?

Avoid questions that may (1) insult the interviewee—"Why was the city sued so frequently for police brutality during your term as chief of police?" (2) invite the interviewee to ramble on—"What do you think of youth today?" (3) elicit short yes/no answers—"Should the Indian Point reactor be closed down?" Instead, ask the interviewee to support an answer in some way—"Why should the Indian Point reactor be closed down?"

A checklist for planning an interview

- Determine your exact purpose, and check it with your research question and hypothesis to be sure they all relate.
- Set the interview up well in advance, specifying the amount of time it will take and asking permission to tape if you wish to do so.
- Prepare a written list of questions you can use to structure the interview. Brainstorming or freewriting techniques can help you to come up with questions (see 2e).
- If possible, try out your questions on one or two people to determine how clear and precise they are and how long answers will take. Revise and edit the questions as need be.
- Prepare a final copy of your questions, leaving plenty of space for notes after each one.
- Check out all equipment beforehand—pens, tape recorder, and so on. Record the subject, date, time, and place of interview at the beginning of all tapes.
- Take several pencils or pens and a notebook.

Conducting an interview

Be prompt, and dress appropriately. If you bring a tape recorder, ask the interviewee again for permission to record your conversation. Even if you use a recorder, bring a notebook with your questions, and write down the answers and any other notes you wish to make. Do not feel bound to the exact structure of your prepared questions, as long as the interview proceeds in a direction that seems fruitful. Be flexible. Note the time, and be careful not to take up more time than you said you would. End the interview with a thank you—and follow up with a letter thanking the person for taking the time to meet with you. (See 44e for a discussion of follow-up letters.)

3. Surveying opinion

One kind of large-scale interviewing surveys a number of people about an issue and provides one means of determining public opinion.

Surveys can take the form of interviews (see 38a2), but more often they depend on **questionnaires**. For an introductory language course, for instance, one student decided to investigate the variety of terms used to refer to grandparents. To gather this information, she prepared a simple questionnaire and distributed it to the members of five sections of the linguistics class she was taking.

The student investigating campus parking for motorcycles surveyed his dormitory's residents, asking how many owned motorcycles and how many of them had difficulty finding parking spaces. Though he sent questionnaires to everyone in the dorm, such extensive surveying is often unwieldy and even unnecessary. What you need is a representative sample of people, enough so that your survey accurately reflects opinion within the group you are discussing.

Preparing a questionnaire

To be effective, a questionnaire asks questions that will elicit the information necessary to accomplish your purpose. Questions should be clear and easy to understand and should be designed so that you will be able to analyze the answers easily. For example, questions that ask respondents to say yes or no or to rank something on a five-point scale of most to least desirable are easy to tabulate.

A checklist for designing a questionnaire

1. Write out your purpose, and review your research question and hypothesis to determine the kinds of questions to ask.
2. Determine the audience for your questionnaire, and figure out how you will reach them.
3. Using brainstorming, freewriting, or another strategy from 2e, draft some potential questions.
4. Check each question to see that it calls for short, specific answers.

5. Test the questions on three or four people—including your instructor, if possible. Note which questions are hard to answer and why, and how much time the answers require.
6. Revise the questions as necessary to make them clear and specific.
7. Be sure to state a deadline as well as a place for returning the form.
8. Consider adding a question that asks for any other comments.
9. Type the questionnaire so that it is easy to follow, leaving adequate space for all answers.
10. Proofread your questionnaire.

▌ 38b. Exploring library resources

The library is one of a researcher's best friends, for answering a research question and exploring and testing a hypothesis most often begin there. Libraries provide two necessary kinds of information: general background, which will give you an overview of your topic and place your research question in context, and particular support, which helps answer your research question and develop your hypothesis.

▌ 1. Beginning your library research

Start by reviewing your research question, hypothesis, and knowledge you already have about your topic (see 37d). Where did that knowledge come from? Do you own any books about your topic? Have you recently read any magazine articles about it? Do your textbooks help? This is the place to begin a working bibliography, your list of possible sources, jotting down whatever sources you can think of.

When you have exhausted your own resources, turn to acquaintances who may be able to point you in useful directions. If, for instance, you are writing about computers, and a student down the hall knows everything about computers, go and talk to her. What books does she recommend? Does she have any computer magazines? How can she help get you going? Call that biology major you met last weekend, and ask her about genetic engineering. Take notes on what she says. Look up the teaching assistant you had for chemistry lab, and ask him for a reading list on radioisotope decay. If your library offers an orientation tour, go along and ask about sources on your topic.

Finally, talk to your instructor. Even if you are researching a topic you yourself selected, your instructor may be able to suggest where to begin looking for sources.

Choosing note-taking materials

Many researchers like to gather and organize information on index cards because they are easy to carry, and can be easily rearranged and grouped. Others prefer to use a tablet or notebook. Whichever form you choose, using it systematically will later help you to locate data and can serve as the basis for endnotes or a list of sources.

Identifying key words

Looking through card catalogs, databases, or indexes can be accelerated if you have identified **key words** to look for—synonyms for your topic, broader terms that would include it, or appropriate subtopics. Information on ice cream, for instance, might appear under the heading of frozen desserts, dairy products, or sherbet.

Choosing sources

Where to start? You may decide to begin with an overview, looking first, for example, at an encyclopedia. This strategy may be especially useful if you need a better focus on a research question or want to check for basic bibliographies. On the other hand, you may already have ideas about where to begin. Before you plunge in, however, ask yourself a few questions.

- *How current do your sources need to be?* If you must investigate the "cutting edge" of a field, you will want to check current periodicals (rather than books, which take longer to reach publication). On the other hand, if you want broader, more detailed coverage and background information, you will look more to books.

- *How much time do you have to spend?* If you have only two weeks to do your research, you will want to be selective about how broadly you cast your net. In fact, you probably will need to discipline yourself to move quickly along a fairly narrow research track. If you have several months, however, you can follow a broader course, perhaps even consulting materials beyond those available in your library.

- *How many sources should you consult?* You can expect to look over many more sources than you actually end up using. Your best guideline is to make sure you have enough sources to support your hypothesis or to prove your point.

Consulting the library staff

Your most valuable source at the library is the highly trained staff, especially the reference librarians. To get the most helpful advice, you should pose *specific* questions. "Where can I find information about computers?" will not give a librarian much specific information to go on, but "Where can I find information on the history of computers?" should help the librarian to lead you more directly to the sources you need. The more precise your question, the more useful an answer you will get.

If you find yourself unable to ask clear and precise questions, you probably need to do some general background research into your topic. Then work again on narrowing and focusing, defining a clearer issue, asking a more specific research question, and finding a sharper hypothesis. On your second trip, you will be ready to ask more specific questions and to find appropriate sources. (See 37c for more information on asking a research question and formulating a hypothesis.)

▌ 2. Selecting reference books

Your library's reference collection includes two broad types of **reference materials**: those that are general in scope and those that deal with specific disciplines (music, zoology, political science, and so on). Guides to reference books can help you identify sources that suit your purpose. Your research question can then help you choose the best references to use. Among the types most often consulted are encyclopedias, biographical dictionaries, almanacs, and periodical indexes.

Guides to reference books

Whether your interest is in nuclear physics, baseball history, or agricultural economics, you can probably find it in one of the two guides to reference books listed below. These guides group reference books by fields, including specialized bibliographies—lists of books and articles about a particular issue or discipline. Because these guides list other reference books—not actual sources—a few minutes with them can be a shortcut to the books that match your interests and purposes.

> *Guide to Reference Books*, 10th ed., 1986. Edited by Eugene P. Sheehy, this large book is usually just called "Sheehy." It supplies annotated lists of general reference works and specialized bibliographies. Sheehy is divided into five sections: General Reference; Humanities; Social and Behavioral Sciences; History and Area Studies; and Science, Technology, and Medicine. Each of these sections is further subdivided into areas and then into special approaches. Full bibliographic information, including the Library of Congress call number, is provided for each entry.

Walford's Guide to Reference Material, 4th ed., 1980–1987. "Walford" consists of three volumes: Volume 1—Science and Technology; Volume 2—Social and Historical Sciences, Philosophy, and Religion; and Volume 3—Generalia, Language and Literature, the Arts.

Encyclopedias

For general background on a subject, **encyclopedias** are a good place to begin. Though some encyclopedias do provide in-depth information, more often they serve as a place to start, not as a major source of information.

GENERAL ENCYCLOPEDIAS

Collier's Encyclopedia, 24 volumes. *Collier's* presents many topics and illustrations chosen to meet the needs of current student research.

Encyclopaedia Britannica, 15th ed., 32 volumes. The *Britannica* has a two-part structure; the *Micropaedia*, which contains general knowledge and short entries; and the *Macropaedia*, which contains longer entries that treat selected important subjects in depth. For fine essays on subjects in the classics and humanities, see if your library has the famous eleventh edition of the *Britannica*, published in 1911 and considered by many to be the most thoughtful and scholarly encyclopedia ever produced.

Encyclopedia Americana, 30 volumes. The *Americana* pays particular attention to American public figures, institutions, and places.

Encyclopedia Canadiana, 10 volumes. The *Canadiana* coverage of Canadian people, places, and institutions is more comprehensive than that of any other work.

SPECIALIZED ENCYCLOPEDIAS

Compared with general encyclopedias, **specialized encyclopedias** usually provide more detailed articles by authorities in the field as well as more extensive bibliographies for beginning research. These volumes are often located in the reference area or reading room for the particular discipline. Here are just a few examples.

Encyclopedia of Anthropology
Encyclopedia of Banking and Finance
Encyclopedia of Bioethics
Encyclopedia of Chemistry
Encyclopedia of Computer Science and Technology
Encyclopedia of Crime and Justice

Encyclopedia of Earth Sciences
Encyclopedia of Economics
Encyclopedia of Education
Encyclopedia of Educational Research
Encyclopedia of Management
Encyclopedia of Philosophy
Encyclopedia of Physical Education, Fitness and Sports
Encyclopedia of Physics
Encyclopedia of Psychology
Encyclopedia of Religion and Ethics
Encyclopedia of Social Work
Encyclopedia of the Biological Sciences
Encyclopedia of World Art
International Encyclopedia of the Social Sciences
McGraw-Hill Encyclopedia of Environmental Science
McGraw-Hill Encyclopedia of Science and Technology
McGraw-Hill Encyclopedia of World Drama
New Illustrated Encyclopedia of World History

Biographical dictionaries and indexes

The lives and historical settings of famous people are the topics of **biographical dictionaries** and **indexes.** Before you use these sources, consider whether you need a volume covering people who are living or people who are dead. If the latter, decide if you want a current volume covering deceased people or an older volume covering living people that was published during the person's lifetime. Here are a few examples of biographical reference works; many others, particularly volumes specialized by geographic area or field, are available.

Biography Index, 1946–. This quarterly index lists biographical material found in current books and over 1,500 periodicals.

Current Biography, 1940–. This monthly publication carries informative articles on men and women in current events. It includes photographs and useful short bibliographies.

Dictionary of American Biography, 1928–1937 plus supplements. Usually called the DAB, these volumes contain biographies of over 15,000 deceased Americans from all phases of public life since colonial days. The entries include bibliographies of sources.

Dictionary of National Biography, 1882–1900 plus supplements. The DNB covers deceased notables from Great Britain and its colonies (excluding the postcolonial United States).

Who's Who in America, 1899–. Published every other year, this is the standard biographical reference for information about famous living Americans. Notable Americans no longer living are included in *Who Was Who in America,* covering from 1607 to the present. Similar specialized reference works include *Who's Who of American Women, Who's Who in Government,* and so on.

Who's Who, 1849–. Published annually, this reference supplies brief biographical listings for well-known living British people. *Who Was Who,* with volumes covering about a decade each, lists British notables who died between 1897 and the present.

International Who's Who, 1935–. Published annually, this source contains biographies of persons of international status.

Sources for current events and statistics

Almanacs, yearbooks, and other sources provide information on current events and **statistical data.** In addition to the following works, each of the general encyclopedias listed earlier in this section publishes an annual yearbook surveying events and developments of the preceding year in various fields.

Editorial Research Reports. Each of the weekly reports in this series consists of a twenty-page survey of a current issue and includes a current bibliography. The reports for each six months are gathered and published in hardcover volumes.

Facts on File. This weekly publication summarizes and indexes facts about current events, making topical information easy to find.

Statistical Abstract of the United States. This annual publication of the Bureau of the Census presents government data on population, business, commerce, industry, immigration, and other subjects.

World Almanac and Book of Facts. This annual publication presents data and statistics on business, education, sports, government, population, and many other topics. It covers institutional names and addresses and reviews important public events of the year.

Information Please Almanac. This annual publication includes many charts, facts, and lists as well as short summaries of the year's events and accomplishments in various fields.

Statesman's Year-Book. This source contains facts and helpful current statistics about agriculture, government, population, development, religion, and other topics in different countries of the world.

Periodical indexes

Periodical indexes provide guides to articles published in periodicals—journals, magazines, or newspapers. Each index chooses a group of periodicals to analyze and usually identifies them at the beginning of the volume. A general index for periodicals lists articles from current general-interest magazines, a newspaper index lists articles from a particular newspaper or selection of papers, and a specialized index covers articles in the scholarly journals of a particular discipline. These indexes will be among your most useful reference books for current articles and information.

GENERAL INDEXES

Readers' Guide to Periodical Literature. A good place to begin for any topic of general or popular interest is the *Readers' Guide*, which indexes articles from over 170 magazines. It is particularly helpful if you need to investigate social trends, popular scientific questions, and contemporary political issues. The *Readers' Guide* appears semi-monthly, with quarterly and annual cumulations. Entries are arranged by author and subject, with cross-references leading to related topics. Here is a typical *Readers' Guide* entry, covering entries under the subject heading *Divorce*.

> **DIVORCE**
>> *See also*
>> Children of divorced parents
>> Custody of children
>> Palimony
>> Support (Domestic relations)
> Johnson Products president hit with divorce petition after 37-year marriage. il pors *Jet* 74:32-3 My 23 '88
> Judgment call [Barnstable County (Mass.) Judge S. Lewis charged with favoring women in divorce proceedings] C. Colbath. il *Ms.* 16:81 Ap '88
> Mum's the word as Di's mom's marriage to a wallpaper heir comes unglued after 19 years [F. Shand Kydd] B. Johnson. il pors *People Weekly* 29:107+ Je 20 '88
>> **Statistics**
> Divorce insurance: have a son [effect of sons on marital stability; study by S. Philip Morgan] M. Adessa. *Psychology Today* 22:14-15 My '88
> Labor and love lost [relationship between hours worked and divorce rate for women; study by Julia Heath] V. Bozzi. *Psychology Today* 22:16 Ap '88
>> **Kenya**
> Divorce of two women tests Kenyan system. *Jet* 74:36 Je 13 '88
>> **United States**
>> *See* Divorce

The New York Times Index. Now extending back to 1851, this index appears twice a month, is accumulated yearly, and lists, by subject, every article that has appeared in the *Times*. For most articles of any length, short summaries are given as well.

Book Review Digest. This index contains excerpts from reviews of books along with information for locating the full reviews in popular and scholarly periodicals. Published yearly, this is the place to look for critical reviews and commentary on a book. When looking for reviews of a book, be sure to check for not only the year of the book's publication but also the next year.

Some libraries own **microfilm indexes** that cover many of the same entries as the printed indexes listed above. Microfilm are strips of film showing reduced pages of information. Each microfilm index covers only a limited period of time, usually several years, but for the recent past they are very efficient. Microfilm run on motorized projection machines that make the task of searching fast and easy. Ask the librarian for help in locating the microfilm and in running the machine. Here are three popular microfilm indexes.

Magazine Index. This index, updated monthly, analyzes four hundred general-interest magazines.

National Newspaper Index. This index, appearing monthly, covers the *New York Times,* the *Los Angeles Times,* the *Washington Post,* the *Wall Street Journal,* and the *Christian Science Monitor.*

Business Index. This index covers more than eight hundred business publications.

Special indexes and abstracts

Many disciplines have **specialized indexes** to help researchers find information in great depth. In general, such indexes list journal articles in periodicals but may include other publications as well. (Check the beginning of the volume for an explanation of what it includes.) Those with **abstracts** also briefly summarize entries, thus supplying more than a title to help you judge an item's potential usefulness. Here is a list of specialized indexes.

America: History and Life
Applied Science and Technology Index
Art Index
Biological Abstracts
Biological and Agricultural Index
Business Periodicals Index
Chemical Abstracts
Communications Abstracts
Computer Literature Index

Cumulative Index to Nursing and Allied Health Literature
Current Index to Journals in Education
Dissertation Abstracts International
Ecology Abstracts
Education Index
Essay and General Literature Index
General Science Index
Historical Abstracts
Humanities Index
Index Medicus
Index to Government Periodicals
Index to Legal Periodicals
MLA International Bibliography
Music Index
Philosopher's Index
Physical Education Index
Physics Abstracts
Psychological Abstracts
Public Affairs Information Service (PAIS)
Science Abstracts
Social Sciences Index
Sociological Abstracts

▌3. Using the card catalog or circulation computer

A library's **card catalog** lists all the library's available materials, or holdings. Many libraries are gradually transferring the holdings in their card catalogs to **circulation computer** systems, which allow patrons to use public terminals to ask the computer to search for material on a topic. Most libraries with circulation computers, however, maintain card catalogs as well.

Finding author, title, and subject cards

In card catalogs, separate cards are prepared for each item—one headed by the author, one by the title, and others by subject. Thus you can look up a book by the last name of the author, by the first main word in the title, or by the subject of the book. Here are examples of author, title, and subject cards.

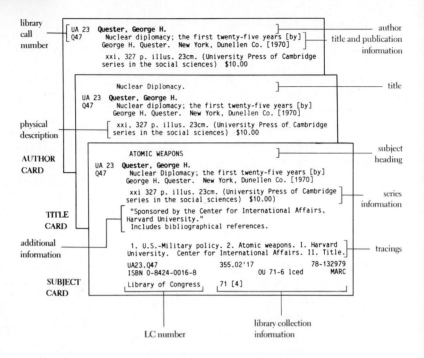

Identifying subjects

The card catalog provides an important source, but searching only subject cards is likely to be inefficient. Subjects are usually identified and arranged according to the system presented in *Library of Congress Subject Headings*. This large reference book may be kept at the reference desk or near the catalog so that you can check the exact wording of subject headings of interest to you.

Problems arise when the Library of Congress heading does not match your particular needs or when it is so broad that it lists hundreds of books, only a few of which will be helpful to you. If you were doing research on nuclear power plants, for instance, and looked up the Library of Congress heading "Nuclear Energy," you would find many books about nuclear weapons that had nothing to do with the nuclear generation of energy. For this reason, you need to screen subject entries carefully. In addition, use other leads—bibliographies, reference books, periodical indexes, notes in other publications, and so on—to identify potentially useful authors and titles. Though demanding more background work from you, such leads are likely to be much more specific and helpful.

Using the call numbers

Besides identifying a book's author, title, subject, and publication information, each catalog card also lists a **call number**—the book's identification number. For these numbers, most academic libraries now use the Library of Congress System, which begins call numbers with letters of the alphabet. Some libraries, however, still use the older Dewey Decimal System with all numerals, while others combine both systems. Once you have written down the complete call number, look for a library map or shelving plan to tell you which section or floor houses your book. When you find the area where your book is shelved, take the time to browse through the books shelved around it. Very often you will find the immediate area a more important treasure trove than any bibliography or index.

If your book is not on the shelf, ask about it at the circulation desk. You may be able to find out if someone has checked it out and if it is due soon. Very often a library will recall a book when another patron needs it. Allow for the time required for the library to notify the patron to return the book and then to notify you that it is available. Your deadline will determine whether it is realistic to request a recall.

❙ 4. Searching computerized databases

Although libraries differ in type and extent of computerization, more and more college libraries are subscribing to **databases,** highly specialized electronic indexes listing thousands of books and articles by authors, titles, and key words describing subjects. Currently, databases are available in the sciences, the social sciences, and the humanities. To use a database service, you provide a list of authors, titles, or key terms, and the computer searches the database for all references to them and then prints out a list of every reference in the database.

To use most databases, you will need the help of a librarian. Usually you must pay a fee for access time, so you will probably want to discuss with the librarian the available services, your needs, and the cost before deciding to consult an electronic database.

Selecting key words

Sometimes the key words for which you will ask a database to search its memory will be authors or titles, but more often they will be subject headings. Choose key words carefully, making them as precise as possible. The key word *brain*, for example, would yield many bibliographic items, probably thousands, but your task would be no easier as a result, and your bill might be tremendous. Using key words such as *neurological disorders* or *neural networks* would be much more helpful and cheaper. Often the most useful items you can give a librarian helping you are one or two good sources you have already found on your topic. The librarian can then determine some key words.

Reading a printout

After your search has been run, you will receive a printout of the results. As the following example printout demonstrates, each entry includes the author, title, publication information, subject, and index.

```
Subjects covered
----------------
Neural nets
Computer research

1    (GENERAL SCIENCE INDEX)
Bower, Bruce
Neural networks set sights on visual processing in brain
Science News 133:149 Mr 5  '88

Subjects covered
----------------
Neural network computers
Brain/Localization of function

2    (GENERAL SCIENCE INDEX)
Zipser, David; Anderson, Richard A.
A back-propagation programmed network that simulates
response properties of a subset of posterior
parietal neurons
Nature 331: 679-84 F 25  '88

Subjects covered
----------------
Neuran network computers
Brain/Innervation

3    (GENERAL SCIENCE INDEX)
Anderson, Alun
Neural networks: learning from a computer cat
Nature 331: 657-9 F 25  '88

Subjects covered
----------------
Neural network computers
Brain/Innervation

4    (GENERAL SCIENCE INDEX)
Farnat, Nabil H.
Optical associative memories: first step
toward neuromorphic optical data processing
Physics Today 41:S62-S63 Ja '88
```

39. Evaluating and Using Source Materials

All research builds on the astute, judicious, and sometimes inspired use of sources—that research work done by others. As Isaac Newton noted, those researchers who see the farthest do so because they "stand on the shoulders of giants." And while researchers cannot always count on a giant's shoulders to stand on, the quality of their insights is often directly related to how well they have understood and used the source materials—the shoulders—they have relied on. As a reader, you will want to make the most of your sources, using the insights you have gained from them in creating powerful prose of your own. This chapter will guide you in considering your use of sources in research.

39a. Choosing sources

Experienced researchers know that all sources are not created equally useful, that some are infinitely more helpful or provocative than others. One of your goals, therefore, is to learn to recognize which sources will be most helpful, which ones will allow you to see the farthest.

The following sections will provide some guidance to help you decide when to delve more deeply into a work and when to set it aside. Not all sources you examine will prove useful to you, so you need to learn how to judge, in Francis Bacon's words, which are to be tasted, which swallowed, and which chewed and digested.

1. Assessing the usefulness of a source

Several characteristics of a book or article can help you assess its usefulness.

Date of original publication

The more recent the source, the more up-to-date you can generally expect its information to be. Recent sources are often more useful than older sources, especially in the sciences, which change so quickly. Be cautious, however, about judging a source only by age. Some older sources in any field are still the most authoritative works of the discipline. Thus, age must be balanced with other factors such as the quality or current acceptance of the material.

Level of specialization

Determine quickly whether a source provides a general overview or whether it is specialized in a way that is useful to you. General sources read easily and may be helpful as you begin your research, but they often lack the authority or up-to-dateness of the more specialized sources you may need later. Extremely specialized works, on the other hand, may be too technical to be read or understood easily.

Relevance to your topic

The most helpful sources are those most closely related to your research area. Look beyond the title to the subtitle, preface, introduction, and table of contents to determine just how directly a particular source addresses your topic.

Cross-referencing

Note those sources that are cited again and again in your reading. The more a source is referred to in other works, the more you can assume it to be a standard work whose content and approach are widely respected.

2. Looking through a source

Researchers can often pick up a book or article, look it over quickly, and decide within a few minutes whether it merits more careful study. Here are some elements to check for in looking over a source to help you use it most efficiently.

- *Title and subtitle.* If you are investigating coeducation in the nineteenth century and find a book called *Women in Education*, the subtitle *The Challenge of the 1970s* will tell you that you probably do not need to examine the book.

- *Abstract.* Abstracts are concise summaries of articles or books. They routinely precede articles in some journals and are included in certain periodical or bibliographic guides. The purpose of an abstract is to help readers decide whether to read the entire work, so if you run across a source that includes one, you should read it.

- *Table of contents.* Part and chapter titles can often give you a good idea of what a book contains, so turning directly to the table of contents is an efficient first step. Try to determine whether the chapter topics seem *specific* enough to be useful to you.

- *Preface or foreword.* Very often the preliminary pages of a book specify in detail the writer's purposes, range of interests, intended audience, topic restrictions, research limitations, and thesis. If the book contains either a preface or a foreword, check to see whether either summarizes what is to come.

- *Conclusion.* Some books and articles end with a summary of the contents and a statement of significance that could help you decide how appropriate that source is for your project.

- *Index.* A good index is like a cutaway drawing of the book's contents. Turn right away to the back of the book and check the index for words and topics key to your project. Then see whether they seem to have much importance in the book. Are the listings for your key terms many or few?

- *Bibliography and/or footnotes.* Lists of references on a subject, usually at the end of a book or article, show how carefully a writer has investigated the subject. In addition, they may help you find other sources for your study.

3. Skimming

If your investigation suggests that a source is potentially useful, take time to skim through it. Skimming a source can tell you a great deal about its approach and tone. Just by quickly reading over a few pages—or even a few sentences—of several parts of a source, you can get an idea of whether or not the book or article will be truly useful for your purposes. Look at the subheadings and at the first sentences of paragraphs. Then check the index for one of your key terms, turn to two or three pages listed, and skim them with the following questions in mind:

- Does this source cover material you need?
- What is the author's perspective—as advocate, critic?

- How does this perspective relate to your own?
- Are there facts, examples, research data, or expert opinions that you can use as evidence?

EXERCISE 39.1

Work in the library for an hour or so, using the techniques explained in 39a to evaluate several possible sources for a topic you are considering. Choose two sources and assess them carefully, entering your comments in your writing log if you are keeping one. Note the sources you examined, what you looked for, what specific elements helped you decide whether or not the sources would be useful, what use you expect to make of the sources, and how long you spent evaluating them. Finally, summarize where the research seems to be headed and what you now most need to do.

39b. Reading sources

Research calls for active, aggressive reading. "Active" readers take up conversation with the books they read, responding to the text with questions and comments. The more attentively you read, and the more you respond to what you read, the better your research will be. This section will guide you through some steps that will help you to become an active, questioning reader.

1. Building a working bibliography

One of the most basic requirements of reading for research is the creation of a working bibliography—a list of books, articles, and other sources that seem likely to address your research question. The emphasis here is on *working*—for this list will continue to evolve as you go along. Your working bibliography will include materials that may end up *not* being useful—one path will lead to another, and you will probably go in a few directions before you can know the one that's right. Keeping a working bibliography can help you to chart your course—and from this bibliography will evolve the list of works you finally use and cite in the essay.

As you use periodical indexes, the card catalog, or the circulation computer, make a bibliography card or notebook entry for each source you expect to be useful. At this stage, you need not be too selective; if you think you *might* use the source, make up an entry. As long as you have a bibliography entry for it, a source is easy to find a second time if you need to.

Some researchers prefer to use cards for bibliography entries because they can easily be arranged and rearranged—alphabetically for your list of sources, or by subtopic for the content of your essay. Other researchers prefer to keep bibliography entries in a notebook. Whichever format you choose, bibliography entries must contain all of the information necessary to produce your final list of sources—author, title, publisher's name and location, year of publication—plus the library call numbers of books or journals, in case you need to retrieve them. When you look at the actual source, be sure to check the accuracy of your entry by consulting the title and copyright pages of a book and the table of contents and first page of an article in a magazine or journal. Here are examples of bibliography cards or notebook entries for a book and a magazine article.

Pn 1992.3
u 5G57
1983

> Gitlin, Todd. <u>Inside Prime Time</u>.
> New York: Pantheon, 1983.

> Swertlow, Frank. "Hollywood's
> Cocaine Connection." <u>TV Guide</u> 28
> Feb., 1981: 6-12.

The entries shown above follow the Modern Language Association (MLA) style, the system for citing sources most widely used in English courses, but different disciplines use other systems (see Chapter 41). Writing the entries on the cards in the exact form you will use in your final bibliography will save you considerable time.

EXERCISE 39.2

If you have been making a working bibliography during your current research, take time now to check your entries for accuracy and fullness of information. If you have not yet made any entries, do so now for the sources you evaluated in Exercise 39.1, following the appropriate citation style.

2. Reading your sources with a critical eye

Researchers read with a strong sense of purpose: how does this source relate to my research goals? does it support my ideas, develop them further, or challenge them? Reading with a purpose calls for examining your sources with an astute, critical eye. Because of time constraints and the wealth of material available on most topics, you probably will not have time to read completely through all of your potential material. Thus, reading with a critical eye can make your research process more efficient; and the following considerations can guide your critical reading:

Reading with your research question in mind

A very good way of focusing your attention on the information most necessary to your research is to read with your research question in mind. Use the index and the table of contents to zero in on the parts of books that will help you answer your research question. Consider the following questions as you read:

- How does this material address your research question?
- In what ways does it provide support for your hypothesis?
- How might particular quotations help support your thesis?
- Does the source include counterarguments to your hypothesis that you will need to answer? What are they? What answers can you provide?

Identifying the author's perspective and tone

Every author holds opinions that affect his or her discussion of an issue, which you as a reader must try to recognize and understand.

Even the most seemingly factual report, like an encyclopedia article, is necessarily filled with implicit, often unstated, judgments. Read with an eye for the author's overall **perspective**—is he or she an advocate, in favor of something, or a critic, at odds with it?—as well as to seek out facts. In addition, identify the author's **tone**, or attitude toward both issues and audience. Is it cautious, angry, flippant, serious, impassioned? (For more on tone, see Chapter 26.) Alertness to perspective and tone will help you fully understand a source and, as a result, better decide how (or whether) to use it. The following questions can help you to read for perspective and tone:

- What is the author's perspective?
- What has persuaded the author to take this perspective? Does the author have a particular orientation toward the subject area?
- In what ways do you share the author's perspective?
- In what ways do you question or differ with the author's perspective?
- What is the author's tone? What words express this tone?

Assessing the author's argument and evidence

Every piece of writing has what may be called an argument, a position it takes. Even a report of scientific data implicitly "argues" that we should accept it as reliably gathered and reported. As you read, then, try to identify the author's argument, for it is his or her main point. Then try to decide *why* the author holds this view. Considering the following questions as you read can help you to recognize—and assess—the points being argued in your sources:

- What is the author's main point?
- How much and what kind of evidence supports that point?
- How persuasive do you find the evidence?
- Can you offer any counterarguments or refutations to the evidence?
- Can you detect any questionable logic or fallacious thinking? (See 4e.)

Questioning your sources

Because all sources make an explicit or implicit argument, they often disagree with one another. Disagreements among sources arise sometimes from different factual understandings, sometimes from different perspectives—ways of looking at things. For instance, if an authoritative source says that the chances of a nuclear power plant melting down are 1 in 100,000, two different commentators could interpret that statistic very differently. A critic of nuclear power could argue that nuclear accidents are so terrible that this chance is too much to take, while a supporter of nuclear power could argue that such a small chance is essentially no chance at all.

The point is that all knowledge must be interpreted subjectively, by people. As a result, a writer may well tell the truth and nothing but the truth; but he or she can never tell the *whole* truth because people are not all-knowing. Thus you must build your own informed opinion, your own truth, by seeking out and assessing many viewpoints as you read. Not all disputes can be solved by appealing to "neutral facts" because there *are* no neutral facts in the world of meanings. You must examine all sources critically, using them not as unquestioned authorities but as contributions to your own interpretation.

▌ 39c. Taking notes

Once you have decided a source might be useful to you, you will want to take notes on what you read. Note-taking requires reading carefully and purposefully, approaching a source with some general questions in mind. What do you expect the source to say about the subject? What will the source help you to demonstrate or prove? What part of your research is the source most relevant to? What else do you need to know?

Notes may be recorded either on index cards or in a notebook. Many writers like cards because they can be arranged in the order in which the notes are to be used in the essay. If you use cards, try to put only one piece of information or quotation on each one, so you can move it easily if necessary.

Because the bibliography entry (see 39b1) for a source fully identifies it, writing the author's last name and a key word from the title at the beginning or end of each note is usually enough to identify it for you. Then your note-taking can begin. Record the exact page reference for the note. If the note refers to more than one page, indicate the page breaks so that if you decide to use only part of the note in your essay, you will know which page to cite.

As you complete each note, read it over carefully. Recheck quotations, statistics, and specific facts for accuracy. Avoid abbreviations that may be confusing, especially in quotations, which should use the exact wording, spelling, and punctuation of the original.

Most of your notes will take the form of direct quotation, para-phrase, summary, or key terms. These forms can be combined; for example, you may want to summarize a passage but to quote one particular phrase or sentence from the same passage. In addition, you can photocopy material that you do not have time to take handwritten notes on.

Quoting

Quoting involves noting down direct quotations, a source's *exact words*. As a general rule, use direct quotations when the quotation is so memorable or expresses a point so perfectly that you cannot improve or shorten it without destroying the meaning you need. Because they represent a source's words exactly, direct quotations give special weight to their author's opinion. Quotations from those directly involved in an issue (crime victims, political leaders) are effective in social science essays; quotations from primary sources (literary works, eyewitness accounts) are especially important in humanities essays.

In any research essay, however, quotations from reliable and re-spected authorities can help establish your credibility as a researcher and thus increase your audience's confidence in your research and your conclusions. In addition, well-chosen quotations can broaden the appeal of your final essay by drawing on emotion as well as logic, appealing both to the reader's mind and heart. A student writing a research essay on the ethical issues involved in bullfighting, for ex-ample, might introduce an argument demonstrating that bullfighting is not a real sport by quoting Ernest Hemingway's striking comment that "the formal bull-fight is a tragedy, not a sport, and the bull is certain to be killed." (See 4e and 4f for more on logical and emotional appeals.)

In beginning research on traditional distinctions between *mind* and *brain*, a student writer came across the following sentences. The first could easily be paraphrased; the second, however, seemed partic-ularly memorable, so the student recorded it exactly.

ORIGINAL SOURCE

Mind is nothing more than a term we employ to describe some of the functions of the brain.

And further brain research isn't going to define further the matter of "mind" any more than turning over all the turf in Ireland is likely to turn up a colony of leprechauns. —RICHARD RESNICK, *The Brain*

553

Copy direct quotations *carefully*, with every punctuation mark, capital letter, and spelling exactly as in the original. Be sure, as the student does in the sample card below, to use brackets to introduce any words of your own and ellipses to show where you have cut material from a long quotation (see 32b and 32f). Of course, you will need to transfer the brackets or ellipses directly into your paper if you use the quotation. Here is the student's note card for the second sentence above. Notice that he uses both brackets and ellipses.

> Resnick, The Brain, p. 343
>
> "And [more] brain research isn't going to define... 'mind' any more than turning over all the turf in Ireland is likely to turn up a colony of leprechauns."

EXERCISE 39.3

Select one or two striking or especially authoritative quotations from a source listed in the working bibliography you created in Exercise 39.2, and enter them on note cards or in a notebook. Explain briefly why you consider each quotation noteworthy—why, in other words, you would quote rather than paraphrase or summarize.

Paraphrasing

A **paraphrase** accurately and thoroughly states all the relevant information from a passage *in your own words*. Paraphrase passages whose full meaning you want to include in your note.

ORIGINAL   Mind is nothing more than a term we employ to describe some of the functions of the brain.

PARAPHRASE   The term *mind* often simply denotes some of the brain's activities. (Resnick, 343)

If the paraphrase read "Mind and brain are the same thing," the paraphrase would have been less than accurate and thorough; if it read *"Mind* is nothing more than a word for some of the functions of the brain," it would risk the danger of plagiarizing by relying too much on the original author's own words.

Here is a longer example and a student's paraphrase as noted on a card.

ORIGINAL SOURCE

Certainly the site of the Popham colony was not the best choice. A few miles upriver from the mouth of the Kennebec, the site was on an open bluff which may have looked splendid in August and September when they landed, but during winter it was exposed to bitter weather and biting winds. This caused suffering, and the colonists later complained that winter was their downfall. Indeed, that winter of 1607 was a severe one, even in England. But if the weather had been terribly bad, the colony could have moved farther up the Kennebec, which they explored as far as Augusta, or to the sheltered islands in Muscongus Bay, which Weymouth had suggested. The site near the mouth of the Kennebec, however, offered a good location for trading with the Indians and good fishing grounds.

The prime reason for failure lay not with the weather or sickness or site, but with the character of the colonists and their leaders. They were not of the right stuff. They failed to form themselves into an effective, pioneering community.

–BILL CALDWELL, *The Islands of Maine*

Caldwell, <u>Islands of Maine</u>, pp. 56–57

Situated on an open bluff above the mouth of the Kennebec, the Popham colony of 1607 was established in August and September but was then exposed to harsh weather during the bitter winter of that year. Nevertheless, the colonists chose to stay there because the river made fishing and trading with the local Indians possible. When the colony failed, the colonists blamed the harsh winter, but in reality they had poor leaders and were themselves poorly chosen. As a result, they never became a cohesive group.

A CHECKLIST FOR PARAPHRASING

- Include all relevant information from the original.
- State the meaning completely in your own words; if you want to include an especially memorable phrase or sentence from the original passage, enclose it in quotation marks.
- Omit your own comments, elaborations, or reactions.
- Make sure to record the original source of the paraphrase.
- Recheck the paraphrase for accuracy and thoroughness.

EXERCISE 39.4

Choose an important passage from one of the sources you listed in the working bibliography in Exercise 39.2, and paraphrase it following the guidelines above.

Summarizing

A **summary** is a significantly shortened version of a passage, a section, or even a whole chapter or work that captures the main ideas *in your own words*. A good summary conveys the heart of a source with just enough information to record the main points. If you must include any of the original wording, put it in quotation marks. A summary card of the passage about the Popham colony that was paraphrased above might look like this:

> Caldwell, Islands of Maine, pp. 56-57
>
> The Popham colony of 1607 failed because of a poor site subject to harsh winter weather, poor leadership, and the poor character of company members, who were never able to work together as a group.

The length of a summary depends on how long the original is and how much information you will need to use. Your goal is to keep the summary as brief as possible, capturing only the gist of the passage. As a general rule, aim for no more than two sentences of summary for a paragraph. If you must summarize a book, pay particular attention to the preface or introduction, which often states the book's main ideas.

EXERCISE 39.5

Choose a section from a source you listed in the working bibliography in Exercise 39.2, and write a summary of it, emphasizing the main ideas in your own words.

Taking key-term notes

Taking key-term notes is a technique many researchers use. As their name suggests, such notes consist of significant terms jotted down as you read along. They may include names, dates, short statements, or quotations—anything that can jog your memory or be used in drafting the essay. Key-term notes on the passage about the Popham colony that was paraphrased and summarized above might look like this:

```
Caldwell, Islands of Maine , pp. 56-57

Popham colony 1607-failed at mouth of Kennebec
poor site on bluff - col. blamed winter
stayed because could trade and fish
poor leadership & poor character
```

Key-term notes are useful in condensing an article or a source to a "nutshell" of information. But you must be sure that they are complete enough so you can remember what they mean and how they fit together. Be sure to include the author and title, and note the page numbers of the passage to which the key terms refer. Be careful about using abbreviations in key-term notes. In this case, the writer probably would recognize *col.* as *colonists.* Had the writer used *co.*, however, remembering whether the abbreviation meant *company, colony, companions,* or some other word might have been difficult.

EXERCISE 39.6

Review the key-term notes on the passage about the Popham colony, and answer the following questions.

1. What points would you add to the notes?
2. What points would you leave out of the notes?

Then create a few key-term notes from the source that you summarized in Exercise 39.5. Then, ask yourself these questions: Do the notes provide enough information to bring back the original passage? What could you do to make these notes more useful?

Photocopying source material

Nearly all libraries are equipped with photocopying machines, and as a researcher you can use them to photocopy pages or even whole articles or chapters. If you photocopy materials, make sure to write out on the photocopy all the source information you will need to cite in your bibliography (see 39b1). (And check to make sure that page numbers are clearly legible on copies.)

▌ 39d. Interpreting sources

Your task as a reader is to identify and understand sources and sets of data as completely as possible. As a writer, your aim must be to present data and sources *to other readers* so that they can most readily understand the point you are making. Doing so calls for careful thinking on your part, as you work to interpret sources.

Turning data into information

Computer scientists sometimes distinguish between **data**—bits of facts or strings of statements—and **information**—the meaning attached to the data. As a researcher, you will gather a great deal of data, probably more than you need or can use. But those data become information only when their meaning is made clear. You may have gathered two dozen facts about a particular city's finances, for example, but together they form a rather random list of facts. Turning them into information calls for pointing out their significance or meaning—that, for instance, the city is on the brink of bankruptcy.

Synthesizing data and drawing inferences

You can begin turning data into information by **synthesizing**—grouping similar pieces of data together; looking for patterns or trends, identifying the gist, or main point, of the data. Most often, finding the gist of a source or set of data will call for drawing **inferences**—conclusions that are not explicitly stated but that follow logically from the data given. For example, you may have data indicating severe drought in every Midwestern state. Other data report very low levels of crop production in those states. From these data, you draw the inference that farmers in the Midwest face financial crisis. As a researcher, you have turned data into information.

Recording your thoughts and ideas

Perhaps the most exciting part of research occurs when the materials you are reading spark something in your mind and new ideas take hold. As you read, your mind is busy processing all the materials you are discovering with those you have previously discovered, seeking connections and similarities, making distinctions, synthesizing in the ways discussed above. As you work, ideas will occur to you that will become part of your position or argument. *Don't let them get away.* Jot down the ideas that come to you as you read, perhaps in a special section of your writing log if you are keeping one. Do not worry about whether the idea is true or right or even useful—just get it down and think about it later. Some ideas may be thrown away because they do not suit the final shape your essay takes, but others will likely *provide* that final shape.

Disagreements among sources can provide particularly fruitful areas to consider and may provoke you to new insights all your own. Consequently, you need to pay close attention to the arguments put forth by all your sources—those you agree with as well as those you disagree with. Jot down your thoughts as you read—agreements, questions, comments, reactions.

EXERCISE 39.7

Following are two passages about the War of 1812, the first from an American encyclopedia and the second from a Canadian history book. Read each one carefully, and then answer the following questions, noting any differences in the two accounts.

1. What motivated the War Hawks?
2. Who attacked whom at the beginning of the Battle of Tippecanoe?
3. What did the War of 1812 mean in British, American, and Canadian history?
4. Why did the Treaty of Ghent end up restoring the prewar boundaries?

Then, answer these questions about *both* passages.

1. What is the perspective, tone, and argument of each passage?
2. How does each passage make clear its point of view?
3. Can you find at least one example in each passage that seems to show how the author's point of view accounts for or affects the interpretation of events?
4. Why do you think each passage takes the view it does?
5. How would you, as a researcher, evaluate and use these sources?

Compare your analysis with those of other students in your class, and be prepared for a full class discussion.

From the *World Book Encyclopedia*

War of 1812

The War of 1812 was in many ways the strangest war in United States history. It could well be named the War of Faulty Communication. Two days before war was declared, the British Government had stated that it would repeal the laws which were the chief excuse for fighting. If there had been telegraphic communication with Europe, the war might well have been avoided. Speedy communication would also have prevented the greatest battle of the war, which was fought at New Orleans fifteen days after a treaty of peace had been signed.

It is strange also that the war for freedom of the seas began with the invasion of Canada, and that the treaty of peace which ended the war settled none of the issues over which it had supposedly been fought.

The chief United States complaint against the British was interference with shipping. But New England, the great shipping section of the United States, bitterly opposed the idea of going to war. The demand for war came chiefly from the West and South, although these sections were not really hurt by British naval policy.

When we add that both sides claimed victory in the War of 1812, it becomes clear that the whole struggle was a confused mass of contradictions. These must be explained and cleared up before we can understand why the democratic United States sided with Napoleon I, the French dictator, in a struggle for world power. . . .

The War Hawks. A group of young men known as "War Hawks" dominated Congress during this period. Henry Clay of Kentucky and John C. Calhoun of South Carolina were the outstanding leaders of the group. Clay was then Speaker of the House of Representatives. Like Clay and Calhoun, most of the War Hawks came from western and southern states, where many of the people were in favor of going to war with Great Britain.

The people of New England generally opposed going to war, because war with Great Britain would wipe out entirely the New England shipping trade which had already been heavily damaged. Another reason New England opposed war was because many New Englanders sympathized with Great Britain in its struggle against the dictator Napoleon.

Many historians believe that a leading motive of the War Hawks was a desire for expansion. The people of the Northwest were meeting armed resistance in their attempt to take more land from the Indians, and they believed that the Indians had considerable British support. An American army was attacked by Indians at the Battle of Tippecanoe in the Wabash Valley in November, 1811, and British guns were found on the battlefield. The Westerners, therefore, were anxious to drive the British out of Canada. Southerners looked longingly at Florida, which belonged to Great Britain's ally, Spain. The South had also suffered a serious loss of markets. But the deciding motive for war seems to have been a strong desire for more territory.

Progress of the war

Declaration of war.   On June 1, 1812, President Madison asked Congress to declare war against Great Britain. He gave as his reasons the impressment of United States seamen and the interference with United States trade. He charged also that the British had stirred up Indian warfare in the Northwest. Congress declared war on June 18, 1812. Two days earlier, the British Foreign Minister had announced that the Orders in Council would be repealed, but word of this announcement did not reach America until after the war had begun.

Because President Madison asked for the declaration of war, many Federalists blamed him for the conflict, calling it "Mr. Madison's war." But it was more the War Hawks' war than it was Madison's. . . .

Treaty of Ghent.   The British public was tired of war and especially of war taxes. The British Government therefore proposed discussing terms. Commissioners of the two countries met at Ghent, Belgium, in August, 1814.

The British at first insisted that the United States should give up certain territory on the northern frontier, and set up a large permanent Indian reservation in the Northwest. But American victories in the summer and fall of 1814 led the British to drop these demands. A treaty was finally signed on December 24, 1814, in Ghent, Belgium. By its terms, all land which had been captured by either party was to be given up. Everything was to be exactly as it was before the war, and commissions from both of the countries were to settle any disputed points about boundaries. Nothing whatever was said in the treaty about impressments, blockades, or the British Orders in Council, which supposedly had caused the war. The treaty was formally ratified on February 17, 1815.

Results of the war

One important result of the War of 1812 was the rapid rise of manufacturing in the United States. During the war, United States citizens were unable to import goods from Great Britain, and had to begin making many articles for themselves. The war also increased national patriotism, and helped to unite the United States into one nation.

The war settled none of the issues over which the United States had fought. But most of these issues faded out during the following years. In the long period of peace after 1815, the British had no occasion to make use of impressments or blockades. Indian troubles in the Northwest were practically ended by the death of the chief Tecumseh and by the British surrender of Detroit and other posts. The United States occupied part of Florida during the war, and was soon able to buy the rest of it from Spain.

One indirect result of the War of 1812 was the later election to the Presidency of Andrew Jackson and of William Henry Harrison. Both of these men won military fame which had much to do with their elections. Another indirect result was the decline of Federalist power. New England leaders, most of them Federalists, met secretly in Hartford, Conn., to study amendments to the Constitution. Their opponents charged that they had plotted treason, and the Federalists never recovered. . . .

Chief battles of the war

The War of 1812 was not an all-out struggle on either side. For the British, the war was just an annoying part of their struggle with Napoleon. For many Americans, it was an unjustified attempt to gratify the expansionist ambitions of the South and West.

From *Canada: A Story of Challenge*

Danger on the western border

From the Treaty of Versailles in 1783 until the outbreak of a second war with the United States in 1812, the western border of young Canada was never secure. Trouble arose in the lands south of the Great Lakes; in the Ohio country which had been officially granted to the United States in 1783, but which had remained tied to the St Lawrence fur trade. The final consequence was open war. The trouble began almost with the signing of peace in 1783, when Britain quickly came to regret the ready surrender of so much of the West, and sought at least to delay its transfer to the United States.

The chief reasons for delay arose from the fur traders and the Indians who were still the masters of the unsettled Ohio West. The Canadian fur merchants of the St Lawrence drew most of their trade from that country, and they asked that the transfer be postponed for two years until they could adjust their business to this heavy loss. The Indians supplied the major reason, however. They declared that they had been ignored in the Treaty of Versailles and that Britain had handed over their lands, which they had never ceded, to the United States. There was danger that if the West was transferred and opened to American settlement the Indians would, in revenge, attack the thinly held and almost unprotected British settlements in Upper Canada.

Taking advantage of vague wording in the peace treaty, therefore, the British held on to the military and trading posts in the West below the Lakes, giving as their reason the failure of the Americans to carry out the term of the treaty that called for the restoration of Loyalist property. It was a sound reason, but not the chief one for failing to transfer the West.

This situation dragged on into the 1790's, while the Americans feared that the British were arousing the Indians against them, and the British feared that the Indians would become aroused. Dorchester, as governor, darkly expected a new war with the United States, and had some hope of building an Indian state in the Ohio country that would stand between the Americans and the Upper Canadian frontier and help to protect the latter. The Americans, meanwhile, were pressing forward from the region south of the Ohio, and sending forces against the Indians in order to break their hold on the western country. In 1794 one of these expeditions completely defeated the tribes at the battle of Fallen Timbers, and hope of an Indian 'buffer state' collapsed. The tribes ceded their lands to the United States. . . .

The rapidly advancing western states of the American union made good use of the growing warlike spirit in the republic. They held that the place to punish Britain was in Canada. Filled with the forceful confidence and expansive drive of the frontier they wanted to add Canada to the American union: a Canada which American frontier settlement had already invaded. Was not Upper Canada by now practically an American state? The 'war hawks' of the American West clamoured for an easy conquest. Their chance seemed to arrive in 1811.

In that year the western Indians, being steadily pushed back by advancing American settlement, attempted a last stand. Led by the chief Tecumseh, they formed a league to resist further inroads. The Americans saw this as the threat of a new Pontiac uprising, of savage Indian raids on the frontier. They attacked the Indians, and by their victory at the battle of Tippecanoe, destroyed Tecumseh's league. Yet the American West was not satisfied. It was fully convinced that the British had been behind the Indians, although the Canadian government had actually sought to keep the Indian league at peace. It seemed that the West would only be safe when the British had been driven out of Canada. The war hawks cried for blood, the American frontier wanted new lands to conquer, and the American East was newly aroused by fresh skirmishes over the right of search. The United States declared war in June, 1812, and set out to capture Canada.

The second struggle with the Americans

The War of 1812 in British history is only a side-show, not altogether successful, during the huge and victorious contest with Napoleon. In United States history it is a second war of independence, chiefly against the weight of British sea-power. In Canadian history it is above all a land war, a second struggle against American invasion. All these pictures are partly true; and in studying the Canadian version one must bear in mind that it portrays only the War of 1812 as it affected Canada. Yet for Canada the war was vitally important; far more important than it was for Britain, and much more dangerous than it was for the United States. . . .

Thus the war ended late in 1814 in a stalemate, which was probably a good thing for future peace.

It was not completely a stalemate. Britain still held the West and some of the Maine coast, and the British naval blockade was strangling American commerce. But in the peace negotiations the Americans made clear their readiness to go on fighting rather than yield territory. Faced with a revival of Napoleon's power in Europe at that very moment, Britain did not press the point. As a result the Treaty of Ghent of 1814 simply stopped the fighting, restored the pre-war boundaries, and said little about the problems that had caused the conflict.

Nevertheless in the next few years many of these problems disappeared. The question of the right of search ended with the Napoleonic Wars, and vanished in the long years of peace after 1815. The Indian problem declined as American settlement filled in the old West; the tribes had been too weakened by the war to offer any further resistance. The American war-hawks had found Canada no willing mouthful, and the United States was turning away to expand in a new direction, towards the south. . . .

The War of 1812 thus tended to bring British North America together and strengthened the bond with Britain. Any common feelings among the colonists, however, were largely directed against the United States. This anti-American spirit was still a narrow basis on which to build a Canadian nationalism. Anti-Americanism was particularly evident in Upper Canada. Further American settlement was largely prevented there, and American settlers already in the province were in danger of persecution—the Loyalists' case in reverse—if their declarations of British sentiments were not loud enough. Nevertheless, on the whole these reactions to the strain of the War of 1812 were understandable; and not an extreme price to pay for the survival of British North America.   —J.M.S. Careless

EXERCISE 39.8

Identify two sources in the research you considered in Exercise 39.1 that hold different perspectives. Then analyze these sources, using the guidelines in 39b2 for doing so. How can you synthesize the information given from the different perspectives? What inferences can you draw from these sources?

39e. Avoiding plagiarism and crediting your sources

"There is," in the words of Ecclesiastes, "no new thing under the sun." In a way, the biblical saying is true of research as well as of life in general: whatever research we do is influenced and affected by everything we have already read and experienced. Our written research acts as part of a larger conversation, and it reflects and depends on that larger context for much of its meaning. If you try, for instance, to trace the origins of every idea you have had just *today*, you will quickly see the extent to which we are all indebted to others as the sources of information.

Given every writer's dependence on a vast network of sources, giving full credit to those sources presents a challenge. Nevertheless, crediting sources as fully as possible is important for several reasons. First, acknowledging your sources helps you critically examine your own research and thinking. How timely and reliable are those sources? Have you used them accurately? Second, crediting sources helps readers by placing your research into a *context* of other thinking and research; it shows in what ways your research is part of a larger conversation and lets readers know where *they* can find more information on a topic. Finally, crediting your sources allows you to thank those whose work you have built on and thus to avoid plagiarism.

Crediting sources fully and generously, then, provides a means of establishing your *ethos*, or credibility, as a researcher (see 4d for further discussion of *ethos*.) Failure to credit sources breaks trust both with the research "conversation" and with readers; as a sign of dishonesty, it can easily destroy the credibility of both researcher and research.

1. Avoiding plagiarism

Plagiarism is the use of someone else's words as your own without crediting the original writer for those words. As a careful and credible researcher, you want to give full credit to sources both in parenthetical citations and bibliographic entries (see Chapter 41). Doing so for every single idea you build upon is an impossible task, however. In practical terms, where do you draw the line?

Materials not requiring credit

Common knowledge.   If most readers like yourself would be likely to know something, you need not cite it. You do not need to credit a source for a statement that Ronald Reagan was elected to his first term as president in 1980, for example. If, on the other hand, you give the exact number of popular votes Reagan received in the 1980 election, you should cite the source for that figure.

Facts available in a wide variety of sources.   If a number of encyclopedias, almanacs, or textbooks include the information, you need not cite a specific source. For instance, you would not need to cite a source for the fact that the Japanese bombing of Pearl Harbor on December 7, 1941, destroyed most of the base except for the oil tanks and submarines. You would, however, need to credit a source that argued that the failure of the bombing to destroy the submarines meant that Japan was destined to lose the Pacific War.

Your own findings from field research.   If you conduct field research—observation, interviews, surveys—and produce results, simply announce those results as your own.

2. Crediting your sources

For material that does not fall under these three headings, credit sources as fully as possible, using quotation marks and citing the source parenthetically or in an endnote and listing it in a list of sources (see Chapter 41).

Materials requiring credit

Direct quotations.   Whenever you use another person's words directly, credit the source. (If two quotations from the same source appear close together and separate parenthetical citations would sound awkward, use only one, placed *after* the second quotation.) Even if you are quoting in the middle of a paraphrase whose source you intend to acknowledge, set off in quotes and *separately* acknowledge the direct use of the author's words.

Assertions that are arguable or facts that are not widely known. If your readers would be unlikely to know a fact, or if an author presents an assertion that may or may not be true, cite the source. To claim, for instance, that Israel has built atomic weapons, you would need to cite the source of your claim, because Israel has denied doing so.

Judgments, opinions, and claims of others. Whenever you summarize or paraphrase anyone else's opinion, give the source for that summary or paraphrase. Even though the wording may be completely your own, you need to give credit for the idea.

Statistics, charts, tables, and graphs from any source. Credit all graphic material, even if you yourself create the graph from data in another source.

Information or help provided by friends, instructors, or others. A conference with an instructor may give you just the idea you need to clinch an argument. Give credit. Friends may help you conduct surveys, refine questionnaires, or think through a major problem. Credit them, too.

READING WITH AN EYE FOR PERSPECTIVE AND TONE

The following paragraphs come from the opening of an essay about nuclear war published in *Parade*. Read the paragraphs carefully, paying close attention to the tone the author creates and to the perspective he takes on his subject. In one or two sentences, describe the author's tone and perspective. What elements in the paragraphs signal the tone? Imagine that you ran across this essay in research for an essay about nuclear armaments. How would the tone and perspective in this source be useful to you? How, on the other hand, might it prove troublesome?

Except for fools and madmen, everyone knows that nuclear war would be an unprecedented human catastrophe. A more or less typical strategic warhead has a yield of 2 megatons, the explosive equivalent of 2 million tons of TNT. But 2 million tons of TNT is about the same as all the bombs exploded in World War II—a single bomb with the explosive power of the entire Second World War but compressed into a few seconds of time and an area 30 or 40 miles across. . . .

In a 2-megaton explosion over a fairly large city, buildings would be

567

vaporized, people reduced to atoms and shadows, outlying structures blown down like matchsticks and raging fires ignited. And if the bomb were exploded on the ground, an enormous crater, like those that can be seen through a telescope on the surface of the Moon, would be all that remained where midtown once had been. There are now more than 50,000 nuclear weapons, more than 13,000 megatons of yield, deployed in the arsenals of the United States and the Soviet Union—enough to obliterate a million Hiroshimas.

—CARL SAGAN, "Nuclear War and Climatic Catastrophe: A Nuclear Winter"

FOR EXAMINING YOUR OWN PARAPHRASES AND SUMMARIES

Choose a section consisting of two or three paragraphs from one of the passages in Exercise 39.7 on the War of 1812, and write a paraphase of it, following the author's content but using your own words. Reread your paraphrase, and analyze it using the guidelines for paraphrasing listed on page 556. Then try summarizing the same section. Reread your summary, and check to see how well you followed the suggestions for summarizing given on page 556.

40. Organizing, Drafting, and Revising a Research Essay

A nineteenth-century author once remarked that "In research the horizon recedes as we advance. . . . And research is always incomplete." Indeed, we might slightly alter a line from Samuel Johnson and say that a person who is tired of research is tired of living. For in many ways, the process of living constantly demands research. But while you may continue to pursue a research question for a long time, there comes a time to draw the strands of research together and to articulate your conclusions in writing. This chapter will help you at that point.

The processes of research and writing are intimately linked. While you are conducting research, you will also be coming up with ideas, considering organizational possibilities, and recognizing connections among your materials, making notes and perhaps attempting partial drafts as you work. From among these thoughts, you will eventually choose the final form in which to cast your own conclusions.

Probably, you will do most of your final organizing and drafting when your research is largely complete and you have most of the facts, citations, quotations, and other data you think you need. For most college research essays, the process of drafting a final version should begin at least two weeks before the deadline, in order to allow for response to the draft, for further research, and for revision.

▎ 40a. Refining your plans

Throughout your research, you have been generating notes that answer your research question and reflect on your hypothesis. Your growing understanding of the subject, in turn, has no doubt led you to gather other information, which may have altered your original question. This somewhat circular process, which may best be described as a research spiral, is at the heart of all research-based writing.

You should by now have a fair number of notes containing facts, opinions, paraphrases, summaries, quotations, and citations of all kinds. You probably also have thoughts about the connections among the many pieces of information you found. And you should have some sense of whether your hypothesis has been proved and can serve as the thesis of an essay. At this point, you should reconsider your purpose, your audience, and your thesis.

▌ 1. Reconsidering purpose, audience, and thesis

Given what you now know about your research question, consider questions such as the following:

1. Are you addressing an audience other than your instructor?
2. How much about your research question does your audience know already? How much background will they need to be told?
3. What sorts of supporting information are they likely to find convincing—examples? precedents? quotations from authorities? (See 4e.)
4. What tone will most appeal to them? Should you present yourself as a colleague, an expert, or a student? How can you establish some common ground with them and show fair consideration of their points of view? (See 4d.)
5. What is your central purpose? What other purposes, if any, do you have?
6. What is your thesis trying to establish? How likely is your audience to accept it?

▌ 2. Developing an explicit thesis

A useful means of relating your purpose, thesis, and audience before you begin a full draft is to write out an **explicit thesis statement** specifying a number of elements about your essay in advance. Such a statement forces you to articulate all your major lines of argument and to see how well those arguments carry out your purpose and appeal to your audience. At the drafting stage, your explicit thesis statement might take the following form:

> In this essay, I plan to (explain, argue, demonstrate, analyze, and so on) for an audience of _____
> that _____

because or if (1) ———————————, (2) ———————————,
(3) ———————————.

3. Testing your thesis

Writing out an explicit thesis will many times confirm the re-search you have been doing and support your hypothesis. Sometimes, however, it may reveal that your hypothesis is not valid, is unsupport-able, or is insufficiently focused. In such cases, you must then rethink your original research question, perhaps do further research, and work toward a revised hypothesis and eventually a revised thesis. To test and probe your explicit thesis statement at this point, consider the following list of questions:

1. How can you state the topic of your thesis or your comment about the topic more precisely or more clearly? (See 2f for more information about topic and comment.)

2. In what ways will your thesis interest and appeal to your audience? What can you do to make that interest grow? (See 4f.)

3. How could the wording of your thesis be more specific? Could you use more concrete nouns (see 25c) or stronger verbs (see 21a)? Should you add qualifying adjectives or adverbs (see Chapter 10)?

4. Is your thesis going to be manageable, given your limits of time and knowledge? What might you do to make it more manageable?

5. What research evidence do you have to support each aspect of your thesis? What additional evidence do you need?

The goal of such questions is to push your thinking about your research as far as you can, exercising your mental muscles and leading you to a richer, more complete understanding of your subject.

40b. Organizing information

In discussing her own process of writing, Marie Winn talks about the challenge of transforming the tangle of ideas and information "into an orderly and logical sequence on a blank piece of paper." This is the task of organization, of grouping information effectively. Experienced writers differ considerably in the ways they go about this task, and you will want to experiment until you find an organizational method that works well for you. This section will review two common planning strategies—clustering and outlining. Before examining these strategies, however, you should consider whether or not your course discipline has a conventional research-writing format that you will need to follow.

1. Considering conventional formats

In many disciplines, essays tend to follow certain conventional patterns. These formats may be fairly consistent, as in laboratory reports and certain research reports in the natural or social sciences, or fairly loose, as in the great range of historical surveys, literature reviews, arguments, and interpretations common in the humanities. An instructor may, in fact, specify the format expected in your final essay or, less formally, advise you to include certain features without requiring a specific structure. On the other hand, your instructor may simply tell you to shape your research essay as you would any other essay (see 2h) or argument (see 4g). The following formats are intended as rough guides that may serve to get you started thinking about organizational patterns. Your purpose and audience and the kind and number of your materials will be of paramount importance in the final organizational pattern you develop.

Surveying literature

In many disciplines you will have occasion to write a **literature survey,** which orients a reader to some of the significant work that has been done in the field or on your topic. Sometimes called a **review of the literature** or **bibliographic essay,** a literature survey serves as a guide to the major resources in a field or supplies an update or an overview of work done on a particular issue. It may be a section within an essay or an essay in itself. A literature survey may not build on an argumentative hypothesis, but it is interpretive in that the writer provides a perspective on the works discussed. This evaluation is explicit in the running commentary on the works discussed and implicit in the act of selecting what to cover in the survey. A literature survey often includes an *introduction*, a *division section* that explains the method of selection and previews the topics to be covered, a *discussion* of the works surveyed, a concluding *commentary*, and a *list of works cited*.

Reporting research

Experimental or field research is often another conventional report format, which usually includes eight standard sections: an *abstract*, which sums up the study's hypothesis, methods, findings, and conclusions; an *introduction*, which poses the question behind the research and proposes the hypothesis to be tested; a *survey of previous work*, which reviews background studies and discusses how they affect the current hypothesis; a discussion of *materials and methods*, which reports exactly what was done and how it was done; *results*, which summarize findings that relate to the hypothesis; *discussion*, which highlights the significance of the results; *conclusion*, which answers, tentatively, the question posed at the beginning of the study and suggests areas for further research; and a *list of references*.

Interpreting sources

In the humanities and sometimes in the sciences as well, you may have cause to follow a conventional format for essays that interpret sources. Such an essay typically includes the following sections, though not necessarily in this order: an *introduction*, explaining the specific question and its importance; *background of previous work*, surveying some of the literature and perhaps identifying controversies or errors; a *statement of purpose or thesis*; an *exploration of the thesis*, supporting it and introducing additional information; a *conclusion*, pointing out any ramifications or complications; and a *list of works cited*.

2. Clustering

During your research, you have been taking notes and keeping lists of ideas. To organize these materials using a clustering strategy, examine them for connections, finding what might be presented with what, which notes will be more useful and which less useful, which ideas lend support to the thesis and which should be put aside. Brainstorm about your research question one last time, and add the resulting notes to your other materials, looking to see if they fit with any of the materials you already have.

If you have been keeping notes on cards, you can arrange the cards in clusters, putting the ones with your main topics in the center and arranging any related cards around them. If you have been taking notes in a notebook, identify your major topics and write them on a blank piece of paper with a circle around each one. Then "cluster" related supporting ideas, quotations, key words, and so forth around them, as shown in the following diagram:

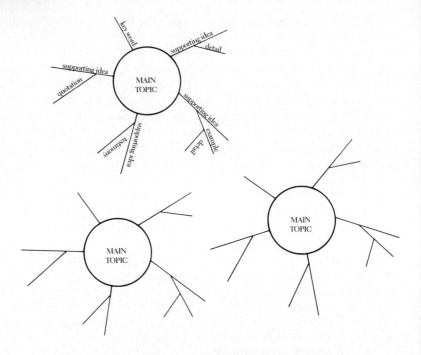

Clustering will help you to identify your major ideas and to see whether you have covered all the necessary areas. It will help you see whether you have too many ideas to manage—or whether you need to do more research in some area. Most important, it will allow you to see how the many small pieces of your research fit together and result in the larger structure of a complete essay.

3. Outlining

Writers use outlines in various ways. Some move from clustering into drafting and then outline the draft to study its tentative structure. Others prefer to use material generated in clustering to develop a working outline, listing the major points in a tentative order with support for each major point. Such a working outline may see you through the rest of the process, or you may decide to revise it as you go along. Still other writers prefer to plot out their organization early on and do so in a formal outline.

574

A formal outline is a double-edged sword. On the one hand, it allows you to see before drafting exactly how all the main parts of your essay will fit together—how your ideas relate, how abstract your ideas are, what the overall structure of your argument will be. On the other hand, most people find a full formal outline devilishly hard to write before they have considered their material in some less formal way. That is why you may decide to make a rough outline *before* a formal outline.

Most formal outlines follow a conventional format of numbered and lettered headings and subheadings using Roman numerals, capital letters, Arabic numbers, and lower-case letters to show the levels of importance of the various ideas and their relationships. Each new level is indented to show its subordination to the preceding level. Following is a model of a typical formal outline:

Thesis statement

I. First main topic
   A. First subordinate idea
      1. First supporting idea
      2. Second supporting idea
      3. Third supporting idea
   B. Second subordinate idea
      1. First supporting idea
      2. Second supporting idea

II. Second main topic
   A. First subordinate idea
      1. First supporting idea
      2. Second supporting idea
   B. Second subordinate idea
      1. First supporting idea
      2. Second supporting idea
         a. First supporting detail
         b. Second supporting detail

Each level contains at least two parts, so there is no A without a B, no 1 without a 2. Comparable items are placed on the same level—all capital letters, for instance, or all Arabic numbers. Each level develops the idea before it—1 and 2 under A, for example, include the points that develop, explain, or demonstrate. Headings are stated in parallel form—either all sentences, or all topics that are grammatically parallel.

Formal outlining requires logical thought and careful evaluation of your ideas, which is precisely why it is a valuable effort. Charting out such an outline allows a writer to see the skeleton of an essay, making sure that all the "bones" are in the right and logical places, that all the relationships make sense. A full-sentence outline will make those relationships most clear, so if you want to give your organization the most rigorous test of its structure, try working it into a full-sentence outline. If the logical relationships seem fully established to you, a topic outline will provide the necessary test of coherence. Remember, however, that an outline is at best a means to an end, not an end in itself. New ideas will almost surely occur as you write, and you should not feel bound to the ideas on your outline. Though an outline serves, on one level, as a plan for your essay, it can also serve to stimulate altogether new thoughts and plans, ones you should feel free to consider and pursue.

Here is a typical topic outline for a literary research essay:

Thesis: F. Scott Fitzgerald helped create the image of the Jazz Age, with all its frivolity and irresponsibility, but at the same time he exposed the corruption and moral decay that were as much a part of the era as were the pursuit of money, youth, and idealized romance.

I. The corruption and tragedy of wealth
  A. *The Great Gatsby*
    1. Ostentatiousness and display
    2. The corruption of Jay Gatz's innocence
    3. The carelessness of Daisy
  B. "The Rich Boy"
    1. Ruin by money
    2. Lack of any moral responsibility
  C. *The Beautiful and the Damned*
    1. Anthony and Gloria's refusal to live without wealth
    2. Total purposelessness
    3. The fight for inheritance
      a. Moral failure
      b. Emotional exhaustion
    4. Hollowness of the material victory

II. The vain attempts to recapture youth and beauty
  A. *The Beautiful and the Damned*
    1. A world for the young
    2. Anthony and Gloria's deterioration with age
    3. Youthful beauty the basis of Gloria's entire personality

B. "Babylon Revisited"
 1. Search for the meaning of youth
 2. Charlie's failure to overcome the mistakes of youth
  a. Aged and alone
  b. Lost and regretful
C. *The Great Gatsby*
 1. Gatsby's failure to recognize the destructiveness of time
 2. His search for the love of his youth
 3. "Vision without youth"
III. The illusory idealization of romance
 A. *The Great Gatsby*
  1. Gatsby's romantic vision of Daisy
  2. Daisy's coldness
  3. The tragic outcome
 B. "Winter Dreams"
  1. Dexter's infatuation with Judy
  2. His sacrifices and disappointments
  3. Judy's ultimate decay

▌ 40c. Drafting your essay

At the point when you are ready to draft your essay, set yourself a deadline and structure all your tasks with that deadline in mind. Gather your notes, clustered or outlined materials, quotations, any sources you may need to consult. Most writers find that some sustained work (perhaps two or three hours) at this point pays off. Begin drafting where you feel most confident. If you have a good idea for an introduction, begin there. If you are not sure exactly what you want to do in the introduction but do know how you want to approach some particular point, begin with that and return to the introduction later. The most important thing is to get started.

The drafting process itself varies considerably among researchers, and much about the way you draft will be up to you. Some writers try to make the first draft as perfect as possible, working meticulously paragraph by paragraph. Others draft as fast as they can, getting all their material down in whatever form and smoothing it out later. Some follow an outline from start to finish; others draft sections separately and arrange them later. Your writing process is your own, and no one else can tell you what works best for you. A few tips, however, may help:

- Draft your material on one point at a time. You may want to plan to draft in several short sessions.
- Don't let yourself get bogged down at this point with individual details. Jot down in the margin notes about any problems or unresolved matters to return to later so that you don't get sidetracked now. Your main objective is to get your draft on paper; later you can revise, fill in the gaps, and refine the details.
- Use any clustering or outlining as a springboard to help you know where and how to start.
- End each writing session by deciding what comes next and making some notes to help you get started when you turn to that topic.

I 1. Drafting your introduction

The introduction to a research essay plays a special role, for it must set the context for what is to come. Like any introduction, it should draw readers into the essay, but also it needs to provide them with any background they will need to understand the discussion. You can find general advice on writing introductions in 3f2 and 5e1, but some specific things you should consider in drafting an introduction for a research essay include the following:

- It is often effective to *open with a question*, especially your research question. Then you might explain what you will do to answer the question and *end with your hypothesis or thesis* (in essence, the answer to the question).
- Because in your essay you will be bringing together several distinct points from various sources, you will probably want to *forecast your main points*, to help readers get their bearings.
- You will want to *establish your own credibility* as a research writer by showing your experience and demonstrating what you have done to become an expert on your topic.
- In general, you may *not* want to open with a quotation—though it can be a good attention-getter, it is probably not a good idea to give any one source such prominence. In a research essay, you may want to quote several sources to support your ideas; opening with a quotation from one source may give the impression that you will be presenting that writer's ideas rather than using them in support of your own.

I 2. Drafting your conclusion

A good conclusion to a research essay helps readers to know what they have learned. Its job is not to persuade (the body of your essay should already have done that), but it *can* leave the reader with a memorable phrase or example that will in fact contribute to the overall effectiveness of your argument. General advice on writing conclusions can be found in 3f3 and 5e2, but following are some specific strategies especially appropriate for research essays.

- A specific-to-general pattern is frequently appropriate, opening with a restatement of your thesis and then expanding to some more general conclusion to remind readers of the significance of your discussion.

- If you have covered several main points, you may want to restate them in your conclusion.

- Try to end with something that will have lasting impact—a provocative question, a vivid image, a call for action, a warning—and that will give readers an idea of what they should think or do.

- Tailor your conclusion to the needs of your readers, both in terms of the information you include and the tone and style of your final appeal.

40d. Incorporating source materials

Once you are at the point of drafting your essay, a new task awaits: how to weave your source materials into your own writing. The challenge is to use your sources yet to remain the author of your paper— to quote, paraphrase, and summarize other voices while at the same time remaining the single dominant voice in your essay. The decision you will often face in using source material is *how* to do so—whether to use a direct quotation, to paraphrase, or to summarize.

1. Using direct quotations

What are the characteristics of a good quotation? They can be boiled down to two: a good quotation should be either necessary or memorable.

Your essay must be your own work, and you should depend on other people's words as little as possible, limiting quotations to those *necessary* to your argument. You can demonstrate that you know the authoritative sources with summary and paraphrase, for instance, but you may want to quote a source if he or she has said something so effectively that the words cannot be paraphrased without altering meaning. Quoting someone's words exactly is also a way of bringing that person into the "conversation" of your discussion, thus linking you to the larger dialogue in the field. Finally, quoting an authority on your subject contributes to your own credibility as a writer.

In addition, you will find some quotations during your research that are so memorable that you may use them largely for effect; to *delight* your audience as much as to inform them.

You can incorporate quotations into your discussion in two ways—by enclosing them in quotation marks within your text or by setting them off as a block. The choice depends on the length of the quotation.

Enclosing brief quotations within your text

Quotations of no more than four lines (MLA style) or no more than forty words (APA style) should be worked into your text, set off only by quotation marks. For example:

> In Chillingworth, Hawthorne shows both good and evil, creating "about as queer a combination as the world has ever witnessed" (Turner 200).

> Technology has become our number one priority. The amount of information continues to grow, making obsolescence a problem for everyone. This pace of change has "magnified the difference between the scientist-technologist and the layperson." Technology is now "specialized, professionalized, and institutionalized" (Pytlik, Lauda, and Johnson 6).

Notice that both of the preceding examples mention the sources of the quotations only in the parenthetical references. Often, however, you will want to mention your source directly, especially when he or she is an authority on your subject. If you introduce quotations in this way you need not repeat the author's name in the parenthetical citation.

> In Russia, however, the men who took control had hardly any experience in military or administrative fields at all. As Edward Crankshaw explained, "They were a disciplined set of revolutionary conspirators who had spent most of their adult lives in exile in Russia or abroad" (44).

Setting off long quotations

Set off long quotations: in MLA style, longer than four lines; in APA style, longer than forty words. Begin such a quotation on a new line, and indent each line of the quotation ten spaces (MLA) or five spaces (APA) from the left margin. This indentation sets off the quotation clearly so that quotation marks are unnecessary. Long quotations must always be introduced in some explanatory way:

A good seating arrangement can prevent problems; however, the technique that Woolfolk calls "withitness" works even better in maintaining effective discipline.

> Withitness is the ability to communicate to students that you are aware of what is happening in the classroom, that you "don't miss anything." With-it teachers seem to have "eyes in the back of their heads." They avoid becoming too absorbed with a few students, since this allows the rest of the class to wander. (359)

This technique works, however, only if students actually believe that their teacher will know everything that goes on.

In general, you should avoid using many long quotations.

Integrating quotations in your text

Quotations have to be carefully integrated into your text so that they link smoothly and clearly with the surrounding sentences. As a writer, you must provide enough explanation so that your readers can follow your meaning. Look, for instance, at the following:

> In *Death of a Salesman*, Willy Loman dreams the wrong dreams and idealizes the wrong ideals. "He has lived on his smile and on his hopes, survived from sale to sale, been sustained by the illusion that he has countless friends in his territory, that everything will be all right. . . ." (Brown 97).

It is possible to figure out the connection between quotation and text, but see how the following revisions make the link far easier to recognize. Note also the slightly awkward shift in verb tenses from text to quotation, which is smoothed out in the revisions.

> In *Death of a Salesman*, Willy Loman dreams the wrong dreams and idealizes the wrong ideals. His misguided perceptions are well captured by Brown: "He has lived on his smile and on his hopes, survived from sale to sale, been sustained by the illusion that he has countless friends in his territory, that everything will be all right. . . ." (97).

> In *Death of a Salesman*, Willy Loman dreams the wrong dreams and idealizes the wrong ideals, living "on his smile and on his hopes . . . sustained by the illusion . . . that everything will be all right. . . ." (Brown 97).

Indicating changes with brackets and ellipses

Sometimes, for the sake of clarity or length, you will wish to alter a direct quotation in some way—to make a verb tense fit smoothly in

581

your text, to replace a pronoun with a noun, to eliminate unnecessary detail. Enclose any changed or added words with brackets, and indicate any deletions with three ellipsis points.

> A farmer, Jane Lee, spoke to the Nuclear Regulatory Commission about the occurrences. "There is something wrong in the [Three Mile Island] area. It is happening within nature itself," she said, referring to human miscarriages, stillbirths, and birth defects in farm animals ("Legacy" 33).

> Economist John Kenneth Galbraith has pointed out that "large corporations cannot afford to compete with one another. Their survival is predicated upon . . . market segmentation. In a truly competitive market someone loses. . . . American big business has finally learned that everybody has to protect everybody else's investment" (Key 17).

Be especially careful that any changes you make in a quotation do not alter its essential meaning. In addition, use these marks sparingly, for too many brackets and ellipsis points make for difficult reading. (For more information on brackets and ellipses, see 32b and 32f.)

┃ 2. Using paraphrases and summaries

When you want to cite ideas from sources but have no need to quote their exact words, you will use paraphrases or summaries. You may find various occasions for paraphrasing or summarizing, but in general these forms will be most necessary for providing background information, presenting facts that may not be commonly known, and explaining various positions on your topic. However frequently you need them, you must work paraphrases and summaries into your essay in a way that both reads smoothly and identifies your sources clearly.

Incorporating paraphrases and summaries

At times, you may choose to introduce a paraphrase or summary with an introduction noting the author of the information (*Professor Karlinsky notes that . . .*). Using the author's name in this way helps to lend authority to the information. Sometimes, in fact, you will want to highlight the source even more prominently. Notice how the writer in the following example focuses on one authority, first introducing him by name and then both quoting and paraphrasing from his work:

> Robert Ornstein, whose book I read during my research on brain lateralization, said he got "vague ideas" over a period of time, ideas that eventually led to the writing of his book. These ideas came from the

right side of the brain; by acknowledging them as valid messages, Orn-stein says he was able to use them to his advantage in his work (68).

In the following example, on the other hand, the writer focuses more on the information paraphrased, using no introductory tag and iden-tifying the authors only parenthetically:

> Three areas of established differences in cognitive abilities are recognized by the majority of researchers: verbal ability, mathematical ability, and spatial ability (Block 517). As shown by current research, a specific cognitive sex difference exists in verbal ability; in general, females are superior to males in this area starting in early childhood (Weitz 99).

Regardless of the method you use to introduce information, indicating the sources of paraphrases and summaries is important. Failure to cite sources for materials that are not in quotation marks but that you could not have arrived at originally, even unintentionally, constitutes plagia-rism. Make certain that you record the sources of general background information as well as specific quotations, facts, viewpoints, and so forth. If your notes are incomplete or your source is unclear, relocate the original to clarify the information. If you are unable to do so, you would be wiser to leave out the material than to risk plagiarism (see Chapters 39 and 41 for further discussion on crediting sources).

▌ 3. Checking for excessive citations

Exactly how much you should cite sources in your essay has to depend on your purpose, your audience, and the section of your essay. In general, however, your essay should not give the impression of being a patchwork of quotations, paraphrases, and summaries from other people. If it does, you will have merely accumulated data; you won't have actually presented information (see 39b2). You need an authorial voice, a perspective that represents you as the author. If you are over-quoting and over-citing, your own voice will disappear. The following discussion illustrates this problem:

> The United States is one of the countries with the most rapid pop-ulation growth. In fact, rapid population increase has been a "prominent feature of American life since before the founding of the republic" (Day 31). In the past, the cause of the high rate of population growth was the combination of large-scale immigration and a high birthrate. As Day notes, "Two facts stand out in the demographic history of the United

States: first, the single position as a receiver of immigrants; second, our high rate of growth from natural increase" (31).

Nevertheless, American population density is not as high as in most European countries. Day points out that the Netherlands, with a density of 906 persons per square mile, is more crowded than even the most densely populated American states (33).

Most readers would think that the source, Day, was much too prominent here. If this passage were a background discussion or a literature survey, with each source being different, such a large number of citations might be acceptable. But all these citations are from the same source, and readers are likely to conclude that the source is primary and the author only secondary.

40e. Reviewing your draft

As with most kinds of writing, taking a break after drafting a research essay is important. Get away from the draft, and try to put it out of your mind. Stay away from it for as long as you can, so that when you reread it you can bring a fresh eye to the task.

When you return to the draft, read it straight through without stopping. Then, read it again slowly, reconsidering three things: purpose, audience, and thesis. You might find that outlining your draft helps you to analyze it at this point (see 40b3).

- From your reading of your draft, what do you now see as its *purpose?* How does this compare with your original purpose? How does it do what your assignment requires?
- What *audience* does your essay address?
- What is your *thesis?* Is it clearly stated?

Answer these three questions as best you can, since they are the starting point for revision. Next, you need a closer reading of your essay. At this point, you might benefit from the comments of other readers. Consider asking friends or classmates to read your draft and respond to the following questions. You can also use these questions yourself as you analyze your own essay in greater detail.

Questions for reviewing the draft of a research essay

1. *Introduction:* How does the opening of the essay gain readers' attention? How does it suggest what readers will learn from the essay?

(Does it forecast the main points?) Does it provide any background information readers may need? How else might the essay begin?

2. *Thesis:* Paraphrase the thesis of the essay in the form of a promise: "This essay will . . ." Does the essay fulfill this promise? Does it express a stand on the topic? How might the thesis be qualified or made more pointed?

3. *Main points:* List the main points made in the essay. Arrange and number these points in the order of their interest to you. Which are most interesting? least interesting? Do any seem extraneous? Which seem incompletely or excessively developed? Does the overall development seem clear and balanced?

4. *Organization:* What is the essay's basic organization? How is this plan made clear to readers? Does the organization seem to work? What, if anything, would you move, cut out, or add?

5. *Supporting information:* Does the essay marshal sufficient support for its case? What kind of support does it offer—examples, precedents, quotations from experts? statistics? Which research materials does it use most convincingly? Which seem less effective? Do any points need more support? What attention is shown to arguments *against* the thesis? Should there be more? Do you accept the essay's argument?

6. *Author's Voice:* Does the writer's own perspective control the tone of the essay, or do the sources cited seem more dominant? What makes the writer's view clear? What sections, if any, are dominated by the sources? How has the writer established his or her credibility on the subject?

7. *Source materials:* Consider the source citations one by one. Is each one smoothly integrated into the text? Can you easily see its connection to the text around it? Are any quotations less than quotable— that is, might they be as well paraphrased? Are any longer than need be? Is any one source relied on too much?

8. *Conclusion:* How does the essay end? What does it tell you to think or do? Does it summarize the essay's main points—and if not, should it do so? How else might it end?

9. *Paragraphs, sentences, and words:* Which paragraphs and sentences seem especially effective? Identify any that you consider strong, and then do the same with those you find weak. Look at the individual words—do any need to be defined? Are any too abstract or vague? Identify any words you find especially vivid.

10. *Final thoughts:* What are the essay's strongest points? What are its weaknesses? What kind of revision does the essay need most? What revision advice would you anticipate an instructor might give?

You may also get helpful advice if you ask questions specific to your essay. Whether you are doubtful about including or omitting discussion of a particular point, unsure about whether to use a certain quotation, or anxious about the impact of an example, ask readers specifically what they think you should do. (For more information on getting critical responses to a draft, see 3c.)

▌ 40f. Revising and editing your draft

Using any responses you have gathered and your own analysis of your draft, turn now to your final revision. It is advisable, at this stage, to work in several steps:

Considering any reviews

Have readers identified any problems you need to solve? If so, do they make any specific suggestions about ways you might or must revise your essay? Have they identified any strengths that might suggest ways of revising your essay—for example, if they showed great interest in a particular point but no interest at all in another point, perhaps you might expand the first and delete the second.

Reconsidering your original purpose and audience

From the above analysis, do you feel confident that you have achieved your purpose? If not, what is missing? Have you made your strongest possible appeal to your readers? How have you established common ground with them? How have you satisfied any special needs they may have?

Gathering any additional material

If you need to strengthen treatment of any points, go back to your notes to see if you have the necessary materials. If not, consider whether you need to do any more research. If you failed to consider adequately any opposing viewpoints, for instance, you may need to go back to the library to find material.

Deciding on any changes you need to make

Figure out everything you have to do to perfect your draft, and write it out. With your deadline firmly in mind, plan your revision.

Rewriting your draft

Do the major work first—changes in content, added examples or citations, paragraph-level concerns. Then turn to sentence-level work, and finally to individual words. Revise for clarity and to sharpen the dominant impression of the essay as a whole. For this part of your work, follow the guidelines on pages 48-53, which will help you examine your paragraphs, sentences, words, and tone.

Reconsidering your introduction and conclusion

In light of your re-evaluation and revision of your draft, reread these very important parts to see that they still serve their purpose. Does anything need refocusing? Do you need to forecast your main points in the introduction or to summarize them in the conclusion? Check to be sure that your introduction captures readers' attention and that your conclusion helps them see the significance of your argument.

Checking your documentation

Are all sources documented, and have you followed the appropriate style consistently? Check Chapter 41 for complete MLA and APA guidelines.

Editing your draft

Now is the time to attend to any problems in grammar, usage, spelling, punctuation, and mechanics. Check for any patterns you have identified as problems in your own writing. It may be fruitful as well to check for the twenty most common errors, listed on page xxxvi, and to consult the editing checklist in 3h. At this point, look very closely at details, checking any spelling, wording, or phrasing about which you are in doubt. You are fine-tuning here, polishing your essay.

Choosing a title

If you have not done so thus far, choose a title, crafting one that is specific enough to let your readers know about your research question and engaging enough to make them want to read *your* answer to it. Following are some examples of working titles that were changed to make them more specific and engaging:

WORKING TITLE	Nuclear Power [too general]
REVISED	Nuclear Power and the Menace to the Seacoast

WORKING TITLE	Testing Minoxidil [too general, uninformative]
REVISED	Minoxidil: A Cure for Baldness or Corporate Snake-Oil?
WORKING TITLE	Don't Lose Your Head—or Your Hand [uninformative]
REVISED	Hard Justice: Law Enforcement in Iran

Preparing your final copy

Your final rough draft may end up looking very rough indeed, filled with cross-outs, additions in the margins, circles, and arrows. So your next task is to create a final, carefully typed, painstakingly prepared clean copy. This is the version of the paper that you will submit, the one that will represent all your work and effort. For information on preparing a final manuscript, see Chapter 46.

Proofreading your final copy

Proofreading is a time for celebration. At this point, you are making your research essay watertight, your very best effort. Many writers look forward to this final reading, often taking time to read through once backwards in order to catch every word-level typographical error. So after proofreading, congratulate yourself and savor the rewards of a job well done. You have produced a solid piece of research, clearly written and cogently argued. You have become a researcher.

READING WITH AN EYE FOR RESEARCH .

The following research essays were written by students, the first for a composition class, the second for a psychology class. Read these essays carefully, and study the marginal annotations. Compare your research essay to these, noting differences in approach, style, format, and use of sources.

½″ from top ↑
Bloise   1 ↓

1″ from top

Heading in
place of title
page

Melissa Bloise
Professor Connors
English 401
4 May 1988

The Strategic Defense Initiative:

Too Good to Be True

Title
centered

Paragraphs
indented five
spaces

→ Proposed by President Reagan in 1983 and
originally estimated to cost $26 billion, the
Strategic Defense Initiative (SDI) has been
touted as a system that will render nuclear
weapons impotent and thus free the world of
the fear of nuclear annihilation, lead to
overall arms reduction, and stimulate the
economy by producing technological innovations useful in the private sector. If even
one of these outcomes were likely, the SDI
project would deserve our careful consideration. Unfortunately, however, it not only
will not lead to any of these desirable goals
but will in fact produce precisely the opposite
effects from those claimed by its proponents.

Abbreviation
introduced

Main points
of argument
presented

Common
ground
established by
acknowledging
desirability of
goals

Thesis
stated

At its most effective, in fact, SDI will
provide an imperfect defense against only one
form of nuclear attack, long-range missiles
that travel through space. Weapons that do
not penetrate the upper atmosphere will, in

First main
point of
argument
(ineffectiveness)
introduced

Bloise 2

essence, fly "under SDI" and will not be de-
terred by the system. At best, therefore, SDI
will "provide a leaky roof on a house with
no walls" (Center for Defense Information
[CDI], "Star Wars" 2).

Short title
used to
identify one
of several
references by
the same
author

Even many of those committed to the development of SDI acknowledge the low probability of achieving the level of technical
development that is needed for a truly effective system. Lieutenant General James A.
Abrahamson, director of the SDI Office, re-
fuses to predict the number of enemy warheads
that would be able to penetrate SDI defenses.
Fred Hoffman, who chairs one of the Pentagon's
SDI study teams, notes that the "likelihood"
of the system's being able to protect "the
bulk of our population" is small. In addition,
the Congressional Office of Technology Assessment reports that "the prospect [of] . . .
a perfect or near-perfect defense . . . is
so remote that it should not serve as the basis
of public expectations or national policy
about ballistic missile defense" (qtd. in CDI,
"Star Wars" 2).

Partial quotation integrated into Bloise's sentence

Authorities cited

Brackets and ellipses used to indicate changes in quotation

Indirect source noted with *qtd. in*

Despite its questionable effectiveness,
many SDI proponents claim that the system would
at least lead to a reduction in the number

Second point of argument (arms reduction) introduced with transition

Bloise   3

of nuclear weapons that the United States and the Soviet Union would need to maintain. By researching and deploying SDI, however, the United States would nullify the Antiballistic Missile (ABM) Treaty of 1972, thus allowing for a buildup of both offensive and defensive arms by both the United States and the Soviet Union. And Gorbachev has specifically stated that if the United States proceeds with SDI, the Soviet Union will increase both the number and sophistication of its offensive nuclear weapons (CDI, "Unravelling" 4).

Cause-effect relationship between SDI and arms buildup explained

Gerard Smith, chief U.S. negotiator for the ABM Treaty, described it in August 1986 as "an essential component of the effort to keep the arms race from going completely out of control" (CDI, "Unravelling" 5). Similarly, former secretary of defense Harold Brown has said, "To the extent that the U.S. is committed to SDI, I think arms control is not going to be feasible. Indeed, I think existing agreements will either erode or be abandoned." Agreeing with Brown are Soviet expert George Kennan and former secretaries of defense Robert McNamara and James Schlesinger, who all believe that SDI and arms control are mutually exclusive (CDI, "Pentagon" 4).

Authorities cited for link between SDI and arms race

Bloise 4

Fueling a new arms buildup without providing adequate protection from the consequences of the old one, SDI would hardly, as its proponents insist, make nuclear weapons obsolete and free us of the fear of a "nuclear winter." Nevertheless, we are being asked to pay dearly for this supposed security shield. Official Reagan administration figures now project research and development costs at $40 billion through 1991, with another $30 billion projected to be spent by 1993. These costs are minuscule compared with projected production and deployment costs. According to a Johns Hopkins University study, a "comprehensive defense" system deployed by 2005 could cost $770 billion (CDI, "Unravelling" 5), and a study conducted for Senators J. Bennett Johnston, Lawton Chiles, and William Proxmire shows that annual maintenance and modernization expenses alone would exceed $200 billion and that total costs could perhaps reach several trillion dollars (Proxmire). According to the House Armed Services Committee, every dollar spent for military research and development creates an additional ten dollars in future defense spending (Shapiro 32). Since at least $70 billion would be spent on SDI research by only 1993, these

Margin annotations:

No source citation needed for information available in several sources

Authorities cited for costs of SDI

Transitional sentence summing up first two points of argument

Third main point of argument (cost-effectiveness) introduced

No page citation needed for one page article

Bloise 5

estimates of total costs do not seem far-
fetched. In comparison, the development of
the B-1 bomber and production of one hundred
planes cost only $28 billion; the Trident
submarine development program and the purchase
of seventeen submarines each equipped with
twenty-four nuclear missiles totaled only $67
billion (CDI, "Star Wars" 4). Clearly, SDI
would ultimately cost hundreds of billions
of dollars that could be used in much more
cost-effective ways.

Comparison used in argument that SDI is not cost-effective

Nor would SDI be likely to prove a boon
to our economy in other ways. Proponents of
the system have often made the claim that SDI
research will produce many spinoff technologies, technologies that will profit the commercial sector. While a few SDI technologies
may have commercial applications, that probability does not warrant the continuation of
the SDI project.

Next point of argument (economic drawbacks) introduced

Limited merit granted to opposing argument (spinoff technologies from military research)

At present, the United States is losing
ground to foreign competitors in just those
industries, such as electronics and aerospace,
in which military research is overwhelmingly
concentrated (CDI, "Military" 1). If significant commercial applications of military
research were occurring, we would expect these
areas to have gained ground instead of losing

Appeals to logic: refutation of claimed cause-effect relationship

DRAFTING AND REVISING A RESEARCH ESSAY

Bloise 6

it. In addition, if spinoffs were common, one would expect successful military contractors to be successful in the civilian sector as well. Instead, dual markets, military and civilian, have developed in the airplane industry and others. The reason is that much of military research is devoted to trying to produce equipment with very particular specifications, such as a refrigerator that can withstand an airplane crash and operate in an unpressurized cabin. Equipment with such rugged and specific performance requirements is too costly and "overdesigned" to have any cost-effective application to the commercial sector of the economy (CDI, "Military" 6).

Finally, the chance of commercial spinoffs is minimal because military research concentrates on the development of weapon prototypes rather than on general technology (CDI, "Military" 2). Far from aiding the civilian sector, in fact, military research actually reduces the amount of civilian research being conducted, a reduction that further hurts our economy. Simon Ramo, former president of TRW, an economic forecasting firm, confirms the adverse economic effects of much military spending, saying,

between military research and spinoffs

Example of military research cited

Authority cited for argument that military spending retards economic growth

Bloise   7

Block
notation
dented ten
paces

> In the past thirty years, had the
> total dollars we spent on military
> R & D been expended instead in
> those areas of science and tech-
> nology promising the most economic
> progress, we probably would be
> today where we are going to find
> ourselves arriving technologically
> in the year 2000 (qtd. in CDI,
> "Military" 6).

Quotation of
more than
four lines set
off

Thus far, over one thousand applications
from American universities have been submitted
to SDI headquarters in search of some of the
$600 million available for university research
on SDI. Many academics worry that important
nonmilitary research will be neglected as a
result of the intense concentration by the
nation's top scientific talent on the SDI
project. As Marvin Goldberger, president of
the California Institute of Technology, says,
"The infusion of such a large amount of money
can distort activities within the university.
It can draw people into research areas they
might not otherwise pursue" (Sanger 135).

Authority
cited for
argument that
SDI will hurt
civilian
research

Even in the event that SDI research does
produce some spinoff technologies, many seriously doubt that the Pentagon would allow the

Refutation of
opposing
position that
had been
granted
limited merit

Bloise 8

private sector to develop them. U.S. university researchers anticipate that key elements of their SDI projects will become
classified. If this occurs, they will be unable to publish their results or discuss possible applications with colleagues (Sanger
134). As early as 1985, the Pentagon began
halting the flow of information by restricting
access to civilian engineering meetings where
unclassified research into SDI was being presented (Marlin and Nimroody). Recently, the
military has become even more concerned about
the flow of technological information and has
imposed tighter restrictions both domes-
tically and internationally, thus further
reducing commercial possibilities.

Chronology of
restrictions on
information
explained

    Finally, the SDI program damages our
economy by allowing a substantial amount of
funding to go to other countries. Since the
project's conception, a steady flow of international defense contractors has visited the
SDI headquarters. In the first six months of
1985 alone, at least seven countries sent
delegations expressing interest in participating in SDI development. Foreign companies
view SDI as a great source of research funds,
and rightly so: up to one-third of funds for
the project could be spent abroad (Griffiths,

Last point of
argument
(American
economic
interests)
introduced

Bloise 9

Taggiasco, Peterson, and Miller 68). The U.S. government, in fact, has been actively seeking foreign company involvement. Abrahamson, Defense Secretary Caspar Weinberger, and Vice-President George Bush have encouraged European participation. In addition to private companies, European universities are climbing on the bandwagon; some are submitting bids at the SDI office's request. In 1986, SDI planned to spend $50 million at foreign educational institutions (Griffiths, Taggiasco, Peterson, and Miller 72). While SDI spending is far from an effective way to spur our economy, spending the money within our borders at least may provide some benefit. By dispersing the funds abroad, we are using U.S. tax revenue to aid other economies.

Figurative language used to clarify idea of enthusiastic foreign participation

Clearly, SDI will not significantly increase the safety of our society from the threat of nuclear annihilation, and in fact, it may well increase our peril. The possibility of greater danger rather than the purported safety should be sufficient to deter a reasoned society from pursuing such a path without thoroughly and reasonably considering questions of secondary benefits. But even the arguments regarding the secondary benefits

Major arguments (military and economic) restated in conclusion

Bloise 10

ostensibly to be gained from SDI are fallacious. Rather than stimulate and strengthen
our economy, SDI would place the United States
in an even weaker economic position in the
world. Development of SDI would reduce research and development in vitally needed
civilian areas while strengthening the econ-
omies of the major economic rivals of the United
States. More important societal issues will
be relegated to a lower priority, with almost
every sector of our society feeling both direct
and indirect negative effects of the cost of
this weapons system. That is assuming, of
course, that there will be anyone left to feel.

Appeal to
emotions in
conclusion

Bloise 11

Works Cited

Center for Defense Information. "Military Research and the Economy: Burden or Benefit?" The Defense Monitor 14.1 (1985): 1-8.

---."The Pentagon Prepares For Nuclear War: The 1988 Budget." The Defense Monitor 16.4 (1987): 1-8.

---."Star Wars: Vision and Reality." The Defense Monitor 15.2 (1986): 1-8.

---."The Unravelling of Nuclear Arms Treaties: Another Step Toward Nuclear War." The Defense Monitor 16.1 (1987): 1-8.

Griffiths, Dave, Ronald Taggiasco, Thane Peterson, and Frederic A. Miller. "The Selling of Star Wars to Businesses Abroad." Business Week 15 July 1985: 68.

Marlin, Alice Tepper, and Rosy Nimroody. "'Star Wars' Benefits Are an Illusion With Mirrors." New York Times 14 Nov. 1986: A34.

Proxmire, William. "When You Talk About 'Star Wars' You're Talking Trillions." Christian Science Monitor 19 May 1986: 16.

Sanger, David E. "Campuses' Role in Arms Debated as 'Star Wars' Funds are Sought." New York Times 22 July 1985: A1+.

Shapiro, Robert J. "A Frightening New Numbers Game." U.S. News & World Report 28 Sept. 1987: 32-33.

Title centered

Entries listed in alphabetical order by author

First line of each entry flush with left margin

Subsequent lines indented ⟶ five spaces

Three hyphens used to indicate additional works by the same author

A Content Analysis of Letters
to the Editor
Leah Clendening

Title and
author
centered

Short title
and page
number

Paragraphs
indented five
paces
    Would people from a large community be
more interested in local or national issues?
In order to answer this question, I conducted
a content analysis of 624 letters to the editor
in two newspapers to discover if community
size affected the subjects of the letters.
One newspaper was from a city with a population
of over 500,000, while the second was from
a city of about 15,000. Issues for both newspapers were read for the same three months
and were compared. Results show a significant
difference between the subjects of letters
and the community size from which they originated.

Passive voice
used to focus
on the
research
rather than
the researcher

<u>Problem</u>

Headings
centered

    Research indicates that the average per-
son who writes letters to a newspaper is a
conservative, well-adjusted, white American
male who is usually middle-aged or older and
a long-term resident of his community (Singletary & Cowling, 1979). One study has concluded that 71.4% of the letters printed were
written by people who wished to inform or
persuade by writing their letters. Most of
the remainder, 27.0%, wished only to use the
letter as a means of self-expression; another
1.6% wished to arouse readers to action (Lemert
& Larkin, 1979).

Previous work
surveyed

Content Analysis 2

But what are the major concerns of these letter writers? Are they more concerned about events in their local communities, or about national issues? And does the size of the community have some influence on what its members write letters about? These questions led to the following hypothesis: people living in a small community (with a population of about 15,000) tend to be concerned more with local than with national issues. People living in a large community (with a population over 500,000) show more concern for national than for local issues.

Research question stated

Hypotheses stated

Method

Newspapers

The two newspapers that served as data sources, the <u>Mount Vernon News</u> and the <u>Cleveland Plain Dealer</u>, were chosen for convenience and availability. Cleveland has a population of 573,822 and a weekly distribution of the <u>Plain Dealer</u> of 482,564. Mount Vernon has a population of 14,380 and a weekly distribution of the <u>Mount Vernon News</u> of 10,936 (<u>1985 IMS/ Ayer Directory</u>, 1985). Each newspaper's letters were read for the months of October 1986, December 1986, and February 1987. Sunday issues were not taken into account.

Subjects of study identified

Short title used to identify source with no author

Content Analysis 3

A category sheet of possible subjects for the letters to the editor was adapted from the coding sheet of Donohew's study on Medicare (Budd, Thorp, & Donohew, 1967, p. 41). One column recorded national issues, and a second local issues. The sheet was constructed with a space for the newspaper's abbreviation, the date, and the letter number(s). The <u>Mount Vernon News</u> was given the abbreviation MVN, and the <u>Cleveland Plain Dealer</u> the abbreviation CPD.

<u>Procedure</u>

After the category sheet was finished and approved, observation began. The newspapers were read and marked for content in a library setting. Each newspaper was skimmed until the Opinion page or the People's Forum section (depending on which newspaper was being observed) was found. Each letter was read and then classified on the category sheet that had been titled with the proper abbreviations, date, and letter number. As observation progressed, constraints of time demanded a change from filling out a separate sheet for each letter to recording each day's letters on the same category sheet. The space left for recording the letter number was used to record the total number of letters for each

Materials described

Page noted for specific source

Steps in carrying out research explained

Content Analysis 4

particular day. After all observation was
finished, the counts for each of the newspapers
were totaled for each month and overall.

Results

Over the 3—month period, 60 letters were
read from the <u>Mount Vernon News</u>. Fifty—three
of these pertained to local issues while seven
pertained to national issues. A Chi Square
test with an adjustment for continuity was
used on these data to find if there was a
statistically significant difference between
concern with local and national issues. Results showed an overwhelming difference between issues, even at the .01 probability
level. A graph was also constructed to show
the number of national issues and local issues
for each month for the MVN.

Results from
first
newspaper
analyzed
statistically

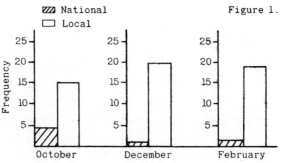

Figure 1.

Graph used
to show
results

Frequency of national and local issues for MVN

Content Analysis 5

From a total of 564 letters read from the <u>Cleveland Plain Dealer</u>, 248 pertained to local issues and 316 pertained to national issues. A Chi Square test with an adjustment for continuity was also used on these data and once again, showed statistically a significant difference. A graph was also constructed to show the frequency of national and local issues for each month for the CPD.

Results from second newspaper analyzed statistically

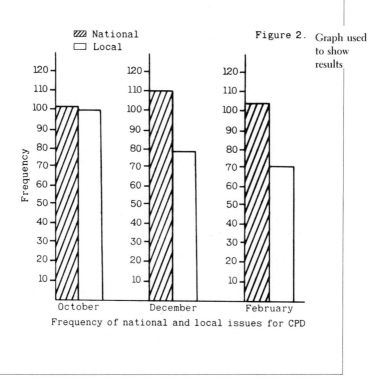

Figure 2. Graph used to show results

Frequency of national and local issues for CPD

Content Analysis 6

One interesting side note is that 21.6% of the letters from the <u>Cleveland</u> <u>Plain</u> <u>Dealer</u> stated grievances or appreciation of some local happenings or people while 36% of the letters from the <u>Mount</u> <u>Vernon</u> <u>News</u> were about grievances or appreciation. These findings differ considerably from those of Lister, who found that only 5% of letters to the editor were of this particular type (Lister, 1985).

Discussion

The findings of this study generally supported the hypothesis, especially in the smaller community where letters concentrated overwhelmingly on local issues. Perhaps residents of such a community do not see themselves as strongly affected by governmental decisions and national happenings. For the larger community, the findings were not quite as clear; current studies do not suggest any apparent reason for this discrepancy, but perhaps further study may reveal the causes.

If more time had been permitted, an entire year's newspapers could have been categorized, thus yielding more accurate information. In addition, a second reader would have eliminated bias on the part of a single reader. It was found as the study progressed that a

Findings counter to previous research noted

Results interpreted

Biases and possible improvements in the study listed

Content Analysis 7

few categories could have been added, such as religion and local and state elections: the lack of these categories, however, did not severely affect the study. Another bias that would be difficult to account for is editorial bias: one study found that only 68% of the letters received by editors were published (Renfro, 1979). The only way to eliminate this bias would be to read all the letters received by editors instead of only those that were printed.

The study raises some interesting questions that further study would probably help to answer. Does gender or age seem to influence whether people are interested in local or national issues? What is the causal relationship between residents of small towns and their greater interest in local affairs? Are the writers local people? Future studies may be able to answer such questions by building on the basic information provided here.

Larger
questions
noted in
conclusion

Content Analysis 8

References

Budd, R. W., Thorp, K., & Donohew, L. (1967). Content analysis of communications. New York: Macmillan.

Lemert, J. B., & Larkin, J. P. (1979). Some reasons why mobilizing information fails to be in letters to the editor. Journalism Quarterly, 56, 504–512.

Lister, L. (1985). An analysis of letters to the editor. Social Work, 30, 77–78.

The 1985 IMS/Ayer Directory of Publications (117th ed.). (1985). Fort Washington, PA: IMS Press.

Renfro, P. C. (1979). Bias in selection of letters to the editor. Journalism Quarterly, 56, 822–826.

Singletary, M. W., & Cowling, M. (1979). Letters to the editor of the non-daily press. Journalism Quarterly, 56, 165–168.

Title centered on new page

First line of each entry flush with left margin

Subsequent lines indented ⟶ three spaces

Entries listed in alphabetical order by author

Last names always first; only initials used for first and middle names

41. Documenting Sources

> Adam-was the only man who, when he said a good thing, knew that nobody had said it before him.   —MARK TWAIN

Adam, in other words, had the luxury of not having to document his sources, but no writer since Adam has been able to make that claim. In your writing, full and accurate documentation is important because it helps build your credibility as a writer and researcher by giving credit to those people whose works influenced your own ideas.

Documentation styles vary among disciplines, with one format favored in the humanities, for instance, another in the social sciences, and another in engineering, but they all require the same basic information. Thus you will want to use the conventions of documentation appropriate to a particular course and field. Correct use of punctuation and format are central to consistency, demonstrate that you have taken pains to follow the conventions of your discipline, and protect you from plagiarizing because of omitted source information (see 39e).

The widely used citation styles presented here have in common two central objectives: to let your readers know what sources you used in your writing; and to help them find the sources, should they wish to. To accomplish these objectives, each style uses specific citations in the text that indicate that source information is being used and corresponding entries in the list of sources cited following the text of the essay that give all the information readers need to find a source.

The **Modern Language Association (MLA) style** is widely used in literature and languages as well as other fields. Revised in 1984, MLA style calls for noting brief references to sources in parentheses in the text of an essay and appending an alphabetical list of sources, called *Works Cited*, at the end. Used in many journals in the field of psychology, the **American Psychological Association (APA) style** is widely followed throughout the social sciences. Like MLA style, APA parenthetical citations within the text direct readers to a list of sources. In APA style, this list is titled *References*. Various versions of the **number style,** whose parenthetical citations identify each work by a number assigned to it in the list of sources (usually titled *Literature Cited*) document work in many scientific papers and journals. Finally, history and some other humanities disciplines still prefer the traditional **note-and-bibliography (Old MLA) style.** This style uses note numbers in the text, keyed to a numerical list of *Notes*; an alphabetically arranged *Bibliography* lists the same sources at the end. Examples of documentation forms, parenthetical citations, and note forms in each of these styles appear in this chapter.

▌ 41a. Modern Language Association style

The MLA style uses parenthetical citations of sources within the text and a list of these sources at the end of the text. This section discusses the basic format for MLA style and shows examples of the bibliographic forms and parenthetical citations for various kinds of source materials. For further reference, consult:

> *MLA Handbook for Writers of Research Papers.* 3rd ed. New York: Mod. Lang. Assoc., 1988.

▌ 1. MLA format for the list of works cited

The *Works Cited* list generally includes only those works actually cited in the paper. (If your instructor asks that you list everything you have read as background, call the list *Works Consulted* instead.)

Arrange this list alphabetically by authors' last names. If your list includes sources for which no author is known, alphabetize them according to their titles. If a title begins with *A*, *An*, or *The*, use its next word to determine its alphabetical placement.

Start your *Works Cited* list on a separate page, with *Works Cited* neither underlined nor in quotation marks, and centered on the page one inch from the top. Quadruple space and start your list. Begin typing the first line of each entry at the left margin, but indent each of the next lines within the entry five spaces so that the author's last names will stand out for easy reference. Double-space each line in the entire list, whether it begins or continues an entry.

Each entry includes the author's name, the title (and any subtitle), and the publication information. List the author's last name first, followed by a comma and the author's first name and any middle initial, with a period. Follow each period in the entry with two spaces.

Underline the titles (and any subtitles) of books and periodicals; put titles (and any subtitles) of articles, short fiction, and poems in quotation marks. Capitalize all major words in the title and subtitle. If a work has a subtitle, place a colon after the main title, one space, and then add the subtitle. Follow the title or subtitle with a period.

The publication information for a book lists the city where the publisher is located (and state or country if your reader is unfamiliar with the city), followed by a colon and one space, a shortened version of the publisher's name (*St. Martin's* for *St. Martin's Press, Inc.*, or *Oxford UP* for *Oxford University Press*), a comma, and the date of publication. For an article in a periodical, you do not need to list the place of publication but simply the name of the periodical in which the article appears, the volume or issue number, the year of publication in parentheses, a colon, one space, and the inclusive page numbers of the article. End the entry with a period.

Consult the various example entries presented in this section for information on where in an entry you should place supplementary information. Here are examples of basic book and periodical entries.

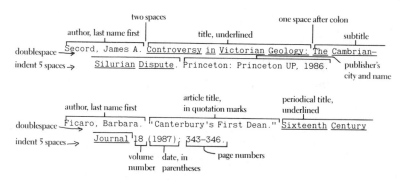

Books and pamphlets

The examples below show how to treat the various parts of information in book and pamphlet entries.

A book written by one author

De Vries, Peter. <u>Peckham's Marbles</u>. New York: Putnam's, 1986.

A book written by two or three authors

List the first author last name first; then list the other author or authors in regular order, with commas between the names.

> McNeill, John T. and Helena M. Gamer. Medieval Handbooks
>   of Penance. New York: Octagon, 1965.

A book written by more than three authors

Name the first author listed on the book's title page, follow it with a comma, and then add the abbreviation *et al.* ("and others").

> Britton, James, et al. The Development of Writing Abil-
>   ities (11–18). London: Macmillan Education, 1975.

A book written by a group

Use the name of a group or organization listed on the title page as the author in place of individual authors.

> Carnegie Corporation on Higher Education. The Academic
>   System in American Society. New York: McGraw, 1974.

A book prepared by an editor

If a work was prepared by an editor, list this person as you would an author and add a comma and the abbreviation *ed.* (for *editor*).

> Parker, Dorothy, ed. Essays on Modern American Drama.
>   Toronto: U of Toronto P, 1987.

If a book has both an author and an editor, your entry should show whose work you cite. If you cite the author's work, name the author first. Then add the editor's name, with the abbreviation *Ed.*, after the title. If you cite the editor's work, such as the variations in the edition or the commentary, name the editor first, followed by *ed.* After the title, add the author's name, introduced with *By*.

A book prepared by a translator

When a book has an author and a translator, your entry should show whose work you cite. If you cite the author's work—the text itself—begin with the author's name. After the title, introduce the translator's name with *Trans.* (for *translator*).

612

Jansson, Sven B. F. The Runes of Sweden. Trans. Peter
    G. Foote. Stockholm: Norstedt Forlag, 1962.

A second work by the same author

If you cite more than one work by a particular author, arrange
the entries alphabetically by title. After the first entry, begin with three
hyphens followed by a period instead of the author's name.

Lasswell, Harold D. The Analysis of Political Behaviour:
    An Empirical Approach. New York: Oxford UP, 1948.
---. The Future of Political Science. American Political
    Science Association Series. New York: Atherton,
    1963.

A republication

If you cite a modern edition of an older book, a paperback edition, or other republication, add the original publication date, with a
period, right after the title. Then give the publication details for the
edition you used.

Scott, Walter. Kenilworth. 1821. New York: Dodd, 1956.

A particular edition

If a book is identified on its title page as a particular edition, add
this information, in abbreviated form, after the title.

Kelly, Alfred H., Winfred A. Harbison, and Herman Belz.
    The American Constitution: Its Origins and Devel-
    opment. 6th ed. New York: Norton, 1983.

A work in two or more volumes

If a work has more than one volume, note the number of volumes
in the complete work before the publication information, if you used
more than one volume. If the volumes were published over several
years, give the inclusive dates.

Braudel, Fernand. The Mediterranean and the Mediterranean
    World in the Age of Philip II. Trans. Siân Reynolds.
    2 vols. New York: Harper, 1972-73.

If you used only one volume, cite only that volume before the publication information; then give the number of volumes at the end of the entry. (Then, because the volume is specified, your text citation needs only the page number.)

> Stevenson, Ian. <u>Cases of the Reincarnation Type</u>. Vol.
> 3. Charlottesville: UP of Virginia, 1980. 4 vols.

A book that is part of a series

If a book is part of a series (as noted on the title page or the page before), add the series name and any number after the title.

> Bloom, Harold, ed. <u>Ralph Waldo Emerson</u>. Modern Critical
> Views. New York: Chelsea, 1985.

An item in an anthology or collection

If you cite a selection in an anthology, name the author of the selection. Then list the selection's title, set off by quotation marks (or by underlining if the selection first appeared as a book), the anthology's title, underlined, and the name of any editor. Finally, note the inclusive pages of the selection, followed by a period.

> Didion, Joan. "Why I Write." <u>The Writer on Her Work</u>.
> Ed. Janet Sternburg. New York: Norton, 1980. 3–16.

An article in an encyclopedia

List the author of the article, often identified by initials corresponding to full names in a list of contributors. If no author is identified, begin with the title. For a well-known encyclopedia, just note any edition number and date. If the encyclopedia entries are arranged in alphabetical order, no volume or page numbers are needed.

> "Traquair, Sir John Stewart." <u>Encyclopaedia Britannica</u>.
> 11th ed. 1909.

A preface, introduction, foreword, or afterword

List the author of the item, then its title, set off only by an initial capital letter, and a period. After the title of the work in which the item appears, introduce the name of the author of the complete work with *By*. (If the same person wrote both, just the last name is needed here.) List the item's page numbers at the end of the entry.

Schlesinger, Arthur M., Jr. Introduction. <u>Pioneer Women:</u>
   <u>Voices from the Kansas Frontier</u>. By Joanna L. Stratton. New York: Simon, 1981. 11-15.

A government document

List government documents as you would books, beginning with
the author, if identified, and giving the name of the government agency
after the title. If no author is given, first list the government and then
the department or agency.

New Hampshire. Dept. of Transportation. <u>Right of Way</u>
   <u>Salinity Reports, Hillsborough County, 1985</u>. Concord: New Hampshire Dept. of Transportation, 1986.

An unpublished dissertation

Set off the title of an unpublished dissertation with quotation
marks. Add the identification *Diss.*, the name of the school at which
the study was done, a comma, and the date.

Kitzhaber, Albert R. "Rhetoric in American Colleges 1850-
   1900." Diss. U of Washington, 1953.

Periodicals

Use the examples below as a guide to the main variations in
journal, magazine, and other periodical entries. (See p. 611 for a sample periodical entry.)

An article in a scholarly periodical that numbers pages consecutively within a volume

If a periodical continues page numbering from one issue to the
next within the annual volume, follow the title of the publication with
the volume number in arabic numerals.

Norris, Margot. "Narration under a Blindfold: Reading
   Joyce's 'Clay.'" <u>PMLA</u> 102 (1987): 206-215.

An article in a scholarly periodical that numbers pages separately within each issue

If a periodical numbers pages in each issue separately, include
the volume number and the issue number, separated by a period.

>   Loffy, John. "The Politics at Modernism's Funeral."
>   <u>Canadian</u> <u>Journal</u> <u>of</u> <u>Political</u> <u>and</u> <u>Social</u> <u>Theory</u> 6.3
>   (1987): 89–96.

An article in a monthly or weekly periodical

For a monthly or bimonthly periodical, abbreviate the month (except May, June, or July), and put the date after the periodical's title.

>   Said, Edward. "Through Gringo Eyes." <u>Harper's</u> Apr. 1988:
>   70–72.

For a weekly or biweekly periodical, note the day, the month, the year.

>   Holden, Ted. "Campbell's Taste of the Japanese Market
>   is Mm–Mm Good." <u>Business</u> <u>Week</u> 28 Mar. 1988: 42.

An article in a newspaper

List the author, article title, and then the newspaper's title (dropping any initial A, *An*, or *The*) as it appears on the front page. Follow it with the city or place in square brackets if this information is not part of the title. Give the exact date of the issue, followed by a colon and the page number. If the page number does not include the section (such as B4 or C1), follow the date with a comma, the section (with *sec.*) followed by a colon, and the page number.

>   Sharpe, Lora. "A Quilters' Tribute." <u>Boston</u> <u>Globe</u> 25
>   Mar. 1988, sec. 2: 47.

An editorial or letter in a periodical

Identify an editorial or letter by adding the word *Editorial* or *Letter* after the title.

>   Magee, Doug. "Soldier's Home." Editorial. <u>Nation</u> 26
>   Mar. 1988: 400–401.
>   Stewart, Francis. Letter. <u>Economist</u> 19–25 Mar. 1988: 4.

A review in a periodical

Give the author's name, if identified, and the title, if the review has one. If not, begin the entry with the phrase *Rev. of* (with just a capital *R*) and the name of the work being reviewed. After this title, add a comma, *by*, and the work's author.

```
Block, J. H. "Debatable Conclusions about Sex Differ-
     ences." Rev. of The Psychology of Sex Differences,
     by E. E. Maccoby and C. N. Jacklin. Contemporary
     Psychology Aug. 1976: 517-522.
```

An article whose author is not identified

Begin with the article title, dropping any initial *A*, *An*, or *The* and place it in alphabetical order. The article below begins on page 20 and continues on pages 23 and 24. To show that the pages are not consecutive, note only the first page number followed by a plus sign.

```
"The Odds of March." Time 15 Apr. 1985: 20+.
```

Other sources

The examples below show how to treat the main types of entries for other sources of information.

An interview

List first the person who has been interviewed. Then list the title, if the interview has one, in quotation marks (or underlined if it is the complete work). If it does not have a title, use the word *Interview*. If the interview comes from a source, identify the source. If you were the interviewer, identify the type as *Telephone Interview* or *Personal Interview*, and note the date.

```
Schorr, Daniel. Interview. Weekend Edition. Natl. Public
     Radio. WEVO, Concord. 26 Mar. 1988.
Berkson, Larry. Personal Interview. 16 May 1989.
```

A letter

If you cite a published letter, enter it like a selection from a book. Note the letter's date and any number used in the source after the title of the letter.

```
Frost, Robert. "Letter to Editor of the Independent." 28
     Mar. 1894. Selected Letters of Robert Frost. Ed.
     Lawrance Thompson. New York: Holt, 1964. 19.
```

Follow the form below if you cite a letter sent to you.

> Diaz, Gloria. Letter to the author. 12 Feb. 1989.

A computer software program

List the writer of the program if identified. Then add the title of the software, underlined, followed by the words *Computer software.* Next identify the company that distributes the software, and the date. Note the computer type, memory required, operating system, format, and any other details.

> Nota Bene. Vers. 3.0. Computer software. Dragonfly Soft-
>   ware, 1988. MS-DOS 2.0, 512 KB, disk.

A film or videotape

For a film, a videotape, or a slide program, include the film's title, underlined; director; the company distributing the film; and the date. Other contributors, such as writers or actors, may follow the director's name. If you are interested in one person's work, such as the director's, list that person's name first.

> The Night of the Hunter. Dir. Charles Laughton. With Robert
>   Mitchum, Shelley Winters, and Lillian Gish. United
>   Artists, 1955.

A television or radio program

Begin the entry with the title of the program, underlined. Add other details (such as narrator, director, writer, and principal actors) after the title as necessary. Then identify the network, the local station and city, and the date. If you are interested in the work of a particular person, begin the entry with that person's name. If you cite a particular episode, begin with the episode's title in quotation marks.

> Hill Street Blues. Writ. Michael Kozoll and Stephen Bochco.
>   With Daniel J. Travanti, Joe Spano, and Charles Haid.
>   NBC. WNBC, New York. 15 Jan. 1981.

A recording

Your research interest determines whether the name of the composer, artist, or conductor precedes the title of the album or tape, which is underlined, or the name of the composition recorded, which is not underlined. Then add the names of any other pertinent people. End with the name of the manufacturer, the catalog number, and the date, all separated by commas.

```
Vega, Suzanne. Solitude Standing. A & M, SP 3156, 1987.
Grieg, Edvard. Concerto in A-minor, op. 16. Perf. Van
    Cliburn. Cond. Eugene Ormandy. Philadelphia Orch.
    RCA, Red Seal LSC 3065, 1969.
```

An artistic work

List the artist, and then give the work's title, underlined. Add the name of the museum or other location, and identify the city.

```
Munch, Edvard. The Cry. Museum of Fine Arts, Boston.
```

A performance

List the title or the name of someone involved if that person's work is your particular interest. Add other appropriate details (such as the composer, writer, director). Then identify where and when the performance took place.

```
Frankie and Johnny in the Clair de Lune. By Terrence
    McNally. Dir. Paul Benedict. Westside Arts Theater,
    New York. 18 Jan. 1988.
```

2. MLA format for parenthetical citations

MLA style uses parenthetical citations in the text following each quotation, paraphrase, summary, or reference to a source. Each citation, made up of the author's last name or key words from the title, and the page reference, refers to an entry in the *Works Cited* list at the end of the essay. The name or key words allow the reader to locate the entry with complete publication information for the source. The page reference allows readers to find the exact material in the source itself. Place the citation, in parentheses, at the end of a sentence or at a logical break in its syntax. Place any punctuation marks—periods, commas, semicolons, or whatever—*after* the closing parenthesis. If your citation refers to a direct quotation, place the citation *after* the closing quotation mark, and *before* any punctuation mark. For longer quotations typed as a block with no quotation marks, place the citation two spaces after the period of the last sentence of the quotation. The parenthetical citation should fit smoothly into your text, interrupting your discussion as little as possible. With this aim in mind, MLA style allows for variations in citing references.

Author and page format

After a quotation, paraphrase, or summary of an author's work, add the author's last name and the page number of the source in parentheses. Note that you do not need a comma to separate the author's name and the page number.

```
In places de Beauvoir "sees Marxists as believing in
subjectivity as much as existentialists do" (Whitmarsh
63).
```

Author named in text

The shorter your parenthetical references are, the easier your essay will be to read. Therefore, you can name the author in your text, then include only a page number as the citation.

```
As Mueller and Rodgers have shown, television holds the
potential for distorting and manipulating consumers as
free-willed decision makers (370).
```

If you refer to a whole work rather than a specific passage, or to a one-page article, include the reference in the text without any page numbers or parentheses.

```
Virginia Woolf's interpretation of Hardy's tragic vision
is very different from Lawrence's.
```

Author of more than one reference

If you cite more than one work by an author in your *Works Cited* list, signal which work you mean by adding a comma and a short form of the title after the author's name.

```
Through Grendel, a "pointless, ridiculous monster,
crouched in the shadows, stinking of dead men, murdered
children, and martyred cows" (Gardner, Grendel 2), readers
are presented with their own silliness.
```

Long quotation

If you use a long quotation (five lines or more), type it as a block indented ten spaces from the left margin, and do not use quotation marks. Skip two spaces *after* the last punctuation mark, and add the parenthetical reference.

```
In similar fashion, the beginning of Being and Time also
raises this problem:
                The question of the meaning of Being must be
                formulated. If it is a fundamental question,
                or indeed the fundamental question, it must be
                made transparent and in an appropriate way.
                We must therefore explain briefly what belongs
                to any question whatsoever, so that from this
                standpoint the question of Being can be made
                visible as a very special one with its own
                distinctive character. (Heidigger 24)
```

More than one author

If you cite a work with two or three authors, list each author's last name in the order used on the title page.

```
"Opinion leaders" influence other people in an organi-
zation because they are respected, not because they hold
high positions (Gortner, Mahler, and Nicholson 175).
```

For a work with four authors or more, use only the last name of the first author, followed by *et al.*

```
As the Schools Council study showed in the 1960s, children
will learn to write if they are allowed to choose their
own subjects (Britton et al. 37-42).
```

Title without identified author

Use a short version of titles with no identified author. Use quotation marks or underlining as you would in the *Works Cited* list.

```
"Hype," by one analysis, is "an artificially engendered
atmosphere of hysteria" ("Today's Marketplace" 51).
```

Indirect sources for quotations

Use the abbreviation *qtd. in* to indicate that you are quoting from an indirect source—that is, someone else's report of a conversation, statement, interview, letter, or whatever.

> As Arthur Miller says, "When somebody is destroyed every-
> body finally contributes to it, but in Willy's case, [the
> end product] would be virtually the same" (qtd. in Martin
> and Meyer 375).

Source with a volume number

If you cite a work with several volumes, note the volume number and the page number, with a colon between the two, after the author.

> Modernist writers prized experimentation and gradually
> even sought to blur the line between poetry and prose
> (Foerster et al. 3: 150).

If you list only one volume of the work in your *Works Cited,* you need only include the page number after the author.

Literary works

To help a reader find a reference to a literary work available in many editions, cite the page number from the edition you used and include such information as part or chapter in a novel (175; ch. 10), the lines in a poem (33; 22-23). If you cite a play, you need only give the act, scene, and line numbers.

> As <u>Macbeth</u> begins, the witches greet Banquo as "Lesser
> than Macbeth, and greater" (1.3.65).

▌ 3. MLA format for explanatory notes

MLA style allows explanatory footnotes for commentary on sources or observations that would not fit readily into the text but are needed for clarification or further explanation. The notes, numbered consecutively, are identified by superscript numbers in the text. The full notes may appear as endnotes (typed in a list headed *Notes* after the text but before the *Works Cited*), or as footnotes at the bottom of the page (typed four lines below the last line of text). (See 41d2 for more information on note forms in MLA style.)

Superscript number in text

```
Stewart seems to emphasize the existence of social con-
tracts in Hawthorne's life so that the audience will accept
a different Hawthorne, one more attuned to modern times
than the figure in Woodberry.³
```

Endnote or footnote

```
    ³Woodberry does, however, show that Hawthorne was
often an unsociable individual. He emphasizes the se-
clusion of Hawthorne's mother, who separated herself from
her family after the death of her husband, often even taking
meals alone (Woodberry 28). Woodberry seems to imply that
Mrs. Hawthorne's isolation rubbed off onto her son.
```

▌ 41b. American Psychological Association style

The APA style cites sources parenthetically in the text and then lists these references at the end of the paper. This section discusses the basic format for APA style and shows examples of the bibliographic forms and parenthetical citations for various kinds of sources. For further reference, consult the following:

Publication Manual of the American Psychological Association. 3rd ed. Washington: Amer. Psych. Assoc., 1983.

▌ 1. APA format for references

In APA style, the list of sources, labeled *References,* appears after the body of your essay but before any appendices explaining your research procedures or results. (If your instructor asks you to list sources read as background as well as those you cite specifically, label your list *Bibliography.*)

Organize your list alphabetically by authors' last names. If a work has no identified author or editor, list it alphabetically by its title (excluding *A, An,* or *The*). If you cite more than one work by the same author, list the works chronologically under the author's last name.

Start your *References* list on a separate page, with the word *References* (neither underlined nor in quotation marks) centered at the top of the page. Double-space, and begin your list. Begin typing the first line of each entry at the left margin; indent the next lines in that entry three spaces. Double-space the entire list.

Each entry includes the author's name, the publication date, the title (and any subtitle), and the publication information, each followed by a period and two spaces. List the author's name with the last name first, a comma, and just the initials of the author's first and middle names. For more than one author, list the others in reverse order as well, with the names separated by a comma and an ampersand (&). Follow the author's name with the date of publication, in parentheses.

Underline titles of books and periodicals, but do not underline nor put in quotation marks the titles of articles. For book and article titles, capitalize only the first word of the title and any subtitle and any proper nouns. For periodical titles, capitalize all major words.

The publication information for a book includes the city where the publisher is located (and the state or country, if your readers are unfamiliar with the city), followed by a colon and one space, and the publisher's name. Like MLA style, APA style calls for a shortened version of the publisher's name, but calls for the names of university presses to be spelled out. In general, just drop any *Inc.*, *Corp.*, or *Publishers*. For an article in a periodical, the publication information includes the title of the periodical in which the article appears, a comma, the volume number (underlined), a comma, and the inclusive page numbers. The entry ends with a period.

Consult the various example entries presented in this section for information on where in an entry you should place supplementary information—particularly for publication information needed for different kinds of periodicals. Here are examples of basic book and periodical entries.

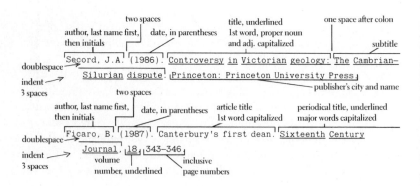

Books and pamphlets

A book written by one author

Coon, D. (1980). Introduction to psychology: Exploration
    and application. New York: West Publishing.

A book written by two or more authors

Newcombe, F., & Ratcliffe, G. (1978). Defining females
    --The nature of women in society. New York: Wiley.

A book written by a group

Institute of Financial Education. (1983). Income prop-
    erty lending. Homewood, IL: Dow Jones-Irwin.

A book prepared by an editor

Solomon, A. P. (Ed.). (1980). The prospective city.
    Cambridge, MA: MIT Press.

A second work by the same author

Macrorie, K. (1968). Writing to be read. New York: Hayden.
Macrorie, K. (1970). Uptaught. Rochelle Park: Hayden.

An item in an anthology or collection

Taylor, R. C. R. (1982). The politics of prevention.
    In P. Conrad & R. Kern (Eds.), The sociology of health
    and illness (pp. 471-483). New York: St. Martin's.

A government document

U.S. Bureau of the Census. (1984). Statistical abstract
    of the United States: 1985 (105th ed.). Washington,
    DC: U.S. Government Printing Office.

Periodicals

An article in a scholarly periodical that numbers pages consecutively within a volume

Shuy, R. (1981). A holistic view of language. Research
    in the Teaching of English, 15, 101-111.

An article in a scholarly periodical that numbers pages separately within each issue

Maienza, J. G. (1986). The superintendency: Characteristics of access for men and women. <u>Educational Administration Quarterly</u>, <u>22</u>(4), 59–79.

An article in a monthly or weekly periodical

Seymour, J. (1988, May 31). Preventing data loss disasters. <u>PC Magazine</u>, pp. 92–96.

An article in a newspaper

Browne, M. W. (1988, April 26). Lasers for the battlefield raise concern for eyesight. <u>The New York Times</u>, pp. C1, C8.

A letter to a periodical

Burney, P. S. (1985, May). Cryptographic message sending [Letter to the editor]. <u>Byte: The Small Systems Journal</u>, p. 14.

An article whose author is not identified

What sort of person reads creative computing? (1985, August). <u>Creative Computing</u>, pp. 8, 10.

Other sources

An interview

Kort, M. (1988, February). Ms. conversation [Interview with Martina Navratilova & Billie Jean King]. <u>Ms.</u>, pp. 58–62.

A computer software program

<u>SuperCalc3 Release 2.1</u> (1985). [Computer program]. San Jose, CA: Computer Associates, Micro Products Division.

▌2. APA format for parenthetical citations

APA parenthetical citations identify each quotation, paraphrase, summary, or reference in your text. These citations generally include the author's last name, the date of publication, and the page number if it is a specific citation. The author's last name is the key to the corresponding full-information entry in the alphabetically arranged *References* list. The year distinguishes one work from another by the same author, and the page reference identifies the exact location of the cited material in the original source. In general, place citations at the end of a sentence or at a logical break in syntax, after the closing quotation mark of a direct quotation, with any punctuation mark *after* the closing parenthesis. For long quotations typed as a block, place the citation two spaces after the period of the last sentence of the quotation. All APA citations follow the same general form, but below are some of the ways to treat variations in form.

Author and date format

The two basic items in a citation are the author's name and the publication date, separated by a comma. Researchers in fields that use the APA style often cite a whole experiment or study rather than quote heavily from specific pages. As a result, APA style citations may refer to whole works without page numbers.

> It takes a 900% increase in profit to offset a 90% decrease so that the company can return to the same profit level as before (Meigs, 1981).

Author, date, and page format

If you need to specify the page, add a comma following the date, and use the abbreviation *p.* for *page*.

> Parents play an important role in building their children's self-esteem because "children value themselves to the degree that they have been valued" (Briggs, 1970, p. 14).

Author named in text

If you name the author in your text, you need only cite the date in parentheses, immediately after the author's name.

> Key (1983) showed how the placement of women in print advertisements was subliminally important.

You can refer to the author and date of the study in your text and eliminate the citation.

> As Mueller and Rodgers demonstrated in 1980, television holds the potential for distorting and manipulating consumers as free-willed decision makers.

Author of more than one reference

When you refer to more than one work by an author in the same citation, use the author's last name and include the dates of all works cited. If you cite two or more works by the same author published in the same year, include the lowercase letter you assigned to each of these works in your *References* list.

> Several other essays continued this exploration of female heroes in science fiction (Russ, 1972a, 1972b).

Long quotation

Type long quotations (more than forty words), as a block indented five spaces from the left margin, and do not use quotation marks. *After* the final punctuation in the quotation, skip two spaces, and add the parenthetical citation.

> Unhealthy cafeteria lunches, full of salt and fat, result from more than just children's love of fast food:
>
>> As mandated by the Child Nutrition Act of 1946, the school lunch program must not only satisfy the nutritional needs of children, but also assist the agriculture industry as an effective farm support program. In 1986, this mandate meant that U.S. schools received more than $1 billion in government-donated agricultural commodities. (Montgomery, 1988, p. 28)

More than one author

If a work was written by two authors, use both names in all citations. Join the names with an ampersand (&) in parenthetical references, but spell out *and* when you name the authors in the text itself.

> While positioning is a successful method for handling students, group focus will also help prevent many problems. "Group focus is the ability to keep as many students as

```
possible involved in appropriate class activities" (Wool-
folk & McCune-Nicolich, 1984, p. 360).
```

If a work was written by three to five people, list all their names in the first citation. In any other citations of the same source, just use the first author's last name plus *et al.* (for "and others"): (Bradley et al., 1979). Only if a work was written by six or more people should you use the first author's name and *et al.* from the first citation onward.

Title without identified author

When the author is not identified, use the first few words of the title in the citation.

```
The school profiles for the county substantiate this trend
(Guide to Secondary Schools, 1983).
```

Indirect sources

Use *cited in* to show when you are using information taken from an indirect source.

```
The entire procedure was replicated with similar results
in Hermosa's study (cited in Poster, 1986).
```

3. APA content footnotes

APA style allows content footnotes for information you wish to include to expand or supplement your text, marked in the text by superscript numbers in consecutive order. The footnotes are listed on a separate page after the last page of your text, under the heading *Footnotes*, centered at the top of the page. Double-space all entries. Indent the first line of each footnote five spaces, but begin subsequent lines at the left margin. Ask your instructor or consult the APA manual for more specific typing requirements for footnotes.

Superscript in text

```
The age of the children involved was an important factor
in the selection of items for the questionnaire.[1]
```

Footnote

```
[1]The advice of Marjorie Youngston Forman and William
Cole of the Child Study Team provided great assistance
in identifying appropriate items.
```

▌ 41c. Number style

In the number style, which is used in many of the natural sciences, parenthetical citations in the text are numbers that correspond to entries in a final list of sources, often called *Literature Cited*. Variations in the number style exist from discipline to discipline, so be sure to ask your instructor which style you should follow. Some common style manuals are the following:

> *CBE Style Manual.* 5th ed. Bethesda: Council of Biology Editors, 1983.
>
> *Handbook for Authors of Papers in American Chemical Society Publications.* Washington, DC: American Chemical Society, 1978.
>
> *Style Manual for Guidance in Preparation of Papers.* 3rd ed. New York: American Institute of Physics, 1978.

For essays using the number style, your list of sources includes only works you actually cite in the essay. The list is arranged either alphabetically by authors' last names, with each entry assigned a number in sequence, or by chronological sequence according to the order in which you cited your sources in the text.

References in the text are identified by a number in parentheses following any quotation, paraphrase, summary, or reference to a source. The numbers refer readers to the corresponding entry in the *Literature Cited* list. If your citation refers to a specific page, include the page number after the entry number with a comma and the abbreviation *p*. Here is sample text reference and corresponding *Literature Cited* entry.

Text reference

```
First of all, the doctor is in the autonomous position
of having a monopoly on the applied uses of medical sci-
entific knowledge, as argued in Freidson (1).
```

***Literature Cited* entry**

```
     1. Freidson, E. Profession of Medicine, Dodd-Mead,
New York, 1972.
```

▌ 41d. Note-and-bibliography style

The **note-and-bibliography style** was the standard format preferred by Modern Language Association (MLA) until 1984 (and thus is sometimes referred to as **Old MLA style**). This style is still used in many fields, particularly in the humanities. In this style, references in the text are noted with superscript numbers that correspond to footnotes or endnotes, which contain full publication information. Sources consulted are also listed in an alphabetically arranged list at the end of an essay, called a *Bibliography*. You may not be called upon to follow this style for essays of your own, but you will want to be familiar with it and understand its conventions because you are likely to see this style in many of the sources you consult during your research. If you need further information, consult *The MLA Handbook for Writers of Research Papers*, 3rd edition.

1. Note-and-bibliography format for the bibliography

The format for entries in the *Bibliography* is the same as the current MLA format for entries in the *Works Cited* list (see 41a1). The *Bibliography* appears on a separate page at the end of the essay, after the list of *Notes* (see 41d2).

2. Note-and-bibliograpy format for notes

The note-and-bibliography style uses superscript numbers ([1]) to mark citations in the text of an essay. Citations are numbered sequentially throughout the essay and correspond to notes that contain complete publication information about the sources cited.

In the text, the superscript number for each note is placed near the cited material, at the end of a quotation, a sentence, or a clause or phrase. The number is typed after any punctuation, with no space between the preceding letter or punctuation mark and the number.

```
As Glueck says, "Most addicts have had dealings with some
type of crime before they became acquainted with nar-
cotics."[5]
```

Notes can be footnotes (typed at the bottom of the page on which the citation appears in the text) or endnotes (typed on a separate page at the end of the essay, before the *Bibliography*). Footnotes are typed four lines below the last line of text on a page, double-spaced between notes but single-spaced within entries. Endnotes are typed on a separate page with *Notes* (neither underlined nor in quotation marks) centered at the top of the page. Endnotes are double-spaced both between and within entries. The format of individual footnotes and endnotes is the same.

The first line of a note is indented five spaces and begins with the superscript number. All remaining lines of the entry are typed flush with the left margin. Before typing your final list of notes, doublecheck that the number of each note matches the correct citation in the text.

Notes follow a rigidly prescribed form, and differ slightly from bibliographic entries: the author's name is listed in normal order, all parts of the entry are separated by commas (instead of periods) and one space, and the publication information is placed in parentheses. The first time you refer to a source in a note you must include all information about it. In subsequent notes, you can list a short form of reference, usually the author's name and the page number. Examples of common variations in entries for different kinds of sources are shown in this section. Corresponding bibliographic entries for these examples appear in 41a1.

Books and pamphlets

A book written by one author

[1]Peter De Vries, <u>Peckham's Marbles</u> (New York: Putnam's, 1986) 25.

A book by more than one author

[2]John T. McNeill and Helena M. Gamer, <u>Medieval Handbooks of Penance</u> (New York: Octagon, 1965) 139.

A book written by a group

[3]Carnegie Corporation on Higher Education, <u>The Academic System in American Society</u> (New York: McGraw, 1974) 56.

A book prepared by an editor

[4]Dorothy Parker, ed., <u>Essays on Modern American Drama</u> (Toronto: U of Toronto P, 1987) xviii–xxiv.

A book prepared by a translator

[5]Sven B. F. Jansson, <u>The Runes of Sweden</u>, trans. Peter G. Foote (Stockholm: Norstedt Forlag, 1962) 38.

A republication

[6]Walter Scott, <u>Kenilworth</u> (1821; New York: Dodd, 1956) 85–86.

A particular edition

[7]Alfred A. Kelly, Winifred A. Harbison, and Herman Belz, <u>The American Constitution: Its Origins and Development</u>, 6th ed. (New York: Norton, 1983) 187.

A work in two or more volumes

[8]Fernand Braudel, <u>The Mediterranean and the Mediterranean World in the Age of Philip II</u>, trans. Siân Reynolds, vol. 1 (New York: Harper, 1972–73) 345.

An item in an anthology or collection

[9]Joan Didion, "Why I Write," <u>The Writer on Her Work</u>, ed. Janet Sternburg (New York: Norton, 1980) 5.

An article in an encyclopedia

[10]"Traquair, Sir John Stewart," <u>Encyclopaedia Britannica</u>, 11th ed.

Periodicals

An article in a scholarly periodical that numbers pages consecutively within a volume

[11]Margot Norris, "Narration under a Blindfold: Reading Joyce's 'Clay'," <u>PMLA</u> 102 (1987): 206.

An article in a scholarly periodical that numbers pages separately within each issue

[12]John Loffy, "The Politics at Modernism's Funeral," <u>Canadian Journal of Political and Social Theory</u> 6.3 (1987): 88.

An article in a monthly or weekly periodical

[13]Edward Said, "Through Gringo Eyes," <u>Harper's</u> Apr. 1988: 71.

An article in a newspaper

[14]Lora Sharpe, "A Quilters' Tribute," <u>Boston</u> <u>Globe</u> 25 Mar. 1987: 47

An editorial in a periodical

[15]Doug Magee, "Soldier's Home," editorial, <u>Nation</u> 26 Mar. 1988: 401.

A review in a periodical

[16]J. H. Block, "Debatable Conclusions about Sex Differences," rev. of <u>The</u> <u>Psychology</u> <u>of</u> <u>Sex</u> <u>Differences</u>, by E. E. Maccoby and C. N. Jacklin, <u>Contemporary</u> <u>Psychology</u> Aug. 1976: 517.

An article whose author is not identified

[17]"The Odds of March," <u>Time</u> 15 Apr. 1985: 20+.

Other sources

An interview

[18]Daniel Schorr, interview, Weekend Edition, Natl. Public Radio, WEVO, Concord, NH, 26 Mar. 1988.

[19]Larry Berkson, personal interview, 16 May 1988.

A letter

[21]Robert Frost, "Letter to the Editor of the <u>Independent</u>," 28 Mar. 1894, <u>Selected</u> <u>Letters</u> <u>of</u> <u>Robert</u> <u>Frost</u>, ed. Lawrance Thompson (New York: Holt, 1964) 19.

A speech or lecture

[22]Virginia F. Stern, "Sir Stephen Powle as Adventurer in the Virginia Company of London," Seminar on the Renaissance, Columbia University, New York, 15 Oct. 1985.

A computer software program

[23]<u>Nota</u> <u>Bene</u>, vers. 3.0., computer software, Dragonfly Software, 1988 (MS–DOS 2.0, 512 KB, disk).

A film or videotape

²⁴The Night of the Hunter, dir. Charles Laughton, with Robert Mitchum, Shelley Winters, and Lillian Gish, United Artists, 1955.

A television or radio program

²⁴Hill Street Blues, writ., Michael Kozoll and Stephen Bochco, with Daniel J. Travanti, Joe Spano, and Charles Haid, NBC, WNBC, New York, 15 Jan. 1981.

A performance

²⁵Frankie and Johnny in the Clair de Lune, by Terrence McNally, dir. Paul Benedict, Westside Arts Theater, New York, 18 Jan. 1988.

Subsequent notes to the same source

After you have given the full information for a source in a note, you can use shortened form, usually the author's name and the page number, in subsequent notes. If you use two works by the same author, add a comma and a short version of the title after the author's name so that a reader will know which source you are citing.

²⁶De Vries 82.

²⁷De Vries, Peckham's 37.

If you need to cite a particular source repeatedly, such as one literary work, mention in your first reference that subsequent references to the work will be found in the text. Then, for subsequent references, simply note the page, line, or act, scene, and line numbers in parentheses after your quotations or references.

¹Kenneth Roberts, Lydia Bailey (New York: Doubleday, 1947) 14. All subsequent references to this work will appear in the text.

▌ 41e. Using common abbreviations

Many research essays and scholarly works use abbreviations, most of them Latin. The use of such abbreviations has been somewhat discouraged today, but you may come across them in sources you consult.

In your own papers, you should use only those abbreviations that are part of your citation style—unless your instructor specifies that you use others. Here is a list of the most commonly used abbreviations.

anon.	anonymous
bk., bks.	book, books
c., ca.	around a given date (*circa*)
cf.	compare (*confer*)
ch., chs.	chapter, chapters
col., cols.	column, columns
ed., eds.	edition(s) or editor(s)
e.g.	for example (*exempli gratia*)
et al.	and others (*et alii*)
etc.	and so on (*et cetera*)
ff.	and the following pages
ibid.	in the same place (*ibidem*)
i.e.	that is (*id est*)
illus.	illustrated by or illustrations
l., ll.	line, lines
loc. cit.	in the same place cited (*loc citato*)
ms., mss.	manuscript, manuscripts
n., nn.	note, notes
n.d.	no publication date
no.	number
n.p.	no place or no publisher
n. pag.	no pagination
op. cit.	in the work cited (*opere citato*)
p., pp.	page, pages
passim	throughout the whole work
q.v.	which see (*quod vide*)
rev.	revision, revised by, review
rpt.	reprint, reprinted
sec.	section
supp., supps.	supplement, supplements
trans.	translated by, translator
viz.	namely or that is (*videlicet*)

PART NINE

Academic Writing

42. Writing in Different Disciplines

How is writing used in various professions? A recent survey asked that question of two hundred members of professional organizations serving the following seven groups: chemists, psychologists, technical writers, city planners and managers, engineers, business executives, and teachers of language and literature. As you might guess, the great majority (98 percent) report that writing is very important to doing their jobs well. More surprising is just how *much* time these professionals devote to writing—an average of 46 percent of their working hours. Other surprises emerged in comparing results by profession; for instance, engineers report spending more time writing than do English teachers. But overall, this survey confirmed that good writing plays an important role in almost every profession, and in some it is crucial to success. As one MBA wrote, "Those who advance quickly in my company are those who write and speak well."

This chapter will lead you to think about the different ways writing works in various disciplines. You may begin to get a sense of such differences as you prepare essays or other written assignments for various other courses. Certainly by the time you choose a major, you should be ready to familiarize yourself with the expectations, vocabularies, styles, methods of proof, and conventional formats used in your field.

This chapter will alert you to ways of analyzing and understanding the writing conventions of any discipline. Only insofar as you can reach such an understanding can you hope not only to use but to assess and perhaps even influence those conventions.

EXERCISE 42.1

Consider how the following topics might be approached in the specified disciplines or fields. What issues might each field see? What approach might each take? How might each investigate and write about the topic?

1. First-grade reading abilities—as seen by reading teachers, librarians, ophthalmologists (eye doctors), or reading-test designers
2. Soccer—as seen by sports physicians, psychologists, recreation department directors, or historians
3. Ancient Egyptian mythology—as seen by comparative literature specialists, anthropologists, archaeologists, or art historians
4. A sunken ship—as seen by engineers, marine biologists, economists, or journalists

42a. Analyzing academic assignments and expectations

Assignments vary widely from course to course and even from professor to professor. You may be asked to prepare one-sentence answers to study questions in history or physics, detailed laboratory reports in biology, case studies in psychology or sociology, or even film scripts in a visual media course. Thus the directions this section offers can only be general, based on experience and on discussions with professors in many disciplines. The best advice is really very simple: make sure you are in control of the assignment rather than the assignment's being in control of you. To take control, you need to understand the assignment fully and to understand what professors in the particular discipline expect in an effective response to the assignment.

When you receive an assignment in *any* discipline, your first job is to make sure you understand what that assignment is asking you to do. Some assignments may be as vague as "Write a five-page essay on one aspect of the Civil War." Others, like this psychology assignment, will be fairly specific: "For your first research assignment, you are to collect, summarize, and interpret data drawn from a sample of letters to the editor published in two newspapers, one in a small rural community, and one in an urban community, over a period of three months. Organize your research report into four sections: problem, methods, results, and discussion." (See the end of Chapter 40 for one student's essay in response to this assignment.) In any case, you must take charge of analyzing the assignment. Answering the following questions can help you to do so.

Questions for analyzing an assignment

1. *What is the assignment asking you to do?* Are you to summarize, explain, evaluate, interpret, illustrate, define? If the assignment asks you to do more than one of these things, does it specify the order in which you are to do them? (Note that the psychology assignment above does specify the activities to be carried out and the general topics to be covered in the report.)

2. *Do you need to ask for clarification of any terms?* Students responding to the psychology assignment might well ask the instructor, for instance, to discuss the meaning of "collect" or "interpret" and perhaps to give examples. Or they might want further clarification of the term "urban community" or the size of a suitable "sample."

3. *What do you need to know or find out to do the assignment?* Students doing the psychology assignment need to develop a procedure—a way to analyze or categorize the letters to the editor. Furthermore, they need to know how to carry out simple statistical analyses of the data.

4. *Do you understand the professor's expectations regarding background reading and preparation, method of organization and development, and format and length?* The psychology assignment mentions no background reading, but in this field an adequate statement of a problem usually requires setting that problem in the context of other research. A student might well ask how extensive this part of the report is to be.

5. *Can you find an example of an effective response to a similar assignment?* If you can, or if the instructor will provide one, you can analyze its parts and use it as a model for developing your own response. One psychology student, when asked to describe what constituted a "good" essay in that discipline, said "Well, for the first two assignments I basically summarized the relevant research data as clearly and briefly as I could and then pointed out weaknesses in the research and implications of it. Since I got A's on both papers I decided I must be doing something right." And indeed she was. By trial and error, she had fixed on an approach to the assignments, a method of organization, and a format that fit into what was accepted as "good" writing in her psychology courses.

EXERCISE 42.2

Here is an assignment from a communications course. Read it carefully, and then use the list of five questions in 42a to analyze the assignment.

Assignment: Distribute a questionnaire to twenty people (ten male, ten female) asking these four questions: (1) What do you expect to say and do when you meet a stranger? (2) What don't you expect to say and do when you meet a stranger? (3) What do you expect to say and do when you meet a very close friend? (4) What don't you expect to say and do when you meet a very close friend? When you have collected your twenty questionnaires, read through your results and answer the following questions:

1. What, if any, descriptions were common to all respondents' answers?
2. What similarities and differences were found between the male and female responses?
3. What similarities and differences were found between the responses to the stranger and to the very close friend situations?
4. What factors (such as environment, time, status, gender, and so on) do you feel have an impact on these responses? How do the factors affect the responses?
5. Discuss your findings, using concepts and theories explained in your text.

▌ 42b. Understanding disciplinary vocabularies

A modern rhetorician describes the way people become active participants in the "conversation of humankind" in the following way. Imagine, he says, that you enter a crowded room in which everyone is talking and gesturing animatedly. You know no one there and cannot catch much of what is being said. Slowly you move from group to group listening, and finally you take a chance and interject a brief statement into the conversation. Others listen to you and respond. Thus, slowly but surely, do you come to *participate* in, rather than to observe, the conversation.

Entering into an academic discipline or a profession is much like entering into such a conversation. At first you feel like an outsider, and you do not catch much of what you hear or read. You may be experiencing this situation right now. Indeed, everyone experiences the same thing when entering a brand-new field. To the new and uninitiated computer owner, the bits and bytes and macros and sidekicks and modem capabilities and other technical terms seem overwhelming. Trying to enter the new "conversation" takes time and careful attention. Eventually, however, the vocabulary becomes familiar, and participating in the conversation seems easy and natural.

▌ 1. Joining the conversation in a discipline

Of course, this chapter cannot introduce you to the vocabulary of every field, nor would it be helpful to do so. The point is that *you* must make the effort to enter into the conversation, and that again means taking charge of the situation. To get started, one of the first things you need to do is to study the vocabulary.

Determine how much of what you are hearing and reading depends on specialized or technical vocabulary. Try highlighting key terms in your reading or your notes to help you distinguish the specialized vocabulary of the field from the larger discussion. If you find little specialized vocabulary, try to master the new terms quickly by reading your textbook carefully, by asking questions of the instructor and other students, and by looking up a few key words or phrases.

If you find a great deal of specialized vocabulary, however, you may want to familiarize yourself with it somewhat methodically. Any of the following procedures may prove helpful:

- Keep a reading log, listing unfamiliar or confusing words *in context*. To locate definitions or explanations, review past reading or check the terms in your textbook's glossary or index.
- Review your class notes each day after class. Underline important terms, review their definitions, and identify anything that is unclear. Use your textbook or ask questions to clarify anything confusing before the class moves on to a new topic.
- Check to see if your textbook has a glossary of terms or sets off definitions in italics or boldface type. If so, study pertinent sections carefully to master the terms.
- Try to start using or working with key concepts. Even if they are not yet entirely clear to you, working with them will help you to formulate questions that will help you come to understand them. For example, in a statistics class, try to work out (in words) how to do an analysis of covariance, step by step, even if you are not sure you could come up with your own precise definition of the term. Or in a biology class, try charting the circulation of the blood even if you do not understand the whole process.
- Find the standard dictionaries or handbooks of terms for your field. Students beginning the study of literature, for instance, can turn to several guides such as A *Dictionary of Literary, Dramatic, and Cinematic Terms.* Those entering the discipline of sociology may refer to the *Dictionary of the Social Sciences,* while students beginning statistical analysis may turn to *Statistics Without Tears.* Ask your instructor or a librarian for help finding the standard references in your field.

Whatever your techniques for learning a field's specialized vocabulary, begin to use the new terms whenever you can—in class, in discussion with instructors and other students, and in your assignments. This ability to *use* what you learn in speaking and writing is crucial to your full understanding of and participation in the discipline.

❙ 2. Writing about literary texts

One example of a special vocabulary is the language of literary analysis, which is used in the fields of English and American literature, literature in other languages, and comparative literature. To analyze literary works and narratives that tell a story, you need to understand the following key terms:

character—the people in the story, who have different motivations and who may act, react, and change accordingly during the course of the story

plot—the events selected by the writer to reveal the conflicts among or within the characters, often arranged in chronological order but sometimes including flashbacks to past events

dialogue—the conversation among characters, which can show how they interact and suggest why they act as they do

setting—the scene of the story, including the time, physical location, and social situation

point of view—the perspective from which the story is told, whether presented by a narrator outside the story, or through the eyes of a character speaking in first or third person

style—the writer's choice of words and sentence structures

figurative language—the use of metaphor, simile, personification, and other figures of speech that enrich description (see 4f3 and 26b2)

imagery—the perceptions and observations created by descriptions and figures of speech that appeal to the senses

symbolism—the use of one thing to represent or suggest other things or ideas

rhythm—the beat or pattern of stresses in a line of poetry, including traditional metrical patterns or the movement of free verse

persona—the perspective and personality through which the events or emotions of the work are presented

tone—the writer's attitude toward the topic, conveyed through specific word choices and structures (see Chapter 26)

Looking for the features identified in the special vocabulary of literary study is one way to begin training yourself to read, to interpret, and criticize literary works—to join the conversation of English studies.

EXERCISE 42.3

Here are the opening paragraphs of *General Chemistry*, a textbook by John B. Russell. Read through the passage, and then analyze it by answering the questions that follow the passage about the special vocabulary in the passage:

> At one time it was easy to define chemistry. The traditional definition goes something like this: Chemistry is the study of the nature, properties, and composition of matter, and how these undergo changes. That served as a perfectly adequate definition as late as the 1930s, when natural science (the systematic knowledge of nature) seemed quite clearly divisible into the physical and biological sciences, with the former being comprised of physics, chemistry, geology, and astronomy and the latter consisting of botany and zoology. This classification is still used, but the emergence of important fields of study such as oceanography, paleobotany, meteorology, and biochemistry, for example, have made it increasingly clear that the dividing lines between the sciences are no longer at all sharp. Chemistry, for instance, now overlaps so much with geology (thus we have *geochemistry*), astronomy (*astrochemistry*), and physics (*physical chemistry*) that it is probably impossible to devise a really good modern definition of chemistry, except, perhaps, to fall back on the operational definition: chemistry is what chemists do. (And what chemists do is what this book is all about!). . .
>
> To make a very long story short, copper and bronze gave way to iron and steel, the latter being an iron-carbon alloy. Metals were very important in early civilization and the practice of metallurgy provided a wealth of chemical information. Egyptians, for example, learned how to obtain many different metals from their ores, and according to some experts the word *chemistry* is derived from an ancient word *khemeia*, which may refer to the Egyptians' name for their own country, *Kham*. However, some experts believe *chemistry* came from the Greek word *chyma*, which means "to melt or cast a metal." . . .
>
> It was not until around 600 B.C. that the beginnings of chemical theory emerged. Thales, a Greek philosopher, proposed that all chemical change was merely a change in the aspect of one fundamental material or *element*. Later, Empedocles, who lived about 450 B.C. proposed that there were four elements: earth, air, fire, and water. . . .

1. What terms are defined? Highlight or circle each one, and underline each definition.
2. What techniques or methods are used to point out or emphasize key terms? Note an example of each.
3. What techniques or methods are used to present definitions of key terms? Note an example of each.
4. How many different ways is *chemistry* defined? What is the function or purpose of each definition?

645

5. Which terms seem most important? Why do you think so?
6. After reading the passage, which of the special vocabulary here is clear to you, and which needs further definition?

▌ 42c. Identifying the style of a discipline

Getting familiar with technical vocabulary is one important way of initiating yourself into a discipline or field of study. Another method is to identify stylistic features of the writing in that field. You will begin to assimilate these features automatically if you take time simply to immerse yourself in reading and thinking about the field. To speed up this process, however, study some representative pieces of writing in the field. Consider them with the following questions in mind:

- In general, how long are the sentences? How long are the paragraphs?
- Are verbs generally active or passive—and why? Do active or passive verbs seem to be part of a characteristic manner of speaking used by writers and researchers in the field?
- How would you describe the overall *tone* of the writing? Is it very formal, somewhat formal, informal?
- Do the writers use first person (*I*) or prefer terms such as *one* or *the investigator*? What is the effect of this stylistic choice?
- Does the writing use visual elements such as graphs, tables, charts, or maps? How are these integrated into the text?
- What bibliographical styles (such as MLA, APA, note, or number style) are used? (See Chapter 41 for illustrations of several styles.)

Of course, writings within a single discipline may have different purposes and different styles. Although a research report is likely to follow a conventional form, a published speech greeting specialists at a convention may well be less formal and more personal no matter what the field. Furthermore, answering questions such as those above will not guarantee that you can produce a piece of writing similar to the one you are analyzing. Nevertheless, looking carefully at writing in the field brings you one step closer not only to producing similar writing but to producing more effective writing as well.

EXERCISE 42.4

The following passage comes from the opening of *The Social Construction of Reality*, by sociologists Peter L. Berger and Thomas Luckmann. Read the passage carefully and answer the questions that follow it.

The term "sociology of knowledge" (*Wissenssoziologie*) was coined by Max Scheler. The time was the 1920s, the place was Germany, and Scheler was a philosopher. These three facts are quite important for an understanding of the genesis and further development of the new discipline. The sociology of knowledge originated in a particular situation of German intellectual history and in a philosophical context. While the new discipline was subsequently introduced into the sociological context proper, particularly in the English-speaking world, it continued to be marked by the problems of the particular intellectual situation from which it arose. As a result the sociology of knowledge remained a peripheral concern among sociologists at large, who did not share the particular problems that troubled German thinkers in the 1920s. This was especially true of American sociologists, who have in the main looked upon the discipline as a marginal specialty with a persistent European flavor. More importantly, however, the continuing linkage of the sociology of knowledge with its original constellation of problems has been a theoretical weakness even where there has been an interest in the discipline. To wit, the sociology of knowledge has been looked upon, by its protagonists and by the more or less indifferent sociological public at large, as a sort of sociological gloss on the history of ideas. This has resulted in considerable myopia regarding the potential theoretical significance of the sociology of knowledge.

There have been different definitions of the nature and scope of the sociology of knowledge. Indeed, it might almost be said that the history of the subdiscipline thus far has been the history of its various definitions. Nevertheless, there has been general agreement to the effect that the sociology of knowledge is concerned with the relationship between human thought and the social context within which it arises. It may thus be said that the sociology of knowledge constitutes the sociological focus of a much more general problem, that of the existential determination (*Seinsgebundenheit*) of thought as such. Although here the social factor is concentrated upon, the theoretical difficulties are similar to those that have arisen when other factors (such as the historical, the psychological or the biological) have been proposed as determinative of human thought. In all these cases the general problem has been the extent to which thought reflects or is independent of the proposed determinative factors. . . .

Neither the general problem nor its narrower focus is new. An awareness of the social foundations of values and world views can be found in antiquity. At least as far back as the Enlightenment this awareness crystallized into a major theme of modern Western thought. It would thus be possible to make a good case for a number of "genealogies" for the central problem of the sociology of knowledge. It may even be said that the problem is contained *in nuce* in Pascal's famous statement that what is truth on one side of the Pyrenees is error on the other. Yet the immediate intellectual antecedents of the sociology of knowledge are three developments in nineteenth-century German thought—the Marxian, the Nietzschean, and the historicist.

1. How long are the sentences and paragraphs?
2. Are the verbs mainly active or passive?
3. What is the overall tone?
4. Do the writers refer to themselves? In what way? What effect do such references have on tone?

42d. Understanding the use of evidence in different disciplines

"Good reasons" form the core of any writing that argues a point, for they provide the *evidence* for the argument. Chapter 4 explains how to formulate good reasons. However, what is acceptable and persuasive evidence in one discipline may be more or less so in another. Observable, quantifiable data may constitute the very best evidence in, say, experimental psychology, but the same kind of data may be less appropriate—or even impossible to come by—in a historical study. As you grow familiar with any area of study, you will gather a sense of just what it takes to prove a point in that field. You can speed up this process or make it more efficient, however, by doing some investigating and questioning of your own. As you read your textbook and other assigned materials, make a point of noticing the use of evidence. The following questions are designed to help you to do so:

- How do writers in the field use precedent and authority? What or who counts as an authority in this field? How are the credentials of an authority established?
- What use is made of empirical data (things that can be observed and measured)? What kinds of data are used? How are such data gathered and presented?
- How are statistics used? How is numerical information used and presented? Are tables, charts, or graphs common? How much weight do they seem to carry?
- How is logical reasoning used? How are definition, cause and effect, analogies, and examples used in this discipline?
- How does the field use primary and secondary sources? What are the primary materials—the firsthand sources of information—in this field? What are the secondary materials—the sources of information derived from others? How is each type of source likely to be presented?

In addition to carrying out your own informal investigation of the evidence used in your discipline, you may well want to raise this issue in class. Ask your instructor how you can best go about making a case in that field.

EXERCISE 42.5

Do some reading in books and journals associated with your prospective major or a discipline of particular interest to you, using the questions above to study the use of evidence in that discipline. If you are keeping a writing log, make an entry in it summarizing what you have learned.

▌ 42e. Using conventional patterns and formats

You can gather all the evidence in the world and still fail to produce effective writing in your discipline if you do not know the field's conventions, the generally accepted format for organizing and presenting evidence. Again, these formats vary widely from discipline to discipline and sometimes from instructor to instructor, but patterns do emerge. In fact, disciplines may share similar conventions for similar types of studies. The typical laboratory report, for instance, follows a fairly standard organizational framework whether it is in botany, chemistry, or parasitology. A case study in sociology or education or anthropology likewise follows a typical organizational plan. And many disciplines share a conventional format for problem-solution reports: statement of problem, background for the problem's formulation, review of the literature on the subject, findings and possible solution, conclusions, and recommendations.

Your job in any discipline is to discover its conventional formats and organizing principles so that you can practice using them. This task is easy enough to begin. Ask your instructor to recommend some excellent examples of the kind of writing you will do in the course. Then analyze these examples in terms of format and organization. You might also look at major scholarly journals in your field, checking to see what types of formats seem most common and how each is organized. Study these examples, keeping in mind these questions about organization and format:

- What types of essays or reports are common in this field? What is the purpose of each type?
- What can a reader expect to find in each type of essay or report? What does each type assume about its readers?

- How is a particular type of essay or report organized? What are its main parts? Are they labeled with conventional headings? What logic underlies this sequence of parts?

- How does a particular type of essay or report show the connections among ideas? What assumptions of the discipline does it take for granted? What points does its organization emphasize?

The following sections illustrate three general patterns common in research essays—surveying literature, reporting experimental or field research, and interpreting sources.

1. Surveying literature in the social sciences

An introductory psychology class was given the assignment to write a brief literature review related to one aspect of child development, summarizing three journal articles addressing the topic, and drawing some conclusions based on their findings. Following are the notes one student made analyzing first the assignment and then the vocabulary, style, evidence, and organizational pattern appropriate for the field of psychology. These notes correspond to the appropriate questions for analysis presented in 42a–42e.

ANALYZING THE ASSIGNMENT AND THE EXPECTATIONS

1. Assignment says to summarize three journal articles. Then, evaluate and interpret their findings.
2. "Literature review" is defined in the assignment.
3. The articles I plan to review each focus on a particular study, so I need to be able to see the strengths and weaknesses of each study. (I also must be able to understand their use of statistics to be able to evaluate the data and then must be able to draw conclusions based upon this evaluation.)
4. No specific format is specified.
5. By examining previous responses to similar assignments, I can determine an acceptable format—will ask professor for some.

ANALYZING THE SPECIALIZED VOCABULARY

1. Articles will have technical vocabulary from psychology and statistics.
2. I will need to know terms such as *variables, inter-rater agreement*, and so on to understanding reading.
3. Terms showing reliability of research need to be mentioned in my summary.

ANALYZING THE STYLE

1. Sentences and paragraphs tend to be short.
2. Many passive verbs are used, especially in the sections presenting data (resembles newspaper style).
3. Overall tone is very formal (although can be slightly less so in the introduction).
4. First person is used very little.
5. Visual elements are used when necessary to clarify the findings. They are first mentioned in text (i.e., *see Table 1*) and then table follows (i.e., at end of paragraph).
6. Professor says journals use APA style; must check out exactly what this means.

ANALYZING THE USE OF EVIDENCE

1. Psychology relies heavily on previous related findings. Credentials are often based upon data alone. Statistically significant findings are very important.
2. Experimental data are very important. Experiments are devised to control for all variables other than the one being manipulated. (If extraneous variables are not controlled, the data will probably be rejected as worthless.)
3. Statistics are very important—results must be within the 0.05 level of significance (only a 5 percent possibility that the results were caused by chance). Probabilities must be presented with results, but tables and graphs are used as necessary.
4. Cause-to-effect logic is very important. Frequently, generalizations are made concerning the "real" world, based upon current research findings.
5. All three articles report on primary research.

ANALYZING CONVENTIONAL PATTERNS

1. In a literature survey, the three articles can be discussed in separate sections. Label each one with a heading. Change to new section for each article discussed, and introduction to each.
2. Arrange articles in chronological order.
3. Summarize each article and include quotations as appropriate to make my main points clear.
4. End with my conclusions about what articles show and about what may happen in the future.

After browsing through her textbook and thinking about the assignment, the student decided to focus on child abuse. A trip to the library turned up many articles on this subject, and she chose three. She summarized the three articles, worked through a draft, and analyzed it, following revision guidelines (see Chapter 3). Here is the final version of her essay, a literature survey reviewing three articles and drawing conclusions about what they show and mean.

Early Detection of Child Abuse*

There is no simple one-word answer to the question of what causes child abuse. The abuse of children results from a complex interaction among parent, child, and environmental factors. This complexity does not necessarily mean, however, that potential victims and abusers cannot be identified before serious damage is done. Researchers have examined methods of detecting potential or actual child abuse.

Prediction of Child Abuse: Interviews

In a study by Altemeier, O'Connor, Vietze, Sandler, and Sherrod (1984), 1,400 women between nine and forty weeks pregnant were interviewed to test their abusive tendencies. Four researchers were present (with an inter-rater agreement of 90 percent or better). The Maternal History Interview included questions about the mother's own childhood, self-image, support from others, parenting philosophy, attitudes toward pregnancy, and health-related problems (including substance abuse). Maternal and paternal stresses during the preceding year were measured with a modified Life Stress Inventory. Any information not included in the standard interview but felt by the researchers to make the mother a high risk for abuse of her child--for example, being overtly untruthful--was also recorded. When the infants were twenty-one to forty-eight months old, the Juvenile Court and the Department

* by Laura Brannon

of Human Services were checked for reports of their abuse
or neglect.

Although the interview predicted abuse (p < .0001),
its ability to predict decreased with time; for example,
although "six of seven families reported for abuse within
the first nine months following the interview were high
risk, . . . after 24 months only one of seven had been
assigned to this group" (Altemeier, et. al., p. 395).
The researchers point out some shortcomings of their study,
particularly the high rate of false positives. (Only 6
percent of the high-risk population was reported for abuse,
22 percent if failure to thrive and neglect were included.)
Although many incidents of abuse may go unreported (which
could account for some of the false positives), this false-
positive percentage should be reduced. Also, it would
be preferable if the role of subjective judgments in the
method for prediction could be reduced as well.

Toward Improving Child Abuse Prediction

A later study by Murphy, Orkow, and Nicola (1985)
was less dependent on subjective judgments. In this study,
587 women between three and six months pregnant were
interviewed using the Family Stress Checklist. This
checklist has ten factors: parent beaten or deprived as
a child; parent with record of criminal activity or mental
illness; parent suspected of abuse in the past; parent
with low self-esteem, social isolation, or depression;
parent with multiple crises or stresses; parent with
violent temper outbursts; parent with rigid, unrealistic
expectations of child's behavior; parent's harsh punishment of a previous child; child difficult and/or provocative or perceived to be by parents; and child unwanted
or at risk of poor bonding. Each item is scored as either
no risk (0), risk (5), or high risk (10); consequently,
an individual's score can range from 0 to 100.

653

Scores of 40 or above represent high risk; 7 percent of the tested mothers were in this range. Although all of the items were somewhat more common among the high-risk group, the following factors were almost totally absent from the low-scoring population and increased as total scores increased: criminal activity, serious mental illness, suspicions of past abuse, violent temper outbursts, rigid expectations of the child's behavior, and harsh punishment of a previous child.

After the children reached an age of one to two years, their medical charts were reviewed. A negative rating meant no signs of abuse. "Mild neglect" was signified by the mother's failure to provide sufficient medical care or her complaint that the baby was spoiled, difficult, or a poor feeder; "child neglect" was signified by the mother's failure to provide food, clothing, shelter, or supervision for the child or by the child's being "accident-prone" or failing to thrive; and "child abuse" was signified by the child's having broken bones, bruises, burns, or welts either verified or strongly suspected to have been inflicted by the parent. The Family Stress Checklist was 80 percent effective at predicting neglect and abuse. There were fewer false positives than in the previous study; the checklist was correct 89.4 percent of the time in predicting which parents would not be likely to be abusive. Variables such as age, marital status, and parenting experience did not significantly differentiate the high-risk mothers from those with low risk.

Early Detection of Child Abuse: Injuries

Johnson and Showers (1985) analyzed 616 child abuse reportings. Boys were reported abused more often than girls (56 percent to 44 percent), and black children were reported abused at a rate disproportionate to their population distribution and general hospitalization rate (p < .001). Also, although more men than women were reported for abuse (51 percent), mothers abuse their children more often. The type, cause, and location of the injuries varied with the child's age and race, but not sex. Johnson and Showers present a table with data on how injuries vary with age and race; this table is reproduced below.

How Injuries Vary with Age and Race

Child's Age	Highest Risk Type	Highest Risk Cause	Highest Risk Location
0–4 years	Broken Bones	Hot Liquid	Skull
	Hemorrhage	Grid/Heater	Brain
	Burns	Iron	Feet
			Genitalia
			Buttocks
			Hips
4–8	Erythema and marks	Cord	Not significant
		Belt/Strap	
8–12	---	Foot	---
		Fist	
12–17	Lacerations	Foot	Scalp
	Pain–Tenderness	Fist	Nose
	Swelling		Neck
Blacks	Lacerations	Cord	Arms
	Erythema	Belt/Strap	Thighs
		Switch/Stick	
		Knife	
		Iron	
Whites	Bruises	Board/Paddle	Buttocks
		Open Hand	Face

Conclusions

Overall, the findings of these studies seem to indicate that tests can be devised to predict potential child abusers. The study by Murphy, Orkow, and Nicola (1985), which relies less on subjective judgments, has a significantly lower false positive rate than the earlier study by Altemeier and associates (1984). Therefore, although such tests have not yet been perfected, they appear to be improving.

The two studies tried to integrate the complex relationships between child, parent, and environmental factors that are involved in child abuse. Ideally, if potential abusers could be identified early enough, they could undergo treatment even before the child is born. Of course, a parent could not be separated from a child on the basis of one test, and therefore, the results should remain confidential to avoid any potential for abuse of the test itself.

Whereas the tests look carefully at the parent's situation, the injury variables analyzed in the Johnson and Showers study (1985) focus attention on the child. If teachers or other people notice that children have frequent injuries (especially with the locations, types, and causes associated with different ages and races), abuse can be detected early and perhaps stopped.

References

Altemeier, W. A., O'Connor, S., Vietze, P., Sandler, H., & Sherrod, K. (1984). Prediction of child abuse: A prospective study of feasibiity. Child Abuse and Neglect: The International Journal, 8, 393–400.

Johnson, C. F., & Showers, J. (1985). Injury variables in child abuse. Child Abuse and Neglect: The International Journal, 9, 207–215.

Murphy, S., Orkow, B., & Nicola, R. (1985). Prenatal prediction of child abuse and neglect: A prospective study. <u>Child Abuse and Neglect: The International Journal</u>, <u>9</u>, 225–235.

EXERCISE 42.6

On the basis of the essay about child abuse, make a list of the characteristics of a literature survey in psychology. Your list will constitute an initial set of criteria that you could use in writing a literature survey of your own.

▌ 2. Reporting research in the natural sciences

An introductory biology class was asked to write a report analyzing a genetic question about a particular species of crayfish: when a female heterozygous for red claws was mated with a male with black claws, the resulting offspring included 154 red claws, 235 black claws, and 43 blue claws. Students were asked to explain the results by constructing hypotheses and evaluating them through the use of the Chi-square test. They were to include in their explanation an elaboration on gene expression, and to refer to at least two scientific journals. In response to this assignment, a student writer produced the following report.

Determining the Genotype of One Parent—
When the Other Is Known—by Evaluation
of the Offspring Frequencies*

INTRODUCTION

The purpose of this experiment was to determine the genotype of a male crayfish with black claws that was mated with a red-clawed female known to be heterozygous for claw color. This determination was made by evaluating the frequencies of three different claw colors observed in the offspring. Hypotheses involving Mendelian principles of genetics and various possible hybrid crosses were proposed and either proven false or recognized as probable

---

* by Julie Slater

by meeting the given stipulations of a black mated to a heterozygous red and the offspring frequencies.

METHODS AND MATERIALS

Two crayfish of a particular species complex were mated. The female, known to be heterozygous for the pheno-type of red claws, was mated with a male that expressed black claws. The offspring were grouped according to claw color and counted. The data were analyzed statistically using a Chi-square test.

RESULTS

In the 432 offspring produced, three phenotypes were noted: 235 crayfish with black claws, 154 with red, and 43 with blue. The observed ratio was 5.4 : 3.6 : 1.

DISCUSSION

The ratio results, which were derived directly from the counting of color patterns, can be accounted for by only one type of mating. Other possibilities were eval-uated, but only one passes the specificities of known female genotype along with the ratio results.

A monohybrid cross with one parent heterozygous for red claws and one homozygous for black produces a ratio of 1:1, which is not in accordance with the three different phenotypes expressed in the offspring. (See Figure 1.) Crossing two heterozygous parents would produce a phenotypic ratio of 3:1. (See Figure 2.) This again does not fit the observed ratio of the crayfish offspring, and it also contradicts the condition that one parent is heterozygous for red claws while the other shows black.

Because neither of the monohybrid crosses accounts for the observed ratio of the offspring, the next probable way to account for the male's genotype was dihybrid cross. A dihybrid cross involving two parents heterozygous for both gene pairs would produce a phenotypic ratio of 9:3:3:1. (See Figure 3.) However, such parents would themselves express the same claw color; in addition, only three different phenotypes were observed in the resulting offspring.

If the parent with red claws is heterozygous on both gene pairs and the one with black claws is homozygous recessive on the first gene pair and heterozygous on the second pair, the expected phenotypic ratio of the offspring would be 1:3:3:1. (See Figure 4.) This cross again produces too many phenotypes for the observed ratio. If, however, epistasis were involved in this cross, the expected ratio would be 4:3:1. (See Figure 5.) Epistasis occurs when a phenotype does not appear because one gene pair hides the effect of the other. In this cross, epistasis was hypothesized to function as follows. If one gene pair includes a dominant gene and the other is homozygous recessive, a black phenotype will be produced. To produce a red-clawed offspring, it is necessary to have a dominant gene on each gene pair. And for the blue phenotype to occur, both gene pairs must be homozygous recessive. The observed ratio approaches the ratio expected under these conditions. To further support this hypothesis, a Chi-square test was performed. The Chi-square value was 4.31 with two degrees of freedom. This value had a significance level between .2 and .1. For all these reasons, the hypothesis was accepted.

Even though a Mendelian dihybrid cross was found to be an acceptable hypothesis for the ratio observed in the offspring, the pigmentations on body surfaces cannot be explained solely by such a cross. There is substantial evidence that the genetic characteristic of coloring in other animals is governed by at least three to five loci (2). (As defined by Gardner (3), a locus is "a fixed position on a chromosome occupied by a given gene or one of its alleles.")

According to Crow (4), it is also possible during meiosis for genes to subvert the process of equal selection by "cheating" so that their own survival is more likely. This cheating, which was shown in experiments with <u>Drosophilia</u> eye pigmentations, throws off the frequencies of the offspring phenotypes and thereby produces more difficult stipulations that have to be met and explained using Mendelian standards.

In addition to these possibilities, the frequencies of the offspring phenotypes can also be affected by the process assumed by the central dogma. (See Figure 6.) This dogma is the idea that information coded in the sequence of base pairs in DNA is passed on to new molecules of DNA, which transcribes codes for the production of mRNA, which then translates, by means of RNA, the information that will be coded into protein (5). At any stage of this process where information is passed on, there can be some form of interference that would prevent the achievement of the expected outcome. There could also be environmental factors that could possibly alter the phenotypes.

SUMMARY

The genotype of the male crayfish was determined as rrBb. This determination was made by using a dihybrid cross of RrBb x rrBb, where epistasis was taken into account, with an expected ratio of 4:3:1. It does not take into account the possibility that the offspring frequencies have been altered by interference during gene replication, transcription, or translation. Other knowledge that should be considered is the evidence that coloring of body surfaces is governed by at least three to five loci and that genes can actually "cheat" to ensure self-survival. Each of these possibilities could create a result that would require further extensive study into the chromosomal makeup of the species. Despite these

possibilities, however, the genotype of the male was
proposed and accepted as rrBb.

MONOHYBRID CROSSES

Figure 1

Rr x rr →   1 Rr red
f,red m,black   1 rr black
f=female, m=male

Figure 2

Rr x Rr → 3 R_ ?
f,? m,? 1rr ?

DIHYBRID CROSSES

Figure 3

RrBb x RrBb → 9/16 R_B_ ?
f,?   m,?   3/16 R_bb ?
                3/16 rrB_ ?
                1/16 rrbb ?

Figure 4

RrBb x rrBb →   3/8 R_B_ red
f,red m,black   1/8 R_bb ?
                 3/8 rrB_ black
                 1/8 rrbb ?

Figure 5 (involving epistasis)

RrBb x rrBb →   3/8 R_B_ red
f,red m,black   1/8 R_bb black
                 3/8 rrB_ black
                 1/8 rrbb blue

CENTRAL DOGMA

Figure 6

replication

DNA →   mRNA   → Protein
        transcription translation
                        involving
                            tRNA

661

LITERATURE CITED
1. Strickberger, Monroe W. 1968. <u>Genetics</u>. New York: Macmillan.
2. Branda, R. F., and J. W. Eaton. 1978. Skin color and nutrient photolysis: An evolutionary hypothesis. <u>Sci</u>. pp. 625–626.
3. Gardner, Eldon J. 1965. Principles of genetics. New York: Wiley.
4. Crow, James F. 1979. Genes that violate Mendel's rules. <u>Sci</u>. <u>Amer</u>.: pp. 134–146.
5. Purves, William K., and G. H. Orians. 1987. Life: The science of biology. Sunderland: Sinauer Associated Inc.

EXERCISE 42.7

1. On the basis of the paper about the crayfish genotype, make a list of the characteristics of a research report in biology. Your list will constitute an initial set of criteria that you could use in writing a report of your own.
2. Based on this paper, what can you surmise about the expectations, vocabulary, style, evidence, and conventional patterns or formats of this field?

▌ 3. Interpreting sources in the humanities

The following paper, written for a literature class, illustrates how a primary source can be analyzed and interpreted in one discipline. Notice that the writer assumes that a reader will need little plot review and will accept the interpretation of character and theme as appropriate concerns.

The Role of Men in <u>The</u> <u>Third</u> <u>Life</u> <u>of</u> <u>Grange</u> <u>Copeland</u>*

Many observers of American society charge that it has created a distorted definition of manhood and produced men who, in their need to assert control of their lives, release their frustration at the expense of women. In her novel <u>The</u> <u>Third</u> <u>Life</u> <u>of</u> <u>Grange</u> <u>Copeland</u>, Alice Walker addresses this theme from the point of view of black men

---

* by Amy Dierst

and women, for whom racism heightens the distortion and its consequences. She suggests that by stifling black men's sense of freedom and control, a racist society creates frustrations that are released in family violence and inherited by their children. Because his wife and children are the only aspect of the black man's life that he can control, they become the scapegoat upon which his frustrations are released. As Walker's title suggests, she sees redemption, or spiritual rebirth into a new life, as the best defense against society's injustice. Though Walker's male characters have been labeled as either heartlessly cruel or pathetically weak (Steinem 37), many of them, like Grange Copeland, do change during the course of a work. Individual transformation stimulates the potential for change in the social system as a whole.

In this novel, Walker shows how the social and economic system of the 1920s offered a futile existence to Southern black families. Grange Copeland, like most Southern black men of his era, lived and worked on a farm owned and operated by a white man. This system, called sharecropping, did not allow for future planning or savings, for everything earned was returned to the white man's pocket for rent. Thus sharecropping, like slavery before it, contributed to the black man's feelings of powerlessness. In his desperation and helplessness, Grange turns to exert power in the one place he is dominant, his home. He releases his frustration by abusing his family in a weekly cycle of cruelty:

> By Thursday, Grange's gloominess reached its peak and he grimaced respectfully, with veiled eyes, at the jokes told by the man who drove the truck [the white farm owner, Mr. Shipley]. On Thursday night, he stalked the house from room to room pulled himself up and swung from

the rafters. Late Saturday night Grange would come home lurching drunk, threatening to kill his wife and Brownfield [his son] stumbling and shooting his shotgun (Walker 12).

At other times, Grange displays his frustration through neglect, a more psychologically disturbing device that later affects Brownfield's emotional stability. Grange's inability to rise above his own discontent with his life and express feeling toward his son becomes his most abusive act. Eventually, he abandons his family completely for a new life in the North. Even when he says goodbye, "even in private and in the dark and with his son, presumably asleep, Grange could not bear to touch his son with his hand" (Walker 121).

Brownfield picks up where Grange left off, giving his father's violent threats physical form by beating his own wife and children regularly. Although he, too, blames the whites for driving him to brutality, Walker suggests that his actions are not excusable on these grounds. By the time he reaches adulthood, sharecropping is not a black man's only option in life and cannot be used as a scapegoat. Nevertheless, he chooses to relinquish his freedom and work for Mr. Shipley.

By becoming the overseer on Mr. Shipley's plantation, Brownfield positions himself for the same failure that ruined his father. Over time, his loss of control of his life turns his feelings of depression and lost pride into anger, and his own destructive nature turns him toward violence and evil (Harris, 240). Unable or unwilling to take responsibility for himself, Brownfield blames his own inadequacies on his wife, Mem, who bears the brunt of his anger:

Brownfield beat his once lovely wife now, regularly, because it made him feel briefly good.

> Every Saturday night he beat her, trying to pin
> the blame for his failure on her by imprinting
> it on her face, and she . . . repaid him by
> becoming a haggard . . . witch. (Walker 55)

Brownfield demonstrates his power by stripping Mem, a former schoolteacher, of anything that would threaten his manhood. Reasoning that her knowledge is a power that he cannot have and therefore she does not deserve, he wants her to speak in her old dialect so that she will not appear to be more intelligent than he does. He also wants her to be ugly because her ugliness makes it easier for him to justify beating her. He wants her to reach a state of ultimate degradation where any strength of her character will be quickly extinguished by a blow to the face or a kick in the side. In fact, "he rather enjoyed her desolation because in it she had no hopes. She was totally weak, totally without view, without a sky" (Walker 59). In a final attempt to release his frustration, Brownfield kills Mem, literally and symbolically obliterating the remainder of her identity—her face (Theroux 2).

But in the face of this brutality and degradation, Walker raises the possibility of a different fate for black men and women. While in the North, Grange undergoes a spiritual rebirth and comes to understand that white injustice is not alone responsible for the cruelty of black men toward their families (Gasten 278). He also realizes that to weaken and destroy a wife and family is not a sign of manhood, saying:

> You gits just as weak as water, no feeling of
> doing nothing yourself, you begins to destroy
> everybody around you, and you blame it on crack-
> ers [whites]. Nobody's as powerful as we make
> out to be, we got our own souls, don't we?
> (Walker 207)

Grange redeems his spirit in his "third life" with his granddaughter, Ruth. His objective now is not to destroy what he loves but to cherish it. When a judge orders Ruth to go back to live with Brownfield after his release from prison, Grange kills him before this horror becomes a reality. Although he is shot to death as he tries to escape the police, he dies a redeemed man and passes his inner strength of hope on to his granddaughter.

The impact of the racist system of the South unquestionably pervades the lives of Walker's black characters. Nevertheless, she does not portray as justifiable the destructive need of black men to exert their strength at the expense of the weak. It is necessary to be aware of societal injustices and their effects but not to use them as excuses for individual cruelty. Through her characters, Walker gives us faith that cruelty turns back on itself. Some meet tragic endings, but the redemption of Grange shows Walker's faith in change. She envisions the children of tomorrow inheriting not hatred and selfishness but compassion and honesty. Her affirmative voice demonstrates the potential for social change through individual transformation.

Works Cited

Gaston, Karen C. "Women in the Lives of Grange Copeland." College Language Association Journal 24 (1981): 276–286.

Harris, Trudier. "Violence in The Third Life of Grange Copeland." College Language Association Journal 19 (1975): 238–247.

Steinem, Gloria. "Do You Know This Woman? She Knows You--A Profile on Alice Walker." Ms. June 1982: 89–94.

Theroux, Paul. Rev. of The Third Life of Grange Copeland, by Alice Walker. Bookworld 4 Sept. 1970: 2.

Walker, Alice. The Third Life of Grange Copeland. New
    York: Harcourt, 1970.

EXERCISE 42.8

1. On the basis of the paper about the Alice Walker novel, make a list of the characteristics of an interpretation of sources in literature. Your list will constitute an initial set of criteria that you could use in writing an interpretation in courses of your own.
2. On the basis of this paper, what can you surmise about the expectations, vocabulary, style, evidence, and conventional patterns or formats of this field?

FOR EXAMINING YOUR OWN WRITING IN A DISCIPLINE

Choose a piece of writing you have produced for a particular discipline—an essay on literature, a laboratory report, a review of the literature in the discipline, or any other assignment. Examine it closely for its use of that discipline's vocabulary, style, methods of proof, and conventional format. How comfortable are you in writing a piece of this kind? In what ways are you using the conventions of the discipline easily and well? What conventions of the discipline give you difficulty, and why? If you are keeping a writing log, make an entry in it on "What I would most like to know about how to write effectively in this discipline." Use this entry as the basis for interviewing an instructor in this field.

43. Writing Essay Examinations

"If you can't write it," says author and former college dean Arthur Adams, "you don't know it." While Adams's statement is debatable in some circumstances, it certainly applies to essay examinations, where writing is the way to demonstrate what you know.

Writing an effective essay examination requires two important abilities: recalling information and organizing the information in order to draw relevant conclusions from it. These conclusions form the thesis of the essay while the information serves as support. While this process sounds simple, writing an effective essay examination under pressure in limited time can be a daunting task. This chapter suggests ways to turn this sometimes daunting task into a perfectly manageable one.

▌ 43a. Preparing for essay examinations

In getting ready for an essay examination, nothing can take the place of knowing the subject well. You can, in other words, prepare for an essay examination throughout the term by taking careful notes of lectures, texts, and other assigned reading. You may want to outline a reading assignment, list its main points, list and define its key terms, or briefly summarize its argument or main points. A particularly effective method is to divide your notes into two categories. In a notebook, label the left-hand pages "Summaries and Quotations." Label the right-hand pages "Questions and Comments." Then as you read your text or other assigned material, use the left-hand page to record brief summaries of the major points made, the support offered for each point, and noteworthy quotations. On the right-hand page, record questions that your reading has not answered, ideas that are unclear or puzzling to you, and your own evaluative comments. This form of notetaking encourages active, hard-headed reading and, combined with careful class notes, will do much to prepare you for the essay examination. Here is an entry from a student's notebook, written in response to Chapter 4 of this book.

Summaries and Quotations	Questions and Comments
-rhetoric—art of language (Aristotle) -all language is argumentative— purpose is to persuade	Maybe all language *is* persuasive, but if I greet people warmly, I don't *consciously* try to persuade them that I'm glad to see them. I just respond naturally (unless they're having an insecure day).
-to identify an *argument*, ask: 1. Does it try to persuade me? 2. Does it deal with a problem without a clear-cut answer? 3. Could I actually disagree with it?	Of all the statements that can be debated, I think the less absolute the possible answers, the more important the question (such as nuclear disarmament) and the harder to solve (otherwise the answer would be obvious—no problem).

In addition to taking careful, detailed notes, you can prepare for an essay examination by writing out essay answers to questions you think are likely to appear on the examination. Practicing ahead of time is usually more effective than last-minute cramming. Late-night cramming for a multiple-choice test may sometimes work, but it is almost sure to be unproductive for an essay examination. On the day of the exam, do ten to fifteen minutes of writing just before you go into the examination to get your thinking muscles "warmed up" and prepare you to do your best job of writing the examination.

▍43b. Analyzing essay examination questions

Before you begin writing, read the question over carefully several times, and *analyze* what it asks you to do. Most essay examination questions contain two kinds of terms, **strategy** terms that describe your task in writing the essay and **content** terms that define the scope and limits of the topic.

STRATEGY ┌──────── CONTENT ───────────┐
Analyze Jesus' Sermon on the Mount.

STRATEGY ┌─────────── CONTENT ───────────┐
Describe the major effects of reconstruction.

STRATEGY ┌───────────── CONTENT ───────────────┐
Discuss the function of the river in *Huckleberry Finn*.

STRATEGY ┌──────────── CONTENT ─────────────────┐
Explain the advantages of investing in government securities.

Words like *analyze, describe, discuss,* and *explain* tell what logical strategy to use and often help set the form of your essay answer. Since not all terms mean the same thing in every discipline, be sure you understand *exactly* what the term means in context of the material covered on the examination. In general, however, the most commonly used strategy terms have standard meanings.

ANALYZE   Divide an event, idea, or theory into its component elements, and examine each one in turn: *Analyze Milton Friedman's theory of permanent income.*

COMPARE AND/OR CONTRAST   Demonstrate similarities or dissimilarities between two or more events or topics: *Compare the portrayal of women in* The Great Gatsby *with that in* Pride and Prejudice.

DEFINE   Identify and state the essential traits or characteristics of something, differentiating it clearly from other things: *Define Hegelian dialectic.*

DESCRIBE   Tell about an event, person, or process in detail, creating a clear and vivid image of it: *Describe the dress of a medieval knight.*

EVALUATE   Assess the value or significance of the topic: *Evaluate the contribution of black musicians to the development of an American musical tradition.*

EXPLAIN   Make a topic as clear and understandable as possible by offering reasons, examples, and so on: *Explain the functioning of the circulatory system.*

SUMMARIZE   State the major points concisely and comprehensively: *Summarize the major arguments against using animals in laboratory research.*

Strategy terms give you important clues for the thesis of your essay answer. Sometimes, strategy terms are not explicitly stated in an essay

670

question. In these cases, you need to infer a strategy from the content terms. For example, a question that mentions two groups working toward the same goal may imply comparison and contrast, or a question referring to events in a given time period may imply summary. Once you understand which strategy to follow, make sure you understand the meanings of all content terms. Particularly in technical or advanced courses, specialized language may need to be clarified. *Romanticism,* for instance, means one thing in the context of an eighteenth-century literature course and something else in a class on modern art. Do not hesitate to ask for such clarification.

43c. Thinking through your answer and taking notes

During an essay examination, you may be tempted to begin writing at once. Time is precious—but so too are organizing and planning. You will profit, therefore, by spending some time—about 10 percent of the allotted time is a good rule of thumb—thinking through your answer.

Begin by deciding which major points you need to make and in what order to present them. Then jot down support or evidence for each point. Craft a clear, succinct *thesis* that satisfies the strategy term of the exam question. While in most writing situations you start from a working thesis in outlining your topic, when writing under pressure you will probably find it easier and more efficient to outline (or simply jot down) your ideas and craft your thesis from your outline. Suppose you were asked to define the three major components of personality, according to Freud. This is a clear question and, assuming that you have read the material and studied your notes, you should be able to make a brief outline as a framework for your answer.

Id
basic definition—what it *is* and *is* not
major characteristics of
functions of

Ego
basic definition—what it *is* and *is* not
major characteristics of
functions of

<u>Superego</u>
basic definition—what it *is* and *is* not
major characteristics of
functions of

From this outline, you can develop a thesis:

> According to Freud, the human personality consists of three major and interlocking elements: the id, the ego, and the superego.

■ 43d. Drafting your answer

Your goal in producing an essay examination answer is twofold: to demonstrate that you have mastered the course material and to communicate your ideas and information clearly, directly, and logically. During the drafting stage, follow your outline as closely as you can. Once you depart from it, you will lose time and perhaps have trouble returning to the main discussion. As a general rule, develop each major point into at least one paragraph. And make clear the connections among your main points by using transitions: *"<u>The last element</u> of the human personality, according to Freud, is the superego."*

Besides referring to your outline for guidance, pause and read what you have written before going on to a new point. This kind of rereading may remind you of other ideas while you still have time to include them; it should also help you establish a clear connection with whatever follows. Write neatly, skip lines, and leave ample margins so you have space for changes or additions when you revise.

■ 43e. Revising and editing your answer

Leave enough time (at least five to ten minutes) to read through your essay answer carefully. Consider the following questions.

- Is the thesis clearly stated? Does it answer the question?
- Are all the major points covered?
- Are the major points adequately developed and supported?
- Is each sentence complete?
- Are spelling, punctuation, and syntax correct?
- Is the handwriting legible?

The more familiar you become with the process of taking an essay exam, the better your answers will be.

▌43f. Considering a sample essay answer

The following example illustrates how one student handled an essay and short-answer examination in a first-year American history course. She had fifty minutes to answer two of three essay questions and three of five short-answer questions. She chose to answer the following question first:

> Between 1870 and 1920, blacks and women were both struggling to establish certain rights in America. What did each group want? Briefly analyze their strategies for improvement, and indicate the degree of their success.

This student began her exam with this question because she knew the most about this topic. With another essay and three short answers to write, she decided to devote *no more than twenty minutes* to this essay.

First, she analyzed what the question asked her to do, especially noting the strategy terms. She decided that the first sentence of the question strongly *implied* comparison and contrast of the two struggles. The second sentence asked for an explanation of the goals of each group, and in the third sentence, she took *analyze* and *indicate* to mean "explain what each group did and how well it succeeded." As it turned out, this was a very shrewd reading of the question. In a post-exam discussion, the instructor remarked that those who had included a comparison and contrast produced better answers than those who did not. Note that, in this instance, the strategy the instructor expected is not stated explicitly in the question. Instead, class members were expected to read between the lines to infer the strategy.

After analyzing the strategy, the student then identified content terms around which to develop her answer: the groups—blacks and women—and their actions—goals, strategies, and degrees of success. Using these terms, she spent about three minutes producing the following outline.

Introduction
goals, strategies, degree of success

Blacks
want equality
two opposing strategies: Dubois and Washington
even with vote, great opposition

673

Women
many ultimate goals (economic, political, educational equality), but focus on vote
use male rhetoric against them
use vote to achieve other goals

Conclusion
educational and economic differences between groups

From this outline, the student crafted the following thesis:

In the years between 1870 and 1920, blacks and women were both
fighting for equal rights, but in different ways.

Guided by these notes, she then wrote the following answer.

The years between 1870 and 1920 saw two major THESIS
groups—blacks and women—demanding more rights, but
the two groups approached the problem of inequality in
different ways. Initially, women wanted the vote, equality WOMEN
within the family, and equal job and education opportunities. Their attempts to achieve all these goals at once GOALS
were unsuccessful, as men countered by accusing them
of attacking the sanctity of the family institution. (Demanding equality in the family meant confronting traditional Christianity, which subordinated women to men.)
With the lead of Carrie Chapman Catt, women narrowed
their goal to a focus on the vote. They emphasized that STRATEGY
they would vote to benefit middle-class Americans (like
themselves), reduced the stridency of their rhetoric, and
said that they would clean up an often corrupt goverment
(they turned the men's strategy against them here by *emphasizing* their own purity and virtue). They also invited
Wilson to talk at their conventions and won him to their
side. Because of their specific focus and reorganization, DEGREE OF
women did finally receive the vote which then gave them SUCCESS
the power to work toward their other reform goals.

Less well organized and less formally educated than BLACKS
middle-class women, American blacks often were unable
to dedicate their full effort to the cause of equality because GOAL
of severe economic problems. In addition, their leaders
disagreed over strategy. Washington told the blacks to STRATEGY
work hard and earn the vote and equality, while Dubois (SPLIT)
maintained that blacks, like all other Americans, deserved
it already. The blacks also had to overcome fierce racial

prejudice. Even after they finally won the vote, whites DEGREE OF
passed laws (literacy tests and grandfather clauses) and SUCCESS
used force (particularly through the Ku Klux Klan) to keep
blacks from voting. Therefore, even after the blacks got
the vote in name, they had to fight to keep and use it.

    Thus both blacks and women fought for (and are still TWO GROUPS
fighting for) equal rights, but the women were more suc- CONTRASTED
cessful in late nineteenth-century America. Educated, organized, and financially secure, they concentrated their
efforts on getting the vote as a means to higher political
objectives, and they got it. Blacks, on the other hand,
had to overcome great financial barriers that reduced access to education and worked against strong organization.
Even after they received the vote, prejudicial laws and
practices kept these Americans subjugated.

Although this essay answer is not perfect, as the student's commentary
and analysis in 43g will make clear, it responded accurately and fully
enough in its allotted fifteen to twenty minutes to receive a mark of A
and only one criticism at the end: "No advances at all for blacks?—
e.g. education."

▌ 43g. Analyzing and evaluating your answer

    Although you will not have time to analyze your answers during
an examination, you can improve your essay examination abilities by
analyzing your own answers later. When the student who wrote the
answer in 43f did so, she decided to go through her answer sentence
by sentence to see how well she followed the guidelines in 43e and
what additional points she might have covered. Lastly, she analyzed
her answer with her instructor's comments in mind.

> *Thesis.* I think my thesis worked pretty well, but it probably would have
> been clearer if I had named specific kinds of rights rather than just saying
> "certain rights."
>
> *Major points.* I included all the points that I listed in my outline, but I
> should have developed more the term *equality* in my discussion of the
> blacks' struggle.
>
> *Spelling, punctuation, usage.* Would have been better to skim essay over
> for spelling and punctuation errors (as in the sixth sentence).
>
> *Additional points.* I could have talked much more about individual
> women's contributions—no time.

Response to instructor's comments. I should have listed the advances made for blacks, which I knew—my interpretation was too negative. I also know much more about Washington and Dubois than I showed on the exam.

Analyzing and evaluating her answer in this way allows her to see whether she tends to stray from the topic and whether she could improve certain elements—such as the thesis and strong topic sentences—in future examinations.

READING AN ESSAY ANSWER WITH A CRITICAL EYE

Here is question 3 on the examination described in this chapter, followed by the same student's answer. Using the checklist in 43e and the suggestions in 43g, analyze and evaluate her answer.

The United States, one might argue, entered the world arena in 1899 and moved to center stage in 1918. What were the landmarks of American entry into the world arena and what, according to George Kennan, were the major mistakes the United States made during those entry years?

The United States grew in power and land during the early twentieth century. We proved our strength in the War with Spain, and in the process, we acquired, at least temporarily, Cuba and the Philippines and tried to shape their governments. We also asserted ourselves in Hawaii, Guam, and Puerto Rico. Our entry into World War I showed our concern with, and entry into, World politics. The war probably would have been lost had we not entered when we did. We provided fresh soldiers who inspired the Europeans. We also provided financial assistance and military equipment to the allies throughout the war (although, initially we sold amunnitions to the Central Powers as well). According to Kennan, the Americans made many mistakes in their approach to the war. First, we did not recognize the importance of European affairs to our own safety. We said that WWI was none of our concern until the neutral rights issue came to a head. When we finally entered the war, we were unprepared. Kennan also states that Americans have a terrible approach to war. Democracies are slow to anger, but once they fight, they go for the kill, forgetting political objectives and focusing on hatred. Also, Kennan feels that we should not have gotten trapped into a war with Spain because of our involvement in Cuba. Finally, Kennan criticizes the Open Door Policy concerning China's regions of influence as being the work of a few elite men. By saying that all of the countries agreed, we took a big gamble. In conclusion, Kennan criticizes American politics because we fail to see the implications of world problems to ourselves; we are never prepared when we enter war; we focus on hatred rather than political objectives; and we take too many risks. Kennan wants us to learn from these mistakes and change our attitudes because, when you're dealing with nuclear war, you can't afford to make *any* mistakes.

FOR EXAMINING YOUR OWN ESSAY ANSWERS

Choose at least two of your recent answers to essay examination questions. Review each question, and then read your answer carefully. How could you improve the organization, content, and correctness of your answer? Make an entry in your writing log, if you are keeping one, noting any new strategies you can use for improving your essay exam answers.

PART TEN

Writing for
Nonacademic
Audiences

44. Writing for Business

Principles of effective business communication are rooted in ideas as old as civilization. In fact, anthropologists now suspect that the very earliest forms of writing record business transactions. Today, much of the world's commerce is conducted in writing—in proposals, reports, and correspondence, particularly memos and business letters. Such correspondence is at its best when it is succinct and clear. Cornelius Vanderbilt was legendary for his ability to write powerfully direct business letters. When the fifty-nine-year-old millionaire took his first vacation, he discovered that a pair of business associates had taken steps that challenged his interests. To them, he wrote this letter:

> Gentlemen:
>
> You have undertaken to cheat me. I won't sue you, for the law is too slow. I'll ruin you.
>
> > Yours truly,
> >
> > Cornelius Vanderbilt

This chapter presents guidelines for effective business correspondence: letters, résumés, and memoranda.

■ 44a. Following business style and format

Business communications are utilitarian documents, intended to produce results. An effective business letter is clear, concise, and polite; it also usually follows a conventional format and speaks in language its reader will readily understand.

▌ 1. Writing clearly and concisely

It is best to use plain, straightforward language, avoiding long words unless they convey meaning precisely and are familiar to your reader.

Look at the following examples of inappropriate jargon—technical language used in unnecessarily complex, vague, or inflated ways. (See 26d5.) The revisions are not only more understandable, but more memorable.

JARGON   The biota marine exhibited a 100 percent mortality response.

REVISED   All the fish died.

JARGON   It is not inappropriate to know that all articles which coruscate do not necessarily possess a high intrinsic monetary value.

REVISED   All that glitters is not gold.

As you read this chapter, keep in mind these general principles of clear business writing.

- Keep sentences relatively short.
- Vary sentence length and structure.
- Prefer simple to complex words—for example *use* instead of *utilize*; *change* instead of *modification*; and *show* instead of *indicate*.
- Use concrete words—picture words and images—where possible, such as "the material springs back" instead of "the material possesses reversible extensibility."
- Use active verbs where possible, such as "waxing brightens the surface" instead of "when wax is applied to the surface, a brightness is achieved."
- Consider your readers at every point, avoiding unnecessary technical terms and relating your information to their experience.
- Write to *ex*press, not *im*press. If your writing is clearly expressive, it will make an impression.

▌ 2. Using a standard format

Business writers use several conventional letter formats which are easy to read and widely recognized. **Modified block** is the format most frequently used for business letters, probably because it is visually appealing on the page, with the whole letter centered vertically as well as horizontally. In this format, except for the return address, the date, and the signature block, all typed elements begin at the left-hand margin. The text of the letter is single-spaced but double-spaced between paragraphs and main sections so that they are clear and easy to read. (See 44b for a sample letter and envelope that illustrate this format.)

When you use the modified block format, first list your return address and the date, beginning each line at the center of the page. Should your stationery have a letterhead, type just the date, starting at the center several lines below the letterhead. Next, skip at least one line (or more to lengthen a short letter), and begin the inside address at the left-hand margin. List the recipient's name, title, and address just as on an envelope. Skip a line before the salutation, and follow the recipient's name with a colon. Skip another line, and begin the body of your letter. Separate paragraphs with double-spacing, but do not indent them.

At the end of the text of your letter, skip a line. Then, aligned with the return address and the date, begin the signature block with your complimentary close (followed by a comma). Four lines below, type your name, adding your title or phone number on the next line as needed. (The space above your typed name is for your handwritten signature.) Then, at the left-hand margin, note on separate lines the initials of the writer (in capitals) followed by those of the typist (in lower case), any enclosures (*Enclosure* or *Enc.*), and any copies (*cc*) forwarded to others. Mention enclosures, such as documents, photocopies, a check, or a résumé, in the text of your letter as well.

Traditional indented format resembles modified block format in every way except that the paragraphs, besides being double-spaced, are indented, generally five spaces. In **full block** format, all parts of the letter, including the heading and the signature block, are flush with the left-hand margin. **Simplified** format replaces the salutation with a subject line (typed in all capital letters) that announces the subject of the letter and omits the complimentary close. Although advocates of the simplified format argue that the salutation and the complimentary close add nothing to the content of the letter, most business people like the personal tone of these features.

▌ 44b. Writing letters of inquiry

Business letters often ask for information about job openings, products, services, fees, or prices. Like all business correspondence,

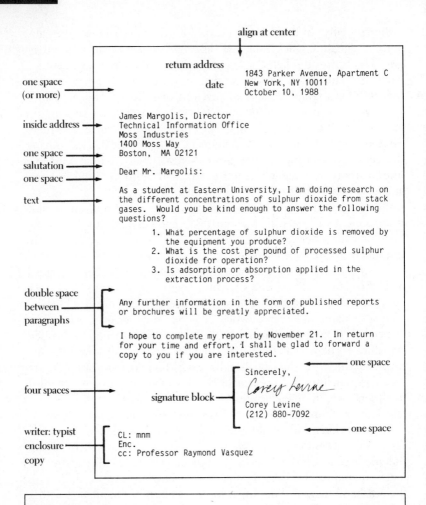

align at center

return address

         date

one space (or more)

inside address

one space
salutation
one space

text

double space between paragraphs

four spaces

signature block

writer: typist
enclosure
copy

1843 Parker Avenue, Apartment C
New York, NY 10011
October 10, 1988

James Margolis, Director
Technical Information Office
Moss Industries
1400 Moss Way
Boston, MA 02121

Dear Mr. Margolis:

As a student at Eastern University, I am doing research on the different concentrations of sulphur dioxide from stack gases. Would you be kind enough to answer the following questions?

1. What percentage of sulphur dioxide is removed by the equipment you produce?
2. What is the cost per pound of processed sulphur dioxide for operation?
3. Is adsorption or absorption applied in the extraction process?

Any further information in the form of published reports or brochures will be greatly appreciated.

I hope to complete my report by November 21. In return for your time and effort, I shall be glad to forward a copy to you if you are interested.

one space

Sincerely,

Corey Levine

Corey Levine
(212) 880-7092

one space

CL: mnm
Enc.
cc: Professor Raymond Vasquez

Corey Levine
1843 Parker Ave., Apt. C
New York, NY 10011

James Margolis, Director
Technical Information Office
Moss Industries
1400 Moss Way
Boston, MA 02121

such letters of inquiry should be clear, concise, courteous, and correct. The most courteous way to begin a letter is to address the recipient by name (correctly spelled, of course). If you don't know the person's name, call the company, or check a business directory in your library. Unless you know that a woman prefers to be called *Miss* or *Mrs.*, address her either as *Ms.* or by her full name (*Dear Beverly Moss*).

Once you have identified the recipient, follow these principles for an effective letter of inquiry:

- Address the recipient politely.
- State your request clearly and specifically, including whatever details will help the reader to respond.
- Explain the reason for your request.
- Express your appreciation.
- Make a response as simple as possible by including your telephone number (with the best time to call if you are difficult to reach).
- If appropriate, include a self-addressed, stamped envelope.

Consider how the sample letter of inquiry on page 684 applies these principles. Note, too, that this letter illustrates standard modified block form.

▌ 44c. Writing letters of complaint

Complaint letters ask for satisfaction of some sort. The most effective complaint conveys the point, however, *without* sounding angry or whining. Such a letter treats the recipient with respect while firmly requesting satisfaction. It aims to evoke in the reader a willingness to please or help the writer without losing good will or violating self-respect. An effective complaint letter is courteous and businesslike, not antagonistic. It tells the recipient exactly what went wrong, what consequences resulted from the mistake, and what action the writer expects. Consider the following guidelines:

- Open cordially.
- Describe the problem clearly and concisely.
- Explain how the problem affected you.
- State what the recipient can do to make things right.
- Express confidence in the reader's ability to remedy the situation.
- Close with thanks.

▌ 44d. Writing business memoranda

Business memos transmit information and record decisions made and actions taken. Like business letters, memos are typed, single-spaced, with double-spacing between paragraphs. They follow a conventional format using one-inch margins and full block form.

Follow these suggestions for any memos you need to write:

- Deal *only* with the subject specified.
- If the subject is complex, requiring a lengthy memo, add subheadings, subtopics, or numbers.
- Begin with the most important information, and move on from there.
- If you expect some action to be taken, end by stating exactly *what* that action should be and *when* it should occur.

The following example illustrates one standard form.

```
Memorandum

Date: May 7, 1988
To: Branch Managers
From: Melinda Russell, Director of Training
Subject: Customer Correspondence Seminars

Any of your personnel who participated in the Customer
Correspondence Seminar should schedule two follow-up
workshops. Please ask all participants to call my office
(ext. 280) during this next week to select dates and times
from the attached list of workshop sessions.

As requested at the last meeting of branch managers, the
workshops will last two hours, rather than three, and are
scheduled for alternating, rather than consecutive, days
to simplify arrangements for released time. Please contact
me personally should any scheduling problems arise.
```

▌ 44e. Writing job applications

Although a job application may contain a number of elements (writing samples, portfolios, autobiographical sketches, and so on), the résumé and the letter of application are part of nearly all applications.

▌ 1. Writing résumés

Résumé comes from the French word for "summary or epitome." A **résumé** summarizes your experience and qualifications and provides support for your letter. A **letter of application** or **cover letter,** on the other hand, emphasizes specific parts of the résumé, telling how your background is suited to a particular job.

An effective résumé is brief—a single, carefully planned page will usually suffice. Begin by brainstorming and taking notes, answering the following questions:

- What skills have you acquired in school, at work, and from your hobbies and interests? Try to find a common thread in all these experiences.
- What can you do well: draw, write, speak other languages, organize, lead, instruct, sell, solve problems, think creatively?
- Are you good at making decisions?
- Are you good at original thinking, at taking the initiative, or at following directions?
- Are you looking for security, excitement, money, travel, power, prestige, or something else?

Research reports that employers usually spend less than sixty seconds scanning a résumé. Remember that they are interested not in what they can do for you, but what you can do for them. They expect a résumé (1) to be typed or printed neatly on clean, high-quality paper; (2) to read easily, with clear headings, adequate spacing, and a conventional format; (3) to provide all the information necessary to make an interviewing decision.

Your résumé may be arranged chronologically or functionally— around your various skills or types of expertise, especially if you have considerable work experience in the field. Either way, you will probably include the following elements:

1. *Name and Address.* Begin with your name, which is usually centered. Supply your home, school, or work addresses, including dates or times you can be reached at each.
2. *Career Objective(s).* List long-range career goals, if appropriate, and specific jobs for which you realistically qualify.
3. *Educational Background.* Start with your most recent school, and list the others in reverse chronological order. Include degrees, diplomas, majors, and special programs or courses that pertain to your field of interest. Consider including your grade-point average if it is high. List notable honors, such as appearing on the Dean's List or receiving scholarships.
4. *Work Experience.* Place any relevant or extensive work experience *before* your education. List your jobs in reverse chronological order,

```
                          Chris Saunders
                         247 Timber Trails
                      Corvallis, Oregon 97330
                          (503) 555-1365


OBJECTIVE:          Public relations position

EDUCATION:          Oregon State University
                    Bachelor of Arts in Journalism, December 1987
                    Major Sequence:  Public Relations
                    Major GPA: 3.0/4.0

COURSES RELATED
TO MAJOR:           Design Graphics
                    Reporter and editor for the campus newspaper

WORK EXPERIENCE:    Supervisor, The Sherwin-Williams Co.,
                    Portland, Oregon, June 1986 to June 1987.
                    Supervised the warehouse operations with
                    eight people working for me.  Ordered
                    supplies and stock with a computer.

                    Inside Sales, The Sherwin-Williams Co.,
                    Eugene, Oregon, summers 1981-1984.  Helped
                    walk-in customers, matched colors of paint,
                    and sometimes stocked shelves.


PROFESSIONAL CLUBS: PRSS:  Public Relations Student Society
                    of America
                    SPJ/SDX:  Society of Professional Journalists/
                    Sigma Delta Chi


REFERENCES:         Available upon request
```

identifying each, noting dates and names of employers, and describing the nature of your duties. If a job is related to the one for which you are applying, give full details. Otherwise, be brief. Include any military experience in this category.

5. *Personal data.* It is illegal for an employer to discriminate on the basis of sex, religion, race, age, or natural origin. You don't need to provide this information or a photograph.

6. *Personal Interests, Activities, Awards, and Skills.* If space permits, list hobbies, offices held, dates and types of volunteer work, and any recognition for outstanding performance.

7. *References.* Choose references who know your work well and for whom you have worked successfully. Then ask these people if they are willing to serve as a reference. On your résumé, list the name, full title, and address of each reference, or note that your references are available on request.

Look at the résumé on page 688, noting in particular the use of space-saving phrases instead of full sentences.

▍2. Writing letters of application

A letter of application is the first "version" of you that a prospective employer will see. As your personal ambassador, it should be absolutely flawless—in format, spelling, grammar, punctuation, mechanics, and usage.

You may want to begin by reviewing your résumé, deciding which areas to emphasize and what information to add. Although each letter will take a somewhat different form, most letters of application consist of three main sections.

Introduction. State your reason for writing, and name the exact job for which you are applying. Tell the reader how you learned about the job.

Body. Describe, as specifically as possible, either your educational or work experience, whichever is more relevant.

Conclusion. Emphasize your interest in the position and your willingness to learn. Request an interview at the employer's convenience. Say when you will follow up with a telephone call if you plan to do so.

At this point you are ready for some constructive criticism. Ask friends, colleagues, or instructors to read your letter and suggest improvements. Read the letter aloud, or have someone else read it aloud to you so that you can listen to its rhythm and flow and catch needless repetitions. Then revise your letter carefully, and prepare the final copy, following these guidelines:

- Use high-quality bond paper and a good electric typewriter or word processor with a letter-quality printer.
- Follow a standard business letter format (see 44a).

689

```
                                    247 Timber Trails
                                    Corvallis, OR 97330
                                    January 11, 1988

    Suzanne Camdon
    Director of Public Information
    Northern California Bureau of Tourism
    1421 Fairfax Street
    San Francisco, CA 94120

    Dear Ms. Camdon:

    In response to the job description sent to the placement
    office at Oregon State University, I am applying for the
    position of public relations writer.

    Having just completed my degree in journalism with a public
    relations major, I am ready to begin a writing job.  Besides
    taking my courses, which included public relations writing
    and case studies, I was a reporter for the campus newspaper
    for two years and an editor in my senior year.  During this
    time, I learned to interview and collect information effi-
    ciently, to write and effective lead, to develop a story,
    to engage a reader's interest, to meet deadlines, and to
    accept an editor's revisions.  Last year my feature on back-
    packing grew into a series of columns, under my byline, on
    student travel.  These columns, and other writing samples,
    are available should you wish to review them.

    Given my background, I would very much enjoy a writing
    position with the Northern California Bureau of Tourism.
    I am available for an interview anytime, and I hope to hear
    from you soon.

                                    Sincerely,

                                    Chris Saunders

    Enc.                            Chris Saunders
```

- Proofread at least twice—once to make sure no words are left out and to check syntax and once to check spelling and punctuation. Then ask at least one other qualified person to proofread your letter, too.
- Make a copy of the letter for your files.
- Prepare the envelope, and proofread it carefully.

Above is a sample letter of application.

3. Writing follow-up letters

Depending on the responses to your application letters, you may need to continue your correspondence with a potential employer. Should more information or materials be requested, send them along with a short letter explaining what you have enclosed. If you are interviewed, a brief thank-you letter, repeating your interest in the job, may work to your advantage. If you are offered a job, you will need to write a letter enthusiastically accepting or tactfully rejecting the offer. On the other hand, if you receive no response to an initial letter, especially to a large company, you may want to draft an inquiry, asking whether the opening remains or whether other jobs are available. You may want to use a similar letter to apply for a different job at a company that especially interests you but has not yet hired you.

Should you want other ideas about effective job-hunting correspondence as well as strategies for developing personal contacts within a business or industry, refer to the job-hunting books available at your college placement office, library, or bookstore. Whatever additional ideas you use, be sure to write clearly and concisely and to follow a standard format as the next letter does.

```
Dear Ms. Camdon:

Thank you once again for your helpful information about
the many services provided by the Northern California
Bureau of Tourism. After my interview with you yesterday,
I am even more enthusiastic about the prospect of applying
my training and experience as a writer on your staff. I
hope to hear from you soon.

                    Sincerely,

                    Chris Saunders

                    Chris Saunders
```

FOR EXAMINING YOUR OWN WRITING

Identify a job for which you think you are qualified and draft a job application letter. Review your letter using the guidelines presented in this chapter, and revise accordingly.

PART ELEVEN

Working with Your Text

45. Writing with a Computer

Imagine this scene: preparing to draft an essay, you begin gathering equipment. First, a quill pen or two. Then pen knives for trimming and sharpening the quill, ink, ink pots, blotting materials and containers, a stack of paper—which is *very* expensive—and perhaps a stationery stand. Finally, you begin. But the ink blots and runs, the quill splits and must be mended, you misspell a word. You will have to start all over again.

Until fairly recently, this scene described the plight of writers and explains why so many tended to concentrate on neatness, on getting things right the first time around. Producing drafts or recopying were very messy, very time-consuming tasks. Then came such advances as ball point pens, typewriters, copy machines, and—most recently and spectacularly—the computer. Today, writers can modify and revise drafts with the touch of a key, can turn out multiple neat, clean copies in a twinkling.

Regardless of its power and efficiency, however, a computer is only a tool. It cannot conduct research, limit a topic, establish a tone of voice, or devise a persuasive argument. Above all, it cannot think (yet). These tasks remain the writer's inescapable responsibility. As a labor saving device, however, the computer can free some of your time and effort—no more mopping up ink or mending pens—so that you can concentrate on the writing process rather than on the mechanics of producing a manuscript. This chapter suggests how to make the computer and three types of writing programs (invention, outlining, and word processing) work for you.

45a. Using a computer for planning

When it comes to writing, the **computer** is essentially a storage device. It takes the material you enter, manipulates it in certain ways, and recalls it quickly. The computer cannot create your text, but it can, with appropriate software, help you plan material for an essay.

1. Using planning programs

Some specially designed **planning programs** can help you with preliminary writing tasks by asking a series of questions and recording your responses. After the questioning session, you can print your answers and use them to guide your composing. Some writers find planning programs helpful, but it is important to remember that the program can only *help* you think, not think for you.

2. Planning with a word processor

If you do not have access to a planning program, you can use your word processor (see 45c) to explore your topic as you would on paper, a technique that is especially helpful if you are accustomed to writing on a keyboard. You can key in notes, freewrite, make lists, write a series of loops, and answer questions (see 2e); you can then store all of these ideas in safe, yet easily accessible **files** on your data disk. By typing the name you have given that file, you return it to the screen and can consult, revise, and even print out **hard copy** if you want to work on it away from the computer, or if you are required to turn in all parts of your writing process.

45b. Using a computer for organizing and outlining

Outlining is an important step in organizing an essay, but it is sometimes difficult to do on paper. By its very nature, planning is a dynamic process, which changes as your ideas mature; often, however, as soon as you write an outline, it seems fixed and hard to change. For this reason, many writers find it convenient to outline with the help of a computer, since they can rearrange headings and subheadings freely.

1. Using outlining programs

Several commercial outlining or "idea-processing" programs can help you create a short, simple outline and gradually expand it into a full, multi-level sentence outline. You can experiment with your ideas, expanding a section of the outline by filling in more sub-levels; or you can condense a section by removing various levels from the screen until you wish to call them up again. Some word-processing programs also have this capability (see 45c).

2. Outlining with a word processor

If you do not have access to an outlining program, you can use word-processing software in much the same way, although it is less flexible. Start by making a list of the main topics you want to cover in your essay, and number them with roman numerals (I, II, III, and so on). Add subtopics as they occur to you, labeling subheadings with letters, the next level down with numbers, and so on (see 40b). Then use the **block insert** and **move** commands (see 45c2) to add, reorganize, or renumber subheadings. With these functions, you can easily move, add, or delete topics, and consider various arrangements of topics.

After completing an outline, you can print it out and examine it at leisure. You may find it helpful to work from hard copy, or printed version, of your outline when you begin to draft your essay. As new ideas come to mind, you can pencil them in. And, of course, you can always access your outline file, make your changes, and print out updated hard copy.

45c. Using the computer for drafting and revising

Word-processing programs, which allow you to enter and edit text in the computer, are most commonly used for drafting, revising, and editing. Ranging from simple data-entry programs to complex systems that can check spelling, display thesaurus entries, and search the text for specific words, word-processing software allows you to manipulate and edit text you might otherwise settle for in its first typed version.

Knowing basic word-processing functions

All good word-processing programs perform the same basic tasks. With them, you can write continuously without hitting a carriage return: the program automatically "wraps" from one line to another. With a single key (often called a **function key**), you can add, delete, or change letters, sentences, and entire paragraphs; move text from one page to another; and even define a block of text you've already typed and ask the computer to underline it or place it in bold letters. After completing a draft, you can store the text on a disk and work with it another time, or print a copy to see how the text looks on paper. Unlike typewriters, word processors allow you to rewrite, edit, and correct a draft without having to retype the entire document—whether you edit hard copy and then make your changes on screen or revise directly on the screen (see 45c3).

Learning the capabilities of your word processor

Many students learn to execute only the basic word-processing commands. Most systems, however, perform many other functions that further simplify your work as a writer. Some word-processing software, for example, can automatically format footnotes or endnotes. Some can generate tables of contents and indexes. Some have a built-in outlining feature similar to the programs described in 44b. While it may take a bit more of your time, investigating the capabilities of your program or those programs available to you on campus can make your writing process more efficient.

Using The St. Martin's Hotline

Accompanying this text is a software package that provides an on-line, abbreviated version of *The St. Martin's Handbook,* called *The St. Martin's Hotline.* Compatible with most word-processing systems, this program is loaded in conjunction with your writing program and "pops up" rules of grammar, punctuation, and style. Should you need to consult the handbook while you are writing, you need only press the "hot key" (**control-home**), and you are presented on the screen with lists (**menus**) of the handbook entries available to you. These lists are arranged hierarchically: each entry you select calls up a more specific list, until you have reached the particular entry, or rule, that you are looking for.

For instance, if you are puzzled about a particular use of the comma in your draft, you can immediately access the main menu, select *Punctuation,* then *Using commas,* and then *Following intro-ductory elements.* Superimposed on your text will be the rule for using commas after introductory elements. After reading the rule, you can then return to your text, make any necessary changes, and proceed with your writing. You can also access the rule you need by typing in key words, in this case *comma* or *introductory element.* The *Hotline* should be especially helpful as you revise (see 45c2); you may even want to wait until you have completed a draft before accessing your pop-up handbook so as not to lose momentum.

▌ 1. Drafting on a computer

Drafting on a computer is much like writing on paper, except that it is easier to make changes—so easy, in fact, that you may be tempted to spend too much time correcting errors during your early drafting. Because the text that appears on the screen and on the printout is neat and clean, mistakes are not hidden in the congenial messiness of a handwritten draft and tend to stand out more glaringly than they would in handwriting. Try not to interrupt your momentum and train of thought, however, by pausing frequently to correct mistakes. Concentrate first on setting down all your ideas, and second on revising and editing.

Once you become comfortable, drafting on a computer is so fast that you may find your eyes and mind getting tired. If so, stop for a moment, relax, and then return to the task. Many writers find that frequent short breaks help them work more efficiently at the computer.

Saving your text

Just as you can walk away from your handwritten or typewritten draft, you can let your word processed draft rest while you relax and revise a bit in your head. But before you step away from the computer or turn the machine off, you must save your text, using the **save** command. In fact, it is a good idea to save your text even after every few new paragraphs. The few seconds it takes you to save your text may save you hours of time and grief in the event of a power failure. Similarly, you should make a **back up copy** of the contents of your disk on another disk after each session at the computer. This way, should your working disk somehow get damaged, you will have another copy of your work.

It is also a good idea to print out your work at the end of each session. By looking over a printout of what you have written so far, you may discover the next point you should discuss or a different organization—ideas that didn't occur to you when you were looking at one page at a time on the screen. When you return to the computer you can incorporate these ideas and have all your changes in one place rather than on numerous handwritten inserts.

2. Revising on a computer

Some of the basic word-processing functions are especially helpful for revision: inserting, deleting, and moving. These functions allow you to reshape your text any number of times until you are completely satisfied with it.

Inserting text

The **insert** function found in most word-processing programs allows you to supply details, supporting evidence, transitional words and sentences, and other material without retyping the entire draft. With this function, added copy merely pushes apart the words and sentences around it, making a place for itself automatically.

Deleting text

When you **delete** text, the rest of the document closes around it so that only the desired copy remains. In some programs, the text is not truly erased, but rather relocated into a temporary memory, off the screen, from which it can be restored on command. If yours does not have this feature, be sure that you really do not want the text you are deleting. Should you want to replace the deleted copy, you must type it again. If you are at all unsure about whether you want to delete the text permanently, you may want to move the text temporarily.

Moving text

The **move** function permits you to move a block of text—a sentence, a paragraph, or an entire page—from one place in the essay to another. Because the original order is easily restored, this feature enables you to experiment with the organization of your draft without any retyping. You can even save the rearranged version under a new file name, print both the new file and the original one, and compare them to see which is more effective.

Revising from hard copy

Because you can print out a neat copy of your essay easily and often, you should use the opportunity to evaluate it often. After you have completed the first draft of your essay, print it out, double-spaced. Remember that the computer-printed draft needs just as much revision as a handwritten or typed draft. You need to scrutinize the printout carefully and reconsider all the decisions you made about content, organization, supporting evidence, transitions, sentence structure, and diction. Working from a clean, legible draft simplifies this task, for you can concentrate on what the paper says, not on how it looks. Revising from hard copy is particularly helpful, for it allows you to mark up the draft, insert notes, and see the entire essay spread out before you.

After marking up hard copy, you can then return to the screen and enter your revisions, taking advantage of the word processor's manipulation commands. You will probably want to save your printed drafts, in case your instructor asks you to turn in your preliminary work in addition to your final draft.

Getting responses to your draft

Another advantage to printing out your early drafts is that you can easily print out several copies, distribute them to some of your classmates, and receive a number of responses at the same time.

3. Editing and proofreading on a computer

Once you have revised your draft and are ready to edit and proofread, the speed and thoroughness with which computers operate can be a great advantage to you, especially through the tasks performed by the *search* and *search and replace* commands. In addition, a spell checker can ease your task of proofreading for misspelled words.

Searching text

The **search** command enables you to identify a character or string of characters, such as a mark of punctuation, a word, or several words. The program then scans the entire text, stopping every time it finds the designated characters, which you can then change or correct. For example, if you tend to place a comma before the word *and*, even when one is not called for, you can execute the search command and enter *and*. The screen will highlight each place *and* appears. You can then check to see if it follows a comma, and then decide whether the use is correct.

Replacing text

The **search and replace** command not only locates a character or string, but also replaces it automatically with another. If you find, for instance, that you have been writing *affect* for *effect*, you can use the search and replace command to find every occurrence of the word *affect* and check to see whether it should really be *effect*. If you want to make the change, a keystroke will allow the computer to replace *affect* with *effect*. With search and replace you can also save time by abbreviating a long title or a phrase that occurs repeatedly in your paper: keyboard the abbreviation while drafting; after finishing the draft, use the search and replace command to find the abbreviation and replace it with the full word or phrase.

Using a spell checker

Spell checkers may be an integral part of your word-processing software; if not, they are available as separate add-on programs. Both work similarly: the program examines all the words in the text and tries to match each one against a word in its memory. If it cannot find a match, the program alerts you to the problem and you must examine the word yourself. Some spell checkers work as you type: the computer buzzes if you type a word it does not recognize. Others you must institute yourself after you have finished typing. A good spell checker not only has a large standard dictionary of words, which you can add to, but also helps you correct errors by displaying a choice of words similar to the one it cannot match. If the program does not have a correction feature, look up the word in a printed dictionary.

No matter how sophisticated the spell checker may be, the full responsibility of correction rests on you. If the program finds a word it cannot match in its memory, there may be several reasons. The word may in fact be misspelled, or it may not be in the program's dictionary. Many errors do not show up in a spell checker because the word, though incorrect in context, is nevertheless a recognizable English word: you may have used a permissible variant spelling, for example, *judgement* instead of *judgment*. The program also cannot tell that you meant to use *their* instead of *there*, *thorough* instead of *through*, or *either* instead of *ether*. Spell checkers can alert you to some misspellings and typographical mistakes, but only your own vigilance can produce an error-free paper.

Editing from hard copy

Even after using a spell checker and editing and proofreading on the screen, you should print out your essay and proofread hard copy meticulously. You may overlook errors on the screen (and so may your spell checker) that you may catch on hard copy. Furthermore, you can share your hard copy with classmates and have them check it over also.

Once you have found and marked all errors and changes on the printed copy, correct them on the screen; then you can print a final copy (see 45c4).

Using a text-analysis program

Text-analysis programs are designed to identify a variety of patterns in sentences. Some programs look for punctuation errors; others look at sentence length, and some even attempt to identify wordy or vague sentences. Some point out sentence fragments; still others search out passive constructions.

To use a text-analysis program, you must have a finished document to feed through the text analyzer. The program then creates a file of comments on your document. Depending upon the capabilities of your particular program, it will isolate long sentences; too frequent use of the verb *be* and other weak constructions; the passive voice; colloquialisms; and so on.

Text-analysis software is restricted, however, by the limited memory of personal computers. A computer is only a mechanism: its judgments are relatively simplistic and may even be wrong; it is not sophisticated enough to judge shades of meaning, tone, the effect of a passage on its intended audience, or other stylistic considerations that only you, the writer, can resolve. If you experiment with a text-analysis program, act on its comments only when your own judgment tells you that they are valid.

▌4. Formatting and printing on a computer

Formatting text

Before you print out your final draft, you will want to format it, or lay it out on the page. Your word-processing program enables you to specify the number of characters per inch, spaces per line, lines per page, justified (even) or ragged margins, and even fonts. Be conservative in the way you use different fonts, however; a mixture of underlining, boldface, and different size type can be dizzying if overdone. Be sure that whatever specifications you choose are in accordance with the style of your discipline and meet with your instructor's expectations.

Printing text

If your printer does not have **letter-quality** (fully formed letters) **capacity,** ask your instructor if he or she will accept **dot-matrix** (letters formed by lines of dots) **printing.** (You may even want to show your instructor a sample of the printing.) If you are printing on tractor-fed paper, always tear off the row of holes along the sides and separate the pages before turning in the paper.

FOR EXAMINING YOUR OWN USE OF COMPUTERS IN WRITING

Take the time to reflect on your use of technology in writing. If you do not yet use a computer/word processor, spend five minutes or so writing a list of those things a computer might help with in your writing. If you are using a computer, spend some time now analyzing how efficient that use is. What does the computer help most with in your writing? What is it the least help with? In what ways has the use of a computer changed or modified the way you go about writing an essay? What would you most like to improve about your ability to use the computer?

46. Preparing Your Manuscript

One of the most satisfying parts of the writing process is the preparation of your final manuscript. This step presents your work in a clean, neat, easy-to-read package, one you are happy to identify as your own.

▮ 46a. Following guidelines

Follow your instructor's guidelines carefully, and ask for more information if these are not clear to you. Most instructors expect typewritten manuscripts, but some may accept neat, legible handwritten papers.

▮ 1. Typing your manuscript

A typewritten manuscript is far easier to read than a handwritten one. You should, therefore, type or print out a word-processed paper whenever possible, even if your instructor does not require doing so.

Selecting paper

Type or print your paper on medium-grade 8½″ × 11″ bond paper. Do not use legal-sized paper (8½″ × 14″), notebook paper, or mismatched, odd-sized sheets.

Onionskin or "erasable" paper is usually unacceptable because it is difficult for your instructor to write on. If you must use erasable paper, submit a photographic copy of your finished paper.

Select an appropriate quality of paper if you use a computer printer. Inexpensive grades are often too flimsy, and many leave stubs when the sheets are separated and the tractor holes are torn off. (Always tear computer-printed pages apart, and remove the tractor holes from the sides.)

Selecting typeface

Use a standard typeface, either **pica** (10-point) or **elite** (12-point). Because special typefaces, such as simulated script, are hard to read, avoid using them.

If you use a computer, a letter-quality printer is best. Check with your instructor before using a dot-matrix printer because some readers strongly object to reading low-quality dot-matrix print.

❙ 2. Handwriting your manuscript

If for some reason you cannot type your manuscript, write as clearly and legibly as you can, forming each word with care. Hand-written papers tend to contain more mechanical errors than do typed papers because they are more difficult to proofread. Thus you should devote extra care to the actual writing.

Selecting paper

Use white, ruled, 8½″ × 11″ loose-leaf notebook paper. Do not use spiral notebook paper, unlined paper, or paper with very narrow lines. Write on only one side of each piece of paper; ask your instructor whether you should write on every other line.

Selecting ink

Write neatly in dark blue or black ink, using a medium- or fine-point pen. Do not use pencil; it is hard to read and smears.

❙ 3. Positioning title and page numbers

The styles recommended for papers written in certain disciplines (MLA for many of the humanities; APA for many of the social sciences) specify the format for the title page. (See pp. 589 and 600 for examples of title pages for each style.) If your instructor does not specify a style, follow the standard format for the first page of a typed paper. One inch down from the top of the paper, type your name at the left margin, followed by the course number, your instructor's name, and the date. Double-space each line as well as your title, which is centered. Capitalize each major word in the title, but don't underline it or enclose it in quotation marks. If the title is very long, divide it into two double-spaced lines, and center each one. Put four spaces between the title and the first line of the essay.

If your essay is longer than two pages, number each page consecutively, beginning with the first page. Place page numbers in the upper right-hand corner, one-half inch from the top and flush with the right-hand margin. Use Arabic numerals, and do not use periods, slash marks, or parentheses with the page numbers. Type your name before each page number in case some of the pages are misplaced.

❙ 4. Including documentation and notes

Credit any sources you researched in writing your essay according to the style required by your instructor. (See Chapter 41 for examples of common documentation and note formats.)

❙ 46b. Using a readable page format

If your instructor asks you to follow a specific style manual in writing and preparing your paper, consult it for more specific details about format. Otherwise, use the following format.

Setting margins

White space helps readers understand how a page is set up. Standard guidelines call for one-inch margins top and bottom, left and right. (More generous margins, even one and one-half inches, make the page easier to read.) Begin each new page by measuring down one inch from the top of the paper.

Indenting paragraphs

Indent each new paragraph five spaces from the left margin. Do *not* leave an extra double-space between paragraphs. If you have only one line left at the bottom of a page, go to a new page to begin a new paragraph.

Double-spacing

Papers for college courses should be double-spaced unless you are specifically asked to do otherwise. Double-spaced type is much easier to read and proofread, and it leaves room for your instructor to make comments and suggestions. (See 31a1 for information about inserting long quotations.)

Binding your manuscript

Unless your instructor asks you to use a binder, a folder, or staples, use only a paper clip to secure the pages of your paper.

46c. Putting your best product forward

Your final copy deserves care; proofread and correct it meticulously. A computer facilitates this job, allowing you to proofread from hard copy or on the screen, make changes, and then print out a clean draft. If you are typing your paper, however, try to make corrections as you go along, using white correction fluid or lift-off tape if your typewriter has a self-correcting mechanism. After you finish typing, go back and proofread each page. If possible, set the manuscript aside and look at it later with fresh eyes.

Correct minor typographical errors by applying correction fluid and retyping. If there is not enough room for the correction, delete the error with a single pen stroke. Then add the correction above the line, marking where it belongs with a caret (∧).

sequence

What Meredith, or any author of a sonnet ∧ tries to do, is to create a whole world of feelings.

If you must make more than two or three such corrections on a page, retype the page. Add any brackets, accent marks, or other symbols neatly in ink if they are not on your keyboard.

Finally, handle the finished product carefully, following those well-known directions: *do not fold, mutilate, or spindle.*

FOR EXAMINING YOUR OWN WRITING

Take a critical look at an essay you have just finished or have recently submitted. Using the guidelines presented in this chapter, assess your use of format and typing conventions. Note particularly those that you have not generally followed or those that are unfamiliar to you. Then annotate your essay, making corrections or noting the appropriate conventions in the margins or above the lines. Keep this annotated essay with your writing log, or make an entry, noting which conventions you need to check carefully when you next begin preparing a manuscript.

Glossaries

Glossary of Grammatical Terms
Glossary of Usage

Glossary of Grammatical Terms

absolute phrase   See *phrase*.

abstract noun   See *noun*.

acronym   A word formed from the first letters of several words, such as RADAR for *radio detecting and ranging*.

active voice   See *voice*.

adjective   A word that modifies, quantifies, identifies, or describes a word or words acting as a noun. An **attributive** adjective precedes and a **predicative** adjective follows the noun or pronoun that it modifies (*a good book, the book is good*). Of the overlapping types of adjectives, **descriptive adjectives** identify a quality that is *common*, such as a type, color, or weight (*research paper, yellow paper, heavy paper*) or *proper*, derived from a proper noun (*English history, Jacobean drama, Homeric epic*). **Demonstrative adjectives** (*this, that, these,* and *those*) point out words acting as nouns (*this paper, those papers*). **Indefinite adjectives** define the specificity of the words they modify (*some research, any research, such research*). **Relative adjectives** qualify words bound directly to a modifying clause (*I know which research is yours*). **Interrogative adjectives** ask questions about the words they modify (*Whose research is finished? What research is she doing? Which research is in progress?*). **Limiting adjectives** are the articles *a, an,* and *the*. **Numerical adjectives** modify words with *cardinal* or *ordinal* numbers (*two girls in their tenth year*). **Participial adjectives** are verbals that act as adjectives (*a waiting car, a damaged package*). **Possessive adjectives** include *my, your, his, her, its, one's, our, your, their* (*her research, our research*) as well as proper possessives formed by adding an *-'s* to a proper noun (*Einstein's research, America's coastline*). See 6b4, 10a, 10b, and 10d.

adjective clause   See *clause*.

adjective forms   Changes in an adjective from the **positive** (simply *tall, good*) to **comparative** (comparing two—*taller, better*) or the **superlative** (comparing more than two—*tallest, best*). Short regular adjectives (*tall*) just add *-er* and

-est, but irregular adjectives (*good*) do not follow this pattern. Most longer adjectives form the comparative by adding *more* or *less* (*more beautiful, less beautiful*) and the superlative by adding *most* and *least* (*most beautiful, least beautiful*). Some adjectives (*only, forty*) do not change form.

adverb A word that qualifies, modifies, limits, or defines a verb, an adjective, another adverb, or a clause, frequently answering the questions *where?, when?, how?, why?, to what extent?,* or *under what conditions?* Adverbs derived from adjectives and nouns commonly end in the suffix *-ly. She will soon travel south and probably visit her very favorite sister.* See also *conjunction.* See 6b5, 10c, and 10d.

adverb clause See *clause.*

adverb forms Changes in an adverb from the **positive** (simply *eagerly*) to the **comparative** (comparing two—*more eagerly*) or the **superlative** (comparing more than two—*most eagerly*). The forms of some adverbs and adjectives are identical (*fast, faster, fastest; little, less, least*). Most adverbs, however, add *more* or *less* in the comparative and *most* or *least* in the superlative (*quickly, more quickly, most quickly*).

agreement The correspondence of a pronoun with its antecedent in person, number, and gender or of a verb with its subject in person and number. *Tina sings, and her fans go wild; the band members play, and the crowd goes wild.* See also *antecedent, gender, number, person.* See Chapter 9.

antecedent A specific noun which a pronoun replaces and to which it refers. The two must agree in person, number, and gender. *Fred Astaire moved his feet as no else has.* The antecedent can sometimes follow the pronoun that refers to it. *Moving his feet as no one else has, Fred Astaire was a singular dancer.* See 6b3, 11a, and 11b.

appositive One noun or noun phrase that parallels another, illuminating it with additional information. *Magic Johnson, the best player in the NBA, scored thirty-one points. The cruelest month, April, is my favorite.* See 6c3 and 27c3.

article *A, an,* or *the,* the most common adjectives. *A* is used before consonants, *an* before vowels. Both are **indefinite** and do not specifically identify the nouns they modify. *A strange feeling came over me* as *an awful specter arose. The* is **definite** or specific. *The awful figure of my long-lost grandfather stood before me.*

auxiliary verb A verb that combines with the base form or with the present or past participle of a main verb to form a verb phrase and to determine tense. The **primary** auxiliaries (*do, have, be*) have different forms and make verb phrases that are reasonably straightforward in terms of tense and mood (*I did think; I had thought; I am thinking*). **Modal** auxiliaries such as *can, may, shall, will, could, might, should, would,* and *ought* [*to*] have only one form and show possibility, necessity, obligation, ability, capability, and so on. Some modals form uncomplicated verb phrases (*I shall (will) think*), but others achieve subtle variations in tense and mood (*I should have agreed with you had I not known better*). See 6b1 and 8a.

cardinal number   A simple number that answers the question *how many?—seven, one hundred fifty*. Distinguished from *ordinal number*.

case   The form of a noun or pronoun that reflects its grammatical role in a sentence. Nouns and indefinite pronouns can be **subjective, possessive,** or **objective**, but they change form only in the possessive case. *The dog* (subjective) *barked. The dog's* (possessive) *tail wagged. The mail carrier called the dog* (objective). The personal pronouns *I, he, she, we,* and *they,* as well as the relative or interrogative pronoun *who,* change form in all three cases. *We* (subjective) *will take the train to Chicago. Our* (possessive) *trip will last a week. Dr. Baker will meet us* (objective) *at the station.* See also *person; pronoun.* See Chapter 7.

clause   A word cluster containing a subject and a predicate. An **independent** clause can stand alone as a sentence. *The car hit the tree.* A **dependent clause,** as the name suggests, is subordinate to an independent clause, linked to it by a subordinating conjunction or a relative pronoun. The dependent clause can function as an adjective, an adverb, or a noun. *The car hit the tree that stood at the edge of the edge of the road* (adjective clause). *The car, when it went out of control, hit the tree* (adverb clause). *The car hit what grew at the side of the road* (noun clause). See also *nonrestrictive element, restrictive element.* See 6c4.

collective noun   See *noun.*

comma splice   An error resulting from joining two independent clauses with only a comma. See Chapter 13 for ways of revising comma splices.

common noun   See *noun.*

comparative   See *adjective forms, adverb forms.*

complement   A word or group of words completing the predicate in a sentence. A **subject complement** follows a linking verb and renames or describes the subject. It can be a **predicate noun** (*Anorexia is an illness.*) or a predicate adjective (*Karen Carpenter was anorexic.*). An object complement renames or describes a direct object (*We considered her a baby and her behavior infantile.*). See 6c2.

complete predicate   See *predicate.*

complete subject   See *subject.*

complex sentence   See *sentence.*

compound adjective   A combination of words (of whatever parts of speech)

713

that function as a single adjectival unit (*blue-green* sea, *ten-story* building, *get-tough* policy, *supply side* economics, *north by northwest* journey). Most, but not all, compound adjectives use hyphens to separate their individual elements.

compound-complex sentence　See *sentence.*

compound noun　A combination of words forming a unit that can function as a single noun (*go-getter, in-law, Johnny-on-the-spot, oil well, southeast*).

compound predicate　See *predicate.*

compound sentence　See *sentence.*

compound subject　See *subject.*

concrete noun　See *noun.*

conjunction　A word or words that join words, phrases, clauses, or sentences. A *coordinating conjunction* (such as *and, but, or,* or *yet*) joins elements that are grammatically comparable (*Marx and Engels wrote* [two nouns]; *Marx writing one essay, but Engels writing the other* [two phrases]; *Marx wrote one essay, yet Engels wrote the other* [two independent clauses]). **Correlative conjunctions** (such as *both, and; either, or;* or *not only, but* [*also*]) are used in pairs to connect elements that are grammatically equivalent (*neither Marx nor Engels, not only Marx, but also Engels*). A **subordinating conjunction** (such as *although, because, before, if, that, when, where,* or *why*) introduces a dependent clause, which it subordinates to an independent clause. *Marx wrote at the British Museum where he did most of his work. Before his association with Marx, Engels was already a social theorist.* A **conjunctive adverb** (such as *consequently, moreover,* or *then*) modifies one independent clause following another independent clause. A conjunctive adverb often generally follows a semicolon or colon and precedes a comma. *Thoreau lived simply at Walden; however, he regularly joined his aunt for tea in Concord.* See 6b7 and 13c.

coordination　The grammatical equality of two or more sentence elements. When elements are coordinate, they seem to express equally significant ideas. *She wanted both to stay and to go.* See also *subordination.* See 18a.

coordinating conjunction　See *conjunction.*

correlative conjunction　See *conjunction.*

count noun　See *noun.*

dangling modifier　A word, phrase, or clause that fails to modify the sentence element that it logically ought to. *Studying Freud, the subject of artistic creativity became complicated* (incorrect; the subject of artistic creativity was not studying Freud). *Studying Freud, the class appreciated the complicated nature of artistic creativity* (correct; the class was studying Freud). See 15c.

declension　See *case, inflection, number, person.*

degree　See *adjective forms, adverb forms.*

demonstrative adjective See *adjective.*

demonstrative pronoun See *pronoun.*

denotation The literal meaning of a term, as opposed to its **connotation** or associations. See 25b.

dependent clause See *clause.*

descriptive adjective See *adjective.*

determiner See *article.*

direct address A construction that uses a noun or pronoun naming whoever is spoken to. *Hey, Jack. You, get moving.*

direct discourse Quotation that reproduces a speaker's words exactly, using quotation marks. *Jesse Jackson has often said, "I was born in the ghetto, but the ghetto wasn't born in me."* See 31a and 31b.

direct object A noun or pronoun receiving the action of a **transitive verb** in an **active** construction. *McKellan recited Shakespearean soliloquies.* See also *indirect object.* See 6c2.

double comparative The incorrect use of a comparative to modify another comparative (*more better; less longer*). See also *adjective forms, adverb forms.*

double negative The incorrect use of more than one negative word to communicate a single negative idea. *I couldn't do nothing; I couldn't hardly do anything.*

double superlative The incorrect use of a superlative to modify another superlative (*most unkindest cut; least profoundest thought*). See also *adjective forms, adverb forms.*

expletive A construction that introduces a sentence with *there* or *it* and a form of *be.* Use *There are good reasons for having a physical exam* rather than *The reasons for having a physical exam are good* in formal writing.

finite verb A verb that can join a subject to form an independent clause without adding any auxiliary verb. *I breathe.* See 6c3, 8d, 8e, 8f, and 8g.

fused sentence An error in which two main clauses are run together without a coordinating conjunction or suitable punctuation. Also known as a *run-on* sentence. See Chapter 13.

future See *tense.*

gender The sexual classification of a noun or pronoun—*god, he* (masculine); *goddess, she* (feminine); *godliness, it* (neuter). To avoid sexist language, use words that can refer equally to members of either sex, as in *police officer* rather than *policeman* or *policewoman.*

gerund A verbal identical in form to the present participle but functioning as a **noun.** *Studying is a bore* (gerund subject). *I enjoy studying* (gerund object). See 6c3.

gerund phrase   See *phrase.*

helping verb   An auxiliary verb. See *auxiliary verb.*

imperative mood   The form of a verb expressing a command or urging an action. An imperative may or may not have a stated subject. *Leave. You be quiet. Do come in. Let's go.*

inconsistent structure   The joining of two or more logically and grammatically incompatible elements in a single sentence.

indefinite adjective   See *adjective.*

indefinite pronoun   See *pronoun.*

independent clause   See *clause.*

indicative mood   The form of a verb expressing a fact, questioning a fact, or voicing an opinion or probability. *Washington crossed the Delaware on Christmas Eve. Did he defeat the Hessians?* See also *mood.*

indirect discourse   A paraphrased quotation that does not repeat another's words verbatim and hence is not enclosed in quotation marks. *Coolidge said that, if elected, he would not run.*

indirect object   A noun or pronoun identifying to or for whom or what a transitive verb's action is performed. The indirect object almost always precedes the direct object; it is usually the personal recipient of verbs of giving, showing, telling, and the like. *I handed the dean my application and told him that I needed financial aid.* See also *direct object.* See 6c2.

indirect question   A sentence pattern in which a question is the basis of a subordinate clause. *Everyone wonders why young people continue to take up smoking.* (The question, phrased directly, is "Why do young people continue to take up smoking?")

infinitive   The base form of a verb (*go, run, hit*), usually preceded by *to* (*to go, to run, to hit*). The *to* form is a verbal that can serve as a noun, adverb, or, occasionally, an adjective. *To go would be unthinkable* (noun, subject). *I do not wish to go* (noun, object). *I shall go to beg, to borrow, or to steal* (adverbs). *I'd like my sandwich to go* (adjective). An infinitive can be active (*to hit*) or passive (*to be hit*). Further, the infinitive has two tenses, present (*to [be] hit*) and perfect (*to have [been] hit*). Frequently an infinitive is preceded not by *to* but by a **modal auxiliary,** such as *can, may, must,* or *would,* or by the **primary auxiliary** *do* (*I can go, I did go*). An infinitive may be modified or take objects or complements as an **infinitive phrase.** See *phrase.* See 6b1, 6c3, and 8a.

inflection   Changes in word forms to indicate person, number, gender, and case in pronouns; number, gender, and case in nouns; comparative and superlative forms in adjectives and adverbs; and person, tense, voice, and mood in verbs.

intensifier A modifier that increases the emphasis of the word or words that it modifies. *I should very much like to go. I'm so happy.* Despite their name, intensifiers are stylistically weak; they are best avoided in formal writing.

intensive pronoun See *pronoun.*

interjection A grammatically independent word or group of words that is usually an exclamation of surprise, shock, dismay, or the like. *Help! We're losing control. My word, what do you think you're doing?*

interrogative adjective See *adjective.*

interrogative pronoun See *pronoun.*

intransitive verb A verb that does not need a direct object to complete its meaning. *The children raced up the path.* See also *verb.* See 6c2.

irregular verb A verb with a past tense and past participle that does not follow the usual *-ed* or *-d* pattern. Irregular verbs may be *strong,* with a vowel change in the past and a past participle ending in *-n* or *-en* (*see, saw, seen*), or *weak,* with other abnormalities (*go, went, gone; get, got, got/gotten*). See also *regular verb.* See 8b.

limiting adjective See *adjective.*

linking verb A linking verb joins a subject with a subject complement or complements. Common linking verbs are *appear, be, become, feel,* and *seem. The argument appeared sound. It was an exercise in logic.* See also *verb.* See 6c2.

main clause An independent clause. See *clause.*

mass noun See *noun.*

misplaced modifier A word, phrase, or clause confusingly positioned so that it fails to apply clearly to the expression intended. *With a credit card, the traveler paid for the motel room and opened the door. The traveler paid for the motel room and opened the door with a credit card.* Unless the writer intended to indicate that the traveler broke into a room already paid for, *with a credit card* should follow *paid* or *room.* See 15a.

modal auxiliaries See *auxiliary verb.*

modifier A word, phrase, or clause that acts as an adjective or an adverb and qualifies the meaning of another word, phrase, or clause. See also *adjective, adverb, clause, phrase.*

mood The form of a verb used to indicate whether an action or a state is a possible fact or to ask a question (*indicative*), to give a command (*imperative*), or to express a wish or condition contrary to fact (*subjunctive*). In other words, mood reflects the writer or speaker's attitude toward the idea expressed in the

717

verb. *The sea is turbulent* (indicative). *Be still, ye seas* (imperative). *Would that sea were calm* (subjunctive). See also *imperative mood, indicative mood, subjunctive mood*. See Chapter 8.

nominal A word, phrase, or clause that acts as a noun.

nonfinite verb See *verbal.*

nonrestrictive element A word, phrase, or clause that modifies but does not limit or change the essential meaning of a sentence element. A nonrestrictive element is set off from the rest of the sentence with commas, dashes, or parentheses. *Quantum physics, a difficult subject, is fascinating. He addressed, acerbically, the failure of the system.* See also *restrictive element.* See 27c.

noun A noun names a person, place, tangible object, concept, quality, action, or the like. Nouns serve as subjects, objects, complements, and appositives. Most nouns form the plural with the addition of *-s* or *-es* and the possessive with the addition of *'s* (see *number, case*). **Common nouns** name one (*rock, child, box*) or more (*rocks, children, boxes*) in a class or general group. **Proper nouns** begin with capital letters and name specifics such as a particular person, place, religion, time period, holiday, movement, or thing (*Angelou, Caesar, Florida, Jefferson Memorial, Elizabethan Age, July, Rosicrucianism, Ramadan*). Some proper nouns can form plurals (*Adamses, Caesars*). **Abstract nouns** name intangible qualities, concepts, actions, or states (*virtue, Virtue, peace, violence, evil, health, haste, time, inertia*). Some abstract nouns may be common or proper, depending on the sense that the writer wishes to communicate. Many abstract nouns have plural forms (*virtues, evils*), and as plurals they become increasingly *concrete.* **Concrete nouns** name people, places, or things and may be common or proper. In addition, **collective nouns** name coherent groups. In its singular form, a collective noun names a body or group of related elements; in its plural form, it names several such bodies or groups (*pride, prides* [of lions]; *family, families; Congress, Congresses*). **Count nouns** name people, places, and things that can be counted (*one woman, two women; one park, three parks; one tree, four trees; one Smith, five Smiths*). **Mass nouns** name concrete things that are not usually counted, although their plural forms are common (*sand, sands* [of Waikiki]; *rain,* [summer] *rains*). See 6b2.

noun clause See *clause.*

noun phrase See *phrase.*

number The form of a noun, pronoun, demonstrative adjective, or verb that indicates whether it is singular or plural: *oak* is singular, *oaks* plural; *I* and *me* are singular, *we* and *us* plural; *he buys* is singular, *they buy* plural; *this book* is singular, *these books* plural. See 6b1, 6b2, Chapter 8 introduction, and 9a.

object A word or words, acting as a noun or pronoun, influenced by a transitive verb, a verbal, or a preposition. See also *direct object, indirect object, object of a preposition*. See 6c2.

object complement   See *complement.*

objective case   See *case.*

object of a preposition   A noun or pronoun connected to a sentence by a preposition, thus completing a **prepositional phrase.** *Johnson went to Pembroke College at Oxford. Thank you for coming.* See 6b6 and 6c3.

ordinal number   The form of a number that expresses order or sequence (*first, seventeenth, twenty-third, two hundredth*). See also *cardinal number.*

participial adjective   See *adjective.*

participial phrase   See *phrase.*

participle   A verbal with properties of both an adjective and a verb. Like an adjective, a participle can modify a noun or pronoun; like a verb, it has present and past tenses and can take an object. The **present** participle usually ends in *-ing,* the **past** participle in *-ed, d, -en,* or an irregular form. Without any auxiliary verbs, the present participle is active, the past participle passive. *Reeling, Spinks hit the canvas. The torn page was a clue.* See 6c3. With auxiliary verbs, present participles form the progressive tenses (I *am making,* I *was making,* I *will be making,* I *have been making,* I *had been making,* I *will have been making*). Similarly, past participles form the perfect tenses (I *have made,* I *had made,* I *will have made*). Further, past participles, with auxiliary verbs, are used to form the passive voice (I *am beaten,* I *was beaten*). These compound tenses are known as verb phrases. See also *adjective, phrase, tense, verbal, voice.*

parts of speech   The eight grammatical categories into which words can be grouped depending on how they function in a sentence. Many words act as different parts of speech in different sentences. The parts of speech are *adjectives, adverbs, conjunctions, interjections, nouns, prepositions, pronouns,* and *verbs.* See 6b.

passive voice   See *voice.*

past participle   See *participle.*

past perfect tense   See *tense.*

past tense   See *tense.*

perfect tenses   See *participle, tense, verb.*

person   The relation between a subject and its corresponding verb, indicating whether the subject is speaking about itself (first person *I* or *we*), being spoken to (second person *you*), or being spoken about (third person *he, she, it,* or *they*). *Be* has several forms depending on the person (*am, is,* and *are* in the present tense plus *was* and *were* in the past). Other verbs change form in the present tense with a third-person singular subject (I *fall,* you *fall,* she *falls,* we *fall,* they *fall*). See 6b1, Chapter 8, and 9a. **Personal pronouns** also change form as subjects, objects, and possessives. See 6b3.

personal pronoun   See *pronoun.*

phrase   A group of words that functions as a single unit but lacks a subject, a finite verb in a predicate, or both. Phrases can be grouped not only by the parts of speech that govern or introduce them but also by their grammatical functions as adjectives, adverbs, nouns, or verbs. An **absolute phrase** modifies an entire sentence and thus is grammatically divorced from the sentence. It uses a noun or pronoun as its subject and a participle (possibly implied) or participial phrase as its predicate. *The party being over, everyone left. The party over, everyone left* (participle implied). A **gerund phrase** serves as a noun, acting as a subject, a complement, or an object. It is built around a gerund, the *-ing* form of a verb acting as a noun. *Exercising regularly and sensibly is a key to good health* (subject). *I dislike exercising regularly and sensibly* (direct object). *I am bored with exercising regularly and sensibly* (object of a preposition). An **infinitive phrase** may serve as an adjective, an adverb, or a noun and is governed by an infinitive. *The Pacific Coast is the place to be* (adjective). *She went to pay her taxes* (adverb). *To be young again is all I want* (noun). A **noun phrase,** including a noun and its modifiers, may serve as a subject, a complement, or an object. *A long, rough road* (subject) *crossed the barren desert* (object). *A raccoon is a resourceful animal* (complement). A **participial phrase** is governed by a present or past participle and functions as an adjective. *Breaking his leg, he stumbled. Having broken his leg, he stumbled.* A **prepositional phrase** is introduced by a preposition and may act as an adjective, an adverb, or a noun. *The gas in the laboratory is leaking* (adjective). *The firefighters went to the lab to check* (adverb). *Out of season is the least crowded time* (noun). A **verb phrase** is composed of a main verb and one or more auxiliaries, acting as a single verb in the sentence predicate. *I should have come to the review session.* See 6c3.

positive degree   See *adjective forms, adverb forms.*

possessive adjective   See *adjective, case.*

possessive case   See *case.*

predicate   The actual or implied finite verb and related words in a sentence. The predicate expresses what the subject does, experiences, or is. A **simple predicate** is a verb or a verb phrase that reflects on the subject. *For years the YMHA has been a cultural center in New York City.* A **compound predicate** has more than one simple predicate. *The athletes swam, cycled, and ran in the triathlon competition.* A **complete predicate** includes the simple predicate and any associated modifiers and objects. *I gave Sarah an engagement ring.* See 6c2.

predicate adjective   See *complement.*

predicate noun   See *complement.*

prefix   An addition (often derived from a Latin preposition or negative) to the beginning of a root word to alter its meaning (*preview, undress*). See 24d1.

preposition   A part of speech that indicates the position of a noun or pronoun in space or time and links it to other sentence elements. *He was at the top of the ladder before the other contestants had climbed to the fourth rung.* See *phrase.* See 6b6.

present participle   See *participle.*

present perfect   See *participle, tense, verb, verbal.*

present progressive   See *participle, tense, verb, verbal.*

present tense   See *tense, verb.*

progressive forms   See *participle, tense, verb.*

pronoun   A single-word noun substitute that refers to an actual or logical antecedent. **Demonstrative pronouns** (*this, that, these,* and *those*) point out particular nouns. *This is the article I read. Those are the books I bought.* **Indefinite pronouns** do not refer to specific nouns and include *any, each, everybody, everyone, some,* and similar words. *Never in the field of human conflict was so much owed by so many to so few.* Some indefinite pronouns have a possessive case. *Everyone's best interests will be served by a cure for AIDS.* **Intensive pronouns** (*myself, yourself, himself, herself, oneself, itself, ourselves, yourselves, themselves*) emphasize their antecedent nouns or personal pronouns, agreeing with them in person, number, and gender. *She herself knew that we ourselves were blameless. The fire did not damage the house itself.* **Interrogative pronouns** (*who, which,* and *what*) ask questions. *Which one would you like? What is going on?* **Personal pronouns** (*I, you, he, she, it, we, you,* and *they*) observe number, gender, and case as they refer to particular people or things. *He knew what was his and also what was best for him.* See also *case, gender, number.* **Reciprocal pronouns** (*each other, one another*) refer to the individuals included in a plural antecedent. *Holmes and Frazier fought each other. The candidates debated one another. Each other* is preferred in sentences involving two subjects, and *one another* in those involving more than two subjects. **Reflexive pronouns,** identical in form to intensive pronouns, refer back to the subject of the sentence or clause. *I washed myself* (direct object). *I gave myself a pat on the back* (indirect object). **Relative pronouns** (*who, whom, which, that, what, whoever, whomever, whichever,* and *whatever*) connect a dependent clause to a sentence. *I wonder who will win the prize.* See 6b3.

proper adjective   See *adjective.*

proper noun   See *noun.*

reciprocal pronoun   See *pronoun.*

reflexive pronoun   See *pronoun.*

regular verb   A verb with a past tense and past participle ending in *-d* or *-ed* (*care, cared, cared; look, looked, looked*). See also *irregular verb.* See 8b.

relative adjective   See *adjective.*

relative pronoun   See *pronoun.*

restrictive element   A word, phrase, or clause that limits the essential meaning of the sentence element it modifies. The restrictive element is not set off from the element that it modifies with commas, dashes, or parentheses. *The tree that I hit was an oak. The oak at the side of the road was a hazard.* See also *nonrestrictive element.* See 27c and 27i1.

run-on sentence   See *comma splice, fused sentence.*

sentence   The grammatically complete expression of an idea. In writing, a sentence begins with a capital letter and ends with a period, a question mark, or an exclamation point. A sentence may be **declarative** and make a statement (*The sun rose*), **interrogative** and ask a question (*Did the sun rise?*), **exclamatory** and indicate surprise or other strong emotion (*How beautiful the dawn is!*), or **imperative** and express a command (*Get up earlier tomorrow.*). Besides having these functions, sentences are classified grammatically. A **simple** sentence is a single independent clause without dependent clauses. *I left the house.* Its subject, predicate, or both may be compound. *Sears and Roebuck founded a mailorder house and a chain of stores.* A **compound** sentence contains two or more independent clauses linked with a coordinating conjunction, a correlative conjunction, or a semicolon. *I did not wish to go, but she did. I did not wish to go; she did.* A **complex** sentence contains an independent clause and one or more dependent clauses. *After he had cleaned up the kitchen, Tom fell asleep in front of the television.* A **compound-complex** sentence contains at least two independent clauses and one or more dependent clauses. *We had hoped to go climbing, but the trip was postponed because she sprained her ankle.* See also *clause.* See 6a and 6d.

sentence fragment   An apparent sentence that fails to communicate a complete thought, usually because it lacks a subject or a finite verb. Often fragments are dependent clauses, introduced by a subordinating word but punctuated as sentences. Fragments should be revised to be complete sentences in formal writing. See Chapter 14 for ways of correcting sentence fragments.

simple predicate   See *predicate.*

simple sentence   See *sentence.*

simple subject   See *subject.*

simple tense   See *tense.*

split infinitive   The often awkward intrusion of an adverb between *to* and the base form of the verb in an infinitive construction (*to boldly go* rather than the preferable *to go boldly*). See 15b1.

squinting modifier   A misplaced word, phrase, or clause that could refer equally, but with different meanings, to words preceding or following it. *Playing poker often is dangerous.* The position of *often* fails to indicate whether frequent poker playing is dangerous or whether poker playing is often dangerous. See 15a3.

subject The noun, pronoun, and related words that indicate who or what a sentence is about. A **simple** subject is a single noun or pronoun. *Owls are nocturnal birds.* A **complete** subject is the simple subject and its modifiers. *The timid gray mouse fled from the owl.* (*Mouse* is the simple subject; *the timid gray mouse* the complete subject.) Further, a subject may be **compound**: *The mouse and the owl heard the fox.*

subject complement See *complement.*

subjective case See *case.*

subjunctive mood The form of a verb used to express a wish, a request, or a condition that does not exist. The *contrary-to-fact subjunctive* using *were* is the most common. *If I were president, I would change things.* The dependent *that* clause expressing a command, demand, necessity, request, requirement or suggestion is also common. *I asked that he come.* The subjunctive also survives in many time-honored expressions. *Be that as it may. Suffice it to say that I have had enough.* See 8h.

subordinate clause A dependent clause. See *clause.*

subordinating conjunction See *conjunction.*

subordination The grammatical dependence of one sentence element on another. *Because the corporal is subordinate to the sergeant, the sergeant is the boss.* When one element is subordinate or dependent on another, instead of being equal to it, the subordinate element seems less significant, and the independent element seems more significant. See also *clause, coordination.* See 18b.

substantive A word, phrase, or clause that serves a noun.

suffix An addition to the end of a word that alters the word's meaning or part of speech—as in *migrate* (verb) and *migration* (noun) or *late* (adjective or adverb) and *lateness* (noun). See 24d2.

superlative See *adjective forms, adverb forms.*

syntax The arrangement of words in a sentence in order to reveal the relation of each to the whole and each to the other.

tense The verb forms that indicate the time at which an action takes place or a condition exists. The times expressed by tense are basically present, past, and future. Verbs have **simple** (I love), **perfect** (I have loved), **progressive** (I am loving), and **perfect progressive** (I have been loving) forms that show tense and, used in sequences, show the time relationships of actions and events. See 8d, 8e, 8f, and 8g.

transitive verb A verb that directs action toward a direct object and may express action done to or for an indirect object. A transitive verb may be in the active or passive voice. *The artist gave me the sketch.* See also *verb*. See 6c2.

verb   A word or group of words, essential to a sentence, that expresses what action the subject takes or receives, what the subject is, or what the subject's state of being is. Verbs change form to show tense, number, voice, and mood. A **transitive** verb takes an object or has passive forms. *Edison invented the incandescent bulb. The incandescent bulb was invented by Edison.* An **intransitive** verb does not take an object. *The bulb glowed.* **Linking** verbs join a subject and its complement. *Edison was pleased.* Depending upon its use in a sentence, a verb may sometimes belong to all three groups. *Evans grew oranges* (transitive). *The oranges grew well* (intransitive). *The oranges grew ripe* (linking). See also *auxiliary verb, irregular verb, mood, person, regular verb, tense, verbal, voice.* See 6b1 and Chapter 8.

verbal   A **gerund, participle,** or **infinitive** serving as a noun, an adjective, or an adverb. *Running is excellent exercise* (gerund/noun). *A running athlete is an exhilarating sight* (participle/adjective). *We went to the track to run* (infinitive/adverb). See also *gerund, infinitive, participle.* See 6c3.

verbal phrase   A phrase using a gerund, a participle, or an infinitive. See *phrase.*

verb phrase   A main verb and its auxiliary verbs. A verb phrase can act only as a predicate in a sentence. *She should have won the first race.* See *phrase.*

voice   The form of a transitive verb that indicates whether the subject is acting or being acted on. When a verb is **active,** the subject is the doer or agent. *Parker played the saxophone fantastically.* When a verb is **passive,** the subject and verb are transposed. Then the grammatical subject receives the action of the verb, action taken by the object of a preposition. *The saxophone was played fantastically by Parker.* The passive voice is formed with the appropriate tense of the verb *be* and the past participle of the transitive verb. See also *verb.* See Chapter 8.

Glossary of Usage

This glossary provides usage guidelines for some commonly confused words and phrases. Conventions of usage might be called the "good manners" of discourse. Just as our notions of good manners vary from culture to culture and time to time, so do conventions of usage. The word *ain't*, for instance, now considered bad manners in formal discourse, was once widely used by the most proper British speakers, and is still used normally in some spoken American dialects. So usage matters, like other choices you must make in writing, depend on what your purpose is and what is appropriate for a particular audience at a particular time. Matters of usage, especially those which are controversial or which seem to be changing, are treated in the body of this textbook. In addition, this glossary provides you, in brief form, with a guide to generally accepted usage in college writing and with a guide for distinguishing between words whose meanings are similar or which are easily confused. For fuller discussion of these matters, you may want to consult one of the usage guides listed in 23c.

a, an   Use *a* with a word that begins with a consonant, (*a forest*, *a book*), with a sounded *h* (*a hemisphere*), or with another consonant sound such as "you" or "wh" (*a euphoric moment*, *a one-sided match*). Use *an* with a word that begins with a vowel (*an umbrella*), with a silent *h* (*an honor*), or with a vowel sound (*an X-ray*).

accept, except   The verb *accept* means "receive" or "agree to." *Melanie will accept the job offer.* Used as a preposition, *except* means "aside from" or "excluding." *All the plaintiffs except Mr. Sneath decided to accept the settlement offered by the defendant.*

advice, advise   The noun *advice* means an "opinion" or "suggestion"; the verb *advise* means "offer or provide advice." *Charlotte's mother advised her to become a secretary, but Charlotte, who intended to become a dancer, ignored the advice.*

affect, effect   As a verb, *affect* means "influence" or "move the emotions of." *Effect* is a noun meaning "result" or, less commonly, a verb meaning "bring about." *A nuclear war would have far-reaching effects. Many people are deeply affected by this realization, and some join groups aimed at effecting arms reduction.*

aggravate Colloquially, *aggravate* means "irritate" or "annoy," but this usage should be avoided in formal writing. The formal meaning of *aggravate* is "make worse." *Having another mouth to feed aggravated their poverty.*

all ready, already *All ready* means "fully prepared." *Already* means "previously." *We were all ready for Lucy's party when we learned that she had already left.*

all right *All right* is always two words, not one.

all together, altogether *All together* means "all in a group" or "gathered in one place." *Altogether* means "completely," "in all," or "everything considered." *When the students were all together in the room, it was altogether filled.*

allude, elude *Allude* means "refer indirectly." *Elude* means "avoid" or "escape from." *The candidate frequently alluded to his immigrant grandparents who had come here to elude political oppression.*

allusion, illusion An *allusion* indirectly refers to something, as when a writer mentions or hints at a well-known event, person, story, quotation, or other information, assuming that the reader will recognize it (*a literary allusion*). An *illusion* is a false or misleading appearance (*an optical illusion*).

a lot *A lot* is not one word but two. Do not use it in formal writing to express "a large amount" or "a large number."

already See *all ready, already*.

alright See *all right*.

altogether See *all together, altogether*.

among, between In referring to two things or people, use *between*. In referring to three or more things or people, use *among*. *The relationship between the twins is different from that among the other three children.*

amount, number Use *amount* for quantities that you cannot count (singular nouns such as water, light, or power). Use *number* for quantities that you can count (usually plural nouns such as objects or people). *A small number of volunteers cleared a large amount of brush within a few hours.*

an See *a, an*.

and/or *And/or* should be avoided except in business or legal writing, where it is a short way of saying that one or both of two items apply. In other formal writing, take time and space to write out *X, Y, or both* rather than *X and/or Y*. If you mean *and* or *or*, use just that word.

any body, anybody, any one, anyone *Anybody* is an indefinite pronoun, as is *anyone*. *Although anyone could enjoy carving wood, not just anybody could make a sculpture like that. Any body* is two words, an adjective modifying a noun. *Any body of water has its own distinctive ecology. Any one* is two adjectives or a pronoun modified by an adjective. *Customers were allowed to buy only two sale items at any one time.*

726

anyplace, anywhere In formal writing, use *anywhere*, not *anyplace*. *She walked for an hour, not going* <u>anywhere</u> *in particular.*

anyway, anyways Use *anyway*, not *anyways*, in writing.

anywhere See *any place, any where.*

apt, liable, likely *Likely to* means "probably will," and *apt to* means "inclines or tends to," but either word will do in many instances. *During an argument, he is* <u>apt</u> *to yell while she is* <u>likely</u> *to slam doors. Liable to* is a more negative phrase that means "in danger of." *That dog is* <u>liable</u> *to dig up my garden. Liable* is also a legal term meaning "obligated" or "responsible for." *The dog's owners are* <u>liable</u> *for any damage that he causes.*

as Avoid using *as* for *because* or *when* in sentences where its meaning is not clear. For example, does *Carl left town* <u>as</u> *his father was arriving* mean *at the same time as his father was arriving* or *because his father was arriving?*

as, as if, like These expressions are used when making comparative statements. Use *as* when comparing two qualities that people or objects possess. *The box is* <u>as</u> *wide* <u>as</u> *it is long.* Also use *as* to identify equivalent terms in a description. *Gary served* <u>as</u> *moderator at the town meeting.* Use *like* to indicate similarity but not equivalency: *Hugo,* <u>like</u> *Jane, was a detailed observer.* In such instances, *like* acts as a preposition, followed by a noun or noun phrase, while *as* may act either as a preposition or as a conjunction introducing a clause. *The dog howled like a wolf, just* <u>as if</u> *she were a wild animal.*

assure, ensure, insure *Assure* means "convince" or "promise," and its direct object is usually a person or persons. *The candidate* <u>assured</u> *the voters he would not raise taxes. Ensure* and *insure* both mean "make certain," but *insure* is usually used in the specialized sense of protection against financial loss. *When the city began water rationing to* <u>ensure</u> *that the supply would last, the Browns found that they could no longer afford to* <u>insure</u> *their car wash business.*

as to *As to* should not be used as a substitute for *about. Phoebe was unsure* <u>about</u> *(not* <u>as to</u>*) Bruce's intentions.*

at, where See *where.*

awful, awfully The formal meanings of *awful* and *awfully* are "awe-inspiring" and "in an awe-inspiring way" respectively. Colloquial speech often dilutes *awful* to mean "bad" (*I had an* <u>awful</u> *day*) and *awfully* to mean "very" (*It was* <u>awfully</u> *cold*). In formal writing, avoid these casual usages.

awhile, a while The adverb *awhile* can be used to modify a verb. *A while,* however, is an article and a noun and can be the object of a preposition such as *for, in,* or *after. We drove* <u>awhile</u> *and then stopped for a* <u>while</u>*.*

bad, badly *Bad* is an adjective, used to modify a subject or an object or to follow a linking verb such as *be, feel,* or *seem. Badly* is an adverb, used to modify a verb. *The guests felt* <u>bad</u> *because the dinner was so* <u>badly</u> *prepared.*

727

because of, due to Both phrases are used to describe the relationship between a cause and an effect. Use *due to* when the effect (a noun) is stated first and followed by the verb *be*. *His illness was due to malnutrition*. (*Illness*, a noun, is the effect.) Use *because of*, not *due to*, when the effect is a clause, not a noun. *He was sick because of malnutrition*. (*He was sick*, a clause, is the effect.)

being as, being that These expressions are used colloquially as substitutes for *because*; avoid them in formal writing. *Because* (not *being as*) *Romeo killed Tybalt, he was banished to Padua*.

beside, besides *Beside*, a preposition, means "next to." *Besides* is either a preposition meaning "other than" or "in addition to" or an adverb meaning "moreover." *No one besides Francesca knows whether the tree is still growing beside the house*.

between See *among, between*.

breath, breathe *Breath* is the noun, and *breathe* is the verb. *"Breathe," said the dentist, so June took a large breath of laughing gas*.

bring, take *Bring* is comparable to *come*; *take* is comparable to *go*. Use *bring* when an object is moved from a farther place to a nearer one; use *take* when the opposite is true. *Please take my prescription to the pharmacist, and bring my medicine back to me*.

but, yet Use these words separately, not together. *He is strong-minded but* (not *but yet*) *gentle*.

but that, but what Avoid using these as substitutes for *that* in expressions of doubt. *Hercule Poirot never doubted that* (not *but that*) *he would solve the case*.

can, may *Can* refers to ability and *may* to possibility or permission to do something. *Since I can ski the slalom well, I may win the race. May* (not *can*) *I leave early to practice?*

can't, couldn't These are the contractions for *cannot* and *could not*. Avoid them, like other contractions, in formal writing. *If I couldn't complete it during the break, I certainly can't now*.

can't hardly, can't scarcely Both *hardly* and *scarcely* are negatives; therefore, the expressions *can't hardly* and *can't scarcely* are redundant double negatives. *Tim is claustrophobic and can* (not *can't*) *hardly breathe in elevators*.

can't help but This expression is wordy and redundant. Use the more formal *I cannot but go* or the less formal *I can't help going* instead of *I can't help but go*.

can't scarcely See *can't hardly, can't scarcely*.

censor, censure *Censor* means to remove material that is considered offensive for political, moral, personal, or other reasons. *Censure* means "formally reprimand." *The public censured the newspaper for censoring negative letters to the editor*.

728

center around   This idiom rarely if ever appears in formal writing. Use *center on* instead. *Their research centers on the disease-resistant hybrid varieties.*

compare to, compare with   *Compare to* means "describe one thing as similar to another." *Hillary compared the noise to the roar of a waterfall. Compare with* is the more general activity of noting similarities and differences between objects or people. *The detective compared the latest photograph with the old one, noting how the man's appearance had changed.*

complement, compliment   *Complement* means "go well with" or "enhance." *Compliment* means "praise." *Several guests complimented Julie on her marmalade which complemented the warm, buttered scones.*

comprise, compose   *Comprise* means "contain" (the whole *comprises* the parts). *Compose* means "make up" (the parts *compose* the whole). *The class comprises twenty students. Twenty students compose the class.*

conscience, conscious   *Conscience,* a noun, means "a sense of right and wrong." *Conscious,* an adjective, means "awake" or "aware." *After the angry argument, Lisa was conscious of her troubled conscience.*

consensus of opinion   Use *consensus* instead of this redundant phrase. *The family consensus was to sell the old house.*

consequently, subsequently   *Consequently* means "as a result" or "therefore." *Subsequently* just means "afterwards." *Roger lost his job, and subsequently I lost mine. Consequently, I was unable to pay my rent.*

continual, continuous   *Continual* describes an activity that is repeated at regular or frequent intervals. *Continuous* describes either an activity that is ongoing without interruption or an object that is connected without break. *The damage done by continuous erosion was increased by the continual storms.*

couple of   *Couple of* is used informally to mean either "two" or "a few." Avoid it in formal writing, and say specifically what you mean.

could of   See *have, of.*

criteria, criterion   *Criterion* means "a standard of judgment" or "a necessary qualification." *Criteria* is the plural form. *Many people believe that public image is the wrong criterion for choosing the next president of the United States.*

data   *Data* is the plural form of the Latin word *datum,* meaning "a fact" or "a result collected during research." Although colloquially *data* is used as either singular or plural, in formal writing it should be treated as plural. *These data indicate that fewer people smoke today than ten years ago.*

different from, different than   *Different from* is generally preferred in formal writing although both phrases are used widely. *Her lab results were no different from his.*

differ from, differ with   *Differ from* means "be unlike" in identity, appearance, or actions. *Differ with* means "disagree with" in opinion or belief. *Mr. Binns*

729

differs with Ms. White over the importance of class discussion. Therefore, the way Mr. Binns conducts his class *differs from* the way she conducts hers.

discreet, discrete *Discreet* means "tactful" or "prudent." *Discrete* means "distinct" or "separate." *The dean's discreet encouragement brought representatives of all the discrete factions to the meeting.*

disinterested, uninterested *Disinterested* means "unbiased" or "impartial." *It was difficult to find disinterested people for the jury.* Uninterested means "not interested" or "indifferent." *Cecile was uninterested in the outcome of the trial.*

distinct, distinctive *Distinct* means "separate" or "well defined." *The experiment involved separating the liquid into its five distinct elements.* Distinctive means "distinguishing from others" or "characteristic." *Even from a distance, everyone recognized Greg's distinctive way of walking.*

doesn't, don't *Doesn't* is the contraction for *does not* and should be used with *he, she, it,* and singular nouns. *Don't* is the contraction for *do not* and should be used with *I, you, we, they,* and plural nouns. In formal writing, however, avoid these and all other contractions.

due to See *because of, due to.*

effect See *affect, effect.*

elicit, illicit The verb *elicit* means "to draw out" or "evoke." The adjective *illicit* means "illegal." *The police tried to elicit from the criminal the names of others involved in his illicit activities.*

elude See *allude, elude.*

emigrate from, immigrate to, migrate *Emigrate from* means "move away from one's country." *Immigrate to* means "move to a foreign country and settle there." *My family emigrated from Norway in 1957. We immigrated to the United States.* Emigration and *immigration* are generally permanent actions; *migration* suggests movement that is temporary or seasonal and either *to* or *from* a place. *Every winter, whales off the Pacific coast migrate south from Alaska toward warmer water.*

ensure See *assure, ensure, insure.*

enthused, enthusiastic *Enthused* is used colloquially to mean "enthusiastic about." Avoid it in formal writing. *The students remained enthusiastic despite the rain and the mud that threatened to flood the excavation.*

equally as good Replace this redundant phrase with either *equally good* or *as good as. The two tennis players were equally good, each as good as the other.*

especially, specially *Especially* means "very" or "particularly." *Specially* means "for a special reason or purpose." *The audience especially enjoyed the new composition, specially written, for the holiday.*

every day, everyday *Everyday* is an adjective used to describe something as ordinary or common. *Every day* is an adjective modifying a noun, specifying which particular day. *I ride the subway every day even though pushing and shoving are everyday occurrences.*

every one, everyone *Everyone* is an indefinite pronoun. *Every one* is a noun modified by an adjective, referring to each member of a group. *Because he began the assignment after everyone else, David knew that he could not finish every one of the selections.*

except See *accept, except.*

explicit, implicit *Explicit* means "directly or openly expressed." *Implicit* means "indirectly expressed or implied." *The explicit message of the ad urged consumers to buy the product while the implicit message promised popularity.*

farther, further *Farther* refers to physical distance. *How much farther is it to Munich? Further* refers to time or degree. *I want to avoid further delays and further misunderstandings.*

fewer, less Use *fewer* with objects or people that can be counted (plural nouns). Use *less* with amounts that cannot be counted (singular nouns). *The world would be safer with fewer bombs and less hostility.*

finalize *Finalize* is a pretentious way of saying "end" or "make final." *We closed* (not *finalized*) *the deal.*

firstly, secondly, thirdly These are old-fashioned and unwieldy words for introducing a series of points. Use *first, second,* and *third* instead.

flaunt, flout *Flaunt* means "show off." *Flout* means "mock" or "scorn." *The teens flouted convention by flaunting their multi-colored wigs.*

former, latter *Former* refers to the first and *latter* to the second of two things previously introduced. *Anna and Kim are both excellent athletes; the former plays tennis, and the latter has won several marathons.* See also *later, latter.*

further See *farther, further.*

good, well *Good* is an adjective and should not be used as a substitute for the adverb *well. Gabriel is a good host who cooks quite well.*

good and *Good and* is colloquial for "very"; avoid it in formal writing. *After Peter lost his sister's camera, he was very* (not *good and*) *sorry.*

half a, a half, a half a Both *half a* and *a half* are standard. *A half a* is wordy. *She ate half a* (or *a half* but not *a half a*) *sandwich.*

hanged, hung Of these two past forms of the verb *hang,* only *hanged* refers to executions while *hung* is used for all other meanings. *The old woman hung her head as she passed the tree where the murderer was hanged.*

hardly See *can't hardly, can't scarcely.*

has got to, has to These colloquial phrases for "must" should be avoided in formal writing. *She must* (not *has to*) *be intelligent.*

have, of *Have,* not *of,* should follow *could, would, should,* or *might. We should have* (not *of*) *invited them.*

731

herself, himself, myself, yourself Do not use these reflexive pronouns as subjects or as objects in a prepositional phrase. *Tamara went with me* (not *myself*) *to see the pottery show.*

he/she, his/her *He/she* and *his/her* are ungainly ways to avoid sexism in writing. Other solutions are to write out *he or she* or to alternate using *he* and *she*. Perhaps the best solutions are to eliminate the pronouns entirely or to make the subject plural (*they*), thereby avoiding all reference to gender. For instance, *Everyone should carry his/her driver's license with him or her* could be revised to *Drivers should carry driver's licenses at all times* or to *People should carry their driver's licenses with them.*

himself See *herself, himself, myself, yourself.*

his/her See *he/she, his/her.*

hisself Replace *hisself* with *himself* in formal writing.

hopefully *Hopefully* is widely misused to mean "it is hoped," but its correct meaning is "with hope." *Sam watched the roulette wheel hopefully*, not *Hopefully, Sam will win.*

hung See *hanged, hung.*

if, whether Use *whether* or *whether or not* to express an alternative. *She was considering whether or not to buy the new software.* Reserve *if* for the subjunctive case. *If it should rain tomorrow, our Tai Chi class will meet in the gym.*

illicit See *elicit, illicit.*

illusion See *allusion, illusion.*

immigrate to See *emigrate from, immigrate to, migrate.*

impact As a noun, *impact* means "a forceful collision." As a verb, it means "pack together." *Because they were impacted, Jason's wisdom teeth needed to be removed.* Avoid the colloquial use of *impact* as a weak and vague word meaning "to affect." *Population control may reduce* (not *impact*) *world hunger.*

implicit See *explicit, implicit.*

imply, infer To *imply* is to suggest. To *infer* is to make an educated guess. Speakers and writers *imply*; listeners and readers *infer*. *Beth and Peter's letter implied that they were planning a very small wedding; we inferred that we would not be invited.*

incident, instance *Incident* refers to a specific occurrence. It should not be confused with *instance* which is an overused, though correct, word for "example" or "case." *The violent incident was just one instance of John's fiery temper.*

incredible, incredulous *Incredible* means "unbelievable." *Incredulous* means "not believing." *When townspeople attributed the incredible events in their town to the presence of a UFO, Marina was incredulous.*

infer See *imply, infer.*

inside, inside of, outside, outside of Drop *of* after the prepositions *inside* and *outside. The class regularly met outside* (not *of*) *the building.*

instance See *incident, instance.*

insure See *assure, ensure, insure.*

interact with, interface with *Interface with* is computer jargon for "discuss" or "communicate." *Interact with* is a vague phrase meaning "doing something that somehow involves another person." Avoid these colloquial expressions.

irregardless, regardless *Regardless* is the correct word because *irregardless* is a double negative.

is when, is where These vague and faulty shortcuts should be avoided in definitions. *Schizophrenia is a psychotic condition in which* (not *when* or *where*) *a person withdraws from reality.*

its, it's *Its* is a possessive pronoun, even though it does not have an apostrophe. *It's* is a contraction for *it is;* avoid *it's* and other contractions in formal writing. *It's* (more formally, *it is*) *important to begin each observation just before the rat has its dinner.*

kind, sort, type As singular nouns, *kind, sort,* and *type* should be modified by *this* and followed by singular nouns. The plural forms, *kinds, sorts,* and *types* should be modified by *these* and followed by plural nouns. Write *this kind of dress* or *these kinds of dresses,* not *these kind of dress.* Use such phrases to classify or categorize, but leave them out otherwise.

kind of, sort of Avoid using these colloquial expressions as substitutes for "rather" or "somewhat." *Laura was somewhat* (not *kind of*) *tired after painting for several hours in the studio.*

later, latter *Later* means "more late" or "after some time." *Latter* refers to the last of two items mentioned and can be used to avoid repeating a subject twice. *Jackson and Chad won all their early matches, but the latter was injured later in the season.* See also *former, latter.*

latter See *former, latter* and *later, latter.*

lay, lie *Lay* means "place" or "put." Its forms are *lay, laid, laying, laid,* and *laid.* It generally has a direct object, specifying what has been placed. *She laid her books on the desk. Lie* means "recline" or "be positioned," and does not take a direct object. Its forms are *lie, lay, lain, lying. She lay awake until two, worrying about the exam.*

leave, let *Leave* means "go away" or "depart." *Let* means "allow." The expressions *leave alone* and *let alone,* however, are generally considered interchangeable. *Let me leave now, and leave* (or *let*) *me alone from now on!*

lend, loan In formal writing, use *loan* as a noun and *lend* as a verb. *Please lend me your pen so that I may fill out this application for a loan.*

733

less See *fewer, less.*

let See *leave, let.*

liable See *apt, liable, likely.*

lie See *lay, lie.*

like See *as, as if, like.*

like, such as Both *like* and *such as* may be used in a statement giving an example or a series of examples. *Like* means "similar to"; use *like* when comparing the subject mentioned to the examples. *A hurricane, like a flood or any other major disaster, may strain a region's emergency resources.* Use *such as* when the examples represent a general category of things or people. *Such as* is often a graceful alternative to *for example. A destructive hurricane, such as Gilbert in 1988, may drastically alter an area's economy.*

likely See *apt, liable, likely.*

literally *Literally* means "actually" or "exactly as it is written" and may be used to stress the truth of a statement that might otherwise be understood as figurative. *Literally* should not be used as an intensifier in a figurative statement. *Sarah was literally at the edge of her seat* may be accurate, but *Sarah was so hungry that she could literally eat a horse* is not.

loan See *lend, loan.*

loose, lose *Lose* is a verb meaning "misplace." *Loose*, as an adjective, means "not securely attached." *Sew on that loose button before you lose it.*

lots, lots of These informal expressions, meaning "much" or "many," should be avoided in formal writing.

man, mankind In the past, *man* and *mankind* were used to represent all human beings, but many people now consider these terms sexist because they do not mention women. Replace such words with *people, humans, humankind, men and women,* or similar all-encompassing phrases. Replace occupational terms ending with *-man* with gender-free phrasing such as *fire fighter* for *fireman, letter carrier* for *mailman,* and *minister* or *cleric* for *clergyman.*

may See *can, may.*

may be, maybe *May be* is a verb phrase. *Maybe*, the adverb, means "perhaps." *He may be the president today, but maybe he will lose the next election.*

media *Media*, the plural form of *medium*, takes a plural verb. *The media are* (not *is*) *going to cover the council meeting.*

might of See *have, of.*

migrate See *emigrate from, immigrate to, migrate.*

moral, morale A *moral* is a succinct lesson. *The unstated moral of the story is that generosity eventually is rewarded. Morale* is the spirit or mood of an individual or a group of people. *Office morale was low.*

Ms. A term invented in the 1960s to give women a title comparable to *Mr.* for men. Formerly, a woman was called either *Miss* or *Mrs.*, each term defining her in terms of her marital status, which is a private matter. Use *Ms.* unless the woman specifies another title. *Ms.* should appear before her first name, not before her husband's name: *Ms. Jane Tate,* not *Ms. John Tate.*

myself See *herself, himself, myself, yourself.*

nor, or Use *either* with *or* and *neither* with *nor. Cindy hopes to study abroad <u>either</u> next year <u>or</u> the year after. <u>Neither</u> her mother <u>nor</u> her father are very encouraging.*

number See *amount, number.*

of See *have.*

off of Use *off* rather than *off of. The spaghetti slipped <u>off</u>* (not *<u>of</u>*) *the plate.*

OK, O.K., okay All are acceptable spellings, but do not use the term in formal writing. Replace it with more exact language. *The performance was <u>unpolished but enthusiastic</u>* (not *<u>OK</u>*).

on, upon *Upon* is an old-fashioned and overly formal substitute for *on. My grade will depend <u>on</u>* (not *<u>upon</u>*) *how well I do on my final examination.*

on account of Use this substitute for *because of* sparingly or not at all. See also *because of, due to.*

or See *nor, or.*

outside, outside of See *inside, inside of, outside, outside of.*

owing to the fact that Avoid this and other unnecessarily wordy expressions for *because.*

per Use the Latin *per* only in standard technical phrases such as *miles per hour.* Otherwise, find English equivalents. *As mentioned in* (not *<u>as per</u>*) *the latest report, our town's average food expenses every week* (not *<u>per week</u>*) *are $40 <u>per capita</u>.*

percent, percentage These words identify a number as a fraction of one hundred. Because they show exact statistics, these terms should not be used casually to mean "portion," "amount," or "number." *Last year, 80 <u>percent</u> of the club's members were female.* Use *percent* after a figure. In formal writing, spell out *percent* rather than using its symbol (%). *Percentage* is not used with a specific number. *A large <u>percentage</u> of sales representatives are single.*

plenty *Plenty* means "enough" or "a great abundance." *Many immigrants consider America a land of <u>plenty</u>.* In formal writing, avoid its colloquial usage, meaning "very." *He was <u>very</u>* (not *<u>plenty</u>*) *tired.*

plus *Plus,* a preposition meaning "in addition to," often is used in the context of money. *My inheritance is enough to cover my debts <u>plus</u> yours.* Avoid using *plus* as a transitional adverb meaning "besides," "moreover," or "in addition." *That dress does not fit me. <u>Besides</u>* (not *<u>plus</u>*), *it is the wrong color.*

precede, proceed Both verbs, *precede* means "come before," and *proceed* means "continue" or "go forward," as in the related word *procession*. *Despite the storm that preceded the hallway flooding, we proceeded to class.*

pretty Avoid using *pretty* in formal writing as a substitute for *rather, somewhat*, or *quite*. *Bill was quite (not pretty) disagreeable.*

principal, principle These words are unrelated but are often confused because of their similar spellings. *Principal*, as a noun, refers to a head official or an amount of money loaned or invested. When used as an adjective, it means "most significant." The word meaning "a fundamental law, belief, or standard" is *principle*. *When Albert was sent to the principal, he defended himself with the principle of free speech.*

proceed See *precede, proceed*.

quotation, quote *Quote* is a verb, and *quotation* is a noun. In colloquial usage, *quote* is sometimes used as a short form of *quotation*. In formal writing, however, use *quotation* as the noun form. *He quoted the president, and the quotation was preserved in history books.*

raise, rise *Raise* means "lift" or "move upward." In the case of children, it means "bring up" or "rear." As a transitive verb, it takes a direct object—someone raises something. *The guests raised their glasses in good cheer.* *Rise* means "go upwards." It is not followed by a direct object; something rises by itself. *She saw the steam rise from the pan just as the soup bubbled into a boil.*

rarely ever In formal writing, use *rarely* by itself, or use *hardly ever*. *When we were poor, we rarely went to the movies.*

real, really The adjective *real* means "true" or "not artificial." The adverb *really*, in informal usage, means "very" or "extremely." Do not substitute *real* for *really*. *The old man walked really (not real) slowly.* In formal writing, avoid using *really* altogether. *The old man walked very (not really) slowly.*

reason is because This expression mixes *the reason is that* and *because*. Use one or the other but not both together. In general, use the less wordy *because* unless you want to give a statement the air of an explanation. *The reason the copier stopped is that (not is because) the paper jammed.*

regardless See *irregardless, regardless*.

relate to Avoid this vague colloquial expression in formal writing. *Relate to* loosely means "understand" or "appreciate." Write *I like the Rolling Stones* and explain why rather than writing *I can relate to the Rolling Stones.* Also see *regarding, in regard to, with regard to, relating to*.

respectfully, respectively *Respectfully* means "with respect." *Respectively* means "in the order given." *The brothers, respectively a juggler and an acrobat, respectfully greeted the audience.*

rise See *raise, rise*.

scarcely See *can't hardly, can't scarcely.*

secondly See *firstly, secondly, thirdly.*

set, sit *Set* means "put" or "place," and it is followed by a direct object—the thing that is placed. *Sit* does not take a direct object and refers to the action of taking a seat. *Amelia <u>sat</u> in the armchair and <u>set</u> her teacup on the table next to her.*

sexist language See *man/mankind; he/she, his/her.*

shall, will Today *shall* is used much more in British English than in American English. Use *shall* for polite questions in the first person ("<u>*Shall*</u> *we buy it?*" "<u>*Shall*</u> *I call a taxi?*"). Use *will* in all other cases involving the future tense.

should of See *have, of.*

since *Since* has two meanings. The first meaning shows the passage of time (*I have not eaten <u>since</u> Tuesday*); the second and more informal meaning is "because" (<u>*Since*</u> *you are in a bad mood, I will go away*). Be careful not to write sentences in which *since* is ambiguous in meaning. <u>*Since*</u> *I broke my leg, I have been doing nothing but sleeping.* (*Since* here could mean either "because" or "ever since." In order to avoid such problems some writers prefer not to use *since* to mean "because.")

sit See *set, sit.*

so, so that In formal writing, avoid using *so* by itself as an intensifier, meaning "very." Instead, follow *so* with *that* to show how the intensified condition leads to a result. *Aaron was <u>so</u> tired <u>that</u> he fell asleep at the wheel of his car.*

some body, somebody, some one, someone *Somebody* is an indefinite pronoun, as is *someone*. *When <u>somebody</u> comes walking down the hall, I always hope that it is <u>someone</u> I know. Some body* is two words, an adjective modifying a noun, while *some one* is two adjectives or a pronoun modified by an adjective. *In dealing with <u>some body</u> like the senate, arrange to meet consistently <u>some</u> <u>one</u> person who can represent the group.*

someplace, somewhere *Someplace* is informal for *somewhere;* use the latter in formal writing.

some time, sometime, sometimes *Some time* means "a length of time." *Please leave me <u>some time</u> to use the computer. Sometime* means "at some indefinite later time." <u>*Sometime*</u> *I will take you to the Orkney Islands. Sometimes* means "occasionally." <u>*Sometimes*</u> *I see him on my way to class.*

somewhere See *someplace, somewhere.*

sort See *kind, sort, type.*

sort of See *kind of, sort of.*

so that See *so, so that.*

specially See *especially, specially.*

stationary, stationery   *Stationary* is an adjective meaning "standing still." *Stationery* is a noun meaning "writing paper or materials." *When the bus was stationary at the light, Karen took out her stationery and wrote a quick note to a friend.*

subsequently   See *consequently, subsequently*.

such as   See *like, such as*.

supposed to, used to   Both of these expressions require the final *-d* indicating past tense. *He is supposed to bring his calculator to class.*

sure, surely   Avoid using *sure* as an intensifier in formal writing. Replace this colloquial expression with "certainly" or "without a doubt," or use the adverb *surely*, which means "it must be so." *Surely* is often used to express a hoped-for situation. *Surely John will go to a doctor.* It is also used persuasively. *We cannot go on a picnic. Surely it will rain.*

take   See *bring, take*.

than, then   Use the conjunction *than* in comparative statements. *The cat was bigger than the dog.* Use the adverb *then* when referring to a sequence of events or emotions. *Jim finished college, and then he joined the Peace Corps.*

that, which   *That*, always followed by a restrictive clause, singles out the object being described. *The trip that you took in Japan was expensive.* ("That you took to Japan" singles out the specific trip.) *Which* may be followed by either a restrictive or a nonrestrictive clause but often is used only with the latter. The *which* clause may simply add more information about a noun or noun clause, and it is set off by commas. *The book, which is on the table, is a good one.* (This *which* clause simply adds extra, nonessential information about the book—its location. In contrast, *The book that is on the table is a good one* specifies or singles out the book on the table as opposed to the book on the chair or the book in some other particular place.)

their, there, they're   *Their* is a pronoun, the possessive form of *they*. *The gardeners held onto their hats as the helicopter flew over.* *There* refers to a place. *There, birds sing even at night.* *There* also is used with the verb *be* in expletive constructions (*there is, there are*). *There is only a short line at the cafeteria right now.* *They're* is a contraction of *they* and *are* and, like all contractions, it should be avoided in formal writing. *They're* (more formally, *they are*) *living in Japan.*

theirselves, themselves   Use *themselves* rather than *theirselves*.

then   See *than, then*.

thirdly   See *firstly, secondly, thirdly*.

'til, till, until   *Till* and *until* are both acceptable in formal writing, but some writers prefer the full word *until*. The older form *'til*, like all contractions, should be avoided in formal writing.

to, too, two   *To* is a preposition, generally showing direction or nearness. *Stan flew to Cleveland.* Avoid using *to* after *where. Where are you flying* (not *flying to*)? *Too* means "also." *I am flying there too. Two* is the number. *We too are going to the meeting in two hours.*

to, where   See *where.*

toward, towards   *Toward* is generally preferred, but either word is acceptable.

try and, try to   *Try and* is colloquial for *try to;* use *try to* in formal writing. *Try to have an expressive face.*

two   See *to, too, two.*

type   See *kind, sort, type.*

uninterested   See *disinterested, uninterested.*

unique   *Unique* means "the one and only." It describes an absolute state and therefore should not be used with adjectives that suggest degree, such as *very* or *most. Malcolm's hands are unique* (not *very unique*).

until   See *'til, till, until.*

upon   See *on, upon.*

used to   See *supposed to, used to.*

very   Avoid using *very* to intensify a weak adjective or adverb; instead, replace both words with one stronger, more precise, and more colorful word. Instead of *very nice,* for example, use *kind, warm, sensitive, endearing,* or *friendly,* depending on your precise meaning. Replace *very interesting* with a word such as *curious, fascinating, insightful, lively, provocative,* or *absorbing.*

way, ways   When referring to distances, use *way,* not *ways. The Trivia Bowl championships were a long way* (not *ways*) *off.*

well   See *good, well.*

when, where   See *is when, is where.*

where   Use *where* alone, not with prepositions such as *at* or *to. Where are you going?* (not *Where are you going to?*) *Where do you shop?* (not *Where do you shop at?*)

whether   See *if, whether.*

which   See *that, which.*

which, who   When referring to ideas or things, use *which.* When referring to people, use *who,* not *which. My aunt, who was irritated, pushed on the door, which was still stuck.*

who, whom   Use *who* if the following clause begins with a verb. *Monica, who smokes incessantly, is my godmother.* (*Who* is followed by the verb *smokes.*) *Monica, who is my godmother, smokes incessantly.* (*Who* is followed by the verb *is.*) Use *whom* if the following clause begins with a pronoun. *I have heard that Monica, whom I have not seen for ten years, wears only purple.* (*Whom* is followed by the pronoun *I*). An exception occurs when a verbal phrase such as *I think* comes between *who* and the following clause. Ignore such a phrase as you decide which form to use. *Monica, who* [*I think*] *wears nothing but purple, is my godmother.* (Ignore *I think*; *who* is followed by the verb *wears.*)

who's, whose   *Who's* is the contraction of *who* and *is.* Avoid *who's* and other contractions in formal writing. *Who's* (more formally, *Who is*) *in the garden? Whose* is a possessive form; it may be followed by the noun it modifies. *Whose sculpture is in the garden? Whose is on the patio?*

will   See *shall, will.*

would of   See *have, of.*

yet   See *but, yet.*

your, you're   *Your* shows possession. *Bring your sleeping bags along. You're* is the contraction of *you* and *are.* Avoid it and all other contractions in formal writing. *You're* (more formally, *You are*) *in the wrong room.*

yourself   See *herself, himself, myself, yourself.*

Answers to Even-numbered Exercises

To help you check your progress as you work, here are answers to some exercises in Chapters 6–36. Specifically, you will find answers to even-numbered items of those exercises with predictable answers. Exercises with many possible answers—those asking you to imitate a sentence or to revise a paragraph, for example—are not answered here.

ANSWERS TO EXERCISE 6.1
The subject is set in italics, the predicate is in boldface.
2. *He* **was an army doctor, with . . . a rough voice.**
4. *The dog* **answered the sound with a whine.**

ANSWERS TO EXERCISE 6.2
2. ran, ran over (two-word verb)
4. can collect; might run; should finish
6. walked
8. will extend

ANSWERS TO EXERCISE 6.3
2. n-plagiarism
4. n-story; a-a; n-tale; n-theft; n-violation

ANSWERS TO EXERCISE 6.4
2. a-crowd; p-that; p-I; a-one
4. a-Celia; p-she; p-herself

ANSWERS TO EXERCISE 6.5
Adjectives are set in italics; adverbs are set in boldface.
2. **anxiously;** *my; long*
4. *Twenty; Italian; strong*
6. *Those;* **quite; happily;** *their; new*
8. **more; pessimistically**
10. *personal; political; relevant;* **not**

ANSWERS TO EXERCISE 6.6 (WILL VARY)
2. The beautiful, athletic heroine marries the charming, bookish prince.
4. Only the best students are using the vast library holdings for scholarly research.

ANSWERS TO EXERCISE 6.7
2. through; across; into
4. from; beyond; toward

ANSWERS TO EXERCISE 6.8
2. conj-nevertheless
4. coor-but
6. corr-not only/but also
8. sub/until
10. corr-neither/nor; conj-therefore

ANSWERS TO EXERCISE 6.9
The complete subject is set in italics; the simple subject is set in boldface.
2. A *two-foot* **snowfall** *on April 13*
4. **Anyone** *who lives in a glass house*

ANSWERS TO EXERCISE 6.10
2. pred-made us a nation; trans-made; do-us; oc-nation
4. pred-shall rise again; intr-shall rise

ANSWERS TO EXERCISE 6.11
2. in his vocabulary
4. of the dugout

ANSWERS TO EXERCISE 6.12 (WILL VARY)
2. Without fear, Socrates faced death.
4. Except for a few of his followers, everyone thought Socrates was crazy.

ANSWERS TO EXERCISE 6.13
2. gerund-saving; n, object of prep
4. part-raised; adj, modifying "I"; part-exploring; adj, obj compl

ANSWERS TO EXERCISE 6.14
2. inf-To listen; prep-to Bruce Springsteen
4. part-Floating; prep-on my back
6. prep-with a mixture; app-a sensitive child; prep-of awe and excitement
8. part-Basking; prep-in the sunlight; prep-in a reminiscence; prep-of golden birch trees
10. prep-of recreation; gerund-taking a nap

ANSWERS TO EXERCISE 6.15 (WILL VARY)
2. After soaking up the sun and eating good food, she looked healthy when he saw her the second time.
4. The Sunday afternoon dragged to an absolute halt.
6. In addition to kissing babies, posing for pictures, and eating boiled chicken, the candidates shook hands with the voters.
8. A late bloomer, Ben often thought regretfully about the past.
10. They lived in a trailer, crowded together like sardines.

ANSWERS TO EXERCISE 6.16 (WILL VARY)
2. Waiting to go through customs, we clutched our passports.
4. To annoy his parents, Michael had his ear pierced.

ANSWERS TO EXERCISE 6.17
2. dep-As a potential customer entered the store; sub conj-As; ind-Tony nervously attempted to retreat to the safety of the back room
4. dep-when she was deemed old enough to understand; sub conj-when; ind-she was told the truth; ind-she knew why; dep-her father had left home
6. ind-Mary and John decided to bake a chocolate cream pie; dep-which was Timothy's favorite; rel-which
8. ind-It was easier; dep-than she had expected; sub conj-than
10. ind-I could see; dep-that he was very tired rel-that; dep-but I had to ask him a few questions

ANSWERS TO EXERCISE 6.18 (WILL VARY)
2. George was worried about his real estate investments because the representatives of the nuclear power plant had come to town for a site inspection.
4. Rob, who had an extensive collection of jazz records, always borrowed money from his friends.
6. We, who remembered the Grateful Dead and wanted tickets for their next performance, stood outside for an hour.
8. Because she was willing to stay home on weekends and study, Erin won the translation contest.
10. The man, whose memorial plaque hangs in the lobby, was killed in that mill in 1867.

ANSWERS TO EXERCISE 6.19 (WILL VARY)
(The entire sentences are of course independent clauses.)
2. dep cl-Either Macmillan takes Strunk and me in our bare skins; ind cl-I want out; prep p-in our bare skins; n p-our bare skins
4. ind cl-Life in a zoo is just the ticket; prep p-in a zoo; n p-a zoo; n p-the ticket; prep p-for some animals and birds; n p-some animals and birds
6. ind cl-The way to read Thoreau is to enjoy him; inf p-to read Thoreau; inf p-to enjoy him; n p-his enthusiasms; n p-his acute perception
8. ind cl-No sensible writer sets out deliberately to develop a style; n p-no sensible writer; inf p-to develop; n p-a style; ind cl-all writers do have distinguishing qualities; v p-do have; n p-distinguishing qualities; ind cl-they become very evident; n p-very evident; dep cl-when you read the words; n p-the words
10. ind cl-A good many of Charlotte's descendants still live in the barn; prep p-of Charlotte's descendants; v p-still live; prep p-in the barn; n p-Charlotte's descendants; n p-the barn; dep cl-when the warm days of spring arrive; n p-the warm days; prep p-of spring; ind cl-there will be lots of tiny spiders; n p-tiny spiders; part p-emerging into the world; n p-the world

ANSWERS TO EXERCISE 6.20
2. complex, declarative
4. simple, declarative

6. complex, declarative
8. compound-complex, declarative
10. complex, declarative

ANSWERS TO EXERCISE 7.2 (WILL VARY)
2. hers
4. his

ANSWERS TO EXERCISE 7.3
2. whoever: subject of *faces*
4. whom: object of preposition, *with . . . whom we wanted*

ANSWERS TO EXERCISE 7.4
2. whom
4. he
6. she
8. whoever
10. whom, who

ANSWERS TO EXERCISE 7.5
2. I———→me
4. correct
6. him———→he
8. me———→I
10. whomever———→whoever

ANSWERS TO EXERCISE 8.1
2. have———→has
4. correct
6. be———→is
8. don't———→doesn't
10. is running

ANSWERS TO EXERCISE 8.2
2. come, found
4. lost/had lost; took/had taken
6. grew/have grown/could have grown
8. met, taken
10. met, thought, known

ANSWERS TO EXERCISE 8.3
2. sang———→sung
4. went———→gone

ANSWERS TO EXERCISE 8.4
2. laid
4. lying
6. sat

8. raise
10. rose

ANSWERS TO EXERCISE 8.5
2. have predicted/have been predicting—action begun in past continues
4. arrived/has arrived—started in past, may continue today
6. rode/was riding—past action, completed
8. will have watched—future action, completed by a certain time
10. rises—general truth

ANSWERS TO EXERCISE 8.7 (WILL VARY)
2. Having left England in December, the settlers arrived in Virginia in May.
4. Having cut off all contact with her parents, she did not know whom to ask for help.

ANSWERS TO EXERCISE 8.8
2. The storm uprooted huge pine trees.
4. For months, the mother kangaroo protects, feeds, and teaches her baby to survive.

ANSWERS TO EXERCISE 8.10
2. was——→were
4. was——→were

ANSWERS TO EXERCISE 9.1
2. am
4. supplies
6. were
8. holds
10. leaves

ANSWERS TO EXERCISE 9.2
2. correct, "talking and getting up" go together
4. correct
6. display——→displays; "neither/nor"
8. correct, "most" refers to a quantity
10. seem——→seems; "either/or" calls for a singular verb
12. correct, "only one" is singular
14. were——→was; *Our Tapes* is singular, a title
16. have——→has; "politics" is a collective noun
18. cause——→causes; "mumps" is singular
20. happen——→happens; "everything" is singular

ANSWERS TO EXERCISE 9.3 (WILL VARY)
2. Although roommates do not always get along, they can usually manage to tolerate each other temporarily.
4. Both Tom and Teresa are willing to lend us a car.
6. Every house and apartment has its advantages and its drawbacks.
8. Our team no longer wear their red and white uniforms.
10. Sometimes she turns on the bathroom fan and the infrared light and neglects to turn them off.

ANSWERS TO EXERCISE 10.2
2. negatively——→reacts
4. really——→cold
6. fully——→grown; well——→eating
8. surely——→have made
10. strictly——→brought

ANSWERS TO EXERCISE 10.4 (WILL VARY)
2. According to the article, walking is more healthful [not healthy] than jogging.
4. Women tend to live longer than men; hence, more of the elderly are women.
6. A research scientist from the Lunar and Planetary Laboratory, University of Arizona, argues that mining asteroids may well prove economically important.
8. The student cafeteria is operated by a college food service, part of a chain.
10. *Oedipus Rex* is a more successful play than *The Sandbox*.

ANSWERS TO EXERCISE 11.1 (WILL VARY)
2. Lear divides his kingdom between the two older daughters, Goneril and Regan, whose extravagant professions of love are more flattering than the simple affection of the youngest daughter, Cordelia. The consequences of this error in judgment soon become apparent, as the older daughters prove neither grateful nor kind to him.
4. New England helped to shape many aspects of American culture, including education, religion, and government. As New Englanders moved west, they carried their institutions with them.
6. Jimmy told Allen that his own mother was ill. Jimmy told Allen that Allen's mother was ill.
8. When drug therapy is combined with psychotherapy, the patients relate better and are more responsive to their therapists, and they are less vulnerable to what disturbs them.
10. If guns cause crimes, outlaw guns.

ANSWERS TO EXERCISE 11.2 (WILL VARY)
2. Texans often hear about the influence of big oil corporations on their political candidates.
4. After having a conversation with a Vietnam veteran, my friend saw the war differently.
6. The chair was delivered three weeks late, which, according to the store management, is a normal practice.
8. Many employees resented the company's no-smoking policy. (the no-smoking policy of the company)
10. A doctor can count on making his or her fortune within ten years of graduation.

ANSWERS TO EXERCISE 12.1 (WILL VARY)
2. Then, suddenly, the big day *arrived*. The children were still a bit sleepy, for their anticipation had kept them awake.
4. A cloud of snow powder rose as skis and poles *flew* in every direction.

ANSWERS TO EXERCISE 12.2 (WILL VARY)

2. I think it better that Grandfather die painlessly, bravely, and with dignity than that he *continue* to live in terrible pain.
4. The consultant recommended that the candidates tell more jokes and that they *smile* more during their speeches.

ANSWERS TO EXERCISE 12.3 (WILL VARY)

2. no change
4. The first thing *we see* as we start down the slope is a large green banner.

ANSWERS TO EXERCISE 12.4 (WILL VARY)

2. Workers with computer skills were in great demand, and a programmer could almost name *his or her* salary.
4. New parents often find it hard to adjust to having a baby around; *they* can't just get up and go someplace.

ANSWERS TO EXERCISE 12.5 (WILL VARY)

2. According to the article, the ozone layer is rapidly dwindling, *and the lives of future generations are endangered.*
4. Oscar Wilde wrote that books cannot be divided into moral and immoral categories, *and that books are either written well or badly.*

ANSWERS TO EXERCISE 13.1 (WILL VARY)

2. Film-makers today have no choice; therefore, they must use complicated electronic equipment.
4. My mother taught me to read, but my grandmother taught me to *love* to read.

ANSWERS TO EXERCISE 13.2 (WILL VARY)

2. The mother eagle called twice *before* the young eagle finally answered.
4. *After* the Soviet Union expelled Solzhenitsyn in 1974, he eventually settled in Vermont.

ANSWERS TO EXERCISE 14.1 (WILL VARY)

2. Americans yearn to live with gusto.
4. The climbers had two choices—to go over a four-hundred-foot cliff or to turn back—but they decided to make the attempt.
6. Westerners objected in particular to a law that limited traffic speed to fifty-five miles per hour.
8. Offering good pay, good working conditions, and the best equipment money can buy, organized crime has been able to attract graduates just as big business has.
10. Wollstonecraft believed in universal public education and in education that forms the heart and strengthens the body.

ANSWERS TO EXERCISE 14.2 (WILL VARY)

2. The researchers saw few, if any, teachers threaten students with bodily harm. Occasionally, though, they saw a teacher *resist* striking a student.
4. She scooped up the fur jacket which had been thrown into a heap on the dirt floor.

ANSWERS TO EXERCISE 14.3 (WILL VARY)

2. *verbal-phrase fragment:* The protagonist came to a decision to leave his family and go to London.
4. *subordinate-clause fragment:* Many senators from the West opposed the bill because of its restrictions on mining and oil drilling.
6. *appositive fragment:* Forster stopped writing novels after *A Passage to India*, one of the greatest novels of the twentieth century.
8. *compound-predicate fragment:* I loved Toni Morrison's *Beloved* and thought she deserved the Pulitzer prize.
10. *subordinate-clause fragment:* Because the younger generation often rejects the ways of its elders, one might say that rebellion is normal.

ANSWERS TO EXERCISE 15.1 (WILL VARY)

2. I heard my friends talk enthusiastically about their great weekends while I tried to finish my assignment.
4. On the day in question, the patient was not able to breathe normally.
6. He sat in his chair very quietly, rolling his eyes.
8. Vernon made an agreement with his father to pay back the loan.
10. The maintenance worker shut down the turbine that was revolving out of control.

ANSWERS TO EXERCISE 15.2 (WILL VARY)

2. I was glad to know that the money I had made for the night would stay in my pocket.
4. His doctor recommended a new, painless examination for heart disease.

ANSWERS TO EXERCISE 15.3 (WILL VARY)

2. The mayor promised that during her first term she would not raise taxes. During her first term, the mayor promised that she would not raise taxes.
4. Doctors can now restore limbs that have been partially severed to functioning condition. Doctors can now restore limbs that have been severed to partially functioning condition.

ANSWERS TO EXERCISE 15.4 (WILL VARY)

2. The exhibit attracted large audiences because it had been heavily publicized.
4. Bookstores sold fifty thousand copies in the first week after publication.

ANSWERS TO EXERCISE 15.5 (WILL VARY)

2. Given the sharp increase in the crime rate, many women feel that their safety is being threatened.
4. Women go to shooting ranges and gun clubs for training in the use of weapons.

ANSWERS TO EXERCISE 15.6 (WILL VARY)

2. While attending a performance at Ford's Theatre, Lincoln was shot by John Wilkes Booth.
4. Dreams are somewhat like a jigsaw puzzle: when put together in the correct order, both dreams and puzzles have organization and coherence.

ANSWERS TO EXERCISE 16.1 (WILL VARY)

2. Your dentist will usually tell you if you need braces. To find out if you need braces, ask your dentist.
4. By not prosecuting white-collar crime as vigorously as we prosecute violent crime, we encourage white-collar criminals to ignore the law. We must prosecute white-collar crime as vigorously as violent crime unless we want to encourage white-collar criminals to ignore the law.
6. People in love want to make each other happy. Love is often characterized by two people who want to make each other happy.
8. Oedipus has the "shock of recognition" when he suddenly realizes that he has killed his father and married his mother. The "shock of recognition" comes when Oedipus suddenly realizes that he has killed his father and married his mother.
10. Europeans discovered Australia, but the British made it into a penal colony. Although it was a European discovery, Australia became a British penal colony.

ANSWERS TO EXERCISE 16.2 (WILL VARY)

2. Argentina and Uruguay were originally colonized by Spain, and Brazil was colonized by Portugal.
4. During the football strike, fans were angrier at the players than they were at the management.
6. The picture made me think about whether Baby M's life would be more difficult than any other children's lives.
8. Nonsmokers and marijuana smokers have different personalities.
10. One way to develop a topic for an essay is to jot down whatever comes to mind on a sheet of paper.

ANSWERS TO EXERCISE 17.1 (WILL VARY)

2. Also notable throughout the story is the image of chrysanthemums.
4. Movies about Indians always conjure up destructive stereotypes of drunkenness, horse thieves, and blood-thirsty war parties.

ANSWERS TO EXERCISE 17.2 (WILL VARY)

2. A prime example was the rescue attempt of the American hostages in Iran that resulted in the death of eight Marines.
4. I put on ten pounds immediately after I stopped exercising.
6. To check the engine, listen for rattling or pinging noises.
8. Randall exposes the injustices that confront American blacks.
10. Waitressing for six hours, followed by mopping and sweeping half a restaurant, can lead to exhaustion.

ANSWERS TO EXERCISE 18.3 (WILL VARY)

2. When Entwhistle and Townshend met singer and guitarist Roger Daltrey, they formed a group called the High Numbers.
4. *Working*, an important book by Studs Terkel, examines the situation of the American worker.

ANSWERS TO EXERCISE 19.2 (WILL VARY)

2. My favorite pastimes include reading, exercising, and talking with friends.
4. I want not only hot fudge but also whipped cream.

ANSWERS TO EXERCISE 19.3 (WILL VARY)

2. Most readers begin reading with an implicit faith that the text will be coherent and that the writer will convey meaning clearly.
4. Needing a new pair of shoes and not being able to afford them is enough to make anybody sensitive.
6. Too many students came to college to have fun, to find a husband or wife, or to put off having to go to work.
8. Her job was to show new products, to help Mr. Greer with sales, and to participate in advertising.
10. Stress can result in low self-esteem, total frustration, sleeplessness, nervousness, or eventually suicide.

ANSWERS TO EXERCISE 19.5 (WILL VARY)

2. There are three ways to apply Ninhydrin to the area to be examined: by brushing, spraying, or dipping.
4. There are two types of wallflowers: the male nerd and the female skeeve.

ANSWERS TO EXERCISE 20.3 (WILL VARY)

2. Once I mastered the problems which I had encountered at the beginning and once I had become thoroughly familiar with the stock, I became the best salesperson in our store.

ANSWERS TO EXERCISE 21.1 (WILL VARY)

2. I work for two brothers who own a hardware store.
4. The sweater feels soft and warm.

ANSWERS TO EXERCISE 21.4 (WILL VARY)

2. They started shooting pool, and before Marie knew it, ten dollars was owed to the kid. [Preference depends somewhat upon the context. The passive voice is unclear about who owes the kid ten dollars. Is Marie alone? Are she and the kid the "they" of the sentence, or is someone else involved? The active is clearer but might be incorrect, if others besides Marie owe the kid money.]
4. I adjusted more easily to living in a dorm than to living in an apartment. [Again, the active is preferred, since the passive adds nothing.]

ANSWERS TO EXERCISE 22.1

2. to; too
4. noticeable; until
6. believe; lose
8. affects; success; than; its
10. develop; truly; successful
12. where; and
14. businesses; dependent

16. experience; exercise
18. categories; final
20. occasion; whether; weather
22. woman's
24. It's; all right; sense

ANSWERS TO EXERCISE 22.3
2. conscience
4. leisure
6. caffeine
8. receive
10. heiress

ANSWERS TO EXERCISE 22.4
2. wholly
4. lonely
6. dyeing
8. continuous
10. outrageous

ANSWERS TO EXERCISE 22.5
2. fatally
4. finally

ANSWERS TO EXERCISE 22.6
2. carrying
4. studies
6. dutiful
8. obeyed
10. coyly

ANSWERS TO EXERCISE 22.7
2. fastest
4. reference
6. regrettable
8. drastically
10. weeping

ANSWERS TO EXERCISE 22.8
2. hooves
4. babies
6. stepchildren
8. miles per hour
10. phenomena
12. beaches
14. golf clubs

ANSWERS TO EXERCISE 23.2

2. student: from ME < L *studere*, to study
4. whine: from ME *whinen* < Indo-European *kwein*, to whiz, hiss, whistle
6. sex: from ME < L *sexus* < *secare*, to cut
8. tortilla: from Sp, diminutive of *torta*, cake
10. video: from L, I see < *videre*, to see

ANSWERS TO EXERCISE 23.5 (WILL VARY)

2. The OED lists to make strange or turn away from, to transfer ownership, and to change or alter something. *Webster's New World Dictionary* adds two slightly different meanings: to cause to be withdrawn from society, and to transfer affection.
4. The OED defines *hopefully* as an adverb: "In a hopeful manner; with a feeling of hope; with ground for hope, promisingly. *Webster's New World Dictionary* lists both adverb and adjective uses but notes that the adjectival use is "regarded by some as loose usage, but widely current."

ANSWERS TO EXERCISE 24.2 (WILL VARY)

2. subterranean: beneath earth; of or relating to under the surface of the earth.
4. monograph: to write one or a single writing; a learned treatise on a small area of learning.
6. superscript: to write over or above; a distinguishing symbol written immediately above or above and to the right of another character.
8. neologism: recent word or thought; a word, usage, or expression that is often disapproved because of its newness or barbarousness.
10. apathetic: without feeling or not suffering; having or showing little or no feeling or emotion, having or showing little or no interest or concern.

ANSWERS TO EXERCISE 25.1

2. rapturous
4. dramatically

ANSWERS TO EXERCISE 25.3 (WILL VARY)

2. *tragic*—distressing, alarming, disturbing; *consumes*—defeats, feeds on, erodes; *displays*—champions, thrives on, builds up, promotes; *drama*—excitement, tension, vitality
4. *held*—breathed; *keenness*—coolness, crispness; *twitch*—perk up; *surprise*—adventure, enterprise; *tremors*—chills; *run*—jet

ANSWERS TO EXERCISE 25.5 (WILL VARY)

2. Cooing, singing, twittering—the early morning beckoning of birds outside my window make it a treat to get up.
4. The valet stepped cautiously yet excitedly toward my Porsche.

ANSWERS TO EXERCISE 26.4 (WILL VARY)

2.   —destroys his victims with flashes of lightning (metaphor)
     —roasted her victims over a fire (metaphor): both of these metaphors suggest the

powerful effect that Pope's and Austen's words could have on the targets of their criticism or attacks; Pope's words were flashes of lightning, Austen's words made her victims feel as though they were being roasted over a fire

4.   –deep and soft like water moving in a cavern (simile): this simile compares the sound of her voice to water in a cavern

ANSWERS TO EXERCISE 26.6 (WILL VARY)

2. All candidates strive for the same results: they strive to discredit the opposition, and to persuade the majority of voters that they are qualified for the position.
4. The more angry she became over his actions, the more he rebelled and continued doing what he pleased.

ANSWERS TO EXERCISE 26.7 (WILL VARY)

2. total annihilation
4. to make peace

ANSWERS TO EXERCISE 27.1

2. Unfortunately,
4. If you follow instructions carefully,
6. no comma needed
8. no comma needed
10. Founded by Alexander the Great,

ANSWERS TO EXERCISE 27.2 (WILL VARY)

2. Immigrants came to the United States with high hopes, *but* their illusions were often shattered.
4. A basic quality of leather is stretchability, *so* it takes on the shape of a foot.

ANSWERS TO EXERCISE 27.3

2. *who laughs last* is a restrictive clause because only the *she* who has the last laugh can laugh best. The person who laughs first or second doesn't laugh best. Laughing best is restricted to the person who laughs last.
4. *smoked over an alder wood fire* is a restrictive appositive phrase because the meaning of the sentence is not complete without it. Only salmon that is smoked over an alder wood fire can have *a unique flavor.*

ANSWERS TO EXERCISE 27.4

2. no comma needed.
4. . . . power wire, which is usually red; . . . the ground wire, which is usually black.
6. The Zunis, an ancient tribe dwelling in New Mexico, . . .
8. . . . was Karl Marx, who believed that his role as a social thinker . . .
10. aid, if one of them . . .

ANSWERS TO EXERCISE 27.5

2. The social sciences include economics, psychology, political science, anthropology, and sociology.
4. The daddy-long-legs's orange body resembled a colored dot amidst eight black legs.

6. Superficial observation does not provide accurate insight into people's lives—how they feel, what they believe in, how they respond to others.
8. I timidly offered to help a loud, overbearing, lavishly dressed customer.
10. These Cosell clones insist on calling every play, judging every move, and telling everyone within earshot exactly what is wrong with the team.

ANSWERS TO EXERCISE 27.6
2. The West, in fact, has become solidly Republican in presidential elections.
4. Fictions about race, not the facts, influence human relations.
6. no comma needed
8. And now, customers, follow along as I demonstrate the latest in video discs.
10. This is imported pâté, not chopped liver.

ANSWERS TO EXERCISE 27.7
2. Ithaca, New York, has a population of about 20,000.
4. The Modern Language Association headquarters recently moved to 10 Astor Place, New York, New York 10003.

ANSWERS TO EXERCISE 27.8
2. no change
4. "Neat people are lazier and meaner than sloppy people," according to Suzanne Britt.

ANSWERS TO EXERCISE 27.11
2. Observers watch and interpret facial expressions and gestures.
4. Our supper that evening consisted of stale bologna sandwiches, soggy cookies, and leftover trail mix.
6. As we sat around the campfire, we felt boredom and disappointment.
8. The photographer Edward Curtis is known for his depiction of the West.
10. Driving a car and talking on the car phone at the same time demand great care.

ANSWERS TO EXERCISE 28.1
2. City life offers many advantages; however, in many ways, life in a small town is much more pleasant.
4. Physical education forms an important part of many university programs; nevertheless, few students and professors clearly recognize its value.
6. Voltaire was concerned about the political implications of his skepticism; he warned his friends not to discuss atheism in front of the servants.
8. My high school was excessively competitive; virtually everyone went on to college, many to the top schools in the nation.
10. Propaganda is defined as the spread of ideas to further a cause; therefore, propaganda and advertisement are synonymous terms.

ANSWERS TO EXERCISE 28.4
2. If the North had followed up its victory at Gettysburg more vigorously, the Civil War might have ended sooner.
4. Our uniforms were unbelievably dingy, stained from being constantly splattered with food and often torn here and there.

ANSWERS TO EXERCISE 29.1
2. Cicero was murdered in 43 B.C.
4. In April 1981, NBC interviewed Dr. Spock.

ANSWERS TO EXERCISE 29.2
2. Are people with so many possessions really happy?
4. Correct, indirect question.

ANSWERS TO EXERCISE 29.3 (WILL VARY)
2. I screamed at Jamie, "You rat! You tricked me!"
4. Get away from that window right now!

ANSWERS TO EXERCISE 30.1
2. *CBS's* acquisition of the guitar company disappointed some musicians.
4. *Carol and Jim's* income dropped drastically after Jim quit his job.
6. Many smokers disregard the *surgeon general's* warnings.
8. The *governors'* attitudes changed after the convention.
10. My *friend's* and my *brother's* cars have the same kind of stereo systems.

ANSWERS TO EXERCISE 30.3
2. That night I was escorted to the front row and placed on the *mourner's* bench with all the other young sinners. . . .
4. Then I was left all alone on the *mourner's* bench.

ANSWERS TO EXERCISE 31.2
2. In Flannery O'Connor's short story "Revelation," colors symbolize passion, violence, sadness, and even "God."
4. The "fun" of surgery begins before the operation ever takes place.
6. "Big Bill," the first section of Dos Passos's *U.S.A.*, opens with a birth.
8. Pink Floyd's song "Time" depicts the growth of technology and its impact on society.
10. This review will examine a TV episode entitled "48 Hours on Gang Street."

ANSWERS TO EXERCISE 31.4 (WILL VARY)
2. What is Hawthorne telling the readers in "Rappaccini's Daughter"?
4. This "typical American" is Ruby Turpin, who in the course of the story receives a message that brings about a change in her life.
6. One of Jackson's least-known stories is "Janice"; this story, like many of her others, leaves the reader shocked.
8. In his article, "How the Freeze Movement Was Born," Michael Kazin states that a freeze's "bilateral nature nullifies fears of a Soviet advantage."[1]
10. One thought flashed through my mind as I finished *In Search of Our Mothers' Garden:* "I want to read more of this writer's work."

ANSWERS TO EXERCISE 32.1
2. During my research, I found that a flat-rate income tax (a single-rate tax rate with no deductions) has its problems.
4. Many researchers used the Massachusetts Multiphasic Personal Inventory (MMPI) for hypnotizability studies.

ANSWERS TO EXERCISE 32.2
2. Even if smoking is harmful—and there is no real proof of this assertion—it is unjust to outlaw smoking while other harmful substances remain legal.
4. Many people would have ignored the children's taunts—but not Ace.

ANSWERS TO EXERCISE 32.3
2. Another example is taken from Psalm 139: 16.
4. Layton, Ed. *Martin Luther King: The Peaceful Warrior*, 3rd ed. Englewood Cliffs, NJ: Prentice-Hall, 1968.
6. Ghandi urged four things: tell the truth, even in business, adopt more sanitary habits, abolish caste and religious divisions, and learn English.
8. *Signs of Trouble and Erosion: A Report on Education in America* was submitted to Congress and the president in January 1984.
10. The article in *Time* reported that at 4:18 p.m. the surgeon, Dr. William DeVries, leaned over the heavily sedated man and said, "Everything went well—perfectly."

ANSWERS TO EXERCISE 33.1
2. Eating at a restaurant, whether it be a fast-food, Chinese, or Italian place, is always a treat.
4. The Council of Trent was convened to draw up the Catholic response to the Protestant Reformation.
6. I wondered if my new Lee jeans were faded enough and if I could possibly scuff up my new Nikes just a little more before I arrived for spring term.
8. In this essay I will be citing the works of Vladimir Nabokov, in particular his novels *Pnin* and *Lolita* and his story "The Vane Sisters."
10. Few music lovers can resist the music of George Gershwin. (*Rhapsody in Blue* and *Porgy and Bess* are two personal favorites.)

ANSWERS TO EXERCISE 34.1
2. An MX missile is 71 feet long, 92 inches around, and weighs 190,000 pounds.
4. In 1955 the Reverend Martin Luther King, Jr., was elected president of the Montgomery Improvement Association.
6. Like black-and-white television, the five-cent candy bar is a relic of the past.
8. The Public Broadcasting System is promoting more and better programs in the arts throughout the country, not just in Los Angeles and New York City.
10. Dostoevsky was influenced by many European writers—for example, Dickens, Stendhal, and Balzac.

ANSWERS TO EXERCISE 34.2 (WILL VARY)
2. Some call it the handbook for the nineties.
4. I am writing in response to a letter submitted to the *Times-Picayune* on December 9, 1984, by George F. Lundy.
6. Educational broadcasting is at present available to 72 percent of the population.
8. In the thirty-five through forty-four age group, the risk is estimated to be about 1 in 2,500.
10. The ancient amulet measured $1\frac{1}{8}$ by $2\frac{3}{5}$ inches.

ANSWERS TO EXERCISE 35.1

2. When people think about the word *business*, they may associate it with people and companies that care about nothing but making money.
4. The word *veterinary* comes from the Latin *veterinarius*, meaning "of beasts of burden."
6. Flying the *Glamorous Glennis*, a plane named for his wife, Chuck Yeager was the first pilot to fly faster than the speed of sound.
8. *The Waste Land* is a long and difficult but ultimately rewarding poem.
10. My grandparents remember the sinking of the *Titanic*.

ANSWERS TO EXERCISE 36.1

2. re*tract; re-tract
4. mil*i*tar*y; mili-tary
6. oth*er*cen*tered; other-centered
8. dim*ming; dim-ming
10. at*ti*tude; atti-tude

ANSWERS TO EXERCISE 36.2

2. pre-World War II
4. correct
6. self-important
8. seven hundred thirty-three
10. correct

ANSWERS TO EXERCISE 36.3

2. McKuen began to write as an escape from his on-the-move life, which included various odd jobs ranging from ditch-digging to cookie-cutting.
4. Suicide among teenagers has tripled in the past thirty-five years, making it the third-leading cause of death among fifteen to twenty-four-year-olds.
6. Since the use of PCB's has been outlawed, environmentalists feel somewhat encouraged.
8. correct
10. The beautifully written essay earned high praise.

Acknowledgments (continued from p. iv)

Emily Dickinson, "A Little Madness in the Spring" and "Much Madness Is Divinest Sense" reprinted by permission of the publishers and Trustees of Amherst College from *The Poems of Emily Dickinson*, edited by Thomas H. Johnson. Cambridge, Mass.: The Belknap Press of Harvard University Press. Copyright 1951, © 1955, 1979, 1983 by the Presidents and Fellows of Harvard College. Also from *The Complete Poems of Emily Dickinson*, edited by Thomas H. Johnson. Copyright 1914, 1942 by Martha Dickinson Bianchi. Reprinted by permission of Little, Brown and Company.

Dictionary of Modern English Usage, Second Edition, by H. W. Fowler and Sir Ernest Gowers, copyright © 1965, by permission of Oxford University Press.

Robert Francis, "The Pitcher." Copyright © 1953 by Robert Francis. Reprinted from *The Orb Weaver* by permission of Wesleyan University Press.

Robert Frost, "Fire and Ice." Copyright 1916, 1923 by Holt, Rinehart and Winston and renewed 1944, 1951 by Robert Frost. Reprinted from *The Poetry of Robert Frost*, edited by Edward Connery Latham, by permission of Henry Holt and Company, Inc.

Robert Frost, "The Road Not Taken." Copyright 1916, 1923 by Holt, Rinehart and Winston and renewed 1944, 1951 by Robert Frost. Reprinted from *The Poetry of Robert Frost*, edited by Edward Connery Latham, by permission of Henry Holt and Company, Inc.

Greenpeace advertisement. Produced by Greenpeace USA, 1436 U Street, NW, Washington, D.C., 20009.

Ellen Goodman, "Holiday Cheer Shouldn't End with the New Year." © 1988, the Boston Globe Newspaper Company/Washington Post Writers Group. Reprinted with permission.

A. E. Housman, "Loveliest of Trees." Copyright 1939, 1940, © 1965 by Holt, Rinehart and Winston. Copyright © 1967, 1968 by Robert E. Symons. Reprinted from *The Collected Poems of A. E. Housman* by permission of Henry Holt and Company, Inc.

Langston Hughes, "Harlem." Copyright © 1951 by Langston Hughes. Reprinted from *Selected Poems of Langston Hughes* by permission of Alfred A. Knopf, Inc.

Mathematics Dictionary, Fourth Edition, Glen James and Robert C. James, © 1976 by Van Nostrand Reinhold. All rights reserved. Reprinted by permission.

The Oxford English Dictionary, copyright © 1976, reprinted by permission of Oxford University Press.

Readers' Guide to Periodical Literature, August 1988, page 206, Copyright © 1988 by the H. W. Wilson Company. Material reproduced by permission of the publisher.

Karl Shapiro, "The Intellectual." Copyright © 1987 by Karl Shapiro. Reprinted from *New and Selected Poems 1940–1986* by permission of the University of Chicago Press and the author. All rights reserved.

John Updike, "Leaving Church Early." From *Tossing and Turning* by John Updike. Copyright © 1976 by John Updike. Reprinted by permission of Alfred A. Knopf, Inc.

758

Webster's New Dictionary of Synonyms © 1984 by Merriam-Webster Inc., publisher of the Merriam-Webster dictionaries. Reprinted by permission.

Webster's New World Dictionary, Third College Edition, copyright © 1988 by Simon and Schuster, Inc. All rights reserved. Reprinted by permission.

Webster's Third New International Dictionary © 1986 by Merriam-Webster Inc., publisher of the Merriam-Webster ® dictionaries. Reprinted by permission.

The World Book Encyclopedia. Copyright © 1988 by World Book, Inc. "War of 1812" entry reprinted by permission.

World Wildlife Fund advertisement. Reprinted with permission of World Wildlife Fund.

Index of Authors and Titles

Subject Index